George Dangerfield was born in England and came to the United States in 1930 after studying at Oxford. After a brief career as an editor, he became a writer and later a teacher of history. *The Era of Good Feelings* won both the Pulitzer and Bancroft prizes in American History. Mr. Dangerfield's other books include *The Strange Death of Liberal England, The Awakening of American Nationalism,* and *Interpreting American History.*

"If [Mr. Monroe] had determined to retire from the public service at the end of his present term, it was now drawing to a close. It was to be considered now as a whole, as a system of administration. It would hereafter, I believed, be looked back to as the golden age of this republic . . ."

John Quincy Adams

NOVEMBER 22, 1823

(Adams, *Memoirs*, VI, 196-197)

"I see nothing but men and factions without caring whether Govt. shall be well or badly administered, the country exalted or disgraced, or anything but the fulfillment of personal views and passions: and they call this an abatement of party spirits, a reconciliation of parties, a species of political millennium."

Albert Gallatin to his daughter, Frances Gallatin

NOVEMBER 26, 1824

(*Gallatin Papers*)

George Dangerfield

THE ERA OF GOOD FEELINGS

Elephant Paperbacks
Ivan R. Dee, Inc., Publisher, Chicago

First ELEPHANT PAPERBACK edition published 1989 by Ivan R. Dee, Inc., 1332 North Halsted Street, Chicago 60622. Manufactured in the United States of America.

Library of Congress Cataloging-in-Publication Data
Dangerfield, George, 1904–1986.
    The era of good feelings.
    Reprint. Originally published: New York: Harcourt, Brace and Co., 1952.
    Bibliography: p.
    Includes index.
    1.   United   States—History—1817–1825.   2.   United States—History—1825–1829. 3. Treaty of Ghent (1814). 4. Monroe doctrine. 5. United States—History—War of 1812—Influence. I. Title.
E371.D3 1989   973.5   89-12031
ISBN 0-929587-14-6

Contents

CONTENTS

3
THE POLITICS OF SLAVERY: 1819-1821

4
THE DIPLOMACY OF COAL AND IRON: 1821-1824

5
THE LURID ADMINISTRATION: 1825-1829

Foreword

THIS book is essentially a description of some of the personalities and experiences, American and European, which assisted in or were necessary to the political transition from Jeffersonian democracy to Jacksonian democracy: from the great dictum that central government is best when it governs least to the great dictum that central government must sometimes intervene strongly in behalf of the weak and the oppressed and the exploited.

All historical periods are, it is true, transitional, nor is any transition ever complete. If I have ventured to apply the word "transition" to the period covered by the administrations of James Monroe and John Quincy Adams, it is because this period passes through three quite well-defined phases.

(I) The first two years of Monroe's Presidency were remarkable for a nationalist exuberance, which arose from the fact that the United States had emerged from the encroachments of the Napoleonic Wars, and the perils of the War of 1812 (see Part I—"The Charterhouse of Ghent"), not only safely but also with an increased prestige.

(II) The exuberance which greeted and acclaimed Monroe, however, was sustained and intensified by a land boom and a cotton boom; and when these booms collapsed in 1819, the Era of Good Feelings properly came to an end. There followed a period of deep economic depression. During this period, Americans sought, by all sorts of strange and desperate expedients, to obtain some brief respite from the waters of debt.

(III) The depression lasted at least until 1823; and when good times began slowly to return, the debtor classes had leisure to ask themselves whether they had not been abandoned by the general government in the hour of their need, and whether they should not look for a new kind of general government—one that would promote, by strong action and not by negative precept, the great "agrarian" ideal of a society of independent property-owners.

This ideal was not opposed to sound business enterprise or to a *laissez-faire* economy; but it insisted that this *laissez-faire* economy should be modified in an "agrarian" manner (that is to say, in favor of the weak, by attacking monopoly wherever it showed its head) rather than in a "capitalist" manner (that is to say, in favor of the strong, by the distribution of subsidies and privileges whenever they were called for). Jacksonian radicals sometimes went a good deal farther than that: Jackson himself never did. If his memory is green today, it is not because of his unattainable ideal of a society of independent property-owners, but because of his valiant faith in the dignity of the individual, the uncommonness of the common man.

II

It was during the last years of Monroe's Presidency, and throughout the four years of the Presidency of Adams, that American agrarians began to define their rights and to formulate their grievances. They demanded a wider suffrage, rotation in office, a greater access to the business of government and therefore to the history of their times: they complained of imprisonment for debt, of insufficient public education, of incorporation by special charter, of fraudulent banks of issue, of too close a connection between the general government and the moneyed interest. It was by listening to and learning from these demands and grievances that Andrew Jackson, who came to the Presidency in 1829 with no program and almost no ideas, became one of the great popular leaders of American history.

It has often been claimed that these demands and grievances were chiefly of Western origin, but it is significant that they were first clearly formulated, in 1828, by a convention of working men meeting in an Eastern city. The influence of the West was very strong in the 1820's, and one of the masterpieces of American historiography, Frederick Jackson Turner's *Rise of the New West* (1906), maintains, with an authority too great to be disregarded, that this was by far the strongest influence that there was. But the fact remains that the Westerner was more concerned with political than with economic equality; that he was not always opposed to a centralizing government of subsidies and privileges; and that problems of economic inequality were more closely examined and more urgently debated in the East and in the South.

III

The phrase "Era of Good Feelings" has customarily been extended to cover the whole eight years of Monroe's Presidency; not simply because of the nationalism which so distinguished its early years and never vanished from its later ones, but also because it was a period of one-party government.

Almost every man called himself a Jeffersonian Republican in those days, and political conflicts on a national scale were apt to be conflicts between personalities and not between principles or programs. This gives the whole period a certain fascination, because the leading personalities were very strong and very brilliant and because they were quite sure, in all but the most opprobrious or secret of their transactions, that what they said and did would be quoted and remembered for generations to come. In this innocent respect, the Era of Good Feelings was pre-eminently the era of the personal myth.

But one-party government cannot continue long in a political democracy without resorting to dictatorship or dissolving into anarchy. It is not flexible, not responsive to the people; it tends to produce a crusty political elite; and it is easily ensnared by any special interest strongly enough organized to make its wishes felt. The rule of the Republican Party under Monroe was seriously shaken by the panic of 1819; its geographical basis was fatally undermined by the free soil–slave soil debates which preceded the Missouri Compromise; and from then onwards it tended more and more to become the party of federal subsidies and special privileges, of high protective tariffs and of strong but potentially irresponsible central banking. Even the Monroe Doctrine of 1823 bore some traces of this tendency; for the Monroe Doctrine was not only a high and resolute challenge to the autocrats of Europe, it was not only a plea for independent governments and open markets in Spanish America, but it was also a distinct rebuff to the friendly advances of British industrialism (see Part IV—"The Diplomacy of Coal and Iron"). It is well to remember that the same Message which contained the Monroe Doctrine contained also a demand for protective tariffs. And so it came about that by the end of Adams's Presidency—itself a curious and instructive example of political anarchy—the old Republican Party was almost completely out of touch with the wishes and aspirations of a majority of the American people. The majority of the American people, therefore, swept Andrew Jackson and his Democrats into office in the election of 1828.

History teaches us that it never repeats itself; and if we turn its vital analogies into precedents or prescriptions we simply disregard what it has to teach. None the less, looking backward from the complexities of our times to the simplicities of those early days, we can at least infer from the administrations of Monroe and Adams, both of them good and sincere men, that good and sincere men may sometimes palliate or advocate very dangerous policies, and that they will often do so from the best of motives. If political democracy is to survive, in these times as in those, it must survive by fighting the policies and not by persecuting the men.

IV

I am much indebted to Mr. Richard Lowitt and to Mr. Cedric Evans for assistance in research; to Mr. R. W. G. Vail, Director of the New-York Historical Society, for permission to read the Gallatin Papers; and to Mr.

Wayne Andrews, Curator of Manuscripts of that Society, for constant friendly help.

And I cannot conclude this Foreword without paying a most heartfelt tribute to that great company of American and British scholars, living and dead, whose minds have illuminated so many of the paths I have been attempting to follow.

G. D.

Carpinteria, California: August, 1951.

1

THE CHARTERHOUSE OF GHENT:
1814

CHAPTER ONE

ℐn the Rue des Champs

I HAVE been most unnaturally occupied," John Quincy Adams wrote to his father on July 7, 1814, "for I have accomplished two voyages by sea, and two journies by land. Have crossed the Gulf of Finland and Baltic from Reval to Stockholm, and the North Sea from Gothenburg to the Texel. Have traversed the Kingdom of Sweden and the *sovereign princedom* of the Netherlands; and here I am in the city of Charles the 5th waiting with my four colleagues, until it shall please the mistress of the world, as she now fancies herself, to send deputies for the purpose, as she imagines, of receiving our submission." [1] The city of Charles V was the city of Ghent; the four colleagues were Henry Clay, James A. Bayard, Jonathan Russell, and Albert Gallatin, Ministers Plenipotentiary and Envoys Extraordinary for the purpose of negotiating and concluding a treaty of peace with Great Britain, "the mistress of the world," for whom John Quincy Adams had already conceived a strong repugnance. "I am well assured," he continued, "that the work to which we have been called, that of conciliating American and British pretensions, will be found *more unnatural* than your and my wandering life."

The Adams capacity for self-commiseration is famous, but any American whose wanderings, in the year 1814, had been more or less intimately connected with the indecisions of Tsar Alexander, the jealousies of the British government, and the lurid destiny of Napoleon, might have had good reason to complain that he wandered in an unnatural manner. Not one of the five American commissioners had had a comfortable passage to the city of Ghent, if uneasiness of mind and uncertainty of destination may be numbered among the discomforts of travel. But the combined experiences of Clay, Russell, Bayard, and Adams could not hope to equal, for mere perversity, the ordeal

[1] The notes will be found on pages 429-492.

3

of Albert Gallatin. Not only had Mr. Gallatin been exasperated in St. Petersburg and chilled in London; not only had he become at one time nothing more than a private gentleman, obliged to seek, in the enemy's capital, the salvage of his political fortunes; not only had he been more than a year upon his journey; not only had he started out as the senior member of one commission and arrived as the junior member of yet another—but also he knew that some of the blame for his odd itinerary and odder metamorphoses was due to a discreditable intrigue in the United States Senate. Ingratitude is a bitter draught, ingratitude from one's adopted country perhaps the bitterest of all, and Mr. Gallatin was forced to swallow it in great gulps. It says much for this equable and patriotic man that now, when his political career was visibly descending the slope that leads to political oblivion, his sense of humor and of proportion remained unimpaired.

Between June 24 and July 7, 1814, the five American commissioners who were to end the War of 1812 arrived by ones and twos in Ghent. All were in that mood of luminous good spirits which often overtakes men who are banded together to perform a task they believe to be impossible. Mr. Adams even told his wife that what she had heard of the character and temper of Henry Clay—that he was "one of the most amiable and finest temper'd men in the world"—exactly coincided with his own experience of that gentleman. In the light of what was to come, the words have a strange sound.[2] But there is a contagion in despair: men who believe that their destiny is to sink together are apt to discover in one another amiable characteristics which, in more fortunate circumstances, might have been totally invisible. All five peace commissioners were convinced that they were doomed to lock horns with their English opposites and then retire from the combat with nothing to show for their efforts. They were disagreed only over the length of time this encounter would consume.

I

These five men, gathered together in that ominous summer of 1814, deserve some particular attention. As a group they displayed, according to one vaguely baffled observer, "all the varieties of American party."[3] Indeed, it would have taken a discerning eye to perceive the difference between the Old Republicanism of Albert Gallatin and that of the more doctrinaire saints of his own party, or to what extent these differences, in turn, diverged from or agreed with the Young Republicanism of Henry Clay; or to gauge the Federalism of Bayard and the ex-Federalism of Adams; or to determine the leanings in either or any direction of a Rhode Island Jeffersonian like Jonathan Russell. One thing, however, impressed their English adversaries—"the Federalists are quite as inveterate enemies to us as the Madisonians."[4] When the occasion called for a display of unity, the Americans were always united.

Conservative political philosophy in Europe entertained as a cardinal maxim the notion that republican governments could not survive if they were asked to adapt themselves to the needs of a great territory and a sprawling population. Smallness and symmetry were essential: the United States of America fulfilled neither of these conditions, and that their career would be stormy and brief was confidently expected.[5] In its outward seeming, the American commission invariably gave these predictions the lie. Moreover, when a young nation, in the hour of danger and agony, could produce a delegation so resolute in defense and so formidable in argument, it might have been well to pause and inquire whether or not that nation had a future. This the British delegation at first neglected to do. With a flat hand, it pushed its adversaries against a wall, only to discover that there was no wall. The more they were pushed, the more the Americans receded in spirit into the unsymmetrical immensity of their own geographical background, converting what was supposed to be a source of weakness into a means of strength. Only imagination and knowledge could have pursued them successfully into such a retreat: nature had not supplied the British delegation with the first, and its superiors in London, busy with innumerable other matters, had failed to provide it with the second.

II

The three most prominent American commissioners were, of course, Adams, Clay, and Gallatin. Of these three, Gallatin was the eldest, and the best equipped for the ordeal of a negotiation. He possessed that rare combination of qualities a copious intelligence and a sunny temperament. He was decidedly aristocratic, and had a strong sense of his own dignity; but he had also a sense of humor and a dry, gentle wit. Substantial but never too solid, firm but flexible, he was the ideal moderator for a gathering which—like the American commission—was apt to experience a series of almost instantaneous transitions from interest to opinion, from opinion to prejudice, and from prejudice to fury; while in the meetings with the British delegation his intelligence and suavity were of the utmost value. He was born in 1761 into one of the best and oldest families in Geneva; and upon this background he had engrafted a close knowledge of the habits of western Pennsylvania and a long and intimate acquaintance with political and executive Washington. He had been a leader in Pennsylvania state politics; he had fought the Republican battle through the *Sturm und Drang* of the Fourth, Fifth, and Sixth Congresses; he had been Secretary of the Treasury under Jefferson and Madison. Once upon a time, with a characteristic modesty, he had described himself as "*un homme sans agréments*" (graces) . . . *qui bredouille l'anglais comme un français*."[6] But it was his graceful European manner which seemed to infuriate his Federalist opponents in the House of Representatives, and which, during his tenure of the Treasury, helped to envenom a small, factious, and disreputable clique in the Senate.

He was proud of his European background. When he was complimented upon being more European than American—as, for example by Henry Goulburn, the British plenipotentiary—he would mutter, in some embarrassment, that the only Americans were the Red Indians.[7] He realized that the Englishman had been insulting, but the insult warmed and flattered some unreconstructed portion of his psyche. Was he not an American through and through—by choice, by experience, by the operation of a hundred subtle influences? And yet he had been born and raised in the midst of one of the most unobtrusive, polite, and cultured societies in pre-revolutionary Europe. It was true that as a child and an adolescent he had been subjected to some disturbing influences. The Calvinist rigidity of Geneva was more evident in its politics than in its parlors, but it existed; and it was threatened to some extent by the mischievous genius of Voltaire, who lived just over the border at Ferney, the mecca of thinking Europe. As a child, Gallatin was a frequent visitor at Ferney.[8] And then another spirit, absent but powerful, ruled by stealth in Geneva. When Gallatin graduated from the Academy in 1779, he was already committed to the teachings of Jean Jacques Rousseau; and it was because of Rousseau that suddenly, at the age of eighteen, he fled to Bordeaux and took ship for America. In 1784, after many adventures, he made that return to nature which his master seemed to require of him, and buried himself in the Pennsylvanian wilderness, on the banks of the Monongahela.

His whole life was a battle between his Gallatin background and his republican principles. Both were undoubtedly satisfied by his admission into a Virginia Cabinet—there was no better society anywhere in the world than that of Jefferson and Madison—but even here his Gallatin past gave an unexpected coloration to his Republican present. One of his greatest papers is his Report on Internal Improvements of 1808;[9] and the Report is distinctly Hamiltonian. He was also a champion of the First United States Bank. As Secretary of the Treasury his financial policies were sound, none sounder; he labored always to expel the fancies and preserve the purity of good Republicanism; and the effect of it all was to make him more and more conservative. By the time he reached Ghent, he was thoroughly exhausted by the rough and tumble of American politics.

Yet public life of some kind was a necessity to him. Years later, as a very old man reviewing his past, he confessed to Sismondi that he believed that no other kind of life would have been possible.[10] He could have used his financial prestige to increase his fortunes. In 1815, John Jacob Astor offered him a fifth interest in his business, and in a singularly candid letter set forth its nature and extent. Altogether, aside from $200,000 in the six per cents— "but this I do not mean to part with"—he had $800,000 employed in trade. He calculated the profits at $50,000 to $100,000 a year, after deducting interest and all expenses; and he proposed to "keep pretty steady to the trade to China with which I mean to connect as much of the fur trade as I can."[11] Astor and Gallatin were on good terms—but Astor, with his crude manners, his fluent illiteracy, his shrewd cold mind: the very incarnation of the acquisitive instinct! To be in trade, and with such an associate! On the whole, Gallatin thought not; and he turned the offer down.

Such was the man who, by sheer distinction and address, was accorded the chief place in the American commission—which place rightfully belonged to John Quincy Adams. Gallatin's appearance was impressive and reassuring: he had a dark complexion, hazel eyes full of humor and sympathy, a long prominent nose, and a fine forehead. One can see him still, poised between the fiery Clay and the empurpled Adams—between Achilles and Ajax—and dropping into the terrible clash of these two personalities some little jest which, as if by magic, turned their wrath aside. He was a noble American, and he deserved well of the state.

III

John Quincy Adams also deserved well of the state, and was to attain an eminence that foreign birth denied to Gallatin. Yet the eminence, once reached, was a thorny one: there are few examples of political mismanagement more instructive than the presidency of John Quincy Adams, unless it be that of his father, John Adams.

He spent his life in the public service, for which he was peculiarly fitted except in one respect—he was almost totally deficient in the art of getting on with other people. He was an independent man, but he wore his independence with a difference. It was like a *tunica molesta*—a shirt of fire—smeared with the inflammable materials of pride and suspicion, awkwardness and singularity, a chemical composition which burst into dull flame at the slightest contact with the outer world. "Of all the men," wrote a prejudiced Englishman who met him in 1812 when he was the American Minister to Russia, "whom it was ever my lot to accost and to waste civilities upon, [he] was the most doggedly and systematically repulsive. With a vinegar aspect, cotton in his leathern ears, and hatred to England in his heart, he sat in the frivolous assemblies of Petersburg like a bull-dog among spaniels; and many were the times that I drew monosyllables and grim smiles from him and tried in vain to mitigate his venom." [12] The writer little guessed at the self-mortifying processes perpetually at work behind that forbidding exterior. "I was not satisfied with myself this day," Adams wrote in his diary, after dining at Philadelphia with the President of the Bank of the United States, "having talked too much at dinner . . . Nor can I always (I did not this day) altogether avoid a dogmatical and peremptory tone and manner, always disgusting and especially offensive in persons to whose age or situation others consider some deference due." [13] Once, after speaking too harshly to a religious maniac called Jenkins, who called on him with some printed sheets of scriptural texts against dueling, he confided to his diary: "I am a man of reserved, cold, austere, and forbidding manners; my political adversaries say, a gloomy misanthropist, and my personal enemies, an unsocial savage." [14] And he confessed to himself that he had not the pliability to reform this "defect."

A bull-dog among spaniels! The tribute is an unconscious one, but it is a tribute none the less. If he could not fawn, he could fight. In the intensity of his self-scourgings one can detect a certain pride. The very lack of pliability that so perplexed him in his moments of self-abasement was also a source of pleasure. "I think I touched them up," he would often say, after some particularly angry scene of his own contriving. He had—he could not help it—the instinct for the jugular.[15] His printed assault upon Jonathan Russell—who had been so ill-advised as to cast doubts upon the patriotism of Adams's conduct at Ghent—was so deadly that for many years afterwards the vocabulary of America was increased, though not enriched, by the transitive verb "to Jonathan-Russell," meaning to pulverize an opponent.[16]

He fought persistently, splenetically—sometimes expending his energies upon the meanest objects, sometimes putting them to the service of purely personal ambitions, but more often dedicating them to what he believed to be the cause of justice and of virtue. For he was, above all things, a moral man; it is, indeed, the clue to his character. And though one hesitates to apply the extinguishing substantive "puritan" to so complex a personality, there were certain aspects of Adams's character which no other word seems to fit. He was a puritan in his distrust of political expedients; a puritan in his hatred of himself; a puritan in his belief—nowhere expressed but everywhere apparent—that this hatred was evidence of an innate superiority; a puritan in his anxious welcome of personal disaster and in his conviction that every great success must be followed by a compensatory failure; a puritan in his individualism; and a puritan in his virulence.

It is perhaps unnecessary to say that a man of this kind would not make a good party politician. In 1808, John Quincy Adams was forced to resign from the Senate, of which he was a Federalist member from Massachusetts, because of a rebellious tendency to support Republican policies.[17] The tendency was a sound one: he deserted the Federalists because he thought that they were degenerating into a treasonable faction; but, somehow or other, this did not turn him into an acceptable Republican. Ostracized in State Street, he was by no means *persona grata* in Virginia. There are few charitable references to him in Jefferson's correspondence. When Madison suddenly offered him, in 1809, the post of Minister to Russia, the fathers of the democratic church were gravely perturbed. "That both the Adams' are monarchists," said John Taylor of Caroline, "I never doubted. Whether monarchists, like pagans, can be converted by benefices, is a problem the solution of which I always feared Mr. Madison would attempt."[18]

But John Quincy Adams was no monarchist. He was a scientific republican, who hoped to advance his country's fortunes in a regular series of rationally planned steps, and who, when at length he became President, ruined what little chances of success he had by actually outlining some such scheme in his First Annual Message. It is typical of the man and of his destiny that he should have dreamed of planned economies long before the time was ripe for them; that he should have taken the American people into his confidence; and that the American people, with a sure instinct, should have hurled him from the seats of power. He himself declared that he had much more confidence in the calm and deliberate judgment of the people than President Monroe had,[19] but one might qualify this statement by adding that he would have had little confidence in the people's judgment, however calm and deliberate, if it did not accord with his own. If to be a Federalist meant distrusting the people and loving strong government, and to be a Republican meant loving the people and distrusting strong government, then John Quincy Adams was always more a Federalist than a Republican. But let us admit that he wore his Federalism, like his independence, with a difference.

That he became, after his labors at Ghent and London were over, one of the greatest of Secretaries of State, has rarely been denied. And here he would not have become great if he had not been gifted with imagination. He longed to put this gift to other uses than those of the public service. It would have been the summit of his ambition, he wrote, "by some great work of literature to have done honor to my age and country, and to have lived in the gratitude of future ages." [20] He tried his hand at poetry—he is one of the very few translators of Horace who has been able to recast that subtle Roman into the likeness of Messrs. Moody and Sankey; at belles lettres; at contemporary history. He confidently believed that his *Report on Weights and Measures* would be his most important literary labor,[21] and the *Report*—a superb example of a gift for generalization working but not lost among the minutiae of scientific research—did, in fact, survive him. But it was not the *Report*, it was his diary [22] which became his monument—his diary which, he thought, if only his intellectual powers had been greater, might have become "next to the Holy Scriptures, the most precious and valuable book ever written by human hands." [23] There was nothing modest about his modesty.

The diary, that vast repository of priceless historical information, has its failings too. Strictly trustworthy as to fact, it is slightly less so when it approaches the interpretation of fact. And when it deals with his fellow Americans, it is not trustworthy at all. It projects us into a scorched and gloomy world where almost everyone is sooner or later engaged in a conspiracy to retard or ruin the career of Mr. Adams. Though it is filled with valuable sketches, and illuminated by flashes of intuition, it has to be read with extreme caution. *Incedo super ignes*—I walk over fires—he wrote at one of the critical moments in his career.[24] Did he realize that the fires, for the most part, shot up from the abyss of his own nature? Perhaps he did. The diary is a testament to his queer, inverted honesty: it proves that at one time or another he successfully misinterpreted almost every character but his own.

For these voluminous pages reveal him with a singular fidelity—his lofty intelligence, his capability, his wide and curious learning, his generous ambitions, his corroding meannesses and more corroding fears. As one reads them one realizes that his spirit was never resigned to the shackles of practical affairs or the mean diet of official routine; that it was always straining at its bonds; that sometimes—not very often, just occasionally—it soared clean away. At such times the appearance was the appearance of a crow or a raven, but the flight was the flight of an eagle.

IV

In 1814, in his forty-eighth year, with most of his career ahead of him, John Quincy Adams had already acquired some experience of European diplomacy. He had not, however, a very diplomatic appearance. He was quite short, rather stout, rather carelessly dressed; he suffered from a rheumy affection of the eyes, so that tears seemed to be perpetually coursing down his cheeks; he had a bald, bold, belligerent head; his mouth was drawn and grim and faintly peevish.[25] One can understand that he might have been, to say the least, somewhat out of place among the luxuries and frivolities of St. Petersburg; one can be equally sure that he was never taken in by them. At Ghent, he was more at home.

Of all his fellow commissioners, John Quincy Adams thought that he most resembled Henry Clay. "There is the same dogmatical, overbearing manner, the same harshness of look and expression, and the same forgetfulness of the courtesies of society in both." [26] The resemblance, it is true, is made to end there, but that it should have been made at all seems extraordinary. What two social *personae* could have been more different? Yet Adams had hit upon the truth. There were times, as at Ghent, when—to use a phrase Clay himself would not have scorned—the chips were down, when the inner Henry Clay revealed himself with startling abruptness. And the inner Clay was quite at variance with the outer one.

Outwardly, Henry Clay was a man born to please, high-tempered and mettlesome, but soothing his way through life with an indolent charm. He was a tall, lanky man, with tow-colored hair, gray-blue eyes, a mouth so wide that he complained that he could never learn to spit, and a long sardonic upper lip.[27] He was a marvelous conversationalist, and would sit by the hour, "his snuff-box ever in his hand," says Harriet Martineau, "discoursing on any one of the great subjects of American policy which we might happen to start." [28] When ladies were not present, his conversations were apt to be more salty.

He was human—too human, perhaps—and the presence of other human beings was a constant necessity to him. He was always attractive to women, and it was inevitable that tales of sexual irregularities should be spread abroad by his opponents: one may believe these political *fabliaux* or not, as one pleases.[29] In this respect, all that emerges from his stay at Ghent is a harmless tale of being rebuffed by a chambermaid, with which he afterwards made them laugh at Washington, and which found its way, oddly enough, into the awful aridity of De Witt Clinton's diary.[30] But that a story even faintly *de sexu* should be found floating, like a shaft of sunshine, among the fustiness of those negotiations is sufficiently astonishing.

Henry Clay carried with him into anything he did a captivating vitality; it was this that made him so much loved by his countrymen, though, for other reasons of a political nature, they did not altogether trust him. Living in an age, and coming from a background, that did not frown upon dissipation, he was not the man to deny himself its pleasures. He would sit up night after night, drinking and gambling—at loo or brag, at old sledge or all-fours. "Isn't it a pity," said a New England lady to Lucretia Clay, "that your husband gambles so much?" "Oh, I don't know," was the tranquil reply, straight from the heart of Kentucky, "he usually wins." [31] As regards his staying powers, he somewhat resembled Charles James Fox, an Englishman of even greater charm and more stupendous appetites—the most riotous nights, the deepest potations, did not interfere with the next day's work. Once when Clay was Speaker of the House, a friend ventured to remonstrate with him after an all-night carousal. "How can you preside over the House today?" "Come and see," said Clay.[32] On at least two occasions at Ghent (there were probably others) the laborious Adams, rising before dawn to begin his day's work, heard a card party breaking up in Clay's chambers: and the careful New Englander makes a note of the time—3.45 and 4.30.[33] To Clay, who took the negotiations just as seriously as Adams did, these were very reasonable hours.

It was ironical that a man who had been as responsible as Clay was for the outbreak of the War of 1812 should have been chosen for the role of peacemaker; and when the news of his appointment was made known in New York, a city much opposed to the war, stocks fell three or four per cent.[34] The merchants and shipowners found it hard to believe that such a man could be up to any good. His motives for accepting were, no doubt, mixed enough: to escape the obloquy that attaches to war-makers when the wars they make prove unsuccessful; to look after Western interests at the conference table; to resign from a Speakership that, in an impotent House of Representatives, must have become tedious and disgusting to a man of his spirit—all these could have been present in his decision. But he was also a patriot, and he may well have put political considerations aside in order to do a service to his country.

Every particle of his curious and attractive composition was, none the less, impregnated with political elements. He was born to make his way through the management of other men; and when he was first elected Speaker, in November 1811, he displayed not only an airy mastery of other people's emotions but also an intuitive grasp of parliamentary law, without which this mastery would have come to nothing.[35] He had, of course, been trained for a lawyer, and, according to Justice Story, he might have attained some eminence at the bar.[36] But he was not deeply versed in anything that required study—and beyond a knowledge of land-suits and a forensic eloquence that brought him fame and profit as a trial lawyer, his legal abilities were probably rather slender.[37]

Impatient and careless in everything but business matters, he looked for higher rewards. His lazy charm was shot through and through with impulsiveness, with aggressiveness; it was weighted with overelaborate courtesies towards anything on two legs which might have a vote; it was shattered with sudden outbursts of towering, irrepressible wrath. No man was more quick or more generous than he in asking for forgiveness after such outbursts; but his friends were perplexed by them. How could a man combine so sweet a nature with so sudden and sharp a tongue, or such easygoing ways with such rages? Albert Gallatin, if anyone, found the answer. "His great fault is," he wrote, "that he is devoured with ambition."[38] It was this that Adams had detected in his behavior at Ghent. Whatever the outer Clay might say or do, the inner Clay wanted but one thing out of life. He thirsted for the Presidency, secretly, persistently, all his life long— and like Tantalus he thirsted in agony and in vain.

He was born in Virginia in 1777, in that low, marshy region between Piedmont and Tidewater known as the Slashes. He got his law training at Richmond under Wythe and Brooke; then he followed his mother and step-father into Kentucky, and settled at Lexington in 1797. Lexington in those days was known as the Athens of the West, though it would have taken a partial eye to discover anything Athenian about it—except that it condoned the institution of slavery. Kentucky was not so far removed in time from the Dark and Bloody Ground of Daniel Boone, and the Athens of the West was never without its gouging affrays, its stabbings, and shootings. Henry Clay duly winged his man, a Federalist who had denounced him as a Jeffersonian demagogue for urging the members of the State Legislature to wear only clothes of home manufacture.[39]

Land was the absorbing topic, land-speculation the very life of that early Kentucky. Lots were briskly sold and resold in paper cities, rising upon the banks of invisible rivers. More cautious purchasers, who were provident enough to examine their land before they bought, were not free from diffi-culties, for there were no official surveys, and the same tract was not in-frequently entered at various times by different purchasers, "so as to be literally shingled over with conflicting claims."[40] Nor was the situation eased by the land-laws, which were, even for land-laws, peculiarly confusing and perverse.

Under these circumstances, it is hardly surprising that most of the society to be found at Lexington should have been of a legal nature; nor that the Kentucky Bar should have been noted for its cleverness. After his marriage to Lucretia Hart in 1799, connecting him more closely with the transplanted Virginians who ruled Kentucky,[41] Clay rose steadily in his profession. But it required something more than a good marriage to succeed in that frontier world—so materialist and so romantic, so candid and so cunning, so utopian, so crass, and above all so egalitarian. One had to be something more than a sharp man or a bold man, or a well-connected man: one had to be acutely sensible, as Henry Clay was, of one's personal myth, and one had to be able to project this myth upon any human situation, however raw. By 1809, when he deserted Kentucky for Washington, he had become the state's favorite citizen. And he had been gathering laurels of another kind as well. He joined the Junto, the Lexington debating society that held its meetings at various taverns: and the marvelous voice, which afterwards thrilled so many Congresses, was first hailed at the "Eagle," the "Sign of the Indian King," and the "Free and Easy."[42]

When he arrived at Ghent, he had already been twice a Senator of the United States and once a Speaker of the House of Representatives. He owned a brick mansion near Lexington, six hundred acres of fertile land, eighteen slaves, and sixty-five horses.[43] He was only thirty-seven years old, and the most famous man west of the Alleghenies. Under his captivating manner there was something of the swagger and hardness of the frontier: something of its simplicity, too. Every night of his life—or every dawn—before he went to bed, Henry Clay recited "Now I Lay Me Down To Sleep." [44]

He was not a statesman and he was never to become one in the full sense of the word. His statesmanship was at best intermittent, and it was constantly giving place to a quality less elevated, perhaps, but fully as interesting. For Clay was, if anything, the archetype of the successful transatlantic politician. Now an archetype cannot be judged by its copies. It does not transmit all its original energies. With all his political shortcomings, and they were many and various, Clay was notably possessed by that vision which Henry Adams has so eloquently described.[45] Show him a barren mountain, and he saw only gold mines and copper mines; show him a forest in whose poisonous shadow men sickened and died, and he filled it with prosperous and happy citizens; show him a snaggy, deceitful river, and he tamed it with wharfs and factories; show him a howling wilderness, and he would instantly translate it into cornfields and meadows. This was the early American vision, which Europeans found so bombastic and repulsive, but which proved, after all, to be somewhere near the truth. He brought this vision with him to Ghent. Here it collided explosively with his purely sectional interests, and with his keen sense of political survival. But as a factor in the negotiation it had at any rate one property that is said to be the property of truth. In the end it prevailed.

V

James A. Bayard and Jonathan Russell were not the equals of the three great men whose characters have just been touched upon. Bayard was a Federalist from Delaware, who had spent eight years in the House of Representatives and nine in the Senate, a substantial and capable man who had refused to follow his party into disaffection and had probably lost its confidence.[46] He had played a decisive part in swinging support from Burr to Jefferson, when the election of 1800 was thrown into the House of Representatives, and though he never approved of Jeffersonian measures, he seems to have been increasingly skeptical as to the efficacy of Federalist nostrums.[47] He was, in brief, a just and moderate man, and even Adams, who mistrusted him at first, declared at last that "the Chevalier has the most perfect control of his temper, the most deliberate coolness . . . I can scarcely express to you how much both he and Mr. Gallatin have risen in my esteem, since we have been here, living together." [48] Jonathan Russell of Rhode Island had been chargé d'affaires at Paris and London, where he had acquitted himself satisfactorily, and was at the moment Minister to Sweden. Though a New Englander, he had "the greatest deference for the opinions of Mr. Clay," [49] but he acted rather a solitary part, rarely joined in the commission's discussions, and had too strong a sense of his personal dignity.

In a famous sentence, Henry Adams has written: "Probably the whole British public service, including Lords and Commons, could not at that day have produced four men competent to deal with Gallatin, John Quincy

Adams, Bayard, and Clay on the ground of American interests." [50] He pays no attention to Russell, perhaps because Russell afterwards traduced his grandfather, John Quincy Adams. But in all justice, he might have added a fifth Englishman to the four whom the whole British public service could probably not have produced, and then placed Russell where he belonged, at the end of the list but on it.

VI

On July 31, the five commissioners moved from the Hotel des Pays Bas on the Place d'Armes to a rented house on the Rue des Champs, known as the Hotel d'Alcantara.[51] Their landlord was a French universalist. He sold millinery, perfumes, and second-hand furniture; and prided himself upon being a fine cook, an admirable judge and purveyor of wines, and an honest man. His name was Lannuyer, and a certain monotony in his deceptions and his cuisine provoked the commissioners into making the inevitable pun. But however weary they might be of their landlord, they had "the satisfaction" —which was short-lived—"of living together in perfect harmony." [52] The house was commodious, and, after all, "It was not so easy to find a contractor who could accommodate himself to five separate and distinct humors." [53]

The humors were certainly distinct; they were also distinctively American. In their vitality and their suppleness, in the competitive methods by which they reached their decisions, in the optimism which was rarely banished even from their darkest hours, in their irritability and their sharpness and their intransigeance, in the unity of their determination and the disunity of their interests—they seemed to body forth, in some fragmentary but effective way, at once the present and the future of the young republic.

CHAPTER TWO

The War Message
of James Madison: 1812

THE forces which decreed that England and America should go to war in 1812, and that five American commissioners should seek for peace in the city of Ghent in 1814, were sufficiently complex, but they have been reduced by a master to a few allusive sentences. It was in the year 1812 that John Adams and Thomas Jefferson opened that famous correspondence which was to soften and finally to annul the misunderstandings of many years. John Adams began it by saying that he was sending by post "two pieces of homespun lately produced in this quarter," by which he is supposed to have referred, with the rather ponderous embarrassment of fatherly pride, to a book of lectures delivered by John Quincy Adams at Harvard College.[1] Of the book itself it would be fair to say that it derived its spirit rather from the rocks than from the flocks of Massachusetts; and, since the book arrived long after the letter, Jefferson was at first taken in. He replied with a brief dissertation upon the homespun of Virginia, and then—for he was truly anxious to renew relations with an old friend and colleague—allowed his pen more scope, taking some liberties with chronology but none with truth.

"A letter from you," he said, "calls up recollections very dear to my mind. It carries me back to the times when, beset with difficulties and dangers, we were fellow laborers in the same cause, struggling for what is most valuable to man, his right of self-government. Laboring always at the same oar, with some wave ever ahead, threatening to overwhelm us, and yet passing harmlessly under our bark, we knew not how we rode through the storm with heart and hand and made a happy port. Still we did not expect to be without

15

rubs and difficulties; and we have had them. First the detention of the western posts, then the coalition of Pilnitz, outlawing our commerce with France, and the British enforcement of the outlawry. In your day, French depredations; in mine, English, and the Berlin and Milan decrees; now the English orders of council, and the piracies they authorize. When these shall be over, it will be the impressment of seamen or something else; and so we have gone on, and so we shall go on puzzled and prospering beyond example in the history of man. . . . As for France and England, with all their preeminence in science, the one is a den of robbers, the other of pirates." [2]

The Napoleonic demon had so disturbed and transformed world relations, and with such haste, that Jefferson's reference to the detention of the western posts was a reference to ancient history. Who cared to remember, in the year 1812, the negotiations of 1791-2, when the British had insisted upon clinging to the frontier posts in open violation of the treaty of 1783, which called for an immediate withdrawal from them? Yet here indeed, and not too obscurely, lay one of the main causes of the War of 1812, for in refusing to withdraw, the British had revealed for the first time what was to develop into a persistent unwillingness to recognize all the implications of American independence.

By the "coalition of Pilnitz," Jefferson evidently referred to the First Coalition against France of 1792-7. When this coalition was instituted, Napoleon was still a lieutenant of infantry, obscure and starless, and dedicated, ironically enough, to the principles of Jean Jacques Rousseau; and he had yet to attain the rank of brigadier—he was more than two years away from the bridge of Lodi—when Great Britain issued her Order-in-Council of November 6, 1793, denying Americans even the direct trade between their own ports and the French islands, and bringing the United States to the verge of hostilities. [3] Thus, as Jefferson indicates, almost from the day of its birth the American republic had been in danger of war. The "rubs and difficulties" existed long before the outbreak of the Napoleonic Wars; they could be attributed directly to the agonies, the encroachments, and the necessities of Europe. And to western Europe's way of thinking, the young republic, clinging so precariously to the fringes of Christendom, was, for all its superb and dangerous pretensions, little more than a European appendage. Great Britain was particularly apt to indulge in this misapprehension, to which the outbreak of the Napoleonic Wars in May 1803 gave an unfortunate but perhaps an inevitable emphasis.

The Napoleonic Wars may justly be said to have constituted, at least in the Thucydidean sense, [4] a world war. Certainly on June 18, 1812, when the Congress of the United States passed a declaration of war against Great Britain, no one could doubt that this gloomy title was deserved. The lofty. shadow, so long impending, so often dismissed by an exercise of intelligence which we cannot but admire and by a passivity in the face of insult and outrage which some have found ignoble, had at last reached out to the smallest of the world's civilized capitals. It was now decreed that the war should extend to the Mississippi. Two days before, by suspending their

Orders-in-Council and thus yielding to the American principle of peaceful coercion, the British Commons had declared this extension to be an unnecessary one. Six days later, the armies of Napoleon crossed the Niemen, and began a march that was to end in the embers of Moscow. Thus, the appearance of helplessness before a blind impulse unworthy of the name of destiny had now established itself: it is one of the characteristics of world wars, perhaps one of the most misleading, as it is also one of the most difficult to analyze or even to comprehend.

The message of President Madison, which he sent to Congress on June 1, 1812, and in which he recommended to the consideration of that body the "solemn question" of peace or war, is full of interest.[5] It presented two points of view which in a domestic sense were complementary and in an international one were wildly contradictory. Considering the circumstances under which it was written, and the man who wrote it, this is not altogether surprising.

I

It is possible that James Madison, the philosopher of the Constitution, might not have suffered in reputation if he had retired from the world at the end of his constitutional labors. He might then have brought to some even more fruitful harvest those gifts which still enchant us in his contributions to *The Federalist:* his reasonableness; his objectiveness; his remarkable gift for treading a path, unscathed, between the clash of passionate extremes; the deftness and the learning with which he holds the balance between the principles of good government upon the one hand and the selfishness of mankind upon the other. Might he not even have produced, amidst the quiet of his Virginia estates and in the fullness of time, what we still lack—a rationale of Jeffersonian political theory?

The Madison who contributed to *The Federalist,* however, was not a Jeffersonian, and the Madison who subsequently became a Jeffersonian was hampered rather than assisted by the gifts that so distinguished him as a contributor to *The Federalist.* It is still difficult to understand by what convulsion the former was turned into the latter. Was it merely a generous reaction to the stimulus of Thomas Jefferson? To listen to his enemies, and not least the enemies within his own party, one might suppose that this convulsion was nothing less than a reversal of the energies of nature: the moth had developed into a chrysalis, the bird into an egg. Some even ventured to suggest, in their rage, that the egg was addled. The truth, however, was somewhat less monstrous. It seems that, within the limits imposed by a studious and reflective temperament, James Madison had a craving for the life of action. The more one examines his career, the more it seems to belie the notion, current in his time and sometimes accepted in ours, that he was a mere "creature of the closet," [6] a student who shrank from the dust of the marketplace, from the harshness and acrimony of early American debate.

Certainly during the nationalist period of his career, which culminated in his great efforts at the Constitutional Convention and in his *Federalist* writings, and which made him one of the most distinguished as he was one of the youngest of the Founding Fathers, he showed no distaste for the give and take of common life. And in his second or particularist period, beginning with the second session of the First Congress and ending with the Virginia Resolutions of 1789, he seemed to flourish most, in Congress or out of it, in an atmosphere of danger. Once a Federalist, a moderate believer in strong central government, he became a leader of the Republican opposition, developed in all its strictness the compact theory of the Constitution, and declared that the Federalist Executive, by an arbitrary seizure of power, was threatening to transform the republican system of the United States into "an absolute, or, at best, a mixed monarchy." In a season of retirement, and in protest against the sinister encroachments of the Alien and Sedition Acts,[7] he drafted the Virginia Resolutions, the most debatable of his utterances, in which, in the urgency of his protest, he seemed to tear down the fabric he had sought to perfect in his *Federalist* writings.[8] It was the turning point in his career.

For when the northern states called these resolutions into question as being secessionist and subversive,[9] Madison replied [10] that on the contrary they were merely hypothetical, intended to produce reflection and not to promote action. And years later, when the apostles of Nullification quoted these resolutions as a precedent for their dangerous manifestoes, the old man, in his extremity, took refuge in the interpretation of a single word.[11] Does not this indicate an innate shiftiness, an unwillingness to subject his thought to the test of action, or, conversely, a willingness to push his conclusions up to but not beyond the point where they actually became logical? Perhaps it does; Madison was not always the most straightforward of men. But he might well have maintained that logic is not the only resource of the statesman; that it is frequently of no use at all; that when the political waters threaten to close over one's head, an aptitude for *a priori* reasoning becomes but a feeble safety-line. These arguments might not have satisfied his Federalist enemies in 1789; and they would have been totally unacceptable to the Nullifiers in 1832. He might, however, have gone even further. He might have said that his writings in *The Federalist* and his Virginia Resolutions were, in either case, a particular response to a special set of circumstances. Each was intended to serve a supremely practical end, and each was successful. Was not the Constitution ratified? And did not the Virginia Resolutions (with the Kentucky Resolutions, which Jefferson had drafted in more fiery language) help to dig the grave of the Federalist party, with the incidental effect of bringing James Madison into the State Department and the Presidency? It is surely foolish to abide by one's reasoning, at the probable cost of one's political life, when that reasoning has done its work.

In any event, in his period of executive power, from 1800 to 1816, when he was either the agent of Jefferson's will or himself the President, he showed a diminishing taste for liberal expedients. He seemed rather to return somewhat to the beliefs he had once held, and to relish, if not actively to promote, the increase of executive power. This was perhaps inevitable. It was the effect of a change from opposition to incumbency. Moreover the Republican-Federalist conflict, in which James Madison, as leader of the Republican Opposition in Congress, had played such a leading part, was not merely a conflict of philosophies or prejudices; it was a battle between kinds of property. On the one side were the merchants and investors, on the other the agrarians. And since agrarian property is generally debt-ridden property, it was the constant endeavor of the Republicans to prevent the general government from becoming what John Taylor of Caroline called a government of "paper and patronage"—to prevent it, that is to say, from falling into the hands of those whose business it was to create and to manipulate debt. Opposition of this kind is likely to be rigorous and extreme. Hence the Republicans' call for economy and a weak executive; hence their hatred of standing armies and efficient navies; hence their declaration that sovereignty was not, in fact, the attribute of an entity called "the nation" (to some extreme Republicans the word "nation" was anathema), but was delegated to the central government by the individual states. It followed necessarily that what had been delegated could also be withdrawn. But once this debtor interest came into power, it discovered that it could not turn itself into a creditor interest without performing such a revolution as would end in the extinction of credit itself. Nor did it wish to do so. It was not revolutionary. It was strongly conscious of the rights of property. Its tendency, therefore, was to make the best bargain that it could with its adversaries: to pare their claws, but not to decapitate or disembowel them; to reduce them to political impotence, to sap their economic strength, but not to emasculate them economically. It could not make such a bargain, of course, without some self-flagellation; and its cries of pain as it trod the path just abandoned by its enemies could be heard in the shrill accents of John Randolph of Roanoke and the solemn periods of John Taylor of Caroline. Its adversaries on the other hand proceeded to borrow when in opposition the language they had so decried when in power; and it was the Federalists who now began to canvass disunion, and to show an extreme solicitude for the sovereignty of the individual states.

The effect of all this upon James Madison was to turn him back to the beliefs of earlier days. He did not go all the way. He continued to profess a belief in state sovereignty and strict construction; but he managed, at the same time, to entertain a certain warmth towards the principles of strong central government. This was the beginning of that philosophical *dédoublement* which makes the perusal of some of his later writings so baffling an enterprise. At the time of his accession to the Presidency, it was barely perceptible; but a hint or two had been enough. The doctrinaire radicals of his own party, the Old Republicans, had already turned upon him in wrath, and tried to elevate Colonel James Monroe, who, however, speedily deserted them when this particular plan fell through. These men were so rigid that even Jefferson himself was scarcely a Jeffersonian to them; but they did not impugn, or rarely impugned, the purity of Jefferson's motives, and they hoped to reform him in time. He resembled one of those local saints whose images a pious peasantry, in times of murrain or pestilence or drought, take from their shrines and flog unmercifully: the blows are not light but they are loving, and they testify in a most dramatic way to a fundamental faith in the efficacy of the smitten saint. But Madison they considered incorrigible. While they compiled a list of his Federalist leanings, they also accused him, with an iron inconsistency, of sins they had committed themselves, among them the sin of Francophilia, which they had demoted from a virtue to a vice, with a singular speed and an even more singular forgetfulness. Madison held on his course, shaken but not intimidated; and whatever one's opinion of his political compromises may be, one has to applaud his political courage. Dangers crowded thick upon the man who succeeded Thomas Jefferson. At home, sullen or vituperative or treacherous enemies and tepid friendships; abroad, the terrible figure of Napoleon Bonaparte and the respectable savagery of the British Cabinet. The principle of peaceful coercion, upon which the Republicans had founded their dealings with the French and British, was about to collapse. Disunion and war, singly or together, were the calculable consequences. It is not surprising that he should have appeared aged and careworn on the day of his inauguration; that he should have trembled as he read his inaugural address: or that the address itself should have been so full of careful qualifications as to mean almost nothing at all.¹²

Whether the principle of peaceful coercion was not, under the circumstances, the best that could be found; or whether James Madison, among the available candidates, was not the best choice for President—these are nice questions. It is easy to answer them in the negative, and extremely difficult to justify the answer. Madison was not equal to the conduct of a war, but who among the Republicans could have taken his place? As for the Federalists, they were prepared to subside, with a sign or a snarl, into the spreading arms of England: a polyp would have proffered a more congenial embrace.

II

"Jemmy Madison—oh, poor Jemmy," Washington Irving wrote in 1812, "he is but a withered little applejohn," ¹³ and this description, which was essentially political, presents the fallacy of mingling political considerations with physical appearances. Madison has suffered in history from the fact that, for all his superior talents, he was not a superior administrator, not a born leader of men, and not equipped with a physical presence that might persuade men to suppose that he could ever, under any circumstances, either administer or lead. He was small, neat, and precise: he was dressed invariably in black, with buckles at the knees of his breeches, silk stockings, and buckled shoes. His hair was powdered and tied at the back. In the company of people whom he did not know or did not like, he was mute, cold, and grave. His appearance, therefore, was not reassuring: it suggested a nature at once retiring, meager, and weak.

But he was not a weak man: he was persistent rather than stubborn. Political enemies and presuming diplomats discovered, too late, that he was most dangerous when he was most demure. And if his public appearance belied his origin and background (for the gentlemen of Virginia affected a carelessness in dress and a cordiality towards the outer world) in private he was a famous conversationalist, full of anecdote, "sometimes of a loose description," but more often dealing with history or politics.[14] He was happily married to the most handsome, the kindest, the most comfortable of women, and their hospitality was abundant.[15] It was from the outer world only that he concealed himself; but the judgment of the outer world prevailed, especially since it was useful to his enemies, and continued to prevail long after it had outlived its usefulness.

He was not afraid of making up his own mind. Yet what kind of mind was it that was then made up? When he recommended to Congress the consideration of the "solemn question" of peace or war with Great Britain, the answer he expected was an answer that ruined the work of years. His deepest predilections were for peace. To the best of his ability he had pursued a policy of commercial restriction as being the only antidote to war. In the pursuit of this honorable policy, he had allowed himself to be deceived by Napoleon in a manner so blatantly dishonorable as to make it quite impossible that he should have been taken in. Perhaps, by playing Napoleon's game and pretending that American commerce had suddenly and strangely been freed from the robberies of France, he had allowed himself to be seduced by the idea of a diplomatic triumph. But a diplomatic triumph that has no reference to the actual events it is supposed to modify or change is never triumphant and is not diplomacy. To a man of Madison's intelligence this must have been obvious from the beginning; nor could he have hidden from himself, as he certainly did not from his contemporaries, the fact that when at length he assumed a warlike posture, its dignity was in inverse proportion to the amount of political pressure which forced him to assume it. He sincerely hoped, none the less, that this posture, once assumed, would alarm Great Britain into ceasing her provocations, and would thus make a war unnecessary. To his eternal credit, it must be allowed that he very nearly succeeded.

III

The so-called War Message, when at length it was sent to Congress on June 1, 1812, may not rank high in polemical literature, but it was, as to four fifths of its contents, a dignified and forcible presentation of the American case against Great Britain. It did not go back beyond the year 1803. It omitted "unrepaired wrongs of inferior magnitude," though these might have thronged its pages. It was content to offer, under five heads, a series of major British acts hostile to the United States as an independent and neutral nation.

> "British cruisers," the President began, "have been in the continued practice of violating the American flag on the great highway of nations, and of carrying off persons sailing under it, not in the exercise of a belligerent right founded on the law

of nations against an enemy, but of a municipal prerogative over British subjects. British jurisdiction is thus extended to neutral vessels in a situation where no laws can operate but the law of nations and the law of the country to which the vessels belong. . . . The practice, hence, is so far from affecting British subjects alone that, under the pretext of searching for these, thousands of American citizens, under the safeguard of public law and of their national flag, have been torn from their country and from everything dear to them; have been dragged on board ships of war of a foreign nation and exposed, under the severity of their discipline, to be exiled to the most distant and deadly climes, to risk their lives in the battles of their oppressors, and to be the melancholy instruments of taking away those of their own brethren."

It may well be argued that, in continuing with the practice of impressing American seamen after the battle of Trafalgar had made her mistress of the seas, Great Britain had committed not only a crime, which was bad, but an error, which was worse. It is surely impolitic to goad with insults a country with whom it is increasingly to one's interest to stay at peace. It is sufficient to say that had Madison been able to allude, not to "thousands" of impressed Americans, but only to one, he would have had, then and there, his *casus belli*. Great Britain, however, had received no warning that America intended to make war on such a ground; and, as one can see from Jefferson's letter to Adams, impressment, though bitterly resented, had up to this point been officially considered as irrelevant to the main issues. It would not have been casuistical in the British had they maintained that, in putting impressment in its rightful place at the head of his list of grievances, Madison had not strengthened his argument but weakened it.

His second complaint was open to the same objection. He went on to say that British cruisers, not content with enforcing their country's muncipal law upon an international highway, had violated the rights and peace of the coasts of America. "They hover over and harass our entering and departing commerce. To the most insulting pretensions they have added the most lawless proceedings in our very harbors, and have wantonly spilt American blood within the sanctuary of our territorial jurisdiction." This was irresistibly true: but this, too, strange as it may seem, had never before been advanced as a ground for war.[16]

The President then presented a third grievance which, upon any consideration, was unexceptionable. "Under pretended blockades, without the presence of an adequate force and sometimes without the practicability of applying one, our commerce has been plundered in every sea, the great staples of our country have been cut off from their legitimate interests." To make matters worse, the British had had the hypocrisy to declare "as the true definition of a legal blockade 'that particular ports must be actually invested and previous warning given to vessels bound to them not to enter.' "

Madison had now reached the heart of the matter. His fourth grievance referred to a gross extension of this system of pretended or "paper" block-ades. "Not content with these occasional expedients for laying waste our neutral trade, the cabinets of Britain resorted at length to the sweeping system of blockades, under the name of orders in council, which has been molded and managed as might best suit its political views, its commercial jealousies, or the avidity of British cruisers." It was against the unflattering pretensions of these Orders-in-Council, which interdicted the coasts of Europe to American commerce and enforced the interdiction outside the harbor of New York, that Jefferson and Madison had aimed their policy of peaceful coercion. The President now permitted himself a display of bad temper not inappropriate to the complex system of robbery, whose ramifications he proceeded to summarize:

> "It has become, indeed, sufficiently certain that the commerce of the United States is to be sacrificed, not as interfering with the belligerent rights of Great Britain; not as supplying the wants of her enemies, which she herself supplies; but as interfering with the monopoly which she covets for her own commerce and navigation. She carries on a war against the lawful commerce of a friend that she may carry on a commerce with an enemy—a commerce polluted by the forgeries and perjuries which are for the most part the only passports by which it can succeed."

Had the message ended at this point, it would have represented the legitimate complaint of a pacific, unmilitary nation which was being forced into war against its own will because of a gross violation of its neutral rights. Although it is not customary for a people against whom a declaration of war is being urged to read with any sympathy the documents that urge the declaration, it is hard to believe that this part of Mr. Madison's message, when at length it was published in England, was not read without some feelings of shame.

IV

How comfortably, none the less, might such feelings have been put to sleep by the President's recital of his fifth grievance.

> "In reviewing the conduct of Great Britain towards the United States *our attention is necessarily drawn to the warfare just renewed by the savages on one of our extensive frontiers*—a warfare which is known to spare neither age nor sex and to be distinguished by features particularly shocking to humanity. It is difficult to account for the activity and combinations which have for some time been developing themselves among tribes in constant intercourse with British traders and garrisons without connecting their hostility with that influence and without recollecting the authenticated examples of such interpositions heretofore furnished by the officers and agents of that government."

In these words, Mr. Madison connected the British with that singular chain of events which led to the battle of Tippecanoe. The diffidence of his language suggests the posturing of a man who is about to take a dive into very dangerous waters; and, indeed, the addition of the fifth grievance was not very wise or very helpful. For though the British record in their dealings with the Indians was an unsavory one—though there was nothing fanciful in the Western belief that they would not hesitate to loose upon the frontier all the horrors and miseries of an Indian war;[17] though their innocence in this particular instance was the innocence of people who were not yet ready to be guilty—it is only just to admit that, if they had had their way, there would have been no battle of Tippecanoe at all.

CHAPTER THREE

Tippecanoe:

1811

IN THE town of Vincennes, in the Territory of Indiana, lived a very respectable personage called John Badollet. Badollet was a Republican of the old school, who spent much of his time in regretting the past, and more of it in hating William Henry Harrison, the governor of the Territory. Some of his correspondence on this subject has survived, and it is to be recommended as much to connoisseurs of invective as to students of the middle years of our ninth President.[1]

Like everyone else in Indiana, Badollet was haunted day and night by the thought of a general Indian uprising; and after the battle of Tippecanoe had been fought on November 7, 1811, his fears, like those of everyone else, became acute. He only disagreed with the majority as to the reason for them. For whereas most Indianians were convinced that British intrigues were at the bottom of the whole thing, Mr. Badollet—"& I am not the only one here," he wrote, "some of the most thinking ancient inhabitants are asserting the same"—inclined to the belief that the Americans and not the British were to blame. This belief was reinforced by the fact that it did not accord with the views of Governor Harrison, whom Mr. Badollet detested, not merely on personal grounds, but because the governor had once tried to introduce into Indiana a modified form of slavery.[2]

"The true cause of the Indian discontents," Badollet wrote in another letter, "was the treaty." [3] This opinion, which would have agitated the West in 1812 almost as much as did the Indians themselves, is generally accepted today: though what interests us today is not simply the cause of the Indian discontents, but the true cause of the treaty.

25

I

The Treaty of Fort Wayne of September 30, 1809,[4] had extinguished the Indian title to nearly three million acres of valuable hunting grounds, and had thrust the Territory nearly a hundred miles up both sides of the Wabash valley. It was concerted between Governor Harrison, on the one hand, and the Miamis, Eel Rivers, Delawares, Pottawatomies and Kickapoos on the other; people who had been decimated and debauched by their contact with Anglo-American civilization, and whom the governor himself had described as "the most depraved wretches upon earth." [5]

A treaty of this kind can be described as the simple product of a land-hunger, though its simplicity, in this instance, was somewhat complicated by the personal ambitions of Governor Harrison. That Harrison was anxious to restore the reputation he had lost as a promoter of slavery admits of no doubt; and it is equally true that he hoped for military employment in the event of a war with Great Britain. An easy triumph over the Indians would be the most likely way of accomplishing both these objectives.[6] Harrison therefore planned a large preliminary purchase of Indian lands, which should gratify all the parties in the Territory, with two exceptions—"the most thinking ancient inhabitants," whose scruples he could afford to disregard, and the Indians, whom he proposed to destroy. But Harrison was also the agent of the United States government, which he was obliged to consult in advance and which had given its approval to the treaty.[7] The government's language was so cautious as to suggest an uneasy mind. James Madison, who had just become President, disliked the idea of being drawn into an Indian war. But Mr. Madison was in no position to disapprove a land purchase, for he was the inheritor of an Indian policy that was beyond alteration and that he was bound to abet.

II

No candid man doubts the benevolence of Thomas Jefferson; and if in Jefferson's attitude towards the Indians there was a curious intermingling of benevolence and fraud, that was due to the inherent impracticability of any transaction between the Indian and the frontier. The Indian had come to terms with his environment, and proposed to remain so forever; the frontier's very existence depended upon modifying its environment, as quickly as possible and by any means that came to hand. Land was at once its luxury and its necessity. There was too much land: it gobbled and abandoned it like a glutton; and yet it could not have too much. Land cession, therefore, was the basis of Jefferson's policy; land cession in terms of *quid pro quo*, that "fair equivalent" so necessary to European diplomats when they executed a treaty, but so meaningless when it entered into an arrangement between men whose minds were plunged deep in Yesterday and men whose minds, however crudely, represented the vast complexities and aspirations of Tomorrow. Jefferson's mind, to be sure, was anything but crude; yet Jefferson in 1803, in the same month and almost on the same day, could write in a very different strain to William Henry Harrison, whose morals were commonplace, and to Benjamin Hawkins who, as agent to the Creek Indians, dispensed a mild, loving, and beneficent influence over an immense territory in middle and lower Georgia, Alabama, and Mississippi.

To Harrison he wrote: "To promote this disposition to exchange lands which they have to spare and we want, for necessaries which we have to spare and they want, we shall push our trading houses, and be glad to see the good and influential individuals among them in debt; because we observe that when these debts get beyond what the individuals can pay, they become willing to lop them off by a cession of lands." But to Hawkins he wrote: "The promotion of agriculture, therefore, and household manufacture, are essential in their preservation, and I am disposed to encourage and aid it liberally. This will enable them to live on much smaller portions of land. . . . While they are learning to do better on less land, our increasing numbers will be calling for more land, and thus a coincidence of interests will be produced between those who have lands to spare, and want other necessaries, and those who have such necessaries to spare and want lands." Did he really believe that the general government could so control the appetites of the frontier? Had he not once confessed that he could not recollect in all the animal kingdom a single species but man which is eternally and systematically engaged in the destruction of its own species? [8] "The wisdom of the animal," he went on, "which amputates and abandons to the hunter those parts for which he is pursued should be theirs, with this difference, that the former sacrifices what is useful, the latter what is not. In truth, the ultimate point of rest & happiness for them is to let our settlements and theirs meet and blend together, to intermix, and to become one people. Incorporating themselves with us as citizens of the U.S., this is what the natural progress of things will of course bring on. . . ." [9] Between the Indian who is forced to "lop off" his debts by a cession of lands, and the Indian likened to the legendary badger who castrates himself in order to escape the fury of his hunters, there was little to choose. The metaphor was as cruel as the simile. Harrison, however, would have read the letter to Hawkins no more happily than Hawkins would have read the letter to Harrison. To plunge a trustee into debt in order to induce him to betray his trust would have seemed to Hawkins a nefarious business; to incorporate the red man with the white man as a citizen of the United States would have seemed to Harrison abysmal nonsense. The two letters indicate that Jefferson's Indian policy was one vast equivocation, which only the underlying passion for land could reduce to a plain form.

III

Tecumseh, or Tecumthe, was a great Shawnee warrior who had lived since 1808 among the Kickapoos and the Pottawatomies, upon lands ceded to the Territory by the Treaty of 1809. This treaty, therefore, gave a renewed impulse to the great project of an Indian confederacy which had long been haunting his extraordinary mind. To form a union of every Indian tribe from Canada to Florida; to abase the chiefs and to raise the warriors; to invest the ownership of all land, and the right to decide all questions of wars and of treaties, in a general congress of Indian representatives—such were the dreams of Tecumseh, and such, in a less hasty world, might have been his achievements. But the world *was* hasty, it *was* dynamic; it could not have endured the enforcement of static principles, of immutable ways of life, or the sight of unanimous anarchies thinly inhabiting vast spaces of immensely fertile land. It was only as a dreamer that Tecumseh was ahead of his times; but the dreamer was also a thinker and a man of action—"one of those uncommon geniuses," said Harrison, in a moment of genial expansion, "which spring up occasionally to produce revolutions and overturn the established order of things." [10] Yet Tecumseh's reasons for opposing a piecemeal cession like the cession of Fort Wayne were by no means revolutionary ones. Had not the government of the United States, at the making of the Treaty of Greenville in 1795, negotiated with all the tribes assembled, and had it not then guaranteed to all the tribes together the title to unceded land? It was useless to cite precedents against Tecumseh, for, except for the Treaty of Greenville, there were no good precedents to cite: and the Treaty of Greenville was clearly on his side.[11]

How far the British had entered into his schemes will never be determined; it is certain that he depended upon them for more than sympathy, that he sought advice and assistance and obtained supplies of arms and clothing from British officials in Canada, and that the British officials in Canada attempted to dissuade him from any warlike action until or unless their own country should be at war with the United States. After the Treaty of 1809, it was clear that he might not be dissuaded much longer; but then it was not Harrison's intention that he should be.

The Wyandots or Hurons, first in dignity among the tribes of the Territory, now joined themselves to his league. Reports of Indian unrest came in from all sides—from Sandusky, from Detroit, from St. Louis. Tecumseh and his brother, who was known as the Prophet, had settled down with their followers at the junction of the Tippecanoe and the Wabash, where they cultivated their fields and abstained from whisky in a manner that would have warmed the heart of Jefferson. But in 1810 the Prophet's Town, as it was called, seemed, for all its peaceful pretensions, to be the center of intrigue. Here the religious exercises, the frenzied prayers, the morbid prophecies of Tecumseh's brother were mingled with the more statesmanlike utterances of Tecumseh himself, who was demanding nothing less than a recession of the lands ceded at Fort Wayne.

In August, Harrison summoned Tecumseh to Vincennes, and Tecumseh arrived on the 12th. In a notable speech delivered to an audience of armed men, Indian and white, Tecumseh declared that he would not himself make war, but that he would resist by force any attempt to possess the ceded lands. But let the United States give up the purchase, let them promise never again to buy lands except with the consent of all the tribes, and he would become their ally in any war against Great Britain.[12] Tecumseh was a great man, and the vision of great men is often so clear as to be innocent; but in playing off the Americans against the British for a stake of three million acres, Tecumseh showed more innocence than is customary even with very great men.

During the winter, there was peace on the Wabash. The Secretary of War wrote to Harrison in November, telling him to refrain from occupying his new purchase, but in language of such fatal inexactitude as to leave to Harrison the final choice of peace or war.[13] The measure of the Secretary's good will may be taken by the fact that he suggested the imprisonment of "this conspicuous personage and his brother" as a means of securing their good behavior. But in truth the government's writ no longer ran in the Territory. From February to June of 1811,[14] rumors of British agitators and tales of stolen horses and of hostile "talks" flew abroad; they circled the Territory and settled upon the Prophet's Town at Tippecanoe Creek. On June 24, Harrison again wrote [15] to Tecumseh. He understood, he said, that the warrior and his brother proposed to murder him. On July 27, with three hundred men, Tecumseh stalked into Vincennes, throwing the town and the governor into an agony of fear.

With a candor that has been practised with success only by uncandid persons, and then only in a world where candor is assumed to be something else, Tecumseh explained to Harrison exactly what he proposed to do. He was going south to cement his confederacy, which was to be a peaceful union of the Indians of the north and the south; when he returned he would go to see the President; and in the meantime, he trusted that his Indians would be left in the undisturbed possession of their hunting grounds. And south he went, within two days, into scenes where he can hardly be followed in fact and not at all in imagination—where, amongst magical songs and dances and the gyrations of extraordinary prophets pronouncing, as they whirled, a doom upon all who refused aid, his figure can be vaguely discerned, tall, lean, magnificent, impassive.[16] Did he hope to impose upon these intoxicating scenes a semblance of order and of intelligence; or had he become part of the intoxication himself? Whatever the answer, he was already a doomed man. He was not to realize his dream of an Indian confederacy. A very different fate was reserved for him. When the War of 1812 broke out, he joined the British and was given the empty title of brigadier general. He distinguished himself in several battles; but the British had promised that they would never yield an inch of their own soil, and when they began to do so, he knew that he was a ruined man. He had fallen into the grip of two forces, an empire and a frontier, neither of which was particularly distinguished for mercy, and both of which were destined to compose their differences by other methods than Indian wars. He died at the Battle of the Thames on October 5, 1813, covering the retreat of Procter's army, for which he had nothing but distrust and contempt. He no longer wanted to live, and he died in the only way that seemed to him appropriate. His epitaph, *aere perennius*, may well be contained in these words, at once compassionate, fatalistic, and biased: "The ruin of these tribes began from the day when Europeans landed on their shores; it has proceeded ever since, and we are now witnessing its completion. They seem to have been placed by Providence amid the riches of the New World only to enjoy them for a season; they were merely to wait till others came." [17]

IV

Tecumseh had scarcely departed before Harrison began his preparations to strike. According to his lights, which were also those of a majority of Indianians, he had no other choice. Tecumseh had swallowed the bait; he had declared himself hostile to an occupation of the purchase; he must be crushed now, in his absence, if he were to be crushed at all. Instructions from the government dated July 17 and July 20 [18] proved to be contradictory; the former seemed to palliate a war; the latter was emphatically for peace, but announced that Colonel Boyd and the Fourth Regiment of U.S. Infantry were descending the Ohio to come to Harrison's aid. When the regiment arrived, early in September, the whole army of perhaps nine hundred regulars and volunteers was dispatched up the river to a point about sixty-five miles above Vincennes and well within the boundaries of the new purchase. On October 6 Harrison joined this force. On October 12 he received a letter from Secretary Eustis,[19] the contents of which, since it has been lost, may be deduced only from Harrison's reply of October 13: "The powers given me in your last letter . . . call for measures of a more energetic kind." [20] And so, on October 28, its numbers having been increased to at least a thousand effectives, the army began its march.

Tecumseh had instructed his brother, the Prophet, to make no hostile move; and the Prophet had done his best to obey.[21] But he did not know of Harrison's whereabouts after October 28, and could not therefore intercept him with messengers. Harrison himself, perhaps, as his army moved up the west bank of the Wabash, over the meditative levels of a great prairie, may have had leisure to think upon the events of the past two years. We know that on November 6, when at last he came within sight of the Prophet's Town, he had an attack of conscience, and ordered a halt.[22] Conscience had never been listed among the impedimenta useful for an Indian campaign, and the representations of his officers were so vehement that the governor, unwillingly, consented to move forward again. He had proceeded for about four hundred yards when he was met by three Indians, messengers from the Prophet, with words of peace.[23] Again his conscience assailed him; again he called a halt; again he was overruled; and, agreeing only to attend a conference with the Prophet in the morning, he permitted his army to resume its irresolute advance. It was almost evening. The fears of the Indians, "already excited by the appearance of that formidable military force, were increased greatly by witnessing their corn field opened, crossed and trampled by the light horse and mounted Riflemen." [24] The place chosen for an encampment was a triangular bench of high land, perhaps a mile to the northwest of the town. Where it fronted the Indians, it rose to a height of ten feet above a marshy prairie; in the rear it dropped twenty feet into an overgrown brook. Whatever its virtues as a camping ground may have been, no spot was better suited to an Indian attack. But only a line of sentinels, drawn about the campfires, protected the soldiers as they slept in their tents that night; for want of axes (so Harrison said) there was neither palisade nor entrenchment.[25]

About the battle that was fought by firelight at Tippecanoe Creek nothing is certain, neither the hour of attack nor the number of attackers. Harrison had just left his tent, at four or four thirty or five on the morning of November 7, and was about to summon his men to arms, as was his habit when on the march, when a sentry fired a shot. Then the Indians, with a yell, came swarming up from the willows and brushwood that choked the brook, and broke into the camp at its farthest angle. As the men stumbled from their tents, they were shot down by the light of the campfires; but the lines were reformed at the point where they had been broken, and the battle became general. And so it went on for about two hours. At last, in broad daylight, the Indians were driven back into the swamp and gave up the contest, leaving thirty-eight corpses on the field. The American casualties numbered one hundred and eighty-eight, of whom sixty-three were dead or dying.[26] Such was the battle that broke Tecumseh's confederacy in 1811; that has been called the first blow in the War of 1812; and that sent Harrison to the White House some thirty years later, where he expired almost immediately from a surfeit of office-seekers.

When the army returned to Vincennes on November 18, having reduced the Prophet's Town to ashes, Harrison was generally hailed as the hero of the West. From the legislatures of Kentucky, Indiana, and Illinois, expressions of praise and delight poured in. There were some dissidents. The Federalists of Kentucky blamed the death of Major J. H. Daveiss, commander of the volunteer dragoons, upon the incapacity of Harrison;[27] but since Harrison was a Republican and Daveiss a Federalist who had been dismissed from his office of United States District Attorney for Kentucky by Thomas Jefferson, owing to a misunderstanding about the prosecution of Aaron Burr, the military value of such criticisms must be open to some doubt. The battle was canvassed in the press and in private,[28] and not always to Harrison's advantage. But, on the whole, it must be admitted that the seeds planted at the Treaty of Fort Wayne had produced a sufficient harvest at the battle of Tippecanoe Creek.

The Prophet crept back to the ruins of his town, Tecumseh returned from the south, but the peace that Harrison so confidently asserted would not be broken, on the premise that the Indians in all their relations with the white man had never before been so thoroughly defeated,[29] lasted only until April 1812. Then a series of scattered murders culminated in the assassination of the seven members of the Herriman family, within five miles of Vincennes. It was the Indians' revenge, wrote Badollet, "for the inhuman burning of the prophet's town. The scattered settlements fall back, a few forts are formed & the country hitherto flourishing is fast returning to a state of wilderness." [80] Harrison, in his report of May 6,[31] confirms the statements of Badollet. "Most of the citizens of this country," he wrote, "have abandoned their farms, and taken refuge in such temporary forts as they have been able to construct." It was now convenient—it was indeed necessary—for the inhabitants of the Territory, while they echoed the predictions of the commandant at Fort Wayne [32] that an Indian war must be expected, to ascribe to British plots what could more directly be ascribed to their own compulsions. From the Treaty of Fort Wayne, which they had so generally applauded, the chain of cause and effect led straight to the murder of the Herrimans and the terror of the countryside. Tecumseh himself, appearing at a grand council at Massassinway on the Wabash, looked not so much at the facts as at the harsh poetry that had given to these facts their rhythm and their inevitability. He said that his intentions were still peaceful, and that the murders had been committed by Pottawatomies not under his control—the same people whose "pretended chiefs" had been "in the habit of selling lands to the white people that did not belong to them." [33] In his mind, it all went back to the land cession, but with this difference—that those who had connived with the white man in the first instance had murdered the white man in the last.

Such, then was the "warfare just renewed on one of our extensive frontiers" that, in his message of June 1, the President made the ground of his fifth complaint against Great Britain.

The President and the Secretary of War had in every instance but one—and that is uncertain—followed and not led the governor of the Indiana Territory. But if they could not direct his movements, they could divine his motives; or rather they could see behind him a larger motive, a more irresistible impulse.

The spirit of the agricultural frontier exerted upon such various bodies as the British, the governor, Tecumseh, and the general government itself an almost catalytic power: it formed them into a new compound, itself remaining untouched. From this compound all personal characteristics, all guilt or innocence, all nobility or meanness, all conflicting interests, seem to have been precipitated out. What is left is nothing more or less than the means whereby a very powerful ambition hoped to accomplish its ends.

Had this ambition of the agricultural frontier been confined to the seizure of Indian lands within the territorial limits of the United States, then the British might have been guilty of an Indian war, even though they tried to prevent it from breaking out when it did. The British certainly resisted the advance of the frontier, upon mercantilist considerations, and for the sake of fur-trading interests; and they were not particularly nice as to their methods of resistance. But the spokesmen of the frontier openly declared that their real objective was to drive the British not merely from the farming lands of upper Canada but from the face of the continent. In the light of these declarations, the President's fifth grievance was an unhappy contradiction of all the other four. For the spokesmen of the frontier controlled the Twelfth Congress, and exercised a decisive influence upon the President and his Secretary of State; and it was the representatives of the frontier—voting in a wide arc from Vermont to Georgia—who saw to it that the Twelfth Congress declared war against Great Britain.

When the war broke out, this hollow imperialism of the frontier sprang up and withered along the Canadian borders; but had there been none of this imperialism there might not have been a War of 1812.

CHAPTER FOUR

The Twelfth Congress:

1811

THE Twelfth Congress, which met on November 4, 1811, was the embodiment and very nearly the embalmment of a rebellion against the peaceful system of Jefferson. What is interesting is not the success of the rebellion but the defeat of the system; for this defeat, whether measured in votes or in time, was a very narrow one. The Twelfth Congress was not driven before the will of a united majority, for the majority was never united: acute differences interpenetrated its cohesions, so that the miracle is that these cohesions cohered. Often the most important decisions were reached only with the help of those to whom such decisions seemed either nonsensical or ruinous or both, and who offered their help for that reason. The Congress was shot through with treason, if one may ascribe treason (as surely one may) to men who sincerely put their own interests before those of the country at large, and who believed that if the former were in peril the latter must be endangered also. If the rebellion succeeded, and the peaceful methods of Jefferson were finally subverted, it is because energy dominated the Twelfth Congress, just as theory had enfeebled the Eleventh.

This energy can be measured in a very simple way—that is, by the youth of the men who transmitted it. These men were few in numbers; their leaders can be counted on one's fingers. From Kentucky, Henry Clay and Richard M. Johnson; from New York, Peter B. Porter; from South Carolina, John Caldwell Calhoun, William Lowndes, David R. Williams, Langdon Cheves; from Tennessee, Felix Grundy. The oldest of these men was 36, the youngest 29. Some of them were the representatives of the West or of the frontier of the older sections; almost all of them had been trained to the law, not a hard taskmistress in those days but a most fecund mother of political sons. They were personable, they were self-confident, they were remarkable, even among Congressmen, for their willingness to make speeches. But it was not these qualities, impressive though they were, which give these men in retrospect their rather terrible charm. It meant little that they appealed to the Founding Fathers, whose philosophies they had never bothered to study and whose basic controversies they were too young to remember: all that we can see in this appeal is the emergence of a fetish. It meant little that they harangued the Congress on the subject, already stale, of free trade and seamen's rights. What mattered was that they were endowed with a full share of political astuteness; and that, before they loosed upon Congress their ideas and their oratory, they had taken care to seize the most important committees in the House of Representatives.

On November 4, after maturing their plans in caucus the previous evening,[1] they succeeded in electing Henry Clay to the Speakership of the House. Clay was already famous in the West, and deserved to be: the elevation of such a man to such a position meant that the House had turned its back upon the principle of peaceful coercion. This posture was, to say the least, an irreverent one; for though the Twelfth Congress was the result of a political landslide, nearly half the members of the former Congress having failed of re-election in 1810, it was still nominally in the grip of the party of Jefferson and Madison, to whom the principle of peaceful coercion was very dear. Whether the Congress would maintain this posture was always doubtful; but that it *did* maintain it was largely due to the election of Henry Clay to the Speakership, and the consequent organization of the principal committees.

The chairmanship of the Committee on Foreign Relations was given to Peter B. Porter, whose appearance was as commanding as his past was doubtful. Born in 1773, he was educated at Yale and at Judge Reeve's law school at Litchfield, Connecticut. He became clerk of Ontario County in western New York, and was removed from this position in 1805 because of his leanings toward the faction of Aaron Burr.[2] In Congress from 1809 to 1813, he represented the interests of the Niagara frontier, "was perfectly familiar with the needs of the people,"[3] and, as senior partner in the transportation firm of Porter, Barton, & Co., advocated the granting of public lands in aid of road and canal projects. It was not likely that such a man would have too nice a regard for strict Republican principles, but then Mr. Clay was not in search of strict Republican principles when he appointed Porter to the chairmanship of the Committee on Foreign Affairs. The committee on Military Affairs was given to David R. Williams of South Carolina, an honest and independent planter, who in the Ninth and Tenth Congresses had supported a peace policy against what he believed to be the interests of his section, and was thereafter disgusted with party regularity and peaceful submission.[4] He was somewhat overbearing in temper, and his manners were theatrical. Langdon Cheves, the new chairman of the Naval Committee, was born in the up-country of South Carolina, in a fort where his mother had fled from the Cherokee Indians after the British attack on Charleston.[5] Largely self-educated, he was admitted to the Charleston bar in 1797, and soon afterward plunged into politics. He had served in the Eleventh Congress, where his massive form and his gift for dignified and sometimes brilliant oratory had already made an impression; and where he had already admitted that he longed to force a conflict with England.[6] He was also a member of the Committee on Ways and Means, which contained no Federalists at all, and where he could stiffen the resolution of the somewhat wavering Ezekiel Bacon of Massachusetts.[7]

The Third Annual Message of President Madison,[8] which Congress heard on November 5, seemed to indicate an almost equal dissatisfaction with France and England. In the face of their "hostile inflexibility in trampling on the rights which no independent nation can relinquish," the President suggested that "Congress will feel the duty of putting the United States into an armor and an attitude demanded by the crisis, and corresponding with the national spirit and expectations." [9] But what were the national spirit and expectations? The elections of 1810-11 had certainly indicated that the country was dissatisfied with the fumbling methods of the Eleventh Congress; this dissatisfaction was no more evident than in Massachusetts, where Elbridge Gerry had defeated his Federalist opponent for the governorship by a majority of three thousand votes, and where the Republicans for the first time controlled both Houses in the state legislature. Moreover, Timothy Pickering, whose addiction to extreme Federalism was suitably recognized by the number of times his opponents burned him in effigy, was not permitted by this legislature to succeed himself in the United States Senate; and the vacancy was awarded to Joseph Bradley Varnum, a man of mild and correct Republican beliefs, which did not restrain him from conspiring with the young extremists of the House of Representatives. But it was never safe to trust to the political emotions of Massachusetts. Already a reversal of grave significance was under way; and in April 1812 Gerry was to lose the election to ex-governor Strong, thereby restoring the state to its old masters. Indeed, the elections of 1810-11 might be described as the effect of a war fever that burned itself out; or as a reflex action, a mere instinctive response to the dull pressure of the times, which precipitated into Congress a certain number of belligerent men, and could do no more. It was the actions of these young men, the "Young Republicans" or "War Hawks," and not the elections of 1810-11, that announced the arrival of a new era: [10] and their actions were due to the fact that they alone represented the dominant energy of the United States.

I

It is in the Report of the Committee on Foreign Affairs,[11] presented by Porter on November 29, and in the debate that followed it, that this energy found its voice. The report did no more than recite the wrongs France and England had committed against the neutral commerce of America; how each had been invited by the Non-Importation Act of 1810 to give up, in return for trade advantages, the retaliatory systems under cover of which they perpetrated their robberies; how France had apparently accepted this invitation, while England had continued in her bad ways, had even demanded new concessions, and had accompanied these demands with further impressments of American seamen. It closed with six resolutions, recommending an addition of ten thousand men to the regular army, a levy of fifty thousand volunteers, the putting of the Navy upon a war basis, and the arming of merchant vessels.

The language of this Report has been called "concise and often pungent," [12] though pungency was certainly lacking from its allusion to impressment, and it was most concise when it seemed to admit that the national sensibilities could easily be deadened by reiterated recitals of wrongs and injuries. None the less, its whole tone was warlike. And its true significance can be found in its attempt to correct the indecisions of the President's message; for the message was unable to decide whether England or France was the more to blame, and the committee's report put the blame squarely upon England.

Then, at length, opening the debate upon this Report, Peter B. Porter revealed the inner meaning of all that had gone before. The committee was determined, he said, to recommend open and decided war, and with these objectives: the destruction of British fisheries, the destruction of British commerce with America and the West Indies, and the conquest of Canada. Nor was the greed for land to be satisfied merely with the conquest of Canada. "This war," said Felix Grundy, the brilliant young criminal lawyer from Tennessee, "if carried on successfully, will have its advantages. We shall drive the British from our continent. . . . I am willing to receive the Canadians as adopted brethren. It will have beneficial political effects; it will preserve the equilibrium of the government. When Louisiana shall be fully peopled, the Northern States will lose their power and be at the discretion of others; they can be depressed at pleasure, and then the Union might be endangered. I, therefore, feel anxious not only to add the Floridas to the South, but the Canadas to the North of this Empire." [13]

What could be more reasonable? The farmers of the West coveted the lands of their Canadian brethren; the planters and land speculators of Georgia and Tennessee, gazing across the Spanish border, saw in the Floridas not only a base for marauding Indians and a refuge for runaway slaves, but also a broad belt of land cutting off the gulf on a long coastline. [14] And where might not the acquisition of the Floridas lead? The empire of Mexico lay beyond.

The President himself had already gone as far as, and perhaps somewhat farther than a President could go in nibbling off a portion of West Florida. [15] The convenient fact that the Spanish monarch was now an ally of Great Britain, and that the British would be sure to use the Floridas in any war against the United States, seemed to justify a seizure of the whole domain.

Moreover, the Spanish were in debt to the United States for damages done to American trade. The Administration itself was thus inextricably involved: for while Madison, as a good Virginian, saw nothing to please him in the acquisition of Canada, as a good Virginian he could not resist the allurement of Florida. Incantation alone could ward off the spell, but that had been tried in the Third Annual Message; and the answer to the Third Annual Message was the speech of Felix Grundy.

That a representative from Tennessee should display such solicitude towards the Northern states as Grundy had shown in his speech might seem odd to the point of improbability, if we did not know that those who prepare for war are not averse to strange combinations, and that these combinations are often the harbingers of distant and more fatal divisions. Grundy's healing words presaged not the solidity but the solubility of the Union. His speech was one of those frequent inseminations of the womb of time which produced, at length, the Civil War. The same prophetic aspect was worn by James Madison, who was being forced into the likeness of the war-god Janus, with one face looking north and one south; and who did not relish the northern view.[16]

II

It remains only to record that the Report of the Committee on Foreign Relations was delivered on a date almost coincidental with the arrival at Washington of the news of Tippecanoe. These two events are connected simply by the fact that they had the same origin: the victory of Harrison and the six resolutions of Porter's committee were equally the products of a land-hunger. The coincidence was, none the less, a fateful one. On the evening after Porter's speech calling for a conquest of Canada, James Monroe, the Secretary of State, ate his supper at the boarding house where Clay, Cheves, Lowndes, Calhoun, and Grundy lodged together. This boarding house was known as the War Mess.[17] Here Monroe promised that if there was no redress of grievances before the 1st of May 1812 the government would declare war.[18] When Monroe had entered the Administration in 1811 it was upon Old Republican principles that he did so: that is to say, upon the belief that Americans were not placed between desperate alternatives; that, having endured all the humiliations England and France could heap upon them, they should now peaceably extract whatever profits there were to be extracted. But whereas to the Federalists the profits of peace were material ones, to the Old Republicans they were largely spiritual. War was a great contriver of strong governments: and strong governments were anathema to the Old Republicans. Why should they construct, perhaps in a permanent form, what they had spent the best years of their lives in pulling down? And what would happen to the liberal movement in Europe if they did so? [19] These arguments were certainly forcible; and Monroe, in lending himself to the opposing councils of the War Mess, revealed not only an inherent disposition to attach himself to the strongest influence, but revealed also the strength of the influence to which he now attached himself. Having captured the Secretary of State, imperialism could go no further, and scarcely needed to.

III

It is no doubt merely truistic to state that imperialism has a conscience: or rather, that it cannot indulge its appetites without first proving that these appetites have been justly provoked. When the justice of the provocation requires no proof, the imperialist does not conceal the nature of his appetites. "*For what are we going to fight?*" Andrew Jackson wrote on March 7, 1812. "To satisfy the revenge or ambition of a corrupt and infatuated ministry? . . . No. Such splendid atchievements as these can form no part of the objects of an american war. But we are going to fight for the reestablishment of our national charactor, misunderstood and vilified at home and abroad; for the protection of our maritime citizens, impressed on board British ships of war and compelled to fight the battles of our enemies against ourselves; to vindicate our right to a free trade, and open market for the productions of our soil now perishing on our hands because the *mistress of the ocean* has forbid us to carry them to any foreign nation; in fine, to seek some indemnity for past injuries, some security against future aggressions, by the conquest of all the British dominions upon the continent of North America."[20] A simple imperialism of this kind does not require a defender. No nation had been more grossly provoked than the United States had been by Great Britain and by France: and since France had already yielded Louisiana, and had nothing more to give, there was no point in declaring war against her. "I should not wish to extend the boundary of the United States by war," said Richard Mentor Johnson of Kentucky in the House of Representatives, "if Great Britain would leave us the quiet enjoyment of independence; but considering her deadly and implacable enmity, and her continued hostilities, I shall never die contented until I see her expulsion from North America, and her territories incorporated with the United States." The conscience of Kentucky was thus easily quieted, and the conscience of Kentucky was a good example of the conscience of the West.[21]

That impressment should have been advanced as the chief British injury by a cotton-planting militia general, rallying the spirits of a border state, shows to what extent the agrarian interest had seized control of events. Impressment had never been a mercantile argument. True, it had nearly wrecked Jay's Treaty in 1794, and had certainly ruined Monroe's and Pinkney's Treaty in 1805, but thereafter it had loomed in the background, a vast and powerful irrelevancy, biding its time. When men like Andrew Jackson and Henry Clay brought it out, they did so in all good faith. Their high spirit was affronted, and when they said that they longed to re-establish the national character they meant every word of it. The owners of tonnage and cargoes, on the other hand, had never shown any grave concern about the impressment of their seamen into the British navy; and if they were bitterly mortified, as no doubt they were, they hid their mortification with a very good grace. The price of their silence was the profit of neutral trade. The price the frontier demanded for not keeping silence was every inch of British soil upon the North American continent. Thus the conflict seemed to lie between the American West and the London government; and the remainder of the United States, with the general government as an uneasy arbiter, seemed to be caught in some intermediate position, now blowing hot, now cold, now offering trade advantages, now threatening war. The struggle in the Twelfth Congress shows the violence and uncertainty of this conflict. There were times when the Young Republicans barely held their own; there were times when old dogmas and half-forgotten allegiances suddenly thronged up, and the Young Republicans split apart. The debate on the Naval Committee's proposal to appropriate seven and a half million dollars to build twelve seventy-fours and twenty frigates is full of interest.[22] Clay, Lowndes, Calhoun, and Porter recognized the importance of this measure and boldly supported it; but Johnson and Grundy appealed, and not in vain, to the awful examples of Tyre and Sidon, of Athens and of Carthage, which had lost their liberty when they sought to extend their power upon the ocean. These impressive *non sequiturs,* and the classic Republican distaste for an efficient navy, won the day; by a vote of fifty-six to fifty-two, the United States was condemned to face the mistress of the seas with a force of sixteen frigates, ships, and armed brigs, and some hundred and sixty-five totally useless gunboats.[23] What the fate of Athens or of Carthage would have been, under similar circumstances, was not discussed.

Whether the energies of frontier imperialism would exhaust themselves in an attempt to manage the Congress, or whether the stubborness of British mercantilism would yield to the combination of commercial restrictions and a threat of war—this was always the question. If the British had yielded in time, all the efforts of the Young Republicans would have gone for nothing; if the Young Republicans had given way, the British might have retained some part of their depredating system. It was a singular combat. The commercial and navigating interests of New England naturally sided with the British. They regarded their losses—the confiscation of cargoes, the burning of ships, the theft of sailors—as the unfortunate but inevitable accompaniments of a successful neutral carrying trade in time of war. Such matters could be adjusted, both amicably and by overlooking them. For their domestic opponents, on the other hand, they expressed the contempt that naturally goes with an extreme divergence of interests. "Proclaim an honourable neutrality!" was the admonishment of the Reverend Elijah Parish of Massachusetts, in a fast-day sermon in July 1812. "Let the southern *Heroes* fight their own battles. . . . Once more breathe that free, commercial air of New England which your fathers always enjoyed."[24] In other words, why fight for the acquisition of wild lands and the formation of new states, which would drain capital from the seaboard without an adequate return? Those who in wealth or dignity or learning constituted the pillars of the commercial system of New England entertained a deadly aversion to their fellow countrymen upon the frontier. "In mercy, therefore, to the sober, industrious, and well-disposed inhabitants," said Timothy Dwight of Connecticut, concluding a long argument in dispraise of the pioneer, "Providence has opened in the vast wilderness a retreat. . . . We have many troubles even now; but we should have many more, if this body of foresters had remained at home." [25] Nobody was more familiar with the mind of Providence than a good Federalist Connecticut divine; but never had the mercantile spirit expressed itself more clearly. The wilderness was a retreat, providentially designed for the improvident and the ungodly: to fight a war, which might result in the extinction of trade, in order to satisfy the ambitions of this horrid region was manifestly absurd. But, as matters fell out, the British yielded too late: and when impressment took its rightful place at the head of President Madison's war grievances, and even the battle of Tippecanoe was found at the bottom of the list, it was clear to what extent the "foresters" had had their way.

CHAPTER FIVE

Moscow, St. Petersburg, London

PRESIDENT MADISON'S War Message was not merely a response to the pressure of the frontier: it was also the result of a choice between two aggressors. In a time of world war a neutral nation is usually forced to make this somber choice. The French and the British had been competing for the favors of the United States: not with kind words and seductive offers but—it is always the way with great belligerents—with menaces and aggressions. For the United States possessed an immensely lucrative carrying trade, and it was most unlikely that its argosies could sail unscathed between the clashing systems of England and of France. Napoleon, whose Berlin (November 21, 1806) and Milan (December 17, 1807) Decrees had closed the ports of Europe and of Europe's colonies to British commerce, proposed by the same decrees to confiscate every neutral vessel that came within his grasp and that had had relations of any kind with the British; and, since the British controlled the high seas after Trafalgar, relations of some kind were unavoidable. The British, in their Orders-in-Council of November 11, 1807, announced that there should be no neutral trade with Europe and Europe's colonies except under British license and toll, thus hoping to use a world war as a means of recovering a monopoly of trade. If Napoleon could have enforced his Decrees upon the ocean, the American carrying trade would have disappeared: if the Orders-in-Council had succeeded, the American merchant marine would have been reduced to a state of vassalage.[1]

The details of the trade relations between Great Britain and Napoleon— the efforts of the British to force their goods upon their great enemy and their great enemy's tragic realization that ruin would come to him because he was being fed and not famished—would require another book. It is sufficient to say that the Napoleonic Wars were a gigantic trade war. And how could so successful a trader as the United States hope to stay out of them? Thomas Jefferson believed that this could be accomplished by mingling certain plain commercial considerations with some of the eternal principles of the Sermon on the Mount. As regards the Freedom of the Seas, his principles may be summarized as follows: Free ships make free goods except for contraband of war; neutrals may trade between port and port of a belligerent, except in contraband of war; lists of contraband must be carefully defined and restricted and must exclude foodstuffs and naval stores; blockades must be maintained by a sufficient number of ships, so as really to prevent access to an enemy port. Now these were luminous principles, and it is only right that Jefferson should be hailed as one who opened a new epoch in the development of the usages of neutrality. It would not be unfair to add, however, that these usages could have been developed only by a philosopher, one who welcomed the profits of neutral trade but who was resolutely determined not to protect them with a show of armed force. When Jefferson realized that France and Great Britain were unwilling to recognize his concept of Neutral Rights, he resorted to a supreme measure of peaceful coercion. His Embargo Act of 1807 was a self-blockade, which confined the Americant merchant to port or to the coasts, and which by previous legislation forbade the importation of the more profitable British goods: but every effort was made to violate its provisions (which certainly did not square with the Jeffersonian belief in weak central government); and the swift paralysis its terrible austerity inflicted upon the farming, planting, mercantile, and shipping interests brought it to an end in 1809. That it was responsible for the British panic and depression of 1809-10 can, however, hardly be doubted; and the panic and depression of 1809-10 fatally undermined the popularity of the Orders-in-Council. When James Madison tried less forceful measures of peaceful coercion, these too were successful, for Napoleon was obliged to pretend, in 1810, that his Berlin and Milan Decrees were revoked; and in 1812 the British, realizing that their markets in the United States were more important than a monopoly of the carrying trade, suddenly repealed their Orders-in-Council.[2]

It may be argued that a success which comes too late is not a success but a peculiarly bitter form of failure. Before the news of the repeal of the Orders could reach the United States, the United States had already been sucked into the war. Whether the British Orders had been more piratical and destructive than the French Decrees was a question that, then and thereafter, could not be decided; and it is certainly true that Madison had great difficulty in making up his mind. In the final paragraph of his War Message, he was obliged to confess that the French were little better than the British. Why, then, had he chosen to fight the latter? The pressure of the War Hawks in the Twelfth Congress could be held responsible. But was this the only reason? It might have been maintained—and in Massachusetts *was* maintained—that Great Britain was less outrageous, less despotic, more virtuous than Napoleonic France. This argument is somewhat vitiated for us by the fact that Spencer Perceval, as Chancellor of the Exchequer in 1807, summarized the objectives of the Orders-in-Council in words that were singularly brutal. "Our Orders say to the enemy, 'If you will not have *our* trade, as far as we can help it you shall have *none*; and as to so much of our trade as you can carry on yourselves, or others carry on with you through us, if you admit it you shall pay for it.'" Did not this fully justify James Madison's complaint that "Great Britain carries on a war against the lawful commerce of a friend that she may better carry on a commerce with an enemy"? [3] But it is well to remember that Perceval had prefaced his summary with the sentence, "This is a formidable and tremendous state of the world." It was, indeed.

In the winter of 1807, Napoleon was at the height of his power. The Tsar had become a member of his Continental System; Spain was his; from Trieste to the Baltic he was master of the coasts of Europe. It is axiomatic that the British have always become, to say the least, extremely uneasy when the ports of the Channel and the North Sea are in enemy hands. The Channel was, of course, a barrier, perhaps an impassable one. We have only to recall the difficulties that beset Julius Caesar, when there was no fleet to oppose him, and the disaster that overcame the Spanish Armada when there was an opposing fleet, to realize why Napoleon abandoned his camp at Boulogne and with it all notion of a military invasion.[4] Yet the fear of Napoleon remained. The Channel was something more and something less than a physical barrier. It was a state of mind, all the more sensitive because the coast of France was visible in good weather from the cliffs of Dover. The channel made the British the least European of European peoples; it also made them the most homogeneous. Yet their very homogeneity was difficult to define. It was crossed by social distinctions so complex and exclusive that beside them the protocol of the Hapsburg court would have seemed like a child's lesson-book. "The straits of Dover were too narrow, the shadow of a hostile continent too oppressive, the English sod was soaked with too many dews and cut by too many hedges, for each individual, being quite master of himself, to confront every other individual without fear or prejudice." [5]

But in times of national peril, the whole nation seemed to think alike. There were differences, and very acute ones, on matters of detail or of policy; and it is one of the peculiar triumphs of the English people that these differing voices were not hushed. On matters of first importance, all were agreed. Napoleon was a threat to English liberty, and would remain a threat until he had been utterly overthrown. Exactly what English liberty consisted of was a question of extreme delicacy. The English criminal code in the year 1807 was a savage embodiment of the jealousy of classes; the English army was overflogged and underpaid, and officered by gentlemen who purchased their promotions; the English navy was a living hell; yet that liberty of some kind existed, and that it must be defended, was an article of English faith. From one end of the country to the other, in the loftiest nurseries and the lowest cottages, children who disobeyed were sent to bed with the threat that "Boney would get them"; and it would be too great a compliment to the commercial publicists of the time to suppose that these little ones were threatened in the interests of a monopoly of trade. Some fashionable and doctrinaire Whigs, it is true, professed, not without justice, to see in Napoleon the last champion of the French Revolution—men who, eight years later, received the news of their country's victory at Waterloo with genuine chagrin. Yet these men were not numerous; nor, oddly enough, were they ever traitorous. And so, when Prussia and Austria repented before Napoleon in sackcloth; when Russia submitted; when Sweden sank into impotence—the Lords and Commons, the gentlemen and peasantry of England still remained, fearful, defiant, unconquerable, and alone.

It is no wonder that the Emperor, when at last he fled before the remnants of his army retreating from Moscow, should have dinned into the ears of his traveling-companion, de Caulaincourt, his rancorous, reiterated hatred of England.[6] Of all the modern conquerors of Europe, he came the nearest to understanding that country, possibly because he neither admired nor envied it. But he, too, was baffled: by representative institutions that did not represent, by aristocratic governments with acute commercial susceptibilities, by a constitutional monarchy without a constitution, by a liberty that enslaved. Somewhere behind these contradictory appearances, something, a torch of freedom, was being handed on from generation to generation—battered, blackened, almost unrecognizable, but still alight.

If Napoleon was baffled, was there not some excuse for James Madison? Moreover, English liberty was a concept confined in its operation solely to England. Napoleon's attitude towards the United States was ambiguous enough—there were times when he behaved not like an Emperor but like a pettifogging provincial lawyer with a taste for larceny—but after the sale of Louisiana he never impressed the Americans as being opposed to their independence. The British, on the other hand, rarely failed to give this impression. A humiliating semi-independence seemed all that they would permit. Their forcible impressment of at least six thousand American seamen into the British Navy; the insulting language of Foreign Secretaries like Lord Harrowby and George Canning; the impossible instructions delivered to their Ministers at Washington; the vicious attack upon the unready U.S.S. *Chesapeake* by H.M.S. *Leopard* in 1807; the resistance to American expansion to the west, the warships hovering around the harbors of the East, the determination to control American shipping—all this seemed to proclaim a decision to reduce the United States to the position of a colony that paid its own expenses.[7] This was not true, of course, of enlightened British opinion; but under the administrations of the Duke of Portland and of Spencer Perceval enlightened British opinion was in abeyance. Under these circumstances, James Madison's choice became almost a necessity. The pressure of frontier imperialism was not the only nor the most efficient cause of the War of 1812: it was, rather, the most immediate and obvious one. Indeed it was so obvious that the British complained, not unjustly, that they had been stabbed in the back: with a characteristic reticence, however, they refrained from suggesting that they themselves may have been responsible for the stabbing.

When the question of war or peace came before the House of Representatives, the whole interior, and particularly the frontier voting in its great arc from Vermont to Georgia, said "aye"; the navigating interests said "no." They were ready enough to suffer the confiscations of the French and the British, to move around the world under the capricious protection of the Royal Navy; even to lose their seamen to that protectress: for they had become a kind of left wing of the British navigation system. The profits of a single successful voyage compensated for any number of losses. But landsmen who lived by remote rivers and in the shade of almost fabulous forests were now talking of free trade and seamen's rights; and their hunger for Canadian farmlands and Florida real estate, sharpened by a long diet of British insults and threats, carried the day. The vote on June 4, 1812, was seventy-nine to forty-nine: in the Senate on June 18 it was even closer —nineteen to thirteen.[8] It was with a depleted Treasury and a divided nation that James Madison went to war.

Few events in American history are more disarming than the unwillingness of Jeffersonian statesmen to prepare for the war before it broke out, or their optimism after it had done so. On June 19, James Madison visited "in person—a thing never known before—all the offices of the Departments of War and Navy, stimulating everything in the manner worthy of a little commander-in-chief, with his little round hat and huge cockade." [9]

I

Optimism, indeed, was needed, though optimism alone would prove fatal. The United States in 1812, as it faced its war with England, was a country whose mass far outweighed its energy or capital. On the north, the frontier lost itself in wilderness; one could trace it perhaps as far as the Lake of the Woods, but from then onward all was mysterious, indefinite, and controversial. In the Straits of Mackinac between Lakes Michigan and Huron the solitary Indian, traveling from his summer meeting with Canadian factors at the falls of Saulte Ste. Marie, might descry an American flag flying on the island of Michilimackinac—a lonely symbol, forlorn and wonderful, of early American pretensions. Except for Astoria, clinging like a fragment of commercial prose to the great rhythms of the Oregon coast, Michilimackinac was the most distant landmark of the United States. At Fort Dearborn by the foot of Lake Michigan, Fort Wayne on the Maumee, and Fort Harrison on the Wabash, there were feeble military garrisons; but Detroit was the only formidable fortress in the whole Northwest. East of Detroit lay two short rivers, three great lakes, and no adequate defenses except for the forests between Lake Champlain and Eastport, a tangled and whispering barrier into which no army, however desperate or determined, would ever venture to plunge.

The land frontier of continuous settlement slanted southwest from Lake Champlain to the mouth of the Ohio, and then southeast to St. Mary's River on the northern border of Spanish Florida, two thousand nine hundred miles in all. The War of 1812 dipped its fingers into most of the pockets of settlement outside this immense frontier—Detroit, Michilimackinac, Fort Dearborn, New Orleans, and Forts Mims and Bowyer, watching the approaches to the Tombigbee settlements.[10]

On the northern lakes there was no navy, until Perry conjured one out of the green woods of Erie; on the southern frontier there were soldiers here and there—at New Orleans, at Fort Stoddard—but there were also forts and townships within the Spanish border which British troops would probably occupy; and, after Tecumseh's southern visit, no one knew what the remnants of his Confederation might do either in the south or in the west.

Yet the plight of the land frontiers was as nothing when compared to that of the Atlantic seaboard. From Passamaquoddy to the St. Mary's River, through fifteen degrees of latitude, this seaboard wooed the attentions of the British Navy; fine harbors winked and beckoned, great bays and rivers opened their arms and their mouths in invitation. The estuaries of the Patapsco and the Patuxent solicited a manly thrust against Baltimore and Washington; the kindly Potomac yearned, and not in vain, to bear the British fleet to Alexandria. Only a fine but exiguous navy, and that singular phenomenon, the Jeffersonian gunboat, represented an opposition: and the gunboat, as often as not, left its anchorage merely to retreat. The very sandreefs of North Carolina were a more adequate defense. But had the navy been ten times larger than it was, it would have suffered from a lack of proper bases. The British had Halifax, the Bermudas, Santa Lucia, Barbados, Jamaica. From here they were to blockade as they pleased: to ruin the fisheries of New England and all the commerce of the eastern states; or depredate in Chesapeake Bay from Norfolk to Havre de Grace on the Susquehanna; or plunder at will along the coasts of South Carolina.

The war, therefore, expressed itself most forcibly on the Canadian border, which for military purposes ended at Detroit. The incandescence of Young Republican oratory was only a feeble glow when it encountered daylight, or fact; for though the inhabitants of French Canada were indifferent, the inhabitants of Upper Canada would favor America only in the event of an American success—a reverse would of course remind them that they were, after all, loyalists, the refugees and victims of the Revolution. Moreover, until some navy could be created to operate upon the lakes of Ontario, Erie, St. Clair, and Champlain, the main action would have to be upon the land, and here the fate of Hull at Detroit was to show, too clearly, what could be expected when the invasion of Canada was entrusted to the direction of Virginia. While Dearborn lingered at Albany, Hull was overwhelmed. A concerted attack along the short detached lines of the Niagara and Detroit Rivers might have produced an effect; but to the difficulties of communication was added the calamity of administrative incompetence. "Perverse stupidity," snarled Sir James Yeo, commenting three years later on the American failure.[11] Sir James, who had been the British naval commander on the Great Lakes, seems conveniently to have forgotten the names of Macdonough and Perry; but, in any case, his words had no application to the true nature of the American dilemma. Its origins lay deep in the realm of the unconscious and the uncontrollable. The ambitions of the West were forced to operate through the medium of a government headed by a Southern President—a man of unquestioned patriotism, but a man whose inmost being shrank away from a conquest of Canada. The result was disordered thinking, divided counsels, lethargic action, inane cheerfulness—in short, all the symptoms of a failure of nerve.

Upper Canada was tempting; in some respects, it resembled a ripe fruit, dangling in the very jaws of lakes St. Clair and Erie, and offering itself to anyone who owned these waters. To bite it off by land—that was another question. Indeed, considering the strength of the British position, flanked by lakes Ontario and Erie, and protected by two short and controlling rivers, it might rather have been likened to an arrow, thrust into America, with Fort Malden at the tip. The sacrifice of Hull, and the scarcely more respectable campaign on the Niagara, demonstrated to what extent the government was blind to the true nature of the problem. Everything needed for the defense of Canada came from England. Arms, munitions, soldiers, seamen, naval stores—all arrived by way of Montreal and the St. Lawrence River. There was no other means of communication. If this could have been severed, Upper Canada—like an apple cut off from its stalk, or an arrowhead from its shaft—would have fallen into American hands without a blow.[12] No western mind, no military commander, no planner in the Virginia Cabinet seems to have realized the necessity of concentrating every man upon the Plattsburg line of operations, of striking at the eastern section of the long Canadian line, and leaving the Detroit and the Niagara to the militia.[13] At last, in October 1814, Colonel Monroe drafted a scheme for such an attack; but even then, with the enthusiasm of the amateur strategist, brushing aside all considerations of logistics and of communications, he seems to have meditated a combined operation by way of Sackett's Harbor as well as by Lake Champlain.[14] The mere rumor of such a plan, however, startled the British into a desperate exploration of the route from Montreal to Kingston by the Rideau Lakes and the Ottawa River.

II

The navy was very small; but it was marvelously efficient and its spirit was high. The army was in a less fortunate position. Its senior commanders were old, and to age they added inexperience; or, in the case of General Wilkinson, a settled habit of corruption. Its ten regular units were scattered all over the country; and the new regular regiments that Congress had authorized between January and June were still little more than paper regiments. Of the fifty thousand twelve-month volunteers whom Congress had also voted into existence, perhaps four thousand had offered. The quality and scope of the militia were unknown. None the less, looking back on his situation in later days, James Madison declared that it could have been much worse. Had not Napoleon, five days after the American declaration of war, marched his armies across the Russian frontier?

"It was a fair calculation," Madison said, "when war became inevitable, or rather after it had commenced, that Napoleon, whether successful or not against Russia, would find full employment for her and her associates, G. Britain included. . . . The moment chosen for the war would, therefore, have been well chosen, if chosen with a reference to the French expedition against Russia; and although not so chosen, the coincidence between the war and the expedition promised at the time to be as favorable as it was fortuitous." [15]

These arguments were undoubtedly sincere, but they would never have borne a hostile inspection. Madison had been forced into war by Western influences, but what other influences, unbidden by the West, contributed to this pressure? If he believed in 1812 that a French attack upon Russia would be favorable to American chances against Great Britain, then the words "coincidence" and "fortuitous" could be used only with the limited meaning that no man was able to predict the exact moment when Napoleon would cross the Russian frontier. Everything else was common knowledge. The last American vessel to escape the Russian winter of 1811 was the *Dolphin*, Captain Latham, bound for New York. She sailed from Kronstadt on October 15, and she carried with her dispatches from John Quincy Adams, the American Minister at St. Petersburg. The latest of these, dated October 11, 1811, declared: "If war should not commence soon there is, I believe, nobody who thinks it possible it should be postponed longer than until next summer. The Emperor Napoleon's confidence of success . . . is founded on the consciousness of his strength, and his conviction that Russia has no general officer capable of commanding armies in opposition to an enemy like France. In this opinion he is not singular." [16] Indeed, Adams's whole correspondence with the State Department from August 2 onward was filled with premonitions of a Franco-Russian war. As far back as April 1810 he had reported the beginnings of a rupture; and by midsummer of 1811 it was generally believed in Europe that war could not be put off beyond the spring of 1812.[17] It is a fairly safe assumption that, when America declared war against England, all well-informed persons on both sides of the Atlantic knew that such a moment was very near.

Enmeshed in paradox, Madison did not burden his conscience with the most outrageous paradox of all. The Decrees of Berlin and Milan were revoked, as the last paragraph of the War Message declared; and yet—it was odd, but it was true—Napoleon was going to war with Russia in order to maintain those very Decrees. The more one examines that paragraph, the more its obscurity deepens into inspissated gloom.

III

The Franco-Russian quarrel arose from the Tsar's refusal to exclude American ships from his harbors. Since Great Britain could sell to the Americans and the Americans to Russia, the exchanges thus effected between Great Britain and Russia were bound to undermine Napoleon's continental structure, as shaped by the Berlin and Milan Decrees. In order to make London costly as a market, Napoleon had already attempted to destroy the British fleet, as a preliminary measure to the invasion or isolation of the British Isles. This attempt had been ruined at Trafalgar. He then proposed to afflict Great Britain with insolvency by stopping up the Continent: when this began to fail in 1810, he was forced by the logic of competition to undertake a more stupendous, a more desperate enterprise. For more than a century England and France had been competing for the same trade routes between the same termini, with India at one end and America at the other; and France had steadily been losing ground. The Napoleonic Empire was an elaborate, glittering, and formidable effort to readjust this situation. Once England had obtained the command of the seas, there was no alternative but to command the overland routes to India, and thus to conquer her Asiatic base and sever her communications. If the Tsar would submit to Napoleon's Decrees, and close the Baltic, then the Tsar would become his agent in this deed. In any case, Moscow was the converging point of the roads that connected the Baltic with the traffic of Asia. Towards Moscow, therefore, Napoleon directed his Grand Army on June 23, 1812.[18]

Madison made no alliance and entered into no understanding with Napoleon, but he believed, in 1827 at least, that Napoleon carried with him into Russia the fortunes of the United States of America. "Had the French Emperor not been broken down, as he was, to a degree at variance with all probability, and which no human sagacity could anticipate, can it be doubted that Great Britain would have been constrained by her own situation and the demands of her allies, to listen to our reasonable terms of reconciliation?" [19] It would seem that he considered Napoleon's career to have been ended at Moscow in 1812, rather than at Leipzig a year later; and the point is arguable.

At any rate, Napoleon's invasion of Russia was conducted in the grand style. For the last time, the Grand Army swept forward, in all its magnificence: in crested helmets, and jaunty shakos, and floating plumes; with laced dolmans and brilliant facings; with silks and with eagles, with trumpets and kettledrums, and long retinues of coaches and kitchens. It was led by a commander of transcendent genius, only forty-four years old, whose visions matched and outmatched the visions of Alexander the Great. And yet— somewhere, something was wrong.

The Emperor carried with him, as an expert on Russian affairs, his late ambassador at St. Petersburg, Armand de Caulaincourt, Duke of Vicenza. A nobleman of the old regime, handsome, elegant, engaging, but impetuous and dogged in argument, Caulaincourt had, above everything else, the gift of loyalty.[20] He was one of the most faithful of the Emperor's servants; and he occupied the position of a licensed Greek chorus, whose function it was to comment upon defects, to extol the virtues of enemies, to criticize, to encourage, and to mourn. It is not uncommon for autocratic personages to tolerate and even to require the advice of such dependents: as one listens to the voice of one's servant, to the oddly mingled accents of doom and of deference, one is projecting a personal insecurity, or sharply criticizing a transferred weakness—above all, one is displaying one's own power. Caulaincourt was Napoleon's personal whipping-boy. He was rewarded with splendid appointments and with a ducal title that meant nothing; he experienced the lash of Napoleon's sarcasm, the weight of his suspicion, the bruising of his rage; he received those little tweaks of the ear which were the signs of imperial affection. Through it all, storm and shine, his loyalty had never wavered. For years he had wished to marry Madame de Canisy, and for years Napoleon had forbidden the match. At last, at Fontainebleau in 1814, when all was over, the fallen Emperor gave his permission. With a gesture of superb faithfulness, Caulaincourt bent down to kiss his master's hand.[21]

It was still in the spirit of a Greek chorus that Caulaincourt wrote his memoirs of the Moscow campaign. Like all memoirists who write in the first person, he was tempted into omniscience; and he displayed—more than even historians do—a certain facility in the making of *ex post facto* judgments, in viewing the past as if its successive denouements were always in the future, unknown yet foreseeable. But he was a trained soldier and an honest man; and what he saw, or says that he saw, cannot be disregarded. He noted everything, even the supernatural. On the very day of the crossing of the Niemen, the Emperor tumbled from his horse. What a bad omen! So thought Berthier, the Prince of Neufchâtel, and Caulaincourt agreed. But worse was to follow. Almost from the beginning the transport broke down. The horses, floundering in the sandy Russian roads, perished of exhaustion, of colic, and of neglect; the overweighted wagons collapsed and were abandoned; the supplies vanished through loss or theft, or were scattered along the roads far in the rear. There was a shortage of harness, of spare parts, of ambulances; there were no forges, no nails, no smiths; the hospitals were deficient, and the doctors too few. The Grand Army, already sick and threatened with starvation, began to look out for itself; beneath its dazzling appearance and its swift advance disorder and indiscipline were everywhere apparent. Far ahead, Joachim Murat, the king of Naples, a fantastic confection of jewels and ostrich plumes, frittered away his cavalry in taxing maneuvers and unprovoked skirmishes. The greatest of cavalry leaders in a battle, he was one of the most intemperate in an advance. Perhaps he wished to prove that he was really a king, to show his courage, to flaunt his uniform under the noses of the Cossacks; perhaps war to him was merely an escapade, and life itself a jest. At any rate, the cavalry was half destroyed before it ever came into action. Thus the Grand Army rushed upon its doom.[22]

When Hull surrendered at Detroit, Napoleon was in sight of the walls of Smolensk.[23] Sometimes he had grumbled, or raged, or fallen into a surly preoccupation; but for the most part he displayed the intoxication, no longer of genius, but of delusion and infatuation. When Smolensk went up in flames, self-immolated, a mournful prelude to Moscow, he could hardly contain himself. "Isn't that a fine sight?" he shouted to Caulaincourt, clapping him on the back. "Horrible, Sire!" "Bah!" he replied. "Gentlemen, remember the words of a Roman Emperor: 'A dead enemy always smells sweet!' " "The Emperor's remark," wrote Caulaincourt afterwards, "long haunted my inmost thoughts." [24]

On October 13, Van Rensselaer recoiled from Queenston, and except for the absurdities of Smyth, the campaign at the Niagara was at an end. On October 19, Napoleon and the Imperial Guard vanished from Moscow, and the fearful retreat was under way: on November 3, at Slavkovo, the snow began to fall. [25]

Thus the "fair calculation" of James Madison, when at length it was cast up, amounted to the collapse of Western imperialism at the American end of the immense front and a huge and terrible retribution at the Russian end. A solitary human being seems to connect these two extremes. Joel Barlow, the American Minister at Paris, having wrestled in vain to extract some sense from the double-dealings of Napoleon, was invited on October 11 to come to Wilna. Here, it seemed, he was to be given proof that the Decrees of Berlin and Milan had actually been revoked. The journey appealed to his taste for adventure and for movement. His whole career, indeed, had been singularly *mouvementé*, in thought and in action. Born and educated in Federalist Connecticut, he became a Physiocrat and a Jacobin, the friend of Robespierre and of Tom Paine. He was able, like all early nineteenth-century liberals, to combine with perfect ease the concept of human liberty with that of freedom of enterprise. [26] Handsome, likable, and enthusiastic, he had been made a citizen of France in the days of the National Convention; he was very close to the Directory; he enjoyed the double honor of being eulogized by Fox and proscribed by Pitt. After a life of satisfying adventures in London, Paris, and Algiers; of luminous radical thinking; of shrewd financial operations; he returned at last to America with $200,000, and settled himself in luxury upon the outskirts of Washington, where he was able to rejoice in the companionship of Jefferson and the remoteness of Connecticut. He produced a revised and lengthened version of his early poem *The Vision of Columbus;* and *The Columbiad*, as it then became, had in it some of the preservative from oblivion. It survived the jests of Hawthorne and Byron; not because its poetry was good, but because its heavy images and doubtful prosody could not conceal an ardent temperament and a generous mind.

Ardent, indeed, and generous he was to the end. The last American envoy to attempt to solve his country's neutral problems by the application of Jeffersonian methods, he performed the disheartening task with a high spirit and an indomitable pertinacity. He was in his sixtieth year when, on November 11, he plunged into the wintry desolation of Poland. The roads were hideous with the litter of Napoleon's advance; and Wilna, when he arrived

there on November 18, was already horrified with the news of Napoleon's
retreat. He stayed until December 4 and then, upon the insistence of the
Duc de Bassano that it was no longer safe to remain, he left for Paris. The
cold was fearful, and after traveling night and day, he was forced by exposure, fatigue, and incipient pneumonia to halt at the little village of Zarnovitch, near Cracow. And at Zarnovitch, on Christmas Eve, he died.[27]

At some time in December, perhaps at Wilna, or as he lurched back to
Paris, or even, it may be, stretched on his bed of death, he wrote a last poem,
"Advice to a Raven in Russia." Do not, he told the raven, attempt to pick
out the dead soldier's eyes.[28]

> "The frozen orb, preserving still its form,
> Defies your talons as it braves the storm,
> But stands and stares to God, as if to know,
> In what curst hands he leaves his world below."

The sentiment of this poem—a reasonable but feeling malediction upon all
wars and war-makers—was distinctly Jeffersonian; but so, too, was the writer
and the victim. In the hurry of events, the government did not find time to
pronounce an official *requiescat* on Joel Barlow. Perhaps, like most gallant
persons, he needed none.

IV

James Madison, more fortunate than Barlow, was not required to follow or
to wait for Napoleon. Almost from the beginning of the War, long before
any news of Russia had found its way back to America, he empowered his
chargé d'affaires in London to propose an armistice—for which the conditions precedent should be the repeal of the Orders, suspension of impressment, the dismissal of impressed seamen, and the abandonment of paper
blockades.[29] The War of 1812 was attended by so many curious circumstances that the additional oddity of a maintenance of diplomatic relations
while the war was actually in progress passed almost unnoticed. On August 24
Jonathan Russell duly made his proposal, with its four conditions precedent
now reduced to three, and a further assurance that a law would be passed prohibiting the employment of British seamen in the public or commercial
service of the United States.[30] In his reply, Lord Castlereagh intimated that
he found the conditions insulting and the assurance equivocal; and protested,
in language no more involved than was usually the case with him, that His
Majesty's government "cannot consent to suspend the exercise of a right
upon which the naval strength of the Empire mainly depends, until they are
fully convinced that means can be devised and will be adopted, by which
the object to be obtained by the exercise of that right can be effectually
secured." [31]

A second attempt was made on September 12, 1812, when Russell, on
receipt of a dispatch from Monroe, proposed an armistice without any
formal declaration of the points at issue.[32] These offers to end the war before
it had fairly begun did much honor to Madison as a Republican, and afford

a pretty accurate measure of the swift decline of Western influence. But impressment was now the single issue between the two countries; and the British would have nothing to do with an armistice that might involve the discussion of that subject. They had already dispatched Admiral Sir John Borlase Warren with the offer of an armistice based upon the repeal of the Orders alone. This, too, came to nothing.[33] Jonathan Russell left London and went on board *The Lark*. Though nobody knew it at the time, impressment—the only *casus belli*—was not to be discussed again until after the war had ended.

V

Nine months after the outbreak of the war, the Russian *chargé d'affaires* in Washington, André Daschkoff, informed the Secretary of State that the Tsar Alexander I was anxious to act as a mediator between the United States and Great Britain.[34] The story of Napoleon's retreat from Moscow was now known; the British blockade was growing daily more severe; the Eastern states were sullen, though not yet actively hostile; the country's finances were already in great disorder. The government had every reason to accept the offer, and Monroe's reply to Daschkoff was full of compliments to the Tsar.[35] In order to quiet the growing clamor of the peace party, it was decided to act without finding out what the British response to the Tsar's offer would be. President Madison appointed Albert Gallatin (at his own request), John Quincy Adams, and James A. Bayard as Envoys Extraordinary and Ministers Plenipotentiary to treat with British persons similarly appointed, at St. Petersburg, under the mediation of the Tsar. Monroe composed a set of instructions which proved to be an elaborate recapitulation of all the old arguments against impressment.[36] He also quoted the new Foreign Seamen Act of March 3, 1813, which excluded all but United States citizens from the public and private vessels of the United States; and he offered to extend this Act even further and to forbid the calling of the sea to any native-born Briton who should henceforth be naturalized in America—an extension which very nearly if not quite conceded the right of impressment.[37] But the Foreign Seamen Act was to take effect only after the war; its constitutionality was doubtful; and it was open to the double objection that, while it seemed to offer too much from the American point of view, it pressed upon the British terms they had already rejected and would in all probability reject again.[38] On May 9, without waiting to discover what the Senate would have to say to their appointment, Gallatin and Bayard embarked at New Castle on the *Neptune*, and dropped down Delaware Bay.[39] They arrived in St. Petersburg on July 21.

They little knew that they had fallen into the hands of a man who, with the best intentions, was to prove a sore embarrassment. The Tsar Alexander's gifts were admittedly great and his qualities were good: but decisiveness and consistency were not to be found among them. He would often attempt to give simultaneous operation to two or even three totally conflicting sets of plans. Psychological generalizations are dangerous; but perhaps one might venture the statement that this kind of thing might be expected from a monarch who came to the throne over the body of his murdered father, and whose conscience was thereafter burdened and overburdened with daily deposits of accumulating guilt, until in his latter days his veering moods gave way to a dark and cruel melancholy.

In the year 1812, however, Alexander I was still an engaging man—tall, handsome, amorous, affable—who seemed anxious only to do good. When John Quincy Adams arrived in St. Petersburg in 1810 to take up his duties as American Minister, he received the most gratifying attentions from the Tsar, and he had every reason to believe that here, indeed, was a liberal prince. To some extent, Alexander's education had been designed to produce just such a result. His tutor had been Frederic César de la Harpe, a Swiss philosopher who, like Albert Gallatin, had imbibed the doctrines of Jean Jacques Rousseau. But La Harpe perceived that there was a fundamental incompatibility between the principles of Rousseau and the society and character of the Russians: and, being also greatly attached to the political theories of Plato's *Republic*, he decided to mold his young pupil more into an Athenian than a Genevan form. Today, we may doubt that Plato's *Republic* could ever, on any terms, produce a republican: but the Tsar grew up in the belief that he could bestow upon his subjects all the blessings of the free life. He never realized that the free life cannot in fact, devolve upon the human race from above, at the will of a single man, but must arrive from below, through the slow and possibly exasperating process of popular government. As the years went by, the disappointed Alexander changed from a despot to a bewildered mystic and from a bewildered mystic to a tyrant—as dull and ferocious, in his way, as any of that species.

This process had not begun in 1810. The Tsar was still benevolent. He was genuinely kind-hearted. Nothing could have been more encouraging than his attitude towards the United States and their envoy. The Adams diary for this period is notable for its accounts of chance meetings with Alexander as he strolled on the quay or the Admiralty Mall, when the Autocrat and the New Englander discussed now the vagaries of international politics, now the financial difficulties of republican diplomats, now the advantages and disadvantages of warm flannel underwear. His Imperial Majesty, it would seem, did not wear any, even in the sharpest cold of winter. Such were the condescensions of this philosophical prince. His attitude towards the maritime principles of the United States was unexceptionable—chiefly, it is true, because Russia could extract no profit from the maritime principles of the British. When he was attacked by Napoleon in 1812, it was because he would not exclude American shipping from his ports. He was, said his Chancellor, Count Roumanzoff, America's single support: "Our attachment to the United States is obstinate, more obstinate than you know of." For the rest of his life, and in spite of much disillusioning evidence, John Quincy Adams revered the memory of Alexander.[40]

But when Gallatin and Bayard arrived in St. Petersburg in 1813, Europe was once again, and more noticeably than ever, in a state of disequilibrium; and nowhere was this condition reflected more vividly than in the mind of Tsar Alexander. Napoleon had not been overwhelmed by the terrible outcome of his Moscow campaign. He had gathered together another *Grande Armée*, and in April 1813 he had advanced into Germany. There followed the battles of Lutzen (May 3) and Bautzen (May 20), in which he defeated the Russians and the Prussians—not completely: Bautzen was celebrated with *Te Deums* on both sides—but thoroughly enough to justify the assertion that if only he had followed the allies as they fell back upon Pilsen, he would have gained a decisive victory and might have dictated his own terms.

The Tsar's actions at this point can be explained only upon the supposition that he was trying, out of a sense of honor too delicate or perhaps too psychotic for us to understand, to keep faith simultaneously with Napoleon and with Great Britain; with a new enemy whom he had never ceased to admire and with new allies whom he did not really like. And it so happened that he had at hand two advisers, or instruments, who conveniently personified these divergent aims. In St. Petersburg the Chancellor, Count Roumanzoff, favored Napoleon and was hostile to England: while at the imperial headquarters the obedient Count Nesselrode, who acted as Foreign Minister in the field, was known to entertain strong British sympathies. Like the figures of Noah and his wife, which alternately emerge from and retire into the recesses of those old-fashioned clocks which profess not only to tell the time but also to predict the arrival of dry or rainy weather, these two personages appeared or vanished, according as the Tsar's strange inner mechanism responded to a French or a British sentiment.

When the British heard of the Tsar's offer of a mediation, they immediately—with many expressions of gratitude—informed the Russian Ambassador, Count Lieven, that they would have nothing to do with it. They did not wish to submit their maritime principles to the scrutiny of a Baltic power notoriously unsympathetic to them.[41] When the news reached England that Gallatin and Bayard had landed on the coast of Sweden, the British language was repeated in stronger terms; and on July 13 Lord Castlereagh, the British Foreign Secretary, wrote to Lord Cathcart, at the Tsar's headquarters, to tell him that the Prince Regent was now ready to appoint plenipotentiaries to treat with the Americans directly, either at Gothenburg or in London.[42] But while the Tsar let it be known through Count Nesselrode that he was perfectly satisfied with this arrangement, he continued to instruct Count Roumanzoff to press the offer of a mediation, and he did everything he could to conceal from the Americans at St. Petersburg the fact that the British were ready to treat with them directly. Even after Napoleon's victory at Dresden had been annulled by his defeat at Leipzig on October 18, Alexander continued his mysterious silence. As late as November 15, Adams was complaining that no official communication had been received from the Russian government.[43] By this time, of course, both fact and rumor had penetrated to the American watchers in St. Petersburg.

They knew that England was ready to commence a direct negotiation. They had no power to treat with England except under a Russian mediation, nor could they close their mission without some authority from the Tsar. They could only watch and wait, while the great winter closed down on St. Petersburg, and the unhappy Roumanzoff, in the midst of his own disgrace, tried with his uneasy attentions to make them feel at home. One can hardly resist the conclusion that the Tsar had blandly sacrificed his American friends to his own indecisive policy; that he had kept them idly lingering, month after month, at St. Petersburg; and that he had made it as difficult as possible for Lord Castlereagh to open a direct communication with Madison and Monroe.

At length, however, Lord Castlereagh decided to pay no more attention to the feelings of the Tsar, but to communicate directly with President Madison. His letter was dated November 4, the very day upon which the news of the battle of Leipzig collided in London with the news of Perry's victory on Lake Erie.[44] The collision was not a resounding one; it was drowned by the bells that pealed for Napoleon's defeat. But Castlereagh's offer to Madison was a necessary extension of the repeal of the Orders-in-Council, and betrayed nothing but the uneasiness of the industrial, commercial, and shipping interests. As for Castlereagh himself, he, almost alone among Foreign Secretaries, had shown no animosity towards America. His energies were devoted to the settlement of Europe; and continued to be thus devoted for the rest of his life, until the settlement of Europe became so charged with difficulties that it unsettled his reason.

VI

In addition to the mere ennui occasioned by his futile sojourn in St. Petersburg, Albert Gallatin was further inflicted with the news, which arrived on October 19, that the Senate had turned down his nomination as envoy to Russia. This event took place on July 16. It was due, partly to a Federalist assertion that the functions of Secretary of the Treasury and Envoy Extraordinary were incompatible; partly to the machinations of a particularly discreditable set of Republican dissidents, headed by Senators Giles, Leib, and Samuel Smith.[45] Gallatin, however, received no official notification; the Tsar had just recognized by letter his position as envoy; and Roumanzoff was decidedly of the opinion that he could not leave until official advices were received from America.[46] Up to the very moment of the Senate's action, President Madison had been unable to decide whether Gallatin would prefer the Treasury without the nomination or the nomination without the Treasury.[47] He now seems to have expected Gallatin to return home and resume his duties.[48] But Gallatin felt that his return under such circumstances would be humiliating and disastrous, and that he could retrieve his political fortunes only by rescuing the negotiation. Though he thought of himself as a private gentleman, and no longer as a member of the commission, he lingered on in St. Petersburg, meditating upon the alternatives of a journey to London or an expedition to the Tsar's headquarters, and growing, as was only to be expected, daily more depressed in spirits and health.[49]

VII

The journey to London began on January 25, 1814.[50] On that day, despite the remonstrances of Roumanzoff, Gallatin and Bayard set out for Amsterdam by way of Berlin, hoping to take ship from Holland to England, and there "to ascertain in a manner involving no responsibility what the views of the British government are in relation to a peace with the United States." [51] At Berlin they learned that word had just been received in Amsterdam from Great Britain that the United States had accepted the British offer to treat directly, and that Great Britain had fixed Gothenburg as the place of meeting.[52] Meanwhile, John Quincy Adams, "still bound up here in these 'thrilling regions of thick ribbed ice,'" was writing to them to complain that "it now appears likely that we shall never be told by the Russian Government how their ally treated their offer of Mediation," and to speak harshly of Russia's "eversion [sic] to communicate a fact which ought to have been made known to us months ago." [53] Nor was the Tsar's exasperating silence ever to be broken.

At Amsterdam, whither they had struggled through one of the harshest winters in the history of Europe, the two Americans learned, on March 20, that Madison had appointed a new commission to treat with the British, and that Gallatin's name was not on the list.[54] None the less, Gallatin felt that he had no choice but to proceed to London, and having obtained the permission of the British government, through the good offices of Alexander Baring, he and Bayard arrived in their enemy's capital on April 9.[55] It was probably here that Gallatin received word of his appointment to the new commission. Here they attempted to pull what strings they could, but the British public was convinced that the Americans were the aggressors, and though the Cabinet was less hostile, and Lord Castlereagh almost friendly, the defeat of Bonaparte had obviously weakened the American position.[56]

VIII

Little is known of the commissioners' actions during this period. At first they lodged together in Seymour Street, where they were peppered with invitations more inquisitive than friendly. Then, it seems, they moved—Mr. Gallatin to Oxford Street, Mr. Bayard to Albemarle Street. The great Jeremy Bentham offered his services. The egregious Cobbett, much to Gallatin's private delight, attempted to force his opinions upon Bayard. There were dreadful dinner parties, which passed off in silence and constraint, with Lord Bathurst and Lord Liverpool.[57] But on May 16 a series of discussions of great significance reached their conclusion. On that day, Lord Bathurst wrote to Bayard and Gallatin, formally proposing the city of

Ghent, "in the Low Countries," as the meeting place; and on May 17 Bayard and Gallatin agreed.[58]

"*Pourquoi Gand?*" asked Emperor Alexander, when this change of meeting-places was brought to his attention.[59] But the question was a rhetorical one. The change from Gothenburg to Ghent was merely the topographical formula for a change in British sentiments. For whereas Ghent was little better than a British garrison, Gothenburg lay well within the sphere of possible Russian influence.

With the abdication of Napoleon, the Fourth Coalition (1812-1814) began to disintegrate. Vast flaws and cracks—political, economic, geographical, dynastic—appeared upon its surface, which, like some plaster hastily applied, had never been either smooth or convincing, and could not stand the seismic jarring of this sudden peace. It was inevitable—more inevitable, even, in those times than in ours—that this disintegrating process should express itself in terms of personalities, and that the Tsar's personality should become an integral part of it. In the last few months of Napoleon's downfall, the figure of Alexander had dominated the scene like some prepotent, living myth. A prince who had discovered the secret—hitherto, oddly enough, never revealed—of Christian liberalism, and who exercised an autocratic rule over a huge, semicivilized, mysterious realm! One would have to be an exceptionally gifted person either to reconcile these conflicting roles or to persuade others that the reconciliation was not a sham. To the outside world, which saw him not at all, to those who were admitted to his kindly presence only occasionally, he might still remain "the darling of the human race," at once the harbinger and the architect of a new era.[60] But the few personages who saw him frequently, and who were able to subject his actions to a keen and intimate scrutiny, had already commenced to distrust and even to despise him. A Christian liberal! Where did the libertine end and the liberal begin? And what confidence could one place in a man who was a sort of latter-day Nostradamus, a prey to mystical impulses and peculiar superstitions, who subjected questions of the highest policy to such prophetic intimations as might be found in the pages of Virgil? Moreover, he was already bringing to perfection the art he had practiced upon the Americans. He used his ministers as the vehicle of his indecisions, and would withdraw in person in the evening what he had solemnly pledged by proxy in the morning.

The Americans, none the less, were forced to rely upon him. Who else, among the crowned heads and the crowding ministers, could be trusted to plead their cause? The Tsar was "half an American," said Lord Castlereagh.[61] Perhaps he was; and, in London, Gallatin and Bayard eagerly awaited his arrival. But William H. Crawford, the American Minister in Paris, who had been intentionally excluded from the list of envoys to be presented to Louis XVIII, could not get near the Tsar.[62] Lafayette became America's intermediary—and Lafayette, agreeable, famous, gullible, and a marquis, was not the kind of liberal upon whom Alexander could turn his back. They met at Madame de Staël's, and the conversation turned at once upon American affairs. Alexander remarked that the Americans had not properly improved their internal situation, by which he was understood to refer to the disaffection of the Federalists. Lafayette replied that political parties were necessary in a commonwealth. Whereupon the Tsar, relenting, declared that he would use his influence in the cause of peace. "My journey to London," he said, "affords opportunities." [63]

He had already sent ahead of him a most dubious emissary—the Grand Duchess Catherine, his sister and confidante. She arrived in London at the end of March, a short, ugly, intensely female woman; and almost from the beginning, out of pure mischief, she took care to excite and to increase the hatred of the Prince Regent. This was easy enough to accomplish; a few well-timed, malicious remarks would serve the purpose; but it was most unwise. The Prince Regent was a constitutional ruler, but not in the sense in which we understand that phrase today. He could and did exercise a considerable influence upon his ministers. Moreover, though the most selfish and disreputable of men, he was not a fool. There may well be some connection between the barbed remarks of the Grand Duchess and the change of venue for the American negotiation from Gothenburg to Ghent. In any case, when the Tsar arrived at the beginning of June, Anglo-Russian relations had been damaged; though of course not beyond repair. Tact and courtesy could have mended them, and never were these qualities more needed. The Tsar, naturally affable, walked freely among the Londoners, almost as if he were anybody else; the Prince Regent, engaged in a discreditable and unpopular effort to divorce his wife, scarcely dared show himself in the streets. This disparity in their relative positions was one that Alexander would have done well not to emphasize. But the Tsar did everything he could to enhance his popularity with the Londoners, and the Prince Regent grew daily more sullen and somber. Nor was this all. Alexander never seems to have understood either the peculiar jealousies of Englishmen or the nature of political parties. His attentions to the leaders of the Whig Opposition were marked, too marked; and they excited, oddly enough, not only the rage of the Tories but that of the Whigs, too. His unpopularity in higher circles communicated itself, in some mysterious fashion, to lower ones; the huzzas grew less frequent in the streets; the admiring crowds, which had gathered around his headquarters at the Pulteney Hotel in Piccadilly, dwindled; and when he left London on June 27, it was in an atmosphere of coolness that he did so.[64]

Nothing could have been more unfortunate from an American point of view. The Tsar was the living embodiment of a resistance to the maritime pretensions of England. Anglo-Russian cordiality might have done something—it might have done a great deal—to bring the British and the Americans to an understanding; and the Tsar and his malicious sister had succeeded in bringing about a condition of Anglo-Russian mistrust. When Gallatin had an audience with Alexander on June 16, the Tsar confessed that he had made three attempts at intervention since he had been in London, but that he feared they had been of little use. Tall and splendid in his uniform and stars, he was infinitely kind and condescending. He patted young James Gallatin on the head. "You are rather young to be in diplomacy," he said. But that, in effect, was all he had to offer.[65]

With this interview, Alexander passed from the scene as an active agent in American affairs. His intentions had been good, and his actions invariably harmful. And yet, after all, his attitude towards the United States—whatever its immediate outcome—was not unjustifiable. The British attempted to keep their American imbroglio free from the affairs of Europe; and as the Congress of Vienna drew nearer, all the sovereigns of Europe, the Tsar alone excepted, either overlooked the United States or regarded them with mistrust.[66] After many years, the circumstances and direction of American growth allowed this separation from the affairs of Europe to become, for long periods, almost an article of American faith; one that, frequently reinforced by liberal misquotations from the Farewell Address of George Washington, survived even the World War of 1914-1918. The past cannot repeat itself. Everything changes, daily, hourly, by the minute, and beyond recall. But just as the physical world is full of images and similes which can be employed for the instruction of man as he passes through, so is the past full of analogies. When the Tsar attempted, in his half-hearted way, to mingle the American negotiation with the affairs of Europe, was he not illustrating the truth that when any one part of the world is in disorder or trouble, all parts of the world are affected? The early history of America displays this truth, just as its contemporary history has come to do. It was not merely impressment, or the nature of Anglo-American trade, or the greed of the frontier imperialists, though these were important factors, it was a whole world movement that brought the American commissioners in the end to Ghent. And another lesson was evidently inculcated by the Tsar's interference. It is most impolitic to trust to the good will of despots, however benevolent. All that the Tsar bestowed upon the Americans was a series of delays; and what he altered, he altered for the worse.

IX

Lord Castlereagh's offer of a direct negotiation traveled to America on the British schooner *Bramble*, which also carried the news of the battle of Leipzig. The conjunction was an ominous one. If Napoleon had been defeated, then the ports of Europe would once again be thrown open to British commerce; the British navy would be able to pay more attention to the American coast; and the British army, released from Spain, would be directed towards America. President Madison did not hesitate, therefore, to accept the offer of Lord Castlereagh. The *Bramble* arrived at Annapolis on December 30; on January 14, Madison nominated J. Q. Adams, J. A. Bayard, Henry Clay, and Jonathan Russell as commissioners to negotiate directly with Great Britain, and the Senate confirmed these nominations four days later. On February 8, realizing at last that Gallatin was determined to stay in Europe, Madison nominated him as a fifth commissioner, and offered the name of George W. Campbell as his successor at the Treasury. These nominations were also accepted. "Your name being restored to the Mission, has revived the hope of its success," wrote A. J. Dallas, who was soon to succeed the inept Campbell.[67]

Clay and Russell set sail on the sloop of war *John Adams* on February 27, and after a tempestuous voyage reached Gothenburg on the 14th of April. The appalling winter had not yet broken, and the Texel was full of ice. A silence settled down upon the movements of all five commissioners, at least as far as America was concerned: as late as May 22, Madison believed that all five were at Gothenburg and in the midst of their negotiation, which, he wagered, would not last a month.[68] The commissioners themselves with difficulty discovered one another's whereabouts. On April 16, Clay and Russell addressed a joint communication to John Quincy Adams, saying that they did not know whether or not he had left Russia, and that they believed Gallatin and Bayard to be in Amsterdam.[69] On April 20, they told Monroe that they had discovered that Gallatin and Bayard were in London, but they had lost all track of Adams.[70] The severity of the winter and violent passing of the war had made communications even worse than they normally were at this season. As the spring slowly arrived, their situation became a little clearer. By May 1, Russell had gone on to Stockholm to take up his duties as Minister, and Clay had learned that there was a possibility of removing the negotiation to Holland.[71] Adams left St. Petersburg for Gothenburg on April 28, took ship from Reval, and after battling with the winds and the ice of the Gulf of Finland, arrived at Stockholm on May 25. Here for the first time he learned that Gallatin and Bayard had remained in London and had written to propose a removal from Gothenburg to Ghent, of which he heartily disapproved, although "it may have been carried so far that I shall be under the necessity of acquiescing in it." [72] He lamented that if he had not been detained at Reval by dangerous weather, he would have arrived in Gothenburg in time to greet Colonel Milligan, Mr. Bayard's secretary, who brought the proposal to remove the negotiation from Sweden, "and in that case none of us would ever have come to Ghent." [73] On June 2, in no very good temper, he set out for Gothenburg.[74] Believing that the British government had not yielded an inch on impressment, he saw nothing but wasted time in these journeys across Europe.[75] At the third post-house out of Stockholm he was met by a messenger from Clay, telling him that the negotiation was now officially transferred to Ghent, "on a proposition by Lord Bathurst, assented to by Messrs. Gallatin and Bayard"; but when he arrived in Gothenburg, Clay had conveniently vanished.[76] The rest of Adams's journey was pleasant, and his spirits rose, for "we have all the time been approaching summer, as the summer has been approaching us." At Amsterdam he went to the theater to hear Cherubini's "*Les Deux Journées*" and "*Ambrose, ou violà ma Journée*" of D'Alayrac, thus missing Mr. Clay, who had also arrived, but who, for once, had gone to bed early.[77] While Clay lingered in Amsterdam, and Russell at The Hague, Adams went on ahead to Ghent, and "you are sufficiently acquainted with my disposition," he told his wife, "to know that it was no inconsiderable gratification to my feelings to find myself the first here." [78]

X

Ghent was little better than a British garrison, crowded with scarlet uniforms and not very much in love with them.[79] The key to the rivers and waterways of Flanders, it had known British garrisons before.[80] If tradition counts for anything in such cases, and perhaps it does, the citizens of Ghent instinctively cared little for eminent personages, less for warriors, and much for independence and for peace. The American commissioners, with their modest retinue, and their unpretentious clothes, satisfied both these latter requirements. The interest was extreme. "Never in my life," Adams wrote on June 30, "did I find myself surrounded by so much curiosity." [81] From then on his letters and his diary are filled with evidence of the kindly feelings of magistrates and people.

All through July, a stream of secondary personages flowed through the city—the two sons of the King of Prussia, his two brothers, the second son of the Prince of Orange, Count Nesselrode, Field Marshal Blücher. But the British commissioners did not arrive. They had been appointed in May—Lord Gambier, Mr. Henry Goulburn, Dr. William Adams. What could be keeping them? The Americans waited for them for days, for weeks, for a whole month. During the course of a debate in the House of Commons on July 20, of which a garbled version was received in Ghent on July 29, Lord Castlereagh protested that the departure of the British commissioners was being regulated so that they might find all the Americans at Ghent when they arrived there, and that by his latest advices from Paris Mr. Gallatin was still in that city. "Now, my dear friend," wrote Adams to his wife, "we have the most substantial reason for knowing that . . . Lord Castlereagh had special and precise information that he had been here at Ghent, a full fortnight, on the day of that debate. So much for Lord Castlereagh's candor." [82] The debate seems to have hastened matters, and the instructions to the British commissioners were handed them on July 28.[83] They had an audience of the Prince Regent to kiss hands on their appointment. They set out for Ghent. Upon their arrival they took up their quarters at the Chartreux, or Charterhouse, a former Carthusian monastery. The date was August 6, 1814.

CHAPTER SIX

The Charterhouse of Ghent

IT SEEMED, at the time, surprising that the three British commissioners should have been men of such mediocre attainments. But they were never their own masters. Their function was to respond to the manipulation of the strings in London; and since their superiors in London were engaged in a series of European negotiations of a most difficult and delicate nature, the strings were sometimes pulled in a very jerky manner, and the puppets danced uncomfortably, awkwardly, with preposterous stops and starts. They were, however, very useful servants, if only because they were men of little consequence. They could be disavowed or scolded without creating so much as a ripple in the political waters of England. For this reason they were permitted to display, in a most masterly fashion, an attitude towards the present and future of America which was old-fashioned, which had helped to bring about the war, and which was destined to pass away forever within the compass of the next decade.

James, Baron Gambier, was an admiral in the British Navy. Around his nice, white, rather handsome head there lingered an aura, if not of sulphur and brimstone, at least of smoke and flame: for he had commanded the British fleet that bombarded the helpless city of Copenhagen in 1807. This ghastly exploit was almost his sole claim to fame, and had earned him his peerage. He had also been court-martialed, and acquitted, for incompetence in 1809. His appointment as the senior plenipotentiary in a negotiation that would presumably deal with maritime questions was slightly ominous and far from tactful. James Gallatin describes him as "a fire cracker which would never go off but was always spluttering." [1] The firecracker never did go off. In the diary and the correspondence of John Quincy Adams, never a merciful commentator, Lord Gambier appears as, on the whole, a courteous and convivial old gentleman. If he possessed any talents as a negotiator, there is no proof of it.

Henry Goulburn, the second plenipotentiary, was more adequately equipped. He had been Under-Secretary of State for War and Colonies, in which position he had acquired a useful knowledge of Canadian affairs. He was essentially a useful man, and could be relied upon—as one learns from the correspondence of his chief, Lord Bathurst—to undertake, not without grumbling, those disagreeable tasks to which useful men are so often condemned. In later years, he attained some eminence in the Tory party. He enjoyed the confidence of Peel, never an easy thing to earn; and was once Home Secretary and twice Chancellor of the Exchequer. Those who rummage in that marvelous warehouse of Tory gossip and history, the *Life of Benjamin Disraeli*, will discover him there: "an old piece of dusty furniture," said Disraeli in 1850, "under whom we might all have served without any great outrage of personal feelings." [2] But it is clear that he had some talent in debate; [3] and that, from long sittings on the Front Bench, he came in the end to enjoy the prescriptive rights of an elder statesman. [4]

Persistence would seem to be the leading characteristic of such a career. At the time of his appearance at Ghent, he was still a young man, just thirty years old. He was very reserved, but his reserve appears to have been in a perpetual state of hasty repair. Under any great pressure from the Americans it would, like a deficient dam, leak little dribbles and freshets of ill temper. But he had much to put up with, for he alone seems to have suffered from the notion that he was, after all, little more than a puppet; and when the Americans quizzed him—as they sometimes did very rudely—upon the inability of his commission to make its own decisions, he would remonstrate pathetically with his superiors. [5]

Of the third plenipotentiary, Dr. William Adams, an expert on maritime law, Henry Adams has written that he was "an unknown man, and remained one." [6] His grandfather has been more explicit. "This personage," wrote John Quincy Adams, in a passage indicating that he knew his Smollett, "has pretensions to wit, and wishes to pass himself off as a sayer of good things. The Chevalier [Bayard], who is a sportsman, was speaking of a fowling piece on a new construction, price fifty guineas, which was primed with one grain of fulminating powder. The Doctor thought that no fowling piece could be good for anything that cost more than five guineas. He hinted to the Chevalier that his fifty guinea musket was a gimcrack—a philosophical whimsey, better for shooting a problem than a partridge; and he was [as] liberal of his sarcasms upon *philosophy* as he could have been, if delivering a dissertation upon gun-boats and dry-docks. The choice of the person upon whom this blunderbuss of law discharged its volley of ridicule against philosophy diverted us all. . . . The Chevalier pronounced our namesake to be a man of no breeding." But Dr. Adams was a scholar of some repute; and scholars are not always well-bred. [7]

In their headquarters at the Chartreux, the British commissioners lived the lives of men to whom sequestration from society was no punishment—almost, one would say, the lives of monks, except that Mr. Goulburn had his wife with him. Their acquaintance in Ghent, said Lord Gambier, was confined exclusively to the Intendant's family.[8] Two immense scarlet sentries trod a clockwork vigilance before their inhospitable doors.

I

On the evening of August 8, the American commissioners received dispatches from Monroe, dated June 25 and June 27, which instructed them to postpone the subject of impressment to a future date, or even to omit it altogether.[9] Their original instructions had insisted that, if they could not procure the abolition of impressment, "all further negotiations will cease, and you will return home without delay." [10] Thus, in a silence that was almost furtive, this great question was smuggled out of the negotiation; and with it went the first of James Madison's war grievances, and all the rodomontade of the West. It was a great concession, and only the state of the war, which was bleak, and the condition of the United States, which was bankrupt, saved it from being a shameful one.[11]

Yet, even when armed with this concession, the Americans learned during the course of their first three conferences with the British—on August 8, 9, and 10—that unless some miracle took place the negotiation was doomed from the start. They had been instructed not to bring the question of fishing privileges into the discussions; and the British explained that these privileges, granted by the Treaty of 1783,[12] would not be renewed without an equivalent.[13] The commissioners had been told to explore the definitions of blockade and the question of neutral rights; but the British had been instructed to shy away from these subjects as if they were some kind of cactus. The British explained that they were obliged to make the matter of Indian pacification and Indian boundaries a *sine qua non:* upon these dangerous topics the Americans had no instructions at all. At the second meeting on August 9, Dr. Adams went a little further, and, with a diffidence and imprecision upon which no admiration need be wasted, sketched out a scheme for an Indian buffer state which filled the Americans with horror. A third meeting on August 9 was taken up with an unseemly wrangling on questions of protocol; and then both commissions retired, to communicate with their governments. It is not surprising that at a dinner given to the Americans in the city—twenty-two in all—on the 12th, Mr. Adams should have proposed the toast: "Lawrence's last words." [14]

On August 18, Lord Castlereagh, with Lady Castlereagh and her sister, and a considerable retinue of carriages, couriers, and secretaries, arrived in Ghent. The British Foreign Secretary was on his way to Paris and Vienna. The Americans did not visit him, and he thought that a decent regard for his own commissioners would not allow him to approach the Americans.[15] In private, he seems to have lectured his underlings on the peremptory tone in which they had conducted their end of the discussion, and to have suggested that perhaps in the future a little politeness might be in order; but they had demurred to this suggestion. They could not, they said, appear to weaken. He protested no further, but proceeded to discuss with them a new set of instructions he had brought with him from London.[16]

It was, therefore, in a mood of increased asperity that the British commissioners approached their American opponents on the 19th.[17] And their proposals were of such a nature that no politeness could have softened them. Reading from Lord Castlereagh's instructions, Henry Goulburn asked that a permanent barrier be erected between British and American territory, beyond which neither government should acquire land; and that this barrier should be the Indian boundary fixed by the Treaty of Greenville in 1795. If we draw a line from Cleveland through the State of Ohio, and extend it to the mouth of the Kentucky River, this would represent the boundary fixed by the Treaty of Greenville; beyond it lay the whole northwest, from which the British thus proposed to exclude the Americans forever. They also proposed a "rectification" of the Canadian frontier of such a kind as to give the British a line from Lake Superior west to the Mississippi, and a direct communication between Halifax and Quebec. The treaty right of the British to the navigation of the Mississippi was to be continued.[18] The Americans must keep no armed vessel or naval force upon the western lakes from Ontario to Superior, inclusive, and must agree neither to build new fortifications along these lakes nor to maintain such fortifications as were already there.[19] The Americans heard Mr. Goulburn out in silence, and then asked if the proposition respecting the Indian boundary was to be considered a *sine qua non?* "Undoubtedly," was the reply. And American disarmament upon the lakes. "One *sine qua non* at a time is enough," said Dr. Adams roughly; but the British envoys admitted, upon further questioning, that they reserved for themselves the right to keep both forts and naval forces on the lakes. What of those Americans who lived beyond the line of the Treaty of Greenville, in Ohio and Indiana and Illinois and Michigan? There were perhaps a hundred thousand of them. They must shift for themselves, said Mr. Goulburn and Dr. Adams.[20]

This is substantially all that remains to us of that conference at the Chartreux on August 19, 1814.

In history, as in legend, there are occasions where time itself seems to have been arrested in its course: when certain events, previously unrelated except as a chronological sequence, seem to come together and present themselves, in a hushed immobility, to the astonished observer. So it is with this conference. Here, at last, one of the leading motives in early Anglo-American relations is finally and irrevocably captured. The coldness of Lord Harrowby, the insults of George Canning, the *Leopard's* feral assault upon the *Chesapeake*—they are all here, no longer as fragments of behavior which can be fitted together only with difficulty, but as the several elements of a single state of mind. The list is endless; but one need add to it only that curious passage from a London newspaper which called for the "deposition" of President Madison, as if he were some savage chieftain lurking in a kraal behind a thorn-hedge, or a nawab rioting in the recesses of his palace. For it was not a set of proposals, but a state of mind, that the British presented to their American opponents. It had been maturing for nearly three decades; it had broken out here and there in irritating rashes and sudden eruptions; and now it had drawn to one preposterous head.

The British commissioners had, in fact, exceeded their instructions; and they exceeded them because they believed in the possibility of one of two alternatives. Either the American commissioners would provisionally accept their proposals, and this acceptance would be ratified by the Executive and the Senate—this they thought the more likely—or the same result could be attained in another year or so of war. In either event the United States, whether united or not, would become that most useful of phenomena—a colony that, being nominally independent, paid its own expenses. For a colony the United States would become, in everything but name. Unable to expand to the west or the northwest, threatened by navies and forts along its undefended lakes, deprived of a part of Maine and of the very sources of the Mississippi, enjoying its fisheries only as a gift to be withdrawn at will, with its merchant marine enmeshed in the complicated nets of the British Navigation Laws—this, evidently, was America, in the mind's eyes of Lord Gambier, Mr. Henry Goulburn, and Dr. William Adams on August 19, 1814.

Only men who were lacking in imagination could have offered with such dull precision so dismal a future; but then only men who lacked imagination could have given a visible shape to such a congregation of unformulated ideas and half-conscious emotions. Indeed, their formulation of August 19 represented all that was unimaginative in the British attitude towards America. It was never to appear again in so palpable a form; for it was essentially old-fashioned, the product of a mercantilism already being undermined by the doctrines of Adam Smith and the energies of British coal and iron.

Lord Castlereagh himself, it is almost needless to say, though he had written the instructions upon which the British commissioners founded their cases, had never intended them to bear such an interpretation. He told Lord Liverpool on August 28 that the whole territorial question was one of expediency, not to be insisted upon to the point of a rupture. Precisely what interpretation he did intend them to bear is more difficult to decide.[21] Although the military situation was such that the British had every hope of a successful invasion from Canada and a successful attack on Baltimore and New Orleans, it is extremely doubtful—it is, in fact, quite improbable—that Lord Castlereagh or his colleagues in London proposed to use these successes as a means of preventing the westward expansion of the United States: *unless, of course, the United States was willing to yield to this crippling restriction.* Even their choice of the Greenville Treaty line as the furthest extent of American growth to the northwest was not as formidable as the British commissioners had made it appear to be; for Indian treaty lines were, to say the least, rather elastic, and to say the most, quite meaningless; and the Greenville Treaty line may well have represented a means of retreat and not of restriction. Perhaps Lord Castlereagh wished to test the resistance of the Americans. Or perhaps, in the spirit of the bazaar, he offered his highest price on the understanding that he would come much lower. In any case, he was quite ready to disavow his underlings at Ghent if they should seem to have placed themselves in a false position; and disavow them he did. On August 19 they spoke their own minds for the last time.

II

The American commissioners, retreating to the Hotel d'Alcantara, began at once their task of replying to the British demands. John Quincy Adams prepared a draft—as head of the commission this was his duty—upon which his colleagues fell without mercy.[22] Mr. Gallatin wished to strike out all offensive phrases; Mr. Clay thought that figurative language was improper in a state paper; Mr. Russell's objections were of a syntactical nature; and Mr. Bayard was passionately addicted to his own vocabulary. From August 21 to August 24 they sat—sifting, erasing, patching, amending—"until we were all wearied, though none of us yet was satiated with amendment." [23] Like the Empress Messalina—*lassata . . . nondum satiata*—the commission at length, at eleven o'clock on the night of August 24, completed its labors.

The intensity of the commissioners was not, of course, due to the niceness of their literary tastes. They were profoundly moved by what seemed to them—as it seems to us—a deliberate attempt to cripple the future of their country. Upon this they were united, and they strove to dress their unity in dignified, decisive, and permanent language. In this they were successful. Their note of August 25 shows no signs of its diverse origin.[24]

It declared that no principles of reciprocity, no maxims of public law, no maritime rights of the British Empire required the establishment of an Indian boundary. "To surrender both the rights of sovereignty and of soil over nearly one-third of the territorial dominions of the United States to a number of Indians, not probably exceeding twenty thousand, the undersigned are so far from being instructed or authorized that they assure the British plenipotentiaries that any arrangement for that purpose would be instantaneously rejected by their government." As for the rest of the British demands—"they were above all dishonorable to the United States in demanding from them to abandon territory and a portion of their citizens; to admit a foreign interference in their domestic concerns, and to cease to exercise their natural rights on their own shores and in their own waters." This reply, Adams wrote in his diary, should bring the negotiations very shortly to a close. Bayard had already warned the British that their conditions would prolong the war.[25] "It has not made the least impression upon me or my colleagues," reported Goulburn to Bathurst.[26]

Some impression, however, had been made upon the London government and its Foreign Secretary in Paris. When Lord Castlereagh received Mr. Goulburn's report, he realized at once that the commissioners had gone too far. He wrote to Goulburn, telling him to say nothing more until he had received further instructions from London.[27] The Prime Minister was more explicit: "Our commissioners," he told Lord Castlereagh, "[have] taken a very erroneous view of our policy." But what was his policy? "I think it not unlikely," he continued, "after our note has been delivered in, that the American commissioners will propose to refer the subject to their Government. In that case the negotiation may be adjourned till the answer is received, and we shall know the result of the campaign before it can be resumed. If our commander does his duty, I am persuaded that we shall have acquired by our arms every point on the Canadian frontier which we ought to insist on keeping." [28] Thus everything was made to depend upon the formidable expedition already moving towards Plattsburg under Sir George Prevost. It would almost seem as if Lord Liverpool disagreed with his commissioners only upon a point of language, not of intention. But if we examine the agitated correspondence that flew to and fro between London and Vienna, and between the Prime Minister and his Secretary of State for War and Colonies, we see that this was not the case. By September 14, the Earl of Liverpool had already abandoned the Indian boundary, and was anxious only not to abandon the Indians. If the Indian question could be arranged, he asked, "might we not then make a demand for Niagara, Michilimackinack and Sackett's Harbour, and, if they were granted, propose to waive any question about the territory of Maine?" The Americans, he believed, would direct their whole reasoning against the claim to Sackett's Harbour. "This would give us time. We might hear from America in the interim. If we did not, we might then decide whether we would insist on Sackett's Harbour or be contented with the other positions. At all events it is material that they should be informed that we have agreed to modify the principle of the *exclusive* military possession of the Lakes. . . ." [29] With these broad strokes, the Prime Minister outlined an astonishing picture of diplomatic retreat. He did not know that, even while he was making it, another and equally significant retreat had taken place. Sir George Prevost was already in full flight from Plattsburg.

III

Mr. Goulburn and his colleagues received their new instructions on September 3, and communicated them in a long note dated September 4.[30] It was, of course, a reply to the American note of August 25, which Lord Liverpool had already denounced as "a most impudent one, and, as to all its reasoning, capable of an irresistible answer." [31] The irresistibility of Liverpool's reasoning must, however, remain in some doubt; for the British commission, while maintaining the spirit of its new instructions, on this occasion transgressed the letter of them. It accused the Americans of having pursued a policy of acquisition and aggrandizement—in Florida, in Louisiana, towards the Indians; and, "it is notorious to the whole world that the conquest of Canada, and its permanent annexation to the United States, was the declared object of the American Government." [32] The use of the word "declared" was a fatal error. It was fortunate, indeed, that the British commission never learned of the existence of certain paragraphs in Mr. Monroe's instructions—paragraphs of so compromising a character that they were never published—in which the Secretary of State made it abundantly clear that nothing less than the seizure of Canada would content him. [33] Mr. Clay had many times declared in Congress that Canada must be seized; but the British commissioners had no more right to give an official character to what had been said in Congress than the Americans had to search the speeches of private members of the House of Commons for official arguments. Whom then did the British have in mind? In a private conversation with Mr. Adams, Henry Goulburn had already confessed that General Hull was the culprit. Whereupon Mr. Adams protested that no government could be held responsible for the manifestoes of generals, issued on remote frontiers; though he refrained from expressing any surprise at the choice of so discredited a general as William Hull. [34]

Upon no question was the United States so vulnerable as upon that of Canada. Wherever one examined the American past—in Congress or out of it, in the acquisitive oratory of Republican representatives or the denunciations of New England preachers, in the proclamations of generals or the grumbling of Federalist merchants—the conquest of Canada, in one form or another, had been on everybody's lips. Even the American commission was open to attack. Had not Mr. Clay, as Senator and Speaker, proclaimed himself an imperialist? And, on the wider question of a policy of aggrandizement, had not Senator Bayard attacked the government's policy towards Florida? Indeed, where Florida was concerned, the President himself had used language that might now have been turned against him with great effect. But it so happened that never, upon any public occasion, had a President or a Secretary of State declared himself in favor of the conquest of Canada. When the British note was examined, Mr. Clay was for answering it by a note of half a page: its language, he thought, was stupid. Mr. Adams, who had made no expansionist speeches in Congress, disagreed. "I neither thought it stupid," he said, "nor proper to be answered in half a page." Mr. Adams was doubtless thinking of those paragraphs in Monroe's instructions which the American commission had tacitly decided not to use; and his conscience was bothering him. [35] The American reply, however insecure as to its foundations, was not lacking in force, and, where it touched upon the Indian problem, attained all the eloquence that might be expected from men who had just been released by their opponents from a very awkward trap. [36] When Lord Liverpool read it, his spirits were sensibly dampened. "It was impossible to read their last note," he admitted, "without admitting that upon this one point [of the Indians], as far as it was an *argumentum ad homines*, they had the best of it." [37] "Goulburn and our other commiss.," he went on, "evidently do not feel the inconvenience of the continuance of the war. I feel it strongly, but I feel it as nothing now to what it may be a twelve-month hence."

IV

While peace thus dawned upon the mind of Lord Liverpool, the British commissioners strove to unite their opponents in the cause of war. The strings had been pulled rather sharply, and the puppets were condemned to a jerky obedience: but they were, unfortunately, articulate, and while their thoughts could be controlled their language could not. Lords Liverpool and Bathurst had been listening, it is fairly safe to assume, to Spanish voices in London, and their new instructions contained more specific references to Florida.[38] But the Spanish ambassador, Count Fernan Nuñez, demanded not only the evacuation of the occupied sections of Florida, but also the return of all of Louisiana; and Liverpool and Bathurst were not the men to encourage such pretensions.[39] Their references to Florida were perfunctory, a mere discharge of obligations, but the eager gentlemen in Ghent converted them into language so insulting that Mr. Adams was determined to explore the whole question.[40] Mr. Gallatin, however, was now the head of the commission in all but name, and he let it be known that this must not go on. He himself had fought the government's Florida policy in the Cabinet, and he knew very well that both Monroe and Madison were open to the charge that they had nourished a clandestine plot to revolutionize East Florida.[41] Mr. Adams was not familiar with the secrets of Madison's Administration: but he had a great respect for Mr. Gallatin—"he keeps and increases," he said, "his influence over us all"— [42] and he turned from this fruitful topic to the even more agreeable one of lecturing the British upon the striking evidences of Divine Providence and of attention to public law which might be discovered in the American behavior towards the Indians. His colleagues struck this language out: it was mere cant, said Mr. Clay, between whom and Mr. Adams all cordiality had long disappeared. The result was a reasonable statement upon Indian pacification, which, while it maintained the principle of American sovereignty, did something to allay British fears as to the fate of their Indian allies. "The style of the papers we receive," said the dissatisfied Mr. Adams, "is bitter as the quintessence of wormwood—arrogant, dictatorial, insulting—and we pocket it all with the composure of the Athenian who said to his adversary, 'Strike but hear!' " [43] The American reply was sent to the British on the 25th, and forwarded at once to London.[44] "Neither pacific nor conciliatory," was Lord Liverpool's comment. Could not Lord Bathurst ask Sir Christopher Robinson to look up all the instances in which "stipulations have been made in treaties by one belligerent, not for individuals, but for parties, sects, tribes, &c., residing within the dominions of another?" But his mind was already occupied with different thoughts. "The Americans," he wrote, "took more than a week to answer our last note. We need not, therefore, be in any great haste about our reply. Let them feast upon Washington." [45] The news of the capture and burning of Washington had just arrived in London.

It is only just to Lord Liverpool and the members of his government to say that they did not maintain this note of triumph for very long. The burning of the public buildings at Washington on August 24 and 25 by a British force under Major-General Robert Ross and Rear Admiral Sir George Cockburn was an act of vandalism for which nobody has been able to find an excuse. After a brief and somewhat shamefaced celebration, the British themselves condemned it. It certainly diminished to the point of invisibility what was left of the prestige of James Madison, who had been obliged to fly into the Virginia hills while his capital burned behind him; but it seems to have enhanced that of the capital itself. Hitherto regarded as a remote and unfortunate necessity, Washington—in some quarters at least—was promoted to a symbol of union and resistance. In a negative way, its new prestige was immediately disclosed by the depressing effect that its capture had upon the already tottering banks; and this influence radiated far beyond the United States. When the news reached Paris on September 30, for example, it was speedily carried to the Rue de Grenelles, where Madame de Staël (though so ardently American in her sympathies that she bored the Duke of Wellington, not easily bored by admiring ladies) sat down at once to write to Gallatin for advice as to the immediate disposal of her holdings in American lands and funds.[46] Not for nothing was she a banker's daughter.

On October 1, the news was brought to Ghent.

CHAPTER SEVEN

Peace

M R. GALLATIN, writing to Madame de Staël, gave it as his opinion
that the British had blown up or burned the Capitol and President's
House (*faire sauter ou brûler les palais du Congrès et du Président*) because,
with the exception of certain cathedrals, England had no public building to
compare with them.[1] This extravagant thought, a compound of grief and
rage, represents the state of mind of the commission when the news became
known. Even the high spirits of Mr. Clay, who was by nature inclined to
regard each American disaster as the aphelion of a comet, the furthest midnight point at which it turns again towards the sun, were sadly abashed.

I

If cometary analogies are permissible, then the capture of Washington was
indeed an aphelion. At that point the United States must either vanish from
all calculation or turn upwards on its great ellipse. To the watchers at Ghent,
either event was possible, and the former more likely than the latter. The
expedition that had raided Washington would presumably move on to the
capture of Baltimore; another armada, under the general command of Lord
Hill, was said to be preparing to cross the ocean towards New Orleans;
while Sir George Prevost, as far as was then known, was moving towards
Plattsburg and the great invasion route of Lake Champlain. The Americans
had captured Amherstsburg and Erie, the British held Michilimackinac and
Niagara and all of Maine east of the Penobscot. The American navy ruled
Lake Erie, but Captain Downie and his British warships seemed to be the
power upon Lake Champlain. Whatever balance existed in this state of
affairs would be fatally upset by a success on the part of Prevost or Ross.
On October 14, the British commissioners sent the Americans a copy of

the London *Times* of October 10, and another of October 11, containing official accounts of the capture of Machias and other towns on Passamaquoddy Bay, the destruction of the frigate *Adams*, the failure of Lieutenant-Colonel Croghan at Michilimackinac, and the siege of Plattsburg by the British-Canadian army. Mr. Clay, visibly more upset than his colleagues, as he was always more mercurial, railed "at the commerce and the people of Massachusetts."[2] He would have done better to rail at the British, who on October 8 had already presented their opponents with the best-written of all their notes.[3] In this they made some menacing comments upon the illegality of the Louisiana Purchase and the avarice and oppression of the United States in its acquisition of territory in Florida, demanded enough territory to afford a communication between Halifax and Quebec, and presented an article on Indian pacification which they called an "ultimatum." This note was principally the work of Lord Bathurst. Undoubtedly its Louisiana and Florida portions bore some imprint of the pressure of Count Fernan Nuñez, the Spanish ambassador, but it seems principally to have been designed to scare the Americans into submission.[4] In this it was partially successful. Adams pleaded in vain for a full and powerful answer on Florida and Louisiana, and declared that the pacification of the Indians represented a concession so great that he was prepared to break off upon it rather than yield. But he was in a minority of one.[5] Oppressed by the news from home, his colleagues accepted—*sub spe rati*, subject to the ratification or rejection of their government—the Indian ultimatum, believing that it was reciprocal, did not include the Indians as parties in the peace, and that it obliged them to concede little or nothing. Their note, which was sent on October 18, also contained a request for a British *projet* that should include all the points considered essential by Great Britain, and promised to submit a *contre-projet*.[6]

Thus, though the Americans could not recognize its approach, the peace came a step nearer.[7]

It came nearer still in the British reply, dispatched from London on October 18. Lord Bathurst's instructions were full of significant changes. He was prepared to discuss or not, as the Americans pleased, the right of naturalization and the question of impressment; he was willing to explore the boundary question on a basis of *uti possidetis* (the "state of possession" or each nation to keep what it had won); and he proposed to deny to the United States the right of drying and curing fish on unsettled British shores. These instructions were embodied in a note that the British commissioners sent to their opponents on October 21.[8] Its tenor was severe, but deceptively so. The British demands up to this point had included half of Maine and all the banks of the St. Lawrence from Plattsburg to Sackett's Harbour; now they were being slowly reduced to a point upon which the whole Empire was prepared to make its stand—the exclusion of American fishermen from British shores, and the right of way to Quebec.[9] The exclusion and the right of way involved, it is true, the dismemberment and ruin of Massachusetts; but the reduction was none the less a momentous one. Nor is the reason for it hard to find. On October 17, while Lord Bathurst and his colleagues were still deliberating upon their answer, news had been received in London that Macdonough had defeated and killed Downie on Lake Champlain and that Sir George Prevost, retiring from Plattsburg, had given up the invasion of Canada.

Sir George had retired from Plattsburg in a manner that suggested rather a rout than a retreat; yet he had scarcely engaged the enemy. In a later report he declared that it was useless for him to continue the fight on shore, once the British navy had been defeated by Macdonough on the lake.[10] The version of Major General Sir Frederick Philipse Robinson was more interesting. Sir Frederick had commanded Sir George's flank attack on Plattsburg, which was supposed to cross the Saranac and take the American works in reverse. By all accounts, he had lost his way, and, hearing the American cheers that announced Macdonough's victory, had halted, while the whole British army waited in vain for his assault. Naturally enough, such a commonplace version of his actions did not commend itself to Sir Frederick. He told Lord Bathurst that he and his "six regiments of Wellingtonians" were *"driving the Doodles in all directions"* when ordered to retire from the redoubts because H.M.S. *Confiance* had struck her colors to U.S.S. *Saratoga*. As for the British gunboats, they had sailed away, wrote Sir Frederick, "in the most shameful manner, without doing anything from the first." In any combined attack, if it fails, the army is apt to blame the navy; but Robinson's conclusions went beyond this, and are worth reporting. "I am sick at heart," he wrote, "this is no field for a military man above the rank of a colonel of riflemen. . . . This country can never again afford such an opportunity, nothing but a defensive war can or ought to be attempted here, and you will find that the expectations of His Majesty's ministers and the people of England will be utterly destroyed in this quarter." Sir George Prevost, who was soon to be recalled, doubtless agreed with this prediction; and from beyond the grave comes the ghostly assent of General John Burgoyne.[11]

These reports had not yet, of course, reached London; but the bare news of Plattsburg was enough, especially when combined, as it was, with the tidings of George Drummond's defeat at Fort Erie, and of the death of General Ross and the retirement of his army at Baltimore. The effect upon the Americans at Ghent was one of reprieve, but that was all. In their notes they had never departed from the high tone set by Monroe in his communication to Lord Castlereagh on January 5, in which he had insisted upon the rights of the United States as a sovereign and independent nation.[12] Now they refused to treat on a basis of *uti possidetis*.[13] Not realizing as yet either the extent or the implications of the British reduction of territorial claims, they were convinced that their reply would bring the negotiation to a close.[14]

But the American war had once again assumed its position as an unassimilable fragment of a world conflict. "If we had been at peace with all the world," Lord Liverpool wrote Lord Castlereagh on November 2, "and the arrangements to be made at Vienna were likely to contain anything very gratifying to the feelings of this country, we might have met the question [of the continuance of the American war] with some degree of confidence." [15] Nothing could be more curious than Lord Liverpool's statement that England could be at peace with the whole world and still continue her American war. A certain confusion of thought, however, might well be forgiven him, for at Vienna everything was in disorder. The month of October had been taken up with questions of procedure, from which only Talleyrand had emerged with credit, and which offered the single assurance that there never would be, in the full sense of the term, a Congress of Vienna.[16] Napoleon was shut up in Elba, where he maintained an eccentric court; Louis XVIII, learning nothing and forgetting nothing, sat upon the throne of his fathers; Europe was at peace. Never had peace seemed less durable. Already the question of an independent Poland shadowed the conferences at Vienna and threatened to produce another war, for which history had many somber precedents. At the heart of this question stood the Tsar and his army, and the Tsar might be tempted to mingle his American sympathies with his efforts to create a constitutional Polish state. He would then be certain to reopen the question of maritime rights, and if he did so the American war might cease to be just an expensive inconvenience; it might become a disaster.

Other considerations, of a financial and commercial nature, perturbed the mind of Lord Liverpool, but where the Congress of Vienna was concerned the government naturally turned to the Duke of Wellington, who had raised common sense to the status of genius, and whose presence in America might make the war respectable in the eyes of Europe. On November 3, the Cabinet decided to ask the Duke if he would not go to the United States, in order to bring the war to an honorable conclusion.[17] The Duke replied on November 9:

> "I have already told you and Lord Bathurst that I feel no objection to going to America, though I don't promise to myself much success there. . . . That which appears to me to be wanting in America is not a general, or a general officer and troops, but a naval superiority on the Lakes. . . . In regard to your present negotiations, I confess that I think you have no right, from the state of war, to demand any concession of territory from America. . . . You have not been able to carry it into the enemy's territory, notwithstanding your military success and now undoubted military superiority, and have not even cleared your own territory on the point of attack. . . . Why stipulate for the *uti possidetis?* You can get no territory; indeed, the state of your military operations, however creditable, does not entitle you to demand any."

This reply is famous, and historians have generally contented themselves with it. It appears, however, that while the Cabinet was writing to the Duke, asking him to go to America, the Duke was writing to the Cabinet, suggesting that he should do so. The earlier letter is not without interest.

"I see that the public are very impatient," Wellington wrote on November 4 from Paris, "about the want of success in America, and I suspect that they will never be quiet till I shall go there. I think that matters are in so uncomfortable a state here, and they are so little settled in Congress [of Vienna], that you could not spare me out of Europe; and indeed it is now too late to think of going to America this year; and I believe that I should not be able to go to Quebec till April. If, however, in March next you should think it expedient that I should go there, I beg you will understand that I have no objection whatever." [18]

Five days had sufficed to bring about an extraordinary change in the thinking of the Duke of Wellington. On November 4, he was willing to go to America in March, and apparently in no doubt as to his success if he should do so. On November 9, he was still ready to go, but doubted his success, because of a lack of naval superiority on the Lakes. We can surely assume that in the interval he had had leisure to meditate upon the battle of Plattsburg, and had come to the conclusion that Macdonough's victory was decisive.[19]

After Wellington's letter of November 9, it was impossible for the British Cabinet to continue with its demands for territory. From then on the whole nature of the negotiation changed. When the *Confiance* struck her colors to the *Saratoga* in Plattsburg Bay on September 11, the effect was felt from Canada to Vienna.

II

Only at Ghent did the turning of the tide of military disaster sound, in the ears of the isolated American commissioners, a jangling note. The Americans believed that their rejection of the *uti possidetis* spelled the end of the negotiation. Even when the British replied on October 31 with a demand for an American *projet*,[20] the Americans suspected that they were simply killing time until they should hear of some British success at New Orleans, whither the expedition of Cochrane was presumed to be creeping after its defeat at Baltimore.

None the less, they set to work writing a *projet* to contain all their demands; and they were faced at once with a terrifying dilemma. If they based their right to the fisheries upon the third article of the Treaty of 1783, then by the eighth article of the same Treaty they must admit the British right to a free navigation of the Mississippi. If one right was indefeasible, so was the other. They dared not accept the British contention that the Treaty of 1783 had ceased to exist with the War of 1812. No doubt that was sound international doctrine; but to the Americans the Treaty of 1783 and the independence of America were very nearly identical. What could they do? The West was not what it had been in 1783: it had become a political force, and Henry Clay was its champion. His very future was involved in a successful resistance to the British claim to navigate the Mississippi, which had been revived in this menacing fashion after lying dormant for thirty years. John Quincy Adams could hardly be described as the champion of Massachusetts. The Adams family was a hissing in State Street, and a dubious mystery everywhere else in the state. But John Quincy Adams was, at least, the champion of the Adams family; and he would never surrender a right for which his father had battled in 1783. Neither Clay nor Adams was a man who took pleasure in silence if it was possible to speak, or who, if speech represented the assassination of an enemy, would speak with less conviction. Now at last, after weeks of enforced restraint, these two articulate personalities discharged their batteries upon each other. There were scenes of towering rage and violent recrimination; and though the wrath of public men is rarely as dreadful as it sounds, it almost seemed as if, in the little sitting-room in the Rue des Champs, there was taking place in miniature that very event which conservative Europe had so confidently awaited—the disruption of the Union. But Albert Gallatin interposed and, with all the delicacy of supreme tact and indomitable patience, brought about a compromise. Both opponents were to keep silence. Trembling with rage—with their best arguments unanswered and their worst epithets still undischarged —they agreed to do so. And so, in the note that accompanied their *projet*, the Americans merely stated that they had no authority to discuss the fisheries; while upon the subject of the Mississippi they said nothing at all. The note and the *projet* were delivered on November 10.[21]

When they received this communication, the British commissioners revealed once again that rather saurian state of mind which had characterized the behavior of General Ross and Admiral Cockburn at Washington. They observed that their opponents were prepared to treat on a basis of *status quo ante bellum*, or the state before the war, but would have nothing to do with the *uti possidetis*, or state of possession. They were undecided whether to break off the negotiation upon this question, or whether to break it off on the question of the fisheries. But to break it off upon one question or the other was their united resolve. Which would be the more favorable? They were not oversensitive men; but the answer they received from London was calculated to cause them extreme discomfort. They were to abandon the *uti possidetis*, and they were *not* to abandon the negotiation.[22]

They could be forgiven for misinterpreting the intentions of Lords Liverpool and Bathurst, for these two noblemen oscillated rather wildly between peace and war. But Lord Liverpool was a solid man and Lord Bathurst a capable one; their oscillations were more perplexing than real; and they had been slowly turning towards a pacific point of view. The British commissioners had neither the temperament nor, to do them justice, the information with which to realize this. High above their heads, the British government labored to make up its mind: now, at last, it was made up. So far from attempting, like its commissioners, to urge the Americans into a continuance of the war, it was determined to force them to make a peace.

III

By the middle of November, Lord Castlereagh's maneuvers at Vienna had lost the confidence of the British Parliament, press, and public, and seemed to be heading, if anywhere, towards a new European war. It is hardly necessary to emphasize the effect this was bound to have upon the negotiations at Ghent; and such emphasis as is needed is readily supplied by a letter Alexander Baring wrote to Albert Gallatin on November 15.

Baring was the London banker for the United States, a position that transcended belligerence. As a Member of Parliament, he had consistently opposed the government's American policy, but for unofficial communications he had always acted as the middleman between the Cabinet and the American commissioners. There was probably no man in England at that time in whom the Americans reposed a more complete trust.

Now he wrote to Gallatin that for the Louisiana dividend, due in January, "we have remittances from the United States Treasury but they are *all* protested." Ordinarily, he continued, he would have made the advances, but now he had some scruples as to the eventual security. Nor was this all. He was about £25,000 in advance on the account for the relief of seamen—this account being now liable to heavy charges for prisoners of war. Here he confessed to scruples of a very different kind. It was not the money that worried him—he stood to lose a few thousand pounds more or less—but could he continue with these payments, or with those connected with the negotiation at Ghent, or even with his payments on the Louisiana dividend, when he was clearly "advancing sums for the service of a Government with which we are at war? . . . I live in hopes," he concluded, "that before the question comes of payment of the January Dividend some favourable change may occur to relieve my anxiety." [23] In other words, if the Americans did not make a speedy peace, Mr. Baring threatened to deprive them of all banking facilities: to proclaim their government bankrupt in Europe, to starve them out at Ghent, and to inflict upon their prisoners of war whatever further miseries there remained to be inflicted. Even the most innocent mind could not fail to see that the British government had asked Mr. Baring to put pressure on the American commissioners, and that Mr. Baring had been only too glad to do so.

Three days after this letter was written, the British Cabinet finally decided to abandon all territorial claims upon the United States, except as regarded certain islands in Passamaquoddy Bay.[24] On November 26, the British commissioners, in the language of reluctant obedience—"the undersigned have foreborne to insist upon the basis of *uti possidetis*, to the advantage of which they consider their country fully entitled"—made it clear that all major obstacles to a peace had been removed except the ominous question of the fisheries and the Mississippi.[25] On November 29 Mr. Baring wrote another and even more curious letter to Mr. Gallatin. No more was said about refusing credit; all was kindness and accommodation. But the kindness of bankers is supremely practical and demands a practical return. Mr. Baring merely pointed out that £21,300 in Louisiana dividends were payable in London in January; that he had £13,800 on hand with which to make the payment; that the United States had sent him for this purpose £33,200 in bills which had been protested and would not be paid, and £7,600 in bills on the north of Ireland which had not yet been returned but which he thought would prove good. If they did prove good, he would be left with a balance of £100, from which he was expected to advance the 300,000 florins due in Amsterdam in January for the payment of the Louisiana dividend there. On the Account of Seamen, the United States owed Mr. Baring £30,100, of which £12,900 had recently been paid in good bills, leaving a balance against the United States of £17,200. The Secretary of the Treasury had also sent a remittance of £22,400 "towards discharging the expenses incident to the intercourse with Foreign nations on the Continent," of which £7,400 were in good bills and £15,000 in bad bills; and from this Baring Brothers were supposed to remit 100,000 florins to the bankers in Amsterdam.[26]

Thus Mr. Baring tormented the financial conscience of the ex-Secretary of the Treasury. The letter of November 29 must have reached Ghent by December 4; by December 14 Mr. Gallatin was ready to abandon the American claim to the fisheries. There remains only one more item in this strange —and, for all we know, one-sided—correspondence. On December 2 Mr. Baring wrote to Mr. Gallatin to explain the character of the protested or doubtful bills, which amounted in all to £48,185 19s. 10d. There was a bill for £17,139 13s. 5d., drawn by Jacob Barker on Messrs. Harard of Liverpool, which had already been protested, and another for £8,046 6s. 5d., drawn by Minturn and Champlin "on ourselves fell due yesterday and protested. The Drawers have failed." There was a bill for £15,000, drawn by Barker on Harard, falling due on January 30, and another for £8,000, drawn by Barker on Mallet and Sons, falling due on January 7—these might still be taken up at maturity, but Baring thought the chance a slight one. "These Bills," he added, "are all connected with some shipments from Amelia Island which we do not exactly understand." [27]

That the United States Treasury should found its credit upon the dubious fortunes of Barker and Minturn was bad; that it should default upon its international obligations was worse; but both circumstances combined were not so astonishing as the disingenuous attitude of Mr. Baring. When two New York merchants, like Jacob Barker and William Minturn Jr., drew bills on a Liverpool merchant in connection with shipments from Amelia Island, everyone knew exactly what those shipments were. Amelia Island was an entrepôt for illegal transactions in cotton between the United States and Great Britain.

The War of 1812 was at least as fruitful in ironies as any other war, but it produced no greater irony than this. The Treasury was attempting to discharge its English obligations out of the proceeds of transactions that officially it was bound to condemn. Mr. Gallatin knew this, Mr. Baring knew it, everyone knew it; no one was prepared to understand "exactly" what he knew. Amelia Island was another Heligoland, where smuggling was carried on with the connivance of both governments. The trade relations between the United States and Great Britain were, indeed, much the same as those which had previously subsisted between Great Britain and France; they were less spectacular, but the political morality was no different. War corrupts all men. "For carrying our produce to foreign markets," wrote Thomas Jefferson at the outbreak of the war, "our own ships, neutral ships, and even enemy ships under neutral flag, which I would wink at, will probably suffice."[28] The notion that war must be made popular with producers by allowing a trade with the enemy was not original to Mr. Jefferson; it had been that of Napoleon and the British Board of Trade. Try as they would, American statesmen could never get around it. In 1812 and 1813, American grain had been shipped to the Peninsula under British license, in order to feed the armies of Wellington, and Congress did not put a stop to this trade until, with the opening of the Baltic in 1813, it had ceased to become profitable.[29] The British who fought at Bladensburg and burned the Capitol were the products, as to their health, of these shipments; so were the "six regiments of Wellingtonians" under Sir Frederick Robinson at Plattsburg, though these might claim that their immediate rations had been provided by American farmers from across the frontier. The British always broke their own blockade when it pleased them and tightened it when it pleased them; private American citizens were anxious to assist them in the former operation, and the efforts of the American government to offset the latter by imposing a new embargo lasted only from December 1813 to March 1814.[30]

From then on, it was a question of which economy would be the first to collapse—or, rather, which country needed the other more. The American degeneration was more rapid. After the fall of Washington in August, bank paper depreciated so swiftly that it soon commanded no more than a very local circulation: the government was unable to transfer its bank deposits from one part of the country to another; and by November 9, 1814, things had come to such a pass that it was obliged to admit itself bankrupt.[31] The last word seemed to be spoken on January 21, 1815, when John W. Eppes, Chairman of the Committee of Ways and Means, read out a communication from the Secretary of the Treasury in which he confessed that "when I perceive that more than forty millions of dollars must be raised for the service of the year 1815, by an appeal to the public credit through the medium of Treasury notes and loans, I am not without sensations of extreme solicitude." When Mr. Eppes had finished reading this communication he threw it on the table "with expressive violence, and turning round to Mr. Gaston [William Gaston, Federalist representative from North Carolina], asked him with a bitter levity between jest and earnest,—'Well, sir! will your party take up the government if we give it to them?' 'No, sir!' said Gaston; . . . 'No, sir! Not unless you will give it to us as we gave it to you!'"[32]

Thus it would seem that the British had merely to wait for the American republic to collapse under its own weight. Yet the British uneasiness, as it filtered its way through the letters of Alexander Baring, was evidently acute. How else could a man whose relations with the American government had been friendly and sincere, and who had consistently profited by his financial dealings with American merchants, have been persuaded to enter upon a course of blackmail, however oblique, and of menace, however veiled? And, in truth, the British did not believe that they could continue the war much longer. The news from Vienna promised little but a renewal of the European war; the press was divided between hatred of the Americans and distrust of the government; Parliament was growing restless; loans were at a discount; the American war was becoming more extensive than had been foreseen; and the public debt was the largest in history. A relatively primitive economy like that of the United States might survive the collapse of the general government: and, indeed, never did armies fight so well as that under General Brown, at Lundy's Lane, in the midst of a disaffected countryside, or that under General Jackson, at New Orleans, with the backing of a penniless and impotent administration. But the British war economy could hardly sustain a re-enactment of the property tax.[33]

Moreover—and this was a paramount consideration, and was to remain so for many years to come—it was clear that British commercial interests needed an untrammeled North American market. The collapse of the money market in 1810 as a consequence of the Jeffersonian embargo had already proved this; the proof was repeated in the repeal of the Orders-in-Council in 1812; and if a further repetition were needed it could be discovered in the letters of Alexander Baring.

And so, with peace a foregone conclusion, the negotiation at Ghent turned more and more towards the question of what kind of United States would emerge from the tribulations of the eighteenth century into the promises of the nineteenth. If the War of 1812 had any meaning, it was to be found in this question and its answer. The British commissioners had originally insisted that no kind of United States, worth considering, would emerge; and by so doing they had united their adversaries beyond the hope of dividing them. They now turned—too late—towards the problems of the fisheries and the Mississippi, and were able only to prove that disunity must, sooner or later, fall to the lot of the American people. The unity of the American commissioners, though they shook it, they were never able to dissolve.

IV

The American commissioners received on November 27 the British reply to their *projet* and note of November 10. As far as the Americans could understand it, which was not far enough, this reply practically conceded the American right to the fisheries, while it insisted upon the British right to navigate the Mississippi. Adams was ready to accept it as it stood; but Clay, with his ally Russell, vehemently opposed it. In 1783, the United States did not own the mouth of the Mississippi, scarcely knew whether or not they owned its source, and laid claim to only one of its banks. A right to free navigation was, therefore, a very different thing in 1783 from what it had since become in 1814. The British commissioners, it is true, had now yielded on the northwest boundary question. The American *projet* of November 10 asked for a boundary along the forty-ninth degree of North latitude, from the Lake of the Woods across the Rocky Mountains; and the British in their reply merely requested free access to the Mississippi over whatever American territory should lie between it and the Canadian frontier. But the demand for free navigation remained: the symbolical significance of that demand was immense; and Clay, whether as an imaginative or as a political man, was bound to resist it. So long as the British clung to it, so long were they unwilling to accept the principle of westward expansion. Moreover, Clay's Western mind was filled with disturbing visions of British traders wandering freely between Canada and the Mississippi, and filling the whole Northwest with corruption and conspiracy.

There were other considerations, though they did not occur to the commissioners at Ghent. In 1807, the steamboat *Clermont* moved heavily up the Hudson; in 1809 there was a steamboat on Lake Champlain, another on the Raritan, another on the Delaware.[34] In 1811, the stroke of the steamboat's paddle-wheel was first heard on the Ohio.[35] The age of wind, and horses, and waterfalls was drawing to a close. How long would it be before British ocean-going steamboats entered the continental waterway from the Gulf of Mexico? And how invaluable would the right of free navigation then become!

Henry Clay, who did not think of steamboats, but to whom the Mississippi was a sacred river, argued his case for three days; and for three days Albert Gallatin sought to effect a compromise. Would it not suffice, merely as a basis for further negotiation, if the Americans agreed to accept the navigation of the Mississippi and the British conceded the right to the fisheries? [36] Mr. Clay said no, Mr. Adams said yes: the assault of the former was scarcely more dangerous than the defense of the latter, who was now unloved by all his colleagues. But at length, over *all* their signatures, the Americans agreed to renew both the rights.[37] It was Gallatin's greatest victory.

A conference was held at the Chartreux on December 1, the first meeting of the two commissions since August. It immediately became apparent that the British had no intention of yielding upon the fisheries. The matter was an imperial one. Canadians had long gazed with jealousy upon the American fishermen who "swarmed like flies" of a Sunday on the Gulf of St. Lawrence, dealing out tea, coffee, clothing, and a hundred other articles on which no duty was ever paid.[38] It was well known that before the war at least three quarters of the dried fish exported from Massachusetts came from the Bay of Chaleur and the coast of Labrador. What *natural* right did the Americans have to dry their fish on unsettled British bays, harbors, and creeks? At a further conference on December 11 the British, instructed from London, declared their willingness to renew, for fair equivalents, both the fishing liberty and the navigation of the Mississippi, thus implying that both rights were forfeited, or subject to forfeit, by war.[39] This was hardly an improvement; and though it implied a British readiness to negotiate on any terms rather than not negotiate at all, its effect on the Americans was appalling.

To Adams, the natural right to the fisheries was an article of faith; to Gallatin and Bayard, an article of pride; to Clay, a matter of obeying instructions; to Russell, a matter of following Clay. A whole dirge might be written upon this descending scale of values. Only the heroic efforts of Gallatin had prevented the conferences in the Rue des Champs from becoming a battleground between the shores of the Mississippi and the seaports of Massachusetts. All five commissioners were champions of the Union. Filled with consternation—for did not this sectional difference prefigure other, more distant, and more terrible contests?—they strove to rescue the fisheries. A further conference with the British on December 12 added nothing to anyone's peace of mind. Adams would not admit that the fisheries were not a natural right; his colleagues could scarcely agree that they were. They believed such a proposition to be untenable; and one by one, during December 13 and 14, they dropped away. In a private conversation with Lord Gambier on December 12, Clay was sufficiently explicit. "Upon Lord Gambier's saying," reported Mr. Goulburn, "that the result of not stipulating in the treaty respecting the fisheries would be the renewal of war whenever we drove off the American fishermen, as we certainly should do, Mr. Clay replied that the United States might remonstrate but that they would never make war on that ground." And yet, even while he abandoned New England to the mercies of the British, there was something in Mr. Clay's demeanor which created the suspicion that he might have said a great deal more than he meant. "To acknowledge that they consider the stipulation of 1783 as no longer in force, or that their right to the fishery depends on the treaty alone, is what I feel convinced the Americans will never consent to." [40] This was the conclusion of Mr. Goulburn and his colleagues; and this conclusion alone saved Mr. Adams, who otherwise, on December 14, stood quite alone.

V

Massachusetts had little use for Mr. Adams; but Mr. Adams clung bitterly to Massachusetts. He did not think it remarkable that the remnants of the British claims should be pointed against that state alone. He was convinced that if Massachusetts had been "true to the Union" the British would never have dared to hinge the question of peace or war upon Moose Island and the privileges of Massachusetts fishermen.[41] But so it was: by the end of November, the navigation of the Mississippi had become a symbol that, however mischievous and menacing, had temporarily lost its usefulness. All now depended upon the fisheries and the Passamaquoddy islands. The chief of these islands was Moose Island, which the British had captured and from which, in happier days, a delegation used to make its way to the General Court of Massachusetts.

Meeting in special session, early in October, the General Court of Massachusetts adopted the Report and Resolutions of its committee recommending the assembly of a Convention of delegates from New England. The language of the Report was frightful. "It is with great concern," it said, "that your committee are obliged to declare their conviction that the Constitution of the United States, under the administration of the persons in power, has failed to secure to this Commonwealth, and as they believe, to the Eastern sections of this Union, those equal rights and benefits which are the greatest objects of its formation." [42]

The project of a Convention—or "this mad project of national suicide" as John Quincy Adams preferred to call it—could be excused only on the assumption that the Union itself was still an experiment,[43] and that, when a great material interest found itself at a disadvantage in the Union, it was apt to conclude that the experiment had failed.[44] New England Federalism was less a right wing of American politics than a left wing of the British navigation system. It saw the War of 1812 as a quarrel between that system and the western and southwestern frontier; and its sympathies inevitably followed its interests. But where does sympathy end and treason begin? New England Federalism answered that question in a typically eccentric fashion, and did not have a chance to complete its answer, for the war ended too soon. Such fragments of its answer as are available are scarcely reassuring.

During the war the manufactures of New England—which had, indeed, been forced upon that section by the exigencies of embargo and blockade—drained specie away from the rest of the country. This specie was locked up in various vaults and found its way, if anywhere, into English hands. It was notorious that the bankers of Boston purchased British Treasury notes at a liberal discount, and sent coin to Canada in exchange; and that by this means they lent more money to England than they did to the United States.[45] Indeed the Boston *Gazette* of April 14, 1814, declared that "any man who lends money to the government at the present time will forfeit all claim to common honesty and common courtesy"; while the government on the same day was reduced to the strange expedient of promising that the names of all Bostonian subscribers to its loan would be kept secret.[46]

A study of the election returns shows that large numbers of New Englanders supported the war; while it is probable that only a small fragment of the peace party wished to end hostilities by an act of treason. But this fragment was composed of wealth and learning, it was veined with theocratic traditions, and it exercised a magnetic effect upon the disorganized mass around it. Thus the voice of New England came to be the voice of extreme Federalism and its movement tended to be more and more a movement towards disunion.

At the very beginning of the war the New England judiciary, as represented by the Supreme Court of Massachusetts, announced that the commanders-in-chief of militia in the various states had the right to decide whether or not they should put their troops at the disposal of the general government; a committee of the Connecticut legislature denied that militia could be ordered into the service of the United States to assist in carrying on an "offensive" war; and Rhode Island and Vermont, through their governors, echoed these doctrines.[47] Such doctrines must be ascribed not to a lack of native courage—the regular troops who fought so savagely at Lundy's Lane were recruited in Massachusetts—but to a lack of conviction, on account of which the energies of the whole section were turned to planning Conventions and taking profits. In December 1813 the President himself reproved the people of New England for the enthusiasm with which they supplied the needs of the British armies and fleets hovering off their coasts or menacing their borders.[48]

The clergy, though their language was grave and restrained in general, preached that active participation in the war would incur the guilt of blood; and a few of the more hotheaded among them drew strange and subversive parallels from the scriptures. The Reverend Elijah Parish of Newbury, for example, told his parishioners that Moses had dissolved the Union with Egypt; he exhorted "a resolute and pious people" to follow in those distant steps.[49] Whether these arguments satisfied the parishioners of Newbury has never been recorded: but if New England needed a Moses, it followed that America already had a Pharaoh; and the comparison of James Madison to that wicked monarch might seem, even to a resolute and pious people, a little far-fetched. New Englanders, however, had been known to compare Napoleon to Anti-Christ. The nature of Evil had few perplexities for them; they spent a good deal of their time combating it, in one form or another. Even the British were not exempt from it: and it was because the most treasonable gestures of the New Englanders had been performed with an air of righteous independence that the British had first extended their blockade to those friendly coasts [50] and then attempted to resolve the scruples of Massachusetts by threatening her with the loss of her fisheries and the curtailment of her territory.

Few outside commentators, then or thereafter, professed to understand the mind of New England during this critical period. A combination of extreme individualism and extreme orderliness, it baffles inquiry. No doubt a man like Timothy Pickering, the disunionist leader, could be placed, if not understood. Like his obvious counterparts—Gouverneur Morris in New York, and Lord Gambier in Ghent—he was historically extinct. He had no more place in the nineteenth century than the dinosaur or the mammoth, and his actions could be relished only by connoisseurs of the out-of-date. But what of Governor Caleb Strong of Massachusetts—Caleb Strong, who was so kindly, so moderate, so humane, and who was the author of *Patriotism and Piety?* We have every reason to believe that in the fall of 1814 this gentleman sent a private agent to Sir John Sherbrooke in Halifax with tentative proposals of armistice and alliance with Great Britain.[51] Sir John was more noted for the violence of his temper than the acuteness of his judgment, and he may have misunderstood the intentions of Caleb Strong; but if so, the misunderstanding was general. Lord Liverpool certainly declared that if the Senate refused to ratify the Treaty of Ghent, "we must immediately propose to make a separate peace with [the Eastern States], and we have good reason to believe that they will not be indisposed to listen to such a proposal." [52] Could he have been correct? While John Quincy Adams fought to preserve the rights of Massachusetts at Ghent, at Hartford in Connecticut twenty-six delegates—"the Wise and Good of those States, which deem themselves oppressed" [53]—were assembling from Massachusetts, Connecticut, Rhode Island, the counties of Cheshire and Grafton in New Hampshire, and the county of Windham in Vermont, for purposes that, whatever else they may have been, were certainly not constitutional. The leaders of the Hartford Convention were, it is true, temperate men; and their Report and Resolutions merely threatened rebellion if their recommendations were not complied with. But disunion is disunion, however mildly asserted.[54] Nathaniel Ames, the Boston radical, triumphantly compared the Hartford Convention to the mountain in labor. It "bro't forth a mouse," he said.[55] If we may trust to classical analogies, such events are always ridiculous; and ridicule was, indeed, liberally heaped upon the meeting at Hartford.[56] It is, however, well to remember that if the war had lasted into 1815 another and more dangerous Convention would have been called; and that in such a case the mouse, however ridiculous, would in its turn have brought forth a mountain.

It is no wonder, therefore, that John Quincy Adams felt himself totally abandoned on December 14, 1814. As "a citizen of Massachusetts," none the less, he was determined not to sign a treaty that sacrificed the fisheries, even if it should be acceded to by his colleagues.[57] There was something ominous about this tendency in the American delegation to resolve itself into the citizens of various states. But, as always, when disintegration set in, unity reasserted itself. His colleagues made one last effort. On December 14 they drew up a note, offering to be silent as to the fisheries and the Mississippi, or to refer them to further negotiations in such terms as to imply no abandonment of a right.[58] Henry Clay continued to grumble—"he said we should make a damned bad treaty, and he did not know whether he would sign it or not"—while no one believed that the British would yield.[59] Had not a similar offer been made on November 10? The offer was sent to London—for nine days the commissioners waited in miserable suspense—and on the ninth day the British messenger returned with new instructions. These were more than startling. The Americans were to have their way. The disputed material on the fisheries and the Mississippi was to be omitted altogether.[60]

"The relief to my mind," said Adams, in a phrase that still echoes with astonishment, "was inexpressible." [61]

At a last conference on December 23, the British proved to be inflexible only on one point: they would not yield the islands in Passamaquoddy Bay until a friendly sovereign and commissioners from both nations had decided who had the title to them. Otherwise silence fell upon all the disputed questions—upon the fisheries and the Mississippi, upon the American claim to a boundary westward from the Lake of the Woods along the forty-ninth parallel, upon impressment and blockades and claims for spoliations. Everything was as it had been when Congress declared war in 1812.

On December 24, 1814, a treaty of peace was signed at the Chartreux in Ghent.[62]

VI

The British, when they yielded, did so with the thudding effect of anticlimax. It was as if a solid piece of masonry had suddenly and softly collapsed, at once startling and depressing the observer. The dramatic effects of the War of 1812 were mostly reserved for its epilogue, the battle of New Orleans, which brought the curtain down in triumph and horror. If there was any drama in the negotiations at Ghent, it was admirably concealed from view, and seemed to insist, by the quality or lack of quality of its conclusion, that it had not existed at all. Yet if we look into those negotiations we can see that the British had, in fact, acted out at Ghent the preliminary steps in the solution of a great argument. Ever since the *Essex* decision of 1805, they had been debating two points of view: one, that it would be more profitable to control and even to crush the commerce of the United States; the other, that it would be more profitable to let it alone. The former was succinctly stated by Spencer Perceval, and rather comically represented by men like Admiral Berkeley, Admiral Cockburn, and General Ross. The latter appeared, always in a very tentative form, in the Parliamentary arguments of men like Brougham and Baring. The first point of view, which we might describe as mercantilist, seemed to be justified by the fact that British foreign commerce flourished particularly between the years 1806 and 1811.[63] Yet in 1811, British economy was on the verge of ruin; the exchanges had turned against Great Britain; her commerce was corrupted; her warehouses were glutted; the normal channels of trade were either dammed or overflowing. Could it be said that commercial monopoly might be ruinous to an industrial nation? It was British industry which ultimately brought about the destruction of Napoleon's Continental System. British industry needed access to the markets of America, not control of the American carrying trade, and this fact was superbly emphasized by the Jeffersonian Embargo and Non-Intercourse. Once it had become clear, the second point of view prevailed, and in 1812 the Orders-in-Council, which were essentially mercantilist, were swept away.

It was mercantilism that burned Washington. Mercantilism lay in bloody windrows before the mud rampart at New Orleans. But the mercantilist spirit fought its greatest battle from its headquarters at the Charterhouse in Ghent, in the fall of 1814. Its territorial demands were designed to cramp the growth of the United States and wither their future; and, when the American commissioners sternly resisted these demands, Lords Liverpool, Bathurst, and Castlereagh abandoned them with what sounds to the modern ear like a sigh of relief. Lord Liverpool, indeed, went on to become one of the earliest and most interesting examples of liberal Toryism, that singular phenomenon which was to have, as will appear in the course of this narrative, such a curious and exciting effect upon Anglo-American relations. Many years were to pass before the British adopted a system of free trade in its entirety; but at Ghent, in 1814, they signed a treaty which demonstrated, if anything, that free trade had a future.

VII

In their antimercantilist decision the British were much assisted by the formidable front presented by the American commissioners at Ghent. Another element in the hastening of the peace was the unwillingness of the British public to submit to a property tax for the sake of rectifying the Canadian border or opposing an Indian buffer state to the northwest expansion of America. Yet another element was the American privateer, who infested even the sacred "narrow seas," accounted for fourteen hundred British ships, and was a most expensive embarrassment to a country that claimed to rule the ocean.[64] The single-ship victories won by the American over the British navy were also intensely mortifying; while the victories of Perry and Macdonough were temporarily decisive. The British Navy was, of course, supreme; British military preponderance was bound sooner or later to bear down all opposition; but the British could not wait for these processes to complete themselves, and the war remained from first to last a peripheral war. They could only hope that some great success at New Orleans, with its consequent threat to the Mississippi Valley, would provide a sword to dangle over the heads of President and Senate should they cunningly refuse to ratify the Treaty . . . for though they were obliged to discard many prejudices at Ghent, they never could rid themselves of the notion that James Madison was not a Virginia gentleman but an elderly knave, with a boorish command—dim, dull, but almost perfect—of all the arts of trickery and malice.

The British fear of a renewal of the European war was, to be sure, a vital element in the hastening of the peace at Ghent.[65] One can isolate the negotiations there for the purposes of examination, but one has always to remember that they are merely a fragment of a larger problem. Lord Castlereagh, for example, always saw them in that light; and if an antimercantilist sentiment formed itself in *his* mind, it was in the manner of a pearl forming itself in an oyster, by a process of irritation. None the less, the emergence of such a sentiment, in so startling and sudden a form, gives to those negotiations a very important place in British history.

VIII

From an American point of view, the Treaty of Ghent left everything to the solution of time. It was a phase in the maturing of a nation, for at Ghent, more even than on any lake or ocean or battlefield, the Americans fought for their chance to grow up. The avowed reasons for the war—the perplexing questions of maritime rights—were never discussed. The hidden reasons,

American land-hunger and British opposition to American ambition in any form, dominated the proceedings from the start. Once these had been settled by a territorial adjustment, or lack of adjustment, which represented if anything a triumph of the West, the negotiation turned, with an unconscious subtlety that still appalls us, towards the problem of American sectionalism. At Ghent British mercantilism withdrew snarling into the background; and at the very moment of this triumph, American sectionalism came snarling to the front. The negotiation abolished vast areas of the past; it opened strange vistas into the future. It was a most curious and instructive moment in history. Its details, together with certain aspects of the troubles that preceded it, are essential to the understanding of the period that followed it.

This period is no less curious and instructive. With its accompaniments of confusion and vigor, of aspiration, uncertainty, division, and ill will, it has come by some odd irony to be known as the Era of Good Feelings.

2

THE ERA OF GOOD FEELINGS: 1817-1819

CHAPTER ONE

The President

ON SATURDAY, July 12, 1817, the following paragraph appeared in the Boston *Columbian Centinel:*

> "ERA OF GOOD FEELINGS.
>
> During the late Presidential Jubilee many persons have met at festive boards, in pleasant converse, whom party politics had long severed. We recur with pleasure to all the circumstances which attended the demonstration of good feelings."

The *Columbian Centinel,* a newspaper whose Federalism was so pronounced that it amounted to a dialect, had not been distinguished during the War of 1812 for any great prescience. With a consistency that never flagged, it had taken the wrong side and made the wrong predictions. It was therefore most improbable in 1817 that this same journal would be tempted into any extensive display of its speculative gifts. When it spoke of an Era of Good Feelings, it probably did not intend to speak for a larger area than the city of Boston and the township of Dedham. But the phrase became popular; it was repeated in ever wider circles, until at last it came to be almost synonymous with the Administration of James Monroe. But the blight of its origin was upon it. While feelings of one kind or another ran high during the Administration of Monroe, they were—except for one brief period that cannot be prolonged into an era—invariably not good.

I

The Presidential Jubilee to which the *Centinel* referred in such feeling terms was the visit of James Monroe to the city of Boston. This visit was part of a tour the President made soon after his inauguration, for the purpose of inspecting coastal fortifications and frontier outposts. Those who read the brief, but somehow too long book that was written at the time about this tour are apt to come away with a sensation of deafness.[1] The applause was tremendous. From every village, every township, every city on his route, the people came forth to salute their President. At Baltimore the good citizens were, it is true, a little touchy about the President's arriving on a Sunday; at Philadelphia the applause was "restrained by the dictates of propriety"; but from then onwards all was crescendo.[2] But the climax was reached at the city of Boston—about whose neck still hung the albatross of secession—and in whose acclamations even the least sensitive ear might have detected a certain uneasiness of conscience. And yet "no human heart can remain unmoved, when an antagonist offers the hand of reconciliation." [3]

Undoubtedly, James Monroe was moved; he may even have been flattered; but the quality of James Monroe was such that flattery, however unsparingly applied, would be most unlikely to swerve him from his lifelong purpose. Like every other public man who had reached a certain eminence, he was not insensible to the allurements of power and fame. But what separated him from other public men was the fact that what he longed for most was public service. Thomas Jefferson, who knew him best, knew this was the chord that must be touched. "I shall tomorrow nominate you to the Senate for an extraordinary mission to France," he wrote in 1803, "and the circumstances are such as to render it impossible to decline." [4] This sentence sums up the predominating trait of a career. To be of service, and under circumstances that made it impossible to decline! Yet there is much danger in such cravings. One may forget, in the delights and ardors of service, the ends to which that service is dedicated; one may be intellectually unable to see the wood for the trees, or temperamentally indisposed to do so. Thus in 1805 Monroe made with Pinkney a thoroughly bad treaty with England. Pinkney might be forgiven, because he had had no previous diplomatic experience; but this was not the case with Monroe. To Monroe, it seems, the first consideration was to make a treaty, and accordingly he made one. Whether that treaty was a good one or a bad one—such thoughts came later. On his return from England, in something lik_ disgrace, Monroe attempted to justify his actions in public and in private, but he never could explain them away. A man of his type is not cut out to be a diplomat: one can say no more than that.

Upon his return he was solicited by John Randolph—as self-appointed spokesman for the Tertium Quids, the dissident Jeffersonians—to run for President against James Madison. For a while he wavered. Like the Tertium Quids, he was supposed to be a man of unquestioned orthodoxy, the strictest of Old Republicans. His part in effecting the Louisiana Purchase in 1803 had made him popular in the West.[5] He felt that Thomas Jefferson, in refusing to submit his treaty to the Senate, had behaved ungenerously—had, in fact, sacrificed him on some political altar. He did not fancy himself in the role of a burnt offering, particularly when the fortunes to be advanced thereby were James Madison's. But something—an infallible instinct—told him that if he made himself the leader of the Quids he would be swept away into an agrarian Utopia, a bourne from which the traveler with difficulty returned, and never returned as President. No man would want to end his life as the governor of a Territory or as a Representative in Congress. He longed to be useful, *conspicuously* useful: and when in 1811 he was offered the Secretaryship of State, he forgot his orthodoxy, forgot the Tertium Quids, forgot his old quarrel with Jefferson, and followed his erring brother Madison towards the seats of power.[6] "Glamis and Cawdor!" was John Randolph's bitter comment.[7]

But John Randolph was wrong. Monroe was no Macbeth. The Presidency when it came was not gulped down with the peculiar zest that would have been Henry Clay's, for example, if the same reward had come to him. Unlike Clay, Monroe was not devoured by ambition; or rather, the ambition that possessed him was of a very different kind. He saw the Presidency as the culmination of a long life of public service, and he proposed to enjoy it as such. He did not meddle very much with local politics; he did not taste, through the use or misuse of patronage, the delicious fruits of power; he did not create a machine or consolidate a party. The Presidency was port after stormy seas; and though the waves rose higher with every year of his Administration, on the whole he rode them equably enough. He had attained his eminence at some cost to his principles; but he was a man who responded more to influences than to principles, and his principles, in any case, had been swallowed up in the grand notion of service. He may well have been one of the few Presidents, or public men, or rulers of any kind, of whom it may be said that he had an easy conscience. Only one thing seems to have troubled him—his intrigue against General Armstrong before and after the battle of Bladensburg; but the memory of that intrigue troubled him until his dying day.[8]

Thomas Jefferson said that if Monroe's soul were turned inside out not a spot would be found on it.[9] The Virginia Dynasty was not backward in self-praise, but Jefferson had an instinct for authenticity. Monroe *was* a good man. His motives were not lofty, but they were pure. Upon a character of extreme simplicity he had engrafted a wide and not very happy experience of men and of events; and this experience, while it did not affect his generosity or his kindliness, had toughly seasoned him.

He was in his sixty-first year when he became President, a tall man, of a rather venerable appearance, who wore the knee-length pantaloons and white-topped boots of an earlier day. Men looked up and took their fill of his obvious presence. It was easy to recall the fact that he had fought with credit in the Revolutionary War; indeed, everything about him was a reminder of a time sufficiently distant for everyone to be proud of it. He was a Virginian, but not an aristocratic Virginian like Jefferson and Madison: he was more awkward and more formal than they; he was also less subtle, original, and intelligent. On the whole, people preferred it that way. The Virginia Dynasty had been noted hitherto rather for complexity than for simplicity, and if the new President had to be a Virginian, which some northern people did not think a necessity, at least it was a consolation to know that he was an understandable one.[10]

II

Two weeks before his inauguration, Monroe received a letter from Boston which has at least the merit of foreshadowing the course of events. His correspondent, William Tudor, Jr., was editor of the *North American Review*, a periodical which became so extremely sectional under his brief sway that it was sometimes called the *North Unamerican*.[11] After congratulating the President-to-be on the "feeling of sovereignty," Tudor—who was, needless to say, a Federalist—went on to suggest that the time had come for a conciliation between Massachusetts and the national government. "I have heard in more than one instance solid respectable citizens express their belief in your magnanimity & generous feelings." These solid respectable citizens were all, oddly enough, Federalists also. As for the Democrats in Boston, they were "utterly contemptible . . . cringing & subservient . . . in reality ready to betray those who have fostered them." In Monroe's case, the writer had it on the best authority that they were determined that he should not enjoy a second term, and that they proposed to unite with the "sorry factions" of Pennsylvania and New York for this purpose. The Federalists, on the other hand, were now ready to support and not oppose the national government. "I think on the principles now acted upon at Washington that they have no dispute to maintain. If it were possible for you gradually to bring about an exchange, take the support of the Federalists and abandon their opponents you would be a prodigious gainer." [12]

Such were the beguilements of Mr. William Tudor. Whether a Jeffersonian President would care to be congratulated upon a "feeling of sovereignty," or whether he would repose much confidence in a party that had delivered the electoral vote of Massachusetts to his rival in the recent election, were questions Mr. Tudor—who can hardly be accused of being oversensitive—seems not to have pondered very deeply. What is more to the point is that the letter revealed, in an irritating but useful manner, both the tactics and sentiments of the Federalist minority.

When the news of peace reached Washington in February 1815, the commissioners from the Hartford Convention, who had come to present their somewhat secessionist resolutions, departed from the capital city as unobtrusively as possible, but pursued by the gibes of their countrymen. With them they carried the ruin of the Federalist Party. It was just strong enough in 1816 to carry the states of Massachusetts, Connecticut, and Delaware against Monroe, but that was the end. Thereafter it clung, in a rather fungoid manner, to certain localities, but as a national party it had ceased to exist.

The Federalist Party might roughly, very roughly, be described as the party of the mercantile, manufacturing, and investing interests. The future of these interests in the nineteenth century was to be a glowing one; and since the party that had hitherto served them had been so factious and disloyal as to lose all influence in the country, it was natural enough for them to look for another one. They looked around. There was no choice but a choice between discredited Federalism and triumphant Republicanism; towards Republicanism, therefore, they gravitated. They were not generally so crude as Mr. William Tudor; they did not suppose that the President would openly seek their support; but they were sure that they could seek the support of the President. For indeed, as Mr. Tudor had so unkindly put it, there was nothing in recent events at Washington to indicate that their ideas would be unwelcome there.

Thomas Jefferson was not a party man. He believed that political parties had to some extent a physiological foundation—that they represented rather a variety in nature than a validity of principle. "The terms of whig and tory," he said, "belong to natural as well as to civil history. They denote the temper and constitution of mind of different individuals." [13] Certainly parties were useful, but how easily did they cease to embody principles and degenerate into factions! "If we can hit on the true line of conduct which may conciliate the honest part of those who are called federalists," he wrote in 1801, ". . . I shall hope to be able to obliterate, or rather to unite the name of federalists & republicans." [14] But Jefferson grew alarmed at the amount of union, or obliteration, that took place under his successor. Before he left office in 1817, James Madison seemed almost to have adopted the program of his adversaries—seemed only to have saved himself, by a last veto, from becoming a convert, by total immersion, to the Federalist Church. True, that church as a physical structure was in ruins; but its spirit was everywhere. When the Republicans, under Madison, chartered a Second Bank of the United States; when their newspapers recited in support of this Second Bank the very arguments Alexander Hamilton had adduced to prove the constitutionality of the First; when they showed a marked solicitude for manufactures, for tariffs, for an army and a navy—where was it all to end? [15]

Where indeed? James Monroe, so susceptible to influences, was not the man to resist the drift away from old agrarian Republicanism. The inferences Mr. Tudor had drawn from the late proceedings of Mr. Madison and his Administration were, no doubt, crudely drawn, but who was to say that they were not correct?

III

President Monroe assumed office under conditions very nearly unique. Every man who hoped to better his interests—it scarcely mattered what those interests were—had begun to call himself a Jeffersonian Republican. A social democracy can survive under, or even require, a one-party government; but a political democracy cannot. Thomas Jefferson had predicted this state of affairs long before, and had outlined also the dangers that might arise from it. "I had always expected," he told Thomas Cooper in 1807, "that when the republicans should have put all things under their feet, they would schismatize among themselves. I always expected, too, that whatever names the parties might bear, the real division would be into moderate & ardent republicanism. In this division there is no great danger. . . . It is to be considered as apostasy only when they purchase the votes of federalists, with a participation in honor & power." [16]

But Jefferson did not take into consideration the fact that "moderate" republicanism might apostatize to the Federalists not by purchasing their votes but by assimilating their views; in short, that it was not political apostasy that was to be feared, but political osmosis. Apostasy had been thrust under Monroe's nose in the letter from William Tudor; and, several months later, was thrust under it again in a letter from George Sullivan, one of the leaders of the Boston bar, who blandly suggested that his intimate friend, Mr. Daniel Webster, could readily be induced to come into Monroe's Administration as Attorney-General, and that if he did so he would prove to be "a rock, on which your administration might rest secure against the violence of almost any faction." Otherwise, said Mr. Sullivan, "your administration will be overthrown; because your Cabinet is weak & discordant." [17]

Monroe was proof against such offers. What confronted him was a more alluring possibility: that inaction might become wisdom. To let things slide; to observe and modify but not actually attempt to shape the course of events; all Monroe's instincts urged him to such a course. It had, it is true, some distressing results. It meant the death of the old—the "ardent"—Republican Party as a national force, and its transfiguration into a sectional one. It meant that Monroe must drift, at a slightly increasing tempo, along the stream of neo-Federalist ideas which had already captured his predecessor. It meant that the clash of parties would give way to the clash of personalities. It meant the most vicious quarrels at the top, and the most peculiar incoherence underneath. But the one-party government of James Monroe gave this very incoherence a chance to develop a shape, however vague, and a direction, however veering. The eight years of his Presidency, and the four bitter and hateful years that followed, were essentially formative years—and for the simplest of reasons. The true direction of events came not from above but from below. Monroe's second election was a mere formality, scarcely concealing the fact that it was in the dusty bickerings, the obscure and almost shapeless maneuvers of state politics, that the future was being formed. Monroe has often been slighted for his negative role during these years. If he transmitted an impulse to his ambitious lieutenants—and he did so with extreme caution—it was towards making a compromise with the principles of Thomas Jefferson. The country was still predominantly agrarian, but the energies of agriculture were diffusing themselves over a wider and wider extent of territory, while the energies of the business community were being concentrated in certain definite localities. Concentration has always a greater political influence than diffusion; Monroe was highly susceptible to influences; Jeffersonians were not, after all, deaf to the claims of property. . . . From these simple premises it is not difficult to derive the relation between Monroe's government and the business community. Under Monroe's successor, John Quincy Adams, this relation became obvious: under Monroe, it was still tentative. For Monroe was always under the spell of those agrarian principles which he was so cautiously deserting. His services as President might be summed up in four words—he personified an interim. The War of 1812, as has perhaps been indicated, was merely the symptom of a profound change in domestic and international relations. After the shock of such a change, an interim was necessary; and if the interim was necessary, the personification was honorable.

IV

From the benign shadows of his Revolutionary past, to which it seemed that his triumphal tour had consigned him, James Monroe looked out into the future and, taking a rather more extensive view than the *Columbian Centinel* would ever have permitted itself, saw nothing ahead of him but party good feelings and sectional harmony. "I indulge a strong hope," he told the Republican minority of the Massachusetts legislature, "that our principal dangers and difficulties have passed, and that the character of our deliberations and the course of the government itself, will become more harmonious and happy than it has heretofore been." [18] Nothing is more apt to befuddle the vision of statesmen than an indulgence in strong hopes; but if President Monroe needed a corrective, the personnel of his Cabinet must surely have supplied it. He had hoped to surround himself with men like himself, respectable men to whom duty was paramount, and who proposed to do as little of it as they conveniently could—not out of a lazy disposition but from a deep respect for *laissez faire*.[19] But Monroe's ambitions were all satisfied and there were scarcely a dozen men in the country of whom the same thing could be said. In Benjamin Crowninshield of Massachusetts, his Secretary of the Navy, and William Wirt, of Virginia, his Attorney-General, he seems, indeed, to have found two such men: but Crowninshield soon retired out of sheer inanition; and Wirt was that rarest of early American phenomena, a lawyer who was actually satisfied with the practice of the law.[20] As for the remainder of the Cabinet—William Harris Crawford, Secretary of the Treasury, John Quincy Adams, Secretary of State, and John Caldwell Calhoun, Secretary of War—here, indeed, the special daimon of the times displayed itself.

The Treaty of Ghent had uncoffered, among other restless spirits, this daimon—this extreme anxiety among men of parts either to be, or to be in important relations with, Monroe's successor. By 1817, it is safe to say, the notion that he might be the next President had dawned upon Mr. Adams,[21] a similar revelation had been vouchsafed, though somewhat earlier, to Mr. Crawford, whom only caution and reverence had prevented from being a serious competitor to Monroe in 1816,[22] while in the case of Mr. Calhoun, it came later, but not without violence. Meanwhile the Speaker of the

House of Representatives, Mr. Henry Clay, furious at being passed over for Secretary of State, a post generally held to be the likeliest route to the Presidency, arranged every detail of his political behavior with reference to his succession to Monroe.

With every prominent man a Republican in name at least, it was natural that the succession to the Presidency should be canvassed with increasing virulence and imprecision. By what set of principles was the country to judge between the claims of these men? The position of Monroe was, to say the least, uncomfortable: three of the most likely claimants were in his own Cabinet; a fourth was in a place where he could do more harm or good to the Administration than any other single man. The fifth was soon to emerge in the formidable and politically equivocal shape of the hero of New Orleans.

With the exception of John Quincy Adams, the Presidential aspirants in the Cabinet had not arrived there through a deliberate choice of Monroe's. Mr. Crawford had been Secretary of the Treasury under James Madison, and was simply too powerful a man, with too many claims upon Monroe's indulgence, to be removed against his will. Mr. Calhoun had reached the War Department by a process of elimination that, whatever else it may be, is certainly not selective. He had fought for the War of 1812 in Congress with dignity and intelligence: he was now, more than ever, a nationalist. A strange and somber destiny awaited him. He was to remain a nationalist to the end of his days—but a nationalist of a most peculiar kind, a nationalist who preached the rankest secession, and who became the architect of civil war. He was and continued to be the most original political theorist of his time, with a supple and steely dialectic at his command: yet the fruit of all his political theorizing was a scheme which, if worked out to its logical conclusion, would have reduced the nation to immobility within a year.[23] He was a man of vision who perceived, long before the publication of the *Communist Manifesto*, that an unrestricted capitalism must reduce larger and ever larger masses of people to virtual slavery; and his remedy for this was not to ponder those measures by which capitalism might be restricted, but to propose for the majority of mankind, and in the name of minority rights, a more and more unrestricted slavery. In 1817, he was not yet that "cast-iron man, who looks as if he had never been born" whom the acute observation of a visiting maiden lady so unerringly transfixed in the mid 1830's.[24] The great reactionary was still concealed in the ardent nationalist. The champion of slavery was still just another slave-owner in a slave-owning capital. Age, mortification, and sickness had not yet converted his face into that terrible mask with which Senator Calhoun, voiceless and dying, confronted the Senate in 1850. In 1817, he was rather severe, rather puritanical, somewhat too introverted, but fascinating; and many were the audiences he captivated with his flow of ideas, uttered in a harsh controlled voice and enlivened by the peremptory glances of his glittering, dark-gray eyes. But even then he lacked to a conspicuous degree the art, not of getting on with other people, but of understanding them.

The metamorphosis of so sincere a man as Mr. Calhoun from a nationalist in 1817 to that unappetizing chimera, a nationalist-particularist, in 1828 indicates the variability of those years. The standing of Mr. Crawford indicates their obscurity.

Mr. Crawford was the standard-bearer of the Old Republicans, a man whom Thomas Jefferson would have selected as Monroe's successor. There seem to have been few grounds upon which Mr. Crawford could have founded a claim to the allegiance of the Old Republicans. He was notably a supporter of the Second Bank of the United States—and the Second Bank of the United States, as every Old Republican knew, bore upon it the mark of Cain. His reports as Secretary of the Treasury showed no outright hostility to a mild protective tariff—and protective tariffs, however mild, did not suit well with agrarian or commercial beliefs. On the question of the right of Congress to spend public money on the building of roads and canals—the vexed question of Internal Improvements—Mr. Crawford was inclined, tentatively at least, to place himself among the ranks of those who believed that Congress had such a right.[25] No strict Republican could have followed him here, for all believed that such a use of public money would be unconstitutional, corrupting, and subversive of State Rights; and it was by his veto of the Bonus Bill, which embodied these corrupting principles, that James Madison, on the very last day of his Presidency, preserved his standing as a Republican Father.

All that could be said for Mr. Crawford as an Old Republican was that he professed himself a believer in State Rights, and in their corollaries—economy, simplicity, and retrenchment. Were these professions sufficient, even when Mr. Crawford and his followers began to call themselves Radicals? His background, like the rest of him, was perplexing. Born in Virginia, he had first practiced law in the Western Judicial Circuit of the State of Georgia, where he came to be the spokesman of the upland planting interests. No man could be a spokesman for anything in those days, in that part of the world, without being prepared to defend his opinions with his pistol. In 1802, Mr. Crawford was called out by Mr. Peter Van Alen, Solicitor General of the Western Circuit, after a dispute in Colonel Willis's tavern in Wilks County—perhaps over a dishonest land scheme into which Crawford refused to enter, perhaps over the election of a new judge for the Western Circuit, perhaps because his enemies had decided that the time had come for him to leave the world. Mr. Van Alan, however, was killed.[26] His opponents, who represented the small democratic farmers of the frontier, continued their assault. A little later, after a lively exchange of letters in the Washington (Ga.) *Monitor* and the Louisville *Trumpet*, a duel was arranged between Mr. Crawford and John Clark, the Indian fighter. Once postponed by a Court of Honor, the duel at last took place on December 16, 1806. Mr. Crawford's left wrist was shattered in the first exchange of shots, and his seconds declared themselves satisfied; but the implacable Clark renewed the challenge. One or the other, he declared, must die—if not at the second encounter, then at the third, if not at the third, then . . . But Mr. Crawford wisely declined this invitation, and soon after disappeared into the more respectable regions of the United States Senate, where he offered a temperate support to Jeffersonian measures.[27]

The quarrel with Clark illustrates—rather violently, it is true—the direction of Mr. Crawford's politics. For the rest of his career he was to be troubled by the enmity of the more democratic elements within his own state. He was a moderate Republican, sensitive to the claims of wealth and respectability, and adept in the use of patronage and the management of Congressmen. In Washington he was extremely popular. A man of immense physique, of a handsome appearance, of a marvelous but faintly coarse affability, he was clearly intended for a successful career in politics.[28] He had a genuine capacity for business and by no standard could he be described as an unworthy man, though it would have taken a rather special set of standards to hold him up as a notably worthy one. It may even be that only an attack of paralysis, which struck him just when he needed all his energies, kept him from the Presidency; though it seems more probable that what he needed—and, in the days before the railroad, could not create —was a national machine.

Yet nothing could illustrate the ambiguity of the times more clearly than the fact that Mr. Crawford was the choice of the Old Republicans; that so rigorous a democrat as Nathaniel Macon should have supported him; that Thomas Jefferson should have lamented in almost unmeasured terms his eventual failure to succeed Monroe.[29] All Mr. Crawford had to offer was a gradual rather than a speedy abandonment of Jeffersonian principles.

V

The phrase "Era of Good Feelings" was originally compounded of Federalist Boston's belief that James Monroe was a good man, and its hope that he was not a party man. Whether or not nonpartisan goodness would be an efficient substitute for creative principle—this was a question the next few years would have to decide.

CHAPTER TWO

The West

THE Peace of Ghent was a victory for the West. No Eastern demand
was satisfied by it; but once the British had withdrawn their claim to
the sources of the Mississippi and the control of the Northwest, the triumph
of expansionism was complete. All serious territorial disputes were now confined to the northeast frontier, about which the West cared little, and the
Oregon country, about which it cared much but knew less. At the same
time, the Peace of Ghent marked the beginning of a release from Europe.
The time was gone when the thunders of a Trafalgar or an Austerlitz, a Jena
or a Wagram, stealing across the Atlantic, could rattle the windows of
American merchants and legislators; when the fortunes of an Administration
seemed to rise and fall with the fluctuations of a campaign in the Spanish
Peninsula; and when some obscure and secret change in the policies of
Whitehall was sooner or later translated into extravagant uneasiness along
the Wabash. The connection was still intricate and sensitive, as the events
of the next few years were to show, and it was never for one instant severed;
but it was evidently loosened, by the pull of the Pacific Ocean and by the
influence of that star which marked the center of population as it ascended
from the coastal plain and climbed toward the summit of the Alleghenies.[1]

What the deliberations of Ghent had proved—and they had done so with
all the elaborate arguments that commonly attend the proving of the truth
of an axiom—was that the United States of America must not be considered
a European appendage. American axioms, to be sure, were not always very
clear to European minds; but if further arguments were needed, one was
immediately supplied by the increase in the velocity of the westward
movement.

I

This movement had been checked to some extent by the War of 1812. Rumors of Indian uprisings halted the pioneer upon his frontiers and even pressed him back; but by 1814 the more potent influence of taxation and commercial depression had reasserted itself. Farmers, mechanics, artisans, and tradesmen, fleeing the ogres of monopoly and debt, turned their faces westward; and the frontier resumed its irregular advance. With the coming of peace, the advance became a migration. It was one of the greatest migrations in history and in its early stages was one of the most imaginative, for its impulse was centrifugal, and a centrifugal impulse favors the imaginative mind. Competition, of course, was the essence of the frontier, and there was probably no place in the Mississippi and Ohio valleys where industry, thrift, and luck were stronger than callousness, cunning, and scoundrelism.[2] The frontier offered many awful examples of what a highly acquisitive mentality can do when it is permitted to change its environment by any means that come to hand. But the means were still crude in the 1820's; and though the implementing of ideals by practices that negated them was an exercise the frontier always performed with a certain adroitness, it cannot be denied that in the 1820's the high ideals were as noticeable as the low practices. The frontier uttered with conviction the language of the great American dream. This dream was essentially the adaptation of political ideals to territorial opportunities; and it was not called into question so long as environment took the shape, or seemed to take the shape, of vast spaces of unoccupied land. It was a dream that foresaw the simultaneous achievement of two dissimilar objectives: a maximum of political liberty and a maximum of material well-being; and those who were possessed by it were always a little impatient of the innumerable adjustments necessary to bring these two great objectives into some kind of focus. Nowadays we have learned through painful experience that the two objectives are on different planes; but in 1817, and for many years after, this fact was more inconvenient than apparent.

The tutelary geniuses of the westward movement were Necessity and Hope, which have always provided the motive force for human beings. It would be wrong to underestimate the importance of the latter. Hope is an instinctive apprehension of the fact that everything is in the process of becoming, that all things change, that nothing can be undone; and it is natural enough that this fact, admitted into the drama of human affairs, should take on some extravagant forms. The westering migrant, for example, was drawn across the Alleghenies by a strand of rumors. Some of these rumors were obviously put out by the land-speculating fraternity; some were old and magical. In very early days, the American West was said to be full of "savannas"—Hesperian meadows of rich grass, bosom-high, and perfumed by exotic flowers and trees. The early Spanish explorer, with his lean and fantastic vision, had looked for them; but no man had ever found them. They retreated as mankind advanced; and when the news came from Lewis and

Clark, and from Zebulon Pike, that beyond the Missouri lay a treeless desert, it was generally conceded that the savanna had passed beyond the reach of the pioneer farmer.[3] In the 1820's the mythical "desert" was like the dragon of the Hesperides, all dry rustling scales and fiery breath, guarding the approaches to the promised land. None the less, the savanna, like a memory or a spell, still haunted the westward movement as it spilled into the Mississippi Valley. Men still cherished the belief that at the end of the journey lay the incomparably good life; and they continued to cherish this belief even after they had arrived at their destination.

Oddly enough, the pioneer farmer avoided the real savanna whenever he encountered it. The prairie was found in Illinois, in Indiana, even among the forests of Ohio; but the westward movement into the Ohio and Mississippi valleys was still in the grip of seventeenth- and eighteenth-century agriculture. For two centuries, or thereabouts, the forebears of the nineteenth-century pioneer had themselves been pioneering in the forest. Girdling, grubbing, log-rolling, burning, and the building of log houses were inherited techniques.[4] William Cobbett has testified to the extraordinary proficiency of Americans with the ax: he said that they could do ten times more work with that tool than any Englishman he ever saw, and they were very active and hardy—"they will catch you a pig in an open field by *racing* him down; and they are afraid of nothing." [5] But he added that they knew little of such delicate skills as hedging or the use of the bill-hook; it was in forest farming that the Americans excelled. They put great faith in their ability to select a soil by the character of its forest cover; hardwood, for example—a heavy growth of it—was certain evidence of a "strong" soil.[6] But at the prairies and treeless savannas they looked askance. They suspected a soil where no timber had ever grown; they feared the open solitude, the exposure to winds and storms. The game they coveted lived in the forests; from the forests they obtained the walls of their houses, their fuel, their fences, the wooden pins they used for nails, the wooden hinges and door latch, the wooden chimney, and the hollow log that curbed their wells. The immense difficulty involved in digging a deep well with picks and shovels made the prairie hateful; and the expense of breaking up the prairie sod, which required three or four yoke of oxen and a heavy plow, was prohibitive, and the return was slow. Prairie soil had to lie fallow for a whole season until the grass roots had thoroughly rotted; whereas in the forest the pioneer, armed only with an ax and a hoe, could girdle the trees, grub out the undergrowth, plant his corn, and have a good crop the first year.[7]

A well-found emigrant would go into the wilderness with an ax, a gun, a few household goods, a cow, a yoke of oxen or a horse, a few sheep, and some pigs. Or he might have acquired the characteristic small wagon, with its blanket "tilt," which Birkbeck noted on his westward journey in 1817, and which was the sure sign of a man with some farming experience and a little capital. Such travelers were the sober realists of the movement.[8] Others, less prosperous, trudged westward with a single pack-horse, carrying all their household effects, while the barefoot wives followed behind with the babies. Or the family cow may have been the beast of burden. More often than not, the migrant was a man with no farming experience—a mechanic, or artisan, or merchant's clerk. A handcart on four plank wheels carried his smaller children and the family clothes, skillet, bed-quilt, and bag of corn meal; or a wheelbarrow would serve this purpose; or in cases of extreme destitution a man would carry all his property on his back.[9] Was he driven by necessity, or drawn by hope?

Early in the spring, in the season of courage and of dreams, the rude pilgrims from the seaboard turned their faces west, and, as soon as they struck the great highways, melted into an almost continuous stream of wagons, carts, and foot parties. The journey that lay ahead was immense and terrible. William Cobbett, who never ventured out of the East, recoiled from it with the instinctive horror of a Surrey yeoman. "The rugged roads, the dirty hovels, the fire in the woods to sleep by, the pathless ways through the wilderness, the dangerous crossings of the rivers." And as for the destination! "To boil their pot in the gipsy-fashion, to have a mere board to eat on, to drink whiskey or pure water, to sit and sleep under a shed far inferior to . . . English cowpens, to have a mill at twenty miles' distance, an apothecary's shop at a hundred, and a doctor nowhere." Few English families, he thought, could put up with such conditions or could even cope with them. Did not an American farmer mend his plow, his tackle of all sorts, his household goods, his shoes? Did he not, if need be, *make* them? Could an Englishman do this? Could he live without bread and, worse, without beer, for months at a time? The whole business horrified him; it was a "transalleganian romance," he said bitterly; and he hoped his countrymen would have nothing to do with it. Let them settle in the Atlantic states, near the great cities on the coast.[10] Many settlers, no doubt, would have agreed with Cobbett. "It was on the 6 of May we came here," an anonymous woman wrote to President Monroe, from Barnsville, Ohio; "we had no other food for our horses nor cows but what they could procure in the woods. It took nearly all the time of one of our grown sons to hunt the cattle (the little ones are of no use for this purpose). Your patience sir will not hold out while I would describe swarms of large flies which inhabit these uncultivated lands and which stinging the cattle nearly drive them to madness. Unsound corn, sick wheat and mills seven miles off and then only going in times of great moisture. Indeed last summer the whole settlement were supported by one hand mill for several months. You will conclude we did not eat much bread—and neither we did." But the Americans had a saying that the cowards never started, and the weak died by the way. Few of them, once they had set out, turned back again. Thomas Jefferson told Adam Hodgson that he never knew a person to leave the coast for the Western country and then return to the seaboard.[11]

The main routes of migration from the East were the Mohawk and Genesee turnpike, which led to Lake Erie; the Catskill turnpike to the headwaters of the Allegheny; the old road from Philadelphia to Pittsburgh by way of Lancaster and Bedford; and the Baltimore turnpike, which joined with the National Road at Cumberland on the Potomac. This was one of the greatest arteries of migration and commerce, passing across the mountains to Wheeling on the Ohio, and connecting at its eastern end with the Shenandoah. Once beside the Ohio, migrants might take a steamboat, or put their possessions on an ark or a flatboat and float down the river to their destination; but the majority could not afford the expense. Those who drove their own teams, and camped by the wayside, could make the journey at an average cost of thirty cents per diem per person! [12]

Beyond the divide between the waters of North Carolina and West Virginia, there were also many passes through the mountains; and to the west, from Kentucky and Tennessee, there were innumerable paths to the Ohio in the vicinity of Cincinnati and Louisville. Farther south, the Saluda Gap led from South Carolina into the valleys of eastern Tennessee. [13]

Meanwhile, the pioneer of the Southwest, following the rivers that flowed towards the Gulf and the lower Mississippi, was closely pursued by the planter and the slave, moving around the southern end of the Appalachian system or westward through the passes into Georgia, Alabama, and Tennessee. Just as the free farmer of the Southern interior had already been replaced in the up-country by the slave-holding farmer, and had become the leading element in the upper Mississippi Valley, so now the Southwestern pioneer was pushed back into the pine hills and the barrens, or out towards Texas. He could not refuse the high price offered for his clearing, or could not survive in the competitive bidding at the public land sales; or else the mere presence of slavery so filled him with disgust and exasperation that he abandoned the "buck-shot" soils of central Alabama and Mississippi and fled into the waste. [14]

II

The words "West" and "frontier" are almost interchangeable for the 1820's. The West was the lurch of Christendom along the shortest route between western Europe and eastern Asia, and it was led by the fur-trade—conducted by men of extreme daring and organized by men of extreme cupidity—the produce of which was still the most likely medium of exchange between China and the United States. The frontier was anywhere across the Alleghenies where subsistence farming predominated: thus in the 1820's the frontier was moving out of Ohio, but could still be found in western Pennsylvania. Or again the frontier could be the barrier—as in western Georgia, eastern Alabama, and the northern two thirds of Mississippi—that Indian lands opposed to the advance of cotton. [15] It was extremely fluid; but it also settled into stagnant pools along the mountain ridges in eastern Tennessee and Kentucky, and away from the rivers and the coast it lingered in the lower South like a state of mind—abandoned, primitive, and obstinate.

In 1817, the frontier was advancing along the lines of least resistance, following the rivers, and thrusting out slender fingers towards the West. If the pioneer had a processional, it was choired by rivers. The great movement hastened up the Wabash and the Kaskaskia; up the Mississippi towards the mouth of the Des Moines; up the Missouri, the Arkansas, the Washita, the Red; and down the Pearl, the Pascagoula, the Alabama, and the Chattahoochee. Behind it, like unsubmerged islands, lay the rough mountain regions of the Adirondacks and the Alleghenies of northwest Pennsylvania; it swerved aside from the swamps of northwest Ohio, western Indiana, and southern Georgia; it recoiled a little from the malarial flood plains along the lower course of the Mississippi.[16] It was a ragged affair, but formidable, inspired, and inspiring. Only where the Missouri crossed the boundary of the present state did it suddenly stop; for here began the arid region, or so the readers of Zebulon Pike believed, where a treeless and waterless prairie swept away into some fearful Sahara that heaved its sands to the feet of the Shining Mountains.

The trapper, the elemental spirit of expansionism, already knew that the stories of the great American "desert" were false. But he did not write books. Although, in 1840, the westward movement had at last completely emerged from the forest into daylight, and had reached and reconciled itself to the prairie region, it waited even then upon the line of the ninety-seventh meridian until the railroad pushed on forward in the decade 1850-60. In the 1830's pioneers had begun to settle the savannas of Ohio and Indiana, and the large prairies of Illinois, Michigan, Wisconsin, and Missouri; but in the 1820's it is safe to say that pioneer farming was, with but few exceptions, forest farming. In the shade of the forest men grew sallow and sickened, but ideals flourished; and it was not until it left the forest that the frontier lost its innocence.

III

A man who traveled from the Alleghenies to the Mississippi for pleasure or for curiosity would find himself comparing the advance of civilization to the stratification in a rock. The Indian trace, the trapper, the backwoodsman, the pioneer farmer, the commercial farmer—such had been its progress from east to west; and each successive stage or wave had left its evidence along the way. The visible termini for most travelers would be the log cabin at the western end and the frame house at the eastern; or the track and the road, the clearing and the meadow. These sightseeing travelers had, with a very few exceptions, the static point of view of men who pass from inn to inn, and who measure their advance by mileage. Their evidence is valuable, indeed essential, for it is often all that we have; but it rarely attains vitality. Because they proposed to return to the orderly life out of which they had ventured, such travelers were only tourists in the underworld.

But the settler who committed himself to the westward migration was like a man entering a whirlpool, who passed as he sank the various stages of civilization, all of them intensely active, and who sank, more often than not, forever out of sight and memory. Sometimes, to be sure, if he had the means he stopped at some already prosperous community along the way, bought a few acres of enclosed and partly cleared land, and acquired a habitation and a name.[17] But the movement was relentless and imaginative, and the backwoodsmen who sold their rude clearings or even abandoned them at the first approach of civilization, and "lit out for the tall timber," were more typical of it than were those who settled in one place for the rest of their lives. The pioneer farmer was a restless man, as in a world of cheap land and dear capital he might well be; and he moved as often as he felt attracted by the thought of better soils just ahead, selling his cleared land for a small profit.[18]

In any case, the majority of settlers, upon reaching a destination, began by hewing out a clearing in the midst of the forest. It may be taken for granted that from the beginnings of settlement until after 1850 the great proportion of farms were cleared out of forest land.[19] After this, if a settler were fortunate enough to have accessible neighbors, which was by no means always the case, he summoned them to a "raising," with whisky and a frolic, and the log cabin was built by a communal effort.[20] He then proceeded to "girdle" or deaden an additional tract, by cutting a ring through the bark around the lower portion of the tree-trunks to prevent the sap from rising. The branches then withered and, after they had been burned, the first crop of corn and vegetables was planted. The new clearing, with its gaunt and menacing trees, wore a dismal look, as if it had been blasted by cannon or withered by fire or disease. Generally, five acres were cleared in this way, half an acre being given to the vegetable garden, half an acre to wheat, and the rest to the corn patch. Corn was the chief support of the settlers, and was almost always the first crop on newly cleared land.[21] Such livestock as there was ran loose in the woods, each owner recognizing his animals by their earmarks; and although careful farmers made up winter feed out of Indian corn and pumpkins, in most cases the animals shifted for themselves.[22] That image of hunger, the "wind-splitter," the fabulous hog of the Western forest, was the product of this treatment.

The pioneer farmer raised his own wool, cotton, and flax for his summer and winter clothing, which his women spun and wove and made into garments; his cap was fashioned out of raccoon fur; he was shod from the skins of deer or cattle. His household furniture, his farming utensils, his harness, were all homemade; and his wooden cart, without tires or boxes, and run without tar, could be heard creaking a mile or more away.[23] The valiant women helped with the planting, the hoeing, and the raking at harvest time; and if there was milking to be done, they did that too—for except in Yankee families no settler, man or boy, could be persuaded to milk a cow.[24]

Such was the Western Arcadia, and had it not been for the fever that flitted through the woods, the ague distilled by the swamps and river mists and the desecrated leaf-mold, the malaria and milk sickness, the loneliness, the corroding poverty, and the inevitable squalor,[25] such an Arcadia might have justified even the optimistic rumors that traveled back from it towards the Eastern seaboard. But the forest left its mark. Where the primitive frontier reigned, as in Indiana, the traveler noticed that the cleared land was rich and valuable, but the people pale and deathly looking. An Englishwoman, traveling up the lower Mississippi in 1827, shrank in horror from the bluish-white complexions of the people who crept from their squalid settlements at every landing.[26]

And yet, unless the sickness seized them with too fierce a grip, the pioneers often impressed the passerby in quite another way. The most shiftless of them—it was odd, but it was true—seemed to be the most buoyant. "Everyone in the West walks erect and easy," said one traveler; "impudent and lazy," said another. Both remarks reflect the independence of the frontier, its belief that no man was its master. As for its imagination, the expression of that was naturally crude and *farouche*. The backwoodsman who dragged his wife and children on and on into the forest, and away from the face of civilization, was a highly imaginative type—"half wild and wholly free"—a curious variant of the classical cenobite. The "generals, colonels, majors" who infested land-office towns like Kaskaskia were not obsessed with some idea of social distinction; while they probably used these self-bestowed titles as a screen for some very sharp practices, they were just as probably expressing their belief in the uncommonness of the common man. For it was the common man who, like a giant, subdued the wilderness, and the frontier never forgot it.[27]

The centrifugal impulse of the frontier can be illustrated by the movements of the Lincoln family. The Lincolns rode and walked from Kentucky into southern Indiana in 1816, moving from the path of slavery, which threatened them with the irremediable status of "poor white." Ten years later Thomas Lincoln, no richer, heard the call of the Illinois prairies, and he and his family crossed the Wabash and the Sangamo. Their struggles and tragedies in Indiana were those of all but the more fortunate migrants. At Little Pigeon Creek, for a whole year, they lived in a "half-faced camp," a three-sided cabin, with two trees for corner posts, and an open face looking south, where a log fire burned day and night. "The sides and roof were covered with poles, branches, brush, dried grass, mud; chinks were stuffed where the wind or rain was trying to come through." [28] After a year, they moved into a log cabin, with a dirt floor, no windows, and a hole for a door, and the young Lincoln slept in a minute loft upon a heap of leaves. Some relatives occupied the half-faced camp, one of them declaring years afterwards that "we lived the same as the Indians, 'ceptin' we took an interest in politics and religion." [29] Then came that mysterious visitor, the milk sickness, and Nancy Hanks Lincoln was taken from her children.

IV

The imaginative mind and the economic mind will be found side by side in any primitive society capable of evolution; but as long as conditions favor the imaginative mind, the economic mind tends to adopt its standards. The predatory and usurious instincts of the frontier—which were very strong—were also gambling instincts, and the predator ruined himself almost as frequently as he despoiled his victim. More can be learned from the early frontier if one examines its imaginative side; and this can be discovered most easily in its religion.

The Deism of Jefferson—tolerant and skeptical—never reached the West, which was, if anything, puritanical. In Ohio, with its leaven of New England settlers, this puritanism was sometimes modified into a religion of steady habits and theocratic ministers; elsewhere, it was a puritanism designed rather to justify the wilderness than to convert sinners. Sinners were openly in the majority, and few of them were amenable to conversion. A "Missouri sabbath" was a byword in the West, when Missouri was still a frontier Territory; and farther back, in Illinois and Indiana, it was hardly more seemly.

The Baptists, therefore, who were in general Arminian, on the frontier discarded this doctrinal mildness for the tenets of Calvin. This was a natural response to a wild region whose superb energies expressed themselves in raw physical labor, in drunkenness and profanity, in mad boasts and murderous combats. A conviction of the utter depravity of man was reinforced by the life along the Western waters—where the terrible flatboat men, "half horse, half alligator," poled the produce of the interior down to New Orleans, and where any minor disagreement might end with one contestant, with a practiced thumb, gouging out the eye of the other, who bellowed in agony but never asked for mercy. In this nightmare world, how evident it must have been that some men were predestined to eternal damnation and some to eternal bliss, and that the number of the elect was small indeed. The doctrine of predestination, and of justification by faith, flattered the individualism of the frontier and did not curb those excesses which alone made its lot endurable; for if, indeed, a man was damned from birth, of what avail was repentance?

The Calvinism of the frontier Baptist had some curious consequences. The extreme Calvinists—who were divided into two groups known as the Primitive Baptists and the Two Seed-in-the-Spirit Baptists—brought dissension to many a Western church by their violent opposition to foreign missions. This did not spring merely from a simple assumption that all heathen were probably damned, and that in any case it was presumptuous to attempt to assist the will of God; it was the expression of a distrust in any social elite—for it was, strange to say, as a social elite, an aristocracy, that the Foreign Mission Board appeared in the eyes of those determined people. "Point out to us," begged the Maria Creek Church (Indiana) of the Wabash Baptist Association, "point out to us the wickedness of the Baptist Board of Foreign Missions." This was in 1820. By 1821 the Baptists of Tennessee, and by 1824 the Baptists of Illinois, were overwhelmingly antimission.[30] It was only natural and right that they should be antislavery as well, for slave-holders tended to become an aristocracy; but their respect for property—something acquired and kept by unceasing labor—prevented them during the 1820's from becoming abolitionists.

The Baptists of the frontier were also, as might be expected, deeply opposed to an educated ministry. Their ministers must be men like themselves. This was equally true of the Methodists, the other great frontier sect, who—

if they did not actively oppose an educated ministry [31]—were extremely suspicious of it. Nor was it just a clerical elite that they feared; they were sure that educated men would never undergo the hardships that fell to the lot of the traveling minister. For the Methodist circuit-rider might ride a circuit of a hundred miles, with as many as twenty-one preaching places.[32] "Multiply colleges, universities, seminaries and academies," said Peter Cartwright, "multiply our agencies and editorships, and fill them with our best and most efficient preachers and you localize the ministry and secularize them, too; then farewell to itineracy." [33]

These words are worth studying, for they express the fundamental prejudice of the frontier, whether religious or not. It was not education, but the vainglory of education that was to be feared and shunned. In a society whose energies were spent in back-breaking toil, there was a distinct connection between learning and leisure; and a display of learning might be as loud an example of conspicuous waste in that world as a display of jewels or carriages or servants in another. The circuit-rider was assuredly not learned; and the circuit-rider did as much as any man to bring order into the chaos around him. He was heroic. He rode those almost trackless solitudes in all seasons and all weathers, bringing the word of God through swamp and torrent to lonely people. He had one of the most persistent characteristics of saintliness: an ability to identify himself with common humanity, to be one with and not apart from his fellow man. And he had another gift that saints have been known to employ with great effect: when the occasion called for it, he could use a very scourging tongue. "Look at that dirty, nasty, filthy tobacco chewer," thundered James Axley, the renowned preacher of Eastern Tennessee, "sitting on the end of that front seat; see what he has been about. Look at the puddles on the floor; a frog wouldn't get into them; think of the tails of the sisters' dresses being dragged through that muck." Judge Hugh Lawson White, the victim of this sensible tirade, vowed that he never chewed tobacco in church again.[34]

Thus the most characteristic religion of the frontier was one that, preaching order and practicing equality, sustained and reinforced its democratic instinct. The vigorous but gloomy doctrine of the backwoods preaching was, and was intended to be, strong spiritual medicine, and was swallowed by its audience with the wry zest of those who believe that the more disagreeable the taste the more powerful the purge. Yet the local or the circuit preacher was not sufficient; the frontier stood in need of thaumaturgy, and every once in a while an "awakening," a fever of revivalism, would sweep it from end to end. Then all dogma was discarded, and all sense, and while the preacher displayed an intimate knowledge of the agonies of hell, while he wrestled and overthrew the Devil with a persistence and success that might easily have discouraged a less athletic demon, the congregation rolled upon the earth, shrieking, writhing, and frothing at the mouth. The effect of the revival was threefold: it satisfied a need for professional entertainment; it had a therapeutic value, bringing a primitive form of shock treatment to those who were emotionally repressed; and it assured men and women who were condemned to live in the harshest of environments that they were not forgotten by a watchful Providence. And their notions of Providence were suited to their environment: it was rather the God of wrath than the God of love to whom they turned. It was only in their tongue-tied hospitality—in their raw sense of the brotherhood of man—that the God of love was permitted to appear.

V

In its most extreme expression the doctrine of the Two-Seed-in-the-Spirit Baptists was "nothing more nor less than a modification of ancient Manichaeism." [35] A man was either born of the divine seed or he was not: if he was not, he was born of the "seed of the serpent," planted in Eve and all her daughters after the Fall, and then he became a child of the Devil. The children of the Devil were, it is needless to say, far more numerous than the children of God, and nothing could save them. This fearful doctrine, which led its exponents into many bigotries and absurdities, did not seem absurd, did not perhaps even seem out of place, in that harsh environment. It was the effect of an energy—strong, superstitious and imaginative—that is characteristic of any primitive community; and it is only natural that such men as Daniel Parker, who was one of the leading spirits of the Two-Seed-in-the-Spirit Baptists, should have confessed himself unalterably opposed to centralizing authority in any form. [36] For centralization would have been the end of him. The frontier, the primitive phase in the advance of a highly centralizing civilization, never had time to develop its imaginative men to their fullest extent. Their business was to get the hard work done, to subdue the original wilderness, or to explore beyond it for the profit of other men; and unless they were capable of evolving into some more complex form, they simply vanished—"exentrique, like the wandering star." The fur-trapper, the secular equivalent (and more than the equivalent) of men like Daniel Parker, was the spearhead of the westward movement. A unique mixture of explorer, trader, and fighting man, usually illiterate but carrying in his head a superbly accurate map of the planetary spaces beyond the Missouri, he was the very embodiment of imaginative energy. He was let loose upon the West for as long as he was needed, and then destroyed. When John Jacob Astor, one of the earliest and cruelest examples of centralizing energy, retired with his profits from the fur business in 1834, he left nothing but ruin behind him.

Thus a fear of centralization must be considered as one of the instincts of the frontier: but it was an instinct only—a fear that is felt by individualists, not a fear that is formulated by doctrinaires. Just as the good people of Maria Creek smelled aristocracy in the Baptist Board of Foreign Missions, so the West in general saw in the Administration of James Monroe the sign of a social elite, of a dynasty of Virginians, with the inevitable entourage of professional office-holders and heirs-apparent. When depression settled upon the West after the panic of 1819 this instinct found its voice in "a general impression that there was something radically wrong in the administration of the Government." [37] But the early West never went farther than that.

It had its own brand of militant nationalism, a potent influence in the 1820's, which was oddly compounded of Jeffersonian phrases, expansionist sentiments, and a sure conviction that there was nothing wrong with centralization when it favored the debtor and the farmer, and everything wrong with it when it did not. When centralizing energy appeared in the form of a contraction of credit, as in 1819, the West was enraged; when it showed itself as a protective tariff, or a national scheme of internal improvements, the Westerner was hard put to make up his mind. There was, he believed, centralization and centralization; and he could say no more.

VI

"Old America," said the English speculator, Morris Birkbeck, in 1817, "seems to be breaking up and moving westward." [38] His statement, on the face of it, is a trifle glib—he had acquired over 26,000 acres in Illinois and was anxious to dispose of them to likely purchasers in England—he had, indeed, written a book for that purpose. But the break-up of Old America—an idea Mr. Birkbeck advanced as a useful and legitimate piece of salesmanship—was, in a limited but extremely important sense, actually taking place. The westward migration represented, if anything, the diaspora of the American Enlightenment; for the westward migrant, trudging along his terrible roads towards his improbable wilderness, carried with him the great principles of Liberty and Equality, the twin torches that had flared and smoked through the eighteenth century and now lighted him fitfully along his way.

The pioneer and the migrant saw themselves not as wage-earners but as property owners; and surely the conflicting philosophies of the Enlightenment agreed at least upon one thing—that the property owner must be free to follow his own self-interest. As an agrarian property owner, the pioneer naturally carried farther and farther into the West some fragments of the enlightened nationalism of Thomas Jefferson, which was essentially an agrarian nationalism, and which believed that an evangelizing nation was fully as important as a self-contained one.

"We feel that we are acting under obligations not confined to the limits of our own society," Jefferson wrote. "It is impossible not to be sensible that we are acting for all mankind." [39] An old gentleman, writing to his Congressman son in 1819, expressed this ideal with equal force. "You must not loose sight," he wrote, "that you are ligislating for a great Nation whose Decisions may be a president for ages to come." [40] All Americans believed that they were setting precedents for ages to come, and none held this belief more firmly than did the Western pioneer. Necessity drove him, it is true: the trails he blazed through the forest were trails that led away from exhausted soils, discriminating laws, limited suffrage, unlimited slavery; but the vitalizing notion that he was the standard-bearer of a new freedom accompanied him all the way. He was convinced that somewhere in the wilderness lay the solution for the ills of the Old World. And so, while the party of Thomas Jefferson slowly disintegrated along the Eastern seaboard, or aligned itself more and more with the interests of the Southern slave-holder, the ideals of Thomas Jefferson were being carried into the wilderness.

The old nationalism of the Enlightenment, however, had already reached its apogee in 1807 with the announcement of the Embargo doctrine—the very gospel of enlightened self-interest. It was never to appear again in so concentrated a form. It was the victim of a lamentable, but oddly enough almost universal, unwillingness of self-interest to be enlightened. Thereafter, dispersed along the roads and streams leading to the Ohio and Mississippi valleys, it lost in power what it gained in mobility; for dispersal is never strength.

The pioneer, after all, was a civilizing influence only to the extent that he modified his environment as quickly as he could. For this essential purpose the Jeffersonian notion that all men are created equal was extremely useful; indeed, the pioneer could hardly have got along without it. It was a very complex notion—it may have originated in John Locke's curious misunderstanding of the nature of perception—but the society the pioneer evolved construed it into an equalitarian democracy that Jefferson himself must have thought alarming. All the new states in the West and Southwest showed a fondness for manhood suffrage which exercised a disturbing but salutary influence on the rest of the country. None the less, there is much peril in the equalitarian doctrine; for its devotees are often lulled into forgetting that political equality does not mean economic equality; and the early West was frequently woken from its social trance by sharp reminders of this simple fact. One might almost go as far as to say that this fact—which is the bugbear of all political democracies—bewildered and provoked the pioneer at every turn.

The pioneer's solution was not a Jeffersonian one. He did not condemn central government—which in those days was taken to be the purveyor of economic inequality—but he sought to dominate it wherever he could. He represented a centrifugal energy, and central government represented a gravitational one. It was there to see that pioneer society did not fly off into space. The laws relating to the public lands are very instructive in this respect. In 1817, when a settler wished to purchase public lands, the minimum purchase allowed him by law was a quarter section (160 acres), and the minimum price per acre was $2.00, one fourth to be paid down, and the rest payable in four annual installments. This was a scheme to raise revenue, rather than a plan to assist the settler, for the credit system encouraged speculation, and the debt on public lands rose from $3,042,613.89 in 1815 to $16,794,795.14 in 1818.[41] The great land boom collapsed in 1819, and the settler was in a fair way to being ruined when a Senate Committee on Public Lands, all of whose members but one were from the West, brought in a thoughtful report recommending the abolition of the credit system.[42] This was accomplished by the famous Act of April 2, 1820, which also reduced the minimum purchasable tract to 80 acres, and set the minimum cash payment at $1.25. A farm of 80 acres could now be purchased for $100. This was the first effort to legislate for the settler rather than for the

Treasury; and on September 30, 1822, the debt on public lands had sunk to $10,544,454.16.[43]

By the apportionment of 1822, the Western representation was increased to forty-seven members in the House of Representatives, which, with a delegation of eighteen in the Senate, made a formidable group: and legislation favoring the settler continued all through the 1820's, culminating in the pre-emption laws of 1830. These laws officially changed the status of the squatter from one of public pest to one of public benefactor. The squatter, supreme individualist who ranged far ahead of the government surveyors, and occupied the best of the unsurveyed lands without going through the formality of paying for them, had always been protected by frontier opinion and to some extent by Congressional sentiment. The pre-emption laws made him free of the whole public domain in the sense that he was given the right to purchase his lands, no matter how valuable they might be, at the minimum price and before anyone else could bid for them in the public auction.[44]

Thus there was a close relationship between pioneer society and the bounty of the general government, which lasted long after the debt on public lands was extinguished in 1832. Yet the relationship was never a comfortable one. The West, considered as a centrifugal force, longed for complete control of the public land system, while the general government, as a gravitational pull, yielded this control with the utmost reluctance. Eastern capitalists, Western speculators, and Southern planters were all opposed to a liberalization of the land laws; and although the movement of American history was towards the Pacific, it was not until 1862 that a Homestead Act finally committed this movement into the hands of the common man. And by then it was too late. No society of free pioneering farmers could survive the attack of the railroad interests or disentangle itself from the nets of price-fixing monopolists.[45]

VII

Meanwhile, in the 1820's, the West maintained an ambivalent attitude towards the general government, and expressed a nationalism that was all its own. The addition of six new states between 1816 and 1821, all but one of them in the West or Southwest, was a visible triumph for the expanding frontier, and indicates, even more than do population figures or ratios of increase, the great velocity of the westward movement.[46] Both those who believed in a strict adherence to State Rights, and those who favored a stronger central government, professed themselves satisfied with this new development.[47] The former welcomed to the fold six new sovereigns who would resist the pretensions of consolidation, while the latter believed that economic nationalism would, as a consolidating force, be increased rather than diminished by the addition of new states with neither the strength nor the traditions to resist it.[48] The issues involved were not academic. Agrarian philosophy contended that if the general government grew too strong, it would inevitably align itself with the financial and investing interests; and

had its professors lived until the 1870's, they would have been amply justified in all their predictions. Even centralizing opinion feared the West. The
conservative financier, for example, thought that the new states were a constitutional sanction of the procreative instinct, an instinct which he was inclined to discourage on economic grounds, for he believed that "the creation
of capital is retarded, rather than accelerated, by the diffusion of a thin
population over a great surface of soil.[49] The West itself oscillated in a most
confusing way between the two points of view. Its several states were the
creatures of the national government, deriving their very existence from an
Act of Congress. It was not likely that they would have such a delicate sense
of State Rights as did the more doctrinaire of their elder sisters; that they
would always resist the rough advances of consolidation; or that when they
did resist them they would invariably do so from the highest motives. On
the other hand, they were all agrarian and debtor states; and in moments of
crisis or depression it was their instinct to suspect that there was some connection between the central government and the creditor interest. This confusion of sympathies was increased by the great drama of the Missouri Compromise, which began to divide the West on the free soil question.[50]

When the Western mind was actually confronted, in the 1820's, with a
program of national consolidation, its response was an odd mixture of enthusiasm and fear. Between 1816 and 1832, Henry Clay was engaged in devel
oping his American System; and by 1824 its main features were evident for
all to see. It was composed of protective tariffs; a national system of internal
improvements financed by the sale of public lands; and the centralizing influence of the United States Bank.[51] Henry Clay was a Westerner, and a man
notably possessed by the great American dream: might not this system be
called an answer to the needs and aspirations of the West? So Mr. Clay
argued. He contended that a protective tariff, by fostering the country's industries, would provide a domestic market for the country's produce; that
the internal market thus provided for could not be organized without a
complex of roads and canals efficient enough to reduce the cost of transportation; and that domestic exchanges could never be regulated without a
stable currency. Did not his system provide for all these things? He advanced
this system with all the warmth and magic of his oratory, which have not,
alas, survived the touch of cold print, and the answer to this question, as it
congeals upon the cold page, would seem to be that Mr. Clay's system was
an adroit commingling of the less precise formulations of the Enlightenment
with some of the more exacting demands of the business community. No
man touched the chords of Liberty and Prosperity with a defter, indeed
with a more sincere, finger than did Mr. Clay; but somehow or other they
did not harmonize with the rest of his music. He was a great man and a generous man, and he never ceased to fascinate his countrymen; but his American
System was consolidation at its brassiest. Certainly, as the 1820's advanced,
the country became more and more aware of the need for internal improvements; and the Western farmer, whose progress depended upon the production and marketing of an agricultural surplus, was more aware of it than

anyone else. None the less, Western farming in the 1820's was still largely subsistence farming. The agricultural market was roughly organizing itself through the increased demand from Southern slave-holders for Western produce, and a program of economic nationalism with a strong financial emphasis could not be expected to find complete favor after the panic of 1819, when the agrarian West was continuously striving, by some piece of frenzied legislation, some stay law or replevin law, to gain a brief respite from the waters of debt.[52] Might it not be said that, if Mr. Clay dreamed the great American dream, he did so with one eye open, and that the open eye was in rapt contemplation of the interests of Eastern monopoly? In any case, the Western instinct against centralization seems to have been aroused, and though Mr. Clay never ceased to command the affection of the West, as was only right and proper, it is safe to assume that after 1824 he began gradually to lose its confidence.

VIII

The West—the flow of human beings from the Alleghenies at one end to the prairies and the Gulf at the other—was a great and wonderful influence upon American life in the 1820's. It was perhaps the last time in all history when mankind discovered that one of its deepest needs—the need to own— could be satisfied by the simple process of walking towards it. Harsh as the journey was, and cruel as the wilderness could be, this movement could not help but be a hopeful one. In the 1820's, the West sank into debt; but still its inhabitants professed, in the midst of their discontents, to see some evidence of promise in the individual human being, and to look for a human being, rather than a set of principles, who should constellate this evidence for them. The Westerner was a Rousseauesque figure. While on the one hand he offered the world an inspiring picture of courage, simplicity, and ingenuity, on the other hand he became the very symbol and representative of the congregated discontents of a nation. He spoke for the Eastern mechanic; for the debtor in his cell; for the rural democrat of New England and New York; for any man who considered himself abused, cheated, or misunderstood. His nationalism, therefore, though exuberant, was a visionary nationalism, speaking with many tongues and little clarity.

The dreams of Mr. Clay were too capitalistic to satisfy this kind of nationalism; the Jeffersonian philosophy, though highly quotable, was held to be too impractical to cope with the imperatives of the practical life; the Virginia Dynasty, lingering on in Washington in the person of Mr. Monroe, was considered too narrowly professional to provide a leadership. To whom could the hopeful and the discontented turn? In the early twenties, Andrew Jackson began to emerge as just such a man. It was true that little was known about him; and that his political beliefs and economic habits, had they been carefully examined at the time, would not have satisfied either the debtor, or the antislavery man, or any of the more exacting of his followers.[53] But the materials for a careful examination were not readily accessible; and what was known against him was always glossed over. The outline was clear, the details were mysterious; and the mystery carried its enchantment. Only one thing was certain about General Jackson—in moments of crisis he invariably behaved as the imaginative man, of the extreme martial type. This type was a Western ideal; and because it was a Western ideal it summoned, like a magnet, all sorts of aspirations that were not Western at all.

When the Monroe Administration, in 1818, turned the General loose upon the Seminoles and Spaniards of Florida, it could not possibly have foreseen all the consequences of this action. The General was a powerful weapon in 1818, and did all that was required of him. It was only later that the weapon turned upon Monroe's heir and dealt him a mortal wound.

CHAPTER THREE

The General

THE most interesting feature in the military career of Andrew Jackson was its brevity; the next most interesting feature was the indomitable spirit of Andrew Jackson. Good fortune would appear to have been the third: the rest were insignificant. Brevity, intensity, good fortune—what more was needed to fix the General securely in the American firmament? The meteor and its fiery track stayed in mid-heaven; the rocket burst into a fountain of stars, but never faded or fell. In 1818, when one spoke of the Military Hero, one did not mean General Jacob Brown or General Winfield Scott or, still less, General William Henry Harrison: Andrew Jackson was the man. He stood poised in the imagination of his countrymen above the mud rampart of the Rodrigues Canal, a position from which no amount of honest alarm or ingenious calumny could ever dislodge him. Here, in fact, on January 8, 1815, he had presided over the defeat of the British, who were kind enough not to attack him where he was most vulnerable but wasted their superb valor on an impossible frontal assault. Yet would the assault have been impossible if Jackson had not been there? His good fortune was obvious: the Battle of New Orleans conspicuously demonstrates that mixture of courage and incapacity which the British generals of that era reserved, to do them justice, only for their American campaigns. No less obvious was Jackson's fierce, intractable spirit. He seemed to hold the battle together, and to draw the British to their doom, not by superior ability, but by sheer will. His energy was the energy of a magnet, which defies gravity.

Behind the Battle of New Orleans lay the storming of Pensacola; behind the storming of Pensacola lay the victories of Talladega, Emuckfaw, Enotachopco, and Horseshoe Bend; and sandwiched between Horseshoe Bend and Pensacola were twenty-three million acres ravished from the vanquished Creeks at the Treaty of Fort Jackson. Such were the military achievements of Andrew Jackson, and they had been crowded into the space of fourteen months.

In 1818, Andrew Jackson was, as it were, a military silhouette, an outline and nothing more. Few people outside the state of Tennessee knew the details of his civilian career—an odd jumble that only upon close inspection resolved itself into the typical progression of a frontier *arriviste*. Horse-coper, lawyer, politician, judge, enterpriser—by these rungs the general had ascended to the position of slave-holder and country gentleman. There was little to set him apart from the rest, except a passionate idiosyncrasy, a conviction that he was always right, which, enforced by an imaginative temperament and a fierce will, transformed him into the most generous of friends and the most remorseless of enemies. His marriage to Rachel Donelson (one can say it without risk of sentimentality) is one of the great love stories in American history. His feelings towards his enemies, in speech or writing or action, commonly expressed themselves in terms of caning, slitting throats, or shooting. He was all tenderness on the one hand, and all savagery on the other; and the events of his daily life, subjected to the impulsive tribunal of his singular conscience, from which there was no appeal, might as easily call forth the one as the other. At the root of his social being lay the simple ethic he had once expounded for the instruction of a refractory Spanish official: "An eye for an Eye, Toothe for Toothe, and Scalp for Scalp." [1] It was the dominant motif of a long and great career.

Feral in his enmities, conservative in his politics, absorbed in the pursuit of wealth,[2] Andrew Jackson might have crouched forever among the lights and shadows of middle Tennessee, perfectly camouflaged against the aim of history. But Andrew Jackson had military ambitions; he would rather be a major-general of militia than anything else; and it was as a major-general of militia, more responsive to the imperialism than to the democracy of the frontier, that he was caught up in the whirl of high events and placed at last upon the mud rampart of the Rodrigues Canal. By then he was already transformed into a major-general in the regular army, and thereafter he was a national figure. The figure was enigmatic: no one could say which path, politically, the General would take, or if he would take any. Only in these days may one assert that he was not an opportunist, willing to head any cause that would sweep him into power. He was shrewd and calculating, as his environment required him to be; one could not otherwise survive on the frontier, or just behind it. But he was essentially an imaginative man, slow to make up his mind on great issues, and responding at length to the depth of his feelings and not to the dictates of his reason. As a rational man, he was a temperate conservative; as a feeling man, he was an intemperate rebel. The imperatives of debtor democracy, grand and confusing as they were, were bound to carry more appeal to such a man than the cold enticements of industrialists, investors, and manipulators of credit. But all that was in the future. In 1818, General Jackson was a rare metal, not indeed free of some natural alloy, waiting for the nineteenth century to stamp upon it an enduring image.

I

That the Virginia Dynasty should have given Jackson the opportunity to increase his military reputation was a little ironical: it was not too fond of military heroes. In 1815, none the less, when Jackson rode to Washington, Thomas Jefferson came down from his inventive mountain to meet him on the way; and at the capital he carried all before him.[3] He had now begun to resemble the Jackson of history. The long, narrow face, lined with pain and passion, the small blue eyes, the surmounting brush of stiff gray hair; the high bony nose, firm chin, and generous mouth; the emaciated body: this was the apparition which startled and delighted Washington. The General's fine manners, when he chose to use them, were decidedly prepossessing. He used them to good effect; President Madison and his Cabinet were all impressed; and with Secretary Monroe his discussions verged upon the confidential.[4] When Monroe became President, however, the relationship thus established was seriously threatened. In an agitated correspondence with the Assistant Secretary of War, the President, and Mr. Secretary Calhoun, General Jackson insisted that he was the sole channel through which the commands of the War Department might be transmitted to his subordinates in the Southern Division.[5] The difficulty was eventually smoothed out; but the commander-in-chief must have realized, if he did not know it before, that whatever the military virtues of the Southern major-general may have been, a nice respect for authority was not among them.

Was it wise to entrust to such a man the conduct of a campaign that involved the chastisement of the Seminole Indians who lived across the border in Spanish Florida? Was it wise, that is to say, if the government wished to remain upon good terms with Spain? Florida politics were rarely easy to understand; and they were never less intelligible than on December 26, 1817, when orders were sent to General Jackson requiring him to assume direction of the Seminole campaign.[6] If anything was ascertainable in the General's composition, beside his magnificent courage and his evident disregard for higher authority, it was his extreme nationalism—the nationalism of the frontier, with its ingrown hatred of Indians and Spaniards. Was it because of this nationalism, or in spite of it, that the General was sent into Florida? The mystery has never been cleared up. Whatever the reason, the results were spectacular: within a few weeks of assuming command on the Georgia border, the General had planted the American flag on two Spanish fortresses, and court-martialed and executed two British citizens.

II

The Seminole Indians were, as to their nucleus, the members of a tribe called the Oconee, affiliated with the Creeks, but always on the outer edge of the Creek confederacy. This tribe may have come to Florida in 1750. It was increased by runaways from the Creek nation—the word "Seminole" was applied by the Creeks to people who removed from populous districts and went to live by themselves—and after the Creek war of 1813-14, and the invasion of sacred grounds at the Battle of Horseshoe Bend, more Creeks fled across the border and transformed themselves into Seminoles. They lived in villages of log and palmetto huts, surrounded by cleared fields of from two to twenty acres of land; and from their custom, which was distinctively Creek, of circulating red war-clubs among these villages as a preliminary to going to war, they were sometimes known as Red-Sticks.[7]

These "Seminoles" were usually at odds with the runaway slaves, who formed another group—perhaps eight hundred in all—in the northern parts of Florida. In the year 1816, most of these Negroes lived in or near a fort that overlooked the narrow, crooked Apalachicola River. The fort was a relic of British adventures in Spanish Florida during the War of 1812, and the British had left it well stocked with arms—ten or twelve pieces of cannon, twenty-five hundred muskets, five hundred carbines, five hundred steel-scabbarded swords, four hundred pistols, three hundred quarter-casks of rifle powder, and seven hundred and sixty-three barrels of common powder.[8] It was a formidable and mischievous legacy. The Negroes who fell heirs to it considered themselves unassailable; and, being always mindful of the inhuman circumstances that had driven them into Florida, not unnaturally behaved in a hateful way. At length they made the mistake of attacking an American convoy ascending the Apalachicola towards Fort Scott, the last outpost of the United States upon the Georgia-Florida boundary. One American sailor was captured, tarred, and burned alive; four others were shot down. On July 26, 1816, the convoy struck back. A cannon-ball made red-hot in the galley of one of its gunboats was fired into the fort and penetrated its larger magazine. There was a fearful explosion; a shower of blood, flesh, and debris descended upon the shallow river and the stunned Americans; and from the ruins of the fort, which had housed three hundred and forty-four men, women, and children, only three wretches crept out alive. They were handed over to the Seminoles for execution; and to the Seminoles, also, were given whatever weapons had been uninjured by the explosion.[9]

This somber event, which casts a shadow upon the name Apalachicola, made a deep impression upon the Seminoles. But the impression was more deep than lasting. Fortified by their new store of weapons, the Indians began to ask themselves whether they had not been cheated of certain lands across the border at the confluence of the Chattahoochee and the Flint. Early in 1817, trouble broke out between the Americans and the Seminoles of lower Georgia, trouble which, as was usually the case upon the frontier, might as easily have been attributed to one side as to the other. The frontiersman, who was adept in all the arts of savage intercourse, such as lifting scalps and cattle, probably gave as much provocation as he received, and may have given more.[10] The Seminoles observed the *lex talionis*, and, according to their reckoning in September 1817, the Americans had slain ten warriors and owed them three: in other words, they admitted to seven murders as against the Americans' ten.[11] Their bookkeeping in this respect was usually accurate.

In November, Brevet Major-General Edmund P. Gaines, who commanded in Georgia, dispatched a force of two hundred and fifty men, under Major Twiggs, to the Seminole village of Fowltown, some fourteen miles from Fort Scott, with orders to bring back the chiefs and warriors for a conference. Major Twiggs's invitation was refused; the village was burned and two warriors and a woman were slain; and the Seminoles in reprisal ambushed an American hospital boat as it crawled up the Apalachicola, killing thirty-four ill soldiers and seven women. The commander, Lieutenant R. W. Scott, was generally believed to have been tortured to death.[12] This was on November 30. On December 16, General Gaines was authorized to cross the border if necessary and attack the Seminoles *"unless they should shelter under a Spanish post."* [13] On December 26, it was decided that General Gaines's presence was needed in Amelia Island, another fragment of the Spanish Empire, which had fallen into the hands of pirates, and offered, among other things, serious competition to the vested smuggling interests of the Atlantic Coast. On December 26, General Jackson was requested to proceed to Fort Scott and assume command, his orders being the same as those given to General Gaines.[14] He had anticipated these orders to this extent—that on January 6, 1818, before they reached him in Nashville, he had already written to the President, suggesting the advisability of a forcible seizure of Spanish East Florida. This could be done without implicating the government. "Let it be signified to me through any channel, (say Mr. J. Rhea) that the possession of the Floridas would be desirable to the United States, and in sixty days it will be accomplished." [15] No one could say that the Administration had not been warned.

III

The confusion of local interests upon those distant, those almost fabled borders is beyond the wit of man to disentangle. The great land cession wrested from the Creeks at Fort Jackson was presumably at the bottom of it all; and since one land cession commonly suggested another, General Jackson's "Rhea Letter" may have been a simple application of frontier logic to nationalist premises. Then again, the slave-holders of Georgia and South Carolina saw in East Florida a mere invitation to their slaves to run away; while certain gentlemen in Tennessee had invested heavily in Florida lands. Land speculation is woven into the texture of American history. General Jackson was not himself interested in Florida real estate; his feelings were as altruistic as they could well be under the circumstances; but the speculations of his relatives and neighbors may have added some yeast to the general ferment.[16] As for the Seminoles, their belief that they had been cheated of their rights at Fort Jackson was not diminished by the promises British officers had made them before the end of the War of 1812. Indeed, a certain Colonel Nicholls, after the war was over, had actually made an offensive and defensive alliance between the Seminoles and Great Britain. This alliance was explicitly disavowed by Lords Bathurst and Castlereagh:

but the Seminole prophet Francis, whom Nicholls took with him to London, was invested with the scarlet coat of a brigadier-general, presented with a ceremonial tomahawk, and received in audience by the Prince Regent, who said some very kind things and gave him a snuff-box.[17] Colonel Nicholls's parting advice to the Seminoles was hardly pacific. "I ordered them," he wrote, "to stand on the defensive, and have sent them a large supply of arms and ammunition, and told them to put to death without mercy, any one molesting them."[18] It is not to be wondered at that the prophet Francis, returning to Florida with his scarlet uniform, his tomahawk, and his snuff-box, believed that he had the backing of the British Empire in any undertaking against the Americans.

The Spanish in Florida were a handful of men too weak to govern and too proud to confess it. Their king was a brute, and his government, with the exception of the honest Pizarro and the ingenious de Garay, was a preposterous archaism. In Washington, the Spanish Minister, Don Luis de Onís y Gonzalez, was engaged in a rueful negotiation with Secretary Adams, respecting the eventual transfer of the Floridas to the United States.

IV

The Floridas, like Canada, had long provoked the appetite of American imperialists; but, unlike Canada, their position justified the appetite. People used to say that whoever possessed the Floridas held a pistol at the heart of the Republic, and the Floridas conveniently shaped themselves to this concept, East Florida representing the butt of the pistol and West Florida the barrel. James Madison had gone so far—too far, perhaps, for a President—as to encourage in 1810 the revolutionary sentiments of the inhabitants of West Florida, with the result that the United States felt obliged to occupy that province as far east as the Pearl River. This was in October 1810.[19] In April 1812 an Act of Congress incorporated this area in the state of Louisiana; while an Act of May 14, 1812, added to the Territory of Mississippi a further slice of Spanish West Florida, extending as far east as the Perdido River.[20] The pistol now had a distinctly snub-nosed look; but it was none the less dangerous for that. The immediate sanction for these two Acts was yet another Act of January 15, 1811, which empowered the President to take custody both of West and of East Florida if they were in danger of occupation by some foreign power other than Spain, and which was based in turn upon a justly famous Resolution.[21] The war passed; the danger of a British occupation of Florida vanished; the United States remained upon the east bank of the Perdido River. It was now clear that Spain would have to cede the Floridas: the question was, upon what terms would she do so? There were claims and counterclaims. The United States contended that Spain had not lived up to the terms of Pinkney's Treaty of 1795, not least in failing to control her Seminole Indians: the Spaniards complained that the United States violated neutrality by openly befriending the rebellious Spanish colonies of South America.

For the Spanish Empire was now in an acute stage of disintegration. The disintegration was nothing new—it had been evident since the seventeenth century—but its acuteness was due to the influence of Napoleon, one of the greatest solvents in all history. When Napoleon planted his brother Joseph like some kind of provocative vegetable upon the imperial throne of Spain, while Ferdinand VII languished in a prison at Valençay, he produced a revolution in the Spanish American colonies, at first in favor of Ferdinand, and then in favor of independence. In April 1810 Simon Bolivar obtained control at Caracas, and from then onwards the huge Spanish Empire began to crumble. The court of Ferdinand VII—a disagreeable combination of grandees, priests, and parvenu favorites—seemed peculiarly adapted to preside over this immense dissolution.

The Spanish Minister at Washington was supposed to prevent the United States from recognizing the rebelling Spanish colonies. He was also, in a way, the guardian of those portions of the Empire which—like the Floridas, Texas, and New Mexico—lay upon the southern and western borders of the Republic. A discussion involving one would involve all: the cession of one implied the cession of the rest. To postpone the inevitable by obstinacy, opaqueness, procrastination, and all the arts of sticking in the mud—this was the duty of the Spanish Minister: and there was much in the temperament and training of Don Luis de Onís which fitted him for this difficult task.

Don Luis came to the United States in 1809. He arrived somewhat surreptitiously as Minister from the Junta Central, a nationalist entity with vaguely Republican leanings, which opposed itself to the Bonapartist regime in Spain. It would, however, be doing the greatest injustice to Don Luis to suppose that he himself had republican leanings of any kind. His loyalty to that undeserving monarch, King Ferdinand VII, was extreme, and must be accounted to him for virtue. Months passed, years passed, and still he could not obtain recognition from the United States. He lingered in Pennsylvania, an industrious intriguer, with a pronounced addiction to Federalist society.[22] At last, on December 9, 1815, his credentials were accepted; and it was as the envoy of Ferdinand VII that he began his career of official service.

Amiable in his private relations, he brought to his public duties certain qualities that can be described only in terms of their opposites. A rigid suppleness, a calcified cunning, a chilly heat—such were the diplomatic properties of Don Luis. Whatever he had learned at the University of Salamanca (for he was well educated by Spanish standards), at the court of Saxony, or in the Ministry of State in Madrid, had been squeezed into the narrow mold of Spanish thought, and had emerged in the shape of a fairly well-informed opposition to the principle of change. He clothed this opposition in language prolix even by Spanish standards, and his dispatches from America during his ten years' residence fill ten thousand good quarto pages.[23]

The cession of the Floridas was, of course, not the only bargaining point at the disposal of Don Luis in his attempt to prevent the United States from recognizing or even befriending the Spanish revolutionaries in South America. He was also ready to discuss the boundaries of the Louisiana Purchase in their relation to the Empire of Spain. As regards the southwestern aspect of this immense and vital problem, he derived his knowledge from a manuscript prepared by two priests—the learned Father Melchior de Talamantes, whose labors had been unfortunately cut short by his arrest for complicity in a revolutionary plot, and the even more learned Father José Antonio Pichardo. It was called *A Treatise on the Limits of Louisiana and Texas,* and it had attained a peculiar sanctity in the eyes of Don Luis and his superiors because it was perhaps a million words in length.[24] It must be evident that only a new and forthright energy—General Jackson's perhaps?—could relieve the Spanish mind of this formidable weight of literature.

Don Luis de Onís began his conversations with Secretary of State James Monroe by asserting that the Louisiana Purchase was, in effect, a gigantic fraud. His government would cede the Floridas, he said, if the Americans would agree to accept the Mississippi River as their western boundary. When John Quincy Adams took up the negotiation in December 1817, Onís was prepared to modify this fantastic proposition, but only to the extent of admitting that a line drawn between the Mermentau and Calcasieu rivers, in the very midst of the state of Louisiana, might be considered the southwesternmost limit of the United States. Mr. Adams, like Mr. Monroe before him, offered the Colorado River of Texas as a possible boundary in the southwest.[25] In spite of many discussions in Washington and Madrid, their positions appeared to be immovable; and little was left to them but the consolations of prose. "Truth is of all times," wrote Onís on January 24, 1818, "and reason and justice are founded on immutable principles. It is on these principles that the rights of the Crown of Spain are founded to the territories eastward and westward of Louisiana." He went on to say that by the Colorado River he assumed Mr. Adams to mean the Colorado of Natchitoches and not the Colorado farther west.[26] Mr. Adams answered that by the Colorado of Texas he meant the Colorado of Texas. "The observation," he added, "that truth is of all times, and that reason and justice are founded upon immutable principles has never been contested by the United States; but neither truth, reason, nor justice consists in stubbornness of assertion, nor in the multiplied repetition of error." [27]

To which Don Luis could only reply that he must send a courier to Madrid.[28]

Perplexities crowded upon him. The United States were preparing to occupy Amelia Island, on the grounds that it was a nest of pirates. What was to prevent them from applying the same reasoning to Galveston in Texas, the home of the notorious Laffite? Or from forcibly seizing the Floridas, where neither Governor Coppinger nor his lieutenant, the commandant of St. Marks, made any pretense of controlling the Seminoles? Then again, Mr. Clay was exercising his arts upon Congress in favor of the independence of the United Provinces of La Plata; and though his efforts were defeated by a large vote on March 15, 1818, it was common knowledge that he would try again.[29] Elsewhere, on the Alabama River, a group of Bonapartist exiles was known to be meditating an incursion into Texas, in order to place ex-

King Joseph of Spain upon the throne of Mexico.[30] This enterprise fore-shadowed, if anything, the curious affinity between later Bonapartism and *opera bouffe;* but everyone took it seriously at the time, and none more than Onís.

Moreover, he realized that in John Quincy Adams he had no ordinary antagonist. He applied for recall; but the Spanish government was relent-less.[31] With a sigh of resignation, he buckled on his diplomatic armor, which was more appropriate in design to the reign of Ferdinand the Catholic than that of Ferdinand VII, but which, after all, fitted him not uncomfortably. When General Jackson burst into Florida, the positions of Mr. Adams and Don Luis had not changed. Mr. Adams still stood upon the Colorado River of Texas; Don Luis was firmly planted between the rivers Mermentau and Calcasieu. Between them lay half the state of Louisiana and half the province of Texas. Their movements in either direction, it seemed, were becoming more and more dependent upon those of General Jackson.

V

Eleven days after he had received his orders from Washington, General Jackson set out for Fort Scott with an advance guard of two mounted com-panies. In the absence of the governor of Tennessee, he had upon his own responsibility ordered the Tennessee mounted volunteers (two regiments of mounted gunmen, or about one thousand men in all) to meet at Fayette-ville on or before the first of February.[32] The population of Nashville turned out to cheer as Old Hickory, at the head of his advance guard, rode out into the future.[33]

On February 14, when he met General Gaines, he discovered that the commissariat, as was commonly the case in remote campaigns, had broken down. General Gaines, by the unusual exertions of his own quartermaster, had kept his troops from starving; but on February 19, the two generals learned that the officer in charge of Fort Scott proposed to abandon that important stronghold if food did not reach him. General Gaines, with twelve men, disappeared down the swollen Flint in a small boat, hoping to arrive at Fort Scott in time to prevent this movement.[34] General Jackson, with his mounted troops, Gaines's nine hundred Georgia volunteers, and a body of Indians, moved on to Fort Early, where he found himself on February 26 without a barrel of flour or a bushel of corn. But he had "pork on foot," and he proposed to continue his march towards Fort Scott. He reached the Fort on March 9, with starvation at his heels and ahead of him a dismal prospect of swollen rivers and swampy grounds.[35] He was now in command of two thousand hungry men.[36] And so the campaign began.

The General did not hesitate on the border, but hurried across towards the ruins of the Negro fort on the Apalachicola, which he rebuilt and re-named Fort Gadsden. For nine days he lingered in this ominous spot, wait-ing for supplies. The remainder of his Tennessee volunteers were still in Georgia, held back by rumors of starvation further ahead. The pangs of his troops were slightly assuaged by a single shipment of flour up the Apalachicola. General Gaines, who had vanished from sight during the previous month, reappeared on March 24 dressed only in a pair of pantaloons: his boat had capsized, he had lost all his baggage and three of his men, and he had been wandering half-naked in the woods for four and a half days. Washington was as distant as if it had been upon another planet. Half-starved in this wet wilderness, in this imperial solitude, the General was preoccupied with visions of the Spanish garrison of St. Marks.

> "The Spanish Government," he wrote, "is bound by treaty to keep the Indians at peace with us. They have acknowledged their incompetency to do this, and are consequently bound, by the laws of nations, to yield us the facilities to reduce them. Under this consideration, should I be able, I shall take possession of the garrison as a depot for my supplies, should it be found in the hands of the Spaniards, they having supplied the Indians; but if in the hands of the Indians, I will possess it, for the benefit of the United States, as a necessary position for me to hold, to give peace and security to this frontier." [37]

With these words, the campaign began to lose its character of an Indian war, and to merge into an intrigue to seize the Floridas—an extension of that Jeffersonian-Madisonian intrigue which had so perturbed the conscience of Mr. Gallatin at Ghent.[38]

The arrival of Captain McKeever on the evening of the 25th, with provisions and gunboats, assured the General of support on his right flank as he advanced towards St. Marks.[39] He was now working out a military theme with a typically Jacksonian tempo, the solution of which was to be made manifest in the council chambers of Washington, London, and Madrid.

VI

The General left Fort Gadsden on March 26. On April 1, he was reinforced by a party of friendly Creeks under the half-breed McIntosh, and by a detachment of Tennessee volunteers under Colonel Elliott.[40] A skirmish on April 1, and a pursuit on April 2, were sufficient to disperse the neighboring Seminoles and to destroy their settlements. "In the centre of the public square, the old Red Stick's standard, a red pole, was erected crowned with scalps, recognized by the hair, as torn from the heads of the unfortunate companions of Scott." [41] About one thousand cattle, and more than three thousand bushels of corn, fell into the hands of the hungry invaders.[42] On April 6, the army halted in sight of the Spanish fort of St. Marks.

The Spanish commandant was helpless before the evident purpose of General Jackson to seize and garrison his fort. On April 7 the protesting official and his garrison were furnished with transport to Pensacola; the Spanish flag was lowered; the Stars and Stripes floated in its place. The Americans discovered, anxiously lingering in the commandant's quarters, an elderly gentleman with long white hair and a reserved but benevolent countenance.

"My love," wrote the General to his wife, "I entered the Town of St. marks on yesterday . . . I found in St. marks the noted Scotch villain Arbuthnot . . . I hold him for trial." [43]

At the same time Captain McKeever of the United States Navy, by the ingenious device of flying the British colors as he brought his gunboat into St. Marks's Bay, lured into his clutches no less a personage than Francis, the Seminole prophet, the ci-devant brigadier-general, who had not lost his faith in the British Empire. With him was another chief, "A savage-looking man . . . taciturn and morose," whose name was Homollimico, and who was believed responsible for the torture and death of Lieutenant Scott.

All now depended, the General thought, "upon the rapidity of my movements." He began by hanging Francis and Homollimico on April 8. On April 9, taking with him eight days' rations, he set out for Boleck's Town, the home of a great chief who was not unkind to refugee Negroes. It was one hundred and seven miles away, on the banks of the mysterious Suwanee. To reach it one had to cross a dim, uncharted forest, dismally rooted in swamps and quagmires. The infantry sank to their waists in the morass; the horses "gave out daily in great numbers"; but the determined General completed his march in eight days. At sunset on April 18 the desperate army rushed upon the town; but the town was empty. Warned in advance, the great chief Boleck (or Bowlegs as he was generally called), his warriors, his women, and the ex-slaves who had sought his protection and entered his service, had vanished across the broad river. Only a few stern souls remained to engage the Americans. Of these, nine Negroes and two Indians were slain. [44] On the next day, General Gaines crossed the river in pursuit, but returned empty-handed. That night, as the army lay encamped on the level banks of the Suwanee, in a silence broken only by "the measured tread of the sentinels and the murmur of the long-leafed pines," there stumbled into the arms of one of its pickets a certain Lieutenant Robert C. Ambrister, late of the British Royal Colonial Marines, his servant Peter B. Cook, and two Negro attendants. [45]

On April 21, Jackson turned back towards St. Marks. He had with him Lieutenant Ambrister and certain documentary evidence—found upon one of Ambrister's attendants—which implicated Arbuthnot in the warning of Boleck. He believed that the Indians were now "divided and scattered, and cut off from all communication with those unprincipled agents of foreign nations who have deluded them to their ruin." [46] He made the return march in five days.

He had always contended that foreign agents were at the bottom of the Seminole disturbances. The capture of Arbuthnot and Ambrister, and the further discovery of suspicious documents on Arbuthnot's schooner when it was captured by Captain Gadsden at the mouth of the Suwanee, convinced him that he had these agents in his power. [47] On April 26, a special court, composed of fourteen officers, was convened at St. Marks to try the two prisoners.

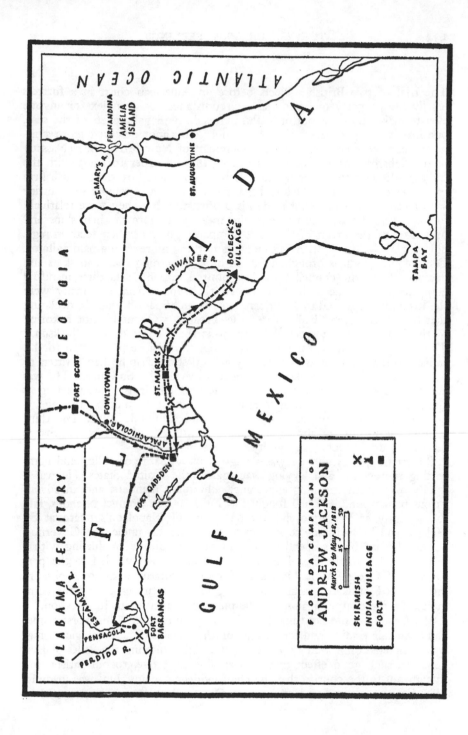

ATLANTIC OCEAN

FERNANDINA
AMELIA
ISLAND
ST. MARY'S R.
ST. AUGUSTINE

GEORGIA

FORT SCOTT
FOWLTOWN

FLORIDA

SUWANEE R.
BOLECK'S
VILLAGE

TAMPA
BAY

APALACHICOLA R.

ST. MARK'S

FORT GADSDEN

ALABAMA TERRITORY

ESCAMBIA R.

PENSACOLA
FORT
BARRANCAS
PERDIDO R.

GULF OF MEXICO

FLORIDA CAMPAIGN OF
ANDREW JACKSON
March 9 to May 28, 1818

0   25   50

SKIRMISH
INDIAN VILLAGE
FORT

VII

The trial of two British subjects before an American court in a fortress
legally the property of Spain was a circumstance too complex for anyone
ever to make any sense out of it. Putting aside the legal aspects of the case,
one may venture to assert that Alexander Arbuthnot deserved more sympathy than recrimination. He was a merchant of New Providence (Nassau)
in the Bahamas, who came to Florida in 1817 in order to trade with the
Indians. Hitherto this trade had largely been conducted by the Scottish firm
of Forbes & Company, which had never been known to temper its injustice
with mercy. Mr. Arbuthnot made his profits, too, but they were relatively
fair ones. So the Indians brought him more and more of their skins and
beeswax; and the agents of Forbes & Company, gnashing their teeth in rage,
noised it abroad that Mr. Arbuthnot was nothing more than a paid agitator.
Certainly the Indians brought to Arbuthnot something else than skins and
beeswax. Over the council fires they poured into his ears their manifold
complaints. He came to be their father, their spokesman; and many were
the letters he addressed to American, British, and Spanish officials, declaring
that the United States had violated the Treaty of Ghent by not restoring
to the Indians the lands ceded by them at the Treaty of Fort Jackson.[48]
The kindly old man had unquestionably conceived a deep affection for his
Indian children; but it is equally beyond question that he had written to
warn chief Boleck of Jackson's advance towards the Suwanee.[49] He was
arraigned upon three charges: inciting the Creek Indians to war, acting as
a spy, and exciting the Indians to attack, with intent to murder, two agents
of Forbes & Company, William Hambly and Edmund Doyle. The third
charge was manifestly absurd, and was not pressed; of the second charge
he was no doubt technically guilty.

Robert Christy Ambrister was arraigned on a charge of aiding and com-
forting the enemy, and levying war against the United States. He was a
young man of an engaging appearance, charming manners, and an adven-
turous background. He had fought in Florida under Colonel Nicholls, and
subsequently at Waterloo; he had been one of Napoleon's guard at St.
Helena; and he had gone to Nassau to stay with his uncle, the Governor,
because he had been suspended from all military duties for dueling with a
brother officer in the East Indies.[50] In Nassau he had yielded to the persuasions of George Woodbine, a professional agitator with some obscure
interests in Florida real estate, and had gone adventuring among the Seminoles. To the charges against him he pleaded "guilty, with justification." [51]

Mr. Arbuthnot did not think himself guilty: and, indeed, his worst crimes
had been fair trading and friendship for the Indians. The case against him
was completed on March 27. He spent the night studying the Rules of Evidence to such good effect that he was able to prove, to our satisfaction
though not to the court's, that the chief evidence against him was inadmissible, because it was based on hearsay. On April 28 he was condemned to

be hanged; while the verdict of death by shooting, passed the same day upon Lieutenant Ambrister, was reconsidered and changed to one of fifty lashes and confinement for a year.[52] On April 29 Jackson approved the sentence of Arbuthnot and the finding and first sentence of Ambrister, and disapproved the reconsideration.[53] The sentences were carried out that same morning.[54]

The two men took their deaths very patiently. No one who ventured into the weird limbo of Florida in those days did so with much thought for the morrow. When the sound of the drum and fife was heard, parading the platoon for his execution, "There," exclaimed Ambrister, "I suppose that admonishes me to be ready; a sound I have heard in every quarter of the globe, and now heard by me for the last time." [55] He had made himself very popular with his captors, and all but one of his judges followed his body to its grave.

Twenty minutes after Ambrister's death, the body of the aged Arbuthnot, decently clad in black, swung from the yardarm of his own schooner, the *Chance*. "It is fair to say," reflected Lieutenant Rodgers of the Tennessee Volunteers, "that in person he would remind the observer of Aaron Burr." [56]

VIII

General Jackson conscientiously believed that his two victims deserved to die; for if he was a relentless judge, he was also an upright one.[57] The fact that he had now seriously wounded the susceptibilities of two empires bothered him not at all; he was already meditating an even more audacious move. Across the border from Fort Gadsden, in the exiguous Spanish province of West Florida, lay the little town of Pensacola, whose wooden houses and ruined gardens bore witness to the decay of Spain. Jackson was beginning to convince himself that the governor of this dismal capital, Don José Masot, had connived with the Indians in certain murders and depredations committed in the Territory of Alabama. (This was not the case: Masot's commerce was chiefly with pirates and slave-traders.) Jackson had already taken Pensacola by assault in the War of 1812, and he was by no means unwilling to take it again. He hoped, he told the Secretary of War in an extraordinary letter written on May 5, that such a measure—"adopted in pursuance of your instructions"—would meet with the approbation of the President.[58] The lights of international law had grown exceedingly dim for the nationalist general in his steamy wilderness.

It would appear from the correspondence Jackson wrote at Boleck's Town that he did not then propose to capture Pensacola; a reconnaissance and a skirmish were all that he had in mind.[59] The idea may have come to him at St. Marks, but not until after the executions of Arbuthnot and Ambrister. On the morning of their trials, he was still talking of an immediate return to Nashville.[60] At Fort Gadsden, however, where he arrived on May 2 and rested for a few days, he seems finally to have decided that an invasion of West Florida was a necessity; and he had crossed the border with what remained of his army, and was already beyond the Escambia River, when a message was received from Governor Masot, requesting him to retire. "Otherwise," said the governor, "I shall repel force with force." [61] Masot had already had some unfriendly correspondence with the General concerning the navigation of the Apalachicola and Escambia rivers; and this challenge, which it was no more than Masot's duty to make, was construed by the General into an expression of inveterate hostility.[62] It was all that he needed. On May 24 he had occupied St. Michael's fort, overlooking Pensacola, and the governor had fled the town and was immured in the fortress of Barancas, commanding the entrance to the harbor, six miles away. From the letters that passed between the two forts it would seem that Jackson's evidence against Masot—accusing him of supplying the Indians with arms and ammunition—was just about as slender as were Masot's chances of defending his stronghold against Jackson.[63] Masot replied, none the less, that he proposed to defend Barancas "to the last extremity." [64] On May 28 Jackson approached the fort with one nine-pound piece and eight five-inch howitzers; there was a spirited exchange of fire; and then, honor being satisfied, Masot hoisted the white flag.[65] On May 29 Jackson seized the royal archives, appointed Colonel King of the Fourth Infantry to the post of military and civil governor of Pensacola, and declared that the revenue laws of the United States were now in force in West Florida.[66] After this proconsular act, there was nothing left to do but to return to Tennessee; and on May 30, accordingly, he did so.

IX

The enthusiasm that greeted the General upon his return home was unbounded. He had conducted his campaign with great speed and incomparable *élan*. The fact that he had mortally offended two foreign governments, or the chance that he had chastised some innocent Seminoles along with the guilty ones—these considerations did not present themselves very forcibly to most of his fellow citizens. The politicians might summon some high arguments against him—Mr. Ritchie of the *Richmond Examiner* might sharpen his Virginian pen; the judicious Mr. Niles of Baltimore might remark that "General Jackson . . . does not sufficiently reflect how intimately the character of the country is connected with his own, now that he is an officer"—but the country as a whole seemed proud of the intimacy of the connection.[67] "As to polecy," said old James Tallmadge, Sr., of Poughkeepsie, "I think it is on the generals side as it will strike a terrow on the Indians and Negros and all the unprincipled scampering traders that harbour about in them regons." [68] Some of the General's supporters were more eloquent; but nobody, really, went very much further than that.

CHAPTER FOUR

The Secretary

THE news of the storming of Pensacola traveled back to Washington with what was, for those days, unusual speed. It was known to the President as early as June 18.[1] On June 24, Don Luis de Onís, having read a circumstantial account in the *National Intelligencer,* was writing to John Quincy Adams to demand "a positive, distinct, and explicit" account of what had taken place.[2] Adams could make no answer, since he was as much in the dark as was Onís. The President left for his home in Loudoun County on June 26; "and though the moment is very critical and a storm is rapidly thickening," Adams wrote, "he had not read many of the papers I left with him, and he puts off everything for a future time." [3] On July 7, the Spanish Minister came in from his summer home at Bristol, demanding an interview. On July 8, both he and the French Minister, the Baron Hyde de Neuville, had been with Adams; both had worn a very tragical expression; and both had been told that Jackson's dispatches had just arrived, and that nothing could be said until the President had read them. But Adams warned the French Minister that, in his opinion, Mr. Monroe would support the actions of General Jackson.[4]

The Cabinet met five times between July 15 and July 21, and it appeared that Mr. Adams's opinion was incorrect. Every member of the Administration, except the Secretary of State, was for disavowing the General!

Mr. Calhoun, the Secretary of War, seemed to be personally offended—his orders had been disregarded. Mr. Monroe thought that there might be justifying circumstances, but that Jackson had not made out his case.[5] Mr. Crawford, the Secretary of the Treasury, feared a war with Spain, with a disastrous effect upon trade and revenue. Mr. Adams alone was prepared to support Jackson on the grounds that he had acted *defensively*. It was possible, he contended, to restore Pensacola to the Spanish and still justify

137

its capture. By the 20th, he had, he thought, impressed Mr. Wirt, the Attorney-General; but Mr. Calhoun and Mr. Monroe were still inflexible; and Mr. Calhoun went so far as to suggest that the General's actions were connected with a speculation in Florida lands.[6] Mr. Adams, though the heat and gravity of the argument had made him so nervous that he was stricken with a "weakness and palsy" of his right hand and could not report it all in his Diary, held his ground: and the upshot of the Cabinet's discussion was that Mr. Wirt wrote a paragraph for the *National Intelligencer*, designed to satisfy all shades of opinion, and Mr. Adams told the Spanish Minister that the forts would be given up but that General Jackson, though acting on his own responsibility, could not be censured for capturing them.[7] He considered this a partial disavowal—"a weakness and a confession of weakness."[8]

I

The Cabinet's discussion is only a fragment in a nationalist mystery; and the mystery is not a Jacksonian one. The General's actions throughout had been simple and direct: he had declared in his Rhea Letter that he was convinced that the Floridas should be seized; and he had seized them. He maintained to his dying day that Mr. Rhea—a Congressman from Tennessee and an old and devoted friend—had in fact written to him to convey the government's private and unofficial approval. This letter, he said, arrived with a packet of mail on February 13, when he was bivouacked at Big Creek, near Hartford, Georgia, and nearly a month before he assumed command at Fort Scott. He declared that he afterwards burned this letter at Mr. Monroe's request; and a notation on his private copy of his own letter of January 6 bears out the first part of this contention.[9]

Mr. Monroe has left his own version of the affair.

> "I well remember," he wrote to Mr. Calhoun on May 18, 1830, "that when I received the letter from Gen'l Jackson, to which you allude, of the 5th (*sic*) of Jany. 1818, I was sick in bed, and could not read it. You were either present, or came in immediately afterwards, and I handed it to you for perusal. After reading it you replaced it, with a remark that it required my attention, or would require an answer, but without notice of its contents. Mr. Crawford came in soon afterwards, and I handed it also to him, for perusal. He read it and returned it, in like manner, without making any comment on its contents, further than that it related to the Seminole war, or something to that effect. I never showed it to any other person, and I am not certain whether it was he, or you, who observed that it related to the Seminole war. Having made all the arrangements respecting that war, and being sometime confined by indisposition, the letter was laid aside, and forgotten by me, and I never read it until after the conclusion of the war, and then I did it on the intimation from you that it required my attention. You ask whether the letter was before the Cabinet, in the delib-

eration on the dispatches received from the General communicating the result of that war, or alluded to by any member of the administration. My impression decidedly is that it was not before the cabinet, nor do I recollect, or think that it was alluded to in the deliberation on the subject. Had it been I could not, I presume, have forgotten it." [10]

The issue is between two men of undoubted veracity.[11] On his deathbed, Mr. Monroe deposed before witnesses that he had never authorized John Rhea to write any letters whatever to General Jackson, and that he had never desired John Rhea to request General Jackson to destroy a letter. He was not the man to carry with him, as his passport into the shades, a deliberate lie.[12] As for Mr. Rhea, it was not until he was a very old man that he began to wonder whether he might or might not have written such a letter.[13] In 1818 he was quite certain that he had not.[14] It is true that on January 12, 1818, Mr. Rhea wrote the General a letter, which could have reached him at Big Creek, and which might have given the idea that the Administration approved of an unofficial seizure of East Florida.[15] Since it took a courier fifteen days to ride from Nashville to Washington, a letter written from Washington on January 12 could not possibly have been an answer to a letter written from Nashville on January 6; but the General may not have been bothering about dates.

In any case, both Monroe and Jackson were telling the truth as they understood it; and the controversy between them merely shows what a very difficult abstraction the truth is. What is more to the point is the attitude of the Administration in 1818. That Mr. Monroe was careless in not reading the Jackson letter when it was first brought to him on his sick-bed can hardly be denied; and his carelessness was equaled if not surpassed by that of Mr. Calhoun. Mr. Calhoun knew something about the character of the general to whom he proposed to entrust the Seminole campaign. Jackson was not only a fervent nationalist: he was also a creature of impulse and of action, overflowing with self-assertiveness, and primed like a pistol with an instinctive hatred of the Spaniard. Surely it would have been the course of wisdom to have implemented the General's orders—if the General was to be restrained from following his instincts—with some very positive instructions as to what he might and might not do. But was the General to be restrained? When the news of St. Marks was brought to the War Department, it was most equably received.[16] Only when the crowning blow had been struck, when Pensacola had been stormed and seized, when the inability of the Spaniard to defend his own possessions had been demonstrated to the whole world— only then did Mr. Calhoun send positive orders into Florida that St. Augustine was not to receive the treatment that had been meted out to St. Marks and Pensacola.[17] It does seem as if the General was being treated like a Francis Drake or a Walter Raleigh—in short, like some man of the extreme martial type who could be let loose upon the Spaniards and then disgraced and ruined.

If this were indeed the case, it would still be unjust to assume that the

Administration had acted from conscious motives. Mr. Monroe had been merely passive: he had not read the General's letter of January 6 until it was too late to do anything about it. He was, it is true, by no means without experience of the stimulating effect of Florida upon the military mind; and as Secretary of State in 1812 he had disavowed General George Mathews for doing to Amelia Island exactly what General Jackson, in 1818, had done to St. Marks and Pensacola. And he had disavowed General Mathews, moreover, under circumstances which suggested that he had first encouraged him.[18] He had not hitherto discouraged General Jackson's nationalist views. "I was not very severe on you for giving the blow," he wrote in 1816, concerning the seizure of Pensacola in 1814, "nor ought I have been for a thousand considerations which I need not mention." [19] Two days after the Florida orders had been sent to General Jackson, he wrote the General a letter which was singularly provocative. "The mov'-ment against the Seminoles . . . will bring you on a theatre where you may possibly have other services to perform. . . . Great interests are at issue." [20] On the other hand, Mr. Monroe always asserted that he had been taken by surprise by General Jackson's deeds in Florida; and his actions certainly indicate that he had been. Could it be that his instinctive desire to seize the Floridas shrank away from a precise formulation of its objectives— shrank so far, indeed, that it was unable to recognize them when it met them face to face?

If Mr. Monroe was innocent of any conscious betrayal of General Jackson during those first Cabinet discussions, what can be said for Mr. Calhoun? He was a nationalist in those days, but he was also an untried Secretary; and as a Secretary he may have deplored what as a nationalist he would have applauded. His immediate reactions were sufficiently equivocal. For while on the one hand he continued to maintain in some quarters that the storming of Pensacola was totally unauthorized, on the other hand he informed Captain Gadsden, who was very close to General Jackson, that he detested the willingness of some of his colleagues to sacrifice "their best friend" in order to protect themselves.[21] General Jackson preferred to believe the latter version.[22] It was not until more than ten years had passed that he was told the whole truth; and then he turned upon Mr. Calhoun in wrath and flame.

II

Mr. Adams had not been a party to the decisions of the War Department. He knew nothing at the time about the orders that authorized General Jackson to pass into Spanish Florida, and he had not been shown the General's correspondence until it was too late to correspond with the General.[23] He had always, however, taken a strong line, and he must have realized that Jackson's sortie into Spanish Florida was bound to dislodge the Spanish Minister and his government from their inert position between the Mermentau and Calcasieu rivers in the state of Louisiana.

Meeting with Mr. Onís on July 11, he still insisted upon the Colorado River of Texas as the western boundary from its mouth to its source; and, according to Mr. Onís, was prepared to draw a line from the source of the Colorado to the source of the Missouri, and thence directly west to the Pacific Ocean.[24] On July 16 he told the French Minister that he was prepared to move eastward from the Colorado River to the Trinity River, take a line north from the source of the Trinity to the Red River, follow the Red River to its source, then cross to the Rio del Norte (the Rio Grande) and follow its course or the summit of a chain of mountains northward and parallel to it, and either stop there or take a line west to the Pacific.[25]

Thus on July 11, he was clinging to the Colorado River, but was prepared to bring the Spanish-American frontier as high as 45° 20′ north latitude, which was where he believed the source of the Missouri to be; while on July 16, he had abandoned the Colorado River for the Trinity River, but proposed to place the Spanish-American frontier as low as 41° 30′ north latitude, the supposed position of the source of the Rio Grande. And in either case, he had suggested to the Spanish Minister the possibility of drawing the Spanish-American line clear across to the Pacific—a superb and, to Onís, a sacrilegious pretension, for to Onís's way of thinking the whole Pacific coast belonged to the king of Spain as far as 56° north latitude.

The map from which Adams and Onís worked, and upon which Adams drew the line he showed to the French Minister, was the January 1, 1818, edition of John Melish's *Map of the United States and the Contiguous British and Spanish Possessions*. It was a remarkable, indeed a great piece of cartography; but if all maps are abstractions, this one was the very abstraction of abstractions. A map is a representation of a portion of the earth's surface, drawn to scale on a flat surface of paper; Mr. Melish's map was drawn to scale, and the surface upon which it was drawn was flat; but it was not yet a representation of a portion of the earth's surface. It was a representation of what a portion of the earth's surface might be, if one knew more about it than one did. Rivers rose far from their actual sources, mountains strode where plains should be. No one with ideas as great and compelling as those which possessed Mr. Adams could have gazed upon it without a feeling of exhilaration. Only a few of the most intrepid of his contemporaries had actually seen those rivers and those mountains or followed the planetary curve of those tremendous plains. To him, and indeed to Onís and to the Baron Hyde de Neuville—though we have no reason to believe that *they* were exhilarated—a study of Melish's great map was still to some extent a plunge into the unknown. Yet the lines he drew upon it were drawn with assurance.

The critical period in Adams's negotiation with Onís would seem to be from July 11 to July 16, 1818, for it was in those days that the United States first began to lose its grip on Texas and win a line to the Pacific. It almost seems as if yet another abstraction were arising from the discussions and proposals of those important days; as if one were being presented, not with a representation of a portion of the earth's surface, but with a representation of the minds of civilian statesmen when they were subjected to the pressure of a military event.

It is now known that President Monroe and Secretary Adams had agreed between them, as early as February 1818, to fix the Spanish-American boundary by the Trinity River from its mouth to its source, then to the Arkansas at its nearest point, then along the Arkansas to its source, and thence due west to the Pacific, "or to leave the limit in the latter instance to be settled by commissioners." [26] On July 11, however, Mr. Adams was still firmly on the Colorado River; but now, for the first time, he proposed to Mr. Onís a boundary line to the Pacific. The line thus proposed was, it is true, most unfavorable: it would appear that the news of Pensacola had simultaneously increased the Secretary's demands and shaken his resolve. On July 13, President Monroe returned to Washington.[27] On July 16, in the midst of the Cabinet's attempts to disavow General Jackson, Mr. Adams withdrew from the Colorado to the Trinity; but at the same time, asked for a line to the Pacific which was infinitely more favorable than the line of the 11th.

These latest proposals, therefore, when reduced to a line drawn upon a map, illustrate the oscillations of President Monroe's mind before the *fait accompli* of General Jackson. Monroe had never been, and never would be, very interested in Texas.[28] On the other hand, though not a deep thinker, his background was that of a doctrinaire Republican, and he was probably more happy with a sweeping generalization than with a set of facts. The line to the Pacific was a magnificent generalization. Wherever it was drawn, all the territory to the north of it between the Rocky Mountains and the Pacific coast was subject to negotiation with Great Britain: all to the south of it was Spanish. The line was simply an expression of belief in the American destiny. Mr. Monroe—it was one of the most touching and most valuable of his simplicities—sometimes believed that republican principles were destined to spread a Saturnian reign from coast to coast: he may even, at times, have fancied himself in the role of Saturn. As a conciliatory man, he was occasionally willing to leave the whole business to a commission; but when his Secretary of State insisted upon drawing a line, the President was ready enough to follow him. His imagination urged him along the same path; and the two statesmen felt their way across the continent together, with Mr. Adams a little in the lead.

Left to himself, Mr. Adams would most probably not have moved the boundary eastward to the Trinity River. On July 16, however, the President was still shocked by General Jackson's deeds, and very much in the mood to abandon the General. In the same mood, he got ready to abandon Texas. But Mr. Monroe was an experienced man and a devoted public servant; and he could not but see that the General had, as it were, twitched aside an old curtain and revealed, in all its dust and disarray, the bankrupt house-keeping of the Spanish Empire. And so, while he yielded in Texas, he pressed on towards the Pacific. Such were the linear consequences of the storming of Pensacola.

III

The French Minister, Hyde de Neuville, now became the channel of communication between Onís and Adams. The channel was, perhaps, somewhat choked with the refuse of French royalism; but the baron—an impressive personage, of a flighty but formidable respectability—was well-intentioned. Moreover he had been instructed to act as a "conciliator"—to discourage either party from running to extremes—to soften the Spanish demands so that they would not irritate the Americans into recognizing the revolutionary governments of South America. For France, no less than Spain, and for scarcely less reason, was abysmally afraid of revolution. The British, on the other hand, were beginning to believe that the profits of trading with a successful revolution might be powerful enough to neutralize the toxic effects of that revolution's success. Moreover, it was thought that they had dangerous ambitions in the Caribbean. De Neuville, therefore, rather favored the Americans than otherwise, in the hope that the Americans, in turn, would disfavor the British. He had already written to Onís, saying that while he could not condone the acts of General Jackson—that "*Napoleon des bois*"—he could not support Onís's cliams. Onís, who had retired to Bristol until such time as St. Marks and Pensacola should be restored to the Spanish Crown, was highly indignant: he had thought better of the Baron Hyde de Neuville. But what, after all, could be expected of a Frenchman who had actually attended a banquet in Washington in honor of that disreputable affair—the Independence of the United States? [29]

In Madrid, meanwhile, the American Minister, Mr. George W. Erving, was engaged in an unequal contest with the Spanish climate, which he thought dangerous, and the Spanish mind, which he found detestable. He was able to report, however, that the mere news that Jackson was to be loosed upon Florida had sent a shiver of apprehension up the Spanish government's spine; and that this news was forcing the government's hand in the matter of the western boundary.[30] In March, Onís had officially transferred the center of the negotiation to Madrid, and Mr. Erving, whose peppery nature and extreme republican susceptibilities made him rather an uncertain diplomat, seriously believed that it should be kept there. Years later, he declared that if it had been, he would have added Texas to the territory of the United States; and that only the "blundering" of Mr. Adams, in keeping the negotiation in his own hands, had prevented this from taking place.[31]

Mr. Erving was always much impressed with the frankness and good faith of José Garcia de Leon y Pizarro, the Spanish Foreign Minister, whom he considered the shining, the solitary exception to the otherwise deplorable

rule of Ferdinand VII. But he never realized, or refused to admit, that
Pizarro could not be trusted—not, indeed, because he was not trustworthy,
but because there loomed behind him that malevolent antiquity, the *Consejo
de Estado*, or Council of State. Whatever decision Pizarro made was subject
to the ratification of this body, which was more likely to overrule him than
not, and which was engaged in an everlasting struggle for the favor of
Ferdinand.

Goya has left an imperishable record of Ferdinand's father, Don Carlos,
and of his mother, Maria Luisa. No court painter before or since has
created so rich, so comic, so searching an indictment of his patrons; no
patrons have ever allowed themselves to be pilloried with a more impenetrable complacency. Goya was a moralist as well as a genius, and he was
doomed to teach the world lessons it was not ready to learn. Brilliant,
cynical, and strong, his portraits destroyed the Spanish Bourbons; but nobody except the painter seems to have realized it. In the course of time,
Don Carlos, with his guns and his *battues* and his grotesque good nature,
and Maria Luisa, with her interminable amours, vanished from the scene;
but Ferdinand VII remained. And Ferdinand VII, even by the standards
of the Spanish and Italian Bourbons, was more than usually dull, sullen,
and ferocious. Hated by his parents, whom he hated in turn, imprisoned
by Napoleon, he developed in solitude all the uglier resources of a futile
mind. When he returned to the throne, he was greeted with an enthusiasm
unintelligible to everybody not Spanish; and he repaid his subjects by depriving them of such constitutional liberties as they had been granted in
his absence. He surrounded himself with men who flattered the worst in
him—"ignorant and stupid *nigauds* (boobies)," Onís told Adams in a moment
of exasperation, "Grandees of Spain, and priests . . . I could have no con-
ception of their obstinacy and imbecility." [82] The most influential of these
was his Minister of Grace and Justice, a former chocolate seller of Cadiz
named Juan Esteban Lozano de Torres, who controlled the police, the law
courts, and the clergy, and who was so ignorant that he did not even know
where the Floridas were. [83] Another was a horsy patrician called the Duke of
Alagón. A third was the Russian Ambassador, Tatischeff, a talented intriguer.

Pizarro was honest and incorruptible, and had no future under such a
master. While he struggled to cede the Floridas under the best terms that
he could get, Ferdinand saw to it that there would be no Floridas to cede.
On December 17, 1817, he granted to the Duke of Alagón and the Count of
Puñonrostro almost all of East Florida except the east coast; and on January 25, 1818, he made a further large cession of Florida land to Don Pedro
de Vargas. [84] The general idea was to take advantage of the rise in land
values which would follow the establishment of American sovereignty in the
Floridas; and the grants were probably worth in the neighborhood of eight
million dollars. [85] Mr. Erving got wind of this pernicious piece of jobbery in
1818, and wrote to the Secretary of State to warn him; but Mr. Adams

read these particular letters with what was, for him, unusual inattention.[36]

In any event, no concession that Erving could have wrung from Pizarro would have been ratified by Ferdinand and his council: that is certain. Only in Washington, with a Minister with full powers to act for his sovereign, could any business be done. Moreover, Pizarro's course was run.

Pizarro had, in fact, remained in office just long enough to receive word of General Jackson's deeds and to write a long and argumentative note to Erving formally suspending all negotiations until the General had been disavowed and punished, the forts restored to Spain, and suitable indemnity made for any damage done to Spanish property, public or private. This note said rather more than it meant; for the news of Pensacola had severely shaken the Madrid government. It was what that government had always dreaded. And so, while Pizarro broke off his negotiation with Erving, he instructed Onís to go if necessary as far as the Colorado River for a western boundary. These instructions were written on August 31. On September 14, Pizarro attended a *corrida* in the bull-ring, worked for a while in his basement office in a palace overlooking the Manzanares, and returned home, an unsuspecting man. At one the next morning, he was woken from sleep by a messenger from General Eguia, the Minister of War, who informed him that he was no longer Minister for Foreign Affairs, and that he and his whole family must leave the capital within five hours, to spend an indefinite exile in a bleak provincial town. Señor de Garay, the Minister of Finance, and the only respectable member of the government besides himself, was dismissed with him and sent into as sudden an exile. What could the reason be? Some people decided that Pizarro was too Anglophile for Monsieur Tatischeff, the Russian Ambassador, who had the ear of the king; and that Pozzo di Borgo, the Russian Ambassador in Paris, had also sedulously intrigued against him.[37] Or it may have been that the king's honor had been deeply wounded by General Jackson; and that he could salve it—characteristically enough—only by sacrificing his most honorable Minister.

IV

Throughout the summer, Onís had resisted the enticements of Hyde de Neuville; he had not budged from the line between the Calcasieu and Mermentau rivers. It was in vain that the President now discovered that he could bring the boundary as far east as the Sabine River; it was in vain that he threatened the seizure of the Floridas, a claim to all of Texas, and war itself, if Mr. Onís maintained his position.[38] The Spaniard was unshaken. He believed that he had saved Texas, as indeed he had for the time being, and that the bacillus of democracy, like a Chinese devil, had been diverted from its flight into Mexico. Perhaps if he delayed—if he raised false issues; if he offered meaningless concessions—he might draw a line safely remote from His Catholic Majesty's city of Santa Fe in New Mexico. He lingered on in Bristol until Pensacola was restored, and then, on October

24, he reopened the direct negotiation with an offer that merely reiterated all that was impossible in his previous demands.[39] When the President heard of this offer on October 26, he declared that his patience was almost exhausted. It was time to bring Onís to the point, he said, or else to break off with him.[40]

Mr. Adams, therefore, prepared and dispatched an offer he himself called an "ultimatum." His line began where the Sabine River emptied itself into the Gulf of Mexico, and ended on the Pacific Ocean at the forty-first degree of north latitude.[41]

He had now retired from the Colorado to the Trinity and from the Trinity to the Sabine; and with what remorse he had done so, only he could tell. But his line to the Pacific now soared along the forty-first parallel, and in fantasy he embraced the whole basin of the great Columbia River.[42] Today it requires an effort of the imagination to realize the grandeur of the Secretary's design, as it appeared to himself and to his contemporaries. All Americans were agreed, no doubt, that the "manifest course of events" could bring the nation to the Pacific coast; not all were agreed as to the wisdom of going there. "Ah Haji," wrote an English poet, "whither wilt thou turn, When thou art there, when thou art there?" What would happen when the Republic reached its western goal? The question has hardly been answered today; but in those days, in the palest dawn of the Age of Steam, many sober persons believed that the United States, stretched out beyond the power of communication, might fly apart from its own size.

These considerations did not disturb the Secretary of State, nor yet the President. What was more to the point was the cunning inertia of the Spanish Minister. Onís had now received his instructions from Pizarro. He knew that the magic of General Jackson had paralyzed the nerve of Madrid, and that it was time for him to desert his preposterous outpost upon the Mermentau-Calcasieu line. He, therefore, accepted Mr. Adams's boundary as far as the Red River at thirty degrees north latitude. From there, he said, let a line be drawn due north to the source of the Missouri, and as for any further boundary questions, they could readily be settled by a commission "in a manner conformable to the titles and documents and possessions respectively exhibited." Everyone knew what the Spanish would be able to do with titles and documents, with what a procrastinating delight they would extract them, one by one, from the bottomless pit of the Madrid archives.[43] Mr. Adams told de Neuville that the American government had now "gone to the wall"; and in his reply to Onís he stated that he withdrew all offers, but would be glad to discuss a treaty that fixed no western boundary of any kind.[44] This was his sword of Damocles. He well knew that Mr. Onís was obliged to fix a boundary that should seal up every aperture through which the virus of American democracy might creep upon his master's languid Empire. The initiative had passed to the United States, and Mr. Adams was ready to crack the whip. It was at about this time that Pizarro's angry letter to Erving reached the Secretary in Washington.

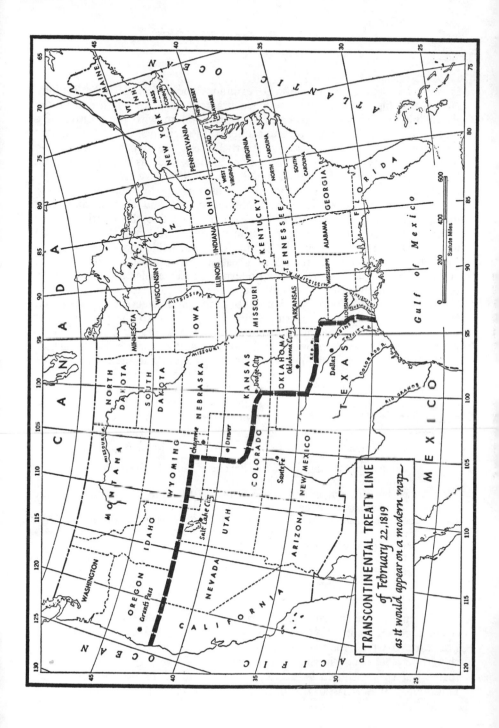

TRANSCONTINENTAL TREATY LINE
of February 22, 1819
as it would appear on a modern map

V

It must be clear to everyone who examines the career of John Quincy Adams that his two most outstanding characteristics were wrath and vision. At their worst, these two combined to present him with the picture of a world that seemed designed by some splenetic Providence solely to frustrate his actions and blacken his name. At their best, the two were a weapon of great potency. To discover them at their best, one has only to read that famous instruction to Erving in which Mr. Adams answered Pizarro's demand that General Jackson should be disavowed and punished. It was written between November 7 and November 28, and though somewhat modified in Cabinet discussions, bears upon every line the imprint of the Secretary's genius. It was designed rather to put the Spanish and the British in the wrong than the Americans in the right; and while it absolved General Jackson from all blame it turned its greatest guns upon the futility of the commandant of St. Marks and the governor of Pensacola, and blasted with ferocious skill and resounding eloquence the various characters of Colonel Nicholls, Captain Woodbine, Mr. Arbuthnot, and Lieutenant Ambrister. It is remarkable among state papers for its adherence to the principle that when one's position is morally unsound it is better to attack than to defend. It proved, or seemed to prove, that Arbuthnot and Ambrister were engaged in "a creeping and insidious war, both against Spain and the United States . . . to plunder Spain of her province, and to spread massacre and devastation along the borders of the United States." As for the activities of Colonel Nicholls in Florida during the War of 1812, did not these constitute a *"shameful invasion"* far more culpable than General Jackson's "necessary pursuit of a defeated savage enemy beyond the Spanish Florida line." And yet, against this shameful invasion of Colonel Nicholls,

> "against the blowing up of the Barrancas, and the erection and maintenance, under British banners, of the negro fort on Spanish soil; against the negotiation by a British officer of pretended treaties, offensive and defensive, and of navigation and commerce upon Spanish territory, between Great Britain and Spanish Indians, whom Spain was bound to control and restrain—if a whisper of expostulation was ever wafted from Madrid to London, it was not loud enough to be heard across the Atlantic, nor energetic enough to transpire beyond the walls of the palaces from which it issued, and to which it was borne." [45]

Mr. Erving was authorized to communicate this document *in toto* to the Spanish government. It was not, it is safe to say, the sort of diplomatic literature to which they were accustomed. It is hard to decide whether it should be placed high in the category of invective or high in that of diplomacy. But that it should be accorded some kind of an altitude can hardly be disputed. It is a classic; and only the general opinion that state papers are outside the pale of letters has prevented it from receiving the recognition it deserves.

But the most remarkable thing about it is not the contempt it pours so openly upon the Spanish government. The Spanish government seems to have been but a secondary consideration. What is truly remarkable about it is the fact that its real challenge is a challenge to the British Empire.

VI

A copy of Adams's great letter to Erving duly found its way to Whitehall, and was perused by Lord Castlereagh, the British Foreign Secretary. The British had previously made it known that they were willing to mediate between the Americans and the Spanish; but they desisted as soon as they realized that the Americans wished to be left alone. As Lord Castlereagh put it, with his usual courtesy, the British had once refused a Russian mediation during the War of 1812, and the Americans had now every right to refuse a British one.[46] When the news of Pensacola reached Europe, and created a "sensation" in Paris and London, the Spanish may have hoped that Great Britain would change her mind and intervene in their favor.[47] Mr. Gallatin, the American Minister in Paris, was seriously alarmed. But even when this news was followed by the story of the execution of Arbuthnot and Ambrister, the London government was oddly quiescent. The British press, to be sure, reacted to this story in a manner very flattering to Spanish hopes. "The publick anger," wrote the American Minister in London to his colleague in Paris, "is exceedingly strong against us. I have never known anything like it since I have been here." But Mr. Rush went on to say that he had had full explanations with Lord Castlereagh, and that "we shall have with the latter no difficulty . . . you may confide in what I say." [48]

It was true. On January 2, 1819, Lord Castlereagh had come to the conclusion that Arbuthnot and Ambrister "had been engaged in unauthorized practices of such a description as to have deprived them of any claim on their own Government." [49] On January 19, at a gathering at Prince Esterhazy's, he told Mr. Rush that "such was the temper of parliament and such the feeling of the country, he believed WAR MIGHT HAVE BEEN PRODUCED BY HOLDING UP A FINGER." [50] The finger was never held up; and the Spanish were forced to realize that they would receive no British support in their boundary disputes or in their efforts to prevent the United States from recognizing the revolutionary colonies of South America.

It was a great moment in Anglo-American relations; perhaps a decisive one. Lord Castlereagh had, of course, been suitably stirred by Adams's note to Erving. It was a challenge to the whole Empire, and if Castlereagh had been a Palmerston, he would have hurled it back in Adams's teeth. Lord Castlereagh, however, preferred to be impressed. He was engaged in the most difficult negotiations concerning the postwar settlement of Europe, and the last thing that he wanted was an American war. Nor was this the only reason; there were other forces at work.

Lord Castlereagh was notoriously European in his thinking; moreover, he was not an economist, and the ties that bound and the interests that severed the United States and Great Britain were all concerned with industry and trade. But the British Foreign Office was well aware of the importance of the South American market, and Lord Castlereagh had already hinted to Mr. Rush that his South American views were nearer those of the United States than those of Spain.[51] And there was another and more vital consideration. The War of 1812, in its sudden solution at Ghent, had revealed the dependence of Great Britain upon an untrammeled North American market. Great Britain did not relish the dependence; but it existed. Asked to choose between Arbuthnot and Ambrister on the one hand, and the North American market on the other, the British government did not hesitate. Arbuthnot and Ambrister were simply written off as a mere item, a necessary loss, in Anglo-American exchanges. The declamations of the press and of the country gentlemen in Parliament—all this was feeding the wind. The United States were, no doubt, socially impossible and politically dangerous; and yet, when Parliament opened in November 1819, and the Speech from the Throne referred to the depressed state of British manufactures, there followed many allusions to the close connection between this state of affairs and the very similar one then existing in America. "What can more show the dependence of countries upon one another!" was Mr. Rush's comment.[52] The defeat of Napoleon had, in fact, brought Great Britain face to face with her own industrial potential; and the whole British economy was turning towards the doctrine of Adam Smith, towards the belief that it might actually be more profitable to compete with a competitor than to crush him. The movement was slow, irresolute, and grumbling; but in 1819 it was well under way. A profound and lasting change in Anglo-American relations was one of its effects.

Nothing could have been more fortunate than the position of the United States. Upon its northern borders lay the domains of a great Empire, which was beginning to demonstrate its belief that there was a certain connection between the expansion of the United States and the growth of British industry.[53] To the south and west lay the Empire of Spain, abandoned by England, powerless to protect itself, and disintegrating rapidly, flagrantly, day by day. Under these auspicious circumstances—a positive pressure from the British north and a negative resistance from the Spanish south—the westward movement of the American people, unless it moved so fast as to defeat itself, was bound to be irresistible. The invasion of Florida by General Jackson, and the resounding challenge of John Quincy Adams, announced this fact as if it had been blown from trumpets.

VII

A great piece of literature, if it takes the form of a polemic, must be judged less by the validity of its arguments than by their effect. Any student of international law could have torn Mr. Adams's arguments to pieces; it was their spirit that was inexpugnable. Mr. Adams took the sensible precaution of having his note to Erving, with its accompanying documents, printed in Washington long before it could reach Madrid. The rather mild tone of the President's Second Annual Message was thus strengthened; and the effect was all that Mr. Adams could have wished for.[54] Even Thomas Jefferson, who could never rid himself of the idea that the Secretary of State was a Federalist in Republican clothing, pronounced the Erving note "among the ablest compositions I have ever seen, both as to logic and style." [55] It made even more of a sensation in Congress, where a noisy debate began on January 12, 1819, with the anti-Administration forces of Mr. Speaker Clay and the anti-Jackson forces of Mr. Secretary Crawford attempting to ruin the General and weaken the Administration. Mr. Clay was much exercised by the hanging of Francis and Homollimico; he entertained the curious notion that Seminole "prophets" were some kind of religious leaders. "When did the all-conquering and desolating Rome," he inquired, in his most thrilling tones, "ever fail to respect the altars and the gods of those whom she subjugated? Let me not be told that these prophets were impostors who deceived the Indians. They were *their* prophets. . . ." [56] The General might have replied that the only altar *he* had come across was a red stick hung with scalps, and that the gods had been conspicuously absent throughout the campaign. Nobody cared to tell the whole truth: that militant nationalism is rarely satisfied with a vegetable diet; that it has a taste for blood; that the real cost of the Floridas had been paid by an undisclosed number of dead Indians and Negroes, and by two gentlemen called Arbuthnot and Ambrister. Mr. Adams's printed words, and the crowding oratory of Jackson's lieutenants in Congress, won the day. After nearly a month's debate, a series of four Resolutions, designed to disgrace the General, were voted down by substantial majorities.[57] Thus the General who had not hesitated to embarrass the government and the government that had almost disavowed the General enjoyed a common triumph.[58] The Secretary of the Treasury, whose supporters in Congress had been badly defeated, now had fresh reasons for not loving the Secretary of State. As for Mr. Clay, his speech had been one of his greatest efforts, but its most striking result had been the enhancement of Jackson's reputation; and the Speaker was soon to learn that, in politics as in legend, it is easier to unbottle a djinn than to seal him up again.

VIII

The Resolutions were defeated on February 8, 1819. On February 15, Mr. Adams and Mr. Onís had narrowed their disagreements down to half the width of the boundary rivers. For weeks past, like two wrestlers in some half-lit ring—with the Baron Hyde de Neuville a dignified, agitated, but impartial referee—they had struggled to and fro across Melish's map. Mr. Adams sought to gain the whole Columbia Basin. Mr. Onís, who had now received instructions to yield a line to the Pacific, strove—and strove in vain—to maintain a fingerhold on the Columbia River.[59] Onís was a doughty grappler, but his grasp was beginning to weaken; and there were times when a mere extra squeeze might have forced him to give up, not only the Columbia River, but the whole of Texas as well. The squeeze was never given. Mr. Adams was battling with his own supporters, and the compromising spirit of Mr. Monroe's Cabinet was forcing him into concessions that, left to himself, he would never have granted. On January 29, he was repeating his "ultimatum" of October 31.[60] Thereafter, with great reluctance, he retired slowly from the 41st to the 42d degree of north latitude for his line to the Pacific, and from the 102d to the 100th degree of west longitude for his western boundary between the Red and the Arkansas rivers.

On February 16, nothing remained to be decided but Mr. Onís's demand that the boundary should pass up the middle of the Sabine, the Red, and the Arkansas rivers.[61] On February 18, Mr. Adams learned that the President, at a drawing-room held the previous evening, had promised Onís that he would make no difficulty about the middle of the rivers. When the Cabinet met on February 19, nothing was said about the President's unconventional behavior, and everyone agreed that Onís should be requested to content himself with the southern and the western banks of the rivers in question. As Mr. Adams afterwards told de Neuville, the President would be most displeased if he thought that a mere politeness, uttered to a foreign Minister at a drawing-room, was to be construed into an abandonment of an important principle.[62] If anyone was being asked to abandon an important principle, however, it was Onís; for by diplomatic custom boundaries invariably ran along the midchannel of rivers. On February 20 Onís, with only a sigh of resignation, took to the river banks, and all was over. On February 22 the great Transcontinental Treaty was signed and sealed.[63]

"It was near one in the morning," Adams wrote, "when I closed the day with ejaculations of fervent gratitude to the Giver of all Good. It was, perhaps, the most important day of my life. . . . The acknowledgement of a definite line of boundary to the South Sea forms a great epocha in our history." [64]

Two days later, the Senate unanimously advised and consented to the ratification of the Treaty.[65]

IX

The Secretary of State was justified in his self-congratulation. His great boundary-line stretched from the Gulf of Mexico to the Pacific Ocean. He had lost Texas, it is true, but he had lost it through no fault of his own. He had gained the Pacific Northwest. Between the Rockies and the Pacific, to be sure, the property of the United States was represented by a line without breadth or thickness, a mere mathematical pretension; but its implications were immense. The Floridas were secure, in return for an assumption of claims upon Spain to the amount of five million dollars; and the Mississippi Valley, the very heart of the Republic, was now safe from foreign control. Certainly, an epoch had been formed.

And yet the Secretary, in the very midst of his fervent gratitude, was anxious and downcast. He distrusted human happiness. It was characteristic of him that he should now be haunted by "a vague, general, and superstitious impression that this treaty was too great a blessing not to be followed shortly by something to alloy it." [66] What blow did Providence have in store for him? He waited uneasily, almost eagerly, and not long. On March 8, Mr. Clay called upon the President with disturbing news. He had heard, and on good authority, that King Ferdinand's grants of land to the Duke of Alagón, the Count of Puñonrostro, and Senor Pedro de Vargas had been dated January 23, 1818.

Such news, and brought by such a messenger! The Speaker, a known enemy to the Administration, a man whom Adams had hated ever since their battles at Ghent! According to Article VIII of the Treaty all land grants in Florida, if made before January 24, 1818, were valid grants. If the Speaker's information was correct, the government had nothing to show for its efforts in Florida but an empty sovereignty. With a sinking heart, Adams hunted up all Mr. Erving's correspondence; and there he discovered the painful truth. Mr. Erving had faithfully transmitted a copy of an order to the Captain-General of Cuba, requiring him to put the agents of the Count of Puñonrostro in possession of his Florida lands. The order was dated February 6, 1818; but it stated very clearly that the Puñonrostro grant had been announced to the Council of the Indies as early as December 17, 1817. Mr. Adams realized that he had made an appalling error; he had examined Erving's correspondence with insufficient care; he had mistaken the date of the order for the date of the grant. [67] He was subsequently able to prove that the De Vargas grant was made after January 24; but it was clear that the Duke of Alagón and the Count of Puñonrostro were now the private owners of the better part of East Florida.

The President was immensely kind. He laid the whole blame on Onís; though whether Onís had or had not consciously deceived Mr. Adams is to this day a matter of some doubt. [68] He declared that the Florida lands were of trifling consequence when compared to the importance of the treaty as a whole. He said that if the worst came to the worst, and the king declined to annul these fraudulent grants, Congress would authorize the seizure of the Floridas and the whole of Texas might then be claimed as an indemnity for the expense of seizing them. But the Secretary of State was inconsolable. He had entered his private purgatory, into which the events of the outer world descended only as ghostly reflections upon his own shortcomings. He had been guilty of "vanity and self-conceit," and his blindness to the dates of the land grants was nothing more nor less than a judgment upon him. [69]

In Washington the Alagón and Puñonrostro grants were considered simply as a piece of royal jobbery; in Madrid, they were convenient excuses for delay. John Forsyth of Georgia, the new American Minister, was instructed when he exchanged the ratifications of the Treaty to demand a full and clear understanding that the grants were null and void. [70] He could not obtain it—and then he discovered something else. He was not to obtain a ratification of the Treaty, either. Captain Read of the sloop Hornet, who had brought

Forsyth to Spain and expected to return with the ratified Treaty, returned empty-handed. Forsyth was a likable, a handsome, an intelligent man; but he spoke no language but English, and he freely confessed that he was a novice in diplomacy.[71] He celebrated his novitiate by accusing the king of conscious baseness, and in language that was scarcely veiled.[72] His language pushed the Council of State a little farther along the path it had already chosen; and it advised King Ferdinand that the Treaty ceded too much land and that it contained no promise not to recognize the revolutionary government of Buenos Aires.[73]

Vattel, von Martens, and other authorities on international law, had always insisted that an absolute monarch was bound to ratify a Treaty signed by a Minister with full powers: and Onís had full powers. But Vattel and von Martens suffered their usual fate: they were disregarded as soon as it became inconvenient to regard them. On June 31, at a midnight session of the Council, King Ferdinand agreed not to ratify the Treaty.[74]

John Forsyth was out of his depth. He told his colleague in Paris, Mr. Gallatin, that his sources of information were few and doubtful. "One mode only is certain here. Bribery & that I am not directed to use." [75] He knew that Alagón and Puñonrostro were intriguing against the Treaty; but he directed his chief suspicion towards the British Ambassador, Sir Henry Wellesley.[76] He was convinced that Sir Henry was a monster of duplicity, and that his government was ready to support the Spanish king in his annulment of the Treaty in return for the cession of Cuba. Others held the same views. The fantastic rumor made the rounds of the cities of Europe during those curious months; but Mr. Rush, who heard it in London, was obliged to confess that—"in spite of the vehemence of our suspicions"—the British government was by no means opposed to the Treaty.[77] Two conversations with Lord Castlereagh in July convinced him, indeed, that the British government was, if anything, a friend to America against Spain.[78] In September, Mr. Forsyth realized that he had done the British Ambassador an injustice: Sir Henry's behavior throughout had been unimpeachably correct.[79] In October he received fresh instructions: he was to accept the Spanish ratification, even if the time limit had expired. But the Spanish government was obdurate. "They insist on the validity of the grants and want some explanations relative to their colonial possessions." In other words, the Treaty was to remain unsigned until the United States agreed not to recognize the revolutionary governments in South America. At this, Mr. Forsyth abandoned all hope of doing anything in Madrid; his sole wish was to be relieved "from a situation irksome to me and in which I am useless to the U.S." [80]

Indeed, a more experienced man than Forsyth might have been forgiven if he despaired of making sense out of what was going on. No diplomat, however gifted, can divine a policy where no policy exists. The dull ferocity of the king, the solemn futility of his Council, the stirrings of mutiny in Cadiz where an army was being gathered for a descent upon South America— all these produced not a definite policy but a vague, misty, sick atmosphere. It was the late autumn of the Bourbon monarchy, and King Ferdinand VII, like some deciduous tree, was beginning to shed his Ministers and cronies. On June 13, the Marquis de Casa Irujo, Pizarro's successor, was suddenly dismissed and vanished into political exile behind the walls of the monastery of Valverde at Avila.[81] The Russian Ambassador, Tatischeff, whose talent for intrigue had been amply satisfied in delicious daily audiences with the king, was no longer *persona grata;* and at the end of October he disappeared, on a permanent leave of absence.[82] In October, too, Lozano de Torres, the ex-chocolate-seller of Cadiz, the king's boon companion, was removed from office—no longer would he dispense Grace and Justice.[83] What could it all mean? Some people still professed to see a British influence behind it all. Tatischeff was notoriously anti-British. But the truth—if the truth was discernible in that melancholy season—seemed to be that the king's dismissals were purely instinctive; that his absolutist sap was shrinking to the root; that he was waiting sullenly for some constitutional winter, which he hoped would not last, but which he could not avoid.

The faithful Onís, who had retired from America full of honors, lingered in England during the summer of 1819. It was said in London that he was to be Irujo's successor.[84] But he showed no great anxiety to return to Spain. Perhaps he feared that he, too, would be exiled to some bleak village or forbidding monastery, there to meditate upon the perils of obedience. When at last he ventured to show his face, he was set to work preparing a detailed statement of the United States naval forces.[85] If the king meditated a war against the Americans, his navy was a doubtful quantity: but his army was beyond control. In January 1820 a military mutiny in Cadiz spread to Madrid, where it became a revolution; and His Catholic Majesty was forced, once again, to accept a constitution.

Thus it became only a matter of time before the Treaty was ratified and the land grants were annulled. When the new Minister to the United States, Don Francisco Vives, drifted into London on his reluctant journey westward, he was bluntly told by Lord Castlereagh that he had better come to terms with the Americans.[86] In St. Petersburg, Count Nesselrode's language was not friendly to Spain.[87] The President's Annual Message of December 7, 1819, was a masterly compromise, since it proposed that Congress might pass a law recommending the occupation of Florida, but suspend its operation until Vives arrived and showed his hand.[88] His special message of March 27, 1820, suggested a further postponement of action, but did not lessen the pressure upon Spain.[89] It is possible that if the equilibrium of the United States had not been disturbed by the Missouri problem some more drastic action might have been taken; but Mr. Clay's resolutions condemning the Treaty died in committee that April.[90] In Europe the revolution spread from Spain to Portugal and from Portugal to the Two Sicilies; and the quasi-liberal Cortes in Madrid was forced to realize that it, too, was considered a revolutionary phenomenon by the great powers, and that it would get no support in any new quarrel with the United States. One last effort was made to obtain concessions for the land grantees; and then at last, on October 5, the Cortes recommended a ratification of the Treaty and declared the land grants null and void.[91] On October 24, the ratification was signed by Ferdinand VII. On February 13, 1821, the Treaty was resubmitted to the Senate for advice and consent, and the Senate, with four dissenting votes, approved it on February 19.[92] On February 22, the ratifications were exchanged with Don Francisco Vives, and the great Treaty was at long last proclaimed in Washington.[93]

X

If the Spanish governments, absolutist or constitutional, had displayed any gift, it was a gift for procrastination. Two years had been wasted; but nothing had been done to weaken the Treaty. It was by no means a perfect Treaty—by excluding Texas, it bequeathed to the United States a legacy of trouble and of war—but it was certainly a great Treaty. The turning-point in the whole complicated transaction had been the British refusal to take issue with the United States over the executions of Arbuthnot and Ambrister; from then on, nothing could prevent the majestic line to the Pacific. Since the days when Lord Gambier, Mr. Goulburn, and Dr. Adams had sought to restrain the United States in the Northwest, a whole revolution in British thinking had begun; and though the Transcontinental Treaty might have been achieved in the face of British opposition, it could not have been achieved so easily, or so well. As for the line Mr. Adams drew upon Melish's map, it did not entirely satisfy but it did most amply symbolize the new nationalism of the West: and, years later, by some majestic coincidence, the pioneers who followed the Oregon Trail followed also the treaty line of February 22, 1819.

CHAPTER FIVE

The Chief Justice

'TIS evening now; beneath the western star
Soft sighs the lover through his sweet segar,
And fills the ears of some consenting she
With puffs and vows, with smoke and constancy.
The patriot, fresh from Freedom's councils come,
Now pleased retires to lash his slaves at home;
Or woo, perhaps, some black Aspasia's charms,
And dream of freedom in his bondsmaid's arms.

In fancy now, beneath the twilight gloom,
Come, let me lead thee o'er this 'second Rome!'
Where tribunes rule, where dusky Davi bow,
And what was Goose-Creek once is Tiber now;
This embryo capital, where Fancy sees
Squares in morasses, obelisks in trees;
Which second-sighted seers, ev'n now, adorn
With shrines unbuilt and heroes yet unborn.
Where nought but woods and Jefferson they see,
Where streets should run and sages *ought* to be." [1]

It was in the year 1804 that Thomas Moore wrote these verses in disparagement of Americans and their capital city. In Dublin, he had been a friend of Robert Emmet, the Irish rebel; but in London he had sung to duchesses. His brief visit to the United States convinced him that he was not at ease with rebellion or democracy. He grew angry; he lost his good manners; he said inexcusable things about Jefferson; but some fragments of the truth stuck to his American poems. His description of the city of Washington might be called a summing up in advance. In 1850, young Henry Adams thought that the columns and fronts of the Post Office and the Patent Office

157

resembled white Greek temples in the abandoned gravel pits of a deserted Syrian city. Very little, except a mere spreading, a proliferation of hotels and of politicians, had occurred between Moore in 1804 and Adams in 1850. Still, here and there, there gleamed in marble or painted sandstone the notion that what was being performed on the banks of the Potomac had some mysterious connection with what had once been attempted beside the Mediterranean; that the human spirit, strangely diverted from its original, its natural task of pursuing happiness, had been directed to commence all over again on the borders of Maryland and Virginia. In 1819, even more than in 1804, the capital questioned the likelihood of success. Something had fled from it—the witty, skeptical ghost of the Age of Reason. The Washington of Jefferson's time offered marvelous discourse in terrible surroundings, and would have enchanted a *philosophe* so long as he did not have to live there. The Washington of Monroe, however, was already touched with the Age of Romance; and, being the most remote of the world's capitals, it was touched but not transformed. Sensibility, enthusiasm, noble unreasonableness—one would have to go elsewhere to look for these as social strategems or canons of behavior. Washington merely became a little more grandiose, within its means, which were small. President Monroe, partly because he was less affably Virginian than his predecessors, partly from a conviction that the nation's new standing in the world required it of him, desired formality. For example, he wished to place the foreign Ministers "upon a footing of form and ceremony," and he even contemplated a uniform dress for the heads of department and the officers of government.[2]

Washington took its tone from the incumbents of the President's House. The new nationalism, which obliged Ministers and Congressmen to visit the President only on stated days of the week, and which imposed a special kind of dullness upon the President's male dinner parties and upon his weekly levees, found other and more pernickety forms of expression.[3] "There has been some change of etiquette among the ladies," Nathaniel Macon wrote in 1818, "which has furnished a subject of conversation; Mrs. Adams expects to be visited first by the wives of congressmen." [4] Senator Macon—it was not unusual with him where the Adamses were concerned—had turned things upside down. It was not Mrs. Adams who expected to be visited first by the wives of Congressmen—it was a matter of indifference to her whether she was visited or not; it was the wives of Congressmen who expected to be visited first by Mrs. Adams. Mrs. Adams—the most correct and agreeable of women—shrank from the prospect. She saw herself a prisoner in her carriage, perpetually leaving cards at improbable addresses; for though upon the plan the city of Washington presented an inspiring appearance, in fact its streets were generally no more than tracks through a forest or pathways beside a heath. None the less, in certain contingencies Congressmen could make Presidents. "This question of etiquette," said Mr. Adams, "is becoming quite an affair of state." And, indeed, a Cabinet meeting had to be called to settle it on a rational basis.[5]

The foreign Ministers strove with balls and receptions to impart a European air to this irretrievably American village; the inhabitants, permanent or temporary, multiplied their routs and fetes and birthday parties. It was all in vain. In vain the ladies descended from their social Sinai, armed with the tables of precedence; in vain they consulted or contrived their rules of etiquette. Other cities had acquired a special patina: they had been glazed over by a million visiting eyes. Visitors to Washington were, it is true, growing more numerous. But the city repelled them with clinging yellow mud or curtains of fine dust; it tormented them with insects; it slew them with malaria. They admired the Capitol and the President's House, now gleaming with white paint to cover the scars of Ross's incendiarism; they gaped at the Southern legislators, jolting in their fine carriages over the unpaved agony of Pennsylvania Avenue; otherwise they scarcely bothered to hide their dismay. Under a light powdering of formality and fine manners, Washington too easily revealed its coarse and simple fabric.

Tom Moore used to say in later years that he was sorry he had written his lampoon on Washington. But, after all, he had only written about a city of the future. Eventually the morasses would become squares, and the trees would make way for an obelisk, an office, a piece of statuary. Eventually, Ambassador Bryce of Great Britain would say that, next to Constantinople, Washington was the most beautiful of the world's capitals. In the meantime, the city resembled a southern village, and never lost this resemblance until the Civil War. What then was the future that one could discern in Monroe's Washington? The slave-block—the capital was already an important slave market—suggested only an incarnate past, with an implacable power of augmenting itself. The future lay somewhere in the huddles of boarding houses, hunched on the ragged skyline, where legislators devoted their spare time to cards and liquor. The future thrust itself into the President's levees, where Mr. Monroe received anyone who had any claim to be there; and where, in consequence, among the ladies in silks and velvets and the gentlemen in laced uniforms and good broadcloth, there was always a sufficiency of muddy boots, stained clothes, and oily uncombed heads "half hid by dirty collars . . . as stiff as pasteboard." [6] This was America's future, her *posterité contemporain*. Its tastes were simple to crudeness, it was given to bragging, and it had no manners at all. It was immensely creative, but the evidence of its power was spread, if anywhere, upon the journals of state legislatures. In Monroe's Washington it was a little out of place.

I

The Washington of Monroe's day generated a good deal of energy, but it was largely personal. The two-party system has rarely if ever produced two distinct parties; in Monroe's time it produced no parties at all. A few old Federalists still moved around the capital, like statues or mummies; their prestige was great, but their power was chiefly the power of locomotion, and the time would soon come when they would move no more. All ambitious men called themselves Republicans, or sought, without undergoing a public conversion, to attach themselves to whatever Republican faction would best serve their interests. The party boss and the political convention were still local phenomena, and national politics arranged themselves around personalities.

The Era of Good Feelings was pre-eminently the era of the personal myth. The nation's destiny was still uncertain: now one man seemed to personify it, now another. Idiosyncrasies still counted for something, and important figures loomed—at least in their own estimation—a little larger than life size. There was a certain innocence in all but the most opprobious of their transactions: they really believed that what they said and did might have some value, not only for future Americans, but for all mankind. For a few years, the tide in the affairs of men was poised at the flood. Anything might happen to anyone. Even the scramble for the succession to the Presidency, which is one of the most disagreeable features of Monroe's regime, was not altogether a scramble for place or power: it was also a scramble for immortality.

When men are thus challenged to exert themselves, the exertions may take some unusual forms. As an example of personal energy, there are few events in American history to equal that great *Report on Weights and Measures* which John Quincy Adams compiled in such time as he could spare from the management of an understaffed department. When he arrived in Washington in 1817, he found upon his desk a resolution of Congress, requiring him to examine the regulations and standards for weights and measures in the several states, and the proceedings in foreign countries for establishing uniformity in weights and measures, and to suggest "the course proper to be adopted by the United States." Congress, like the British Parliament, had been stirred by the new French metric system. Coinage depended upon weights, trade upon measures; did the secret of uniformity and peace lie in the French system? The demands of Congress were certainly not modest. What, for example, was the relation of the foot to the meter? Even a well-trained mathematician and physicist, armed with every appliance and supplied with every facility for research, might have confessed himself baffled by such a question. Mr. Adams was an amateur; and Washington provided neither appliances nor books. For a pair of scales upon which to test his theories, he was obliged to go to the Washington branch of the Bank of the United States; and the scales he borrowed were rusty and unregulated. On another occasion, he could find no one who could tell him the content of an ordinary hogshead of Bordeaux.[7] He was expected, of course, to hand the job over to some underling, who would concoct a précis of the available authorities; no one supposed that he would do the work himself, still less that he would produce a masterpiece.

The Report, which was considered by its author to be his chief claim to renown, contained an historical survey of English, Greek, Hebrew, Roman, and French weights and measures, and a "philosophical account of the moral principles involved in the consideration of weights and measures, and of the extent and limitation of its connection with the binal, decimal, and duodecimal arithmetic." [8] It is a major generalization from history, philosophy, and physics; and its essentially dramatic approach to a subject bristling with technicalities reminds the modern reader that its author was the grandfather of Henry and Brooks Adams. The villain of the piece was King Edward I of England, who coined the pound sterling into 243 silver pennies, and thus took away the standard of all the weights and of all the vessels of measure, liquid or dry, throughout his kingdom. The heroes were the French who, in spite of the "fanatical paroxym" of their revolution, had produced a system of metrology which alone approached perfection.[9] The Secretary doubted whether it would be advisable to disturb the prevailing uniformity between the United States and Great Britain, laden though it was with the crimes of Edward I and the curious mistakes of the Act of 1496.[10] But if the Congress deemed its powers competent and its duties imperative to establish uniformity in its most comprehensive sense, then there was nothing to equal the Definitive French System as established on December 10, 1799. "If the Spirit of Evil," he informed the Congress, "is, before the final consummation of things, to be cast down from his dominion over men, and bound in the chains of a thousand years, the foretaste here of man's eternal felicity, then . . . the metre will surround the globe in use as well as in multiplied extension; and one language of weights and measures will be spoken from the equator to the poles." [11] From the meter to the millennium—what other statesman would have lectured the legislative branch of his government in quite such a way!

What Congress would have made of all this will never be decided; for Congress never bothered to read the *Report*. During Adams's lifetime only one man—an obscure colonel of the Royal Engineers—seems actually to have perused it from beginning to end. He thought it a work of genius, and wrote to say so. Long after Adams's death, Professor Charles Davies and Sir Sandford Flemming reached a similar conclusion. To the observer of Monroe's America it is a singular example of the energy that could be generated by Monroe's Washington. It was published on the very day upon which the great Transcontinental Treaty with Spain was finally proclaimed—February 22, 1821.[12]

Thus, while he was engaged upon this monumental task, Mr. Adams had also been rearranging the continent on Melish's map. At the same time, it was seriously doubted whether Congress could or could not construct a yard of road or dig a foot of canal. The energy contained in Washington can be measured as well by these considerations as in any other way. As has been shown, in the case of Jackson's invasion of Florida, no line of force can be discovered between the capital and the frontier; nor could it have been supplied by an electric telegraph, if one had existed. If the General had been in daily or hourly contact with the War Department, it is still extremely improbable that he could have been restrained from assaulting Pensacola. What influenced him, besides his fervent nationalism, and his inability to distinguish between a campaign and a duel, was the prevailing concept of the powers of the general government. To what extent could it interfere; or, conversely, to what extent could it be disregarded? The General had answered the question in so downright a fashion as to satisfy neither the supporters nor the opponents of strong central government; but the question was of vital significance. It was settled, or its settlement was at any rate adumbrated, in a basement room in the North Wing of the Capitol, where in March 1819 Chief Justice John Marshall delivered his judgment in the case of *McCulloch v. Maryland.* This judgment is at least as extraordinary an example of personal energy as that presented by John Quincy Adams in his *Report on Weights and Measures;* it was also less elevated, and far more influential.

II

Chief Justice John Marshall was a gift sardonically presented to his successor by President John Adams, whose Secretary of State Marshall had been. By nominating Marshall in the last month of his Administration President Adams made it certain that the Federalist cause—defeated in Cabinet and Congress—would at least be maintained upon the Supreme Bench: nor was he disappointed. John Marshall became the great link between the aristocracy of the eighteenth century and the capitalism of the nineteenth. For one brief moment in 1805, during the impeachment of Justice Chase, it seemed as if Marshall himself would fall victim to the just wrath of his opponents: as if disgrace, and worse than disgrace, would be his portion. Marshall himself trembled; but the crisis passed. From then on "the wise, the rich, and the good" knew that, whatever inroads democracy might make upon two of the co-ordinate branches of the government, the third was safe from its invasion.

In 1819, John Marshall was at the very height of his powers; and it is to this year that we must look for the most concentrated expression of his Constitutional views. In February he declared, in his decision on the case of *Sturges v. Crowninshield,* that a New York State bankruptcy law violated the contract clause of the Constitution; and thereupon drew upon his head the objurgations of every debtor in the country.[13] A few days later, in his judgment on the case of *Dartmouth College v. Woodward,* he announced that a corporation charter should be regarded as a private contract, immune from all legislative control.[14] In March, in the case of *McCulloch v. Maryland,* he pronounced the national Constitution and the laws thereof to be superior in every instance to the constitutions and laws of the respective states. To the business community, all this was balm from Gilead.

Of the great figures of Monroe's America, John Marshall has been the one most often wrested out of the context of his times. He then becomes the robed servant of the moneyed interests and the business community; and, of course, to a very great extent he was. There is a close connection between constitutionalism and capitalism; and Marshall has done as much as any man to call attention to it. As Justice Holmes has said, Marshall was not one of the originators of transforming thought: he did not make those decisions which have in them the germ of some wider theory, and therefore of some profound interstitial change in the very tissue of the law.[15] His thought did not transform; it merely sanctioned transformation. It seems to be little more than a judicial gloss upon those doctrines which we commonly associate with the name of Alexander Hamilton. Powerful but unscholarly, olympian but redundant, his decisions inform us that nothing could prevent the advance of capitalism into the empty spaces of America during the early nineteenth century; and that the national Constitution was the very means by which this advance could be expedited. These decisions are so clearly formulated that even the layman can pick his way through them without undue difficulty; but he is apt to find the experience a chilly one. Marshall was no humanitarian. He often had occasion to mention "the people"; but, with very few exceptions, his "people" have neither hearts nor sensibilities nor tears, neither appetites nor satisfactions: they are simply a function of power.[16]

Yet at this point it is necessary to return him to the context of his times. That he was a Virginian Federalist; that he worshiped his father and was obliged, as eldest son, himself to be father surrogate to a large family of brothers and sisters; that his favorite early reading was Pope's *Essay on Man;* that he learned, as a soldier at Valley Forge, to distrust the good faith of the individual states; that he regarded Burke's *Reflections on the Revolution in France* as almost a sacred text—all these were important factors in the life of a man who was a strict, one might almost say a relentless, paternalist, and who strove to inject into the American Constitution a strong dose of English conservative thought. With such a background and such mentors was it likely that John Marshall, when the choice was offered him, would prefer the agrarian to the capitalist? And the choice was offered him over and over again.

At the same time one has to recognize that the business community for whom John Marshall seems so faithfully to have labored was still in its infancy; though it had, to be sure, already given the world some remarkable evidences of an extreme precocity. It would be foolish to assume that the corporation, which Marshall so plentifully blessed in *Dartmouth College v. Woodward,* was the unit of business enterprise it has since become.[17] It could still be regarded as a humble but useful device in the development of a system of free enterprise which was, itself, as yet no more than an eventuality. To Marshall, therefore, the business community was the agent of order and of progress.

There were some men, it is true, to whom the notion of the businessman as a revolutionary, a person capable of subverting society in order to further his own ends, had already presented itself in the most forcible manner: but these men were usually slave-holders, and therefore potential revolutionaries themselves. The prevailing ethos of Marshall's times would have rejected such a notion, because this ethos made it quite impossible for men to sift the evidence that supported it. Land speculation was the focus for financial activity in Marshall's day; and the history of early land-titles is one long record of subverted law, of weird fraudulence, of corrupted legislatures. Marshall's inspection stopped at the legislatures, which he regarded with an extreme suspicion as the repositories of democracy and disorder, two words that were to his way of thinking practically synonymous. He condemned, as it were, the flotsam on the waterline, but not the flood that had deposited it there. He was, indeed, himself still damp from bathing in those waters. He had once been deeply engaged in land speculation, and the consequent litigation pursued him even on to the Supreme Bench. Yet in *Fletcher v. Peck* (1810) he declared that a contract was sacred, regardless of its ethics, and thus appeared to encourage all that was vicious in the land business and to condone much that was dubious in his own past. This was clearly not evident to him; and the fact that it was not evident indicates how deeply land speculation had eaten into the moral fiber of America.[18]

It is true that Marshall subsequently raised the sanctity of contract into a *mystique*, in which Contract appears as a great principle, "anterior to and independent of society"; and that even his obedient colleagues could not follow him into this legal Manichaeism—this effort to provide the business community with a tutelary demon.[19] But Marshall would never have seen things in this light. To him the sanctity of contract was not an ingenious device for transferring the property of the many into the hands of the few, but the very cornerstone of economic stability. It was when he was most mystical that he was also most nationalist.

Indeed, when one attempts to restore him to the context of his times, it becomes exceedingly difficult to separate the business-minded judge from the nationalist statesman. His nationalism was not lovable; it was based on a mistrust of the human *dynamis* of the nation which it strove to create. It was founded upon a defense of artificial property: but it is only just to admit that it did not carry this defense to extremes. In his decision on the case of *Gibbons v. Ogden*, Marshall struck down a steamboat monopoly, and did as much as any single man could do to make the steamboat free upon the western rivers; and the steamboat was not merely an essential factor in the development of the internal market, it was also the very symbol of democracy. Moreover, it was in his judgment in this important case that Marshall, for all his boldness, showed a great deal of caution. The question at the very heart of *Gibbons v. Ogden* was this: Did the mere grant of a power to Congress to regulate commerce "among the several states" automatically prohibit a state from creating a steamboat monopoly? The question was exceedingly difficult, and Marshall himself, in *Sturges v. Crowninshield*, had declared that "the mere granting of a power to Congress did not imply a prohibition on the states to exercise the same power."[20] But he immediately qualified this statement by declaring that whenever the nature of the power required that it should be exercised exclusively by Congress, "the subject is as completely taken from the state legislatures as if they had been expressly forbidden to act on it."[21] Was the nature of the power granted in the commerce clause such that it should be exercised exclusively by Congress? If it was—or rather if the Supreme Court declared it to be—of such a nature, then it was clear that a vast and subtle change had taken place in the relationship between the general government and the individual states. Marshall never answered the question directly.[22] He gained much popularity from his decision, and he might have established the "dormant" power of the commerce clause—that is to say, its *implicit* veto upon state legislation—without too much disagreement from the rest of the Court. Instead, he merely suggested—and in terms that may have been deliberately confused—the existence of the dormant power. He seemed to think that too open a declaration of federal authority would arouse in time an irresistible opposition, and he may well have reminded himself that his own doctrine was, after all, a double-edged affair. If the state authority could be limited by the Court in the interests of the nation, might not the national authority also be limited by the Court in the interests of the states? The Tenth Amendment—not one of Marshall's favorites—always made this possible. Marshall even went further, and began to restore to the states, in the form of a "police power," some of the authority he had elsewhere taken from them.[23] "We must never forget," he once said, "that it is a constitution we are expounding" . . . something organic, capable of growth, susceptible to change.[24]

Indeed his vaguely defined notion that political activity must be co-extensive with economic activity suggests that if he had been born into a late instead of an early stage of liberal capitalism, he might have been as anxious to check the exuberance of business enterprise as he was in fact eager to encourage it. His nationalism was not lovable; but how readily, in another age, under other circumstances, might its terms have been changed!

In 1819, however, his nationalism seemed to place the Constitution at the service of the moneyed interests, and to express a profound mistrust in the ability of the masses to govern themselves—for it was in the state legislatures, in those days, that men chiefly looked for a manifestation of the art of self-government.

It is for this reason that John Marshall with all his advantages—intelligence, conviviality, a prodigious gusto for the simple pleasures of life—has left but a frosty imprint upon American history. There is a perplexing, indeed a terrible disparity between the great mistrusting Federalist judge and the friendly human being who hid himself beneath those judicial robes. John Marshall was a tall man, thin to emaciation, with a head rather too small for his body, and joints so loosely put together that he shambled around like a marionette. His black eyes gleamed with good humor and his characteristic expression was one of great benevolence. As he lounged among the drinkers at a wayside tavern, with his tousled hair and his soiled and shabby clothes, one might have mistaken him—and many people did—for a simple old farmer. There are numberless stories attesting him the most democratic of men: stories of Marshall ambling to market with a basket on his arm and stopping to gossip at every stall; or riding out to his country farm with a stray child on his saddlebow, or with his thumb in a jug of whisky of which he had lost the cork; or crawling on the ground with a straw in his mouth to make some nice decision in a game of quoits; or shouting out a chorus at one of his famous suppers.[25] His chivalry towards women was exalted, even for a Southern gentleman; and Richmond long remembered his romantic devotion towards his poor, distracted wife. Often enough at night he would go downstairs in his bare feet to drive away from their house some errant cow or pig which threatened to disturb her sleep. Or he would send her out for a long country drive while he himself, in his shirtsleeves with a bandanna twisted round his head, would lead the servants in - a thorough scrubbing of the house.[26] The contrast between the man and the judge is so extreme that one is almost forced into mythology for a similar metamorphosis. Does he not resemble the Ovidian Jove, approaching the maiden Democracy in all sorts of agreeable disguises and then only, in the moment of possession, revealing himself as the Thunderer?

Such was the Chief Justice who on March 6, 1819, in his little basement room, pronounced his judgment in the case of *McCulloch v. Maryland.*

III

The facts in the case of *McCulloch v. Maryland* were as follows: Congress had authorized the incorporation of the Second Bank of the United States, and this great institution had set up a branch at Baltimore. In an Act of February 11, 1818, the legislature of Maryland required all banks doing business within her borders, and holding charters she had not granted, to pay an annual tax of fifteen thousand dollars, and to issue notes only of certain denominations. If such banks preferred not to pay the tax, then only they must print their notes only upon stamped paper purchased from the Treasurer of the Western Shore. The Baltimore branch of the Bank of the United States, however, declined to pay the tax, and with complete insouciance continued to issue its notes upon unstamped paper. Whereupon the Treasurer of the Western Shore, John James, sued the cashier of the branch Bank, James W. McCulloch, for the recovery of the prescribed penalties—which, at five hundred dollars an offense, probably ran into many hundreds of thousands.

The Baltimore County Court gave judgment for the state, as did the Maryland Court of Appeals, which then permitted the case to be brought to the Supreme Court of the United States upon a writ of error. Like many other cases involving a Constitutional issue, this was "arranged"; and it was even suggested that there was some collusion in it, and that the Maryland counsel had not presented their strongest arguments.[27]

However this may have been, the issues involved were of great and grave consequence. If one construed the Constitution loosely, then Congress had the right to charter a bank; if one construed it strictly, then Congress had no such right. Obviously, the true significance of the controversy over loose and strict construction lay in the uses to which they could be put by economic interests.[28] The new industrial capitalism needed, or thought that it needed, a national bank in order to send fresh money circulating through all the arteries and veins of trade; while the moneyed interests of New York and New England, though somewhat jealous of the national bank, would not

frown on a judicial decision that threw around financial activity the protecting cloak of loose construction.

A national bank! The words had a distressing sound for all good agrarians,
who believed that the industrialists and financiers were out to crush them
with protective tariffs, and corrupt them with internal improvements. Had
not Alexander Hamilton's child, the First Bank of the United States, been a
deliberate effort to ally the national government with the moneyed interests? And was there any reason to believe that James Madison's child,
the Second Bank of the United States, would be more pure? Mr. Madison,
it is true, had fathered the bank with some reluctance, but the country's
fiscal needs were so pressing, and the currency was in such disorder, that
the government had either to create a national institution or to throw itself
on the mercy of the private bankers. On April 10, 1816, therefore, the
Second Bank of the United States came into existence. It was far more
closely wedded to the government than was the Bank of England, the Bank
of France, or any other similar contemporary institution.[29] The federal government owned one fifth of its stock, whereas the capital of other central
banks was wholly private. The President of the United States appointed
five of the twenty-five directors. No man who disliked the connection between government and banking could possibly approve of such an institution.

It is a little difficult to separate the bank's main functions from the press
of incidental powers surrounding them; from the vast amount of private
business it transacted; from its ability to loan the public money to politicians and newspaper editors; from its control of foreign exchange and its
alliance with foreign banking. But its utility as a keeper of the public deposits and a transferer of the public funds could hardly be denied; and it
was probably true that it alone possessed the power of restoring some kind
of order to the national currency. The government's receipts were principally from taxes paid by importers to customs collectors.[30] These tax payments were generally made in the notes of private banks, for such notes
provided most of the money in circulation in the United States. By receiving
these notes on deposit from the customs collectors, and presenting them to
the private banks for payment, the Bank of the United States became the
creditor of the banks. Thus a private bank that extended credit in a proper
manner, and maintained an adequate gold and silver reserve, could always
meet its obligations, and a bank that overextended itself could not. The
Bank of the United States, therefore, by maintaining a constant pressure
upon the private banks could restrict their lending and their issue of notes,
and curb their tendency to lend too much and so depreciate their circulation. In short, its regulatory powers were exactly the opposite of those
now existing under the Federal Reserve Act. Under the present system, private banks maintain balances with the Federal Reserve Banks, and are their
creditors; in those days, the private banks were the debtors of the Bank
of the United States. It has been maintained that this system, though it

would not be practicable in our complicated economy, was well suited to those simpler times.[31]

Obviously, the private banks disliked this situation—this dependence upon an institution with headquarters in Philadelphia and with four fifths of its board of directors elected by the stockholders of that city, and with all the powers of the national government behind it. Those who examine the doctrine of State Rights in the hopes of finding a rich deposit of idealism in it are generally obliged to confess that this deposit is extraordinarily elusive and sporadic. In the case of *McCulloch v. Maryland* did the state of Maryland propose to tax the branch bank at Baltimore out of existence because it believed such a bank to be a dangerous invasion of its sovereignty, or could the pressure of private bankers have been responsible?

In any case, it is true that the private banks offered very little assistance to the Second Bank of the United States when it first came into being. Its purpose was to create a stable currency, and this in turn could only be effected if the private banks would agree to resume specie payments, if they would consent to contract their credit dealings sternly enough to support the fiction that their paper was convertible upon demand into gold or silver. Since they were making large profits out of inconvertible paper, they were naturally unwilling to make this contraction; and a convention of the associated banks of New York, Philadelphia, Baltimore and Richmond only agreed to do so if the Bank of the United States would extend its credit dealings while they contracted theirs.[32] This was a very harsh, and very early declaration of the view that it is the duty of the central bank to act as lender of the last resort.[33] The bank needed all its caution if it was to discount six million dollars before it called in the balances accumulating against the private banks.

And the bank, as it happened, used no caution at all during the first two years of its existence, with the inevitable result, as will be shown, that when it began to put its affairs in order it was obliged to inflict the country with a ruinous contraction of credit. Thereafter, it performed its functions with a praiseworthy efficiency. And yet there was something dangerous and menacing about it. The strict members of the Republican Party could not forgive James Madison for signing the bill which incorporated the Second Bank of the United States. Had he not fought the first bank tooth and nail? And was there any difference between the first bank and the second? They could not see that, since the monetary policy was national, the means for putting it into effect must be national too; their criticism was just, but it did not go far enough, and it moved in the wrong direction. What was dangerous about the Second Bank of the United States was that it was far too free from government control. The Republicans who created it in 1816 were themselves suspicious of strong government, and they allowed this suspicion fatally to weaken the relation between the government and the bank. Nicholas Biddle, the bank's third president, in those moments of infatuated exuberance to which he was so unfortunately given, made this clear enough; but he made it clear, too, in his sober moments. Writing to Monroe in 1824, he said that certain suggestions of the Secretary of the Treasury "will be most respectfully considered by the Board of Directors, and cheerfully agreed to, *if not inconsistent with their duties to the institution*." [34] What might not be expected from a national bank that would follow the suggestions of the government only when these suggestions did not conflict with the interests of its stockholders?

All this was still in the future. In 1819, the Second Bank of the United States was fighting for its life against the efforts of certain states to destroy it with taxes; while at the same time the nation at large, plunged deep in an economic depression, was beginning to regard the bank as the chief engineer of its misfortunes. It was in this atmosphere that John Marshall was called upon to decide between the bank and the state of Maryland; and this decision permits us to hear, full and resonant, the strange and dangerous voice of early economic nationalism.

IV

The Supreme Court of the United States sat in the city of Washington for one brief term of six or eight weeks every year. Marshall and his associates lived at the same boarding house, where the Chief Justice seemed, says his biographer, to be "the head of a family as much as he was chief of a court." [35] At these close quarters, his singular combination of intelligence, charm, and iron will worked its magic upon his colleagues. The Court was "Marshall's Court," it was said. As the years passed, the political complexion of the justices had changed: a majority of the Court was now Republican. But—it was odd and it was disturbing—these Republicans had scarcely taken their seats before they changed their views. Justice Joseph Story might have been forgiven for such a defection—he was young when he joined the Court, he was impressionable, he came from Massachusetts, and his Republicanism had always been doubtful.[36] But what could one say for William Johnson of South Carolina, once "strongly imbued with the principles of southern democracy," whose leaning towards Federalism now became so pronounced that in some instances—notably in his interpretation of the commerce clause —he seemed to out-Herod Herod himself? [37] Marshall's great decisions, it may safely be said, were generally the result of long discussion between himself and his brethren—they have been described as orchestral rather than solo performances; but there could never be any doubt as to who was the conductor.[38] In legal scholarship, and indeed in richness of mind, men like Story and Johnson were far superior to Marshall; what they lacked was the power to resist his will. Towards the end of Marshall's reign, when nationalism sought to divorce itself from its marriage with private wealth, his Court grew restive; but even after his death there was a Marshall group which, under Justice Story, fought bitterly against the democratic tendencies of Chief Justice Taney.

A Court thus dominated, and by a man who used the "people" as a conceptual means of defeating what little could be ascertained of the people's will, was naturally a dramatic affair. During the hearing of *McCulloch v. Maryland* the Supreme Court basement in the Capitol was "full almost to suffocation, and many went away for lack of room." [39] Probably most people knew that the Chief Justice would declare for the bank and carry the Court with him; what took the country by surprise was the magistral fashion in which he did so. The denouement, then, as far as the bank was concerned, was already known; the drama was prearranged; and what summoned the spectators was a classic interest in the quality of the performance.

Ladies as well as gentlemen elbowed their way into the modest room beneath the Capitol; for Washington was culturally famished and the Supreme Court represented a kind of theater. An eminent counsel had been known to stop in the middle of an argument when ladies appeared, and ask permission to repeat what he had said but in simpler and more amusing language; nor was permission denied him. For the acting out of *McCulloch v. Maryland* a most distinguished cast had been assembled: for the bank, Mr. William Pinkney, Mr. Daniel Webster, and Attorney-General Wirt; for the state of Maryland, Mr. Luther Martin, Mr. Joseph Hopkinson, and Mr. Walter Jones. Luther Martin, "the Thersites of the law," short, broadshouldered, slovenly, seventy-one years old, whose wit had confronted the dull world with conviviality but not with gladness, and whose face was purple from fifty years of brandy-drinking, brought into that room the lurid memories of Justice Chase and of Aaron Burr. Everybody was interested in Luther Martin, who happened also to be making his last appearance before any bar in this world. But the most popular actors were Daniel Webster and William Pinkney. Mr. Webster had already made his reputation as a lawyer and an orator in his arguments before the Court in *Dartmouth College v. Woodward*. His mind had, it is true, not yet revealed its barometric character—its almost perfect registration of the climate of opinion among men of wealth and power. He was not yet a famous man, but much was expected of him. He had at least founded—it is the fate of most orators—a reputation that was to be composed almost exclusively of perorations. At the end of his speech in the Dartmouth College case he had paused, apparently groping for the words that, with a characteristic economy, he had already used in a lower Court. "It is, Sir," he faltered out at last, "as I have said, a small College. And yet, there are those who love it." His voice choked with sobs; the audience reached for its handkerchiefs; and even Chief Justice Marshall began to cry.[40] "Business enterprise," says one disillusioned commentator, "has never had more useful mercenaries than the tears Daniel Webster and John Marshall are reputed to have shed that March day." [41] Such was Webster's magic that the true issue—the demand of private corporations to be immune from legislative interference—temporarily disappeared, and the image of a small college, dedicated to the instruction of the sons of poor men, superimposed itself upon this huge pretension. Certainly, Mr. Webster would go far. His appearance was formidable—the craggy head, the smouldering black eyes, the solid body correctly encased in the blue cut-away with big brass buttons. His opening argument in *McCulloch v. Maryland* was not long, but one would have liked to hear that deep, that thrilling voice as it pronounced the words "the power to tax is the power to destroy"—an argument that Marshall used in his decision and that still booms, very usefully though with less conviction, across the years. He was followed in due time by William Pinkney, the leading actor—one might almost say the leading juvenile—in that gifted cast. The old rip, with his corsets and his cosmetics and his preposterously youthful clothes, was a great favorite with the ladies: when they were present he never failed to scatter little complimentary allusions along the dusty trail of the law. But it so happened that he had one of the finest minds in the profession; and when he spoke—which, on this occasion, he did for three days—the flowery tropes and hircine postures did not interfere with what was, first and last, a masterly exposition of Hamiltonian law. At the end of nine days the audience retired, well satisfied with the performance, and left the Chief Justice to recite, almost to an empty theater, his resounding epilogue.

John Marshall was a master of deductive exposition. No man was happier with a syllogism than he—no man was more adept at separating the "irrelevent" elements from the "significant" facts of the case, and then discovering that this particular case had already been provided for in a general rule of law.[42] Thus it was easy for him to deduce from the "necessary and proper" clause of the Constitution the power of Congress to incorporate a bank, since this power was clearly "incidental" to the great enumerated powers: "to lay and collect taxes; to borrow money; to regulate commerce; to declare and conduct a war; and to raise and support armies and navies."[43] It was, therefore, "the unanimous and decided opinion" of the Court that the Bank Act of February 10, 1816, was Constitutional. The establishment of a branch bank at Baltimore was also Constitutional. Since some of his opponents resolutely refused to believe that the judiciary had the power to declare an Act of Congress either Constitutional or not Constitutional, this announcement was audacious enough. It was nothing, however, to what came after. For in declaring that the Act of the state of Maryland, which taxed the branch bank, was repugnant to the national Constitution, John Marshall readily admitted that the power of taxation was retained by the states and not abridged by the grant of a similar power to the general government. But he went on to say, with all the emphasis at his command, that the Constitution was of so paramount a character that "its capacity to withdraw any subject from the action of even this power, is admitted." In other words, the national government might withdraw from state taxation *any* taxable subject, and not merely those subjects which the Constitution specifically withdraws. And this argument, or assertion, was sustained, not on the language of the Constitution, but on the "great principle that the constitution and the laws thereof are supreme; that they control the constitution and laws of the respective states, and cannot be controlled by them."

Nationalism could go no farther.

Marshall always maintained, as a fundamental premise, that it was possible to fathom the purposes of the framers of the Constitution; and neither his friends nor his opponents disagreed with him.[44] In 1819, it is true, very little was known about the purposes of the framers of the Constitution. The Journal of their Convention had not yet been published; and Mr. Madison's invaluable notes still lay buried in his private archives. None the less, everybody agreed that if one examined the Constitution in the right light one would inevitably descry the purposes of its framers. The great document itself was marvelously brief: even in the late 1880's an English admirer was able to exclaim that it was about half as long as St. Paul's first epistle to the Corinthians, and one fortieth as long as the Irish Land Act of 1881.[45] Few instruments in history have laid down such momentous rules, on such a vast range of subjects, and in so few words. The only question remained—in what light was one to examine it?

Obviously, so much had occurred between the framing of the Constitution in 1787 and the attack on the bank in 1819 that the purposes of the framers, even if they could be discovered, had already become irrelevant. They could not have foreseen the invention of the cotton gin, or the awakening of industrial enterprise under the Embargo. No doubt they intended the Constitution to bestow upon Congress "the capacity to avail itself of experience, to exercise its reason, and to accommodate its legislation to circumstances." Marshall said that they did; and few men in the country could have disagreed with him.[46] Whether Congress should accommodate its legislation to the special needs of bankers and industrialists—that was the question. Marshall carried his generalization one step further. He announced that the framers of the Constitution, when they granted certain specific powers to Congress, did not intend to impede the exercise of those powers by withholding a choice of means. "Let the end be legitimate," he said, "let it be within the scope of the constitution, and all means which are appropriate, which are plainly adapted to that end, which are not prohibited, but consist with the letter and spirit of the constitution, are constitutional." [47] In other words, while Marshall's opponents contended that the national government might only do what it was expressly permitted to do, Marshall himself declared that it might do anything it was not expressly forbidden to do.

What would the framers of the Constitution, with their grave suspicion of the caprice of the majority, have said to *that?* As it happened, one of the Founding Fathers was sitting in Marshall's presence, in the rather saurian shape of Mr. Luther Martin. Mr. Martin, it is true, was not exactly a Father—he had left the Constitutional Convention in a rage, because it seemed to him to be paying too little heed to the claims of the small states. He had subsequently become a Federalist. He was now, once again, pleading the cause of State Rights. If one had asked him what were the purposes of the framers of the Constitution, one would have received a rather confusing answer; but his presence in Marshall's court, as an attorney for the state of Maryland against the bank, suggested that Marshall's interpretation was open to some doubt. On the other hand, no man had more claim to interpret the intentions of the Fathers than had James Madison; and in Number 44 of *The Federalist* Madison himself had written: "No axiom is more clearly established in law, or in reason, than that wherever the end is required, the means are authorized; wherever a general power to do a thing is given, every particular power necessary for doing it is included." [48] Marshall himself had said no more than that.

No sooner had Marshall's decision been published than the attack upon it was commenced; and it was impossible for James Madison to remain uninvolved. He was asked by Judge Spencer Roane for an opinion upon Marshall's decision. "Is there a legislative power, in fact," he replied, "not expressly prohibited by the Constitution, which might not, according to the doctrine of the court, be exercised as a means of carrying into effect some specified power? . . . It was anticipated, I believe, by few, if any, of the friends of the Constitution, that a rule of construction would be introduced as broad and pliant as what has occurred." [49] This was perspicuously stated, as one might expect from that keen and copious mind: it revealed the weak link in Marshall's logic. Whether or not the furibund Roane was satisfied with such an answer has not been recorded; but Madison can scarcely have written it without some misgivings. He can hardly have forgotten Number 44 of *The Federalist*. Moreover, he had signed the bill that incorporated the bank, and his attitude towards Marshall's decision, which protected the bank, must have been, to say the least, ambivalent.

And so it became clear that when the Constitution was challenged by a specific set of circumstances, there would be little comfort in the Fathers, living or dead.

V

The Court's decision in the case of *McCulloch v. Maryland* was read by Marshall on March 6, 1819. The bank was saved. The Chief Justice had said little that had not already been said by Alexander Hamilton in his opinion on the Constitutionality of the first bank, written in 1791. [50] It was not the originality of Marshall's decision that counted: it was its audacity and its resonance. The doctrine of nationalism had been shouted from the highest court in the land; and those who believed, either as ideologists or as economists, that salvation lay with the action of state legislatures, were equally loud in their rebuttal. Even Hezekiah Niles took up the cudgels in his *Register*. [51] Spencer Roane—inadequately disguised as "Amphictyon" and as "Hampden"—pummeled the Chief Justice in the columns of the *Richmond Enquirer*. Judge Roane threatened that Virginia might employ force, if other measures failed her, and Mr. Niles gave it as his opinion that "certain nabobs" in New York, Boston, Philadelphia, and Baltimore had fairly purchased the souls of Congressmen with money in order to secure the passage of the Bank Act. He called upon all the people who hated monopolies and privileged orders to rise in their might and "purge our political temple of the money-changers and those who sell doves." [52] The attack spread. The legislatures of Pennsylvania, Tennessee, Ohio, Indiana, and Illinois voiced their disapproval, asking for an amendment to the Constitution forbidding Congress to incorporate a bank.[58] The Chief Justice was severely shaken; and though he gave his support to the business community in decision after decision thereafter, he never again offered this support in such resounding nationalist terms. It may well be that the reception given to his decision in *McCulloch v. Maryland* taught him a valuable lesson in the art of statecraft, and urged him to pay more attention to the value of local autonomy in his nationalist scheme. For, with all his chilling predilections, Chief Justice John Marshall was a great man.

CHAPTER SIX

Panic

THE months of February and March, 1819, ironically mark the climax
and the conclusion of that nationalist exuberance which had its origins
in the Treaty of Ghent and the Battle of New Orleans. In February, John
Quincy Adams called a new continent into being by drawing lines upon a
map. In March, Chief Justice Marshall conjured a national government
out of the eighth section of the first Article of the Constitution. The connection between these two events was riveted by the Chief Justice himself.
"Throughout this vast republic," he said on March 6, "from the St. Croix
to the Gulf of Mexico, *from the Atlantic to the Pacific,* revenue is to be
collected and expended, armies are to be marched and supported." [1] The
State Department and the Supreme Court took the same confident view of
the future.

As even the negotiations at Ghent had shown, however, there existed in
the United States of America a curious and intermittent taste for disunion.
The nationalism that distinguished the first two years of Monroe's Presidency, and gave to his whole Administration the slightly delusive title of
The Era of Good Feelings, was composed partly of the enthusiasm that
comes from having won, or at least not lost, a war, and partly of the belief
that prosperity was eternal. When the prosperity began to collapse, nationalism as a unifying principle faded with it; and sectionalism, or the
maneuvers of different sets of social and economic arrangements, took its
place. Now in sectionalism there is much that is less agreeable than in nationalism; there is also much that is more interesting.

I

When the War of 1812 ended, the United States of America was still a
poor republic, whose western boundaries frayed out in a mythical desert,

175

and whose standing in the world was not too high. It was not always to be found upon the maps from which European children learned their geography.[2] To some Europeans it was a Utopia; to some a nightmare; and to almost all a place where almost anything might happen. But, distant as it was from the centers of Western civilization, it was not immune from the great movements, the wars and depressions, which afflicted the Western world.

When the Napoleonic Wars ended, the whole Western world began to suffer from a fall in prices. This was probably due to a shortage of specie. The mines of Mexico and Peru, the principal sources of supply of the precious metals, had been disorganized by revolution; and specie was being rapidly drained away into the mysteries of Russia and the limbo of household economy and slave labor east of Suez. In the United States, for example, there was a general decline in wholesale commodity prices, beginning in 1816.[8] In 1816, in other words, the depression in prices ranged from the Bosphorus to the Mississippi. But in America this state of affairs was concealed by a land boom and a cotton boom—two phenomena that, more than any patriotic fervor or party unity, gave to the Era of Good Feelings such cohesion as it possessed.

The economic realities, in fact, were always against the Era of Good Feelings; and one of these realities was the condition of Great Britain. As has already been shown, the political results of the triumph of British industrialism were generally favorable to the growth of the United States: one does not quarrel with a good market. It is better to sell one's manufactures than to go to war over an Arbuthnot or an Ambrister. The economic realities, however, did not go hand in hand with these political gestures. When the great convulsion ended on the hill at Waterloo, Britain found herself the center of world exchanges. Was it not for this, really, that the British redcoats—"the scum of the earth, enlisted for drink"—had endured to the end of that heroic day? She was now forced to cope with the disorganization of the postwar world and with a general decline in prices. The armies, those artificial consumers, melted away; agriculture languished; government orders fell off. Merchants, with vast quantities of goods on their hands, found it difficult to re-establish their old trade connections. Europe eagerly resisted the advances of British industry. But the energies of British industry, which had defeated Napoleon, were great enough to repel the pressure of peace. In 1815, a mass of manufactures from the warehouses of Liverpool and from various depots in Canada, Halifax, and Bermuda descended upon the Atlantic ports of the United States. The first year's imports were readily absorbed; but in 1816, with the next influx of cheap British manufactures, the young industries of the United States were in serious trouble.

The most dramatic arenas for the examination of this state of affairs were the auction rooms of New York, Boston, Baltimore, or Philadelphia. Moreover, it is here that one sees a most remarkable example of distributing enterprise in the early nineteenth century. In the first place, British manufacturers found it easy to circumvent the tariff laws of 1816. The stratagem of the false invoice easily outwitted the vigilance of the American customs officers.

A manufacturer had merely to sell his goods to one agent, at a price apparently below the cost of production, and the invoice setting forth these fraudulent prices, after being endorsed by the American consul at the port of shipment, was sufficient to pilot the goods through the custom house. The goods were then sold to a second agent, armed with a second invoice detailing the correct price of the goods, and this second agent hurried them off to the hospitable auction room. Nothing could have been more convenient; the goods paid a low duty, and the agent was spared all the expenses of warehouse rent, clerk hire, and merchant license tax.[4]

In the auction room itself, the downfall of the American manufacturer was arranged in a most ingenious way. "This business is now so completely systematized," wrote a New York merchant in 1820, "that a great proportion of the goods which are consumed in the country are specially manufactured on the other side of the water for Auction. They are made from the most inferior qualities of raw materials, dressed and finished in such a manner as to show to the best advantage, and in the hurry of sale the deception is not easily detected. The first purchaser finds himself deceived, is tempted and defrauds the next, until finally the loss falls upon the innocent consumer. Hence it is that we rely not only on the foreigners to manufacture for us, but . . . this course throws directly into the hands of foreigners all the profits which are made on importations, as also the profit which used to go into the hands of what is familiarly termed with us the jobbing merchant, without subjecting themselves to any charges other than the state duty and about one percent to the Auctioneer."[5]

The ruin of the jobbing merchant was accomplished in another way, for when with his knowledge of particular markets he placed a judicious order with a British manufacturer, the manufacturer would duplicate this order with similar goods of an inferior fabric and texture, and dispatch them by the very same ship that brought the merchant's order. The inferior goods were then sold quickly at auction, and the honest importer was robbed of his market.[6]

The auctioneers were powerful enough to maintain a grip upon the legislatures; and they were a fruitful source of patronage. In New York state, for example, they were appointed by the Senate, on the nomination of the governor.[7] But, even if there had been no auction system, the deluge of British goods would have proved too much for the American manufacturers. They had been protected by embargoes and blockades, and in the nakedness of the postwar world all but the strongest of them shivered. "It was well worth while," that strangest of Whigs, Henry Brougham, told the House of Commons in 1816, "to incur a loss upon the first exportation in order by the glut to stifle in the cradle those rising manufactures in the United States which the war has forced into existence contrary to the usual course of nature."[8] Indeed, the British manufacturer could hardly do anything else. The ports of Europe were as good as closed to him until he could quote a price attractive to Europe's poverty; and he proposed to reduce the unit cost of his goods by increasing the production and discharging the surplus into whatever channels he could find. The newly reopened trade with the United States was one of the most likely channels, and one of the most natural.

Thus, when James Monroe became President, and the Era of Good Feelings began, the American manufacturer was already in distress. However, the American economy was largely agrarian, and though in manufacturing states the legislatures were deluged with eloquent memorials, their usual response was of a sartorial character. The members announced that in the future they would wear none but American-made clothes. The patriotism of this response was very laudable, but it could hardly have satisfied the manufacturers.[9]

Farmers and shipowners, however, were also temporarily trapped by the reorganization of the postwar world. The ports of the British West Indies were once again closed to them, at a loss of at least six million dollars in agricultural exports, and a consequent unemployment of eighty thousand tons of shipping. British ships in the meantime moved freely from Great Britain to the United States, from the United States to the West Indies, and from the West Indies back to Great Britain; and this triangular trade, denied to the Americans by the closing of the West Indian ports, was immensely profitable. "An English merchant-carrier could even afford to bring goods from Liverpool to New York at an actual loss, inasmuch as he could easily recover on the voyages from New York to the West Indies, and from the West Indies back to Liverpool. . . . The trade between England and America was carried on by Englishmen so much below the cost of the voyage that during the summer of 1816 beef and tallow, butter, hams, and potatoes were actually brought from Galway and Newry to New York, where they undersold our home products." [10]

This state of affairs could not last for long; and it was temporarily hidden from the public, because the public seemed to be living in a bubble, impervious to the realities of the outer world. The price of cotton soared upward in those postwar years until, in 1818, it reached at one moment the staggering eminence of 32½¢ a pound.[11] The British re-export market could not absorb it at such prices, nor could the British manufacturer; and the latter, searching desperately for relief, began to import East Indian cotton, which eventually proved unsuited to the rude machinery of the times. But the proof came too late. In 1817, 117,955 bales were imported into Great Britain from the East Indies; in 1818, 227,300 bales.[12] In 1818 the price of American cotton at Liverpool began to waver, and at the end of the year it fell to 24¢ with every prospect of going lower. When the news reached America in 1819 cotton dropped in one day from 32¢ to 26¢, and plunged on down until it averaged only 14.3¢ at New Orleans.[13]

This disaster, which affected the whole of the South and the Southwest, was nowhere more evident than in the price of lands. The fantasy of high cotton prices had produced and then fed upon a huge inflation in land prices; and as much as $100 an acre had been paid for likely cotton lands in the new Southwest. With the collapse of the cotton market, these lost their value. But the ruin of the cotton market merely completed what had already begun elsewhere: it was no more than the final disruption in an irrepressible landslide.

For the whole postwar American economy had been based upon a land boom. On the one side of the Atlantic were undeveloped soils of an immense fertility; on the other, a Europe denuded and famished by the marching and countermarching of half the armies of the world. From these premises Americans deduced a future which—even for a people notably addicted to flutters in real estate—was more than usually optimistic. Nobody bothered to consider the fact that Europe had an agriculture of its own, and that agriculture was resilient. Aided by a government policy that encouraged the purchase of the public domain on credit, and by the swelling vigor of the westward movement, an immense land speculation began. It was financed by one of the most extraordinary emissions of dubious paper money in the history of the modern world. From 1815 to 1818 the bubble grew and grew; beautiful, iridescent, fraudulent, opaque. For nearly three years it resisted the pressure of a general decline in world prices, of the decay of manufactures and shipping, of the British Corn Laws, of the obstinate resistance of the European consumer. But in the middle of 1818 it began visibly to tremble; and with the collapse of cotton it broke. Land values dropped suddenly from fifty to seventy-five per cent; the prices of staples fell accordingly; speculator, merchant, farmer, migrant were involved in a common chaos.[14] Looking around for a scapegoat, the country saw one institution that seemed to have encouraged and profited by this disaster; and that institution was the Second Bank of the United States.

II

To accuse the bank of creating the Panic of 1819 was to accuse the pistol and not the highwayman, the rope and not the executioner. If it had been wisely managed from the beginning, it could not have prevented the panic; it could only have modified its effects. But it was not wisely managed. In its beginnings under the muddleheaded direction of President Jones, as in its end when President Biddle lost his sense of proportion, it illustrated the dangers that attach themselves to a governmental institution that is not amenable to government control. It also illustrated how pervasive and corrupting is the magic of a land boom.

When the bank made its agreement with the private banks for the resumption of specie payments on February 20, 1817, all was optimism. This was reflected in New York. "It was like magic," wrote John Jacob Astor, "at 10 oClock on the 20 Feby bills on Baltimore were 2½ pct Discount and Specie at 2½ pct Premium for our Banke notes. We oppend here our office and agreed to take Bills on Baltimore Virginia & Phila in half an hour all was at par . . . the U.S. Bank thus far may be called a national blessing." [15]

A year later he had changed his tune. "There has been too much speculation," he complained, "and too much assumption of Power on the part of the Bank Directors which has caused the Institution to becom unpouplar & I may say genrally so." They had been discounting too freely and had made money so cheap "that everything else has becom Dear & the Result is that our merchants instead of shiping produse ship Specie, so much so that I tell you in confidence that it is not without difficulty that specie payments are maintaind the Defferent States are still going on making more Banks & I shall not be surprized if by & by there be a general Blow up among them." [16] The Bank was threatening the very return to specie payments which it had been its main business to promote.

Mr. Astor may be taken as a reliable witness on such a subject as this. From the very beginning the bank had plunged with enthusiasm into the verdant morasses of speculative expansion. Even before it opened its doors, the board of directors at Philadelphia had passed two resolutions permitting discounts on a pledge of stock. Private subscribers to the bank paid for their stock in three installments, the first consisting of $5 in specie and $25 in government stock; the second, coming six months later, of $10 in specie and $25 in government stock; and the third, due twelve months after the second, also of $10 in specie and $25 in government stock. This was the law, and by these means it was proposed to raise seven million dollars in specie and twenty-one million dollars in government stock. By the directors' resolutions, however, stockholders were enabled to pay their second installment on the security of the stock itself; and on August 27, 1817, they were given the extra privilege of discounting on their stock at an advance of twenty-five per cent. As for specie payments, these were easily avoided by forfeiting the first dividend. Under these circumstances it was only natural that those who made large purchases should have been able to retain their stock without paying for it; that the stock should have become a prey to speculators; and that, in the general excitement, the voices of respectable persons raised in protest within Congress and without should have been raised in vain. As Mr. Niles remarked bitterly, Congressmen could be made into stockholders, too.[17]

President William Jones, an appointee of James Madison, was one of those fortunate human beings whose promotions in life seem to depend upon their inability to fulfill them. Inept as Secretary of the Navy in the War of 1812, he had been even more inept as temporary Secretary of the Treasury in 1813; he was therefore raised to the position of president of the bank, where his talent for failure was bound to prove spectacular. He had a kindheartedness which, in his new position, was tantamount to corruption; and a tolerance of other men's peccadilloes which only lacked intent to make it criminal. He immediately precipitated his bank into the dance of speculation, until that respectable institution was revolving like a maenad. Loans were made far in advance of the six million dollars that the agreement of February 1 had made mandatory; and when the government in July 1817 redeemed thirteen million dollars of the public stock in the possession of the bank, the bank's response was to grant further discounts. It was clear that only one consideration counted with Mr. Jones, and that was to secure large dividends for the stockholders.[18]

His geniality in the matter of the branch banks of the United States was particularly striking. By July 1818 there were nineteen of these subsidiary offices; and no effort whatsoever was made to fix their capitals. Moreover the branch directors were, even more than their president, ignorant of the principles of sound banking. They were entirely under the spell of local conditions: they loaned on mortgages, they renewed their notes over and over again, they issued notes and drafts without considering the little matter of redemption; and to them the country owed the appearance of that singular device—the "racer" or "race-horse" bill. This was a bill of exchange paid for by the purchase of another bill of exchange, a form of paper which rushed up and down the country from branch to branch, "ruining the drawers with interest, exchange, commissions for acceptance, and other expenses." [19]

Moreover, his efforts to maintain a uniform currency—which was certainly one of the bank's main reasons for existence—produced some peculiar difficulties. It had been agreed that the notes of any one branch should be paid on presentation at any of the others; and since the course of exchange was almost constantly in favor of the East and the North, the notes of the Southern and Western branches flooded into the East and North for redemption. This "system of drawing and re-drawing carried on by the Mother Bank and all its branches" resulted naturally enough in an overissue of bank notes in the South and West—the Cincinnati branch discounted $1,800,000, the Lexington (Ky.) branch $1,619,000 in July 1818—while specie was drained away from the Eastern and Northern branches.[20] Owing to its stock loan policy, the specie position of the bank had never been very strong; it was compelled to exchange part of its funded debt for specie, which it bought at an advance in Europe and sold at a loss in the United States.[21] As a result of all this mismanagement, Spanish silver dollars sold at a premium of 1½ per cent in October 1817; while in March 1818 they enjoyed a premium of 4 to 4¼ per cent in Boston and New York.[22]

But mismanagement became, at the branch bank at Baltimore, totally indistinguishable from fraud. This branch, like the city itself, was under the thumb of the great firm of Smith & Buchanan—Smith being that same Samuel Smith who had brought about the discomfort of Albert Gallatin in the United States Senate. James A. Buchanan did all the business for his Senatorial partner, was president of the branch bank, and was a director of the mother bank at Baltimore. For the first two years the discounts of this branch ranged from 5 to 12½ millions; the drafts on the other branches were invariably excessive; and the specie holdings, never very large, declined at one time to the exiguous sum of $26,714!

It was in June 1817 that Buchanan and his cashier, James W. McCulloch, began their career of depredation by purchasing 19,940 shares in different lots from D. A. Smith at advances of 19, 20, and 36. In December, they purchased 12,000 additional shares at 155. These purchases, which amounted to $4,451,376, were financed partly by the firm of Smith & Buchanan, partly by loans from the bank on a pledge of stock, and partly by advances to themselves upon no security at all. This did not, of course, escape notice; but Buchanan and McCulloch always replied (when questioned by their board) that they had authority from Philadelphia to make stock loans or (when challenged by outsiders) that their own board had given them permission to go ahead. Even in January 1819, when the bank stock declined to 107, they continued in a kind of delirium to borrow more and more. But they were ruined; and they barely survived Marshall's judgment in *McCulloch v. Maryland* before they threw in their hands. It was subsequently discovered that McCulloch had lent himself $84,000 that even Buchanan was unaware of; that the total of his unsecured indebtedness was $429,049.80; that the firm of Buchanan & Smith was unsecured for $344,212.43; and that even the first teller, Mr. J. S. La Renitrie, had dipped his hand into the till to the extent of $50,000.[28]

The strange anonymity of the law casts over even its most operative names a cloak of obscurity. The case of *Fletcher v. Peck*, for example, is a landmark in the history of Contract; but who was Fletcher and who Peck? The identities of Sturges and Crowninshield are of no interest at all to students of the law of bankruptcy, though their names are at least as immortal as the study of the law can make them. None but a close examiner of the past would care to resolve into their human elements those extraordinary fictions, Fairfax's Devisee and Hunter's Lessee; though here, if anywhere, the human relations between a land speculation and an august court of law are painfully evident. The greater the case, the less human the participants. Only on rare occasions does the spirit of irony—which is never out of place in a court—permit the layman the luxury of a smile. The character of J. W. McCulloch, if any, is quite irrelevant to the issues in *McCulloch v. Maryland;* yet—as if to remind us that even great Constitutional questions are not unconnected with the frailty of human nature—it is surely a remarkable coincidence that the forces of legal nationalism should have constellated themselves around such a name. For a brief moment, the peculating cashier was thrust into the forefront of the battle between the idea of nationalism and the doctrine of State Rights; and the Law, which had used him for its own mysterious purposes, did not prove ungrateful. By the existing laws, his malpractices were mere breaches of trust, not punishable by the criminal law. "This seems a dangerous inequality," thought Mr. Nicholas Biddle—he was writing to President Monroe—"in the punishments inflicted by our legislation. If, for instance, any person employed in the General Post Office embezzles or secretes the smallest amount of property confided to him he may be publicly whipped and imprisoned for ten years—whilst an officer of a Bank in which the revenue of the U.S. is deposited & in the profits of which the U.S. are so largely interested, may defraud the institution of millions & escape the criminal law of the United States."[24] Mr. Biddle, rather against his will, had just become a director of the Bank of the United States, and was soon to be its president, and under him the bank was to become, at any rate, respectable; though, oddly enough, it was none the less dangerous for that.

III

In the meantime, while Buchanan and McCulloch, still undetected, defrauded the branch bank at Baltimore, the directors at Philadelphia were growing alarmed; and even Mr. Jones was forced to ask himself whether his inflationary practices had been altogether sound. He could not help noticing that, while the branches in the West and South paid no attention to suggestions that they might diminish their business, the branches in the East and North had almost ceased to do any business at all. Bankers, speculators, and traders were drawing coin from the vaults of his institution by the simple process of buying its notes in return for state bank paper, presenting these notes for redemption, selling the specie thus acquired at an advance, and buying more notes. In July 1818 the bank's demand liabilities were $22,372,000, and the specie fund with which to meet them had shrunk to $2,357,000.[25] The obvious course was to curtail the issue of bank notes in the South and West; but the whole country was still engaged in the delicious game of overtrading, and Mr. Jones and his board at Philadelphia had no inclination to interfere with it. A large contraction did indeed occur as a result of Mr. Jones's orders; but it seems to have fallen chiefly on good business paper, and scarcely affected the immense sums of money loaned on stock pledges.[26] In August it was decreed that no branch office should receive any notes but its own, except in payments to the United States.[27] In October, a series of eight resolutions suggested every expedient except that of calling the Southern and Western branches to strict account; and though the whole object of the curtailment was to draw funds from those offices, and to summon the bank's capital back to the North and the East, the mother bank continued to purchase and collect drafts on the South and West.[28] In this way, the great curtailment fell on the East, where it was least wanted, and the branches to the South and West continued to expand their business, where they tied up the bank's capital in notes and bills constantly renewed. After December 1818 the bank could obtain no more specie; and had already lost huge sums in buying and importing it.[29]

Thus a curtailment of some seven million dollars had resulted in the prostration of the branch offices in the East and North, and the capital of the bank had been shifted to the South and the West. In October 1818 specie was at 6½ to 7 per cent advance in Boston, and 7 per cent in New York; and panic was very close.[30] For a little while longer, the great land speculation in the South and West maintained the fiction of prosperity.[31] Finally, the government demanded two million dollars of its deposits in specie in order to make a payment in redemption of Louisiana Purchase stock. The bank, searching desperately for some expedient, managed to furnish bills on London in lieu of specie; but this was Mr. Jones's last effort.[32] In January, cotton began its downward plunge; and in January Mr. Jones resigned. The country, by this time, had realized that the bank was no longer in any position to support a land boom, and the popular wrath was rising against it. Such was the state of affairs when Chief Justice Marshall pronounced his judgment in *McCulloch v. Maryland.*

IV

When the Bank of the United States threw in its lot with the speculators, and assisted the country in the business of overtrading itself into bankruptcy, it appears in retrospect merely to have been the superficial symptom of a deep-seated malady. "If we had mines as rich as Potosi," said William Gouge—an authority who cannot be disregarded—"and paper should be issued in excess, we should not be able to retain in the country even that small amount of silver which is necessary to keep Bank notes convertible." [33] As Jefferson put it, the land bubble was a "paper bubble." [34] A country immensely rich in land, but without the capital to develop it, is in danger of sinking into an agrarian apathy, which is the worst of all apathies. But its efforts to create capital may be scarcely less dangerous. If trading had been restricted from the beginning, through a judicious control of the state banks by the national bank, there would have been, it is true, no Panic of 1819; but such a hypothesis is inadmissible. The state banks were beyond control. Americans were engaged in an effort to modify their environment; and, situated as they were, their effort took the form of a land speculation—not merely in 1819, but again and again in their history. From 1815 on, banks multiplied, credit gushed from the printing presses, prices rose, property appreciated: the whole economy was based on paper. A young and vigorous nation cannot escape from overconfidence, greed, and acquisitiveness: they are the diseases of youth, like measles and chicken pox. They generate their favors and deliriums; and after they have struck, they leave the patient with a most disagreeable appearance, spotted over with fraud and corruption, and deeply sunk in debt.

From a world point of view, the advancing West was scarcely within the pale of civilization: and it was perhaps natural that it should solve old problems in fantastic ways. All that was necessary to start a bank, said Hezekiah Niles, was plates, presses, and paper; "a church, a tavern, a blacksmith's shop" was a suitable site.[35] Some of these banks were chartered, some were not; and the state of the former was only a little the more elevated. Charters were obtained from the state legislatures with appalling ease, and their few regulations were easily disregarded: for the local banker was a skillful and persistent lobbyist, and state legislators, strange to say, were not incorruptible. "Few, if any, lawmaking bodies of the States were without officers, directors, or agents of local banks among their membership." [36] Moreover the influence of state banks, even the most respectable of them, was invariably bad: for they assumed that *all* lawmakers had their price, even when they hadn't.[37]

The increase of banks throughout the nation was phenomenal. In 1818 there were at least 392 chartered banks; while the number of unchartered banks, of towns, villages, business houses and individuals issuing paper money, is beyond knowledge. The issuing and borrowing of huge masses of paper money—the eagerness of the country to plunge itself into the vortex of debt—this was the real malady. Its origins lay in a healthy confidence in the future of the country, and it was therefore not incurable: its symptoms were a feverish belief in the price of export staples, followed by a delirium of speculation. The debt to the government for public lands stood at three million dollars in 1815; had increased to nearly seventeen million dollars in 1818; and in 1819 stood at twenty-two million dollars.[38] These figures are at once a measure of growth and a fever chart. But debtors are also voters; and if the national government had been the only creditor, an arrangement could have been made—and, in fact, was made—through a readjustment of the land laws. But the figures were surrounded and interpenetrated by a huge and less malleable debt: debts by individuals to their neighbors, to merchants, to banks; debts among banks unregulated by any sensible credit system; debts expressing themselves in a circulating medium that might have occasioned some surprise even among the inmates of a lunatic asylum. The efforts of local banks to get their paper into circulation were often peculiar, and not infrequently fraudulent. Thus there were banks, with almost no deposits, which placed an infinitesimal sum of specie with a distant bank for the "redemption" of their worthless paper, advertised this fact widely in the neighborhood until the paper rose to par, and then made a special issue, signed with ink of a strange color, which the distant bank was instructed not to redeem upon any terms. Other banks made large accommodations to individual borrowers on the condition that these borrowers were to keep the notes in circulation for a specified time; or lent freely upon the understanding that the debt, when it fell due, should be paid in the notes of other and sounder banks, which the unfortunate borrower was obliged to purchase at a premium from the very institution which had lent him the money.[39] The fiction that bank paper was convertible into specie on demand was feebly supported by the requirement that chartered banks should keep a certain amount of specie in their vaults; and a fixed sum of specie had been known to travel through the forests from bank to bank, resting in each vault in turn just long enough to satisfy the inspector, and then flitting on again. The classic example of this occurred long after the Panic of 1819, but it contains the essence of such transactions. In 1828, the Sutton Bank of Massachusetts was incorporated under an Act that required it to do no business until the capital subscribed and actually paid in, and existing in gold and silver in the vaults, amounted to fifty thousand dollars. On September 27, the day on which three commissioners were to examine the money in the vaults and ascertain that it had been paid in by the stockholders, the Sutton Bank borrowed, on a deposit of fifty-one thousand dollars in bills of the City Bank of Boston, the sum of fifty thousand dollars in specie, for one day only. The commissioners duly examined the specie, received the directors' sworn statement that it represented a first installment paid by the stockholders on their shares, and went their way. The bills and specie were then re-exchanged—the whole business being accomplished in an hour, and all of it within the walls of the City Bank.[40]

Generally speaking, the banks were soundest in New England, less sound in the middle Atlantic States, shaky in the South Atlantic States, and weird to the point of madness in the West and the Southwest, the areas where speculation was naturally most active. Like the fountains in a carnival city, the banks flung up their delusive paper; and the paper choked the very channels that should have carried it off. In October 1818 the notes of the local banks of Cincinnati were "mere waste paper" outside the city.[41] In September of that year, Hezekiah Niles complained that two thirds of the bank bills sent to him in payment for his *Register* could not be passed for money.[42] Local issues, while they dominated their immediate neighborhood by fraud and indeed by violence, were of little value beyond it; and business between district and district, still more between state and state, was hampered at every turn by ruinous fluctuations in the rate of exchange. A man scarcely knew from day to day what the paper he received was worth, or if it was worth anything at all. "I passed away my 20 dollar note of the rotten bank of Harmony, Pennsylvania, for five dollars only," wrote William Faux, at Vincennes, in 1818.[43] At almost the same time the Bank of Vincennes was reduced to the desperate expedient of issuing notes, payable at its branch at Vevay, and inscribed—in print so minuscule that only the most determined eye could have detected it—with the legend "nine months after date." [44] In August 1819, when the panic was at its height in Baltimore, the notes of the District of Columbia were often at 60 per cent discount, the notes of Maryland at anywhere from 1 to 40 per cent, of Virginia from 1½ to 25 per cent, of the Ohio banks from 10 to 50 per cent, and of Indiana, Illinois, and Missouri from 15 to 60 per cent.[45] The exchanges were, of course, thrown into further disorder by the activities of counterfeiters, who presumably enjoyed their most spectacular successes during the spring of 1818, when the thermometer of speculation registered its most frenzied ascent. At any rate, Mr. Niles declared in August that "the notes of at least ONE HUNDRED banks in the United States are counterfeited." [46] The counterfeiters might well have replied that their enterprise differed not at all from that of the wildcat bankers, who industriously emitted the notes of purely imaginary institutions; or they might have retorted, in the words of Warren Hastings, that considering their opportunities they were astonished at their moderation. But, indeed, with money so cheap, counterfeiting was hardly worth while.

The ultimate loser in all this was, of course, the man at the bottom of the chain of debt. We cannot say exactly who he was; in the West, during a land boom, the features of the shark, the speculator, and the honest investor were singularly blended together; but it is not unsafe to assume that the chief burden was borne by those farmers who believed that their loans would be renewed over and over again. This was a Western custom—perhaps not a very sound one—but adapted to the needs of "a large population, with the knowledge, the intelligence and the habits which belong to civilized life, amply supplied with the means of subsistence, but without any other active capital, but agricultural products." [47] The contraction instituted by Mr. Jones was bad enough: it passed from the United States Bank to the state banks, and from the state banks to the merchant, the factor, and the farmer; but the contraction of Mr. Jones's successor, Langdon Cheves, was infinitely worse. We need not follow in all their details the steps Mr. Cheves took to rescue the bank. He became president in March 1819—on March 6, the very day of the Chief Justice's judgment—and he immediately ordered the branch offices to the South and West to issue no more notes, while at the same time he ceased to purchase and collect exchange on the South and West. [48] He decreed that the curtailment instituted by Mr. Jones should continue; he asked permission to pay debentures in the same money in which the duties were paid; and he borrowed two million dollars from Europe. [49] When he assumed control, the bank was, he said, "a ship without a rudder or sails or masts, on short allowance of provisions and water, on a stormy sea and far from land." [50] Within seventy days the storm was weathered and the vessel shipshape: so Mr. Cheves afterwards declared with pardonable pride. [51] Or, as William Gouge put it with equal succinctness, "The Bank was saved, and the people were ruined." [52]

Now, indeed, after the delirium, came what seemed to many the very trance of death. Trade stagnated; the price of staples swooned downward; real property depreciated and its rents or profits vanished; merchants, even the most reputable, were ruined; and in the larger cities, unemployment spread like a plague. [53] In Kentucky, it was said that "a deeper gloom hangs over us than was ever witnessed by the oldest man. The last war was sunshine compared to these times." [54] At Baltimore, rents declined from 40 to 50 per cent. [55] A wharf and several storehouses in Alexandria, Virginia, which had once sold for $17,000, brought only $1,250 at auction in 1820. [56] Mr. Cheves, himself, always declared that he had not ordered a contraction, though obviously this is just what he had ordered. The United States Bank found itself the owner of a large part of Cincinnati—hotels, coffee-houses, warehouses, stores, stables, iron foundries, residences, vacant lots. [57] "All the flourishing cities of the West," said Thomas Hart Benton, "are mortgaged to this money power. They may be devoured by it at any moment." Later on, he was to remember it as "the engrossing proprietor of whole towns." [58] Throughout the land, it was familiarly known as The Monster.

Mr. Cheves was an upright man, who had nothing to gain from the operations of the bank—indeed, he had reduced his own salary from seven to six thousand dollars a year. [59] His predecessor, though considerably less scrupulous, was considered a man of integrity. [60] Yet both had been—unconsciously and no doubt inevitably—the living symbols of the usurious instinct. Credit was freely extended, under Mr. Jones, when it was not needed; and sternly withdrawn, under Mr. Cheves, when it was. The agrarian debtor, caught between falling prices and heavy fixed charges, was obliged to surrender his property because he was denied any opportunity of meeting his obligations. Then credit became easier; property appreciated; and the bank, under Mr. Cheves's successor, recovered and more than recovered its original investment.

The bank, therefore, lay like a wizard at the very heart of chaos; but, like a wizard, it had only exploited chaos: it had not created it. Did the fault lie with the state banks, or with the people who had been seduced by them? Or should one say that the very land greed that had once forced the United States into a war with Great Britain and had so complicated the politics of Florida had now reduced the people to bankruptcy? Moderate men declared that the only solution was patience, repentence, and economy; that the nation had been taught a lesson it would have to ponder in sackcloth and in ashes. The President himself appeared to be gently attached to this school of thought. In his Annual Message of November 14, 1820, he said: "I cannot regard the pressures to which I have adverted otherwise than in the light of mild and instructive admonitions." [61] Instructive they were; but the mildness of admonitions that took the form of corn at ten cents and wheat at twenty cents a bushel might have seemed, to the farmers in the West, open to some question.[62]

Theorists who went into the problem a little more deeply almost unanimously reached the conclusion that the trouble lay with banks of issue. They made a distinction between banks of discount and deposit, and banks that issued notes to circulate among the people as money. Jefferson favored the former, and abhorred the latter.[63] Jeffersonians in general, when they attacked "banking," referred only to the private issue of paper currency; and when, like the great William Gouge, they demanded a "hard money" currency, they did not lay any ban upon bank drafts and bills of exchange.[64] They did not, it would seem, always realize that bank deposits were in themselves currency, since they rarely distinguished between deposits created by the banker in the process of discounting and deposits that arose from the actual lodging of cash in the bank.[65]

And so it came about that the Bank of the United States was the focus of many different assaults. The hard-money theorists were convinced that it was the graven image of the demon of paper money—a private institution with a semi-official status. The worker of the East hated it because it was a bank of issue, and he suffered as much as anyone from banks of issue, since his wages were so often paid him in depreciated paper money. The private banking interests—particularly in New York—were jealous of its power. In the West and Southwest, it was execrated because it restrained the local banks from issuing cheap money. It had its defenders—the legislature of South Carolina, oddly enough, was among them—and, as credit became easier, it was to find friends in unexpected places. But in 1819 it was the scapegoat for all the banks of issue.

The Western states attempted to defeat Mr. Cheves's contraction with stay laws and replevin laws, which have been called "pernicious." [66] The word is rather a shocking one. The farmers and merchants who assembled in the state legislatures were not economists. They lived on the far edge of the world, where democracy and nationalism went hand in hand, and where the debtor was also the creator. It was the debtor who fought the wilderness, who planted the crops, who was turning the great American valley into a region of incomparable fertility and promise. In the West, the debtor was the future. It would have been a grim reflection upon the frontier if—at a time when its most characteristic citizens lay prostrate before the banking interests of the East—some effort, however frenzied and futile, had not been made to protect them. It was in the West, particularly, and particularly from 1819 on, that the various elements of American life seemed to be in solution, ready to form new combinations.

V

In Marshall's judgment in the case of *McCulloch v. Maryland* there were two very different influences at work. On the one hand, the Chief Justice had opposed a legal nationalism to the military nationalism of General Jackson. He had declared, in his resounding if slightly redundant prose, that the national government was an entity to be respected. No longer might generals disappear into the wilderness in a spirit of unmitigated derring-do; nor could the government send them there with a tacit understanding that they were not to obey their orders. Whether generals or governments would respect this implied doctrine was, of course, quite another question. But more could be deduced from Marshall's great judgment. If Congress could charter a bank, could it not also appropriate and spend money upon roads and canals? Could it not raise a tariff wall for protective purposes? Could it not—might it not—in the end emancipate a slave? Marshall's views on slavery were, after all, far more orthodox than his nationalism. In brief, Marshall saw all around him the evidences of chaos and the beginnings of disunion; and he sought to impose upon this vital disturbance the calm and forbidding image of order. He was less a judge than a statesman.

On the other hand, his great decision was—there was no denying it—a decision in favor of Mr. Jones's bank. It sought to rescue from the hands of democracy an institution theoretically pure and implacable, and practically surrounded by a numerous assemblage of sharks, jobbers, and confidence men. It seemed to bind the debtor and the farmer more securely in their chains; it appeared to drop a blessing upon the avarice of Eastern finance.

The state of Ohio, like many other states,[67] had made provisions to prevent the establishment within her borders of any bank chartered outside the state; and Ohio defied the Chief Justice. On September 17, 1819, the state auditor, Mr. Osborn, instructed his agents to invade the Chillicothe branch of the Bank of the United States. They did so. They leaped the counter, seized the vault, and forcibly collected a tax of fifty thousand dollars, which they carried off in a wagon. For this athletic performance they were arrested by a deputy marshal on a *capias* for a trespass *vi et armis;* and were held in prison until January 1820, when a circuit court ordered their release on a technicality. It was not until February 1824 that the case was finally argued before the Supreme Court, which definitely affirmed a circuit court decision that the money seized at Chillicothe should be returned. Among the counsel for the bank on that occasion were Mr. Daniel Webster and Mr. Henry Clay.[68]

The judgment against Ohio, coming after the judgment against Maryland, saved the bank from being taxed out of existence by the individual states, and completed the triumph of the nationalist Chief Justice.

VI

It was not in state actions, however, threatening though they were, that the most formidable attack upon Marshall was to be delivered. In 1820, there appeared a little book called *Construction Construed, and Constitutions Vindicated*, by John Taylor of Caroline, several chapters of which attacked the Chief Justice without naming him, and subjected the Court's judgment in *McCulloch v. Maryland* to the full battery of Virginian Republicanism. John Taylor was one of the great men of his time; one of the first of a long line of American statesmen who flourished only in opposition. Indeed, it might be said of John Taylor that he regarded all government as evil, and that much that is tortuous in his writing is due to this prejudice, which he honestly deplored. The most complex of his arguments are often arguments against himself, in which he seeks—and seeks in vain—to raise his prejudice into a system. The charm of all his reasoning lies in the fact that no system ever emerged from it—that it produced, in prose at once dogged and felicitous, only the landscape of a dream.

John Taylor was one of the greatest agricultural reformers of his day. His plantation at Hazlewood, in Caroline County, Virginia, was famous for its noble cedar hedges, its verdant fields, its healthy crops.[69] His book *Arator* was no less famous in its time. It was founded upon a dislike of tobacco, overseers, and the three-shift system (corn, wheat, pasture), and a belief in deep and horizontal plowing to check erosion, and the supreme virtue of vegetable manures.[70] It advocated a system of "enclosure," or the exclusion of all stock from arable and grass land, and expressed an enthusiasm for Indian corn, which most farmers despised in those days.[71] *Arator* tells of its author's conviction that agriculture is the source of the highest human happiness—"a constant rotation," said Taylor, in one of his noblest phrases, "of hope and fruition." [72] One cannot read such language without being reminded of the great Virgilian *O fortunatos;* but Taylor, like Virgil, was fighting for a lost cause. *Arator* was one of the early bibles of soil conservation; and the economy of the Southern planter was such that it almost obliged him to exhaust his soil.[73]

Taylor's four-course system—corn, wheat, two years of rest without grazing—was gradually abandoned; and *Arator*, as a treatise on agricultural reform, has perhaps only an antiquarian interest. But it was far more than a book on agricultural reform. "There is a spice of fanaticism in my nature," he said, "upon two subjects—agriculture and republicanism." [74] Every now and again in *Arator*—forgetful alike of horizontal plowing, enclosure, the four-course system, and vegetable manure—he turns to rail against the farmer's chief enemy, the "legal faction of capitalists." "This legal faction of capitalists," he writes, in one of his most famous passages, "far from being satisfied with the tythe claimed by the old hierarchy will, in the case of the mechanics, soon appropriate the whole of their labour to its use, beyond a bare subsistence; though in the case of the farmers, it has yet only gotten about four times as much of theirs as was extorted by the odious, oppressive, and fraudulent tythe system. We know death very well when killing with one sythe, but mistake him for a deity because he is killing with four." [75] Here, in the tortured brilliance of this suggestive prose, there emerges Taylor's lifelong foe—the "paper" or money interest—the aristocracy of "artificial property" against which a democracy founded upon "natural" private property must forever defend itself. Wealth, like suffrage, must be distributed widely to sustain a republic: agriculture distributes wealth; but a financial aristocracy appropriates it.

Taylor was held in deep and loving respect by his contemporaries. He had fought in the Revolutionary War, and, under Lafayette, had resisted the Hessian raids in Gloucester County.[76] He had already served twice in the United States Senate, and was to serve a third time. Tall, slender, sandy-haired, and dressed in beautiful brown clothes of an ancient cut, he carried all before him in Washington. "I can hardly figure to myself," wrote Thomas Hart Benton, "the ideal of a republican statesman more perfect and complete than he was in reality." When he walked the streets with Senator Nathaniel Macon, a man fully as noble in character as himself, the pair reminded observers of "two Grecian sages . . . showing that regard for each other which every one felt for them both." [77]

Like many orthodox Republicans, Taylor was not happy near the seats of power. He did not believe in the party system. "I do not recollect in all history," he told Monroe, "a single instance of an administration party being republican." [78] Though he venerated Jefferson—"the old Sachem of our tribe"—he believed that the Virginia Dynasty had been a progressive abandonment of Virginian principle. Did not power corrupt? And what difference was there between Republicans in power and Federalists in power? "Swift's exposition of the couplet, 'Libertas et natale solum. Fine words! I wonder where you stole 'em.' applies very well to the words 'republican and federal' when united with avarice and ambition." [79] As he grew older, he became more and more disillusioned with the national parties. Neither, he said, had overturned un-Constitutional precedents, though they had often charged each other with creating them; and both had waved the flags of party majority before the eyes of the country, which the country had followed into a state of national distress. The Federalists perpetrated the Alien and Sedition Laws; but the Republicans chartered the Second Bank of the United States. "If a man had successively married two wives, one called Lucretia, and the other Penelope; and should believe in their chastity, after having seen both in bed with several gallants of the worst characters, should we call him a blind cully, or an acute observer?" [80]

John Taylor could not be happy in Washington. It was in his own home, among his own fields, near the peaceful Rappahannock, that he had leisure to meditate, to write and to rewrite, to pursue his mazelike thought to its center, and then to find "upon going back a multitude of angles and windings to be streightened." [81] His great *Inquiry into the Principles and Policy of the Government of the United States*, begun in 1799, finished in 1809, and published in 1814, was calculated to baffle even his warmest admirers. Like a master of classical siegecraft, Taylor drew the object of his attack slowly and meticulously into the embrace of his parallels and trenches. He bombarded it with explosive metaphors, with fiery conceits, with hard iron phrases. It is extraordinary prose, hiding its almost painful originality under an appearance of prolixity, and advancing all the time, in a peculiarly relentless manner, towards the inevitable conclusion. It is prose in the high style; for though Taylor hated, he hated like a gentleman; and his most deadly attacks are conducted with an air of eccentric punctilio. "If a president is not enabled to terrify, but only to bribe or influence a legislature into his measures, what would be the difference? That between having one's wife ravished or seduced. Are not men safer against the first evil, and more frequently rendered miserable by the second?" [82]

His *Inquiry* was the evangel of agrarian liberalism and the doctrine of State Rights; and it remains to this day the most searching indictment of the Hamiltonian system. "The course of reasoning pursued in this essay," he said in his chapter on Banking, "results in the definition that *a transfer of property by law, is aristocracy, and that aristocracy is a transfer of property by law*." [83] This definition lies at the heart of all his attacks upon paper money, the funding system, legislative patronage, unjust pensions, exclusive privilege: it is the essence of his distinction between "artificial" private property and "natural" private property. Yet he was far happier—it is often the case with liberal thought—in criticism than in defense. He was devastating in his analysis of the Anglican nature of Hamilton's finance. He perceived that the Hamiltonian system, left to itself, would end in a redistribution of property from above. "Security to private property" were, he said, fine words used to decoy, and "invasion of private property" ugly words used to affright. "The invader, of course, devoutly uses the first phrase, and indignantly applies the second to those who oppose him." [84] But what would he substitute for this pernicious system, once it had been removed—for he wished to remove it all, every last vestige, upon the Voltairian principle of *écrasez l'infâme?* His own program is singularly vague and even contradictory. He cannot tell us exactly what he conceives to be the relation between government and society; his distinction between national rights of self-government and self-defense and the natural rights of the individual is never explained, and perhaps cannot be; nor can we tell precisely what he means by "national." He reduces all government "to the two classes of those founded in good, and those founded in evil moral principles." [85] In the end, this amounts to private property justly acquired and private property unjustly acquired. But there is much danger in applying ethical phrases to economic arguments; the phrases are apt to be double-edged—to fight, as it were, on both sides. Private property that maintained itself by turning the slave into three fifths of a man was fully as weird and artificial a device as private property created by the paper-money "barons" of the banks of issue.

Taylor's arguments are fascinating and must be read in full. If one might presume to reduce them to a sentence it is this: His ideal society was a society of self-interest modified by self-restraint. As he examines with his unremitting intensity the various evils of the Hamiltonian system, there gradually emerges from behind his arguments the glimmering, twilit world in which he believed. It is a world of small freeholding farmers, honest merchants, and independent craftsmen—a world that never existed. Before its portals stands a Jeffersonian angel with a flaming sword, for John Taylor—it is the weakness of all Jeffersonians—was unable to invent a political philosophy including men who owned no property at all. It was therefore necessary for him to banish such men from his earthly paradise—the wage-earner must go along with the capitalist. He saw, as clearly as Calhoun did, that an unrestricted capitalism would produce an unrestricted wage-slavery. His answer was, in effect, *écrasez l'infâme*. Abolish the whole thing. In order to survive, in short, one must cancel the nineteenth century.

Taylor was too wise a man to suppose that he could summon his world into existence by chanting over and over again the operative words "natural private property." He did not believe—as his great contemporary, Robert Owen, believed—that things existed because one *said* that they did. His value for us, and it would seem for himself, was the value of protest. He advocated what today we might call the fifth freedom, the freedom to doubt, without which there may be a contented society but there cannot be a free one. Thomas Jefferson called him "the voice of one crying in the wilderness." [86] Yet Jefferson, had he completed this quotation, might well have asked himself for whom John Taylor was preparing the way. Was he not a forerunner who succeeded the Messiah, a prophet who foretold the past?

VII

Construction Construed was the most forceful of Taylor's writings because it involved the most people. Every debtor believed himself to be the enemy of the Second Bank of the United States; nor was any figure more generally detested in 1819 than John Marshall. Taylor's "democratick republic" was more republican than democratic; he was essentially a minority man, who spoke for a class of planters; now he spoke for the majority. In this remarkable pamphlet he restated with peculiar emphasis—perhaps in the happy conviction that he would obtain, for once, a wide hearing—his fundamental positions. He declared that the state and federal spheres of government were completely separate, that the federal government was the creature of the states, who were wiser and less dangerous, and that no federal department could have a veto over the laws of the states. He maintained in one of the most suggestive of his sentences that "the words of the Constitution are literally *imperious* in reserving to the states, for the *publick good* also, a right of taxation subject only to a positive limitation. The means by which the states may provide for raising a revenue, being expressly bestowed by the people, are surely as sacred, and as constitutional, and as likely to advance the publick good, as any conflicting conjectural means, which can be imagined by congress." [87] Here we have, as clearly as we have it anywhere, Taylor's curious ability to construe the Constitution loosely in terms of its basic philosophy, and strictly in the light of its actual Federalist origin.[88] The "people" became synonymous with the "states," and could be defined only as the "people of each state," a very useful definition for an agrarian who believed that national banks, protective tariffs, and internal improvements were little better than forms of organized theft, which must be defeated in the state legislatures if they were to be defeated at all. Hence he was truly horrified by Marshall's words "the Government of the Union is the government of all, it represents all, and acts for all." To him the United States was an association of separate "nations." The Constitution was powerful, it was imperious, only in a negative sense; it could abridge, it could not increase, the power of the central government. Taylor went even further. "May not a power in the Federal Government to destroy state laws, defeat and render useless, the state power to create laws." [89] Clearly, the state power to create laws was, to Taylor's way of thinking, a power to restrict the operations of the federal government; just as the "natural" right of self-preservation, which he mentions over and over again in his writings, was the right of each individual state to nullify federal laws when it found them oppressive or believed them to be unconstitutional.

In his direct attack upon John Marshall, Taylor addressed himself to Marshall's argument that the Bank of the United States could not be taxed because it was the fiscal agent of the general government. He contended that Congress and the states had a concurrent right of taxation—the single exception being the taxation of imports and exports—and that "congress in virtue of this concurrent right, can inflict no tax, to which the same right in the states does not extend." [90] The argument was unanswerable; or rather, it could be answered only by Marshall's daring assertion that the "same paramount character" that expressly restrains the states from taxing imports and exports may also forbid them, if necessary, to tax anything else.[91] Taylor described this as "verbalizing." "The art of verbalizing single words," he said of Marshall's interpretation, "into a different system, may render the constitution as unintelligible, as a single word would be made by a syllabick dislocation, or a jumble of its letters." [92] If we read Marshall's verdict and then the chapters in *Construction Construed* which attack it, we can see that no amount of argument could ever bridge the abyss that yawned between them.

This was partly, but not wholly, due to the fact that Taylor believed the Bank of the United States to be the creature of a moneyed aristocracy. When Marshall declared that "the power of creating a corporation is one appertaining to sovereignty," Taylor replied that "sovereignty" nowhere appears in the Constitution, and that corporation is an "innately despotick" word.[93]

Marshall said that if the end was within the scope of the Constitution, all means consistent with the letter and spirit of the Constitution are Constitutional too.[94] Taylor replied—as Madison had replied before him—that this was to violate the powers reserved to the states by exalting the means above the ends. "Let us look at a sample of this question," he wrote.

> *"Powers bestowed by the constitution.   Powers claimed as means.*
>
> | Taxation | Incorporating banks |
> | War | Making roads |
> | Appropriating money | Giving it away |
> | Regulating trade | Granting monopolies |
> | Admitting new states | Prescribing state constitutions |
>
> In one column we find objects of general concern to the states: in the other, said to be their legitimate progeny, objects merely personal or local. Now I contend, that the progeny of the parent powers ought to be sui generis." [95]

These arguments were as decisive as the school of State Rights could make them. They pointed out the dangerously close affinity between the nationalist and the capitalist in Marshall's doctrine. But they were arguments in defense of an imaginary world which either defies inspection or, where it impinges upon reality, horrifies the inspector.

VIII

John Taylor declared that there never could be an agricultural aristocracy because the quantity of cheap land and the extent of the country prevented it.[96] His economic thought oddly stopped short at, or circumvented, political facts. The county court system of his own Virginia expressly created an agricultural aristocracy; and this system had its counterparts in other Southern states. Now the agricultural aristocracy of Virginia was a slave-holding aristocracy, and it is not surprising that *Construction Construed* should end with a defense of slavery; that it should declare the slave to be private property not subject to governmental control; and that it should assert, with a daring fully equal to John Marshall's, that when private property is threatened both states and individuals have a natural right of self-defense which is anterior to all political power.[97] Taylor had already maintained that stock-slavery, or slavery to banks, was infinitely worse than chattel slavery, for stock-slavery was "a slavery in which the sufferer is ignorant of his tyrant, and the tyrant is remorseless, because he is unconscious of his crime," whereas in chattel slavery the master is benevolent towards his slave.[98] Taylor was a kind master, and doubtless created the slave-holder in his own image; but this does not excuse his casuistry. He once explained that authority is corrupted by a subjection to authority, "that the influence of Alexander must have operated as strongly upon Aristotle in favor of monarchy, as that of a wealthy and powerful banking aristocracy all around him, undoubtedly did upon Adam Smith." [99] But could not the natural slavery that Taylor implicitly summons into being exercise also its corrupting influence? Might not this truly good man have been *esclave de ses esclaves?* Putting the moral issues aside, one cannot but be horrified at the thought that this redoubtable foe of consolidation in one form should have been quite blind to it in another. Far to the south and southwest the farmer whom Taylor loved and lauded was being driven into the hills and wastes by the very slave power which Taylor defended.

John Taylor was no seer; and his political philosophy, with all its virtues, was a regressive affair: irrevocably shutting doors; opening none. His *Construction Construed*, indeed, had an historical effect one usually associates rather with satire than with philosophy. It inscribed, with a flourish, the word Finis. It announced the end of the Era of Good Feelings.

3

THE POLITICS OF SLAVERY:
1819-1821

CHAPTER ONE

The South

D URING the debates in the House of Representatives concerning the
actions of General Jackson in Florida, one of the most eloquent defenders of the General had been James Tallmadge, Jr., of New York. He
was not then a well man. "He had had," said his father, " a constant diarear
on him all the time he is in Washington . . . until he is so feeble that it
is with the utmost difficulty for him to get threw speaking." [1] His speech
of January 22—one of the most lucid, said the gratified Jackson, ever to be
heard on the floor—was followed by a complete prostration.[2] "I have given
him a little syrup," his wife wrote that evening, "and bathed his breast and
shoulders with brandy, & he is now trying to get a little sleep." [3] A few
days later, his small son died, one of the many little victims of the city of
Washington; his wife retired to Poughkeepsie; and it was a distraught
man who arose on February 13, 1819, to propose an amendment to the
Missouri Enabling Bill which has carned him his small but enviable place in
the history of his times.

"*Provided*," this amendment ran, "That the further introduction of
slavery or involuntary servitude be prohibited, except for the punishment
of crimes whereof the party shall have been duly convicted: and that all
children born within the said State [of Missouri] after the admission thereof
into the Union shall be free, but may be held to service until the age of
twenty-five years." [4]

Of the motives of James Tallmadge in offering this amendment, or of
the maneuvers that preceded it, nothing is known. He was supposed to be
attached to the Clintonian group in New York politics; but this attachment
he subsequently disclaimed; and De Witt Clinton, though distantly related
to the Tallmadges, never showed any fondness for them.[5] If the amendment had had its origin in the ambitions of New York party leaders, it is

clear that Mr. Tallmadge would not have been permitted to introduce it. He seems always to have baffled and exasperated his contemporaries. He was a man of fine presence; an able lawyer, a Republican of conveniently elastic principles, and not averse (as what is left of his correspondence shows) to the picking up of political plums; but these qualities, which should have made him quite at home in the scramble of New York politics, were offset by a curious inability to play the game with any faction. "Politically eccentric and wrong-headed," declared Jabez D. Hammond, the historian of New York, who believed that Tallmadge's real ambition was to form his own party. "The truth is," it was said of him in 1828, "that in regard to political operations Tallmadge is one of nature's *bad bargains*." [6] To be considered one of nature's bad bargains in relation to New York politics was, on the whole, more a matter of praise than of blame: and it may be that when James Tallmadge opposed the admission of Missouri as a slave state, he did so because he abominated slavery and for no other reason.

The amendment, however, was well suited to the political needs of the North and the East. They had never been reconciled to the clause in the first Article of the Constitution which made the Negro slave three-fifths of a man for the purpose of apportioning representatives; and they were now determined to prevent this apportionment from creeping across the Mississippi. The Panic of 1819 was just beginning to show that the economic foundations of the Union were far from sound; and the Tallmadge amendment, which questioned the soundness of its ethical foundations, was a political weapon of the most dangerous kind. When politics, economics, and ethics are all mixed together, the mixture may be confusing, and it is sure to be deadly. During the debate on the Tallmadge amendment, even the most fustian language had a prophetic ring. "You have kindled a fire," shouted Congressman Cobb of Georgia, in response to the arguments of Tallmadge, "which all the waters of the ocean cannot put out, which seas of blood can only extinguish." [7]

The amendment was passed in the House of Representatives by a strictly sectional vote of 87 to 76 (on its first part, prohibiting the further introduction of slavery) and 82 to 78 (on its second part, freeing all children born after the state's admission into the Union). In the Senate, the first part was stricken out by a vote of 31 to 7, and the second by one of 22 to 16; and the Bill, without the amendment, was returned to the House on March 2. The Fifteenth Congress had only two days more to live; the House refused to concur in the Senate's action; the Senate remained obdurate. And so, on March 4, 1819, the Missouri Enabling Bill was temporarily put to sleep. [8]

The paradox—the very complicated and difficult paradox—that slavery could have a legal existence in a land of free men was now, however, fully open to inspection. It would be too much to say that the country as a whole was willing to inspect it; the country as a whole was willing only to be surprised by it. Various Northern cities held meetings in which their citizens expressed themselves as being astonished and horrified at the thought that slavery could cross the Mississippi, though it had been doing so for many years.[9] Southern newspapers and pamphleteers seemed to be outraged by the suggestion that it could be prevented from ranging over the whole Louisiana Purchase.[10] During the framing of the Constitution, during the Burr conspiracy, during the War of 1812, the combination of political grievance on the one hand, and of the anomaly of slavery in a modern republic on the other, had threatened to burst into flame.[11] It had now fulfilled its threat: so much so that people soon began to ask themselves, not whether the fire could be extinguished, but whether it could be banked.

I

In its crudest form, the question raised by the Tallmadge Amendment was that of the control of the Mississippi Valley. Would such an amendment dissolve the old alliance between the free-soil Northwest and the slave-holding South? Here Missouri was little more than a symbol, a geographical ideogram. It could never become a great slave-holding state, because its southern lands were not favorable to cotton as a major crop; while hemp, to which its western soils were well suited, was already crying for protective tariffs. Hemp culture, however, was so disagreeable that it was considered especially appropriate to slave labor: hemp, therefore, was both an attraction and an excuse. Ever since the close of the War of 1812, Missouri's most characteristic immigrants had been slave-owners.[12]

This migration was of grave significance. In the first place, Missouri was a pioneering land, still largely uncleared; and, when cleared, more suited to diversified farming than to a one-crop system. Its manners retained all the innocence or savagery of the frontier; it was a common proverb that when one crossed the Mississippi one traveled beyond the Sabbath.[13] Its closest connections were still with the fur trade. It thrust itself towards the northwest, into distances so vague and along waters so unknown that sober people still declared that there was an active volcano near the sources of the Missouri.[14] Its borders were adjacent to free-soil Illinois and to slave-soil Kentucky and Tennessee. It was, in short, a challenge both to the idea of a democratic West and to the scarcely formulated notion of universal slavery.

It was certainly a matter of great importance to the South that slave-holders should move into this ambiguous Territory; and that the Territory, when it was transformed into a state, should be counted among the slave-holding sisterhood. The Southern states, in terms of population, were now in a minority.[15] Could the Tallmadge Amendment be the presage of an assault upon that strange clause in the Constitution which turned the South's million and a half slaves into nine hundred thousand men for the purpose of apportioning taxes and representatives? Southern politicians had some suspicions that this might be the case. Many years, it was true, would pass before the number of slaves in Missouri would make much impression upon the House of Representatives; but if Missouri were admitted as a slave-holding state, Missouri's legislature could be relied upon to elect proslavery Senators. The admission of Alabama and Maine to statehood being taken for granted, it was necessary for Missouri to be admitted with no restrictions upon slavery in order to maintain an equilibrium in the Senate.[16]

The migrating slave-owner, therefore, seemed to testify to Missouri's right to a slave representation in Congress; he was also the living pledge of an equally balanced Senate, and even of the sanctity of the three-fifths clause in the federal Constitution. As he moved across free Illinois towards the unimaginable West, he left a curious impression upon the casual observer. "I question," wrote Timothy Flint, "if the rich inhabitants of England, taking their summer excursion to Bath, are happier in their journey than these people. About nightfall, they come to a spring or branch, where there is water and wood. The pack of dogs sets up a cheerful baying. The cattle lie down and ruminate. The team is unharnessed. The huge wagons are covered, so that the roof completely excludes the rain. The cooking utensils are brought out. The blacks prepare a supper, which the toils of the day render delicious; and they talk over the adventures of the past day and the prospects of the next. Meanwhile they are going where there is nothing but buffaloes and deer to limit their range, even to the western sea. Their imaginations are highly excited. Said some of them to me, as they passed over the Mamelle prairie, the richest spot that I have ever seen; 'If this is so rich, what must Boon's Lick be?'"[17] Timothy Flint was a romantic soul, a disciple and worshiper of Chateaubriand, whom he pursued, *non passibus aequis*, into some of the longest and most tedious novels ever written. But Flint was a shrewd observer, in the sense at least that his observation ran coolly counter to his overheated imagination: and beneath the inane surface of this cheerful description there drifts and gathers the nightmare of the 1820's . . . the mingling of chattel slavery with the pioneering West. It was this abomination, and not the greater abomination of slavery itself, which shadowed and tainted the political arrangements of the Missouri Compromise.

In the ten states that, in 1819, might roughly be said to have constituted the South, the feeling towards slavery was very mixed.[18] Slavery was held to be an evil, though this opinion diminished through the 1820's, partly because those who held it were inclined to emigrate, partly because it was a burden too great, or too inconvenient, to be borne. Slavery was considered dangerous. Slavery was thought to be profitable. As the decade advanced, men began, with some hesitation, to formulate the proposition that slavery was a positive good.

The fear of slavery—that is, of servile rebellion—was classical; and it arose, as usual, rather from the conscience of the slave-holder than from the contumacy of the slave.[19] Since the passing of the colonial days there was not, after all, a great deal of evidence with which to support it. In 1800, it is true, when James Monroe was governor of Virginia, only a providential thunderstorm, of tropical intensity, had prevented some thousand slaves from advancing upon the city of Richmond with their scythes and clubs. "What has happened," said Monroe, "may occur again at any time." [20] It did not occur again. During the Embargo period, when the agrarian world was almost ruined; during the War of 1812, when the British came as emancipators—the South was peculiarly haunted by the ghost of this revolt, but the specter never materialized. It was in the imagination only that it glowered and strutted. That the Negro slave longed to be free was often denied but never doubted. The conditions of his servitude, however, made it quite impossible for him to organize his forces; and against him, as a revolutionary, there was opposed the sentiment not only of the South but of the whole country. None the less, only a few hundred miles of ocean separated the American slave from the example or contagion of Haiti and Santo Domingo. And so the fear increased, bearing a discernible ratio to the spread of the cotton crop and the natural increase of the slave. During the Missouri debates, it became articulate, and was heard on both sides of the question.

The idea that slavery was profitable had little to do with the question of whether slave labor or free labor was the less expensive. The idea had much to do with social standing, and its political corollaries, on the one hand, and with the forces of industrialism on the other. Nobody would deny that the invention of the cotton gin, which was patented in 1794, was one of the revolutionary events in American history. The gin made its appearance at an inopportune moment. After the War of Independence, it seemed for a while as if neither tobacco nor rice, neither indigo nor sugar, could support the institution of slavery. The Ordinance of 1787, which prohibited slavery in the Ohio country, but by implication threatened it everywhere, was not opposed even by slave-holding Congressmen. Slave-holders, indeed, clung to their slaves only because of the political and social status that attached itself to ownership. Then came the cotton gin, which at first ginned only fifty pounds of cotton a day—an exiguous amount, to be sure, but fifty times as much as a slave woman could do by hand. The ratio of fifty to one revitalized the institution of slavery, which seemed to be dying of sheer inanition.

It is unnecessary to inquire whether Eli Whitney deserves all the credit for the invention of the cotton gin, or whether some should be accorded to Hodgin Holmes, or even to Colonel A. O. Bull of Georgia. For even if there had been no Whitney, nor Holmes, nor even a Colonel A. O. Bull, it is certain that somebody would have produced a cotton gin in the last years of the eighteenth century. The gin was a logical response to the immense development of the British textile industry, which was hungry for cotton. It was a response, moreover, of the simplest kind—in its original form a cylinder fitted with wire teeth, drawing the seed cotton through a wire screen that separated seed from lint.[21] The gin, indeed, did not require—but it certainly excused and even sanctioned—the further accumulation of slaves. Within ten years of its appearance, the cotton crop had quadrupled itself.[22] Only one more development was necessary. The value of the slave remained uncertain, and slavery itself was still deplored as an unpleasant necessity thrust upon the slave-holder by fate, until "upland" or short-staple cotton began to supersede sea-island cotton as the great cash crop. It was not too expensive to cultivate, it was hardy, and (unlike sea-island cotton) it would grow over huge areas of the South. Before 1815, upland cotton was confined to the upper region of South Carolina and the eastern portion of central Georgia: after the peace of Ghent, it spilled over into Alabama, Mississippi, Louisiana; doubled itself within five years; and doubled itself again within another five.[23] Wherever it went, it carried slavery with it: for though it could be cultivated by the slaveless farmer, like the cotton gin it gave a sanction to the accumulation of slaves. And, just as the cotton gin was a logical, so upland cotton was a natural, response to the increased efficiency of British machines, binding the American Negro slave more and more securely to the gross chariot of British industrialism. This somber process had been going on almost unobserved—in Congress or out of it—except for certain Congressional bickerings over the almost neutral question of the external slave trade—until the Tallmadge Amendment called attention to it once and for all.

II

In a sense, the Tallmadge Amendment, with its train of town-meetings, pamphlets, editorials, and debates, summoned the South into being. No man could have said in 1819 what "the South" was; still less could one have spoken of a typical Southerner. Those who dwelt south of the Mason-Dixon line might have been said to have, perhaps, a kind of climatic fellowship. They had the same long hot summers, the violent storms and unpredictable droughts; their winters were always severe, their up-country rivers froze solid from bank to bank, and "at some time or other men froze to death" in every one of their states.[24] Such weather raised their ceilings and pro-liferated their piazzas and balconies; encouraged the growing of staple crops, even while the rains and heats defertilized the soil; and it slowed down the pace of their life. But no generalization could absorb their differences— at least, no generalization based upon climate. The Southern states were a patchwork of political and social distinctions: distinctions between old South and new Southwest, between small farmers and planters, between merchants and manufacturers. Valley warred with mountain, country with town, the Atlantic with the Gulf. There were border states like Virginia, Maryland, and Kentucky, whose cash crops were tobacco, wheat, and hemp, crops that sought a domestic market, and gave their cultivators a certain affinity with the states to the north. East and middle Tennessee and the northern section of North Carolina also belonged to this border region.[25] Below lay the cotton kingdom, which looked abroad for its market, and was almost neurotically swayed by the voice of Liverpool. This kingdom had its frontier states in Georgia, Alabama, and Mississippi, with their unassimilated Indian lands. Here the American savage and the Negro slave still met and touched.

There were regions beyond the reach and almost beyond the imagination of all but a few Americans, like the rice-swamps of South Carolina and Georgia—humid, malarial, moss-hung, interstitially sunlit, where gangs of Negroes painfully toiled beside the sluggish little tidal rivers. There were the sugar plantations of Louisiana, economically separatist because their owners demanded a protective tariff. Everywhere there were contradictions and incompatibilities. "Nature had ruled against the establishment of a single clearing house and control center for the South." [26] And yet all were loosely bound together—the Creole aristocrat of New Orleans, the liberal nationalist of South Carolina, the parvenu cotton-planter of Georgia, the hemp grower of Kentucky, the tobacco magnate of Virginia—all were bound together by the institution of slavery. The Tallmadge Amendment, like a powerful spell, conjured this loose bondage into a tightness and coherence it was never afterwards to lose.

III

The cotton kingdom, as it began its advance towards the southwest, carried with it traditions that had little to do with cotton: and it was these traditions that were threatened by even so oblique an attack upon slavery as the Tallmadge Amendment.

The doctrine of State Rights at its purest implied a belief in local government—that is to say, in very small self-governing communities. Thomas Jefferson always hoped that counties might be subdivided into wards, "little republics, with a warden at the head of each, for all those concerns which, being under the eye, they would better manage than the larger republics of the county or State." [27] Such a plan, he declared, was "the keystone of the arch of our government." But, somehow or other, and try as he might, he never could persuade his own state of Virginia to have anything to do with it. What could the matter be? Jefferson himself was in no doubt. He ascribed the resistance in Virginia to his plan to "the vicious constitution of our county courts (to whom the justice, the executive administration, the taxation, police, the military appointments of the county, and nearly all our daily concerns are confided) self-appointed, self-continued, holding their authorities for life." [28] In Kentucky, too, the justices of the peace held legislative, judicial, and executive sway over local affairs: here, also, they were self-perpetuating. The doctrine of State Rights, so flexible in Jefferson's mind, became rigid and "orthodox" under the influence of this system, which it was designed to protect. The justices of the peace were men of wealth and standing, great slave-owners or good friends of slavery; and although on the higher level of state government there were endless battles between farmer and planter, upland and tidewater, poor and rich, in the realm of the county the influence of the justices was paramount and pervasive.

In North Carolina and Tennessee the county court justices held office for life, but vacancies in their ranks were filled by the legislatures. Since the justices controlled the legislatures, their powers were not much disturbed by this arrangement. And so, in the states that bordered the cotton kingdom, whatever the outward appearance or profession might be, the inner structure was aristocratic.

In South Carolina, local affairs were in the hands of boards, the members of which (with the exception of the sheriffs and the commissioners of the poor) were chosen by the legislature, and usually for short terms of office. This concession to democracy was mitigated by the fact that the legislature of South Carolina—owing to a judicious apportionment of seats between the number of white inhabitants and the amount of taxes paid to the state—was under the control of wealthy men.[29] The cotton kingdom, of course, was already moving out from South Carolina and towards the southwest; and slavery, which was becoming inseparable from cotton, was therefore still seeking for an empire. Ahead of it there lay much virgin forest, or tangled swampy river bottom, or fertile Indian land to be cleared or appropriated. The cotton kingdom still had its frontier in Georgia and Alabama and Mississippi, where local affairs adapted themselves to frontier conditions, and remained in the hands of the people. This was also true of semiseparatist Louisiana.

The aristocratic tradition, none the less, was being carried out of the realms of wheat, hemp, and tobacco and into the new empire of cotton, even to its remotest frontiers. This was because the aristocratic tradition was a slaveholding tradition. No one can deny that in Virginia the opposition to slavery, all through the 1820's, was very strong: but it was powerless to exert its strength. It made little impression upon the General Assembly, which was dominated by the tidewater, and less upon the county court system. A hypertypical Virginian like John Randolph of Roanoke offers a good example of the attitude of the planters: he detested slavery, but he did everything in his power to maintain its Constitutional safeguards. He was a follower of Thomas Jefferson, or had been one so long as Mr. Jefferson's teachings suited his way of life, which was a strange transatlantic version of the way of an English Whig. When Jefferson's teachings ceased to accord with this way of life, by temporizing with the present, or even looking into the future, Mr. Randolph deserted them. "I am an aristocrat," he said, "I love liberty, I hate equality." [30] He did not bother to add that liberty meant liberty for the few.

John Taylor of Caroline, a greater Virginian than John Randolph, maintained that the agrarian South was not aristocratic. He would not admit that the plantation system was blindly following in the path of all new landed aristocracies by pushing the yeoman farmer away from the good land. He, too, and with more conviction than Randolph, sought to build its Constitutional defenses.

These men were, in all innocence, reflecting the dilemma of all the older slave states. They were already "selling" states: that is to say, they were already exporting their surplus slaves to the better markets of the Southwest. Between "selling" and "slave-breeding" there was not, really, very much difference. The static concept of slavery as a mark of social standing was yielding to the dynamic concept of slavery as something from which profit could be extracted. During the prosperous postwar years the average maximum price of a prime field in Virginia was $700, while in New Orleans it was $1,100.[31] This demand from the southwest did much to soften and corrupt antislavery thinking in the older slave states. Nowhere, in fact, was the royalty of upland cotton more evident than in its imperious call for surplus slaves. The older states exported, with their slaves, their aristocratic traditions; and the cotton kingdom, as it spread outwards, carried with it some of the social aggrandizement which had once attached itself to failing tobacco and vanishing indigo, and which was generously bestowed upon their owners by rice, sugar, and sea-island cotton.

IV

As the cotton kingdom grew older and consolidated, its large holdings in land or slaves falling into fewer and fewer hands, it did not discourage the myth that the Southern aristocrat was, in some way or other, a man of gentle descent. Or if not a descendant he was a representative, almost a reincarnation, of the English Cavaliers—the gentlemen who lost their all at Worcester or Naseby, who had charged so impetuously with Rupert at Edgehill, and gasped out their generous lives at Marston Moor and Roundway Down. The myth acquired, as was only to be expected, an appropriate habitation. The cotton planter was furnished with a "great house." Its white columns dreamed through the long summer days over gardens of boxwood and magnolia, of crepe myrtle and Cherokee rose. Inside, in the high polished hallway with the graceful staircase, a tall clock interminably reconstructed the availing past. In the great rooms, under the lofty ceilings, family portraits and patriotic engravings presided over French furniture and English silver. And, to be sure, as the decades passed, more and more of such mansions might have been seen in the cotton states: but they were never typical and always exceptional.

Certainly, the planter who flourished in the cotton kingdom in the year 1819, and the decade that followed, was not yet ready for polish or for grandeur. He may have flattered himself that he had a prototype—an uncertain mixture of the Virginia gentleman, easy-going, unpretentious, well-bred, and the Carolina gentleman, more serious but more cosmopolitan. As the cotton kingdom advanced, the prototype and its copies became more and more dissimilar. The "big house" in a new region was little more than a box with four rooms divided by a hallway upon which was superimposed another box with four rooms and dividing hall-way. It was wind-swept in winter; it was verminous in summer. Its porch was littered with guns and saddles, with whips and farm-tools. The master was a busy man, engaged in extracting a living from a debt-laden crop; the mistress was too preoccupied with her duties to have any leisure for fine clothes or languid airs. In time, if bankruptcy did not supervene, the house would acquire a coat of white paint; a portico, an avenue, a garden, an increasing entourage of stables, offices, and slave cabins. Its inhabitants would be immensely hospitable; they might even become mannered and graceful. But it would never lose its special, original atmosphere, an uneasy mingling of bustle and drift, of purpose and inefficiency.

The slave-holders who, from 1819 on, became the most ardent and uncompromising in the defense of slavery were not, in general, descendants of the eighteenth-century tidewater. It is more likely that they had come up from the eighteenth-century backwoods. They were the products of a continuously evolving frontier, which had never been too merciful to the weak or the unlucky or the pure in heart. The survivors in the battle, which was characterized by all sorts of quick and almost unrecognized changes in fortune, were willing enough to see themselves, when the time came, as the members of a superior class, in birth as in fortune distinguished from their poorer neighbors. As for the poorer or less pretentious classes—the slaveless yoemen of the upper valleys, the small slave-owner who pined in the shadow of the large plantation, the "sand-hiller" or "squatter" of the pine-barrens and sandy hills—the myth took care of these as well. Might not the most desperate and diseased among them, the victims of hookworm and pellagra, the laziest and most slatternly of human beings, actually be the descendants of the indentured servants, the debtors, and the riffraff of colonial days? It is more probable, however, that they, like their economic betters, were simply the products of the competitive frontier; that they had sunk to the bottom, while others rose; and that over large areas of the new South the rich man and the indigent man, the great slave-owner and the poor white, were closer together than they cared or dared to admit.

Moreover the whole South, old and new, was growing attached to the agrarian way of life, as a way of life, not simply as a means of acquiring wealth. Its many incompatibilities were dimly reconciled by the great dream that haunts the correspondence of Thomas Jefferson, and inspired the philosophy of John Taylor of Caroline. It was a dream of independent farmers, who mixed their labor with the soil, and refrained from using legal devices for seizing their neighbor's land; a dream of equality tempered only by an aristocracy of intellect, not of property; a dream of a world whose momentum might be expressed in the proverb *festina lente*, hasten slowly. Let us advance, it admonished, without artificial aids; without the help of financiers, paper-money barons, manipulators of credit, thieves of the public money. If we have property, let it be natural property; if we make profits, let them be profits we have made by our own efforts. The South had already made great sacrifices to this dream. It had given up the manufactures in which, strange to say, it had once been pre-eminent.[32] It had not developed its enormous iron and coal fields, which lay so conveniently adjacent to an abundant water supply. But the sacrifice was made in vain. The agrarian way of life was helpless before the power generated by British inventors like Hargreaves and Crompton, Watt and Arkwright, and financed by the spoils of India. The British textile industry imposed upon the American South a need for production which made the gradual adjustments of agrarianism quite impossible. Under the lash of its demand for raw materials, Southern economy was driven too hard, and in the wrong direction. It was becoming a one-crop, quick-profit, debt-encumbered economy: and its effect could be seen in frayed nerves and exhausted soils.

The dream of course persisted. It was not merely sustained by British demand. It exacted from its votaries a kind of behavior which went a long way towards justifying it. At his best, the Southern white was marked by "a kindly courtesy, a level-eyed pride, an easy quietness, a barely perceptible flourish of bearing, which for all its obvious angularity and plainness, was one of the finest things the Old [antebellum] South produced." [33] Rich or poor, the Southerner believed that he was an independent man, who called nobody his master. And this belief would, indeed, have been wholly admirable if it had not been corrupted by the doctrine of racial superiority. "Manual labor," said John Caldwell Calhoun, in the course of a famous conversation with John Quincy Adams, was "the proper work of slaves. . . . No white person would condescend to that. And it was the best guarantee to equality among the whites. It produced an unvarying level among them. It not only did not excite, but did not even admit of inequalities, by which one white man could domineer over another." Mr. Adams told himself afterwards that this was all perverted sentiment, mistaking labor for slavery, and dominion for freedom. "It is among the evils of slavery," he wrote, "that it taints the very sources of moral principle . . . for what can be more false and heartless than this doctrine which makes the first and holiest rights of humanity depend upon the color of the skin?" [34] What indeed? As for Mr. Calhoun, had he not shown clearly enough that the institution of slavery transcended the imperatives of cotton, rice, and sugar, and that it was already, as it were, a mirror in which the white man saw himself reflected and glorified?

On the county court days, or their equivalents, as the great planters, with their easy-going manners, passed among their poorer neighbors, they seemed to be no more than first among equals. They were careful to foster this misconception. Any white man might, by thrift or luck, rise to their eminence. When Mr. Tallmadge assailed their institution in his Amendment, they let it be known that what he was attacking—this insignificant lawyer from a state that had never bothered to hide its unsavory political squabbles—was not merely slavery, but the whole structure of white supremacy. There were some who never listened to this talk—Quakers, Methodists, up country men—and who, as the feeling in the slavery regions grew more intense, began to move away in large numbers. But of the many who remained, few could resist the insinuation that as white men, no matter how debased their condition, they were somehow naturally and eternally superior to the toiling slave. Only the most distant, only the most determined, could hold out.

V

Moreover, was the South to blame for this institution that was now being attacked in such moral language? Was the Southern slave-owner more at fault, historically, than the Northern merchant who had made such immense sums out of the slave trade? The speech of a certain Rhode Islander, in a distant Congress, was still remembered. "We want money," said John Brown of Providence in 1800, "we want a navy; we ought therefore to use the means to obtain it. . . . *Why should we see Great Britain getting all the slave trade to themselves?*" [35] The Northern merchant, however, might argue that he was less to blame than the Royal African Company, which had foisted the slave trade upon the American colonies. And was not the Royal African Company no more than one example of the harsh commercial enterprise of seventeenth-century Europe? The crime was enormous, the guilt universal.

It is difficult, it is no doubt impossible, to place one's imagination at the service of a slave-holder in 1819: to ask oneself what it must have been like, not merely to own slaves, but to be born and raised in a world where the owning of slaves was taken for granted. When the slave-holder contended that he had inherited an evil for which he was not responsible, did he mean what he said? Undoubtedly he did. But he generally supported this contention by insisting—it was a popular argument in 1819 and 1820, and men like Jefferson and Madison lent their names to it—that if slavery were diffused, the "burden" would be lessened by distribution. This argument had the taint of politics on it. And why was the burden connected with social prestige, unless it resembled the "white man's burden" of a later day, and was called a burden out of mere disingenuousness? When schemes were evolved in the 1820's for a gradual emancipation with full compensation, the slave-holders were generally opposed to it. They had come to believe that their staples could be cultivated only by slave labor.

The proposition was certainly open to some doubt. The bookkeeping of those days, where it existed, was quite unable to cope with the problem of whether or not slave labor was actually profitable. That it was convenient; that it did away with lockouts and strikes; that it made the most of female and child labor—all this was clear enough. Moreover, the slave, unlike the serf, was not bound to the soil; and although slave labor was not very mobile, it could be moved in time towards the points of greatest productive advantage. But was it profitable? Where land was fertile and abundant, and the market not too adverse, the difference between what the slave produced and what it cost to keep him alive while he produced it—the "appropriable surplus"—seemed to answer the question. Certainly, where the maintenance of the slave was concerned, even generous opinion in the South was not very particular. A coarse diet, cheap and inadequate clothes, poor cabins—this was the maximum that any slave could expect. Slave-owners were realists. But the modern bookkeeper would not be too attracted by this "appropriable surplus": he would inquire into the original cost of the slave, and the age at which he had been purchased, and would ask whether or not the price was too high for the necessary amortization. If the slave were inherited or born and raised on the plantation there were the unproductive years of infancy and the semiproductive years of childhood and adolescence to be considered. Then, again, was the planter adequately insured against the old age of his slaves, against accidents, against flight? The planter did not ask these questions. He had some notion that the money he poured into the purchase of human beings represented an overcapitalization, but he comforted himself with the thought that this money was being expended upon a way of life or even (it was a sublime rationalization) upon the care of people who could not otherwise manage for themselves.

He was afraid of armed servile rebellion, though it rarely so much as lifted its head. The rebellion that went on around him, everywhere, all the time, he called by another name. The slave, he said, was incorrigibly lazy, careless, and inefficient. He would not admit that, as rational human beings, slaves could not be made to work well when there was no decent incentive to work at all. Even the house servants, better treated and more secure than the field hands, needed constant supervision. Was not the whole visible world—the land, the tools, the animals, the barns, the house and its furniture—from the slave's point of view, conscious or subconscious, merely the visible sign of a huge conspiracy against him? He was a destructive worker. This should be itemized among the expenses of slave labor—the largest expense and the least amenable to retrenchment.

To wish for freedom, to be resigned to servitude—these are human conditions that can exist side by side. The slave-holder was, it was only natural, willing enough to be seduced by any signs of resignation in his slaves. "Every slave has a comfortable house, is well fed, clothed, and taken care of; he has his family about him, and in sickness has the same medical aid as his master, and has a sure and comfortable retreat in old age. . . . During the whole of his life he is free from care, that canker of the human heart." [36] These words, which were solemnly spoken in the House of Representatives, hardly require a refutation: they are so palpably woven out of a little truth and much falsehood. Yet the man who spoke them so solemnly, solemnly believed that he believed them.

VI

"However deeply it may be regretted," said the Kentucky Court of Appeals in 1828, "and whether it be politic or impolitic, a slave by our code, is not treated as a person, but *negotium*, a thing, as he stood in the civil code of the Roman Empire." [37] This pronouncement may perhaps be fortified by another, the speaker being Chief Justice John Marshall, and the case *Boyce v. Anderson*, in which the owners of the steamboat *Washington* were being sued for the accidental drowning of four slaves. "A slave has volition," said the Chief Justice, "and has feelings which cannot be *entirely* disregarded. . . . He cannot be stowed away as a common package. . . . He *resembles* a passenger." [38] The slave was, therefore, not a man: but a thing that bore the semblance of a man.

As for the system, to which these ghastly definitions were central, it is clear that judicial opinion in the South—in the 1820's at any rate—inclined to the view that it was condemned by natural law and common law, and that it could exist only through municipal regulations.[39] The slave, in other words, was held to be abandoned by natural law and common law.

To what extent were these municipal regulations humane? The pamphleteers, the committees of correspondence, the legislative memorialists who became so active during the summer of 1819 raised this question in a most urgent manner. But there was no federal machinery by means of which a survey of the facts might have been instituted; and, even if there had been, there was so much suspicion on one side, and so much pride and guilt on the other, that no survey could have been impartial or dispassionate. "I was credibly informed," a correspondent wrote to John W. Taylor in 1819, "a man in Culpeper burnt one of his slaves to death deliberately, on the blacksmith's forge: by having him held and the bellows blowed, till it scorched him to death: & got clear by feeing a lawyer without punishment: not even confined till tryal!" [40] This story would probably have been accepted as a truth in New York, and denounced as a lie in Virginia.

It is no longer very rewarding, it is even less necessary, to recite the long list of charges against slavery. Brutality was inherent in the system. Justice Ruffin of the Supreme Court of North Carolina once said that the "harsh *but necessary* discipline of the slave" was "a curse of slavery to both the bond and the free portions of our community." [41] If a master were a brute, there was little to prevent him from indulging himself. Public opinion in the South did not condone cruelty; but public opinion was not very effective. Every slave state protected its slaves from murder; but a distinction was made between wanton murder, for which an owner could be hanged, and murder arising from "undue correction," which in some states required only a statement of the facts and a confession of fault to clear the criminal altogether.[42] If a slave-holder were both a cruel man and an undesirable neighbor in other respects, he might find the neighborhood too hot for him; but mere brutality was held to be its own reward, in that it damaged "the most valuable species of personal property held in this country." [43] Since the slave was never permitted to bear witness against his master, or against any white man, evidence in any case was hard to gather. Only where slaves committed atrocities against one another was mercy extended to them; for juries in such cases were made up of slave-owners, and slave-owners did not much care to send another man's property to prison or condemn it to death.

That many slave-owners were kind and humane towards their slaves cannot be denied; though the kindness was usually capricious, and the humanity was little more than such as is lavished on a pet animal. The innumerable advertisements for runaways, the slave patrols with their hickory switches, the stories of masters and overseers murdered in the dark of the night, show that the system was too inhumane to be really affected by humanitarian practices. The slave-holders used to contend that their slaves were better off than the workers of Europe: that life on a plantation was far more tolerable than, for instance, life in one of the new English factory towns. The contention was just, so much so that it is still heard: it was also quite irrelevant. The factory worker had, eventually, a future: the slave had none. The brutalities of the slave system—or its kindnesses—were of less account than the direction in which the system was moving. Economically, it was moving into debt. Philosophically, it was to proceed by way of Thomas Dew and Chancellor Harper to the final extravagances of George Fitzhugh, who reached the conclusion that *all* American workers should be slaves; but since this conclusion did violence to the doctrine of white supremacy, very few people accepted it. Emotionally, it was drifting into the base assumption that the Negro was congenitally inferior to the white man and had been created for the sole purpose of serving him.[44]

This assumption was the great crime that must be charged against the institution of slavery, which fostered it, strengthened it, and handed it on as a legacy. That it was an unscientific assumption might be forgiven: the lights of anthropology had scarcely been lit. But it also ran counter to natural law, and only the most perverse arguments could reconcile it with the teachings of Christianity. None the less, if men were to hold Negroes as personal property, the assumption was necessary. The more, therefore, that the slave system consolidated, the more eagerly its apologists abandoned their old position that slavery was an unnatural state, "a fixed evil, which we can only alleviate," and the more they asserted that it was in accordance with the Creator's plan.[45]

The imperatives of property, moreover, gave the lie to the slave-holder's favorite assertion that the slave was free from care. The kindest of masters could not prevent his slaves from being sold, after his death, to satisfy the debts of his estate: even a will emancipating a slave would under these circumstances be set aside.[46] "It would be harsh," said a North Carolina judge, concerning the breaking up of a slave family, "to sever the ties which bind *even* slaves together. True, it must be done, if the executor discovers that the interest of the estate requires it." [47] Under these circumstances, formal marriages were not encouraged, and the marriage contract was held to be "dormant" during servitude.[48] Chancellor William Harper said that, while the unmarried mother was an outcast in the North, it was "not so with the female slave. . . . Her offspring is not a burden but an acquisition to her owner. The want of chastity among slaves hardly deserves a harsher name than weakness." [49] From such a statement, from so bland and respectable a source, it is only a step to the lament of a Southern lady—she was James Madison's sister—that "a planter's wife is but the mistress of a seraglio." [50] The slaveowner inevitably took advantage of his female slaves, if his tastes led him in that direction: they could hardly deny him. In short, the slave was afforded only that security which belongs to a piece of property: as a human being he was deeply and tragically insecure.

When the property rights of the slave-owner thus entrenched themselves behind the thickening delusion of Negro inferiority, it was necessary to make the slave, as far as was possible, part of the conspiracy against himself. He was taught only those skills which were useful without being elevating; he was rarely literate; his religion was one that prescribed obedience as the single path to heaven and resignation as the highest virtue; a clownish etiquette was expected and indeed extracted from him. He was told to debase himself; and if he resisted, there was always the lash, or the gallows, or the stake to remind him that, while his masters might break the laws of God and man, he could expiate the assertion of the simplest rights only in stripes and blood.

VII

Such was the conspiracy that Southern property-holders, in the grip of circumstances beyond their control, concerted against the Negro slave. The treatment of the slave, of course, varied with the character of the master, the kind of employment, the state of the market, and the season of the year. Where he was left to the mercy of an overseer, instead of working under the eye of his master, his lot was sometimes intolerable: for overseers were a harsh and disillusioned set of men, who believed themselves to be the victims of the system that employed them, and whose abilities were measured solely by the amount of their production.[51] Most of our information comes from the records of large plantations, however; and there is some reason to believe that a slave on a very small plantation was, as regards his human rights, somewhat better off.[52] The system, in any case, was often tempered by generosity and patience on the one side and by devotion on the other: but neither its patriarchal ways nor its incidental charities could disguise its real character. Mr. Tallmadge, when he offered his amendment, called attention to this character in such a manner as to arouse the guilt of the slave-holder: and from then on the slave-holder was constrained to defend, to excuse, and ultimately to eulogize his peculiar concept of property.

VIII

It should also be remembered that, in cotton regions, the maintenance of the slave was a fixed charge upon what was always a very speculative crop. This undoubtedly affected the slave's treatment, not so much by economies in bad years, as by the influence of the crop upon the character of the planter. The uncertainties of the master's life bred uncertainties of temper, and these were visited upon the slave; for the master was bound hand and foot to one of the most volatile markets in the history of the early nineteenth century, and his life—however easy-going it may sometimes have appeared—was at the mercy of successive waves of optimism and despair.

Liverpool was the center of world exchanges in cotton, and Liverpool was blown upon by rumors that, in the days before trading in futures became customary, made the trade a very hazardous one. Only great planters in the

South, it is true, traded on their own account; and then very rarely. The bondage of the planter to the world market can best be described by defining his relations with his factor.

These relations made it impossible for the planter to protect himself against a bad market, and difficult for him to profit by a good one.

The greater part of the cotton crop was shipped to the ports of Charleston, New Orleans, Savannah, and Mobile on consignment to the factors, who congregated at these ports, and who sold the crop at a 2½ per cent commission. The factors were not simply selling-agents. They kept the planter in funds, which they loaned him at an interest rate of 8 to 12 per cent, to which a brokerage fee of ½ to 2½ per cent was sometimes added. They purchased his supplies for him at another commission of 2½ per cent. In addition, they made themselves responsible for freight, storage, insurance, drayage, weighing, sampling, mending, and repairing; and these charges duly appeared on their accounts of sale, being customarily settled in the form of rebates.[53]

Thus the planter was always in debt to the factor, and this debt was secured in a very interesting way. Loans were usually repaid in kind rather than in money; and, in the agreement he drew up with his factor, the planter was forced to stipulate the number of bales he was to ship, and also the number of acres he was to plant in order to produce these bales. He also agreed to pay a penalty—which sometimes amounted to as much as four dollars a bale—for every bale short of the stipulated number. This forced him into overproduction—and overproduction, unless a bumper crop happened to coincide with a good world market, only drove him deeper into debt.

It was not merely the protection of his loans which made the factor insist upon the penalty clause in his agreement with the planter. Cotton was almost impervious to rough handling and long exposure, and easily survived the crowded conditions at the ports which invariably prevailed between the months of January and April. This made it almost as good as currency; and it was certainly as convertible as the best forms of commercial paper. The factor, therefore, wanted to get his hands upon as much cotton as possible.[54]

Under these circumstances, it was almost impossible for the planter to control the sales of his crop. Some planters, it is believed, did give directions as to the price at which they were willing to sell; but the practice of drawing bills upon the coming crop put such a control well beyond the powers of the majority. "Draw bills!" said a Southern writer. "This bill business is the very thing that ruins us. *Keep out of debt and control your cotton.*"[55]

The planter lived upon intimate and friendly terms with his factor, even though their interests clashed at so many points. Sometimes, it is true, the jealousy inherent in such a situation came out into the open: the factors were accused, for example, of the crime of selling on their own account; and there is evidence that they did so, as early as the year 1822.[56] Such accusations, however, never crystallized into a genuine difference; and the factor retained his mastery until the end.

Now the Southern factorage system itself acted as an agent for American or European concerns situated in New York City. This meant, in effect, that the enormous sums of money which the planter expended on interest charges, brokerage fees, and commissions eventually found their way into the hands of capitalists living north of the Potomac. In the course of time, the planter began to ask himself if he were really anything more than the administrator of the wealth of Northern men, who seemed to be the ultimate receivers of the profits of Southern plantations and Southern slavery.

IX

In 1819, at the time of the Tallmadge Amendment, this process was just beginning. The peculiar relation between planter and factor was, however, already well established. It is easy to see that this relation tied the planter inescapably to a one-crop system. His fortunes were forever mortgaged to the next year's crop, and the next year's crop was at the mercy of any rumor that might disturb the markets of America and England. He did not himself disapprove of the one-crop system; for his notions of agriculture were usually so unscientific, and he was so eager to get out of debt, that he frequently did not observe even the simple rotation of corn and cotton, but put in successive annual cotton crops until the exhausted land no longer paid for the labor. Thus his economy was made to depend upon the possession of a larger acreage than he could till in a single year; and when the price of cotton was high, and the crop was good, he invested his profits in more land and more slaves; and the round of feast and famine, optimism and fear began once again.

His agrarian society, therefore, which put its spare capital into the purchase of land and slaves, was drifting into debt: and its creditor was the capitalist society which was beginning to take shape in the North. There could be only one issue to such an argument. Southern politicians became more and more prominent in national affairs; Northern bankers obtained a firmer and yet firmer grip upon the Southern economy. It was never a fair exchange. It grew embittered, invariably over the question of tariffs: but what really poisoned it was the question of slavery.

As a political man the Southerner was dignified and skillful; as an economic or an ethical man he was irritable and insecure. And all these sides of him first expressed themselves fully in the Sixteenth Congress when the agrarian and the capitalist worlds, emerging from the shadows, came suddenly to grips over the admission of the state of Missouri.

CHAPTER TWO

The First Missouri Debate

FOR the debates on the admission of Missouri there was, as it were, a fresh Capitol. The two rectangular wings, their scarred freestone gleaming with white paint, were to be used for the first time for legislative purposes since the British had put them to the torch in 1814. The Hall of Representatives was particularly striking. Everybody agreed upon the splendor of its appointments, though not all were sure that these appointments answered to that rule of strict simplicity which is required of republics. A fine Brussels carpet was spread over the floor, and a quantity of brass spittoons bore witness to the tastes of the legislators. Crimson curtains were hung beneath the low gallery; crimson curtains imprisoned the windows; above the Speaker's desk with its huge brass candlesticks there brooded an immense canopy of crimson silk with a superimposed gilt eagle. The semicircular Hall was supported by columns of Potomac marble or puddingstone, with white Corinthian capitals. Foreign diplomats, particularly impressed by the damask settees upon which they were invited to lounge, compared it not unfavorably to the legislative chambers in Paris.[1] It was spacious and handsome, but it was harassed by a goblinish congregation of echoes, which hurled the speakers' voices up to the dome, or scattered them among the numerous recesses beneath the gallery; so that, until its last day, few representatives were heard in comfort, and many were scarcely heard at all.

During the course of the Missouri debates a good many words were pronounced that deserved no better fate.

I

From December 8, 1819, until March 20, 1820, Congress discussed in all its aspects—legal, Constitutional, moral, political, economic—the problem of whether Missouri should be admitted to statehood with slavery or without it. Few speeches were made that, as examples of oratory or reasoning, would tempt posterity to read them. Tirelessly the legislators arose to remark that they would not long detain the Senate or the House, and to speak for hours or for days in remorseless reiteration of what had been said before. And yet the debates seem rarely to have lost their air of urgency and their under-tone of disaster. Were they not questioning the sincerity of every profession that had been made in the name of the American Revolution? Great plots were suspected, old alliances threatened, old friendships broken; and when all was over both observers and participants were left with a feeling of mingled anger, dissatisfaction, and insecurity.

II

The House was organized; Mr. Clay took his seat beneath the Speaker's canopy with its superimposed eagle; Mr. John Scott, delegate from the Missouri Territory, moved that the memorials of Missouri be referred to a select committee; and on December 9 this committee—four of whose five members were from slave-holding states—duly reported a Bill for the ad-mission of Missouri without restriction. At the same time, a memorial was presented from the District of Maine, praying for the admission of that Dis-trict to the Union as a state. It now became clear that the supporters of slavery would never agree to admit Maine without the equivalent of an un-restricted Missouri. On December 30, the Maine Enabling Bill came up be-fore the Committee of the Whole, and it was then that Mr. Clay—with the usual accompaniment of shrugs and contortions which no other living orator could have made attractive—declared in the course of a long speech that "equality is equality, and if it is right to make the restriction of slavery the condition of the admission of Missouri, it is equally just to make the admis-sion of Missouri the condition of that of Maine." [2] If this meant anything, it meant that unless the antislavery forces did what they thought was wrong, Mr. Clay had no intention of doing what he acknowledged to be right. [3]

The Maine Enabling Bill was passed after a bitter debate, and was sent up to the Senate on January 3, 1820.

When the Bill left the Senate Judiciary Committee, a curious amendment was tacked on to it by a wafer—nothing less than the Bill admitting Missouri without restriction. Senator Roberts of Pennsylvania immediately moved to recommit this two-headed document, and the battle was joined. [4]

It was evident to everyone who sat in the Senate on that 13th day of January, 1820, that a new spirit was abroad. Senator Macon of North Caro-lina announced that the "appearance" of that chamber was unlike anything he had seen since he had been a member. [5] Senator Barbour of Virginia be-lieved that the subject under discussion was an ignited spark, which would produce an explosion shaking the Union to its center; and Senator Otis of Massachusetts replied that the pine forests of Maine, if set on fire, would probably burn with as fierce a flame as the spire grass of Missouri. [6] These innuendoes—followed by certain remarks concerning the dubious behavior of New Englanders during the War of 1812—were not calculated to restore tranquillity; and when Mr. Roberts of Pennsylvania rather pointedly referred to the Declaration of Independence, and urged his fellow Senators not to admit Missouri "with her features marred as if the finger of Lucifer had been drawn across them," any chance of a peaceful or respectable discussion had vanished forever.[7] Several arguments, however, began to emerge. It was urged that slavery was an evil that could be mitigated by diffusion—to which it was possible to reply, with the Reverend Thomas Malthus, that population always increases up to the limit of subsistence. It was contended that under the treaty with France, ceding Louisiana to the United States, slavery was expressly permitted throughout the Purchase—against which it was argued that the treaty applied only to the condition of territorial government. The three-fifths clause in the Constitution was bitterly attacked, and spitefully defended upon the grounds that no one had ever objected to the slave's being counted as three-fifths of a man for taxation purposes. And finally the Constitutional reference to "*migration* or importation" was construed by the antislavery party as meaning that Congress might forbid the introduction of slavery into new states. The answer to this was that migration referred to the entry of free foreigners into the United States and importation to the slave trade; and that the movement of slaves between state and state was never alluded to.[8]

Malthusian or constitutional arguments would not, in themselves, have produced much uneasiness among the Southern Senators. They felt themselves capable—as indeed they were—of making the Constitution say whatever they wished it to say, and of doing so in a dignified manner. What poisoned the whole debate for them was the statement that slavery was morally wrong from every point of view; and in attempting to rebut this, they were led into some strange extravagances.

It was on January 20 that the debate began to unveil that sinister and distorted aspect which it never lost thereafter. Nor was it any the less disagreeable that Nathaniel Macon of North Carolina should have been the Senator responsible for this.

Few men were more respected than he. His kindly but dignified presence had been known in Washington for more than a quarter of a century. He was one of the strictest of Old Republicans; not so subtle as Thomas Jefferson, not so profound as John Taylor, not so passionately odd as his great friend John Randolph—but fully able to compensate, in simplicity and integrity, for what he lacked in intelligence. His notions of republican behavior were so extreme that he thought his own name too Gallic, and habitually referred to himself as "Meekins." In his old-fashioned clothes of fine blue broadcloth, and his spotless linen, he looked like a statesman of some earlier and purer day—a day that had never existed, perhaps, except in the imagination. He sustained this appearance by his political behavior: no man had so relentlessly recorded so many negative votes, and it is by negative votes that a reputation for unsullied statesmanship is most easily acquired.

Not that Senator Macon voted in this way out of affectation or insincerity: he invariably followed his conscience, and his conscience infrequently reconciled itself to the demands of nineteenth-century politics. At home, on his tobacco plantation beside Hubquarter Creek, he labored as a field hand at the head of his slaves; and "his great object being to live independent," willingly subscribed to the saying that a man should not live near enough his neighbor to hear his dogs bark.[9] In short, he was a model patriarch, a perfect agrarian; and it was upon an agrarian note that he began his speech on January 20. "Why depart," he said, "from the good old way . . . everyone living under his own vine and fig tree, and none to make him afraid?" But what was he afraid of? "A clause in the Declaration of Independence has been read," he continued, "declaring that 'all men are created equal'; follow that sentiment and does it not lead to universal emancipation?"[10] The Declaration of Independence was commonly regarded with extreme reverence by Southern agrarians of the strict Republican school; but, like most manifestoes, its sanctity depended upon the vagueness with which one interpreted it. The clause "all men are created equal" might, if one pursued it back to origins, spring from John Locke's curious notions about the *tabula rasa;* or it might imply no more than that Americans were the equals of Englishmen. But if one took it at the foot of the letter, "will not the whites be compelled to move," said Senator Macon, "and leave the land to the blacks? And are you willing to have black members of Congress? . . . There is no place for free blacks in the United States."[11] The Declaration of Independence, he added, was no part of the Constitution, "nor of any other book." It was, however, a part of the spiritual fabric of the American Republic; and it was a melancholy moment when a man as noble as Macon attempted to tear it away.

As to slavery, "I wish," said Macon, "that he [Mr. Burrill of Rhode Island] and the gentleman from Pennsylvania [Mr. Roberts] would go home with me, or with some other southern member, and witness the meeting between the slaves and the owner, and see the glad faces and the hearty shaking of hands. The owner can make more free in conversation with his slave, and he more easy in his company, than the rich man where there is no slave, with the white hireling that drives his carriage."[12]

Here there was a beginning of the defense of slavery, not as an evil which could not be remedied, but as a positive good. And worse was to follow. On January 26, Senator Smith of South Carolina made a speech which was subsequently characterized by the horrified Mr. Ruggles of Ohio as "going farther than he had ever heard any gentleman go before."[13] William Smith was a strict Jeffersonian, of a severe disposition, a narrow mind, a bitter and sarcastic tongue. Unlike most South Carolinians at this time, he was passionately addicted to State Rights and strict construction; so that his disquisition on slavery must be regarded as the talk of a man who was accustomed to go to extremes. But even with this qualification, the speech is a landmark in the history of Congress, since it was the first open and impassioned justification of the slave system ever to be made upon its floors. Mr.

Smith founded his case, partly upon his belief that since the Deluge it had been the lot of men to serve one another, "in this shape or that"; partly upon an appeal to the most enlightened periods of Greek and Roman history; but chiefly upon Leviticus xxv, 44-6. "This was the law," runs his argument in the *Annals of Congress*, "given by the God of Abraham, the God of Isaac, and the God of Jacob. He was the only true and living God. If we worship the God of Israel, he is our God. It has been said that the law was given to the Jews. So were all the laws of God; and are we left to select such laws for our obedience as we find suited to our inclinations and our policy only, and abrogate the others? Mr. S. said that the holy book of our religion taught us that God was unchangeable; that he had no respect of persons; that he was without variation or shadow of turning; the same yesterday, today and forever. But it is said that slavery is against the spirit of the Christian religion? Christ himself gave a sanction to slavery. He admonished them to be obedient to their masters; and there is not a word in the whole of his life which forbids it. . . . Christ came to fulfill the law not to destroy it. . . . Mr. President, the Scriptures teach us that slavery was universally practiced among the holy fathers." [14]

No other Southern Senator would have been willing to commit himself openly to such a doctrine: but after Senator Smith had finished, it was no longer necessary for any Senator to do so.

III

While the Senate thus reached the first climax in its debate, the House had been discussing its own version of the Missouri Enabling Bill. James Tallmadge, having served his one term in Congress, was now living in Poughkeepsie, and it was John W. Taylor of New York, the seconder of the Tallmadge Amendment, who took on the leadership of the antislavery forces. He was a man of a more conforming type than Mr. Tallmadge, and more easily identified with the capitalist branch of the Republican Party. In his own State, he was securely entrenched in Saratoga County, which regularly returned him to Congress, and was to go on doing so until 1833. But his position among the Republican factions of New York was uncertain: he was neither a Bucktail nor a Clintonian, though the former party regularly opposed him. On the whole, Mr. Taylor was less disliked by the Clintonians. [15] On the slavery question, he was careful to explain, he had merely been carrying on the work started by himself and Tallmadge in the Fifteenth Congress; that it was not until the Missouri Question became a major political issue —in the sense that an ambitious party leader might extract some solid profit from it—that De Witt Clinton had decided to give his endorsement to the antislavery cause. [16]

Mr. Taylor's amendment, offered on January 26, while William Smith was addressing the Senate, was somewhat stronger than Mr. Tallmadge's had been. [17] His speech, made on January 27, addressed itself chiefly to the three-fifths clause in the Constitution. "If you claim it as incident to the power of admitting new states, you may stretch the principle to I know not what lengths. The words of the Constitution may not be violated, but its spirit will be disregarded. No express power is granted to Congress to acquire territory. If it exists at all it is by implication. Thus, on the implied power to acquire territory by treaty, you raise an implied right to erect it into States, and imply a compromise by which slavery is to be established, and its slaves represented in Congress. . . . Your lust for acquiring is not yet satiated. You must have the Floridas. Your ambition rises. You covet Cuba, and obtain it. You stretch your arms to the other islands in the Gulf of Mexico, and they become yours. Are the millions of slaves inhabiting these countries, too, to be incorporated into the Union and represented in Congress? Are the freemen of the old states to become the slaves of the representatives of foreign slaves? The majority may be in your hands. You may have the power to pass such laws, but beware how you use it." [18] The language was stronger than the argument; yet the argument was not weaker, nor the language more inflammatory than what Mr. Alexander Smyth had to offer in rebuttal the next day. For Mr. Smyth declared that the Ordinance of 1787, prohibiting slavery in the Northwest, was not binding upon the people of Ohio, Indiana, and Illinois, because Congress under the Articles of Confederation represented the states and not the people.[19]

To counter an argument that slavery must be restricted by an argument that it could go wherever it pleased might have been more becoming to a schoolroom than a legislature; and Alexander Smyth was just the sort of man from whom such a counter-argument could be expected. He had had a brief career as a Brigadier-General in the War of 1812, a career consisting of a pompous manifesto followed by an inglorious retreat—but this had not deterred his Virginia constituents, mysteriously faithful, from sending him to Congress time and time again. His speeches were dreadfully long-winded —he declared that he spoke for posterity—and this had once forced from the exasperated Henry Clay the remark that he supposed Mr. Smyth intended to go on speaking until his audience arrived. That such a man should have advocated the brushing aside of the Ordinance of 1787 was not surprising. But it so happened that a number of far more sensible men than Mr. Smyth were looking askance at the Ordinance of 1787—and among these was no less a figure than ex-President James Madison.[20] Madison's arguments, it is true, were more cautious and more subtle than those of Smyth; but they showed that even Mr. Smyth would have to be taken seriously, and that when Southern members spoke of the diffusion of slavery they meant that it should be allowed to cross the Ohio as well as the Mississippi. As to diffusion, Mr. Smyth—who came from a tobacco region—was ready enough to admit that slaves in cotton, rice, or sugar areas were subjected to "incessant toil . . . hard worked and ill fed," and that they should be moved into a country "where bread and meat are produced in profusion, with little labor." With this argument—which must have been equally disgusting to either side —and with a threat that restriction upon Missouri would produce either servile insurrection or civil war, Mr. Smyth at length resumed his seat.[21]

Many more able men spoke in the days that followed—Clay, Randolph, Hardin of Kentucky, who "fought with a cleaver, or kitchen knife, sharpened on a brickbat," the reasonable John Sergeant, the dialectical Philip Pendleton Barbour—yet it must be admitted that their arguments were far less convincing than their anger. Over and over again they questioned or defended the validity of the three-fifths clause; or inquired what the Constitution meant when it alluded to "migration"; or maintained, on the one hand, that the Treaty of 1803 specifically permitted slavery throughout the Louisiana Purchase, and, on the other, that the State of Louisiana had not been admitted unconditionally.[22] Over and over again, one side advanced and the other combated the notion that if slavery were thinly spread over a large portion of the Union, its evils would be diminished without any increase in its numbers. One cannot pursue this debate through the pages of the *Annals of Congress* (not the most accurate of reports, but almost all that we have) without realizing that the Southern members would have been happy to chop logic with their opponents through an eternity of speeches. What angered them was the statement that slavery was incompatible with the democratic way of life; what terrified them was the thought that they were losing control of the Republican Party; what they endeavored to conceal was their simple desire to rule the West. In spite of their threats of disunion and civil war, both sides were willing to compromise; and, indeed, as far as their economic differences were concerned, a compromise might have been effected then and at any time during the next forty years. But slavery admitted of no compromise, and at heart everyone knew it. It can still be discerned, like a palimpsest writing, beneath all these desiccated speeches, imparting, even to the weariest argument, the presence of an unwearying doom.

IV

During this early stage in the House debates, it had been suggested, by Mr. Holmes of Massachusetts, that the real purpose behind the movement to restrict Missouri was a new alignment of parties.[23] He hinted darkly that some master conjurer was even then preparing "to ride into the Chief Magistracy of the nation." Mr. Holmes was something of a conjurer himself, having transformed his ardent Federalism into an ardent Republicanism in 1811; and he had now apostatized into the proslavery ranks for the simple reason that he lived in the District of Maine, and was anxious to disentangle Maine's admission from that of Missouri. Holmes, of course, was not the first man to suspect that some political rearrangement lay behind the assault upon Missouri; he was merely the first man to say it openly in the House in 1820. Ever since the decay of Federalism, it had been clear that the Northern Republicans no longer had a reason for allowing themselves to be dominated by their brethren from the South; that they were growing tired of Virginia presidents; and that, with their more numerous population, they might decide to strike out for themselves. Their economic interests were more varied, and their consciences were particolored. Would they follow a leader from

New York—a Federalist leader? On February 11, Mr. Holmes was accused by Mr. Ezra C. Gross of New York of designating that state as the center of the conspiracy. He denied the accusation, but in such a way as to show that it was perfectly true.[24] And there is no doubt that when he had spoken vaguely of "certain great men from the North" he had meant to cast suspicion upon two men and two men only—Senator Rufus King, and Governor De Witt Clinton, of New York.

It was De Witt Clinton's fate, and perhaps his deserts, to be suspected of everything; but Senator King of New York was a man who upheld all that was best in the Federalist tradition. He "had the appearance of one who was a gentleman by nature and had improved all her gifts"; he was courteous, but definitely not a man with whom it was safe to take liberties.[25] In 1789, the legislature of his adopted state of New York elected him Senator; in 1796, George Washington appointed him Minister to Great Britain; in 1804, and again in 1808, he was Federalist candidate for vice-president. Elected to the Senate in 1813, he was one of the leading antiwar members of that body; but he knew how to wear his Federalism with a difference, and before the war ended he was earnestly speaking in favor of it. In 1816, he was the Federalist candidate for President against Monroe. And all through his career, no man had ever questioned his public virtue. To the observer in Washington he had some of the monumental qualities of a John Taylor or a Nathaniel Macon: and never appeared in the Senate except "in full dress; short small-clothes, silk stockings, and shoes." [26] In 1818, however, he had spoken with great warmth in the Senate in favor of Mr. Tallmadge's amendment; and from then on it was believed that he hoped to lead a new party, composed of all that was left of Federalism and all that was dissident in Republicanism, and climb to the Presidency on the slavery issue.

His unanimous re-election to the Senate in January 1820 might have given some force to these ambitions, if he had ever had them; for the New York legislature was largely composed of his political enemies, and why should they give him this extraordinary mark of their confidence? The answer was that New York politicians were at the time more concerned with the success or failure of Daniel D. Tompkins' campaign for the governorship than they were with the virtues of Mr. King; and that it was because each faction in the New York Republican Party hoped for Mr. King's influence in this campaign that both had voted for his re-election.[27] But the country at large could not have known of this, though there is every reason to suppose that Mr. King himself was aware of it. When he heard the rumors that were being spread around, he seems to have been rather alarmed; and he cautiously attempted to transfer the odium to his fellow New Yorker, De Witt Clinton. "In the course of our debate in the Senate on the Missouri Bill," he wrote to his son, "a great deal has been said having no sort of Relation to the subject—one object assiduously aimed at has been to divide the Northern men, by inculcating the notion that the exclusion of slavery in Missouri is not the true object but that the revival and reestablishment of Federalism was the real purpose—that it is a plan devised by & for Mr. De Witt Clinton and intended to advance him to the Presidency." [28] A little later, he confessed that the Virginia papers were accusing *him* of wishing to rise to the Presidency—"views and motives which I in no manner am influenced by—my sole and only object being to oppose the extension of slavery." [29] Martin Van Buren, who had done as much as any man to secure King's re-election, had insisted before throwing his support to the Senator that "the Missouri question conceals *as far as he is concerned* no plot." [30] And, what is more to the point, in all Mr. King's correspondence, published and unpublished, there is no indication at all that he was using the Missouri crisis to advance his own fortunes. That he must secretly have felt some promptings of ambition can hardly be doubted; there was not a leading man in the country in 1820 who did not hope that he might, by some means or other, become Monroe's successor. But this was very different from conscious plotting, either to restore the Federalist Party, or to create a new one. The New York antislavery leaders in the House—Mr. Tallmadge in the Fifteenth Congress and Mr. Taylor in the Sixteenth—if they were in league with Senator King, have left no record of it.[31]

None the less, on the very day that Mr. Holmes was being accused in the House of spreading rumors against the great men of New York, Mr. King had arisen in the Senate to make the first of two speeches that were to bring those rumors home to him. His language was grave, dignified, and earnest, and "the great slave-holders in the House gnawed their lips and clenched their fists as they heard him." [32] This speech was followed by a second, on February 16, and the effect of this second speech was even more enraging, if one may judge by the virulence of the replies. Yet Mr. King had, for the most part, confined himself to Constitutional arguments, and with Constitutional arguments the Southern Senators were perfectly at their ease. Why then were they so enraged? Partly, no doubt, because they believed that Mr. King was bent on forming a new party designed to crush them; partly because, when he did venture beyond the theoretical pale of the federal and state Constitutions, he was either understood too well or not understood at all. When he declared that slavery was contrary to natural law, he was hated for saying it because he was the first Senator to do so, and because it was true. Natural law, to many educated Southerners, meant the law, not only of nature, but of nature's God; and while they did not object to Senator Smith's proclamation that nature's God was only a figment of the French Revolution and that the Scriptural God was on the side of slavery, few of them were altogether easy with such a doctrine. Some even professed to believe that on a distant day—a very distant, millennial day—slaves might be emancipated and take their place as citizens in good standing. To all of them the introduction of natural law was, to say the least, a piece of exceedingly bad taste on the part of Senator King.[33] And then they understood Mr. King to have said, during the course of his second speech, that he felt himself degraded at having to sit in the same chamber with men who represented slaves as well as freemen. What Mr. King had really said was that he felt inferior, because "the citizens of the states where slavery prevails possess a greater portion of political power, than the citizens of states in which Slavery is excluded," and that he did not wish to increase the humiliation by extending slavery. This argument was so confused that his opponents may be forgiven for not having understood it.[34]

Mr. King, indeed, had rarely advanced beyond a position any old-fashioned Northern Federalist might have occupied. He had always been deeply jealous of the West, which he regarded as some kind of imperial possession, to be held in reserve; and towards the pioneers who were flooding into it his feelings were those of suspicion and dislike. But now that the West had crossed the Mississippi, and was threatening to form new states, he was determined that it should not fall into the hands of the agrarian South. He was himself a man of wealth; he was well thought of in financial circles; and in the Senate he was the spokesman for the Bank of New York, of which his son Charles was a member. Upon anything dubious in the way of finance, however, he had always turned a very cold shoulder; and on January 7, 1820, he had declined an offer from Messrs. Leroy and Bayard to take a quarter share in a flutter in government three per cents on the grounds that "it had been spoken of that I may be rechosen a Senator of the U.S." Moreover, he had declined, not only for himself, but also for his son Charles.[35] But he was always a Hamiltonian, if a moderate and circumspect one; and to such a man the Missouri question presented itself chiefly as a capitalist-agrarian dispute.

Not that he was hypocritical in his attacks upon slavery as a moral evil. Even in the Constitutional Convention, where he was a delegate from Massachusetts, he had been one of the leading antislavery speakers. But his sense of slavery as a moral evil was not, on the whole, nearly as strong as his respect for slavery as a form of property. He had no wish to disturb it in those places where it had taken root. Those who turn over his unpublished correspondence will find there an anonymous letter from a certain "Humanitas," begging him to set on foot the abolition of slavery in the District of Columbia. Mr. King's handwriting at this period was rather shaky; but on the back of this letter he wrote, so firmly that the ink seems to bite into the page—"I shall take no measures on this project." [36] The calligraphy is fully as revealing as the sentiment: and both together explain, as well as anything can, the central weakness of Mr. King's position and the ultimate meanness of the Missouri Compromise. Mr. King would not uproot slavery from the national capital; he would not interfere with it in any state east of the Mississippi, nor yet in the state of Louisiana. In these regions, also, he would allow the three-fifths clause to rule forever. Any other course would have seemed to him an unwarrantable interference with the rights of property. It was the extension of slavery—and the extension of slavery alone—which he felt obliged to fight.

With Texas still unassimilated, with Arkansas still a Territory, the battle to keep slavery east of the Mississippi might have been a very noble one. Not a man in the Sixteenth Congress, however, seems to have had more advanced views than Senator King's. These were antislavery men in that assembly: there were no abolitionists. Under those circumstances, the Northern forces were bound in the end to give way. Abolitionism alone—radical in its thinking, fervent and fanatical in its expression, ethical in its origins—was capable of turning the conflict into something less adjustable than a capitalist-agrarian dispute, because abolitionism alone recognized the fact that with slavery there could be no compromise. Abolitionism, however, was still in the future. The present belonged to the slave power.

V

The proslavery forces in the Sixteenth Congress were irritated beyond measures by the attacks being made upon their institution. They were also afraid that some opponent might hurl himself over the barrier of Constitutional argument into the very heart of their position, and declare that their whole system must be swept away. As the debate wore on, they must have realized that this would not happen: the enemies had occupied the suburbs, but would never invade the citadel. When Mr. William Pinkney arose on February 15, in a Senate overflowing with female visitors, he behaved like a man who was very sure of his position. His delivery was, as usual, "alternately loud and low, like some of our methodist preachers, impetuous, theatrical and overbearing"; his language was, as always, "elegant, forcible, & commanding"; his argument, if it has been correctly reported, was singularly mild. He seemed well content not to sally beyond the wording of the Constitution; except on one or two occasions, as when he ventured to assert that "the self-evident truths announced in the Declaration of Independence are not truths at all, if taken literally." [37] He was more than happy to use "the machinery of syllogism" and to assail his opponents with arguments such as this: "The proposition contained in the clause [of the national Constitution, giving Congress the power to admit new states] is universal in one sense only. It is particular in another. It is universal as the power to admit or refuse. It is particular as to the being or thing to be admitted, and the compact by which it is to be admitted. The sophistry consists in extending the universal part of the proposition in such a manner as to make out of it another universal proposition. It consists in confounding the right to produce or refuse to produce a certain defined effect, with a right to produce a different effect by refusing otherwise to produce any effect at all. It makes, in a word, lawful power the instrument of unlawful usurpation." [38]

To men of Mr. Pinkney's way of thinking these arguments, which had all the fascination of irrelevance, were unanswerable. "I was not, however," wrote Rufus King, "of this opinion." [39] He answered with his famous speech upon the law of nature. Yet in the end, he was obliged to confess that the Northern members of Congress "fight Militia against Regulars." [40] The Southerners were better organized, more learned, more supple in debate. On February 16, as was expected, the Senate adopted the Maine-Missouri Bill by a vote of 23 to 21. On that day, too, as had been expected, Senator Thomas of Illinois offered an amendment to the Bill, prohibiting slavery in all the Louisiana Purchase—except the proposed state of Missouri—north of

36° 30′ north latitude. Other amendments were offered, but all were voted down; and on February 17, the Thomas Amendment was added to the Missouri-Maine Bill by a majority of 34 to 10.⁴¹ Mr. King was not among the ten dissidents, eight of whom were Southern Senators; but he thought the amendment an unworthy compromise, "a mere tub to the whale." Was it not clear, he said, that in the western country north of 36° 30′ only one free state could be formed? That all the rest was "a prairie, resembling the steppes of Tartary, without wood or water excepting the great River and its few branches?" And could not one see, south of 36° 30′, room for at least five new slave states? "We have been put," he wrote to Oliver Wolcott, "under a Govt. of the privileged order of men who are henceforth to be & forever to remain our Masters." As for the pretended Southern concession, it was "revocable at pleasure." Thus, for a moment, a long vista of future years was opened up, down which the Missouri Compromise was propelled towards its fatal extinction in the Kansas-Nebraska Act.⁴²

VI

The House received the Senate's Maine-Missouri Bill while it was still debating its own Missouri Bill with John W. Taylor's antislavery amendment. On February 23, by a vote of 93 to 72, it decided to disagree with the Senate amendment to the Maine Bill.⁴³ On February 28, the Senate having sent a message that it *insisted* upon all its amendments to the Maine Bill, including the amendment to annex the Missouri Bill, the House declined by votes of 97-76 on the first eight sections, and 160-14 on the ninth, or Missouri section.⁴⁴ On February 29 it was agreed to hold a conference, and while this was going on, the House's Missouri Bill, with Mr. Taylor's amendment, was sent up to the Senate on March 1, by a vote of 91 to 82.⁴⁵ Within twenty-four hours the Senate had returned this Bill with a message, in which it agreed to separate the admission of Maine from the admission of Missouri, asked the House not to persist in its antislavery amendment, and suggested that both houses should accept the Senate Missouri Bill with the Thomas Amendment. And now, resistance in the House began to weaken, to crumble, to dissolve. By a vote of 90 to 87, it struck the Taylor Amendment out of its own Bill, and by a vote of 134-42 inserted the Thomas Amendment in its place. The Bill was passed in this form. "As usual," wrote John Mott to Rufus King, "Southern management in every struggle comes off victorious." ⁴⁶ But was it Southern management? Might it not rather have been said that antislavery *feeling* in the House was simply not strong enough to hold the line? Three Northern men stayed away on the final day; fifteen more voted with the South; and there were others, said John Randolph, who would have changed their votes if necessary.⁴⁷ And so the first great free soil battle was fought and lost.

To John Randolph was left the last word in this debate. This singular Virginian admitted that all the misfortunes of his life weighed light in the balance when compared with the single misfortune of owing slaves; but he was totally opposed to the restriction of slavery, not merely in Missouri, but anywhere.[48] He voted with the majority on March 2, solely for the purpose of making a motion on the next day to reconsider the House's vote by which it struck out the restriction of slavery in Missouri. This would have reopened the whole question. He was twice ruled out of order by Henry Clay, who still had the Bill in his possession, and who wanted nothing less than a new debate. At last the business of receiving and referring petitions was done; and it was then that Mr. Clay innocently announced that the Bill had already been carried to the Senate by the clerk. He had signed it surreptitiously, and had had it smuggled away. It was an "outrage . . . an unprincipled artifice," said John Quincy Adams, when he heard the story.[49] John Randolph never forgave Mr. Clay for this disgraceful trick; and six years later their quarrel culminated in what Thomas Hart Benton described as the last high-toned duel he was ever to witness. Mr. Clay, on that occasion, put a ball through Mr. Randolph's coat, but Mr. Randolph, paradoxical as ever, shot straight into the air.

VII

Thomas Jefferson was never in doubt as to the significance of the great Missouri contest. He wrote to John Holmes, saying that the question to him had been a "fire-bell in the night." He declared that he considered it at once as the knell of the Union, hushed by the Compromise, but hushed only for the moment. He perceived that a geographical line, coinciding with a marked principle, moral and political, had been held up to the angry passions of men; and that it would never be obliterated.[50] As to slavery, "the cession of that kind of property, for so it is misnamed, is a bagatelle which would not cost me a second thought, if, in that way, a general emancipation and *expatriation* could be effected; and gradually, and with due sacrifices, I think it might be. But as it is, we have the wolf by the ears, and we can neither safely hold him, nor safely let him go." [51] He believed that the diffusion of slavery was more likely to lead to emancipation than the confinement of slavery would ever do; and James Madison agreed with him.[52] Of the three Presidential Virginians, only James Monroe expressed himself as satisfied with the Compromise. He believed that the contest, so far as the Northern leaders were concerned, had been one for power only; and that they had been willing—may even have intended—to dismember the Union. He thought that the Compromise was "auspicious" because it would give passion on both sides time to subside, and because, in such a controversy, it would have been dangerous for either side to come off victorious.[53] These were his second thoughts; he had originally intended to veto the Compromise Bill, and had actually written out a veto message.[54]

The question had caused him the acutest anxiety, for he was by nature inclined to maximize dangers first, and minimize them afterwards. He had not attempted to interfere in any way while the question was still under debate; but, despite his best endeavors, he had not been able to prevent the question from interfering with him. In Virginia, in February, the Republicans were about to select candidates for electors, and it was openly announced in Richmond that if Mr. Monroe allowed the Bill to pass, they would look elsewhere for a President.[55] In his perplexity, he sent a letter to his son-in-law, George Hay, a Richmond attorney, in which he indicated hesitation and doubt: and this letter was certainly intended for communication to the Richmond caucus. Mr. Hay sent it back. It would, he said, be "fatal." It was believed in Richmond that the President would put his veto on "the infamous cabal & intrigue in all its forms & shapes. This I would certainly & promptly do. You may be injured in the N & E States, but you will be amply repaid by the gratitude of the South." [56] Mr. Monroe's silence was interpreted by the Richmond caucus as indicating a veto; and although the Central Committee was dominated by the unfriendly Andrew Stevenson, "everything went on at the caucus last night as it ought to do. . . . Stevenson & . . . his lot . . . will be obliged to go right." [57]

When the Bill appeared for his signature on March 3, Monroe was still undecided. If he signed it, he would be going against the wishes of the caucus, which had nominated electors friendly to him. As was his invariable custom, he did not act until he had consulted his Cabinet. The question he propounded to his Secretaries on March 3 was twofold. Had Congress the power to prohibit slavery in a Territory? And did the word "forever" in the eighth section of the Missouri Bill, interdicting slavery in a Territory north of 36° 30′, apply only to the territorial condition, or extend to the Territory after it had become a state? The argument that followed was prolonged and bitter; and it was clear that, of the whole Cabinet, only Mr. Adams was an antislavery man. Even Smith Thompson, the Secretary of the Navy, and a New Yorker, inclined to the belief that Congress had no right to exclude slavery from a state. At last it was agreed that the Cabinet members should answer in writing, and that the President should change the wording of the second part of his question. He was now to ask merely whether or not the eighth section of the Missouri Enabling Bill was consistent with the Constitution. Both those who believed that it might restrict slavery in a state, and those who were convinced that it might not, could, with an equally good conscience, reply in the affirmative. Thus the Cabinet engineered its own Compromise. Years later, a search was made among the archives for the written answers to Monroe's question; but all that could be found was the envelope, ironically empty, that had once contained them.[58] On March 6, Monroe signed the Enabling Bill, no doubt against his own feelings. As a statesman, which he always believed himself to be, and so often was, he could not have done otherwise.

Mr. Adams publicly favored the Missouri Compromise because it was all that could be effected under the Constitution; but in private he wondered if it would not have been the wiser and bolder course to have persisted in the restriction on Missouri. This would have terminated, he thought, in a convention of the states to revise and amend the Constitution, and from such a convention there would have appeared a new union of thirteen or fourteen states, unpolluted with slavery. He told himself (but himself only) that if the Union had to be dissolved, slavery was the question upon which it ought to break.

VIII

Certain newspaper editors in the North, who believed that they could make Presidents, but who were in no danger of being Presidents themselves, openly vilified the Missouri Compromise. In Carlisle, Representative Fullerton of Pennsylvania was burned in effigy, and Senator Lanman of Connecticut was similarly treated in Hartford.[59] The image of Rufus King was to be put to the flames in St. Louis, but cooler counsels prevailed; and the little city gave itself over to festivities and illuminations. It then became the center of electioneering for delegates to the Constitutional convention. There was a restrictionist ticket, headed by Judge John B. Lucas, a man who was much embittered by the death of his son Charles in a duel with Thomas Hart Benton, editor of the St. Louis *Enquirer*, which lent its support to the pro-slavery ticket. The duel, fought in 1817, was one that young Lucas had sought every honorable means to avoid; and it was generally believed that Benton's part in it had been that of a political bravo. "It is well known," said one of the antislavery party, "that he called Lucas to the fatal spot armed with patent breech'd pistols, instruments so curiously made as to throw a ball into the victim, before poor Lucas' ball could reach him. . . . Mr. B. wishes to fill a Senator's chair and will go through thick and thin to obtain it." [60] This odd version of the duel is no doubt as political as were Benton's motives for fighting it; but Benton at this time—with his land-claim activities and his close connection with Astor's American Fur Company—was at the very lowest point in his career, and it is only just to recall that his later years were as honorable and useful as his early ones were dubious. He was certainly never more than lukewarm in his support of slavery, while Edmund Bates—who, with David Barton, was the leader of the proslavery party in Missouri—finished his career as Attorney-General in the cabinet of Abraham Lincoln.[61] These facts lend some color to the belief that Missourians were moved at least as much by their anger with Congress as by their vehemence for slavery; and the election returns for delegates to the Constitutional convention would seem to show that proslavery sentiment was little better than two to one.[62] However, these returns were so arranged that only one restrictionist—Benjamin Emmons of St. Charles—was actually elected: and even Mr. Emmons did not dare suggest any alteration in the status of the slaves already within the Territory.[63] In short, the mixture of pioneering with slave-owning—which gives this particular phase of western expansion such a nightmare look—makes it difficult for us to determine the state of mind in the Territory as its delegates met to write their constitution. All that we can say is that the Constitution, once written, was little better than a slap in the face of Congress.

Taken as a whole, this new Constitution for Missouri had nothing in it to excite the curiosity of the lawyer and the historian: the delegates, it seemed, had so admired the Constitution of the state of Kentucky that they had almost copied it *verbatim*. Almost, but not quite. In the 26th Section of the 3rd Article they spoke for themselves; and what they had to say—and to submit to Congress for its approval—was little better than a calculated insult. In the first paragraph of that section it was declared illegal for the state assembly to emancipate slaves without their owners' consent: and this, considering the bitter debates of the Spring, was bad enough. But the first clause of the fourth paragraph was far worse. In this clause the Missouri Assembly was enjoined to pass such laws as might be necessary "to prevent free negroes and mulattoes from coming to and settling in this State, under any pretext whatsoever." [64]

Now there were states in which Negroes were free men and citizens, and the federal Constitution stated that "the citizens of each State shall be entitled to all the privileges and immunities of citizens of the several States"; so that it was difficult indeed to maintain that the first clause had anything to recommend it but its brevity. Indeed, if ever the federal Constitution had been grossly and wantonly violated by a group of responsible men, it was so violated in the city of St. Louis by the assembled delegates of the Constitutional convention.

Yet the question involved was that of the status of the free Negro, and the status of the free Negro, in turn, challenged the conscience of the whole nation. If the free Negro was not, in fact, really free in the North, was this due to the existence of slavery in the South? Or was the North preaching a doctrine of human rights which it had no intention of putting into practice? This problem puzzled and confounded, as well it might, the second Session of the Sixteenth Congress.

CHAPTER THREE

The Second Missouri Debate

IN NEW JERSEY," said the Supreme Court of that state, "black men are *prima facie* slaves." And again, "It is a settled rule . . . that the black color is proof of slavery . . . which must be overcome." [1] These mournful dicta had not yet been pronounced when the Sixteenth Congress met again on November 13, 1820; but they might just as well have been. For it was now to be shown that the status of the free Negro in the North was bound to deteriorate in proportion to the increase of slavery in the South: that he was condemned to be a living reminder of the servitude of his fellow men.

I

On November 14 the Missouri Constitution was communicated to the Senate, and submitted to a select committee, which reported a resolution declaring the admission of Missouri into the Union.[2] On December 7 there began a full dress debate upon this resolution, to which Senator Eaton of Tennessee had offered the proviso: "That nothing herein contained shall be so construed as to give the assent of Congress to any provision in the Constitution of Missouri, if any such there be, which contravenes that clause in the Constitution of the United States which declares that 'the citizens of each State shall be entitled to all privileges and immunities of citizens of the several States.' " [3] The proviso was completely toothless, as Senator Eaton had intended; and, reduced to a plain form, seemed to declare that Congress might admit a state to the Union and at the same time withhold its assent from that state's Constitution. It did not touch—it was intended to avoid— what appeared to be the central question: Could the people of Missouri prohibit from entering that state a class of persons who were, for example, citizens of the Commonwealth of Massachusetts?

As Mr. Burrill of Rhode Island pointed out, one could find in the federal Constitution not a single word that recognized color as a bar to citizenship.[4] There was, of course, no answer to this argument: all one could urge in rebuttal was the practice of the several states. Even in Massachusetts, there was a law that forbade the marriage of a white person to an Indian, Negro, or mulatto; and did not this prove, said Senator Smith, that "we must look for the reason of this law, as in all the other states, in the universal assent to the degraded condition of that class of people, and from which none of the States would, perhaps, ever think it expedient to raise them?"[5] No such reason was evident. What Senator Smith seemed to mean was that the Constitution must be interpreted rather in terms of its infractions than of its silences. It had said nothing about color as a bar to citizenship; but since numerous states had broken its rule that the citizens of each state were entitled to the privileges and immunities of citizens of the several states, he argued that this rule could be honored only in the breach. The argument was weird; but the evidence he brought to its support was certainly formidable. In the Constitution of Kentucky it was laid down that "every free white male (*negroes, mulattoes, and Indians excepted*) shall enjoy the right of elector"; in the Constitutions of Ohio and Connecticut the same provision appeared. Vermont and New Hampshire would not admit free Negroes to their militia. Indiana and North Carolina gave them the franchise but would not let them appear as witnesses in any suit against a white man. An Act of Congress of May 15, 1820, made only free white males eligible for the office of Mayor of Washington—although, during the twenty years that Congress had sat there, "a swarm of mulattoes have been reared in the city, many of whom, no doubt, had as illustrious fathers as any in the nation."[6] Senator Smith's list was only a fragmentary one; but he had said enough to show that, where free Negroes were concerned, every state in the Union had discriminated against them in one way or another. Such a general discrimination, he thought, could be construed as a general acquiescence in their degradation; and though this degradation was technically un-Constitutional where the franchise was concerned, acquiescence placed it within the pale of the Constitution. And, indeed, few members of the Sixteenth Congress would have disagreed with the Constitution of Missouri if it had admitted free Negroes and mulattoes under any degrading condition: it was their expulsion from that state which had provoked the whole argument.

If Senator Burrill's appeal to the Constitution was unanswerable, Senator Smith's appeal to custom was no less so. The crime against the Negro was, to some extent, shared by the whole nation. The only reply was that as long as slavery was confined to men of color, who were debased by every means in order to sustain the fiction that they were incapable of rising, then all men of color would suffer as long as any of them were enslaved. The institution must be abolished before the discrimination could be dealt with. But this reply was never made. Even Mr. Morril of New Hampshire, who made the most liberal speech to be heard in that Congress—"it is *citizens* only, and *not* color, that comes into consideration. . . . Color has no share in characterizing an inhabitant or a citizen" was its refrain—even Mr. Morril could not save his arguments from becoming fearfully disingenuous. "Says the gentleman [Senator Smith] 'New Hampshire excludes negroes from training.' . . . This only places them among the exempts, generally the first class in society. And from this very circumstance, they have the privilege of walking about with the other gentlemen and seeing the soldiers train."[7]

Thus the second debates upon the Missouri question, while fully as passionate, suggestive, and portentous as the first, rather stupefy the mind because of this inherent disingenuousness. All were involved in the miserable delusion that the Negro race was inferior to the white: not one man upon the antislavery side dared admit it, or deny it. The Southern contention that the whole question was not one of slavery but of political power was partially justified by the Northern speeches on the Missouri Constitution. There was less insistence upon the moral evil of slavery; and when Mr. Charles Pinckney told the House of Representatives that Negroes were "*created with less intellectual powers than the whites, and were most probably intended to serve them, and be the instruments of their cultivation,*" no man arose to give him the lie.[8] This positive denial of the assertion "all men are created equal" occasioned, of course, no surprise; from the beginning of the Missouri debates, the Declaration of Independence had been under attack. Nor did the fact that Mr. Pinckney had undermined the whole Jeffersonian creed of the equality of man really matter: the Southern Jeffersonians (though not so boldly) had been undermining it in every speech. Even Jefferson, who agonized over the status of the Negro, had been obliged to confess that the Linnæan hypothesis that all men were descended from the same ancient parents might break down when it was confronted with the Negro.[9] Here he spoke and thought as a Virginian and a slave-owner; and though to the end of his days he longed for some proof to set his doubts at rest, and was a more sincere abolitionist than most men to the North of him, he never could reconcile these doubts with his belief in the axiomatic unity of the human race.

Thus we can hardly blame the members of the Sixteenth Congress if, their first assault upon Missouri having broken down because they were too respectful of the rights of property, their second assault should have failed because they could not bring themselves to believe in the equality of the Negro. The most humane philosophers had been unable to reach this conclusion. This was the grievous paradox that remained embodied in American politics, in American economy, in American social behavior: while most state Constitutions declared that all men were created equal, all states, to a greater or less degree, denied this equal creation to some of their inhabitants. The paradox was strengthened by the Missouri debates, and was handed on from one generation to another, growing more steadily in power until Emancipation itself could not set it at rest.

II

The Senate debate upon the Missouri Constitution was virtually at an end on December 12, 1820, when the resolution of November 20, with Mr. Eaton's proviso, was passed without a vote and sent to the House for concurrence.[10] The House had been deprived of the services of Mr. Clay, who found himself obliged (through the pressure of gambling debts, it was uncharitably rumored) to attend to his private affairs in Kentucky until after Christmas, and who had resigned the Speakership. He was succeeded by Mr. John W. Taylor, after a series of ballots which threatened to extend into infinity. Mr. Taylor's success was undoubtedly a triumph for the antislavery forces; but otherwise it was not very inspiriting. Whatever Mr. Clay's political virtues or defects may have been, his presence in the Speaker's chair was always galvanic. Mr. Taylor, on the other hand, though his political management was less open to reproach than Mr. Clay's, had little taste and less talent for his new office. And if ever talent was needed, it was needed for the control and organization of the coming debates on the Missouri Constitution.

Antislavery feeling in the House was, of course, strong enough to resist the resolution of its own select committee that: "The State of Missouri shall be, and is hereby declared to be, one of the United States of America, and is admitted into the Union on an equal footing with the original States, in all respects whatever." [11] The resolution is chiefly memorable because it was moved by William Lowndes of South Carolina, in almost the last speech he was to deliver in that chamber. Lowndes was one of the original War-Hawks of 1812; and, like most of the War-Hawks, he was a man of commanding presence.[12] His voice was low, and there was a great clatter as the members left their seats to cluster round him "whose every word was to be luminous with intelligence, and captivating with candor. This . . . was more than usually eager on this occasion, from the circumstances under which he spoke—the circumstance of the Union verging to dissolution; and his own condition, verging to the grave." [13] The speech itself was a dispassionate exploration of the theory that the people of Missouri, having been authorized by Congress to form a constitution and a state government, and having assented to that proposition, were already constituted a state; and that the act of declaration, now proposed to the House, was mere surplusage.[14]

Mr. Lowndes was only thirty-nine years of age, but he already stood visibly in the shadow of death. A year later, he was nominated by his own state legislature for the presidency; but he showed little interest in this; and six months later he was dead. When he spoke in the House on December 6, 1820, he was a man who had little to prompt him in the way of personal ambition. That his wisdom should have brought him in the end to apply the doctrine of State Rights to so unworthy a cause as that of slavery, was a melancholy conclusion. It seemed to prefigure the other uses to which, down the years, that doctrine—once so republican—was to be put. We must not question the sincerity of Mr. Archer of Virginia when he cried that the essential defenses of the states were giving way before the steady and powerful current of federal authority; nor that of Mr. Floyd of Virginia when he declared that "these independent nations (the states)" could never have imagined that they were granting any power "but that which was necessary to act upon foreigners—in war, to defend the whole—in peace, to regulate the commerce of the whole." [15] The doctrine of State Rights was dear to them, because it represented freedom from the tyranny of centralizing interests: but it had gradually begun to dawn upon them that Congress might—if it exercised powers that were Constitutionally implied but not Constitutionally explicit—become not merely a centralizing but an emancipating body. Thus the doctrine of State Rights became mingled with the defense of slavery. Mr. Lowndes, however, came from a state that had hitherto been nationalist rather than particularist: and his championhip of State Rights was unblushingly a championship of cotton and of the peculiar labor by which it was cultivated.

Now the doctrine of State Rights, since it demanded that the central government should exercise a rigidly limited set of powers, had always been connected with a very strict interpretation of the language of the Constitution. On very special occasions—the Louisiana Purchase and the Embargo Act were perhaps the most outstanding—its advocates yielded to necessity and disregarded the Constitution altogether. Was the Missouri problem so imperative as to demand a similar concession? Apparently it was; for to declare that the Constitution of Missouri was in accordance with the Constitution of the United States was to construe the latter document very loosely indeed. From that time on, the question of "strict" construction or "loose" construction became—what it has subsequently always been—a question of interest and not of principle. Nor can we deny that Mr. Lowndes of South Carolina—the former nationalist of the War of 1812 —pointed the way to that still ardent nationalist, John Caldwell Calhoun of South Carolina; and that it was during the Missouri debates that the seed of nullification, so long embedded in the Virginia and Kentucky Resolutions, began to stir and spring.

III

Mr. Lowndes was well equipped to lead the slavery forces through the second stage of the Missouri Debates; but after his resolution had been defeated on December 13 by a vote of 93 to 79, he had not the health to carry on the battle.[16] The extremists on either side now ranged themselves around the propositions (a) that Missouri was still a Territory, (b) that it was already an independent state or nation. Nothing, it seemed, could dislodge them from these positions. But with the New Year came Mr. Clay, and it was into Mr. Clay's hands that the difficult task was committed.

In the last session, he had been satisfied with the compromise that kept slavery south of 36° 30′; but he had spoken out against restriction in Missouri; and when slavery itself was attacked as a moral evil, he had warned the attackers "with stern tones and repulsive gesture not to obtrude upon him with our New England *notions*." [17] He was a slave-owner himself, committed to the doctrine of a gradual emancipation at a very distant date, and inclined to believe that owners and slaves would get along very well if only they were left to themselves. When the Missouri Compromise was threatened by this new conflict on the Missouri Constitution, he found it easy to persuade himself that the infamous provision excluding free Negroes from Missouri was not repugnant to the federal Constitution. But he believed that the Union was in danger, and he set himself, with all the address at his command, to play the role of peacemaker.

Since his great services at Ghent, Mr. Clay had been something of a stormy petrel in American politics, distinguished chiefly as the champion of South American freedom and the enemy of General Jackson—two causes, not unconnected, to which he had devoted as much disinterested passion as is consistent with strong political ambitions. No one doubted that he hoped to overthrow the Administration with his South American speeches. Few people supposed that his attack upon the General had had any other purpose than the advancement of Mr. Clay. Fascinating and casual, he seemed indifferent to the enmities he incurred or the divisions he caused in his efforts to promote his fortunes; but his sunny temperament was darkened by sudden rages that showed—even to not very discerning eyes—how unremitting, how intense, how desperate these efforts were. He now appeared in the role of peacemaker—not a petrel but a halcyon—and this role, which he played with great success, was to be re-enacted again and again in his long career.

There is no doubt at all that Mr. Clay was a Union man, with a fervent belief in the future of his country; that he was a patriot, in brief, with as good a claim to that title as anyone in the Congress. But there are very few patriots—perhaps there is none—who can entirely dissociate their patriotism from personal ambition on the one hand or from environment on the other. Mr. Clay came from a slave-holding state upon the borders of the South, and with strong affinities with the North and the West: affinities that were embodied in his American System of tariffs, internal improvements, and a national bank. This system required Union at any cost; and Mr. Clay was therefore determined to effect a compromise. His opponents were never quite able to decide where compromise ended and sorcery began.

Compromise is necessary to all political democracies; but in young, eager, and expansive political democracies it never wears a very agreeable look. What the American people required in the 1820's was not someone who could reconcile their differences, but someone who could transcend them. Just how this could be done they did not know, and were never to learn, but Mr. Clay, with his Southern sensibilities and his Northern views and his Western enthusiasms, seemed at least as untrustworthy as he was lovable. His American System was not fully developed, but he was already speaking the language of Northern capitalism with courage and conviction, and was attempting to make it palatable to the West and South; while in the Missouri debates he tried to make the views of the slave-holder not too disagreeable to the West and North. He succeeded in his compromise, and, by the end of February, seemed to tower like a Colossus over the lesser figures of that disordered Congress; but anyone might have been forgiven for the pun that, whatever the head of the Colossus might have been composed of, the feet were feet of clay.

In short, he expected to achieve peace and succeeded only in laying the foundations for civil war. Mr. Lowndes's resolution having been defeated on December 13, the question remained whether or not the House would accept the Senate's resolution as a substitute. On January 29, 1821, Mr. Clay proposed that this resolution be accepted—more in the interests of peace, he explained, than of truth, for he could not believe that it was really necessary.[18] On the same day, Samuel Foot of Connecticut moved to strike out the Eaton proviso from the Senate resolution, and to insert in its place the following language: "That it shall be taken as a fundamental condition, upon which the said State is incorporated into the Union, that so much of the 26th section of the 3d article of the Constitution which has been submitted to Congress, as declares it shall be the duty of the General Assembly 'to prevent free negroes and mulattoes from coming to, or settling in, this State, under any pretext whatsoever,' shall be expunged, within two years from the passage of this resolution, by the General Assembly of Missouri, in the manner prescribed for amending said Constitution." [19] These words were unduly tactful, but they asserted the dignity of Congress; and had they been accepted, they would at least have told the slave-holding interest that it could not do what it pleased with the rights of man. They were not accepted. The same ambivalence that had weakened the antislavery position in the first debates undermined it in the second. "Nothing," said Mr. Cushman of Maine, after a violent attack upon slavery, "nothing can be farther from the free States than the design to meddle with the subject of slavery where it exists by Constitutional compact. But, to consent to its extension, is revolting to all the principles of liberty in which they have been educated." [20] As a political fact, however, was it not clear that if slavery were not abolished, slavery would extend itself? Every amendment to Mr. Foot's motion, therefore, begged this question by mollifying proslavery opinion; every amendment, in short, declared that the excluding section in the Missouri Constitution should never be construed in such a way as to contravene the Constitution of the United States. But in what other way could it be construed? As the debate dragged on, nothing seemed to remain but the figure of Mr. Clay, exerting all his powers to bring the Congress to accept this feeble solution.

IV

Mr. Clay's efforts were about to be crowned with success, when another event intervened, to plunge the Sixteenth Congress into its final and most disorderly exhibition. In the previous November, James Monroe had been re-elected President of the United States; he had secured the electoral vote of every state; and only the adverse vote of William Plumer of New Hampshire in the Electoral College prevented his election from being, like George Washington's, unanimous. But, unlike George Washington, Mr. Monroe had been elected by what might be called an act of unanimous indifference. Even in Philadelphia, where he was opposed by an antislavery ticket headed by (of all people) De Witt Clinton of New York, only two thousand persons went to the polls as compared to forty-seven hundred in the earlier contest for governor; and in the city of Richmond, it was said, only seventeen people bothered to record their votes.[21] Like Tocqueville's Indian, Mr. Monroe was merely to wait until others came. This was not so much a reflection upon his character, as a comment upon the flaccidity of one-party politics.

On February 14, 1821, the electoral votes were counted before the Congress. The ceremony was generally invested with a formal dignity—the president of the Senate, attended by its secretary and sergeant-at-arms, and followed by the whole Senatorial body, entering the Hall of Representatives and taking his seat in the Speaker's chair, with the Speaker on his left hand. After a short pause, the president of the Senate would then open the ballots of the states and hand them one by one to the tellers.[22] The House and the Senate, realizing that this ceremony would take place while the status of Missouri was still undecided, had agreed upon a plan for preserving the dignity that attached to it. The president of the Senate would first declare what the result would be if the vote of Missouri were counted, and then what it would be if the vote of Missouri were not counted; after which he would announce: "But in either case James Monroe is elected President of the United States." The plan was not a very good one, but it was the best that could be devised.

No sooner, however, had the president of the Senate opened and read the vote of Missouri, and handed the paper to the tellers, than a member of the House called out that he objected, because Missouri was not yet a state. There followed a tremendous din. Some called for Order, some seconded the objection. Amidst the tumult, the voice of a Senator could be heard entreating his colleagues to withdraw. The president of the Senate at length pulled himself together, put the question in an inaudible voice, and declared it carried without bothering to ask for a show of hands. One by one the Senators withdrew, leaving the House in an uproar that lasted for more than an hour. At length Mr. Floyd of Virginia arose to move that Missouri was one of the states of the Union, and that its vote should be counted; and it was solely through the exertions of Mr. Clay that this motion was tabled, and the clerk sent to the Senate to inform that body that the House was now ready to go on with the count. The candles had long since been lit. The Senate returned. The president of the Senate read the vote of Missouri and announced, according to the formula agreed upon, that James Monroe had received 231 electoral votes in one case and 228 in the other. He was preparing to add "I therefore declare that in either case James Monroe is elected President of the United States." when Mr. Floyd again asked whether the vote of Missouri had or had not been counted. He was still on his feet, the target of objurgations and cries of "Order!" when John Randolph arose to address the Speaker. By now the noise was terrific, and poor Mr. Taylor, already hoarse from shouting, was hard put to it to declare Mr. Randolph out of order. He then tried to make it known—for members were addressing him from all sides—that Mr. Floyd was also out of order, and that the same would be true of any gentleman who rose to his feet for any purpose. At length, the members of the House contented themselves with mere grumbling, and the president of the Senate was able to announce that James Monroe of Virginia was President, and Daniel D. Tompkins of New York was vice-president for the next ensuing term.[28]

V

This unseemly incident is worth recording only because it showed that the Presidency itself had been made a symbol, not of party warfare, but of the very dissolution of parties.

VI

Mr. Clay had already succeeded in having the Senate's resolution referred to a committee of thirteen. This committee was composed of eight members from free states and five from slave states, and it was therefore unlikely that its report and amendment would satisfy anybody.[24] The amendment was no improvement upon the resolution that it proposed to amend, and on February 12 it was voted down by 83 to 80.[25] Two days later there came the incident of the electoral vote, which exhausted the energies of Congress. Mr. Clay had already won a victory by having a committee appointed at all; and although Mr. Brown of Kentucky—in a speech that introduced the new verb "to be yankied"—moved the repeal of such parts of the Missouri compromise as restricted slavery north of 36° 30', it was now clear that Mr. Clay would have his way.[26] On February 22, he moved for the appointment of a joint committee. The House agreed by a vote of 101 to 55.[27] On February 26 the resolution of the joint committee was passed by a vote of 87 to 81; and the long, tragic, and unseemly struggle was over.[28]

This was the resolution, which differed little from that which had been offered by the committee of thirteen: "*Resolved, by the Senate and House of Representatives of the United States of America in Congress assembled,* That Missouri shall be admitted into this Union on equal footing with the original States in all respects whatever, upon the fundamental condition that the fourth clause of the twenty-sixth section of the third article of the Constitution submitted on the part of said State to Congress shall never be construed to authorize the passage of any law, and that no other law shall be passed in conformity thereto, by which any citizens of either of the States of this Union shall be excluded from the enjoyment of any of the privileges and immunities to which such citizen is entitled under the Constitution of the United States: *Provided,* that the Legislature of the said

State, by a solemn public act, shall declare the assent of the said State, to the said fundamental condition, and shall transmit to the President of the United States, on or before the fourth Monday in November next, an authentic copy of the said act; upon the receipt whereof the President, by proclamation, shall announce the fact: whereupon, and without any further proceeding on the part of Congress, the admission of the State into this Union shall be considered as complete." [29]

Thus it became a "fundamental condition" of the admission of Missouri that, while her Constitution continued to order her legislators to pass laws excluding free Negroes and mulattoes, her legislators should, by a solemn public act, declare that this order did not authorize the passing of any law that contravened the federal Constitution. The solemnity of such a public act might well be doubted; and on June 26 the legislature of Missouri duly passed a most extraordinary bill, which declared itself unnecessary, on the grounds that Congress had no right to require it, and not binding upon the state. This insulting language was deemed sufficient, and on August 10, 1821, President Monroe announced by proclamation that the admission of Missouri was declared to be complete.[30]

This submission to the insults of slave-holders became part of the American way of life until such time as chattel slavery was no longer held to be protected by the rights of property. Its effect upon Missouri may be judged by the State Act of 1825 "concerning negroes and mulattoes," which excluded such persons from the state unless they were the citizens of another state, in which case they were required to present their naturalization papers. This they could not do, since the states in which they were regarded as citizens had not naturalized them. An Act of 1847 went even further, and openly flouted the "fundamental condition" upon which the state had been admitted. This Act provided that "No free negro nor mulatto shall under any pretext emigrate into this State from any State or Territory." [31] Such was the hold upon the future of Mr. Clay's first great compromise.

VII

The alarm that the whole quarrel had aroused was justified in every particular. It was now evident that the old alliance between Pennsylvania and Virginia was at an end. It was even possible that the understanding between the Northwest and the South, which had been the geographical basis for the rule of the Republican Party, was to be changed into a union between the free states of the East and the West. It was certainly true that a geographical ditch had been dug by the Thomas Amendment which could not be bridged by so frail a structure as the resolution of the joint committee. The grievances of industrialists and planters, of capitalists and agrarians, had been raised from the levels of self-interest and inseparably connected with the hatred of slavery as a moral evil or with its defense as a religious and economic blessing. Above all, the whole nation had been shown that it must either accept the undemocratic dogma that the Negro had not been created the equal of the white man, or it must confess that something was seriously amiss with every part of its democratic structure. It has often been said—though without any specific evidence—that the second debate upon Missouri was more embittered than the first; and since this second debate touched not merely the conscience of the slave-holder but the conscience of the whole Congress, this may well have been the case.

It has also been said that the Missouri Compromise put the question of slavery to sleep for many years. But this is not true. It never slept again.

VIII

The effects of this controversy upon the Southern slave-holder might be judged, to some extent, by the fact that his literary representatives now began to defend slavery, not as a necessary evil, but as something historical, Christian, and humane.[32] At the same time, enthusiasm for that dubious though respected enterprise, the American Colonization Society, increased throughout the South, although proslavery extremists already suspected it of having some connection with abolitionism. Since its avowed object was "to promote and execute a plan for colonizing (with their consent) the Free People of Colour residing in our country, in Africa, or such other place as Congress shall deem it most expedient," these suspicions were hardly well founded; and the opposite point of view, that it was designed to enhance the value of slaves by getting rid of free competition, obtained some justification from the fact that a number of slave-holders appeared on the list of its vice-presidents. Nobody commented upon the undemocratic nature of the argument that free Negroes could never improve their lot in America; or upon the curious notion that Africa was such a cultural and climatic unity that any American Negro could be happy in any part of it. By December 1821 the Colonization Society had acquired a tract of land near Cape Montserado in exchange for gunpowder, tobacco, muskets, iron pots, beads, looking-glasses, pipes, and cotton; here the emigrants battled with malaria and the enmity of the neighboring chieftians, to which, but for the efforts of the heroic Jehudi Ashmun, who arrived in 1822, they must have succumbed. Between 1828 and 1830 some 1,430 emigrants were transported to these inhospitable coasts. These exiguous figures mark the beginning of Liberia and the end of the belief that free Negroes wanted nothing better than to return to Africa there "to sing, in the language which records the constitution, laws, and history of America, hymns of praise to the common parent of man." [33]

The free Negro, whose miseries had been exposed in the second Missouri debate, clearly needed some other solution to his difficulties. In the 1820's, in those states where slavery had more or less ceased to exist, could he look for education, opportunity, enfranchisement? On the whole, he could not. Such states, said one acute observer, "usually do what they can to render their territory disagreeable to the Negroes as a place of residence. . . . A kind of emulation exists between the different states in this respect." [34] In the South, though his treatment was sometimes more humane, he was regarded as a potential troublemaker among the slaves.[35] In the 1820's the Negro, bound or free, was almost voiceless in American history; but the Denmark Vesey insurrection must be regarded as having spoken, directly and with a dreadful eloquence, concerning the impact of the Missouri debates upon one fragment of this silent and isolated group.

Denmark Vesey was a free Negro, a carpenter of Charleston, an intelligent man who had amassed a considerable fortune during his twenty years' residence in that city. Whether or not he had several wives, and was infuriated by the slavery his children inherited from their mothers, must remain in some doubt; it is probably true that he was admitted to the Second Presbyterian Church in 1817, and attached himself to the African Methodist congregation, where he became a leading instructor of religious classes, and made much of the story of Exodus.[36] He had everything to gain from remaining on good terms with the whites, but he was profoundly moved by the servitude he saw around him in the city and in his travels to and fro among the neighboring plantations. When he read of the Missouri debates, he seems to have persuaded himself that they represented (which they evidently did not) a concerted attack from the North upon the whole institution; and he was all the more encouraged to plan a revolt.[37] Meetings were held at his house on Bull Street in 1821; contributions were levied; arms were fashioned. By May 1822 all was ready. In such cases as this, figures are notoriously unreliable; and one can mention only as a rumor that 9,000 were supposed to be involved, and that the number of insurrectionists outside the city was estimated at 6,600.[38] No doubt the figures represent an exaggeration, numerically though not spiritually. The nature of the plan, which called for a number of intricately concerted attacks upon the city from different points; the fact that it was known to have been given away before it could be put into execution; the wild hope that it would spread revolt through the South if it succeeded in Charleston—all these particulars prove how desperate were Vesey and his slave collaborators.[39] Vesey, indeed, had been driven so hard by his feelings that he was ready for any expedient that could prevent him from gazing any longer at fellow human beings in servitude—any expedient, that is, except the obvious one of leaving the country. The contemplated revolt might be called a sortie out of bondage; or it might more fairly be described as an unconscious suicide. Knowing that their movements were watched, and their plot known, the leaders persisted; they merely set the date back from the night of July 14 to the night of June 16.[40] On the morning of June 16, the authorities struck. One hundred and thirty-one arrests were made; and of those arrested, thirty-seven were executed between June 18 and August 9, forty-three were transported, and forty-eight were discharged with a whipping.[41] Vesey himself was captured on June 22, and hanged on July 2.

The outcome of all this was, of course, to make the position of the Negro in the South somewhat less endurable than it had been before. Religious exercises among the slaves were more closely supervised, as to matter and manner and place. The slave-holder was confirmed in his suspicion that skilled or educated Negroes were dangerous men; had not the majority of Vesey's collaborators been mechanical workers—carpenters, blacksmiths, harnessmakers, and so forth? The fear of servile rebellion, which had been measurably increased by the language and direction of the Missouri debates, was now, as it were, made visible by the abortive Denmark Vesey affair. Who would dare deny that it was a possibility—even a probability? "Our Negroes," said Edwin Holland, "are truely the *Jacobins* of the country." [42] The fear was useful as well as psychological, strategic as well as guilty; it bound the slave-holders together in vigilance, in a distaste for manumission, and above all in an effort to render the Negro less aspiring by impressing upon him, by every means that came to hand, the belief that he was incapable of aspiration. In his manners, his appearance, his illiteracy, his religious beliefs, he was required to enact, every day of his life, the wretched myth of racial inferiority.[48] If he did not, the reward for his contumacy was sale or torture or death.

IX

The authorities of Charleston, none the less, must be credited with mildness: they could have exacted a far more terrible revenge than they did. The newspapers, of course, gave the whole affair as little publicity as possible. That is one reason why so little is known of the Denmark Vesey rebellion; another is that the leaders, almost to a man, declined to betray their followers. "Die silent," said Peter, the slave of James Poyas, "as you shall see me die." [44] They had planned to visit upon the city of Charleston all the horrors of massacre; but in their deaths, which were dignity itself, they behaved like men who considered themselves martyrs. And perhaps they were.

4

THE DIPLOMACY OF COAL AND IRON:
1821-1824

CHAPTER ONE

A Cloud over the West Indies

ON MONDAY, March 5, 1821, James Monroe was inaugurated President for the second time. It was a day of wind and sleet, and the capital city, never kind to wayfarers, was drowned in mud; so that few people had gathered outside the President's House, and fewer still lined the wayside to see him drive to the Capitol. A little procession was formed. At the head was the President in his plain carriage, with its single colored footman and four horses; it was followed by the carriages of the Secretaries of State, of the Treasury, of War, and of the Navy. There was no escort. Though the streets were deserted, a large crowd stood shivering outside the Capitol, and the avenues to the hall of the House of Representatives were so choked with humanity that Mr. Monroe had great difficulty in forcing his way through.[1] Half buried in the mob, wet and angry, in lace coat and silk stockings, stood the British Minister, Mr. Stratford Canning and Mr. Antrobus, his Secretary of Legation. "We were stuck about ten paces from the door and were utterly unable to get in until the arrival of the President, who to our great concern and satisfaction was squeezed as handsomely and detailed as long as ourselves. . . . In addition to the squeezing and shoving which the poor *Prezzy* experienced at the door, his speech, which was rather long, was occasionally interrupted by queer sounds from the gallery."[2]

Mr. Monroe was dressed in a full suit of black broadcloth, of a somewhat antiquated cut, with shoe and knee buckles, and with his hair, as usual, powdered and tied in a queue at the back. He delivered his speech in a grave and low voice. Dressed, like the President himself in his broadcloth and knee breeches, in the rather stiff phraseology of an earlier day, it sounds to the modern reader less like an inaugural address than a valedictory one. The President looked back to the smiling landscape of what had been the Era of Good Feelings. He recalled the passing of the War of 1812, the building

249

of coast fortifications from the St. Croix to the Sabine in a spirit of "peace and goodwill," the ratification of the Florida Treaty, the "peculiar felicity" of the United States in being altogether unconnected with the causes of war which seemed to menace Europe. He noted that he had been able to repeal the internal taxes, and he expressed his belief that "the present depression in prices" would be temporary; while, as a proof of the "extraordinary prosperity" of the nation, he offered the payment of nearly $67,000,000 of the public debt. He declared that no serious conflict had arisen between the national and state governments, and announced that "there is every reason to believe that our system will soon attain the highest degree of perfection of which human institutions are capable." [3]

Such sentiments were familiar and, no doubt, expected. To have sketched the outlines of the past with a critical or wavering pen—to have looked into the future with doubtful or even speculative eyes—would have been thought most inappropriate on such an occasion. Moreover, the President who had publicly described the Panic of 1819 as a mild and instructive admonition was not the man to do it. He was content to invest the whole scene of his past Administration with the shimmerings of an inveterate optimism. All was sunlit . . . or very nearly all. Here and there, in the interests of art or of common sense, the President had sketched in a patch of shade. But of the ruined farmers, the anxious manufacturers, the angry slave-holders, the furious partisans who were so densely congregated in these little patches he had said not a word. Under these circumstances, it would be interesting to know more about the nature of those "queer sounds from the gallery."

I

Yet to a man of James Monroe's character—a man, that is to say, who was deeply attached to tranquillity ("the pole-star," said Mr. Adams, "of his policy"), and who, more than any other President before or after, seemed peculiarly able to personify and even to impose it—the situation of the country might not have appeared alarming.[4] The ratification of the Florida Treaty, on the one hand, and the conditional admission of Missouri, on the other, suggested that an equilibrium had been reached. And the admission of Missouri had been preceded by another event that did much to keep that question from becoming more embittered, more difficult to solve, than was actually the case. In April 1820 the manufacturing interest made a serious effort to burden the country with protective tariffs; but, lacking support west of Ohio, and with New England quite divided in its sentiments, the tariff bill barely scraped through the House of Representatives and was defeated in the Senate. The debates had been brief and dignified—so much so that one might safely assert that neither the supremacy of cotton nor the future of manufactures was assured enough to bring about a quarrel.[5] The Southern agrarian was not yet able to say that the foreign goods he purchased with his staples were unfairly taxed.

It is true that the confusion of state politics scarcely justified the tranquil optimism of the President. This seminal confusion—in which democratic sentiments sought to express themselves in all kinds of strange combinations —defeated reason and has since defied analysis; if anything could be deduced from it, in a national sense, it would be a general dissatisfaction with the Administration of James Monroe. But this dissatisfaction had not reached the stage of a concerted opposition; it was local, fragmentary, introspective.

It was, therefore, not incorrect for the President to assume—as he seems to have assumed in his Second Inaugural—that a state of temporary equilibrium had been reached. Upon this assumption, moreover, we can understand how it was possible for the second Administration of James Monroe to attempt, step by step, that definition of the relation between the New World and the Old which has come down to us in final form as the Monroe Doctrine. This attempt was, to be sure, in a sense forced upon Mr. Monroe and his advisers. As the War of 1812 had illustrated in the most obvious manner, whatever happens in one part of the civilized world must sooner or later affect every other part; and the vital and portentous fragment of Western civilization which had crossed the Alleghenies and the Mississippi was not immune to this law. The history of the United States in the nineteenth century is the history of the advance of Western Christendom and Western capitalism towards the Pacific; and the particular phase of it which is now to be examined illustrates, with a certain eloquence, the hollowness of the word "isolation." The American people were already turning their backs upon Europe in the 1820's; but they could not turn their backs upon the world. It was in the 1820's that the United States called attention to its future as a world power and proposed (in a negative and premature way, no doubt) to play a leading part in world politics. The Monroe Doctrine professed an unwillingness to interfere in the affairs of Europe; but it is well to remember that it threatened interference if the ambitions of Europe ran counter to its concept of world relations. It contained certain elements of isolationism and of economic nationalism; but, as regards the possible future, it was not really isolationist at all.

Its formulation was due partly to the pressure of world events, partly to the courage of James Monroe, partly to the genius of John Quincy Adams. It was also much indebted to a most singular set of coadjutors—the "Liberal" wing of the British Tory Party, the leader of which was the second Earl of Liverpool, an old enemy of the War of 1812.

II

Once upon a time, in a forgotten essay, Thomas Babington Macaulay described the right wing of the Tory Party as "stern and unbending." [6] Unlike the essay, the description was remembered; and it was subsequently applied, not merely to the right wing of the Tory Party, but to the whole organization. This was a solecism that Macaulay himself—though a great Whig and by no means unwilling to sacrifice the truth to an epithet—would never have perpetrated. He knew very well that Tory leaders, however stern, were not always unbending. There were times when pliability—a very discreet pliability—was their foremost characteristic.

This was peculiarly noticeable after the War of 1812, when Great Britain was brought face to face with her destiny, when she began to realize that she was to be the industrial leader of the world. Destiny may terrify even those whom it favors. The corollary of this leadership was free trade, or the unimpeded exchange of cheap manufactures for cheap raw materials; and the necessary consequence of free trade was that the idea of competition should displace the idea of monopoly. There were interests in Great Britain—landed interests, shipping interests, colonial interests—which would resist such a displacement with a bitter and apprehensive obstinacy; and even the industrialists had grave doubts about it. It was the "Liberal" wing of the Tory Party which first attempted to persuade them all.

That there should be a Liberal Wing at all was curious, because the Tory Party was ostensibly in the grip of great landed noblemen, to whom free trade was anathema, and to whom a majority of the members in Parliament owed their seats. Another and lesser Parliamentary group—"the country gentlemen"—was independent and, except for its unalterable allegiance to the out-of-date, politically unpredictable. A third group was composed of conservative bankers, shipowners, and manufacturers. All were held together by an ill-defined belief in the symmetrical relationship of King, Lords, Commons and people, each in an allotted sphere; all acknowledged the intellectual pre-eminence of Burke and Pitt, both of whom were relapsed Whigs; all were convinced that public opinion, while a good enough thing in its way and in its place, had no right to interfere with the mysteries of government. From this common basis, however, they diverged. The majority was composed of High Tories, or Ultras, who strongly suspected anything that savored of progress; their leaders were such men as the Duke of Wellington, Lord Eldon, and Lord Westmorland. The minority, which gained control during the 1820's, was Liberal: its members had some feeling for administrative, legal, and commercial reform.[7] Robert Banks Jenkinson, second Earl of Liverpool, and Prime Minister from 1812 to 1827, was just such a Liberal.

He was not, of course, a Liberal in the sense in which we would construe the term. He had no sympathy for the plight of industrial workers, though he had been known to express a mild disapproval of child labor.[8] He did not believe that a representative system that allowed decayed old boroughs to return two members to Parliament and denied a franchise to the new towns was at all susceptible of improvement. He was opposed to Catholic Emancipation. He was as responsible as any man for the infamous Six Acts with which his Administration, in 1819, responded to the outcry of a sorely distressed people. It was not in improving the conditions of the poor, or in widening the franchise, or in promoting the advance of civil liberties that Lord Liverpool showed himself a Liberal; such considerations left him cold. But when it came to a sympathetic understanding of the needs, energies, and future of commerce and of industry, there it must be admitted that Lord Liverpool was a Liberal indeed.

He was an amiable, awkward, retiring man who often succeeded in giving an impression of himself which was quite at variance with the facts. When he was seized with a paralytic stroke in 1827, which compelled him to resign, Charles Greville noted in his journal that "It was remarked how little anybody seemed to care about the *man*." [9] Indifference is a great preservative, and many of Greville's *obiter dicta* have become truths because nobody has bothered to question them. In the same way the remark of a Frenchman, who had some pretensions to wit, that if Lord Liverpool had been present at the Creation he would have cried out in a panic "*Mon Dieu, conservons le chaos*," was for a long time inseparable from the Liverpool legend.[10] But Lord Liverpool was neither a nonentity nor a rigid conservative. It is only of recent years that a successful attempt has been made to penetrate the veil that prejudice, tradition, and his own modesty have thrown about him; and this most fidgety and uninspiring of statesmen has now been hailed as "one of the architects of the nineteenth century." [11] The phrase is more excessive than inexact.

He was a professional man—one of those professional men to whom the Tory Party, in spite of its heavy leavening of great landed proprietors, and its aristocratic taste for amateur statesmanship, so often committed its affairs. The Jenkinsons were a respectable family, and when the first Earl died he left his son, according to the *Annual Register*, about £15,000 per annum, of which about £3,000 was derived from land.[12] By the standards of those days—when it was said that "a man can *jog along* on £40,000 a year"—the second Earl was neither very wealthy nor very much of a landed proprietor. Of the eight peers in his Cabinet, moreover, only two had titles that went back for more than a generation, and these two alone belonged to the landed aristocracy. Lord Liverpool was very careful not to break with the High Tory Wing of his party; but the drift of his policy became less and less favorable to the landed interest, and he received into his Cabinet men at whom the great Tory magnates looked askance—reformers and parvenus who would hardly have stayed in office a month if it had not been for his consistent and unwavering support. In short, there were others who loomed larger in the public eye than did Lord Liverpool, but it was Lord Liverpool who pulled the strings.

Madame de Lieven, the Russian Ambassadress in London, who liked to exercise her rather cerebral fascinations upon great men and who was so often bored into fits, confessed that Lord Liverpool bored her but that she was very impressed by him. "The great Liverpool," she called him; and she was not being ironical.[13] She had an instinct for power, and power—a very discreet power—is what Lord Liverpool represented. He was, in fact, a man to whom it is well to pay attention; a man who had learned, while his commissioners were treating with the Americans at Ghent, the unique value of the United States as a market for British manufactures; and who was not the sort of statesman to forget what he had learned.

III

When the Peace of Ghent was signed, all the great issues between Great Britain and the United States (the various boundary questions, the fishery dispute, the navigation of the Mississippi, and all the problems connected with the Freedom of the Seas) were left *in statu quo ante*—in other words, to the arbitration not only of men but of time. And time—or change—was, indeed, the best of arbitrators. The British Empire that emerged from the Napoleonic Wars was already very different from the Empire that had undergone a peripheral break-up in the American Revolution. War is the *ultima ratio* of competition; and war used also to be one of the ways in which economic competition most successfully disguised itself. Even after Waterloo, many Englishmen believed that their Empire was still the old mercantilist Empire—that they had defeated Napoleon through a combination of sea power, colonial produce, a trade monopoly, and European coalitions. That Waterloo had been the consummate expression of the victory of early and competitive British industrialism, they were not prepared to admit. But British manufactures were vigorous and suggestive, and their unwieldy magic fumbled alike at the thinking of Whitehall, the alliances of Europe and the fears of Washington.

British industrialism is a constant factor in the events now to be described—in the affairs of Europe as they encroached upon the New World, and more particularly in the shifts and changes in Anglo-American relations. Its presence can be found, more often as a guiding instinct than as a formulated policy, where it might least be expected. It lay, for example, at the heart of an argument that gradually came to epitomize Anglo-American relations during the Administrations of Monroe and Adams—to crystallize by a kind of molecular affinity all the elements of agreement and disagreement, all the warring particles of tradition and interest in either country. This was the dispute that centered itself around the West Indian carrying trade. Other disputes were larger and apparently graver; this was the most illuminating but the least remembered. It deserves to be examined because it brings into sharp focus the various encounters of the administrations of Monroe and Adams with the governments of Liverpool and Canning.

The beginnings of this dispute lay in the old British foreign policy, based upon sea power and monopoly. When the War of 1812 ended, and the two countries agreed to establish a reciprocal trade between the United States and the British European ports, it was discovered—to the chagrin of the Americans—that the British had no intention of changing their colonial system, which decreed that only an enumerated list of American products could be imported into the British West Indies and British North America, and then only in British ships. The American plenipotentiaries in London protested, and protested in vain. The British merely replied that this was their old policy, which had been laxly administered during the late war, but was now to be reinstated in all its vigor.[14] Thus the British enjoyed a triangular trade from Great Britain to the United States to the West Indies and back; while the Americans were restricted to the direct trade between the United States and Great Britain. The competition thus established—if competition it could be called—was ruinous; and by 1816 more than half the tonnage of the United States was lying in its docks, rotting and useless.[15]

The British, of course, were still thinking upon the old mercantilist lines that a trade monopoly is one of the sinews of national strength, and that a flourishing carrying trade is vital to the existence of a strong Navy. The Americans, however, were not as they had been in the days when there was no choice between the extortions of England and the piracies of Napoleon. Napoleon was in St. Helena; and Spencer Perceval was—where? Congress replied with the Navigation Act of March 1, 1817, which retricted the importation of British West Indian produce to the vessels of the United States or vessels belonging to West Indian merchants.[16] Since the Act did not prohibit the exportation of United States goods to the British West Indies in British vessels, it was not very strong. But the tide of nationalism was running high; President Monroe's First Annual Message demanded firmer measures; and on April 18, 1818, Congress passed another Bill, closing the ports of the United States to all British vessels arriving from a colony that was legally closed to the vessels of American citizens. "We have passed the age of childhood," said Hezekiah Niles.[17]

The Commercial Convention of 1815 was due to expire in 1819, and arrangements for a new negotiation were already being made in London. The British, it seemed, were now prepared to make concessions; and the Americans, on their side, were actually suggesting that nothing would satisfy them but a complete equality and reciprocity in the West Indian trade —in other words, the British must begin to discard their colonial system. The British, needless to say, were not prepared for so sudden a departure from their old ways; and when a new commercial convention was signed in October 1818 the whole question of the West Indian trade was left undecided.[18]

In the proposals and counterproposals which followed it became clear that the British were still clinging to their mercantilist beliefs. "Our colonies," Lord Castlereagh told Mr. Rush, the American Minister, "are, in many respects, burdensome, and even liable to involve the country in wars. Garrisons, and other establishments, are constantly maintained at a heavy charge. In return, it is just that they should be *encumbered with regulations,* the operation of which might help to meet, in part, the expenses which they created. *The great principle of these regulations is known to be the reservation of an exclusive right to the benefit of all their trade.*" [19] The British had already designated St. John and Halifax as free ports, to which the Americans might carry their goods in their own ships; they thus hoped to make New Brunswick and Nova Scotia an entrepôt for an indirect trade between the United States and the British West Indies; and they had made arrangements whereby the Danish and Swedish West Indies could be used as entrepôts for the reception of American tobacco, rice, grain, peas, beans, and flour, which would be transported thence in British ships to the British West Indies.[20] But these arrangements, which were received with acclamation in New Brunswick and Nova Scotia, only exacerbated the feelings of the United States. The Americans contended that there was a natural exchange between their farm products and the rum and molasses and coffee of the British West Indies; and cries of anguish from the planters of those islands indicated that this might, indeed, be the case. For an indirect trade merely increased the price of those necessities which they could get most readily from the United States; and it seemed to them that their very existence was being sacrificed to the British navigation system and to the prosperity of New Brunswick and Nova Scotia.

As matters stood in 1819, the United States had the best of it. The Navigation Act of 1818 had, at least, ruined the triangular trade which had once been the monopoly of British shipping; and British tonnage entering American ports had shrunk from 174,935 in 1817 to 36,333 in 1819.[21]

The issue, on the surface at least, had now narrowed itself down to the simple question of which side could hold out the longer. "I recommend to the consideration of Congress," said President Monroe in his Third Annual Message of December 7, 1819, "whether further prohibitory provisions in the laws relating to this intercourse may not be expedient." [22] Congress acted with commendable speed. On May 15, 1820, Monroe gave his approval to an Act that closed the ports of the United States, on and after September 30, against British vessels coming from ports in Lower Canada, New Brunswick, Nova Scotia, Newfoundland, St. John, Bermuda, the Bahama Islands, the Caicos Islands, or any British possession in the West Indies or in South America. No goods could be imported from these prohibited places unless they were wholly the growth, produce or manufacture of each, imported directly from itself. It was a complete nonintercourse in British vessels with all the British-American colonies; so complete that colonial articles might not even be taken to England and then exported to the United States.[23]

There were many curious circumstances to be discovered both in the framing and in the effect of this new Act. It had owed much to Senator Rufus King, who had just made himself hateful to the Southern members of the Senate because of his Missouri speeches; yet the Senate passed it with only one dissenting vote, and that from a northern Senator.[24] John Quincy Adams believed that it was the first time we had had a chance of trying our strength since the Constitution. President Monroe, on the other hand, had always been unhappy about calling for firm measures in his Annual Messages, and he had signed the Navigation Acts with great misgivings.[25] When the Senate Bill reached the House, it was passed by a vote of 94 to 25, and only eight Southern members were found in the minority. Yet it is these eight Southern votes, and the reluctance of James Monroe, which mark the beginnings of an opposition that was, less than eight years later, to complete the downfall of President John Quincy Adams. The new Act did not affect the tonnage of the United States then engaged in an indirect trade with the British West Indies by way of the Swedish and Danish islands; and it actually enhanced the price of American exports and decreased that of West Indian exports, which the desperate planters sold for whatever they could get. None the less, by 1822 the few dissenting voices of the Sixteenth Congress had swollen to a chorus. The South was beginning to protest that these restrictive measures on British shipping were having a sad effect upon the agriculture of Maryland, Virginia, and North Carolina, and upon the lumber of the Carolinas and of Georgia. Were they not being taxed to maintain a commercial experiment that would promote only the manufactures and the coasting trade of the United States? And was it not obvious that the manufactures and the coast trade were Northern interests? [26] This agrarian protest, coinciding with the decline of postwar nationalism, was an omen even those who were most expert in political haruspicy scarcely noticed. The protest, however, changed the whole complexion of the controversy. It was no longer unanimous on the American side: it had become involved in the passions of farmers and of planters, and was one day to be a test, not of the political strength of Northern shipping, but of the political persuasiveness of Northern industry.

When the news of the Act was brought to the British Foreign Secretary, Lord Castlereagh, he told Mr. Rush, with his usual courtesy, that it did not seem to him "incompatible with the relations of harmony existing between the two nations." [27] Lord Castlereagh was always too preoccupied with the affairs of Europe to have much time to spare for those of the United States; and in any case, though no friend of the Navigation Laws, he would probably have been willing to let the West Indies starve to death rather than go to the trouble of upsetting them. Others were of the same mind. The American Navigation Acts, said a London newspaper, "affect, in truth, so small and inconsiderable a portion of our general trade, as to be worthy of no other notice than as indicating the spirit in which they originate." [28]

Lord Castlereagh, scanning the surface of events, was right; and the London newspaper was right. The volume of West Indian trade was but a small item in British exchanges. But Lord Castlereagh had failed to notice a little cloud—like the Biblical cloud, no larger than a man's hand—which had just arisen on the very edge of the horizon. The Navigation Laws—the ancient underpinning of British foreign policy—were being questioned in Parliament. A storm was arising for which the American Navigation Acts could, to be sure, claim no responsibility. And yet, within two years' time, they had moved to the very center of it. The navigation controversy, in England as in America, was part of the great battle between industry and tradition: with effects of incalculable importance upon both countries.

IV

During the month of May 1820, several petitions of an unusual import were presented to the Houses of Parliament. The merchants of London, "a most extensive and respectable body," the Chamber of Commerce of Glasgow, the woolen manufacturers of Howick, the merchants, manufacturers, and other inhabitants of Manchester, were all petitioning for free trade.[29] They did not propose to remove all the intertwisted restrictions that, in the course of centuries, had grown like a hedge around British commercial enterprise. On the principle of first things first, and with the understanding that freedom of trade is impossible without freedom of intercourse, they concentrated their attack upon the Navigation Laws . . . a mass of acts, dating from the reign of King Edward III, many of which would have been repealed if anyone had bothered to remember them, and all of which were supposed to have come to a head in the great Navigation Act of 1660. This Act provided that no goods could be transported from British colonies into England except in British or colonial ships; that no goods the growth, produce, or manufacture of Africa, Asia or America should be imported into England, Ireland, or Wales except in English, Irish, Welsh or colonial ships, with a British master and a crew three-quarters British; that the foreign goods of Asia, Africa, and America must be brought directly from the place of growth or manufacture; and that no alien ships should be engaged in the English coastal trade. Such were the chief provisions of this monumental Act; and their original purpose was to monopolize colonial trade on the one hand and to ruin the Dutch carrying trade on the other. They were occasionally modified as the years passed; and the American Revolution, which broke their territorial basis in North America, forced their revision to the extent of allowing American goods to be brought directly to England in American ships.[30]

William Pitt, indeed, tried to go further: he wished to allow American ships to bring American goods to the ports of the West Indies, and to bring back to the United States any goods whatsoever. But the outcry from the shipowners was so great that he was obliged to give way. The Navigation Laws remained inviolate—a huge mass of legislation which would have been more intelligible to the seventeenth than to the nineteenth century—founded upon the proposition that the colonies were the nurseries of seamen. When the United States demanded entrance into the ports of the West Indies, they went straight to the heart of this antique, obscure and formidable system; and when the free traders in the House of Commons demanded that this system be either relaxed or done away with altogether, they were being forced by economic distress to add a mighty counterpoint to the American theme.

When the same question was aired in the House of Lords on May 26, 1820, Lord Liverpool committed himself to a very illuminating statement. He did not believe, he said, that the disastrous falling off in exports had much to do with the trade to Europe. It was to the United States of America that it could be "principally, if not exclusively" attributed. The distress in the United States was greater than anywhere else, for the United States was now feeling more acutely than any other country the effect of the Napoleonic Wars. "And how has she felt it? During the whole of the late war, America was the principal neutral power. During a part of that war she was the only neutral power. She enjoyed the most extensive carrying trade.

She supplied this country, and she supplied other countries with many articles, which, neither this country, nor other countries could at that time obtain elsewhere. What was the natural consequence? That America increased in wealth, in commerce, in arts, in population, in strength more rapidly than any nation ever before increased, in the history of the world. In twenty years, the United States of America made a greater progress than the same nation, in the ordinary and natural course of events could have accomplished in forty years. But now all the world is at peace. . . . The state of America, my lords, at this moment is not so much the effect of present positive distress, as of extraordinary past prosperity. She must retrograde to a certain point. . . . I am far from saying this invidiously— On former occasions I have sufficiently stated my conviction that there is no country more interested than England is, that the distress of America should cease, and that she should be enabled to continue that rapid progress which has been for a time interrupted; for, of all the powers on the face of the earth, America is the one whose increasing population and immense territory furnish the best prospects for British produce and manufactures. Everybody, therefore, who wishes prosperity to England, must wish prosperity to America."

What would an American have thought of this description of the "neutrality" of the United States, falling from the lips of a man who had once done as much as anyone to turn that neutrality into belligerence? Yet the words Lord Liverpool spoke on May 26, 1820, were only a logical extension of what he had thought during the negotiations at Ghent. For the turning point in those negotiations had been Lord Liverpool's realization that England could hardly survive without her American market. "My lords," he now continued, "we are now in a situation in which it is impossible for us, or any nation, *but the United States of America,* to act unreservedly on the principle of unrestricted trade. The commercial regulations of the European world have been long established, and cannot suddenly be departed from." [31]

Nothing could have been clearer. The United States might attack the Navigation Laws at their most vulnerable point, but they would not lose the good will of England as long as their market was not hampered with a protective tariff. This doctrine, so openly announced in this historic speech, permeated Anglo-American relations for the next few years to such an extent that they can hardly be understood without a reference to it.

For if the speaker was the Earl of Liverpool, the voice was the voice of British industrialism.

V

It was not until 1822, when some measure of prosperity was returning to the British Isles, that the attack upon the Navigation Laws was concerted. It was then that Mr. Frederick J. Robinson, the president of the Board of Trade, and himself a Liberal Tory, proposed that British vessels and vessels belonging to countries in America ("belonging either to European sovereigns, or to Independent States") should be allowed to carry into certain free ports in the West Indies all articles that could be legally imported into these colonies; and to carry away all articles the produce of the British dominions, and all articles legally imported. "Recent circumstances," he said, "arising out of our restrictions on the one hand, and retaliatory restrictions by the United States on the other, have led to a much more extended use of corn, flour, and lumber from Canada, Nova Scotia, and New Brunswick into the British West Indies." He proposed to protect this trade with a moderate duty "so justly apportioned as not to deprive the people of the United States of their fair proportion of this necessary supply." The foreign vessels thus admitted to the West Indian trade were to be on the same footing, as to duties and charges, as British ships, but the provisions of the law would not apply to the vessels of any foreign states that did not grant equal and reciprocal advantages to British shipping.[32]

Never since the days of Pitt had the United States been so openly courted. On June 24, 1822, a bill was enacted containing all the recommendations of Mr. Robinson.[33] It was, in effect if not in wording, exclusive to the United States; for European shipping was not admitted, and the new countries of South America had not yet been recognized by the British government.[34] It was not, to be sure, anything like a complete repeal of the Navigation Laws. Even with its pendent, the Colonial Trade Bill, it left huge areas of legislative jungle untouched. "It did not imply," said William Huskisson, who supported Mr. Robinson from the Tory back benches, "a sudden or entire departure from our former system, bad as it might be, but such a modification as, it was hoped, would accomplish gradually the desired end, with as little individual hardship, or disturbance of existing interests, as was possible." [35] But its wording, for those times, was almost revolutionary. It was the very nearly first piece of legislation since the days of Richard II which placed navigation or commerce (said the *Edinburgh Review*) on the basis of "a fair principle of reciprocity." [36]

What could have accomplished such a feat? The American Navigation Act of 1820, and the pressure of West Indian interests in Parliament, were generally considered responsible. "The controversy," wrote George Canning's secretary, "turned upon the question, whether we should first be starved into compliance, or they first be tired of the loss of a profitable trade. The victory was theirs, we yielded." [37] This was undoubtedly the official view, and there was much to be said for it. George Canning himself, in later years, however, declared that the best way to meet the American interdiction, and to satisfy the clamor of the West Indian planters, would have been to open to other commercial and maritime powers the trade refused by the United States.[38] This was never even considered. And it was not considered because the instinct of a vigorous and expanding industrial system is always to woo, if possible, its best and easiest market. This instinct was the deepest and most compelling force behind the British "American Trade Act" of 1822.

When William Huskisson arose to support Mr. Robinson's courtship of the United States, he as much as any man in Parliament was the personification of this instinct. In 1821, as a member of a Parliamentary committee on agricultural distress, he had been the leading enemy of the Corn Laws, Protection's Holy of Holies; for he was a moderate but erudite free trader. One could not brush Mr. Huskisson aside as a fanatic or condemn him as a crank; his knowledge of finance, his familiarity with the intricacies of commerce and of industry, were unequaled; and when he spoke in the House of Commons—though his appearance (said Greville) was "slouching and ignoble-looking," and his diction far from pleasing—he was always heard with attention.[39] Here surely was a man whom the new tide of Liberalism would sweep into office, and no one had worked harder for it. Yet in 1822, though one of the most respected members of the ministerial party, he was no more than colonial agent for Ceylon. He was often consulted by the government, and often placed in the forefront of the battle when economic questions were debated, but only minor employments had fallen to his lot. When he spoke in support of Mr. Robinson, he did so with more than the usual caution of a Tory reformer. Though it behooved all reformers to walk delicately in the 1820's, few if any of them, it may safely be said, needed to walk more delicately than did Mr. Huskisson. He was a man of no social standing, in an age when social connections were of far more value than brains or ability. The Tories, it is true, were kinder to such men than the Whigs. The Earl of Eldon, for instance, the Tory Lord Chancellor, was the son of a coal merchant; but the Earl of Eldon had risen to his eminence by applying a monumental legal knowledge to the agreeable task of repressing useful innovations. Mr. Huskisson was not trained to the law. He was not, like the Earl of Liverpool or Mr. Robinson, born into the inner circle of professional politicians. He was simply a man of decent family, who had been brought up in Paris by his uncle and patron, the worthy Dr. Gem, the friend of Jefferson and Tom Paine; and Dr. Gem, who was physician to the Embassy, had got him his start.

Nothing, perhaps, showed more clearly the course of events in 1822 than the fact that Lord Liverpool began to consult an unofficial Cabinet on fiscal and commercial matters; and that Mr. Huskisson was a member of it.[40] Towards the end of the year, Huskisson was offered the post of president of the Board of Trade. But the king disapproved of him, and even Lord Liverpool scarcely ventured to suggest that Cabinet rank should be bestowed upon such a man. Huskisson was deeply pained. If someone had to be deprived of a Cabinet position, surely it should be a man (he wrote) "in a different (I mean a higher) sphere of life from myself. . . . I cannot be what Robinson now is in office and be excluded from the Cabinet."[41] No man was more sensitive than Lord Liverpool to the feelings of others; and although he could placate George IV only by smuggling Huskisson into the government by the back door, he promised that within twelve months he would admit him by the front one. Huskisson's services, moreover, were too badly needed for anyone to take chances with him. By August 1823 the Chancellor of the Duchy of Lancaster was bribed out of the Cabinet with a peerage; the Master of the Mint was demoted to Master of the Buckhounds; and thus, in spite of the grumblings of the King, Mr. Huskisson was maneuvered into the Cabinet.[42]

With this appointment, the tide of Liberal Toryism was truly at the flood. In the meantime, the American Trade Act, with which this tide had been so characteristically freighted, had been received in Washington, and in reply the President had issued a Proclamation on August 24, 1822, which seemed on the face of it to be even more generous than the Trade Act itself.[43] But those who examined it more carefully were surprised to note that the Proclamation had not removed the tonnage duty of one dollar a ton, nor the light money, nor the ten per cent levied on importations of foreign vessels not privileged by treaty stipulations.[44] Mr. Stratford Canning, the British Minister, hurried off to John Quincy Adams with his protest, but got no satisfaction. And worse was to follow. On March 1, 1823, a bill was enacted that had been drafted by the Senate Committee on Foreign Relations to meet the American Trade Act of 1822. Its language, though involved, seemed harmless enough; and only a close scrutiny of its second section revealed how extraordinary it really was. According to this section, British vessels trading from the enumerated West Indian ports would be treated, as regards duties of impost or tonnage, exactly like American vessels trading from the same ports "on proof being given to the President of the United States, satisfactory to him, that, upon vessels of the United States, admitted into the above enumerated British ports, and upon any goods, wares, or merchandise, imported therein, in the said vessels, no other or higher duties of tonnage or impost, and no other charges of any kind, are levied or exacted than upon British vessels, or upon the like goods, wares, and merchandise, imported into the said colonial ports from elsewhere." [45] The sting was in the tail. The word "*elsewhere*," so modest in its appearance, had a most immodest significance. If it meant anything, and it did, it meant that the United States demanded that their vessels and goods should be admitted into British colonial ports on the same terms as British vessels and cargoes from all other parts of the British Empire. The Tory government was sufficiently alive to the needs of British industry to relax the Navigation Laws; but it could not relax them as far as that. It could not remove all the old foundations before it had built new ones. The energies of British industry were great and persuasive; but they were not yet great enough to persuade any government, Whig or Tory, into taking such extreme measures; and years were to pass before any government did so. When Mr. Huskisson heard of the new American Act he called it "a pretension unheard of in the commercial relations of independent states." How would the Americans behave, he inquired, if Great Britain demanded that West Indian sugar should be admitted into New York upon the same terms as the sugar of Louisiana? [46] The analogy was inexact; but the question was, considering the times in which it was asked, exceedingly pertinent.

The genesis of the word "elsewhere" is somewhat blurred, but there is every reason to believe that the Secretary of State was the man responsible for it.[47] Thomas Hart Benton said that only a very few Senators "in the secret" appreciated its drift; to the rest of that body it seemed harmless enough.[48] When the British Minister got wind of it, while the Bill was still in the Senate Committee on Foreign Affairs, he wrote in haste to Mr. Adams, begging to be told that it did not mean what he feared that it meant. And Mr. Adams bluntly replied that the American government did, in fact, interpret *elsewhere* as meaning *anywhere else;* and that it was proposing to trade in British colonial ports on equal terms with the Mother Country and the rest of her dominions.[49]

Up to this point, the United States had merely been protecting the interests of its carrying trade, and should have been fully satisfied with the British overtures in their American Trade Act of 1822. With the "elsewhere" Act of 1823, an entirely new situation was created. Adams, with his keen and prescient mind, knew perfectly well that the British government would never accept the proposal—or rather the challenge—contained in the word "elsewhere"; that they would never jettison their system of colonial preferences for the sake of the American merchant marine. He says that the word "elsewhere" was fully discussed in the Cabinet and the Senate; but we know from Benton, and from remarks dropped in subsequent debates, that this was not the case with the Senate; and of the Cabinet discussions Adams has left no record at all. We are forced to conclude that the British overtures in their American Trade Act of 1822 were not rejected solely from considerations of practical or even of idealistic statesmanship—for the sake of the carrying trade, that is to say, or in behalf of the Freedom of the Seas. No doubt these considerations, particularly the latter, were present in Mr. Adams's mind; it is difficult to believe that they were the guiding ones. It seems that in 1823 Mr. Adams was also moved by an instinct—one can scarcely use any other word—fully as persuasive as the instinct that prompted Liberal Toryism to meddle with free trade. The capital of New England was being diverted from shipping to industry; and although Daniel Webster, that barometer of conservative Massachusetts wealth, was not yet prepared to advocate protective tariffs, Mr. Adams was already convinced of the importance of domestic manufactures in the American economy.[50] The British sought American friendship not so much for the sake of the West Indian planters as because in the United States they recognized and were courting a lucrative and unprotected market for their manufactured goods. They proposed to compete with American manufacturers on their own terms, and they concealed this competition in the seductive language of their American Trade Act. The courtship was not well received; the wooer was rebuffed. Just as British industrialism was moving painfully but inevitably towards free trade, the industry of the United States was preparing to move away from it: and the word "elsewhere" emerges in 1823 not as a practicable device for the promotion of the carrying trade—it was never that—but as the first symbol of this divergence.

CHAPTER TWO

George Canning and the Soft Infection

THE year 1823 was in many larger and more dramatic respects a crucial year in the relations between the New World and the Old. It was the year when the conquerors of Napoleon came to a definite parting of the ways—the British constitutionalists moving towards the principle of nationalism (or competition) and the great reactionaries of Austria, Prussia, and Russia marching in a disorderly fashion towards the principle of Order (or monopoly). It was partly if not chiefly because of this immense disagreement in Europe that the United States was able to define its position in the world in the famous Message that has come down to us as the Monroe Doctrine.

I

In order to appreciate the influence of Europe upon the thinking and actions of American statesmen, it is necessary to recall three arrangements following the overthrow of the Napoleonic Empire.

The first of these was the Final Act of the Vienna Congress—a complex of dynastic and territorial adjustments designed to restore that persuasive form of imbalance known as the balance of power. The men responsible for these adjustments—Castlereagh of Great Britain, Metternich of Austria, Hardenberg of Prussia, Talleyrand of France, and the ministerial apprentices of the sorcerous Tsar Alexander—were not altogether dissatisfied with what they had done; and those who study the Congress of Vienna know that it was only by the surmounting of almost unsurmountable difficulties that anything had been done at all. But these men had paid insufficient attention to what, for lack of a more precise word, we must call the *Zeitgeist*, the spirit of the times—the stirrings of nationality, the longings for self-determination, the passionate and unappeasable unrest which Napoleon had left behind him: for Napoleon, though the most flagrant of despots, exported across his borders, not only death, famine and rapine, but also some of the more stimulating principles of the French Revolution. The statesmen at Vienna, however, preferred to restore a Europe which had been shaken almost to pieces by the marching and countermarching of Napoleon. Theirs was a superb piece of patchwork—it may well have kept the peace (in a general way) for forty years—but one must still ask whether it is practicable to remodel the interior of a house or to refashion its façade, when its foundations are already beyond repair.

The second arrangement was known as the Quadruple Alliance, concerted between Great Britain, Russia, Prussia, and Austria. It was originally formed at the Treaty of Chaumont (March 1, 1814) when Napoleon was still in the field before Paris; and history is full of coalitions formed in the face of a common enemy which begin to crumble as soon as that enemy has been defeated. The Quadruple Alliance was renewed on November 20, 1815, in order to preserve the territorial provisions of the Vienna Treaties and to prevent the Napoleonic dynasty from returning to France. Its sixth article, which was really the operative article, provided that the Four Powers should continue their meetings at fixed periods to discuss such measures as should be "most salutary for the repose and prosperity of nations and for the maintenance of the peace of Europe." Thus was originated the conference system that has continued, on and off, until our own day.

The third arrangement—if arrangement it could be called—was a quasi-mystical compact known as the Holy Alliance, concluded in the first place between Russia, Austria, and Prussia on September 26, 1815, by which the sovereigns of these three countries pledged themselves to base their reciprocal relations upon "the sublime truths which the Holy Religion of our Savior teaches," and to consider themselves and their subjects as "members of the same Christian nation." Other sovereigns were invited to join, and most of them did so. The Prince Regent of England (though this sort of thing was very much to his rococo taste) was obliged to refuse, because he was a constitutional ruler whose signature was valid only when accompanied by that of a responsible minister. The Pope declined, because he was not a hereditary ruler, and because he failed to descry any holiness in an agreement between Protestant and Catholic princes. The Sultan of Turkey, whom the Tsar had wished to include from motives that were certainly mischievous, readily convinced himself that the Holy Alliance was the first step towards a *jehad* or holy war against Islam; and he too refrained from appending his signature. No European statesman at first took the agreement seriously. Lord Castlereagh described it as "sublime nonsense." Prince Metternich dismissed it as a "loud sounding nothing." [1] Five years later, Metternich changed his mind.

II

The Congresses that were held under the aegis of the Quadruple Alliance— at Aix-la-Chapelle (1818), Troppau and Laibach (1820), and Verona (1822) —ended with the Quadruple Alliance virtually in dissolution. At Aix-la-Chapelle Lord Castlereagh had been obliged to make it clear that Great Britain, though she favored a mediation between Ferdinand VII and his disaffected Spanish-American colonies, would never assist in the restoration of these colonies to Ferdinand either by force of arms or by commercial boycott.[2] He had no affection for republics or revolutionaries; but he was not his own master: the British commercial interests demanded that there should be no interference with their Spanish-American trade. At Troppau, two years later, Prince Metternich issued a *Protocole Preliminaire*, putting forward the suggestion that any state that had been subjected to revolution should no longer be considered a member of the Holy Alliance, and that the remaining members had a right to bring it back to the Alliance by force of arms. The British government resisted this reactionary doctrine in a strong dissenting circular; but the three original Holy Allies—Prussia, Russia, and Austria—moving on to Laibach, rephrased the *Protocole* in even more insolent language. The Holy Alliance had lost all pretensions to holiness; but it had at last become an alliance.[3]

The reasons for this were, obviously, fourfold. In 1820 four revolutions had broken out in Europe: in Naples, in Piedmont, in Spain, and in Portugal. It was to underpin this sagging of the foundations of the Vienna Treaties that Metternich had issued his *Protocole Preliminaire*. The Tsar, whose liberalism was now a thing of the past, and who had a million men under arms, proposed to detach a part of this somber horde and send it overland to the Peninsula. He was with difficulty dissuaded. But an Austrian army was let loose upon Naples; and, having once tasted blood in this tigerish manner, the Holy Alliance would probably want more. If revolution could be suppressed by force in the Old World, why not in the New? It was this consideration which, even before the Congress of Aix-la-Chapelle, had haunted Mr. Monroe and his advisers; for while they were not yet ready to recognize the independence of the Spanish colonies, they were most unwilling— for reasons of security, of trade, and even of morality—to see them restored to their old masters.

And then, in 1821, the Greek War of Independence broke out, and the unfathomable Eastern Question entered the nineteenth century. The Tsar, to whom revolutions were commonly anathema, was in two minds about this one. The "peace" of Europe required, no doubt, that subject peoples should remain obedient to their rulers, even when the peoples were Christian and the rulers Moslem; but was he not an Orthodox monarch, with a traditional mission to lead a crusade against the Turk? Did not the Russian Empire require an outlet into the Mediterranean? By now his kindly nature had suffered a fearful eclipse. It was almost swallowed up in gloom and horror. He was becoming—he had already become—a suspicious, solitary, and dangerous man. When the Sultan, terrified by the rebellion of his subjects, suddenly found himself obliged to massacre all the Greeks in Chios, it was believed that the Tsar would make use of this horrifying atrocity as a pretext for raising the whole Eastern Question. It was in order to discuss this problem, along with the problem of French intervention in the affairs of Spain, that another Congress was arranged for the fall of 1822; and Lord Castlereagh—hoping against hope to salvage the Quadruple Alliance and the conference system—promised to attend it in person.

III

Lord Castlereagh's reign at the Foreign Office had not, of late years, had a very stimulating effect upon the policy of the United States. The Americans entered into his calculations only as an afterthought; his policy towards them had been a drowsy compound of appeasement and indifference. His gaze, which was a brilliant one, was concentrated upon the Europe that had vanished with William Pitt, and in his eagerness to restore this spectral continent he wanted no irrelevant troubles along the Canadian-American border. During the negotiations preceding the Anglo-American Convention of 1818, therefore, his manner had been most conciliatory; and he invariably made a good impression upon American diplomats. A terrific grandee, a man of wide experience and immense distinction but not a man of the world, shy, cold, handsome, and infinitely courteous, Lord Castlereagh entertained the private belief that the United States was, socially speaking, inadmissible to the family of nations. It would have distressed him to make these sentiments known to an American, and he went to great lengths to conceal them. Moreover, he was not blind to the value of the United States as a market for British goods; and his behavior during the Arbuthnot-Ambrister crisis, and throughout the final stages of the ratification of the Florida Treaty, bore witness to this fact. But whenever he was asked to declare himself on the question of Spanish-American independence, he maintained an impenetrable reserve, and this disposition of his had more than once a stultifying effect upon American foreign policy.[4]

None the less, his reluctant drift away from the Quadruple Alliance and his cautious resistance to the Holy Alliance did not escape the attention of the American Secretary of State. John Quincy Adams was the first man to see that, with a Europe divided into two camps, constitutional and autocratic, the position of the United States had grown more secure. His diplomatic experience did not permit him to be seduced by British courtesies, but he realized that the British government was averse to a quarrel, and would go a long way to avoid one. It was in January 1821 that he made his position unusually clear to the British Minister, Mr. Stratford Canning— a gentleman who united physical beauty and proconsular dignity in so strange a way that Lady Hester Stanhope used to say that he reminded her of the permanent president of a society for the suppression of vice. Stratford Canning had come stalking into the State Department to inquire about certain Congressional and newspaper statements concerning an American settlement at the mouth of the Columbia, to which (he maintained, erroneously) Great Britain had a claim. It was towards the end of the second day that the conversations reached their climax.

> " 'I do not know,' said I [Mr. Adams writes in his diary] 'what you claim nor what you do not claim. You claim India; you claim Africa; you claim—' 'Perhaps,' said he, 'a piece of the moon.' 'No,' said I; 'I have not heard that you claim exclusively any part of the moon; but there is no spot on *this* habitable globe that I could not affirm you do not claim; and there is none which you may not claim with as much color or right as you can have to the Columbia River or its mouth.' 'And how far would you consider,' said he, 'this exclusion of right to extend?' 'To all the shores of the South Sea,' said I. 'We know of no right that you have there.' 'And in this,' said he, 'you include our northern provinces on this continent.' 'No,' said I, 'there the boundary is marked, and we have no disposition to encroach upon it. Keep what is yours, but leave the rest of the continent to us.' " [5]

Now this was a remarkable statement, both for its scope and for its vision. It was full of the doctrine of Non-Colonization, which Adams was to make peculiarly his own. The whole two-day conversation with Canning—set down in the diary with all the dry relish of an Anthony Trollope—is one of the most important as it is one of the most hilarious passages in that great book. Both men lost their tempers. Mr. Adams's wrath, however, was purposive; Mr. Canning's was simply perplexed. Why was he being lectured in this extraordinary fashion?

Six months later, Adams was invited by the citizens of Washington to address them on July 4, accepted the invitation, and, before a packed and startled audience in the Hall of Representatives, delivered a violently anti-British harangue. He had draped himself for the occasion in a professor's gown; but the Professor inadequately concealed the Secretary of State. There was much criticism, not of the matter, but of the manner of this discourse. "I suppose," wrote Christopher Hughes to Albert Gallatin, "that you have highly *relished* and *approved* the meek *spirit*, kind *temper*, and good taste with which [our Boston *Demosthenes*] treats our *harmless* friend, John Bull." [6] Mr. Adams defended himself in two letters to Robert Walsh, and one to Edward Everett.[7] He said that the British had been responsible for the crimes that provoked the Declaration of Independence, and he did not see why he should have frosted this wormwood with sugar, or neutralized it to insipidity. "The vulgar and malevolent critics upon the address" had failed to discern its meaning. It was intended to demonstrate "from the moral and physical nature of man that *colonial establishments cannot fulfill the great objects of government in the just purpose of society*." It also presented (he said) a principle of duty—the duty not to intervene directly in foreign wars, "even wars for freedom," because such intervention changed "the very foundations of our own government from *liberty* to *power*."

Any critic, however malevolent and vulgar, might have been excused for not discerning in Adams's July 4 rodomontade the transient presence of these two great doctrines of Non-Colonization and Non-Intervention. Non-Colonization meant that the American hemisphere should not be considered open to further colonization by European powers; its implications were both territorial and commercial; it sought to clear the path for the Republic as it strode westward, and to relieve its commerce from exclusive trade practices. Non-Intervention was rather more subtle; it was Intervention standing on its head. In the end it would have to mean that the United States would not intervene directly in foreign wars, even wars for freedom, if foreign nations did not intervene directly in wars affecting the freedom or interests of the United States. Any nation professing Non-Intervention as a global policy will be obliged, sooner or later, and somewhere or other, to intervene.

IV

If Mr. Adams assailed the British, it was not simply from anti-British prejudice, nor was it altogether out of conviction: it was because he knew that the British would not resent his words to the point of making an issue out of them. Stratford Canning duly reported the explosive conversations of January 1821, and was instructed to make no protest; and Stratford Canning, oddly enough for such a man, seems to have found more matter for praise than blame in the July 4 oration. Mr. Adams, indeed, was not attacking the British and their institutions so much as making them "a trumpet whence he blew": the doctrines he communicated through this singular channel have not yet lost their resonance.

With the Florida Treaty ratified, moreover, and the Missouri Compromise safely out of the way, the time had come for Monroe and his advisers to take another step into the future. Hitherto, although Congress had shown itself willing to support them in such a move, they had not been prepared to recognize the revolutionary governments of Spanish America. But the news of the battle of Carabobo, which was fought on June 24, 1821, and resulted in the overthrow of the royalist forces in Colombia, was probably decisive.

On March 8, 1822, President Monroe wrote a special Message, recommending to Congress the recognition of the independence of Buenos Aires (or the United Provinces of the Rio de la Plata), Colombia, Chile, Peru, and Mexico. Since the war still flamed or smoldered here and there—Peru was not actually liberated until the desperate and bloody engagements of Junin and Ayacucho had been fought in August and December 1824—the President suggested that the United States should observe "the most perfect neutrality" between the contending parties.[8] Congress replied to this temperate communication by appropriating $100,000 to maintain the expenses of "such missions to the independent nations on the American continent as the President might deem proper"; and an Act to this effect was signed on May 4, 1822.[9]

The recognition, the first ever accorded to the patriots by any government, was more important as an omen than impressive as a fact. The United States promised the colonists neither money nor arms, neither ships nor men. The United States simply recorded an opinion that the Spanish Crown had lost its hold upon the American colonies. It was by no means prepared to back this opinion with force. And force, or the threat of force, could alone make an impression upon the constitutionalist government of Spain or upon the neo-Holy Allies, who were still in hopes of coming to an accommodation with the revolutionaries—though whether this accommodation would take the form of an agreement or an extermination they were unable to decide.

The revolutionaries themselves received the news with joy: for it portended, after all, the lifting up of day. Moreover, it was a message from the whole American people. There is no doubt at all that the cause of the Latin American patriots was popular throughout the northern republic. There was a superficial resemblance between the resistance to George III and the risings against Ferdinand VII. The efforts of publicists like Brackenridge, Duane, and Niles had given the sagas—they deserve no less a word—of Bolivar, San Martín and their associates and armies a wide circulation. Then (as now) the mind was staggered by that scene of vast revolting provinces, of dissolving vice-royalties and captaincies-general: of the just but agonizing death of an imaginative age. And then something enormous but precise would occur, like the march of San Martín over the Upsallata Pass and into Chile. Or Bolivar would lead his international brigades, tormented with frost and sun, across the Andes into Nueva Granada. It was a tremendous story. American sympathies received their amplest expression in Henry Clay's great speech of March 24, 1818, when he pleaded with Congress for the recognition of the United Provinces of the Rio de la Plata.

Mr. Clay was a politician first and a statesman second: he could not resist the opportunity to advance his own cause while he championed that of the South American patriots. But this does not mean that his speech was insincere. He was a Westerner, with a Westerner's hatred of the Spaniard. He had an honest, instinctive horror of despots and monocrats. His generous feelings responded easily to the heroic issue he then attempted to describe. But he ended by describing a governing class: he could not summon up a picture of the submerged masses whom this class would presumably govern. "It is sometimes said," he remarked, "that they are too ignorant and too superstitious to admit of the existence of free government. This charge of ignorance is often urged by persons themselves ignorant of the real condition of the people. I deny the alleged fact of ignorance; I deny the inference from that fact, if it were true, that they want capacity for free government; and I refuse assent to the further conclusion, if the fact were true and the inference just, that we are to be indifferent to their fate. All the writers of the most established authority, Depons, Humboldt, and others concur in assigning to the people of Spanish America great quickness, genius, and particular aptitude for the exact sciences, and others which they have been allowed to cultivate. . . . The fact is not, therefore, that the imputed ignorance exists; but, if it do, I repeat, I dispute the inference. It is the doctrine of thrones, that man is too ignorant to govern himself." With the broad and noble generalizations in this passage no one would quarrel; but it would have been indiscreet to ask Mr. Clay what he meant by the "people" or by "free government," since he was actually preoccupied with a certain kind of leadership, which he had evolved almost entirely out of his imagination. "I am strongly inclined to believe," he continued, "that they will in most, if not all parts of their country, establish free governments. We are their great example. Of us they constantly speak as of brothers, having a similar origin. They adopt our principles, copy our institutions, and, in many instances, employ the very language of our revolutionary papers." [10] Reading the last sentence, one remembers Simon Bolivar, prone in his canoe upon the bosom of the Orinoco, writing a constitution for Venezuela which combined the monarchial principles of eighteenth-century England with the moral pretensions of the Athenian Areopagus in the fifth century B.C.! [11]

The myth of free government, as expounded by Henry Clay, required that there should be a fairly close resemblance between the American Revolution and the Spanish-American revolts. The Fifteenth Congress was thrilled by his speech—and rightly so—but declined, for practical reasons, to plunge too deeply into his mythology. Its gaze at the time was fixed on the Spanish borderlands. But the publication of the reports of President Monroe's fact-finding commission, which returned from South America in 1818, showed what huge areas of space and time interposed themselves between the North American republic and the South American patriots. The Spanish Empire was unable to produce the mercantile and skeptical type of man; and when it suddenly crumbled all over Mexico and South America, its very ruins seemed to be impregnated with the harsh imagination of the soldier and the theocrat. The new governments had to build upon these ruins, and neither the great scriptures of the American Revolution nor the great slogans of the French Revolution could provide them with a workable plan. Only the Portuguese province of Brazil could have been said—from its seventeenth-century resistance to the Dutch—to have a national past of any kind; and the province of Brazil was then a great mystery, hovering between imperial independence and colonial status.[12] It could not gain admittance to President Monroe's recognition Message of 1822.

The Spanish-American patriots could not easily be wished into the orbit of bourgeois revolution. In 1821, John Quincy Adams told Henry Clay, in the course of a notable conversation, that they would never establish free or liberal institutions. "They had not," he quotes himself as saying, "the first elements of good or free government. Arbitrary power, military and ecclesiastical, was stamped upon their education, upon their habits, and upon all their institutions. Civil dissension was infused into all their seminal principles. War and mutual destruction was in every member of their organizations, moral, political, and physical. I had little expectation of any beneficial result to this country from any future connection with them either political or commercial." [13]

This harsh and illiberal language was designed in part to irritate Mr. Clay, an open rival for the Presidency. In part it was founded upon Mr. Adams's respect for facts—as the facts may have revealed themselves to him, for example, in the rather contradictory reports of the President's fact-finding commission. [14] He used similar if milder language in his instructions to Richard C. Anderson, first Minister to Colombia, though he was obliged to expunge it from his final draft; and if he had been granted a comprehensive view of the next forty years of Spanish-American history, he would have stoutly declared that he was right. [15] He would never have admitted that he had fallen into the rather Machiavellian error of assessing the character and future of whole peoples in accordance with what he believed to be the character and future of their elite.

Between Henry Clay, who gave the heroes of the Liberation an Anglo-Saxon cast of features, and John Quincy Adams, who saw them as the founders of *caudillismo*, there would seem to be an abysmal difference. Surely only willful blindness on the one side, or gross prejudice on the other, could account for such conflicting views. And if we were to take their words literally, we would have to accept one or the other of these alternatives. Actually, they were drawing closer together. Each man believed that the independence of Spanish America (that is to say, its freedom from the public law of Europe) was necessary to the well-being of the United States. Their disagreements as to the future of an independent Spanish America were disagreements of temperament, not of philosophy; and after the Recognition Act of 1822 these disagreements merely charted the distinction between a warm heart and a cool head.

The posture of the Administration towards Spanish America can be discovered in the feelings and actions of James Monroe. The time has long since passed when James Monroe was held to be almost an otiose supporter, or indeed observer, of the foreign policy of Adams. The Adams diary shows that Monroe intervened persistently and anxiously; and the fact that he is one of the few eminent men to escape from those mordant pages relatively unscarred proves that Adams did not think his intervention either unnecessary or obstructive. Mr. Monroe's feelings towards the Spanish-American patriots were at least as warm as those of Mr. Clay; their exploits had blown upon the embers of his revolutionary past. Nor would he ever forget the discourtesies of the Madrid government, in 1804, in the midst of his unfortunate diplomatic career. But his warmth was tempered by the contradictory reports of his fact-finding commissioners on the one hand, and by a certain tenderness for European feelings on the other. Up till 1821, he was usually in agreement with Adams that nothing should be done to interfere with the Florida Treaty; and even after that Treaty had been ratified, a prompting from Congress was necessary before he brought himself to write his Recognition Message.[16] The temperate character of this Message may have been due, in some degree, to the fact that the trade with Cuba, still a Spanish possession, was considerably larger than that with all the revolutionary colonies put together.[17] But his correspondence throughout this anxious period shows that he was a convinced if pragmatic neutral: it was useless to intervene if intervention would not turn the scale, but *would* increase the obstinacy of the Spanish Crown. The true warmth of his feelings burst out when, in an infinitely touching scene, he received the dying Manuel Torres as *chargé d'affaires* of Colombia.[18] But his moral and emotional commitment to Spanish-American independence was always a secondary consideration: like Adams, he was determined that the dissolution of the Spanish Empire should not threaten the Continental Republic as it strode westward; and he waited almost a year, in order to test the reactions of Europe, before he appointed Caesar Augustus Rodney Minister to the United Provinces of the Rio de la Plata and Richard C. Anderson Minister to Colombia.[19]

The Administration's policy, as laid down in the instructions to these two Ministers, was to encourage the new states to adopt not merely republicanism (which might mean anything) but a republicanism of "*civil, political, commercial* and *religious* liberty." This language may have been optimistic, but it was not mere verbalizing. With common sense as a reagent, its precipitates would seem to be: total separation from Europe; trade with the United States on the most-favored-nation terms; and acceptance of the State Department's version of the Freedom of the Seas.

V

With the Greek War of Independence, revolution in one form or another had spread from the Near East to the Andes; the leaders of Europe were in two minds as to the proper way of dealing with it; and the United States had taken advantage of this division to declare itself, morally, commercially, territorially. This was the state of affairs when Lord Castlereagh began his preparations for the Congress of Verona.

He was never to get there. For several years he had been made the scapegoat for the afflictions Lord Liverpool's government (anything but Liberal when it considered the rights of man) had visited upon the miseries of postwar England. Lord Castlereagh was considered the very image and agent of oppression; though, in actual fact, he was something worse than that—he was a man who did not recognize oppression when he saw it. Openly contemptuous of public opinion, he was secretly haunted by the hatred that pursued him. Moreover, he was grossly overworked; Parliament had sat late and had proved unusually difficult; and early in August 1822, standing by the river bank at his home at North Cray, he told his secretary, "I am quite worn out *here*." And he touched his forehead.[20] On August 9 he returned to London. His first visit was to George IV. "Have you heard the news, the terrible news?" he exclaimed, seizing the king's arm. "I am a fugitive from justice." The dismayed monarch held both his hands and begged him to be calm.[21] His next visit was to Apsley House where, lying upon a sofa in the Duke of Wellington's library, he accused himself of every crime. "From what you have told me," the duke replied at last, "I am bound to warn you that you cannot be in your right mind." [22] Wellington wrote a note to Dr. Bankhead, Lord Castlereagh's physician, and Dr. Bankhead and Lady Castlereagh followed the poor madman back to North Cray. He was bled, he was given sedatives, his pistols and razors were taken away from him. But he had managed to conceal a little penknife in the drawer of his washstand. Early on the morning of August 12 Dr. Bankhead received a message from his patient, summoning him to his bedroom. He found the Foreign Secretary standing at the window, staring at the sky, with his head thrown back, and his throat cut from ear to ear. . . .[23]

The news was brought to George Canning just as he was preparing to depart into an illustrious but extinguishing exile as governor-general of India. The ship was waiting to carry him away from England, but he postponed the date of his sailing. He waited for days, for weeks, in an agony of indecision: Should he sail or should he not sail? His greatest rival in the Tory party was dead, and surely now power would come to him. On September 9, 1822, Lord Liverpool offered him the post of Foreign Secretary together with the leadership of the House of Commons. With this appointment, Liverpool's Liberal Tory administration was at last complete.

VI

Canning's return to the Foreign Office, a portentous event in European and American history, came at a time (even more portentous) when the British Industrial Revolution was well on the way to completing the middle stage of its development. The problem of the application of steam power to manufacture had almost been solved. The "Malleable Iron Period" was approaching the top of its climax in James B. Neilson's discovery of the use of hot air in smelting. The Age of Steam was in its dawn, but the age of horses and waterfalls and charcoal was manifestly passing away. The statistics of coal and iron production would tell the tale; but the most striking and eloquent version was provided by the cotton industry. The figures (which are of course very rough ones) show that in the period 1819 to 1821, for example, English mills spun 106,500,000 lbs. of cotton yarn, while in the period 1829 to 1831 they spun 216,500,000 lbs. Weaving was less progressive than spinning—the hand loom in 1830 still outnumbered the steam loom by more than four to one—but the cost of labor in the first period was said to be 15½d., and in the second only 9d. per pound of goods. The organization of the English factory system was, therefore, well on its way by 1830, though it still had a long distance to travel; and the relation between the growth of the English factory system and the rise of English liberalism is so obvious that we need hardly remind ourselves that the period 1819-21 coincided with the first Parliamentary clamor for free trade, and the period 1829 to 1831 with the great agitation for a middle-class Reform Bill.[24]

There have always been spectacular, extraneous personages in the story of British industrialization. Besides the great names of early inventors, for example, we have to place those of Robert Clive and Warren Hastings, who looted the treasuries of Hindustan for the capital with which the great inventions were financed. And the middle stage of the British Industrial Revolution is inseparably connected with the name of George Canning.

VII

Mr. Canning, like William Huskisson, was not popular with the more rigid members of the Tory Party. The reasons for Mr. Huskisson's unpopularity were not far to seek: he was a man of middle-class origin whose views on economic questions were both decided and advanced. Mr. Canning was less of an economist and his origin was not exactly middle class. His father, the disinherited son of an old and honorable family, died in poverty when Canning was only one year old; and his mother had been forced to become an actress in order to support him. He was rescued by an uncle from this untidy life; he was sent to Eton and to Oxford; but he was never forgiven for his mother's imprudence. Years later, Earl Grey asserted that "he regarded the son of an actress as being de facto incapacitated from being premier of England." [25]

Earl Grey, of course, was a Whig; and the Whigs were notoriously cold to ambitious young men of dubious upbringing. Canning, whose uncle had strong Whig feelings and who was known at Oxford as a great radical, early deserted the fold, fled the purlieus of Devonshire House and Carlton House, became one of that group of brilliant young men who contributed to the Anti-Jacobin, and entered Parliament in the Tory interest. It would be wrong, however, to suppose that this move was entirely opportunistic. The friendship of Pitt, and the writings of Burke, had much to do with it. And it was certainly a wise move. Under the Tories his rise was spectacular; he was an Under Secretary of State before he was thirty, and Foreign Secretary at thirty-seven; and in society, as in politics, he carried all before him. Yet even from the beginning he was accused of being a faithless colleague and an industrious and tireless intriguer. Even his cousin, Stratford Canning, could say no more of him than that he was "in the main an honest man." [26]

No evidence has been unearthed convincing enough to sustain these accusations. Certainly Canning was ambitious, and probably he was not overscrupulous; but he was no monster of duplicity. If he was mistrusted, the reason for that lay elsewhere, in the very depths of his personality, not on the surface of his politics. He was a devoted husband, an excellent father, an affectionate friend, a charming and convivial acquaintance: he was also a hypersensitive egotist with one of the sharpest tongues in England, and with a nervous distaste for pomposity and dullness, amounting

almost to exasperation. His gibes were famous, and they were more fitted
to a clever undergraduate than to a seasoned statesman. Lord Westmorland, the hard-drinking Lord Privy Seal, snarled when he heard that he was
now "le sot (sceau) privé"; the shrill-voiced Mr. Wynn, while he was a
candidate for the Speakership, did not relish his nickname of "Mr. Squeaker";
and the Duke of Buckingham, who was sensitive about his corpulence, was
not pleased to be given the title of Ph.D., of Phat Duke. One is tempted
to believe that Canning, who loved his mother, could not help but revenge
upon society in this boyish fashion the slights society had inflicted on her.

He longed to dominate and succeeded in dominating those circles in
which—with all his power, his skill, and his supreme capability, and in spite
of a very good marriage—he was little better than a parvenu. He liked to
strike attitudes and to fabricate scenes. He was admirably equipped to do
so. He had a noble forehead, eloquent eyes, a beautifully chiseled mouth,
and a wonderful voice. "I never saw Canning but once," said Disraeli, who
heard him make his last speech at Parliament. "I remember as if it were but
yesterday the tumult of that ethereal brow. Still lingers in my ear the
melody of that voice." [27] The Vicomte de Marcellus, the French *chargé
d'affaires*, recalled a spring evening at Gloucester Lodge, when Canning
took him into the gardens and recited the strange, melancholy and beautiful
lines with which Virgil concluded his story of the battle of the bees:

> "Hi motus animorum, atque haec certamina tanta,
> Pulveris exigui jactu compressa quiescunt." [28] *

And then he added, "Desire of fame, which cannot at my age be called ambition, drives me back to public affairs"; and so they went off together to
the House of Commons.[29] No doubt he knew that Marcellus was impressionable and that he kept a diary; but who would say that his "desire of
fame" was insincere?

Lord Liverpool, with his impeccable instinct, needed Mr. Canning at
the Foreign Office even more than he needed Mr. Huskisson at the Board
of Trade. Both men were sensitive to the scarcely formulated claims of the
middle classes. But if Huskisson was disliked by George IV, Canning was
hated by him. He had resigned the presidency of the Board of Control in
1820 because he could not agree to the divorce proceedings against Queen
Caroline, Mrs. Canning's lifelong friend. George IV, whose disordered
imagination led him to believe that he had personally headed a cavalry charge
at Salamanca, easily conceived the notion that Canning had been Caroline's
lover. The Ultra Tories in the government—the Duke of Wellington, Lord
Eldon, Lord Sidmouth, the Earl of Westmorland—did not share this delusion, but they were equally dismayed and angered at the thought that
Canning was to come among them again. Lord Liverpool persisted, and
Lord Liverpool had his way. Canning's "first letter from the Foreign Office
was dated 6.18 p.m. on September 16, 1822. 'So here,' he wrote, 'I am.' " [30]

* "These storms of passion, these mighty conflicts, are quelled and put to sleep
by the tossing of a little dust."

VIII

He had long since withdrawn from the society in which he had once been so prominent and assiduous a diner-out. But the greater his seclusion, the more anxious he seemed to be to take the public into his confidence. His colleagues, who had not disapproved of Castlereagh's secretiveness, were appalled at Canning's willingness to publish Blue Books at appropriate moments in order to influence public opinion and mobilize it behind the government.[31] Foreign statesmen were even more disgusted. "To acquire a sort of popularity," said Metternich, who shared with Canning an enmity of long standing, "is a pretension misplaced in a statesman." He was convinced that Canning was a dangerous radical.

Here he was totally mistaken. Canning was a student and disciple of Edmund Burke, and only a very devious mind could discern in the author of *Thoughts on Scarcity* and *Reflections on the Revolution in France* any taint of radicalism. Canning was ready enough to carry Burke's "disposition to preserve and ability to improve" as far as but no farther than it could safely be made to go in the second decade of the nineteenth century. He instinctively desired to release the energy that lay buried in English coal, English iron, and the English factory system. But his attitude towards the industrial and agricultural worker resembled Burke's, though he lacked Burke's dazzling flashes of compassionate insight. It was a combination of eighteenth-century optimism and Malthusian despair. He did not believe that the workers would greatly improve their position; but then he did not think that it was necessary to the national welfare that they should do so. Few early Liberals, Tory or Whig, went much further than that.[32]

Lord Liverpool was already summoning to one or another of his country houses—Combe Wood, or Kingston, or Walmer Castle—that unofficial "economic Cabinet" which was to make the last years of his rule so very suggestive.[33] William Huskisson was undoubtedly, next to Liverpool, the dominant figure at these discussions. They laid the foundations for Mr. Robinson's Free Trade Budgets of 1823 and 1824, for the famous assault upon the Silk Trade monopoly, for the Warehousing Bill and the Reciprocity Duties Bill, and the tentative attack upon the Corn Laws. Huskisson was a friend of Canning's and exercised a great, though by no means a controlling, influence upon his thinking.[34] He became, as it were, the Mercury between the "economic Cabinet" and the Foreign Office; and Canning's policy gave a large and resounding utterance to the domestic Liberalism of the Prime Minister.

He emphasized and underscored that cautious movement towards *laissez faire* which gave Lord Liverpool's domestic measures their singular importance in Tory history. He was faced at the outset with the Congress of Verona, to which the Duke of Wellington proceeded, a chilling emissary, within forty-eight hours after Canning had taken office. A great effort had been made at Verona to give the Congress—which was doomed to be the last one—a personnel equal to its pretensions. Two emperors were present, three kings, three reigning grand dukes, a cardinal, a viceroy, three foreign secretaries, twenty ambassadors, and twelve ministers; and these potentates and dignitaries went in state to a performance of "Romeo and Juliet" in the old Roman amphitheater. At first, all eyes at this spectral conference were turned upon the Duke of Wellington. The Tsar invited him to dine with him alone, as if he were a brother monarch. Metternich dragged Marie Louise out of her retirement to play cards with Wellington; and Napoleon's conqueror noted with surprise that Napoleon's widow was heavy with child by her paramour, the Count von Niepperg.[35]

But events were too much for these amenities. A French army stood upon the borders of France and Spain, with the evident design of rescuing Ferdinand VII from the revolutionary government that held him prisoner.[36] Canning instructed the duke to let it be known that England would be no party to a collective interference in the affairs of Spain—thus driving a wedge, so he hoped, between France and the Neo-Holy Allies.[37] It was noticeable thereafter that Wellington, though surrounded by all the outward signs of consideration and respect, was no longer admitted to the secret deliberations of the Congress. When he left Verona on October 30 he was, none the less, convinced that the Neo-Holy Allies would content themselves with putting moral pressure upon Spain; while his icy representations in Paris, on his way home, had been enough, in his opinion, to keep the French army on its own side of the border. He was not accustomed to contradiction. Mr. Canning, however, thought differently. On December 26, the French government declined a proposed British mediation; on December 28, the great Chateaubriand allowed himself, with becoming reluctance, to be promoted to Foreign Minister. His genius was ill suited to this office; but to Englishmen his promotion seemed to presage another *Pacte de Famille* of the two Bourbon monarchs, and another attempt to reconquer Spanish America for Ferdinand. The French king's speech from the throne on January 28, 1823, with its solemn reiterations of extreme legitimist doctrine, made Englishmen no easier; and it was followed by something like a panic on the Stock Exchange. Canning took the almost unprecedented step of writing a letter to the Comte d'Artois to set before him the outraged feelings of the people of England.[38] D'Artois, Louis XVIII's brother and heir—"old, pale, adorable," and as vain as he was mischievous—returned an evasive answer. There was nothing left for Canning to do but to lift the embargo on arms to Spain and Spanish America; to let the French government know that England would not submit to a permanent French occupation of Spain, or a violation of the neutrality of Portugal, or an armed attempt to recover the Spanish colonies; and to make one of his rare public appearances at the opera, arm in arm with the Duke of San Lorenzo, the Spanish Ambassador who had been summarily dismissed from Paris. On April 6, 1823, the French Army crossed the Bidassoa and plunged into Spain.[39]

IX

The French Bourbons, who learned nothing and forgot nothing, and who had been humiliated by the conditions of their Restoration in 1814 and 1815, disliked the Holy Allies only a little less than they disliked the English. The collapse of the Quadruple Alliance at Verona, and the rising tide of unlimited monarchy all over Europe, convinced them and their ministers that the time had come to free themselves from all foreign control. The Holy Allies desired an Ambassadors' Conference in Paris, to express, as they put it, the moral solidarity between themselves and the French: but the French army moved too soon. Down the bleak Spanish roads, through lines of cheering villagers, whose priests were admirably versed in the art of organizing "spontaneous" welcomes, preceded by flower maidens and guitarists, seduced by banquets, delayed by bull-fights, and pursued by shouts of "Down with the Jacobins and the Jews," the Duc d'Angoulême and his army marched into Madrid. The constitutional government, with the protesting Ferdinand still in its grasp, retired to Seville and then to Cadiz. A Regency of Spanish notables was set up in the capital. Even the Tsar, who had hoped to overrun Spain with Russian troops; even Metternich, who had planned to make King Ferdinand of Naples (temporarily unemployed, since his capital was occupied by Austrian soldiers) the new Regent of Spain—had to admit that the French had been too many for them.[40]

The fall of the constitutional government was now only a matter of time; and the question of the Spanish-American colonies, once more, began to vex the mind. The most powerful man in France was the Prime Minister, Comte Jean de Villèle; and Villèle had let it be known, openly and often, that he favored the creation of Spanish-American monarchies under Bourbon princes. This chimerical scheme was a compromise between France's legitimist dreams and her commercial needs—an effort to mingle the imperatives of trade with those of tradition. Villèle himself had disapproved of armed intervention in Spain: he told the French parliament a year later, *"qu'il falloit attaquer le midi pour échapper au Nord"*—the army had gone into Spain in order to defeat the designs of Russia. This was certainly not Chateaubriand's view, but it was probably the correct one; and in any case Villèle was never prepared to develop his armed intervention in Spain into a grand attack upon Spanish America.[41] This does not mean that the French Council of State had not considered and approved the idea of sending Spanish princes to South America with the backing of the French fleet and army; but it was to be a limited support only, and it was always dependent upon Ferdinand's assuming a reasonable attitude. Since Ferdinand VII was never reasonable, and since he would be satisfied with nothing less than the absolute restoration of Spanish America to his own personal rule, it cannot be said that the French offered any serious threat to Spanish America. But the French had suppressed a revolution in Spain by force of arms; to this extent, whether willingly or unwillingly, they had drifted into the orbit of the Holy Alliance. As the summer of 1823 advanced any reasonable man might have asked himself whether or not the Holy Allies intended to annihilate revolution in Spanish America as they had annihilated it all over western Europe. He would have reminded himself, however, that intention was one thing and action another.

X

On April 14, 1823, George Canning made a great speech in Parliament which publicly reiterated the arguments he had already made to the French government in his dispatch of March 31. "I earnestly hope and trust," he declared in his peroration, "that she (constitutional Spain) may come triumphantly out of the struggle." [42] His neutral policy was approved by the Commons, a mild victory for common sense, since England had no troops ready and her fleet could have been of no assistance to the Constitutionalists. But his hopes for the triumph of revolutionary Spain were dashed by the event; and his views were certainly not well received by the king or the Ultra members of the Cabinet. The Duke of Wellington had been obliged to say things at Verona which he did not altogether believe; and—what was worse—after he had said them they had been disregarded by the French and the Allies. His mortification took the form of an intrigue against Canning. Those who examine the letters of Madame de Lieven to Prince Metternich can watch it grow. It consisted of a series of attempts to humiliate Canning into resigning, and of a confidential correspondence between Metternich, Wellington, and George IV which was never shown to the Foreign Secretary. Canning was immovable. He knew that his policy was a popular one, he commanded a majority in the House of Commons, and above all he enjoyed the steady and unflinching support of the Earl of Liverpool. "My Lord Liverpool is neither more nor less than a common prostitute," Wellington blurted out at a dinner party; but hard words break no bones. [43]

Canning had hoped that the prestige of England would keep the French out of Spain, and that the Holy Allies would listen to his warnings and cease to meddle with the independence of Spanish America: his neutral policy was always directed towards the preservation of the Central and South American market. In the summer of 1823, it did not appear that he had been successful. At his own dinner table, surrounded by Holy Alliance diplomats, George IV rallied his Foreign Secretary. "There is nothing more contemptible and clumsy than half-measures and half-tones. I hate them. *Don't you, Mr. Canning?*" [44] Mr. Canning was silent. But, indeed, his diplomatic defeats were only on the surface. An instinct, too profound for formulation, urged him to shatter the Quadruple Alliance and to dissociate England from the Holy Allies. A British statesman, he said in 1826, "in internal as in external affairs [will] hold a middle course between extremes, avoiding alike extravagancies of despotism, or the licentiousness of unbridled freedom." [45] Even in 1823, he was groping his way towards that kind of world liberalism which is most agreeable to an expanding industrial economy—the liberalism, that is to say, not of free men but of free markets. "With painful steps and slow" Lord Liverpool and his "economic Cabinet" were moving in the same direction. Needless to say, these pioneers did not reach their destination: they were not too sure—they could only hope—that it existed. While Lord Liverpool and Mr. Huskisson hacked away at the jungle of tariff schedules and navigation laws, Mr. Canning succeeded in discrediting the Holy Alliance. All loom together in British history as the heralds of a new era.

XI

John Quincy Adams, like George Canning, did not believe that the Spanish-American republics were in any real danger of physical invasion, either from France, the Holy Allies, or both together. He was far more worried about the island of Cuba, "an object of transcendent importance to the political and commercial interests of our Union." [46] A British naval squadron was hovering close to its shores, ostensibly to protect British shipping against pirates; and it occurred to Mr. Adams, as the Spanish crisis grew in intensity, that Great Britain might rush to the defense of revolutionary Spain and demand in return the modest gift of Cuba. He had different ideas about the future of that island. "It is scarcely possible to resist the conviction," he wrote in his instructions to Hugh Nelson, the new Minister to Spain, "that the annexation of Cuba to our federal republic will be indispensable to the continuance and integrity of the Union itself. It is obvious however that for this event we are not yet prepared. . . . But there are laws of political as well as physical gravitation; and if an apple severed by the tempest from its native tree cannot choose but fall to the ground, Cuba, forcibly disjoined from its own unnatural connection with Spain, and incapable of self-support, can gravitate only towards the North American Union, which by the same law of nature cannot cast her off from its bosom." In the meantime, "you will not conceal from the Spanish government the repugnance of the United States to the transfer of the island of Cuba by Spain to any other power." [47] Here was the No-Transfer Principle in all its glory. It is not altogether surprising that similar ideas, in reverse, should have presented themselves to the fertile mind of Mr. Canning. In October 1822 he was convinced that the United States had designs upon Cuba; and he instructed Stratford Canning to use all his endeavors to ascertain "how far such suspicions are justified." [48] Stratford Canning replied in January 1823 that there was not the slightest foundation for them. In March Lord Liverpool told Mr. Rush, the American Minister, that Great Britain would not agree to any change in Cuba's sovereignty, nor would she dream of seizing the island for herself.[49] In the same month, President Monroe informed his Cabinet that he would be willing to enter into a mutual agreement with Great Britain not to take Cuba. This was thought unnecessary; but it was obvious that the air was clearing.[50]

Aside from the Cuban problem, there was every reason for Monroe and Adams to be satisfied with the actions of Great Britain. At Verona, she had broken with the Holy Alliance. She had made it clear that she would countenance no outside intervention between Spain and her American colonies. Mr. Canning had warned France against invading Spain, and, when the French disregarded his warning, had sped his good wishes to the revolutionaries from the very floor of the House of Commons. That May, in Washington, Stratford Canning was surprised and delighted at the new feeling towards

Britain. "The course which you have taken in the great politics of Europe," he wrote his cousin, "has had the effect of making the English almost popular in the United States. The improved tone of public feeling is very perceptible, and even Adams has caught a something of the soft infection. . . . On the whole, I question whether for a long time there has been so favorable an opportunity—as far as general disposition and good will are concerned—to bring the two countries nearer together. France for the moment is quite out of fashion." [51] In June, Mr. Adams seemed to justify this optimism by suggesting to Stratford Canning that a suitable occasion had now arisen "for the United States and Great Britain to compare their ideas and purposes together, with a view to the accommodation of the great interests upon which they have hitherto differed." [52] The British Minister was convinced that something like an alliance was being suggested to him. But when Adams reported this conversation to the American Minister in London, as giving the general idea of a negotiation which he was to propose to the British government, his language was, to say the least, slightly ominous. "From the many recent indications of the policy of the British Government," he wrote, "we had seen cause to hope that the *rights* of neutrality were more favorably viewed by them than heretofore, and we thought it probable they would not be unwilling to review the doctrine heretofore held by them with a disposition more favorable to neutral interests. . . . But I observed our desire to discuss these collisions of neutral and belligerent rights reposed on the assumption that the views of Great Britain concerning them were not exactly the same that they had been when we discussed them with her heretofore. If we were mistaken in that, if she would enter upon the negotiation only to adhere to the doctrine which she had maintained heretofore, we should prefer postponing again the discussion to a future period." [53]

It would seem that what Mr. Adams had in mind was not so much a negotiation as a challenge to the whole British concept of maritime rights. Just as Lord Castlereagh's first break with the Quadruple Alliance had emboldened Mr. Adams to give his violent July 4 oration, so now was he being pushed by Mr. Canning into a mood of aggressive nationalism. It must be remembered that he had only recently endorsed, and perhaps originated, that extraordinary word "elsewhere," which demanded for the United States equal trading rights with Great Britain in every part of the British Empire. One is tempted to ask whether the "soft infection," which so pleased Stratford Canning, did not come from a virus rather less agreeable than that of friendship.

CHAPTER THREE

The Great Flirtation

WHEN Mr. Canning began his battle with France and the Neo-Holy Allies, Great Britain was climbing out of her postwar depression. The fall in world prices, owing to a shortage of specie and an absence of an elastic credit system, did not hurt her industrial system with its exportable surplus. Her manufacturers were learning those technical refinements which reduce costs. As the collapse of the American cotton market had shown, raw materials were becoming cheap; and though wages are said not to have fallen as low as prices, the English industrial worker of those days was one of the most cruelly exploited people in the world. The British manufacturer, therefore, was able to quote prices that could attract even the misery of postwar Europe: but his chief single market was still the United States of America. As Lord Liverpool had told the House of Lords in 1820, whoever wished prosperity to England must wish prosperity to the United States. In 1822, 95 per cent of all its imports of woolen goods and 89 per cent of its imports of cotton goods were of British manufacture; in 1823, the percentages were 96 and 84. In 1822, 47 per cent of its total imports, and in 1823, 42 per cent were of the growth, produce, or manufacture of England and her colonies.[1] From the British side, this meant that roughly one sixth of Britain's export was consumed by the United States.[2] It was easy for the American merchant to avail himself of the banking and credit facilities open to British merchants and manufacturers; this fact and the basic Anglo-American exchange—raw cotton for textiles—gave the United States a somewhat colonial position in British economy.[3] This exchange had not begun to worry American agrarians; but the manufacturers were growing restive. In 1823, however, they had not yet been able to do what Lord Liverpool so earnestly suggested that they should never do—and that was to persuade Congress to impose a protective tariff.

When the American Navigation Act of 1823, with the word "elsewhere" in its tail, was known in England, there was more surprise than pain. It was thought that an Order-in-Council, which took immediate retaliatory measures, would speedily bring the Americans to their senses. Their Act, in short, was regarded rather as a temporary aberration than as a deliberate policy. The Order-in-Council was, of course, exceedingly firm. It provided that the shipping of the United States, when entering the ports of British colonies in North America and the West Indies, should pay a duty of 4s. 3d. per ton and of ten per cent upon their cargoes.[4] This Order, it was thought, would soon remove the American one dollar per ton and ten per cent on the cargo, levied upon British ships: it was simply tit for tat. The Americans now seemed anxious to settle matters with a convention; and George Canning, who did not know the precise nature of Mr. Rush's instructions, probably thought at the time that this would be as good a way as any to get everyone out of their difficulties.

His behavior towards Minister Rush was, indeed, extremely affable. In July, he asked Mr. Rush to send copies of his speech of April 16 against repeal of the Foreign Enlistment Act to Mr. Monroe and Mr. Adams. These copies were corrected in Canning's own hand. In the course of the speech, he had said: "If I wished for a guide in a system of neutrality, I should take that laid down by America in the presidency of Washington and the secretaryship of Jefferson."[5]

Now it was quite well known that Mr. Canning did not care for Americans and that he had no love for republics. He had never, in all his private correspondence, shown any more disposition to understand or appreciate the United States than Sidney Smith had offered in his famous and bitter article in the Edinburgh Review.[6] In society, American gentlemen and English gentlemen did not as a rule hit it off together: and there are few examples of misunderstanding more complete than the comments privately passed upon each other by Charles Greville and Washington Irving, or by Sir Walter Scott and James Fenimore Cooper.[7] But in the summer of 1823, Mr. Canning's formal courtesy—which he had not always been too careful to maintain—became suffused with an extraordinary warmth. The rather snobbish and rather voluble Christopher Hughes, now chargé d'affaires at Stockholm, happened to be passing through Liverpool on his way to St. Petersburg with dispatches; and here he met the Foreign Secretary, who had come up to his old constituency to make a speech. Canning went out of his way to shower kindnesses upon the American, and at the Mayor's banquet, where Hughes was a guest, he said of the United States and Great Britain that "the force of blood again prevails, and the daughter and the mother stand together against the world." Mr. Hughes was enchanted: he was even more enchanted when Canning passed him on to the hospitality of the Duke of Buckingham, the Ph.D. When he arrived in St. Petersburg, the British Ambassador reported that he "was not yet recovered from his delight and astonishment." [8]

Mr. Hughes, had he read these words, might have remarked that any American diplomat would be astonished and perhaps even delighted at being so cordially received in England: it was not the usual experience.

Canning now carried his "flirtation" with the United States—as he afterwards called it—one step further.[9] On August 16 he had a conference with Richard Rush, in the course of which Mr. Rush asked him "transiently" for his opinion on the state of affairs in Europe, adding that he derived much consolation from the thought that England would never allow France to interfere with the emancipation of the Spanish colonies, nor would she remain passive if France attempted to acquire territory there by conquest or cession. Canning listened gravely, and then asked what the American government would say to going hand in hand with England in such a policy. He did not think that any concert of *action* would be necessary; the simple fact of the two countries being known to hold the same opinion would, by its moral effect, check the French government in any design upon Spanish America. To this astonishing proposal the American Minister replied that he could not say in what manner his government would look upon it, but that he would communicate it in the same informal manner in which it had been thrown out. He went on to remark, very shrewdly, that much depended upon the precise situation in which the British government then stood towards the Spanish-American colonies. Were they taking, or did they think of taking any step towards the recognition of those states? This was the point, said Mr. Rush, "in which we felt the chief interest." Canning was unable to give a direct answer. He said that Great Britain was contemplating a step, not final, but preparatory, which would leave her free to "recognize or not according to the position of events at a future period." To an American, whose country was already committed to the independence of Spanish America, this would not have seemed a candid reply.[10] Mr. Rush's very cool report of this momentous conversation was dispatched from London on August 19, and reached Washington on October 9.

On August 17, the Russian Ambassador, Count Lieven, had a long conference with Canning, in which he sought to impress upon the Foreign Secretary the foolishness of his attitude towards France. Could he not see that the French fortunes were not, after all, at a low ebb? That, on the contrary, their expedition in Spain had succeeded, and that the absolutist cause throughout Europe had received a corresponding impetus? Mr. Canning listened eagerly, and yet—it was very strange—he did not strike Lieven as being at all despondent. He replied that the time had come for him to take an active part in the new arrangements which would be made in Spain. Lieven hurried back to his wife with this news, and Madame de Lieven pondered over it, and pondered in vain. "Will his part be to arrange or to upset?" she wrote to Metternich. "We shall see." [11]

She did not wait to see. The fact was that the plot against Canning, in which she had been so industriously engaged, had failed. Neither the secret letters of Metternich, nor her own representations with Wellington and the king, nor the persistent intrigues of Count Lieven and Prince Paul Esterhazy, the Austrian Ambassador, had succeeded in dividing the government against itself. Wellington, she declared, was "stupid," and the king, though his sympathies were entirely with the Holy Alliance, was incurably lazy. As for England, "her domestic prosperity justifies her behavior. . . . We do not like her foreign policy; but what does John Bull mind? He has his mug of beer. And what do the Ministers mind? They are at peace among themselves." [12] Really ill with mortification, she went to Brighton and made plans to recruit her strength in the Italian sunshine.

Her eager, astute, and restless mind, so brilliantly at home in the Age of Castlereagh, was still imprisoned there. She understood the politics of reaction, but the politics of the middle class entirely eluded her. She was nothing if not aristocratic. She perceived that the Liverpool-Canning-Huskisson wing of the government was firmly in the saddle, but, for the life of her, she could not realize how it had come to get there. With all her cleverness, it never occurred to her that the power now so visibly departing from Windsor Castle and the Brighton Pavilion might perhaps one day be rediscovered in the Manchester Chamber of Commerce.

II

Mr. Canning, therefore, was well established at home. He had defeated a very foolish but very dangerous plot. At the same time, his diplomacy, there was no denying it, had suffered an obvious setback. In September, the French army was approaching Cadiz where Ferdinand VII, the prisoner of the Constitutionalists, lay idly meditating revenge and tribulation. On August 20 Mr. Canning wrote a note to Mr. Rush, in which he stated in "unofficial and confidential" terms that

> "1. We conceive the recovery of the Colonies by Spain to be hopeless.
>
> 2. We conceive the question of the Recognition of them, as Independent States, to be one of time and circumstance.
>
> 3. We are, however, by no means disposed to throw any impediment in the way of an arrangement between them and the mother country by amicable negotiations.
>
> 4. We aim not at the possession of any portion of them ourselves.
>
> 5. We could not see any portion of them transferred to any other Power with indifference."

"If these opinions and feelings are [he added], as I firmly believe them to be, common to your government with ours, why should we hesitate mutually to confide them with each other; and to declare them in the face of the world? . . . Do you conceive that under the power which you have recently received, you are authorized to enter into negotiation, and to sign any Convention upon this subject? . . . Nothing would be more gratifying to me than to join with you in such a work, and, I am persuaded, there has seldom, in the history of the world, occurred an opportunity, when so small an effort, of two friendly Governments, might produce so unequivocal a good and prevent such extensive calamities." [13] The flirtation had become a courtship.

Mr. Rush replied, three days later, that his government fully agreed with the sentiments in Mr. Canning's note, but that the paramount consideration must be the reception of the Spanish-American states into the family of nations by the powers of Europe, "and especially, I may add, by Great Britain." His instructions, he said, did not permit him to commit his government in advance; and he contented himself with remarking that it would give him particular pleasure to bring Mr. Canning's views before the President as promptly as he could.[14] Mr. Canning, however, had just received word that, as soon as the French campaign was over, a new European Congress would be called to deal especially with the affairs of Spanish America. "I need not point out," he said in a letter from Liverpool, which crossed Mr. Rush's in the mail, "all the complications to which this proposal, however dealt with by us, may lead." [15] All he received by way of answer was the familiar hint that if the British government would fully acknowledge the independence of the Spanish-American states, "it would accelerate the steps of my government (and) it would also naturally place *me* in a new position in my further conferences with you, on this interesting subject." [16]

If Rush had succeeded in forcing the British to recognize the Spanish Americans, he was then honestly prepared to go through with his part of the bargain—that is to say, "to make a declaration in the name of my government that it will not remain inactive under an attack upon the independence of those states by the Holy Alliance," and to make this declaration explicitly and avow it before the world.[17] He was well aware that, in thus exceeding his instructions, he might be disavowed by his own government; but he was prepared to take all the blame upon himself, and to sweeten his disgrace with the thought that he had acted for the best. In these very anxious days, with no one to advise him, his actions were astonishingly cool and brave. Canning answered from Westmoreland that he could not bind himself and his colleagues—whose sentiments he had been expressing as well as his own—simply on the American Minister's word without the support of positive instructions from Washington: in other words, that the British government was not yet ready for an immediate recognition. Mr. Rush at first seemed to think that this unwillingness to negotiate on the basis of equivalents—recognition for co-operation—would bring the whole business to an end.[18] But as day followed day without another word from Canning, who was due to return to London in the middle of September, he changed his mind; he thought that the Foreign Secretary would renew his conversations with all his former urgency; and, while preparing his mind for this encounter, he wrote a very strange letter to President Monroe.

He told the President that he deeply mistrusted the Tory government. It was true that they had lately become very liberal in their foreign-trade policy, and he believed that they would become more so. But he did not think that they had changed in their attitude towards political freedom, or that a change, if it took place, would be of a sort to invite the confidence and co-operation of the United States. Great Britain had fought the Napoleonic Wars, ostensibly in support of the freedom of other states, but actually against the people of France. She had aided the Holy Alliance, either positively or negatively, until the Alliance seemed to threaten her commercial interests in Spanish America and her political sway in both hemispheres. She would continue to act the part "which she acted in 1774 in America, which she has since acted in Europe, and is now acting in Ireland. . . . I shall therefore find it hard," he wrote, "to keep from my mind the suspicion that the approaches of her ministers to me at this portentous juncture for a concert of policy which they have not heretofore courted with the United States, are bottomed on their own calculations."

Mr. Rush knew as well as anyone that diplomatic approaches are rarely if ever "bottomed" on anything else. He hastened to add that he did not accuse the British Cabinet, "as it is now composed," of any sinister motives toward the United States. On the contrary, he believed that Lord Liverpool and Mr. Canning would advocate an even more intimate and friendly policy towards them, "no matter from what motives arising." He did not think that the Whigs or the Radicals would ever offer such good terms.[19]

This letter, with its odd alternations of suspicion and speculation, is an admirable example of the effect of the new Liberal Toryism upon a shrewd observer. Mr. Rush was not, like Madame de Lieven, simply bewildered. He saw very clearly that a government might have no respect for civil liberties but still might show a high regard for commercial advantages. He perceived rather less clearly that a British foreign policy based on the conservation of wealth was gradually being superseded by a British foreign policy dedicated to the enlargement of opportunity. He did not believe that the friendly overtures of Mr. Canning were due entirely to a British anxiety for South American markets. He was not sure what other motives might lie behind these overtures, and he was evidently surprised that a Tory Cabinet should be making them—so surprised, indeed, that he could only suppose that a Whig or a Radical Cabinet would be "the decided opponents of such a policy." He did not realize that British statesmen were not their own masters; that all would follow, willingly or unwillingly, wherever the Industrial Revolution led them. In 1823, the Industrial Revolution was not a recognizable concept.

Mr. Rush never lost his head, but he grew more puzzled and suspicious. It is well to remember that he was to become a Protectionist Secretary of the Treasury under John Quincy Adams, and that it was a Tory Prime Minister, Sir Robert Peel, who, years later, dealt the final blow for British Free Trade. There was a prophecy in Rush's letter to Monroe but, like most prophecies, it was indistinct.

III

At any rate, when George Canning reappeared in London he did fulfill one of Richard Rush's predictions. He renewed his overtures and he imparted to them a degree of warmth which still surprises us, coming as they did from a man who disliked republics only a little less than he despised republicans. He said that the United States were the first power established on the American continent, "and now confessedly the leading Power. Had not a new epoch arrived in the relative position of the United States toward Europe, which Europe must acknowledge? Were the great political and commercial interests which hung upon the destinies of the new continent, to be canvassed and adjusted in this hemisphere, without the co-operation or even knowledge of the United States? Were they to be canvassed and adjusted, he would even add, without some proper understanding between the United States and Great Britain, *as the two chief commercial and maritime states of both worlds?* He hoped not, he would wish to persuade himself not." These were seductive words; but the cautious Rush still hung back. He replied that if he were to take the risk of entangling the United States in the affairs of Europe, he must have some justification beyond any that had yet been laid before him. At this, Mr. Canning grew lyrical. "Why . . . should the United States, whose institutions always, and whose policy in this instance, approximated them so much more closely to Great Britain than to any other power in Europe, hesitate to act with her to promote a common object approved alike by both?" No British statesman, while in office, had hitherto been able to detect a close resemblance between the institutions of the United States and those of Great Britain. It only remained for Mr. Canning to declare that if he were invited to the European Congress, he would decline to appear unless the United States were invited also. He could go no further. But he received the same stubborn answer: if he would pledge his government to an immediate recognition of the South American states, Mr. Rush would sign a joint declaration on Spanish America.[20] But the economic wing of the British government, strong as it was, was not yet strong enough to force the whole Cabinet into such an open break with the Powers of Europe; nor would it do so, in any case, as long as the Spanish Constitutionalists were in the field. Eight days after this remarkable interview, which took place on September 18, Canning made a last effort: he summoned Rush to Gloucester Lodge and asked him if "a promise by England of *future* acknowledgment" would satisfy his scruples; but the answer was the same as before. When they met again on October 8 and October 9, not a word was said about co-operation with regard to Spanish America: nor did they ever speak of it again.[21]

The great courtship was ended, and for a very simple reason: there was no longer any time for dalliance. On September 30 Cadiz fell to the French, and the Revolution was over. This news did not reach London until October 10, but Canning had already taken steps to soften its consequences. He believed that the French contemplated a direct interference in Spanish America, certainly with ships and perhaps with soldiers.[22] He did not think for a moment that they could succeed in this venture against the opposition of British sea power.[23] But, as Foreign Secretary, he could not watch with complacence or without fear this resounding victory for the reactionaries of Europe. On October 3, he began a series of conversations with Prince Jules de Polignac, the French Ambassador, which resulted in the great Polignac Memorandum of October 9 to 12, 1823. In this Memorandum, the British government declared that they regarded the reduction of Spanish America to its ancient submission as hopeless; that they would not interfere in any practicable negotiation between Spain and the colonies; but that "the junction of any Foreign Power in an enterprise of Spain against the Colonies, would be viewed by them as constituting an entirely new question, and one upon which they must take such decision as the interests of Great Britain would require." To this exceedingly strong language there were added certain trade requirements of vital significance. The British government maintained that ever since 1810 the trade with the Spanish colonies had been open to British subjects, and that the ancient coast laws of Spain were "as regarded them at least, racially repealed." Great Britain did not ask for a separate right to this trade: the force of circumstances and the "irreversible progress of events" had already made it free to all the world; but if her claim were disputed she would immediately recognize the independence of the Spanish-American states. The Prince de Polignac replied that France, on her part, disclaimed any intention or desire to appropriate to herself any part of the Spanish possessions in America; that she asked for nothing more than the right to trade in Spanish America upon the same terms as Great Britain ("to rank, after the Mother Country, among the most favored nations"); and that she "abjured, in any case, any design of acting against the colonies by force of arms." [24]

It is evident that here was at least as much of an agreement on trade rights as of a warning to France against aggression.[25] None the less, its language was decisive. Nor would it be just to Canning to regard it as anything but a personal triumph for him. The details of those conversations are lost, but we can imagine that imperious manner and that persuasive voice as they laid before M. Polignac the young commands of the British middle class. Canning's belief that he had won a great victory is evident in the curious, the almost menacing exultation of a speech he made at Plymouth on October 28. He compared England's neutral quiescence to the sleep of a battleship:

> "one of those stupendous masses now reposing on their shadows in perfect stillness—how soon, upon any call of patriotism, or of necessity, it would assume the likeness of an animated thing, instinct with life and motion—how soon it would ruffle, as it were, its swelling plumage—how quickly it would collect all its beauty and its bravery, collect its scattered elements of strength, and awaken its dormant thunder." [26]

The Memorandum had not been made public; so that this imagery, however gratifying to the taste of naval Plymouth, must have been designed especially for M. Polignac and M. Villèle and the ministers and autocrats of the Holy Alliance.[27]

IV

Richard Rush maintained that Canning's first overture was a "fortuitous" one.[28] In one sense, no doubt, it was. He seems to have consulted the Cabinet after and not before making it. But, in another sense, it was not fortuitous at all. It was the culmination of those friendly advances towards the United States which had been evident in the settlement of the Arbuthnot-Ambrister affair, and which had been intensified on the one hand by distress in the West Indies and on the other by the Spanish crisis and the optimistic reports of Mr. Stratford Canning.

The drama of the Rush-Canning conversations—for they *were* dramatic—lies in the interplay of the conscious and the unconscious motives in Canningite diplomacy. Consciously, no doubt, Canning wished above all to extract from the United States, in the course of the joint declaration, a pledge never to seize the island of Cuba. Then again, he thought that he could offset his diplomatic defeats in Europe by coming to a public understanding with America. He also feared that the French might revive their colonial empire and their old sea power; and he perceived in the purchasers of Louisiana the most eloquent opponents, with England, of such an ambition. He was concerned about the freedom of the South American trade and he knew that the United States, more than any other nation except France, shared this anxiety. And he was eager to "prevent the drawing of the line of demarcation which I most dread—America versus Europe."[29]

All these were powerful reasons for an overture to the United States; all were unquestionably present in his mind; yet all together do not quite satisfy the conditions necessary for so urgent a plea to Rush. He had learned from Stratford Canning that the United States did not intend to seize Cuba, either then or in the near future. He could hardly have persuaded himself that the United States meant a great deal to the Powers of Europe. He was quite convinced that British sea power could sink any expedition, whether French or Holy, long before it reached Spanish America. As for the future of the South American market, how much better to stand forth as the single defender of Spanish America, not by an act of recognition, but by simply threatening the aggressors with the British navy! Nor could he have concealed from himself that a line of demarcation would be more easily drawn by tariffs than expunged by joint declarations. Every reason had a counter-reason; but Mr. Canning pressed on.

The very essence of Lord Liverpool's government can be discovered in its instinctive response to the demands of industry; and this was strange, since Lord Liverpool's party was a party of landed proprietors, to whom the demands of industry meant less than nothing. The manner of this response was one of arid paternalism: Lord Liverpool's government led the way, it did not conceive itself as yielding to pressure. Its reforms were practical, common-sense reforms; and if they were tentative, that was because it was a pioneer and an experimenter, working against immense obstacles and in an economy not fully developed. Lord Liverpool had always to calm the Ultra Tory members of his own Cabinet. William Huskisson's assault upon the silk monopoly was conducted in despite of the best manufacturing opinion.[30] And even Huskisson proposed no more than a modification of the Navigation Laws and the tariff schedules; even his free trade opinions, vigorous and transforming though they were, were only the leaven in a lump of mild protectionism.[31] In one respect, moreover, all the leading reformers in this singular government—Liverpool, Canning, Huskisson, Robinson—were very Tory indeed: all were opponents of Parliamentary reform.

None the less, the instinct of an industrial economy, hovering upon the edge of an unparalleled expansion, is always to make friends with friendly, free, and subservient markets; and this instinct seized upon Lord Liverpool and his liberal colleagues, using them for its own mysterious ends. When the merchants of London, the Chamber of Commerce of Glasgow, the woolen manufacturers of Howick, and the manufacturers of Manchester and Birmingham appealed to Parliament in 1820 for a greater freedom of trade, Lord Liverpool replied with his blunt suggestion that the prosperity of England depended upon the prosperity of a tariff-free United States. He did not direct the foreign policy of George Canning, but he supported and encouraged it, in Parliament and out. And George Canning approached Richard Rush not only as the conscious diplomatist but also as the partly unconscious servant of the energies of British coal and iron, of British spindles and furnaces. Nor was his plea simply directed towards the safety of Cuba or the enlargement of South American trade: it was also, and more so, a wooing of the free North American market—a diplomatic extension, in a moment of crisis, of Lord Liverpool's 1820 speech. It was aimed, in brief, ultimately and instinctively at the agrarian mind of the United States; or at that portion of the agrarian mind which was contented with the exchange of staples for manufactures.

The Polignac Memorandum was known to France, Austria, Russia, and Prussia by the end of the third week in October; and it was circulated definitely to all the European Cabinets at the beginning of November. It was communicated to Mr. Rush, by word of mouth only, on November 24, and not circulated to him until December 13.[32] It seems that Canning was still trying to effect in Washington, through his *chargé d'affaires*, the joint declaration he was unable to extract from Mr. Rush in London.[33] But the answer he received was President Monroe's great Doctrine of December 2, 1823; and this Doctrine, whatever else it may have been, was not agrarian at all.

CHAPTER FOUR

President Monroe's Message: December 2, 1823

AUGUST of 1823 found Washington City a steamy tribute to the isolation of America. Even Secretary Adams, impervious to the crises of Europe, had fled from the heat into Massachusetts. There he remained buried and oblivious while the Duc d'Angoulême took Cadiz and Ferdinand VII was let loose, to teach his people the meaning of amnesty; while the Holy Allies meditated a new Congress and Canning made his final appeals to the American Minister. Returning on October 11, he found awaiting him Mr. Rush's first two dispatches concerning the Canning overtures. The President gravely showed him these communications, asked for copies to be sent on to him, and left for his farm in Loudoun County.[1]

Mr. Monroe had two anxious and affectionate mentors—Jefferson at Monticello, and Madison at Montpelier. The three venerable men drew closer together as the dusk gathered around the Virginia Dynasty. If Monroe's Administration seemed to be moving further and further away from early Republicanism, all three agreed to blame it upon judges and Congressmen. When the two ex-Presidents discussed Monroe, they did so on a strangely elegiac note. Now he turned for advice to them, sending copies of the Rush dispatches to Jefferson on October 17, with a request that Jefferson send them on to Madison. "Many important considerations are involved in this proposition," Monroe wrote in his covering letter.

> "1st Shall we entangle ourselves, at all, in European politicks, & wars, on the side of any power, against others, presuming that a concert, by agreement of the kind proposed, may lead to that result? 2d If a case can exist in which a sound maxim may, &

ought to be departed from, is not the present instance, precisely that case? 3d Has not the epoch arriv'd when G Britain must take her stand, either on the side of the monarchs of Europe, or of the U States, & in consequence either in favor of Despotism or of liberty . . . My own impression is that we ought to meet the proposal of the British govt." [2]

Jefferson's reply was exceedingly suggestive. "The question presented by the letters you have sent me," he wrote,

"is the most momentous which has ever been offered to my contemplation since that of Independence. That made us a nation, this sets our compass and points the course which we are to steer through the ocean of time opening on us. . . . While [Europe] is laboring to become the domicil of despotism, our endeavor should surely be, to make our hemisphere that of freedom. One nation, most of all, could disturb us in this pursuit; she now offers to lead, aid, and accompany us in it. By acceding to her proposition, we detach her from the bands, bring her mighty weight into the scale of free government, and emancipate a continent at one stroke, which might otherwise linger long in doubt and difficulty. Great Britain is the nation which can do us the most harm of any one, or all on earth; and with her on our side we need not fear the whole world."

After all, he argued, if the issue came to war it would be "not her war, but ours. . . . But I am clearly of Mr. Canning's opinion, that it will prevent instead of provoking war." He was prepared even to sacrifice his dearest wish—that of adding Cuba to the United States—if this would produce a similar self-denial on the part of England. Sooner or later Cuba would become independent and then—by something like Adams's "law of political gravitation"—it would attach itself to the northern republic. "I could honestly, therefore, join in the declaration proposed." [3]

Mr. Madison was more cautious. He replied that the success of France against Spain "would be followed by an attempt of the Holy Allies to reduce the revolutionized colonies of the latter to their former dependence. . . . It is particularly fortunate that the policy of Great Britain, though guided by calculations different from ours, has presented a co-operation for an object the same with ours. With that co-operation we have nothing to fear from the rest of Europe. . . . There ought not, therefore, to be any backwardness, I think, in meeting her the way she has proposed." [4] Unlike Jefferson, however, he did not think that Great Britain had undergone some miraculous conversion. She would prefer not to fight alone, he thought, because that would allow the United States, as a neutral, to extend its commerce and navigation at her expense. If he favored a joint declaration, it was because this was "due to ourselves and to the world." He thought that such a declaration should censure France for her interference in Spain and that it should come out strongly in favor of the revolutionary Greeks.

With these two letters in his pocket, Monroe returned to Washington on November 4. He was prepared to go all lengths with Great Britain.

I

The Cabinet that met on November 7, 1823, had temporarily lost one of its most influential members. William H. Crawford, Secretary of the Treasury, had been taken ill in September while on a visit to Virginia. The nature of his disease has never been determined: it was possibly erysipelas. The local physician administered a deadly nostrum—perhaps calomel, perhaps lobelia—which fettered the Secretary to his bed, half paralyzed and almost blind. A man of vast physique and invincible ambition, Crawford did not resign; he even made a partial recovery in 1824; but he was never the same man again.[5]

Crawford was certainly Jefferson's choice for successor to Monroe; he was the favorite of the Old Republicans; and he had the support of a group of men who, though they rejected the pure Pierian of Old Republicanism, were prescribing for the electorate a somewhat less heady brew called Radicalism. Radicalism was compounded partly of a fondness for economy and partly of an aversion to Calhoun and Adams. Another Presidential aspirant, Smith Thompson of New York, had just decided that his chances were too slim and had left the Navy Department for the Supreme Court; his place had been taken by Samuel L. Southard of New Jersey. The potential successors to Monroe in Monroe's Cabinet, therefore, had now been reduced to Calhoun and Adams. It is to be remarked that, in the anxious days that followed Monroe's return, they forgot their differences and worked, each according to his lights, solely for the public good. Had Crawford been present, he would have done the same. (The facts in the Adams memoirs support this contention; his interpretations do not. He was convinced that Calhoun was a troublemaker.) It is significant that Southard, who was known to be a Calhoun supporter, invariably though silently followed Adams's lead in this critical time.[6] William Wirt, the Attorney-General, philosophically opposed to strong executive action, and inclined to shift the responsibility to Congress, was more vocal than Southard; but his sunny disposition prevented him from sowing discord, and he, like his colleagues, was dominated by a common feeling of profound responsibility.

No set of men, detached from Europe by time and space, had more reason for anxiety and dejection than the Cabinet that met on November 7. Three weeks earlier, on October 16, Secretary Adams had received a note from the Baron de Tuyll, the Russian Minister, which announced that the Tsar positively would not receive any agents from the South American states, and that he congratulated the United States on their *neutral* position towards South America.[7] This ominous communication, coinciding with the news of Canning's overtures, was enough to convince anyone that a new Holy plot, or an old one refurbished, was in the making against the South Americans.

The famous discussions which began on November 7 reached one significant conclusion, possibly the most significant, at the very outset. Calhoun suggested that Rush should be given a discretionary power to make a joint declaration with Canning, even if it pledged the United States never to acquire Cuba or Texas. He had not then been shown Jefferson's and Madison's letters. This suggestion was undoubtedly agreeable to Monroe, since he brought it up two weeks later, and since it was in line with the advice of the two ex-Presidents. Adams vehemently disagreed. He said that we had no designs upon Cuba or Texas, but that they might one day exercise their primitive rights and join the Union; moreover, and above all, he thought that we should not tie our hands by a joint declaration. Monroe, deeply impressed, remarked that he did not wish to take any course that might make the United States subordinate to Great Britain—thus abandoning the Jeffersonian position that Great Britain should take the lead. Adams went on to say that the communication from Tuyll gave the United States an opportunity to take a stand against the Holy Alliance and at the same time decline the overtures of Great Britain. It would be more candid, he said, as well as more dignified to avow American principles explicitly to France and Russia "than to come in as a cock-boat in the wake of the British man-of-war." [8] Speculations are hazardous where there are no facts to support them; we know only that all agreed with him.[9] We are left guessing at the amount of authority with which he made his formidable statement.

This was the first response in Cabinet—a response entirely dictated by Adams—to the overtures of Canning. Though Monroe wavered towards the British thereafter, it was also the final one.

II

On November 13, word was received in Washington that Cadiz had fallen, and the President, alarmed beyond anything Adams conceived possible at the thought that the Holy Allies would immediately attack Spanish America, talked once again of a joint declaration with Great Britain. "He will recover from this in a few days," Adams wrote, "but I never saw more indecision in him." [10] On November 15 the President at length showed his Secretary of State, as a final argument, his two letters from Jefferson and Madison; but Mr. Adams was unimpressed. The Cabinet met at one that afternoon, and Secretary Calhoun—"perfectly moon-struck at the surrender of Cadiz"—gave it as his opinion that the Holy Allies with ten thousand men could restore all Mexico and South America to Spanish dominion. He was all for plunging into war, with Great Britain's help or without it. "They will no more restore Spanish dominion on the American continent," said Adams, "than the Chimborazo will sink beneath the ocean." [11] On November 16 Mr. Rush's dispatch arrived, announcing that George Canning had lost interest in a joint declaration; and the tension immediately lessened.[12] On November 17 Baron de Tuyll called upon Adams to thank him for his amicable reply to the note of October 16, and to present him with two extracts from dispatches from Count Nesselrode. The second of these spluttered like a firecracker and concluded with a loud explosion. It contained an " 'Io triumphe' over the fallen cause of revolution," and a further panegyric upon the "liberation" of Naples, Piedmont, and Spain. It ended with the sinister remark—which concerned the Americas alone—that the Tsar wished to "guarantee the tranquillity of all the states of which the civilized world is composed." [13] This might well have been one of those vague generalizations to which Alexander was so notoriously addicted. Or could it have meant that he hoped to return Spanish America, by force, to the rule of Ferdinand VII?

So Calhoun construed it. He was now confirmed, he said, in his views regarding the designs of the Holy Alliance. "It quite confirms me in *mine*," retorted Adams. He noted coldly that Monroe was extraordinarily dejected; "there must be something that affects him," he wrote, "beside the European news." [14] On the next day but one, Monroe suggested again that Rush should be given discretionary powers to make a joint declaration with Great Britain; and once again Adams opposed him. When the Cabinet met on November 21, and the instructions for Rush were discussed, no further mention was made of such powers. The joint declaration was a dead issue. And no voice was raised against Adams's proposed reply to the Baron de Tuyll, Count Nesselrode, and the Tsar of Russia. He intended, he said, to announce in a moderate and conciliatory manner his government's dissent from the principles set forth in the second extract; to assert those upon which his government was founded; and, while disclaiming all intention to propagate these principles by force, and all interference with the political affairs of Europe, to declare "our expectation that European powers will equally abstain from any attempt to spread their principles in the American hemisphere or to subjugate by force any part of these continents to their will." [15]

This ends the first phase of these renowned discussions. The original tension was undoubtedly created by Canning's offer of a quasi-alliance. It was increased by the incongruous menaces of that kindly and bustling gentleman, the Baron de Tuyll. Throughout, John Quincy Adams was the leader, imposing his will upon his overwrought and discouraged colleagues, partly by the force of a diplomatic experience none of them could equal, partly by the sheer weight of his dour and valiant personality.

III

The second phase began during these same discussions of November 21. It might be called the resurgence of Monroe—the final, the almost tragic utterance of the Virginia Dynasty. Adams had always intended that his assertion of all the principles of foreign policy (including Non-Intervention) upon which the government of the United States was founded should be confined to a diplomatic correspondence only. Monroe was of a different opinion; and Monroe, once he had brought himself to decide upon a course of action, was by no means the sort of man whom one could brush aside. Now he quietly produced a sheaf of papers and remarked that he intended to assert these principles of foreign policy, not in a private and confidential correspondence, but in his annual Message to Congress on the state of the Union. In a tone of "deep solemnity and high alarm" he read his draft to the Cabinet.¹⁶ For a while, Secretary Adams listened to it with a certain degree of complacency; it was more or less the sketch of foreign affairs which he himself had submitted to Monroe a week before.¹⁷ Then, suddenly, the President departed from his Secretary's text. He reprobated France for her late invasion of Spain; he denigrated the principles upon which it was undertaken; he acknowledged the independence of the revolutionary Greeks; and called upon Congress for the appropriation necessary to send a Minister to Greece.

It was typical of Monroe, whose antique dignity and revolutionary courage made such a deep though intermittent impression upon his contemporaries, that, after days of alarm and indecision, he should have decided upon a course that was singularly bold. We must not suppose, however, that he intended to support the revolutionary Greeks—still less the Spanish Constitutionalists—with a show of force. His words were simply ethical. They were filled with the innocence of Old Republicanism, which believed that it was the mission of the United States to transform the Old World, not by fleets and subsidies but by the magic of example and the force of morality.

Mr. Adams knew very well that he could not divert the President from his intention of committing his statement on foreign policy to the Annual Message. But he earnestly besought him not to take so strong a line. Like gouts of water falling upon a blaze, like an extinguisher descending upon a candle, his arguments quenched all that was visionary, and, indeed, Virginian in the President's statement. It would imply, he said, a grave departure from the principles of George Washington. It would be a call to arms and for what causes? For the cause of the Spanish Constitutionalists, whom even the British had abandoned; and for the cause of the Greeks, who were already supported by Russian autocracy. It would result in a diplomatic rupture with Spain, France, and even Russia.¹⁸

On the next day, closeted alone with Monroe, he reiterated his case with even greater urgency. "The ground that I wish to take," he said, "is that of earnest remonstrance against the interference of the European powers by force with South America, but to disclaim all interference on our part with Europe; to make an American cause, and adhere inflexibly to that." This was practical statesmanship before which mere visions silently retire. Two days later, when Monroe showed Adams his revised paragraphs on the Greeks, Spain, and South America, the Secretary found them "quite unexceptionable, and drawn up altogether in the spirit that I had so urgently pressed." Adams's reasons, given to the President in secret, were charged with an irony as deep as it was unconscious. He said that Monroe's period of service could now be considered as a whole, as a system of administration. "It would hereafter, I believed, be looked back to as the golden age of this republic." Let the Holy Allies be the aggressors; let the Administration end as it had begun, in peace and amity with the whole world.[19] Thus the Secretary of State, who had just extracted all traces of Old Republicanism from the doctrine that was to bear Monroe's name, pronounced a last epitaph upon the Era of Good Feelings, itself the graveyard of Old Republicanism.

The second phase in the discussions that preceded the writing of the Monroe Doctrine was now complete. Monroe had decided to give the Doctrine to the Congress, the people, and the world; but he had agreed to do so upon Adams's terms. In the end the advice of Jefferson and Madison, and Monroe's own predilections, had been discarded as impracticable; and the Monroe Doctrine, construed sentimentally rather than doctrinally, pronounces—as it were, between the lines—a grave farewell to the Virginia Dynasty.

IV

The Monroe Doctrine, as given to the world on December 2, 1823, was not a formulation of new principles, but a summing up of old ones, re-edited to suit the times. Nor did it contain, in its written form, the whole of itself. It had one corollary and two pendents, all of which were committed to separate documents. The third phase in the pre-Doctrine discussions is taken up with the writing of these documents.

The draft of certain observations upon "the Communications recently received from the Minister of Russia," to be delivered to Tuyll, was read to the Cabinet by Adams on November 25. It was immediately attacked by Calhoun as being too ostentatious in its display of republican principles, and all too likely to offend, not only the emperor, but Great Britain as well. Would not the relevant paragraphs in the President's Message serve as an answer to Tuyll? Wirt and Southard disagreed: the stranger had come into our house, they said, to proclaim the principles of despotism. He must be answered explicitly. But Wirt objected to the aggressive hostility of Adams's language—one of the paragraphs, he said, was "a hornet". He did not believe that the country would support the government in a war for South America; and, in any case, he had scruples against the use of warlike language when the question of peace or war rested with Congress.[20]

Adams admitted that this was indeed "a fearful question." Congress could not be expected to support the President in a warlike posture if it was not shown all the papers: and both Canning and Tuyll had communicated their views in the strictest confidence. But with his wonderful prescience Adams assumed—and historical scholars have since agreed with him—that the Holy Alliance did not seriously intend to attack Spanish America in 1823.[21] With the utmost reluctance, he agreed to modify his language—"the cream of my paper"—so as to bring it within the pale of the severest Constitutional scruple; but it took several remonstrances from the President before it acquired this shape. As read to Tuyll on November 27, the Observations declared that the United States would remain neutral between Spain and her colonies, so long as the European Powers did so. They went on to say that the President took it for granted that the Russian emperor's remarks, about restoring tranquillity to all the states of which the civilized world was composed, were "not intended to embrace the United States of America, nor any portion of the American Hemisphere." They concluded with this resounding sentence:

> "The United States of America, and their Government, could not see with indifference, the forcible interposition of any European Power, other than Spain, either to restore the dominion of Spain over her emancipated Colonies in America, or to establish Monarchical Governments in those Countries, or to transfer any of the possessions heretofore or yet subject to Spain in the American Hemisphere, to any other European power." [22]

This was a grand reiteration of the No-Transfer Principle which, more than ten years before, Congress had applied to the Floridas.[28]

Adams assumed that these Observations, and the instructions to be given to Rush in answer to Canning's overtures, were, with the President's paragraphs in the forthcoming Message, "the various parts of one system." The instructions, which were dated November 29, 1823, made only an oblique reference to a joint declaration, but said that if Great Britain acknowledged the independence of the Spanish-American states, then and only then would the United States move in concert with her. It is perhaps unnecessary to remark that a movement in concert is not a joint action.[24] By the time these instructions were received in London, indeed not long after they were written, Canning had transmitted to Rush a copy of the Polignac Memorandum. He had then referred to his late courtship of the United States in terms of wistful regret.[25] Rush duly communicated his instructions of November 29. All that Canning said in reply was that intervening events had put an end to the state of things on the basis of which he had made his first approaches.[26]

It is necessary to the understanding of this third phase to examine one sentence in the supplementary instructions Adams sent to Rush on December 8, six days after the President's famous Message had been given to Congress. "The President is anxiously desirous, that the opening to a cordial harmony, in the policy of the United States and Great Britain, may be extended to the general relations between the two countries." [27] Adams meant by these words, whose friendliness was only on the surface, that the British government should be asked to review its traditional policy on Maritime Rights, in order to bring it into line with the views of the United States. He had no reason for supposing, and probably did not suppose, that the British government would actually do so.

It is sometimes maintained that George Canning was willfully blind to this opportunity of making a new and progressive Anglo-American entente. But this is to misunderstand the nature and limitations of Liberal Toryism. Lord Liverpool's government, as an economic innovator, attempted to set certain practical Benthamite doctrines into the framework of the thinking of Burke. That is to say, it strove to release the energies of industry and commerce without departing from its fundamental belief that society was a compact between the living and the dead. It was not yet ready—nor would it have been permitted—to make the break with tradition which Adams demanded of it. In its American Trade Act of 1822 and in Canning's overtures to Rush in 1823 it had gone as far as—and indeed somewhat farther than—it could be expected to go. The response of the United States, whether we examine it in Rush's instructions or in the Monroe Doctrine itself, was an unequivocal rebuff.

V

It would be a poor tribute to James Monroe not to repeat in full the paragraphs in his Message which constitute the Monroe Doctrine. It would be wanting in respect to him not to mention that it was he who took the very bold step of rescuing this doctrine from the secrecy of diplomatic correspondence and giving it to the nation and to the world.

The first significant paragraph was as follows:

> "At the proposal of the Russian Imperial Government, made through the Minister of the Emperor, residing here, a full power and instructions have been transmitted to the Minister of the United States at St. Petersburg, to arrange by amicable negotiation, the respective rights and interests of the two Nations on the North West Coast of this Continent. A similar proposal has been made by His Imperial Majesty, to the Government of Great Britain, which has likewise been acceded to. The Government of the United States has been desirous by this friendly proceeding, of manifesting the great value which they have invariably attached to the friendship of the Emperor, and their solicitude to cultivate the best understanding with his Government. In the discussions to which this interest has given rise, and in the arrangements by which they may terminate, the occasion has been judged proper, for asserting as a principle in which the rights and interests of the United States are involved, that the American Continents, by the free and independent condition which they have assumed and maintain, are henceforth not to be considered as subjects for future colonization by any European Power. . . ."

The language of this paragraph and its doctrine of Non-Colonization were both the work of John Quincy Adams. The Message now dealt at length with a number of domestic issues before it returned to the subject of foreign affairs. It then spoke as follows, and the language was Monroe's:

> "It was stated at the commencement of the last session, that a great effort was then making in Spain and Portugal, to improve the condition of the people of those countries; and that it appeared to be conducted with extraordinary moderation. It need scarcely be remarked, that the result has been, so far, very dif-

ferent from what was then anticipated. Of events in that quarter of the Globe, with which we have so much intercourse, and from which we derive our origin, we have always been anxious and interested spectators. The Citizens of the United States cherish sentiments the most friendly, in favor of the liberty and happiness of their fellowmen on that side of the Atlantic. In the wars of the European powers, in matters relating to themselves, we have never taken any part, nor does it comport with our policy, so to do. It is only when our rights are invaded, or seriously menaced, that we resent injuries, or make preparation for our defense. With the movements in this Hemisphere we are of necessity more immediately connected, and by causes which must be obvious to all enlightened and impartial observers. The political system of the allied powers, is essentially different in this respect from that of America. This difference proceeds from that, which exists in their respective Governments, and to the defence of our own, which has been atchieved by the loss of so much blood and treasure, and matured by the wisdom of their most enlightened citizens, and under which we have enjoyed unexampled felicity, this whole nation is devoted. We owe it therefore to candor, and to the amicable relations existing between the United States and those powers, to declare that we should consider any attempt on their part to extend their system to any portions of this Hemisphere, as dangerous to our peace and safety. With the existing Colonies or dependencies of any European power, we have not interfered, and shall not interfere. But with the Governments who have declared their Independence, and maintained it, and whose Independence we have, on great consideration, and on just principles, acknowledged, we could not view any interposition for the purpose of oppressing them, or controuling in any other manner, their destiny, by any European power, in any other light, than as the manifestation of an unfriendly disposition towards the United States. In the war between those new governments and Spain, we declared our neutrality, at the time of their recognition, and to this we have adhered, and shall continue to adhere, provided no change shall occur, which in the judgment of the competent authorities of this Government, shall make a corresponding change, on the part of the United States, indispensable to their security.

The late events in Spain and Portugal, show that Europe is still unsettled. Of this important fact, no stronger proof can be adduced, than that the allied powers should have thought it proper, on any principle satisfactory to themselves, to have interposed by force, in the internal concerns of Spain. To what extent, such interposition may be carried, on the same principle, is a question, in which all Independent powers, whose Governments differ from theirs, are interested; even those most remote, and surely none more so than the United States. Our policy in regard to Europe, which was adopted at an early stage of the wars which have so long agitated that quarter of the Globe, nevertheless remains the same, which is, not to interfere in the internal concerns of any of its powers; to consider the Government *de facto;* as the legitimate for us; to cultivate friendly relations with it, and to preserve those relations by a frank, firm and manly policy, meeting in all instances, the just claims of every power; submitting to injuries from none. But, in regard to those continents, circumstances are eminently and conspicuously different. It is impossible that the allied powers, should extend their political systems, to any portion of either continent, without endangering our peace and happiness, nor can anyone believe, that our Southern Brethren, if left to themselves, would adopt it of their own accord. It is equally impossible, therefore, that we should behold such interposition in any form with indifference. If we look to the comparative strength and resources of Spain and those new Governments, and their distance from each other, it must be obvious that she can never subdue them. It is still the true policy of the United States, to leave the parties to themselves, in the hope, that other powers will pursue the same course." [28]

We can see, therefore, that the Monroe Doctrine was concerned with two principles:

I. Non-Colonization. No European power could, in future, form colonies either in North or South America.

II. Non-Intervention. The United States would abstain from the wars of European powers, since their political system was quite distinct from that of the American hemisphere. Conversely, the United States would regard as an unfriendly act any attempt on the part of a European power to oppress or to control the destiny of any of the independent states of the New World.

And to these two great principles should be added:

III. No-Transfer. The United States would not submit to the transfer, by one European power to another, of any possession in the New World.

These principles must be considered first as the best guardians of a nation with a great continental expansion still before it—as the natural foreign policy of what was afterwards to be called Manifest Destiny. Then, again, in their resolute challenge to the Holy Alliance and the champions of absolutism, they may properly be described as contributions to the cause of world progress. The Doctrine, it is true, had no force behind it. Even if he had been supported (and he was not) by a resolution of Congress, Monroe could not have made good his words without the support of the British fleet. He did not himself believe that he was addressing these words to anything but an immediate crisis; that they would one day be called the Monroe Doctrine would have filled him with at least as much surprise as gratification. This does not mean that he was deaf to the insinuations of fame. All Americans in those years had a touching belief in the force of language; and Monroe may well have hoped that his words would live after him. But he would hardly have expected them to play the part they did in American foreign policy; and, indeed, it is not until Polk's first Annual Message in 1845 that they were again made to play this part, and then only as regards the North American continent.[29]

As part of the literature of republicanism and self-determination the Monroe Doctrine, none the less, and regardless of its future, would have commanded respect. As an example of Presidential courage—for it must be remembered that Monroe had no knowledge of the Polignac Memorandum—it would certainly have been applauded. Nor would the future have ignored John Quincy Adams, who stiffened and guided the resolution of his President. Whether the Message would or would not have had a nobler appearance with the addition of Monroe's original phrases in support of Spanish and Greek revolution—whether Non-Intervention is not really a form of intervention—these are questions that could be debated forever.

VI

The continental European Powers did not take the President's Message very seriously as regards its physical force. Their statesmen uttered the expected epithets—"blustering," "monstrous," "arrogant," "haughty," and so forth.[30] They still thought of the United States as a littoral republic, poor, disreputable, unprovided with a fleet or an army. No formal protests were made. The Baron de Tuyll was told by his government that "the document in question . . . merits only the most profound contempt. His Majesty therefore invites you to preserve the passive attitude which you have deemed proper to adopt." [31] This Russian attitude was shared by the other Powers, every one of whom regarded the Polignac Memorandum as being the decisive document for the time being. As to the moral effect of the Message, however, they were of a different mind. Political morality to them was a question of Order and of suppression; and they paid the Message the unanimous and enduring compliment of assuming that it was highly immoral—that it would help to advance the cause of republicanism and of popular government.[32] Since the European peoples most interested in these causes had at the time little or no access to recorded history, we are left guessing whether it did or whether it did not.

In Latin America, it was cordially received by liberal thinkers.[33] The governments of Colombia and Brazil immediately endorsed it. But second thoughts, and particularly the second thoughts of conservative leaders, were not too favorable. The advances of five of the new states, either for actual alliance or for provisional assistance, were declined by the United States in language that must have seemed both chilling and evasive. The American delegates to the Panama Conference of 1826 never arrived there.[34] "The declaration of the late President," said Secretary of State Henry Clay in 1828, ". . . must be regarded as having been voluntarily made, and not as conveying any pledge or obligation, the performance of which foreign nations have a right to demand. When the case shall arrive, if it should ever occur, of such an European interference as the message supposes, and it becomes consequently necessary to decide whether this country will or will not engage in war, Congress alone, you well know, is competent, by our Constitution, to decide that question. In the event of such an interference, there can be but little doubt that the sentiment contained in Presiden Monroe's message, would still be that of the People and Government of the United States." [35] Such were the small echoes of Monroe's words.

To the Latin American states, therefore, the Polignac Memorandum, duly and sedulously circularized, must also have seemed the decisive word. And did not England have more to offer—cheap manufactures, loans, a protecting fleet? It was by no means either cynical or ungrateful to prefer these to a trade that was still embryonic, and to promises that grew yearly more lukewarm.

VII

The reaction of Great Britain to the Message was quite another story. At first, it seems, George Canning was very pleased with it. He assumed, quite rightly, that his overtures to Rush had been responsible for its appearance; and he was at first disposed to interpret it, quite wrongly, as the obedient reflection of his own diplomacy. "The Congress," he said, "was broken in all its limbs before, but the President's speech gives it the *coup de grâce*." [36] What actually gave the projected Congress on Spanish-American affairs its *coup de grâce* was Canning's refusal, on January 30, to send a British representative to attend it. [37] This refusal was a logical outcome of his foreign policy, and the President's Message had little if anything to do with it.

As he examined the Message more carefully, however, Canning was infuriated by the Non-Colonization portion of it. "It is Mr. Monroe's declaration in his famous message," Christopher Hughes wrote, three years later, "that it was time for the old world to be taught, that the new was no longer to be regarded as a region open to future colonization (or to that effect) that sticks in their [the British] throats. I know, to use the word of a great British employee, 'there was not a man in the British councils, whose blood did not tingle at his fingers' ends, on reading that proposition of President Monroe.' " [38] Huskisson asserted that the unoccupied parts of America were "just as much open as heretofore to colonization by Great Britain as well as by other powers." [39] Canning found himself unable to continue his plans for a joint representation with the United States at St. Petersburg regarding Russia's pretensions on the northwest coast. [40] It is quite evident that, by the end of January 1824, British statesmen had reached the conclusion that the Message—however useful its Non-Intervention passages may have been—had not been written in a spirit friendly to Great Britain.

But the United States had set themselves forward as the protector of

Spanish America; and it was urgently necessary for Canning to assert himself. He had first to overcome his own predilection for Spanish-American monarchies: this seems to have occurred about the middle of 1824.[41] He was much assisted in this respect by a Memorial from Sir James Mackintosh in favor of recognizing the independence of the South American states. It presented on June 15, 1824, and it bore some of the great City names— Montefiore, Baring, Ricardo, Benjamin Shaw. He then had a more difficult task—he had to persuade the king and the Ultra Tories in the government to consent to this step. His great supporter, the Earl of Liverpool, was a very sick man, who now put both his legs upon his seat in the House of Lords; and never did Canning need support more desperately. If Liverpool failed him, he knew that he would succumb. Once again the hopes of Madame de Lieven and Metternich revived. Wellington would not speak to Liverpool except in the Cabinet, and George IV announced that Canning was a scoundrel.[42] But their hopes were dashed by the resolution of Lord Liverpool. Towards the end of November 1824 he circulated a Memorandum to the Cabinet, advising the recognition of Colombia and Mexico; and, when Wellington threatened to leave the government, came back with yet another Memorandum to the effect that he and Canning would themselves resign if their wishes were not attended to. Wellington's great political virtue was always to realize when a successful counterattack had been delivered. He now came to the conclusion that his position was untenable and, calling for a retreat, carried with him the grumbling figures of Lords Eldon, Westmorland, and Bathurst, and of George IV.[43]

Colombia, Mexico, and the United Provinces (Buenos Aires) were recognized by Great Britain on December 31, 1824. This was made known to Parliament in the King's Speech on February 7, 1825. Lord Eldon, as Lord Chancellor, was obliged to read this speech, which he did with a very bad grace; the king himself declined to have anything to do with it. His Majesty said that he had a bad attack of gout and that, in any case, he had mislaid his false teeth.[44]

More than a year and a half later, Canning came down to the House of Commons to defend his continued toleration of the French occupation of Spain. He based his defense upon his new concept of the balance of power, and concluded with some words that seemed to annihilate history . . . the heroisms and agonies of Bolivar, San Martín, and Sucre, the recognition of Spanish America by the United States, the President's Message. "Contemplating Spain," he said, "such as our ancestors had known her, I resolved that if France had Spain, it should not be Spain 'with the Indies.' I called the New World into existence to redress the balance of the Old." [45]

We are told that after he had pronounced these empty words there was a silence, a titter, and then a great cheer. Afterwards, however, there was not a little criticism of them. But it was not the singularity of Canning's boast which disturbed the House of Commons: it was his use of the first person singular.

VIII

The original overtures of Canning to Rush must be held responsible for the appearance of the Monroe Doctrine in the President's Annual Message of 1823. These overtures, as has been indicated, were more directed towards the safety of Cuba and the diplomatic rebuttal of the Holy Allies than concerned with the preservation of Spanish-American continental markets. It was easier for Great Britain to protect these markets on her own: more dramatic, more suited to the robust genius of Canning. As the Polignac Memorandum showed, they were never in much danger, so long as Great Britain was the commander of the seas. No doubt these markets entered into Canning's calculations when he first approached Rush, but it is difficult to believe that they held a leading place there, or even a very considerable one.

It is, of course, delusive to look beneath the surface of events into those depths where everything becomes dim, mysterious, and wavering. None the less, no one can study the Liverpool-Canning-Huskisson era in British Toryism without realizing that these statesmen were, in some degree, the instruments of early British industrialism. Their motives were complicated and various, but they had been deliberately seeking the friendship of the United States in the belief that its free market was necessary to the prosperity of Great Britain. In the same spirit they shrank away from antirevolutionary Europe—not because they were friendly to revolution, or because their institutions were founded upon the gentlemanly Revolution of 1688—but because the autocrats of Europe were in a sense the symbols of exclusive trade practices. Aside from their obvious reasons for a diplomatic understanding with the United States, they sought to transcribe into friendly language the dominant energies of British coal and British iron.

The reaction of the United States in this respect is suggestive. Jefferson, who was a convinced agrarian, and who saw no reason to object to the free exchange of American cotton and British manufactures, was willing to go all the way with Canning. Madison, at best a moderate agrarian, was also willing, but far more mistrustful of the motives of Great Britain. Monroe originally agreed with his two predecessors, but subsequently allowed himself to be persuaded by Adams into taking an opposite course: and Monroe's whole Administration is marked by a gradual abandonment of agrarian principles. Calhoun, who was both a South Carolinian slave-holder and, at the time, a nationalist, oscillated between submission to Great Britain and a confused belligerence. Southard supported Adams, and Southard was to become a pillar of the Whig Party. Adams, who took Henry Clay for his Secretary of State, and whose Presidency was an honest but tragic commitment to economic nationalism, invariably opposed any joint declaration with Canning.

This strain of economic nationalism in the President's Message is worth isolating only because it provides a clue to the politics and tragedies of the next five years. The Message was followed, in 1824, by a protective tariff that seemed to complete the answer to the friendly gestures of Lord Liverpool and George Canning. At the same time the navigation controversy, which constellated around the word "elsewhere," increased in bitterness. This was the American response to the courtship of British industry.

The Message itself, becoming in the fullness of time the Monroe Doctrine, passed beyond these considerations. Interpreted at times in accordance with its expressed aversion to European politics, it was never able to lose its original and valiant quality of committing the United States—prematurely, indeed, in 1823—to a leadership in world politics. This gives it its singular claim to the attention and indeed to the veneration of all those who ponder the American past.

CHAPTER FIVE

Lord Liverpool Is Answered

THE reception given to the President's Message in the United States was on the whole cordial. It was not enthusiastic. The press, with a very few exceptions, and those mostly from Federalist organs in New England, took the President's words at their face value and assumed as a matter of course that the United States could oppose the Holy Allies singlehanded.[1] From these self-confident editorials we may deduce that the Era of Good Feelings had not altogether vanished from the land. Congress was less impressed. Henry Clay, who approved the Message and was not above telling Adams as much, brought forward a Resolution that would have committed Congress explicitly to the Non-Intervention Principle.[2] But it never came to a vote. A request was made for further information on South American affairs; but when the President let it be known that such information could not be disclosed without injury to the public good, the matter was quietly dropped. It is significant that in the debate upon the construction of additional sloops of war, nothing was said of the Spanish-American struggle; and even more significant that no additional sloops of war were voted.[3] The Executive itself responded to Spanish-American appeals with something less than warmth. The Message was a stone dropped into a pool—only in the course of time would men notice that the ripples had not ceased to spread.

I

It was a nationalist document, the Magna Charta of Manifest Destiny: but Manifest Destiny itself, as a phrase, had not yet been born; and the truth was that in 1823 and 1824 Americans did not know to what kind of political thinking their destiny was to be committed. They saw only that Monroe's period of service was coming to an end without offering the electorate the solace of an issue, a platform, a party cry—those necessary lubricants of a political democracy. Monroe, who hated party spirit, and who thought of himself as everybody's President, was the last man to do so. Five men struggled together for the succession—John Quincy Adams, Henry Clay, Andrew Jackson, William H. Crawford, John Caldwell Calhoun—all distinguished men, all Republicans.[4] Since all were Republicans, the choice between them became more than usually obscure and discouraging. "It is true, Mr. Calhoun is a southern man," said one of his supporters, "but he forms the remarkable exception to this class of citizens—whilst he has the principles of the South— he holds the policy of the North, in other words he unites them." [5] These words were practically meaningless; but no other candidate could have offered anything more helpful.

The day of the Presidential caucus, which surrendered the final choice of Presidential candidates to a group of Congressmen in Washington, was manifectly waning; the day of the national convention had not yet arrived. In the interval, in the darkness and confusion of one-party rule, men strove to rally the electorate around names and personalities, rather than principles and issues. Indeed, upon all the great domestic questions—tariffs, internal improvements at Federal expense, a national bank—the five candidates differed only in shades of emphasis. Even Crawford, who had declared his conversion to Old Republican simplicity, did not exactly put himself in opposition. Nor did Jackson, the most enigmatic of the five; though Jackson, to be sure, was still waiting for a revelation.

On the whole, the campaign for the succession—or the dusty skirmishes that passed for a campaign—turned upon the question of the Presidential caucus. The Presidential caucus was certainly republican, but it was not exactly democratic. The same might be said of the Republican Party. It had lost its spiritual freshness; its philosophy had retreated into the cabalistic books of John Taylor of Caroline; it had become too closely identified with the apologists of slavery; and, what was even less endurable, it was apparently dedicated to the self-perpetuation of Virginia Presidents. Its organization was an intricate, indeed an antique affair, beginning with the more old-fashioned leaders of Congress, and passing down from them to the leaders of the state legislatures and of the Southern county courts. It was known to be for Crawford, who had been born in Virginia; and, of course, it proposed to work its will through the Presidential caucus. The other four candidates were, to be sure, Republicans too, but it was very much to their advantage to give the caucus system a name fully as disagreeable as its sound, and if they were agreed upon nothing else, they were agreed upon the ruin of Crawford.

That heroic man had somehow or other heaved his huge bulk out of the bed to which the physician of Orange County had condemned it, and was ready to resume the contest. He could not transact any business at the Treasury Department; he rarely ventured outside his house; and, although his friends steadily maintained that he would soon be himself again, it was noised abroad that he was still unable to read or write, that his speech was indistinct and his mind wavering. At Monroe's reception for Lafayette in October 1824 he put in an appearance, but rumors had it that he behaved very oddly. "He took a seat nr the President who was standing, still keeping on his hat. Judge Anderson . . . requested him to take off his hat. He did so—but shortly after, again placed it on his head. Mr. Anderson then remonstrated with him and said, Mr. C take off your hat, this is not a proper place to wear it. He complied reluctantly, and said, What, cannot I wear my hat here? These are facts and others might be stated." [6]

But it was not, really, through the circulation of "facts" like these that Mr. Crawford's defeat was accomplished. By the day of Monroe's reception, though still in the race, he had already been defeated. When the Congressional caucus met in Washington on February 14, 1824, it duly nominated Crawford for President, and Albert Gallatin for vice-president; but only sixty-six men dared to put in an appearance. What had become of the rest? Some, at any rate, were "afraid of their constituents," wrote Senator Lowrie of Pennsylvania.[7] It was a sad admission for a caucus supporter. The friends of the other candidates—though not above using a state or county caucus if it happened to come out for their man—had employed their newspapers, circular letters, and committees of correspondence to such good effect that the caucus system was, indeed, in very bad odor. They themselves had gone more directly to the people. Thus the friends of Calhoun instituted a whole series of straw ballots at court days, or at militia musters, or when men assembled for grand jury duty; and only gave up when they discovered, to their horror, that most of the straw ballots were in favor of Jackson.[8]

In March 1824 a nominating convention was held in Harrisburg, Pennsylvania, the state that, next to New York, was the great political catch. It was a strictly anticaucus convention; it had been most carefully canvassed beforehand by the friends of Calhoun; but on February 18 Calhoun's manager threw in his hand, and on the day of nomination, March 4, the convention came out for Jackson as President and Calhoun as vice-president. Calhoun accepted the verdict, retired from the Presidential contest, and decided that he would run for the vice-presidency, which was certainly his for the asking.

The defeat of Calhoun might well have been due to the fact that he was, after all, that meaningless at any rate chimerical mixture—a man of Southern principles and Northern policies. As an administrator he had done brilliantly at the War Department; but he had antagonized the powerful fur-trade interests in the West by his efforts to prevent the Indians from being cheated; and his contracts had been dishonestly, but successfully, attacked in Congress by the friends of Crawford. As a slave-holder, he was not popular in the North; as a moderate protectionist, he was already suspect in the South. But above all—like many leading politicians before and after him—he was deficient in what one must call the public personality. He could not attract to himself in sufficient quantities the priceless fragments of loyalty or sentiment or self-interest; or, having attracted, could not hold them. Mr. Clay, on the other hand, was certainly magnetic—he was the supreme example of a public personality—and he was once again Speaker of the House, the airy and fascinating master of men and of events. And yet—it was strange but it was true—Henry Clay was not trusted, not even in the West, where he was deeply loved. Perhaps he was too charming, or too obviously ambitious; or perhaps the spirit of compromise—which was Henry Clay's familiar spirit—was ill adapted to the mood of the times. It is true that his American System was too close to Eastern banking to please a Westerner or a Southerner; and that his personality was too highly spiced with Western condiments to suit the palate of the East. Mr. Adams was not charming, and only an infatuated admirer would have suggested that he had a public personality; but Mr. Adams, who kept his ideas to himself and stood squarely upon his record at the State Department, had a certain attraction for conservative men everywhere. It should be noted that even John Taylor of Caroline had ceased to mistrust him.[9]

No conservative man, it is safe to say, outside the state of Tennessee, had any faith in Andrew Jackson, who had not exactly enriched his reputation by his disputatious term as governor of Florida. His political managers tried to bestir his inertia by securing him a Presidential nomination from the legislature of Tennessee; and the General remarked that "as the Legislature of my state has thought proper to bring my name forward without consulting me, I mean to be silent—and let the people do as seemeth good unto them." [10] Silence meant consent; but the General did not show much interest in the campaign until he discovered that the reforming Governor Carroll of Tennessee, ostensibly his friend, was secretly supporting Henry Clay. Then his wrath blazed up, and his ambition with it. "Should the people take up the subject of my nomination in the south, and west . . . they will soon undeceive Mr. Clay's friends, if the people of Alabama, Mississippi, and Louisiana, follow the example of Pennsylvania, they will place Clay and Crawford where they ultimately will be, *Dehors the political combat.*" [11] When he spoke of the example of Pennsylvania, the General was specifically referring to a mass meeting held in Harrisburg in February 1823, which made him its unanimous choice for President. And when he spoke of "the people" he was apparently using the word in a sense that George Canning always deplored—that is to say as "applied to a portion of the community." [12] For the meeting at Harrisburg was limited to the small farmers, miners, rivermen, mechanics.[13] Their nomination was conveyed to Jackson in a letter from H. W. Peterson, a barkeeper; and Jackson, for the first time in the case of such invitations, wrote a reply. The Presidency, he said, should not be sought; but it could not, with propriety, be declined.[14] This answer was published in the Harrisburg *Commonwealth* and soon spread all over the country. The combination of Carroll's duplicity and the good will of the farmers and artisans of Pennsylvania had brought Jackson out into the open. It is true that Jackson had invariably taken the conservative side in economic issues in Tennessee; and it might seem odd that he should now stand forth as a popular leader. But he was not simply opportunistic. In Tennessee, class lines were not rigidly drawn, and the self-made men, like Jackson, who were given all sorts of political offices by their less fortunate fellow citizens, had a profound respect for the popular judgment, for was it not wise in its choice and generous in its gifts, at once an oracle and a cornucopia? On national issues, Jackson had no known opinions. Conservatives feared him as a military firebrand; but the men who spoke about him in the cross-road taverns, the blacksmith's shops, and the backwoods meeting-houses called him the Hero and the People's Friend. The Hero was obvious—he had beaten the British and the Indians. But why the People's Friend? They could not say; but they had some suspicion that he was different from the crusty political elite that had run the country for so long. Jackson, meanwhile, had got himself elected to the Senate—a job that he hated but one that was necessary to his political fortunes—and (it was always the case when he went to Washington) was astonishing people with his beautiful manners and his readiness to forget old quarrels. They were prepared, he said, "to see me with a Tomahawk in one hand and a scalping knife in the other." [15] Instead, he spread around him all the kindness and courtesy of a Christian gentleman. General Scott was forgiven, Mr. Clay was forgiven, even Colonel Benton of Missouri—whose brother, with Benton's assistance, had nearly killed the General in a bloody scramble at Nashville years before—was shaken by the hand.[16] Jackson, however, did not do these things from political motives; it was as natural to him to be kind as to hate—and he continued to hate the invalid Crawford, whom he accused of having tried to ruin him during the Florida crisis, and whose election, he said, "would be a great curse to the country." [17] The intrigue for the Presidency he called an "unclean procedure," and he lived a retired life in the capital.[18] With his colleague and political manager, Senator John H. Eaton, he lodged at the house of Major O'Neale, "whose amiable and pious wife and two daughters . . . take every pains in there power to make us comfortable and agreable . . . Mrs. Timberlake the maryed daughter whose husband belongs to our Navy, plays on the Piano delightfully, and every Sunday evening entertains her pious mother with sacred music, to which we are invited, and the single daughter who is also pious and sings well unites in the music." [19] An unshakable belief in female virtue was one of Jackson's most lovable characteristics: but it was not Mrs. Peggy O'Neale Timberlake's sacred music that attracted Senator Eaton.

II

The intrigues for the Presidency did indeed increase to a point where they overcame even the rectitude of John Quincy Adams. Washington in 1824 was a loud political bazaar. The bargaining among the friends of the various candidates had become so frenzied that it scarcely bothered to be surreptitious. This frenzy has somewhat concealed the fact that the campaigns of 1824 were devoted to the overthrow of an old and oppressive political structure. Since nobody knew what was to be put in its place, the campaigns have a negative character; but they were none the less useful for that, and they did produce, on the positive side, the beginnings of an invasion of

American history by "the people," not as rebels but as voters. Access to history through polls was a truly creative event in the early nineteenth century.

Certainly this access was incomplete in 1824. Property qualifications based on real estate were unpopular, and were being abandoned in one state after another: even conservative Maine, when it entered the Union in 1819, did not impose a property test; and the new states in the Mississippi valley gave property no relish of privilege at all. On the other hand, it was not fully realized that those who increase the social wealth, whether they are taxpayers or not, are the real supporters of the government; and taxpaying qualifications, in many states, still barred the way to the polls. The New York and Massachusetts Constitutional conventions, held in 1821, show how unwilling men were to advance beyond what Martin Van Buren called, with approval, "the verge of universal suffrage." Though the champions of property were defeated in both conventions, each retained a tax qualification.[20] Moreover, when a man cast his vote in a Presidential election, he might find that the will of the majority was distorted or negated by a system of district voting; or, what was worse, that the choice of Presidential electors was still in the hands of the legislature.[21] The drift towards manhood suffrage—(white manhood suffrage, for the position of the free Negro voter was steadily deteriorating)—was unmistakable; but it was not yet strong enough to sweep away the various devices that stubbornly impeded or diverted it.

Thus, while Jackson, more than any other candidate, had the good wishes of the people, it was still a little hard for the people to express their good wishes.

III

Then, too, the year 1824 was the great year of indecision, which found both candidates and voters struggling in the same cobweb. The question of a protective tariff had been put off from year to year; but when Henry Clay returned to the Eighteenth Congress and was elected in triumph to the Speaker's chair, it was clear that it could be put off no longer. The issues were comparatively simple. Should the country be satisfied with the prevailing free exchange of raw materials for foreign manufactures, or should it attempt to relieve distress in the grain-growing and industrial areas by creating a home market based on a protected industry? Ever since the Napoleonic Wars the exports of Western grain, in whatever form, had been declining; for European agriculture, trampled and devastated by Europe's armies, soon recovered, and Great Britain's Corn Laws barred the way to American surpluses. The Western farmer was not unwilling to listen to the home-market argument, advanced in Congress with all the eloquence of Henry Clay—and with all his powers in the formation of committees and the management of men—and voiced outside of Congress by such advocates as Mathew Carey and Hezekiah Niles. The beauty of the arguments of Carey and Niles lay in the fact that they were able to invent their own statistics. They pursued their readers with abstractions, and stunned them with computations. Niles, whose *Weekly Register* was more widely read than any other paper, was able to prove to his own satisfaction that the nation's annual export of animal and vegetable foods in 1823 amounted to $9,622,300; whereas the 500,000 persons, "employed in or fed by the products of manufactures," consumed animal or vegetable foods of domestic origin to the amount of $13,700,000. "So we see," said Niles triumphantly, "by the force of plain practical arithmetic, that the support of the 500,000 manufacturers of whom Mr. Floyd speaks so indifferently consumes about one half more than the whole exports of the products of 15 states, and more than seven-eights of all the exports raised by the free agriculturists of the United States." [22] This plain practical arithmetic ignored the fact that the "500,000 manufacturers" were not gathered into a factory system which made them dependent upon agriculture, but were largely engaged in household manufactures, and subsisted themselves to some extent upon produce of their own raising. The industries of the United States were still infant industries; and it might well be argued that protection was as likely to stifle their initiative as to hasten the day when they actually would provide a home market. The iron industry, for example, was very unwilling to make use of the improved processes that were making such headway in England; partly from lack of capital, partly because the supplies of bituminous coal were too far from the regions where the industry was located, partly because the blacksmiths and farmers preferred charcoal iron, which could be more easily worked up into simple tools and ironware, and partly, it would seem, from inertia. Puddling was not generally introduced until 1830-40, and the use of anthracite coal for blast furnaces was unknown until 1836; and by 1836 protective duties were beginning to disappear. Nobody has been able to decide to this day whether the iron industry would have been ruined if it had not been protected, or whether protective duties did not simply postpone the day of improved techniques. The chances are that if they did not actually retard, they certainly did not stimulate the resourcefulness of the ironmaster. [23]

Nobody would deny that the deluge of British manufactures and the Panic of 1819 had threatened the American manufacturer with ruin. Indeed the whole period from 1815 to 1830 was a trying one, excusing and even justifying a demand for protective tariffs. Yet the textile industry seems to have recovered by 1824. Waltham was flourishing. The works at Lowell started production in 1822. Nashua was founded in 1823. From the Providence-Pawtucket regions, factories were creeping up the Blackstone River into Massachusetts, or along the Pawtucket towards Connecticut, or were drawing upon the tremendous water-power of the Fall River. Outside New England and the Hudson, Mohawk, and Delaware river valleys the progress of the cotton industry was slow; but within its own areas it was advancing rapidly, because it did not lend itself to an extensive household manufacture. Hand spinning-wheels could not make good cotton warp. [24] The woolen industry, on the other hand, was still sunk deep in the household manufacturing stage. In 1824, woolen manufacturers might justly have complained that without protection they were doomed. They were unfamiliar with the new machinery, their methods were out of date, their domestic supply of raw materials was inadequate, and they could not compete with the flood of cheap goods from overseas. The weakest were, indeed, overwhelmed. Yet in 1824 the survivors did not receive much in the way of protection, and in 1828, when protection was given them, they had already reached a position where they no longer needed it.[25]

It is difficult to resist the conclusion that the protective tariff imposed by Congress in 1824 was the simple result of persistent and successful lobbying. "There has been more outdoor than indoor legislation with regard to the bill," said Hamilton of South Carolina, "all sorts of pilgrims have travelled to the room of the Committee on Manufactures." [26] Mr. Clay had already seen to it that the Committee on Manufactures—with James Tod of Pennsylvania, a fanatical protectionist, as its chairman—would not turn a deaf ear to these devout men. The Committee on Agriculture was equally friendly.[27] Of the debate, which began on February 12, 1824, it may be said that the protectionists were superior in numbers and the free traders in dialectics. The eloquence of Clay sounded hollow and the persistence of Tod seemed brittle when compared with arguments of men like George McDuffie and James Hamilton of South Carolina, Philip Barbour of Virginia, and Daniel Webster of Massachusetts in the House, and of Robert Hayne of South Carolina in the Senate.

The debate on the new tariff bill began in February 1824. As is generally the case when gentlemen try to erect a tariff wall, there was a good deal of uncertainty as to the materials of which it was to be composed. The home-market argument and the infant-industry argument did not always agree. The wool-growers were demanding a high duty on imported raw wool which was very disagreeable to the woolen manufacturers, who ingeniously supposed that nothing more was needed than a high duty on imported woolens. The ironmasters believed that their very existence depended upon a thumping tariff on Scottish pig iron, though it was said to be peculiarly—indeed uniquely—fit for the small castings used in machinery.[28] And so it went. Even free traders did not always scorn protection where their own interests were affected. The whale fishery of Massachusetts asked for a high duty on tallow, in the rather extravagant hope that the ninety-five per cent of the people of the United States who used candles would be persuaded to follow the example of the five per cent who were content with whale oil.[29] The delegation from Louisiana were free traders to a man, but they did not propose to give up protection for Louisiana's sugar—which in 1824, at the average specific rate of three cents a pound on foreign sugar, amounted to an ad valorem duty of 62.07 per cent.[30]

In the very center of the protectionist army, however, there was a great gap. Massachusetts was turning to manufactures; but not enough Boston capital had yet been diverted from shipping and commerce. The financiers, the merchants, and the shipowners of that city were still true to the old faith. They declared that the proposed tariffs on iron, hemp, and flax would be the ruin of the shipbuilders; and that the new duty on molasses would bedevil New England's rum industry and its basic exchange of fish, provisions, and lumber for the molasses of the West Indies.[31] Daniel Webster, the voice of State Street, who honestly believed that "the wise," "the rich," and "the good" were synonymous terms, was returned to the Eighteenth Congress; and on April 1 and 2, 1824, he made a speech that has been called, with justice, the finest free-trade speech given to that Congress or to any Congress.[32] Webster himself was not satisfied: he thought it ill prepared. Something—perhaps a premonition—made him uneasy. If it was a premonition, it was fully justified. In 1825, the firm of W. & S. Lawrence of Boston turned from importing to domestic manufactures, and carried the opinion of State Street with them. In 1828, standing in the Senate, Daniel Webster took back.every word that he had uttered in the House of Representatives in 1824.

It is not surprising that the protectionists should have failed to penetrate the one really weak spot in the free traders' position; for this was not revealed until the legislature of South Carolina assembled later in the year. Then the South Carolina Senate declared that a protective tariff was un-Constitutional and inoperative, and the South Carolina House of Representatives replied, in three notable resolutions, that state legislatures had no right to question the acts of the federal government.[33] Looking back over the debate of 1824 one can see, of course, how this difference of opinion was reflected in the speeches of the representatives of South Carolina. James Hamilton, for example, raised the question of the constitutionality of protective tariffs: he argued that neither the power to lay and collect imposts nor the power to regulate commerce gave Congress the right to protect domestic manufactures. But his colleague, George McDuffie, was forced to confine his arguments only to the injustice of protective tariffs, as they affected men who sold their cotton abroad and exchanged it for foreign manufactures. McDuffie was a nationalist who had written a pamphlet in "Defence of a Liberal Construction of the Powers of Congress," and just before the opening of the tariff debate he had told the House that "the Constitutional Convention did not regard the State governments as sentinels upon the watchtowers of freedom or in any respect more worthy of confidence than the General Government." [34] This was the language of loose construction; and it is not surprising that McDuffie should have been made uneasy by the arguments of some of his colleagues. He and Hamilton, however, very skillfully concealed their differences from immediate inspection. The South Carolina delegation was unanimous for free trade. But South Carolina was now the intellectual leader of the cotton kingdom, and she had not made up her mind how far she could push the doctrine of State Rights. John Caldwell Calhoun, McDuffie's mentor, was still wavering; and it was not until the South Carolina House of Representatives changed its mind in December 1825, and officially condemned the protective tariff, that Calhoun began to meditate a conversion to free trade.[35]

Over all this heaving confusion of doctrines and interests one can still see, as one reads those interminable debates, the figure of Henry Clay, questing, like a dove of peace, for a patch of dry land. His great speech of

March 31 differs from the majority of his printed speeches in that it is still readable. It has survived the loss of Mr. Clay's ephemeral magic—the strange glidings about the floor, the pointed finger, the punctuating pinches of snuff, the unforgettable smile, and all the charm of that wonderful voice. One cannot doubt the sincerity with which he committed the Western farmer to a system that gave "our capitalists," as Churchill C. Cambreleng of New York put it, "the exclusive privilege of supplying our country with manufactures." His own motives were wonderfully mixed, but not, one is tempted to believe, his cravings for peace. His final appeal to the South, though dismaying in its economies, was far from disingenuous in its emotions. "I appeal, to the South," he cried, "to the high-minded, generous and patriotic South—with which I have so often co-operated, in attempting to sustain the honor and to vindicate the rights of our country. Should it not offer, upon the altar of the public good, some sacrifice of its peculiar opinions? Of what does it complain? A possible temporary enhancement in the objects of consumption. Of what do we complain? A total incapacity, produced by the foreign policy, to purchase, at any price, necessary foreign objects of consumption. In such an alternative, inconvenient only to it, ruinous to us, can we expect too much from southern magnanimity?" [36]

Magnanimity, however, is rarely to be found in tariff debates, whose main interest is that they preserve, in almost perfect form, the dry skeleton of self-interest. The South had already answered Mr. Clay, and it had done so with an argument distinctly *ad hominem*. It had pointed out that Mr. Clay's state and Mr. Clay's district were deeply involved in the production of hemp; and it had not failed to remark upon the coincidence between this state of affairs and the proposed new tariffs on foreign hemp and foreign cotton-bagging. Its representatives observed that Kentucky hemp, which was dew-rotted, was altogether inferior to the water-rotted hemp of Russia: that it was unfit for the manufacture of cotton-bagging. "The bagging of Kentucky," said Brent of Louisiana, "is so inferior that we prefer paying forty cents per yard for the foreign article to making use of the bagging of Kentucky at twenty-five cents." [37] It would be sad, indeed, if at the bottom of all Mr. Clay's arguments there was found to be nothing more than a pile of dew-rotted hemp.

In the end, the House of Representatives, by a vote of 107 to 102, passed the tariff bill; and so earnest were its members that "some attended who were so much indisposed as actually to have left their beds for the purpose of giving their votes." [38] An analysis of these votes shows that the grain, wool, and manufacturing states (with the exception of Massachusetts) were in favor of a tariff, and that the planting, navigating, and fishing states were opposed. The mixture of the home market with the infant industries had a strange appearance. "The merchants and manufacturers of Massachusetts, New Hampshire, the province of Maine and Sagadahock repel this bill," said John Randolph, "whilst men in hunting-shirts, with deer-skin leggings and mocassins on their feet, want protection for manufacturers." [39] When the Bill reached the more conservative Senate, it was severely amended be-

fore being passed by a vote of 25 to 21. Even then, though it did not satisfy
the high protectionists, it was a very protective piece of legislation.[40] The
average rate of all the new duties was 37 per cent; and only the woolen
manufacturers, who had been gratified with 33⅓ per cent on imported
woolens, found themselves hamstrung by another duty of 30 per cent on
imported wool.[41] The new Act was signed by James Monroe on May 22,
1824.[42]

IV

The Act had little effect upon the coming election, since all the candidates
were known to favor it, with the possible exception of William H. Crawford.[43] Its international meaning was equally obscure. All through the debate, gentlemen had mentioned the economy of Great Britain; but they had
been unable to make up their minds in which direction this economy was
moving. As the great purveyor of manufactured articles, Great Britain
would be more affected by the new Act than any other nation. Mr. Clay
thought that she was protectionist; Mr. Webster, more far-seeing, declared
that she was coming more and more to favor free trade.[44] Actually, she reduced her duties on wool to a nominal amount in 1824; and in 1825 there
was a further great reduction in the duties on cottons, woolens, glass, earth-
enware, iron, copper, zinc, tin, and lead. "Prohibitory duties," said Mr.
Huskisson on that occasion, "are a premium on mediocrity." [45] But these
were only preliminary moves, and her confusing situation, as she changed
from the old mercantilism to the new free trade, might well have baffled
the gentlemen in Congress. What is more to the point is the answer she had
now received to her friendly advances from 1820 to 1823. It is often forgotten that in the very Message that carried the Monroe Doctrine there
were also the following sentences: "Having communicated my views to
Congress at the commencement of the last session respecting the encouragement which ought to be given to our manufactures and the principle upon
which it should be founded, I have only to add that those views remain
unchanged, and that the present state of those countries with which we have
the most immediate political relations and greatest commercial intercourse
tends to confirm them. Under this impression, I recommend a review of the
tariff for the purpose of affording such additional *protection* to those articles which we are prepared to manufacture, or which are more immediately
connected with the defense and independence of the country." [46] Thus, the
President's message had greeted Great Britain's advances with the doctrine
of noncolonization and with a call for protective tariffs. When James
Monroe signed the Tariff Act in 1824, the answer to Lord Liverpool and
George Canning was complete or very nearly so. In London, meeting with
Mr. Huskisson and Mr. Stratford Canning, Richard Rush continued to cling
in the most courteous but determined manner to the word "elsewhere." And
so the answer was complete.[47]

CHAPTER SIX

Postscript: "Ave Atque Vale"

JAMES MONROE'S signature to a protective tariff was an obituary in itself. The Virginia Dynasty was dead. There would be no more Old Republicanism in high places. "Congress had just risen," Thomas Jefferson wrote angrily on June 5, "having done nothing more remarkable except the passing of a tariff bill by squeezing majorities, very revolting to a great portion of the people of the states, among whom it is believed that it would not have received a vote but of the manufacturers themselves." [1] He had forgotten, or he did not choose to recall, that Monroe had himself invited Congress to impose the tariff, and that he had done so without any reference to Constitutional scruples. Monroe had persuaded himself, one must suppose, that he was yielding to a popular sentiment; and he had been unable to summon from his dying Republicanism a spirit strong enough to resist it. Did he remember—had he read—what John Taylor of Caroline had written against the argument that manufactures must be protected because they were in their infancy? "How long will the world be persuaded that it is an infant and ought to be scourged into knowledge?" [2] Three months after the signing of the Act, however, the druidical conscience of Virginia was stilled forever. . . . John Taylor died on August 21, 1824.

Monroe's Presidency may have constituted a "golden age," as John Quincy Adams put it; but one would have to admit that its gold had some base of alloys in it. Monroe had given the country an honorable and efficient administration, to which no real scandal had attached itself; but his policy had been in its domestic aspects a policy of drift. He had underwritten, unconsciously at times, unwillingly perhaps, large portions of the American System of Henry Clay. Did this system, which was feared in the South, really satisfy the small farmers of the West and Northwest, whose representatives had voted for it in Congress? Would it please the working man

320

of the East? Or would it appear to be an effort to inscribe the wishes of the industrialist and the financier firmly across the statute book? Whatever the answer, the system was certainly flourishing in 1824. The national bank was stronger than it had ever been. Protective tariffs had arrived in such a form as to whet the appetites they failed to satisfy. There remained the question of internal improvements.

James Monroe, like James Madison before him, had attempted to save his Republican name by the veto of an internal-improvements bill.[3] On May 4, 1822, he had returned unsigned a bill bearing the title "An act for the preservation and repair of the Cumberland road." His reasons were that Congress might appropriate money for the repair of the road, under its appropriation power, but that it could not establish turnpikes with gates and tolls, or enforce the collection of tolls by penalties, as the bill required, for that would imply "a complete right of jurisdiction and sovereignty for all the purposes of internal improvement," and where in the Constitution was such a right to be found?[4] No one doubted the importance of the Cumberland Road, which reached as far as Wheeling on the Ohio, though many people wondered how Congress had come to build it in the first place.[5] The precedent was a dangerous one: it suggested an invasion of the states by the general government, armed with contracts and patronage, and all the panoply of consolidation. Monroe accompanied his veto message with an immense annex, which he had not submitted to his Cabinet, and which set forth the arguments for and against the powers of Congress in regard to internal improvements. Those whose business it was to read this formidable document, entitled "Views of the President of the United States on the subject of Internal Improvements," may well have come to the conclusion that if the veto message shut the door gently in the face of Congress, the "Views" as gently opened it again. Monroe admitted that he had altered his old beliefs. He was now convinced that Congress might grant and appropriate money for internal improvements, for "my idea is that Congress have an unlimited power to raise money, and that in its appropriation they have a discretionary power, restricted only by the duty to appropriate it to purposes of common defense and of general, not local, national, not State, benefit."[6] But who among the sons of men could tell the difference between general and local, national and state benefit? He added that the internal improvements themselves could not be executed by Congress, but only by local agencies. And his expressed belief—and here he was in line with Old Republican thinking—was that the question could best be settled by Constitutional amendment.[7]

The Western states, with no money to spare for their own improvements, may well have thought this the merest splitting of Constitutional hairs. Too much time and money was being spent on getting the farmers' produce to market. A system of internal improvements, combined with a low tariff, might have moved the surplus cheaply to the ports and then sold some of it abroad. Combined with a high tariff, it offered only the industrialists' promise of a home market. These considerations failed to disturb the farmers or their representatives in Congress; and the Tariff Act of 1824 had been preceded by a General Survey Act the evident purpose of which was to prepare the way for a program of appropriations for internal improvements on a national scale, and of subscriptions to the stock of companies engaged in these enterprises.[8] Clay, who led the argument for internal improvements with all his skill and all his vigor, savagely attacked the Administration for its policies. "A new world has come into being since the Constitution was adopted," he said. "Are the narrow, limited necessities of the old thirteen states, of indeed, parts only of the old thirteen states, as they existed at the formation of the present Constitution forever to remain the rule of interpretations?"[9] But, indeed, it was Monroe's "Views" which opened the way for the General Survey Act.

Once again Monroe had been reacting to a popular sentiment. The fever for internal improvements reached its height in 1824. The whole West and Southwest longed to repeat, in some form or another, the triumph of the Erie Canal. The Canal was almost complete. It owed, it is true, nothing to the federal government, much to the promotional genius of De Witt Clinton, and even more to geography. There was a happy, indeed almost a miraculous, propinquity between the upper reaches of the Hudson River and the one real break in the Appalachian system. This was by way of the Mohawk River valley, which led by imperceptible gradations to the Finger Lakes district of central New York, whence the Oswego and the Genesee ran northward into Lake Ontario. The Canal was to be a final blow in the long battle that the Mohawk and the Hudson had fought with the St. Lawrence. This kind of scheme tempted De Witt Clinton out of the obscurities of his personal politics and turned him into the great public servant that nature— whose designs in this respect he so frequently thwarted—had evidently intended him to be. As soon as the necessary legislation had been passed in 1816 and 1817, the Canal (with the additional Lake Champlain canal) was blessed with good fortune. Its complicated finances—the necessary eight million dollars was raised by land sales, taxes on salt and auctions, lotteries, appropriations, and tolls—were neither corrupted nor entangled. Its engineers learned as they went, and the terrain was such that they were not obliged to pay for this experience. At one spot east of Syracuse there was a level of sixty-nine and a half miles without a single lock; and at no point along the whole 363 miles was the route more than six hundred feet above sea level. The very stone they dug up could be used for making locks. Machinery was invented for pulling up trees; matted roots were cut up by a specially constructed plow. Ingenuity flourished; only the wretched human beings who labored at this wonderful ditch were harmed, for most of the route lay through virgin forest and foul marsh, and these, as usual, slew their violators with agues and bilious fevers, with typhus, with pestilences that never found names. In 1823 the eastern section, from Rome to the Hudson, was finished, and the other two sections, from the Seneca River to Rome, and from

Lake Erie to the Seneca River, were beyond the chance of failure. By 1824 it was clear that the great trans-Allegheny route was to be shifted away from the Potomac, away from the slave-holding agricultural South, and towards the industrial North. The fantastic destiny of New York City was already inscribed across the state in the great stone aqueducts and the wonderful fills. It was natural enough for the citizens of Ohio to think of canals that, connecting Cincinnati with the Maumee and Portsmouth with Cleveland, should wed themselves to the system created by New York and make the Western surpluses available in the markets of the East. Indiana, too, had thoughts of a remarkable highway to be formed by joining the headwaters of the Maumee and the Wabash. In such ways the produce of the old Northwest could reach the avenue of commerce now taking visible shape along the Great Lakes and the Erie Canal.[10]

Other states, with perhaps less feasible schemes, were fired by the example of New York. New York, to be sure, had done her own financing; she illustrated this in the most practical manner by opposing all internal improvements at federal expense. So did New England, with the Erie Canal safely at the back door. Some fragments of the Old South resisted the new impulse, partly because they feared that they would be taxed for the benefit of others, but chiefly for the reason John Randolph advanced in Congress—a federal government that could dig a canal could also emancipate every slave in the South.[11] Nevertheless, the Potomac valley, with western Virginia, western North Carolina, and a considerable fragment of South Carolina and Georgia, voted with Pennsylvania and the entire West to pass the General Survey Bill,[12] signed by Monroe on April 30, 1824.

It does not seem very strange that a general government should come to the help of its citizens in the matter of improving their impassable roads or of clearing or contriving their waterways: and the new Western states, themselves the creatures of the general government, did not think it strange at all. But at the same time there still existed a deep instinctive horror of strong central government. The American republic had come into existence by overthrowing a tyrant who ruled from afar: was it now to put itself into the hands of another tyrant, ruling only a little less remotely on the borders of Virginia and Maryland? Was it not always true that political power vested in remote hands was almost certain to be abused?[13] Before the dismayed eyes of those who still remembered and cherished the warnings of Thomas Jefferson, and before the eyes of Jefferson himself at Monticello, there spread the vision of a mass of internal-improvements legislation, entangled in local schemes, confused by jealousies, and saturated with greed and with corruption. And, indeed, the great danger in the internal-improvements movement was that it attempted to centralize too swiftly and too prematurely. In a society still largely agricultural, centralization would benefit the enterpriser, but it might doom the agriculturalist.

I

Moreover, the very embodiment of unsubsidized communication was now moving freely along the waterways of the United States. By 1824 the steamboat had come into its own. There were, for example, as early as 1820, seventy-nine steamboats running on the Ohio between Pittsburgh and St. Louis. As early as 1816 the *Washington* had been equipped with the new high-pressure engine, which connected directly with the crankshaft of the two side-wheels, and which compensated in cheapness and power for what it lacked in safety—for it was very likely to explode, and after such an explosion the vessel, with its ruined cargo and its freight of dead and dying passengers, usually burned to the water line. In 1824 the steamboat was released from all fear of monopoly, if not of explosion, by Chief Justice Marshall's great decision in the case of *Gibbons v. Ogden*. On every navigable stream, on every lake, it was free to make its wonderful progress—a flat-bottomed box, with a deck built only a little above the water, and the bow a square platform above the sharp concealed prow. Its superstructure climbed skyward to the hurricane deck, thirty feet above the water, topped by a pilot house, with the great twin smokestacks towering over all. Its hoarse whistle broke the silence of the wilderness, and the dwellers beside the remotest waters came down to the landing places to marvel at it as one of the miracles of progress. Its upper deck, with the great ornate cabin and the luxurious staterooms, crowded with the fair and the rich and with other beings even more remarkable, seemed like some vision from the Arabian Nights to the simple folk along the Mississippi and the Ohio. The great ark, laden with cattle and grain, with tobacco and cotton and furs, with merchants and gamblers and fine ladies on the upper deck, and stranger and more resolute travelers crouched amid the squalor of the lower one, was in its way a symbol of the new nineteenth-century democracy. It went against the current; it was always in danger from its own mechanism; it was threatened by snags and sawyers and the weird shiftings of the river bed: but it has survived in memory as the greatest and most loved adventure that America ever produced. Above all, it was the purveyor not only of unity but also of independence; for though Congress began to make regular appropriations for the removal of snags and the improvement of river beds, the steamboat required no more help than that. Having triumped over monopoly in 1824, it went on to triumph over space and loneliness. It was one answer to the General Survey Bill, and certainly the most eloquent; but no enemy of internal improvements thought to use it for an argument in Congress.

In any case, James Monroe signed the General Survey Bill without scruple. It was the logical extension of his own "Views"; and more was to come. It is sometimes forgotten that Monroe's last deed as President was to put his signature to a bill that authorized Congress to subscribe three hundred thousand dollars to the Chesapeake and Delaware Canal Company.[14]

This was signed on March 3, 1825. And so it would seem that, from the time when James Madison signed a bill incorporating a national bank until the last day of James Monroe's Administration, when Congress was permitted to buy stock in a canal company, the movement of Virginia Presidents had been away from Jeffersonian principles. These had scarcely survived Jefferson's own Administration, as the revolt of the Tertium Quids, the Jeffersonian fundamentalists, amply proves. But Jefferson's belief that society was divine and that political institutions were ephemeral did not permit him to set up any hard and fast standards; and his great dogma that "the earth belongs to the living generation" absolutely forbade him to do so. Jefferson himself was perfectly capable of qualifying his own aversion to strong government by supremely energetic acts—but these were always to be regarded as exceptions or deviations. The Jeffersonian myth, constellated in all its majesty around the proposition that "that government is best which governs least," somehow survived such Jeffersonian deeds as the Louisiana Purchase and the Embargo Act. But it was an awkward legacy.

Monroe, particularly, who came to the Presidency at the high noon of postwar nationalism, was in a very difficult position. The question that confronted him, as soon as nationalism had been dampened by the Panic of 1819, was a question inseparable from all phases of liberal capitalism, early as well as late. Even the creative labors of pioneers and woodland farmers, even the rise of the cotton kingdom, even the magic of the frontier could not suppress the business community's claim to be the most vigorous and transforming element in the nation. The question then became—should the business community rule the state, or should the government devise means of checking the political ambition of the business community? The question was more insistent in the thirties and forties, but it was at least formulated in the twenties and with sufficient clarity. No sooner had agrarian nationalism suffered its eclipse in 1819 than another kind of nationalism was to be descried—in Chief Justice Marshall's defense of the national bank, in Henry Clay's eloquent economics, in tariff legislation, in internal-improvements legislation.

James Monroe, who literally bankrupted himself in the public service, was not dazzled by material wealth. But James Monroe was sufficiently opposed to strong government not to be able to resist a centralizing tendency even if he secretly mistrusted it. The weakness of anti-statism is that it defeats its own ends because of its ethical distaste for government intervention; and this was complicated, in Monroe's case, by his belief that it was his duty rather to listen and interpret than to lead. In his "Views," scarcely concealed by a cloud of Constitutional arguments, lies the central fact that he was changing his mind because of an agitation in Congress—not because the agitation was sound, but because it existed. He saw no way of combining the public servant with the strong President; he thought the two roles incompatible, and the former more honorable than the latter; and his sense of duty obliged him to follow the line of least resistance. Thus it came about that his foreign policy was always more forthright than his domestic one—not merely because he was guided by a most forthright Secretary of State—but also because foreign policy was clearly within the competence of the Executive.

II

Monroe, retiring into private life, was confronted with bankruptcy, the one tangible reward for his long years of public service. Congress eventually voted him thirty thousand dollars; but it was not enough. He left Virginia in the spring of 1830; he was forced to sell his Loudoun home; and in 1831, in New York City, he died. The day of his death was July 4—but even the patriotic coincidence of such a death upon such a day had been pre-empted by John Adams and Thomas Jefferson. He was given, it is true, a splendid public funeral; an Episcopal bishop read the service over him, the President of Columbia pronounced the eulogy; and all the bells in the city tolled as thousands followed his hearse, solemn and resplendent in black and gold, up Broadway to the Marble Cemetery.[15] But one wonders if it was the man they followed, or just the show.

Every student of Monroe's Presidency must sometimes discover that he has lost sight of the President. After his triumphal tours were over, Monroe assumed a less and less festive place in the minds of his countrymen, until at last he seems almost to have been forgotten, or, what was much the same thing, to have been taken for granted—an essential piece of furniture, but faded, old-fashioned, and destined for the attic or the cellar. Only in John Quincy Adams's diary, where his decisions and indecisions were so accurately recorded, does Monroe appear as he may have been; for Monroe was one of the few men, one feels, whose character was not distorted by that strabismic diarist. Here we see him, both the pacifier and director of the angry and brilliant men who formed his Cabinet. It gives us some idea of his qualities as an administrator—some notion that, if the times were often chaotic, they would have been more so under another more ambitious and less watchful President. Moreover, James Monroe was deeply respected by those who were most closely associated with him. Rather shy, rather formal, very kindly, he was not self-effacing; and he knew very well what was due to the dignity of his position and the weight of his experience. He was simple, but not simple-minded, and his simplicity seems to have been the effect of a quality which is very hard to define, but which one is forced to define as sheer goodness.

The Englishman, Adlard Welby, tells how he and his party, calling on Monroe by appointment in the winter of 1820, were ushered by a servant in plain livery into the study upstairs, where they found the President at work upon a mass of papers—"a plain quiet man [wrote Welby] with a deeply reflective face." Monroe rose and himself placed the chairs for his visitors. There was a brief conversation; and then for each visitor as he left there was a warm handshake and an unaffected "God bless you." This is one of the tersest accounts of the President that has come down to us: it is also one of the most moving.[16]

III

That the phrase "Era of Good Feelings" bears any moral content is a doubtful proposition; but if it can be maintained at all, one may claim that some part of this moral content was due to the character of James Monroe of Virginia.

5

THE LURID ADMINISTRATION:
1825-1829

CHAPTER ONE

A Cup of Hemlock

JOHN QUINCY ADAMS was elected President of the United States by the House of Representatives on February 9, 1825. Thirteen states had given him their vote on the first ballot; seven states had voted for Andrew Jackson; and four states for William H. Crawford.

To be elected indirectly, by the House of Representatives, is not the happiest way of becoming President—particularly when, as was the case with John Quincy Adams, one has not previously obtained even a leading moiety of the popular vote or of votes in the electoral college. When a Committee of the House called on Mr. Adams on February 9, to inform him that he was President-elect, it was received by a man who appeared to be in a veritable agony of mind. Sweat poured from Mr. Adams's stricken face as he listened to the words of Daniel Webster, the Committee's chairman. It almost seemed as if Webster were proffering not the Presidency but a cup of hemlock. Then Adams asked leave to use the precedent set by Thomas Jefferson, and to answer in writing. The answer was not very gracious. If it were possible, wrote Mr. Adams, by declining the office to cause an immediate election that would bring about a clearer result, he would gladly do so. But since this was not Constitutionally permissible, he accepted the Presidency. To his diary he confided that the election had not taken place in "a manner satisfactory to pride or to just desire; not by the unequivocal suffrages of a majority of the people; with perhaps two-thirds of the whole people adverse to the actual result."[1]

This private candor and public hesitancy did honor to the New England conscience; but it did not augur well for the new Administration.

I

History, regarded as a teleological entity, as something displaying a purpose and capable of passing judgments, must be said to have condemned the Administration of John Quincy Adams. It is not a verdict that one would care to dispute. As his grandson, Henry Adams, put it: "To me the old gentleman's Presidency appears always as lurid." [2] Henry Adams, to be sure, did not blame his grandfather for the failure of his Administration; the claims of family were not to be sacrificed to the claims of fact. But the Presidency does seem to be a rather conspicuous example of a great man in the wrong place, at the wrong time, with the right motives, and with a tragic inability to make himself understood.

II

Looking back on the election of 1824-5, Mr. Adams—quite apart from his temperamental unwillingness to welcome good fortune—had good reason to be dissatisfied, plaintive, and conscience-stricken. Not to have obtained "the unequivocal suffrages of the majority" was no doubt bad; but how much worse was it, for such a man as he, to have been obliged to make promises, to flatter editors, to hobnob with contrivers and connivers, to electioneer! Despite his best endeavors, Mr. Adams had been forced to descend to these expedients.[8] The passion for the Presidency in those days was a fever that gave its victims no rest. Its cause was, in part, social malnutrition—society had few rewards to offer, aside from political ones; so that those who hoped to be Presidents, and those who hoped to make something out of making Presidents, were seized with an anxiety amounting almost to desperation. And the fever had another cause, more honorable and less easy to isolate. Everyone still believed that the United States was setting an undying example to the whole world; so that the Presidency was not only a focus of power and a fount of patronage—it was also a kind of apotheosis. Andrew Jackson was (comparatively) immune to this fever in 1824, though not in 1828; but in 1824 it literally blasted Henry Clay's career, and it left John Quincy Adams a sick and shaken man.

Mr. Adams disliked what was being done by himself or with his knowledge in this election; and what was performed behind his back was sometimes so obscurely crooked that, when he learned of it, he could not bring himself to acknowledge it. A good example is the way in which his "friends" obtained the electoral votes of New York.

The story has all the complexity one associates with New York politics of those days; but, reduced to a plain form, it is the story of the rise of Thurlow Weed. Thurlow Weed was a tall, rather awkward-looking young man, with an extraordinary capacity for inspiring confidence, who had been sent from Rochester to Albany in order to lobby for a bank charter. He obtained his charter without any difficulty, and, having nothing else to do, decided to devote his talents to the cause of Mr. Adams. They were talents of no ordinary kind. Thurlow Weed was destined to become the greatest political manager of his day; he had a disinterested, almost a dedicated, passion for political manipulation. The ends of politics he left to others: he was concerned solely with the means. Like Baron Stockmar, he was quite selfless in allowing others to enjoy the rewards of office, notoriety and fame; but unlike Baron Stockmar, there was not a trace of idealism in his extraordinary composition. Henry Adams, who met him years later in London, and was immediately fascinated by him, said that he played with men as though they were only cards, but seemed incapable of feeling himself one of them.[4] Power, not the emblems of power, fascinated him: power, anonymous, pervasive, and inconsequential. In Albany, which was then the greatest and probably the grubbiest school of political intrigue in the United States, he was both a neophyte and a master: or, what was much the same thing, passed from the former status to the latter with something more than the speed of light.

The choice of Presidential electors for New York was still in the hands of the legislature; and three candidates—Adams, Crawford and Clay—were in the field. Jackson counted for little in New York; he had a large and scattered following that was unable to coalesce. As for the legislature, it was under the control of the "Albany Regency," a group of highly efficient men led by United States Senator Martin Van Buren. Their efficiency was sometimes impaired, if not altogether devoured, by a consuming greed for office. They were the brains of the Bucktail or liberal wing of the Republican Party in the state, and they had recently reduced their great enemy—the quasi-Republican De Witt Clinton—to a condition of temporary quiescence.

Thurlow Weed took in the whole scene with the relish of a connoisseur. We can imagine that, having learned in Rochester the political arts that gained him, a young newspaper reporter, the chance to go lobbying for bank charters, he was only too anxious to test them out in the larger, more complicated, but transparently manageable world of Albany. He realized that the Regency had fatally undermined its position by setting its face against giving the choice of Presidential electors directly to the people. This was obvious. Even the scarecrows in the fields, that spring of 1824, bore cards stitched to their coats and inscribed with the word "Regency."[5] But, on the last day that the legislature was in session, the Regency committed a more appalling blunder. It introduced and passed a resolution removing De Witt Clinton from the office of canal commissioner, which he had held without remuneration and to the satisfaction of everyone. Now to demolish Clinton as a politician was one thing—almost everybody had tried his hand at it, with intermittent success, for many years: for Clinton's politics consisted chiefly in demanding a personal allegiance to Clinton, which he rewarded with patronage but not with courtesy. But to attack him as a public servant was quite another. His efforts on behalf of the Erie Canal, in the days when it was still mocked at as "Clinton's ditch," were remembered with gratitude and even with veneration. What divine, or Acherontic, rage had seized upon the Regency, we shall never know for certain; but Martin Van Buren, who was busy in Washington, knew nothing about this deed until it was too late to prevent it.[6] An immediate tempest burst about the heads of the Regency; and the result of it all was that the "People's Party," which favored electoral reform, and the Clintonian Party, its inveterate enemy, joined forces in the November elections, just long enough to bring in Clinton for governor and James Tallmadge for lieutenant governor, over the Regency choices of Samuel Young and Erastus Root.[7]

The Regency's candidate for President was William H. Crawford; but it had long since admitted that much depended on the election for governor.[8] Now the election was lost; and though the choice of Presidential electors was still in the hands of the old legislature, that body was very demoralized. Since the votes for governor were still being counted as it went into session on November 2, the Senate, under the direction of Van Buren, who had returned from Washington to rally his dispirited followers, obediently voted for a list of Crawford electors with six moderate Clay men as a political sop to that faction.[9] Everybody realized by this time that not one of the four candidates would obtain a clear majority in the electoral college and that the ultimate choice for President would rest with the House of Representatives. The picking up of stray electoral votes, therefore, became of the first importance: particularly to the followers of Clay who believed that their candidate, though far behind in the popular race, could still carry the day in the House of Representatives if he could get himself presented there. The New York Assembly, now shaken by the news of Clinton's victory, was not likely to follow the Senate's lead and vote for a list of Crawford electors with six Clay men. Its members seemed almost equally divided among Adams, Crawford, and Clay. According to the somewhat cumbrous electoral law, the final decision would have to be made by a joint ballot of the Senate and the Assembly, to which no name would be admitted which had not already been voted for by one or the other body. Weed, who had silently taken the leadership of the Adams forces away from the eloquent but unpredictable James Tallmadge, immediately circulated the rumor that if the Crawford supporters would eliminate Clay in the Assembly, the Clay men would vote for the Crawford ticket on the joint ballot, thereby securing six electoral votes for their own man. Why the Crawford leaders swallowed this bait is beyond understanding, but swallow it they did; and when the Assembly voted for electors, they threw their support to Adams. Now amidst the cloud of midnight meetings, of subtle bargains, of open threats, of the secret printing of sample ballots, only the figure of Weed stands forth at all clearly —the supreme virtuoso of the campaign of 1824. In private conclave with the Clay leaders, he persuaded them that they should desert the Crawford cause and make a unified Adams-Clay ticket, with the promise that eight electoral votes would thereby be assured to Clay. These tactics were completely successful at the joint ballot. The Regency forces, taken by surprise by Weed's fusion ticket, howled with rage and threatened to withdraw the still obedient Senate; but order was at last restored and the voting was completed. By that time, the Clay leaders were equally mortified. Somehow or other, four of their men on Weed's fusion ticket failed to receive the required majority; and four good Crawford supporters were chosen in their place. It seems that Weed had been unwilling, or possibly unable, to keep his promise.[10]

Van Buren, before retiring from Albany "as completely broken down a politician as my bitterest enemies could desire," wrote a letter to Crawford, attempting to explain "our disastrous contest." Even Crawford, who was as clever as any man at deciphering political codes, might have had some difficulty in making head or tail of Van Buren's explanation; but its conclusion was that the Adams and Clay factions "saw their interest in depriving the state of its vote; we had no interest in such a result & under the circumstances were bound to prevent it." [11] In other words, the fusion ticket was an attempt, not to choose Adams electors, but to create such a furor that no electors would be chosen at all. Van Buren never seems to have realized that he had been outmaneuvered by a young man called Thurlow Weed. Adams would not recognize Weed's existence; and, though he knew that the electoral vote of New York had not been bestowed upon him in a very straightforward manner, tried to pretend that it was simply a tribute to his merit. Clay took the result without rancor; he could not have realized that he was never again to come so close to the Presidency.[12]

III

This story might not have been worth relating if it did not sum up the essential elements of the election of 1824-5. It was not an election that expressed the wishes of the electorate. General Jackson, no doubt, had demonstrated that he was the popular choice: he had been given 153,544 votes to Adams's 108,740, Crawford's 46,618, and Clay's 47,136. His sudden success in North Carolina, where his People's Ticket was a protest against poor crops, economic depression, and the domination of politicians and aristocrats through the caucus system, shows—as clearly as anything could show—what was the nature of his following.[13] Moreover, his influence spread from New Jersey to Alabama; whereas Adams's stronghold was New England; Clay controlled only Kentucky, Ohio, and Missouri; and Crawford was supported by Virginia, his native state, and Georgia, his adopted one. But little could be deduced from an election that had been cooked in the legislatures (as in New York), hampered by district systems, tax qualifications, and the slow death of old political machines, and finally vitiated by an evident feeling among the voters that, even if they could make a choice among this constellation of candidates without platforms, the old-line politicians in the end would be too many for them. As, in the end, they were.

One victim of the election—or at any rate of the Presidential caucus system the election destroyed—was almost unnoticed. Albert Gallatin had returned from Paris (where he had performed his ministerial duties to everyone's satisfaction, and had been flattered by French royalists with the family title of Count) in order to run for vice-president on the Crawford ticket. The Washington caucus duly nominated him; but then it was discovered that his name no longer meant very much, even in Pennsylvania. The glories of Jefferson's Cabinet, the long service under Madison, the great battle at Ghent—all were forgotten. He was only a figure from the past, who had chosen to ally himself with a system which was the past incarnate. There were mutterings about his foreign birth and his aristocratic leanings. At length, on September 25, Senator Walter Lowrie of Pennsylvania—in a letter that cost him the utmost pain to write—asked Gallatin to withdraw. Gallatin, as it turned out, was more than happy to do so. His nomination, he told Van Buren, "was a misfortune founded on a miscalculation." [14] It was also, as to its effects, a straw in the wind: and the wind, it would seem, was blowing from the left.

IV

According to an Act of Congress, the various states in 1824 might vote for Presidential electors on any day that suited them between October 27 and December 1. This statutory imprecision was, in its way, charming; but it turned every steamboat, every stagecoach and courier, every sailing vessel into a purveyor of rumors that were wildly inaccurate. These rumors were not always without effect upon the different electoral colleges as they met to record the choice of the people or the legislatures, so that the election was removed one degree further from the popular verdict it was supposed to represent. It was not until December 16 that the choice of the Louisiana legislature was known in Washington: three electors for Jackson, two for Adams. The final result could now, and only now, be tabulated: 99 electoral votes for Jackson, 84 for Adams, 41 for Crawford, and 37 for Clay. The first three gentlemen would, therefore, be presented to the House of Representatives as Presidential candidates. The four votes of which he had been deprived in New York, by larceny or by luck, had cost Henry Clay his chance of making one of the three. At the same time they had thrust him into a position from which he, more than any man, could extract whatever there was to be extracted. "It is in fact very much in Mr. Clay's power," William Plumer of New Hampshire wrote unhappily to his father, "to make the President." [15]

The friends of Adams and Jackson looked fearfully at this disposer of their fortunes—the gay, the insouciant, the portentous Clay, as he wandered from boarding house to boarding house, from banquet to banquet, with his air of power and his professions of impartiality. [16] In the House of Representatives each state would have exactly one vote: Illinois would have as much power as New York, Missouri as Pennsylvania. Mr. Plumer was perfectly correct. In such a situation what might Mr. Clay not do, with his immense prestige as Speaker, and his popularity in the West? As far as personal relations went, he was nobody's man. He and Mr. Adams had never been on good terms since the day when they had shouted insults at each other, at Ghent, across the little table in the Hotel d'Alcantara. He had broken with General Jackson on the Florida question, and superficial courtesies could not mend the breach. With the radicalism of Mr. Crawford he had nothing in common at all.

Before he left Kentucky for Washington, Mr. Clay had told a few friends that he would never vote for Jackson; and even before December 16, he warned his friend and lieutenant, Thomas Hart Benton, who had become a Jacksonian, that he could not follow his example. So that it is not surprising that, by Christmas, the whole of Washington should have been saying that Clay was leaning towards Adams.[17] On December 17, Robert P. Letcher, Clay's friend, and a representative from Kentucky called on Adams and heard from the Secretary's own lips that he "harbored no animosity" against the Speaker. Clay would support him, Adams noted afterwards, "if he could serve thereby himself"; but Mr. Letcher had not been unkindly received.[18]

Returning to the attack on December 23, Letcher said that everything depended upon the first ballot in the House; and that this could be secured for Adams by the votes of Kentucky, Ohio, Indiana, Missouri, and Illinois. "Impracticable," answered the wavering Adams. By this time, it was common gossip that Clay was looking for the State Department, and therewith the succession; and Mr. Adams was guilty of political innocence when he described Letcher's gross hint as "among the whimsical results of political combination at this time." But he added the ominous words "*incedo super ignes.*" His conscience, always his worst enemy, was beginning to tell him that he could not be President without some fearful loss of self-respect. Nevertheless, on January 1, he agreed with Mr. Letcher that the time had come for him to have a conversation with Clay; and that night the Speaker and the Secretary, sitting together at a banquet for Lafayette, decided upon a conference in the near future. Thus the year began with Mr. Adams walking, not over the fires, but into them.[19]

V

The friends of Adams, Jackson, and Crawford had been approaching one another with all manner of offers; they had courted Henry Clay in a manner which even that gentleman thought ludicrous; and they had watched the friends of Calhoun, who divided their allegiance between Adams and Jackson, with something like envy—for the friends of Calhoun were at liberty to make what bargains they could. But these maneuvers were simply the dust concealing the real conflict; and this can only be examined in the words and actions of the principles themselves.

James Buchanan, a representative from Pennsylvania, was a young, wealthy, and plausible personage who defied plausibility, though not politics, by calling upon General Jackson with a singularly improper suggestion. If Jackson, said James Buchanan, would publicly state that he would never make Adams his Secretary of State, then Mr. Clay and his friends would put an end to the Presidential contest within an hour. Buchanan was a Jacksonian Federalist, with a certain fondness for Clay, though he was not Clay's emissary. He spoke for himself. A smooth and handsome man, with a tall stoutish body, wavy hair, and dainty feet, he was afflicted with an involuntary winking of one of his charming blue eyes, which was said to fascinate the ladies of his acquaintance. On this occasion it can hardly have fascinated General Jackson: it may even have suggested that Buchanan's words were not only improper but impudent. According to Buchanan, however, Jackson simply replied that the secrets of his Cabinet-making were ones which he would conceal "from the very hairs of his head." Such an answer, though negative, was not entirely discouraging; and young Mr. Buchanan hastened to Clay with the intimation that the State Department was as good as his. Clay, according to his own version of this meeting, turned the subject off with a jest.[20]

General Jackson's account of his interview with Buchanan was very different. He was appalled by the notion that he could gain Clay's support by declaring in advance that he would never keep Mr. Adams in the State Department, with the inevitable implication that he *would* put Mr. Clay there. Buchanan was curtly bidden to tell Mr. Clay and his friends that before Jackson would condescend to reach the Presidency by such means he "would see the earth open and swallow up Mr. Clay and his friends and myself with them." [21] This issue between the fifteenth and the seventh Presidents of the United States might today be decided on the relative merits of their respective Administrations, in which case the verdict would go to Jackson. But sentiment and prejudice, fortunately, need not enter into the question. Buchanan's account was manifestly embarrassed and apologetic, and he excluded from it all mention of his subsequent visit to Clay: Jackson's was forthright. One is tempted to believe that Jackson, whatever his friends might say and do behind his back, was personally determined either to have the Presidency without a bargain, or not to have it at all.[22]

Mr. Adams, unfortunately, was too debilitated by Presidential fever to resist an understanding with Henry Clay. If he had resisted it, Jackson would have been elected; and the course of American history would have been—not changed, nothing could have done that—but retarded; for Jackson was less ready for the Presidency in 1824 than he was in 1828, and the people were less ready for him. But Mr. Adams sincerely believed that he was fitter for the Presidency than the moribund Crawford or the military Jackson. Daniel Webster, who had recently paid a visit to Monticello, was carefully circulating the sage's judgment. "I feel much alarmed," Jefferson had said, "at the prospect of seeing General Jackson President. He is one of the most unfit men I know of for such a place." [23] Did not these words count for something? Mr. Adams knew that his Administration could not get along without Western support; he thought Mr. Clay the likeliest man to rally this support; and then, too, in spite of their personal incompatibility, their policies were becoming almost identical. After the recognition of the Spanish-American republics, the Monroe Doctrine, and the signing of the Tariff and the General Survey Bills, there was no longer any reason for Clay to rail against the Administration, "the golden age" of American politics. For these reasons, it would seem, John Quincy Adams stifled his conscience and prepared to come to an understanding with Henry Clay.

And so it came about that the mild theme of Monroe's domestic policies had its solution in the Administration of John Quincy Adams. The solution was a strident, indeed a violent, one: it offered one or two very valuable lessons; and it offered them in a very economical manner—that is to say, almost entirely at the expense of John Quincy Adams and of Henry Clay.

VI

The two men met on the evening of January 9, a Sunday. Adams had been to church and had heard the Reverend Mr. Little discourse on Ecclesiastes vii, 23: "I said I will be wise; but it was far from me." With a wonderful irony, he made a note of this text in his diary. But his diary was otherwise almost silent about what took place on that momentous occasion. All we know is that Clay arrived at six and stayed all evening; and that "he wished me, as far as I might think proper, to satisfy him with regard to some principles of great public importance, but without any personal considerations for himself. In the question to come before the House between General Jackson, Mr. Crawford and myself, he had no hesitation in saying that his preference would be for me." Adams could not quite allow his diary to stop there; he wrote that Clay had told him that he had been approached by friends of Crawford's in a manner so gross as to disgust him, and that certain friends of Adams—without Adams's authority—had urged "considerations personal to himself." [24] In this oblique fashion, the "personal considerations" remained in the picture. We are forced to conclude that the two men came to an understanding—but an understanding only, not a bargain: not the Presidency for the State Department in so many words. Mr. Clay would have thought such a bargain naïve, and Mr. Adams would have condemned it as sinful. But no bargain, after all, was necessary; for an understanding, like charity, covers a multitude of sins.

And never was an understanding more needed. Two days later it was known that the Kentucky legislature had ordered Henry Clay and his colleagues to vote for Andrew Jackson. Henry Clay felt himself capable of persuading a majority of his own delegation to disregard these commands; and as for the legislature, he explained in after years that he did not consider that it had expressed the "wish" of the people of Kentucky. Had not the people of Kentucky, by an overwhelming majority, decided against General Jackson? [25] But the results of the November election might have been interpreted in another way. Kentucky had cast 17,321 votes for Clay and only 6,455 for Jackson: but for Adams Kentucky had not voted at all.[26]

In any case, the alliance had been made; both partners went to work. Mr. Clay, exercised his powers upon the single representatives from Missouri and Illinois and the fourteen from Ohio; Mr. Adams received visitors. The influence of Daniel Webster was considered necessary if the Federalists of

Delaware and Maryland were to be brought into the Adams camp, and Mr. Webster was known to have a craving for the post of Minister to England; so William Plumer of New Hampshire duly called upon the Secretary of State, and was informed that Webster's wishes "might be gratified hereafter." [27] John Scott, Missouri's only representative, came to talk about his brother, the federal judge, who had resented a fellow judge's dissenting verdict to the point of killing him in a duel, and who was reasonably afraid that he might lose his post. Adams reassured Mr. Scott on this point, and intimated that Mr. Clay would have some post in the next Administration.[28] Representative Reed of Massachusetts came to speak of Daniel Webster's fears that Adams, if elected, would proscribe all Federalists; and Reed was told that no person would be excluded for political reasons.[29] Bradley of Vermont, who said that the Connecticut delegation was wavering and would be held in line only if Adams promised not to dismiss the Crawfordite Collector at New London, was assured that no man would be turned out for his opinions in the late election.[30] On January 25, it was known that Clay and the majority of the Ohio and Kentucky delegations had declared their intention of voting for Adams.[31] On January 28, the Jacksonian *Columbian Observer* of Philadelphia printed an accusation that the friends of Adams had offered Clay the State Department in return for his support: the accusation was said to have been written by a representative from Pennsylvania. It was a deadly blow: for if Adams were elected, and Clay were to accept the State Department, he would justify the accusation, but he would also justify it if he stayed out of the Administration, for then he would be called faint-hearted. On January 31, Clay published a card in the *National Intelligencer* which called upon the author to reveal his identity; and the moralists of Washington professed to be horrified at this Western habit of summoning a man to a duel through the medium of a newspaper. But alas for Mr. Clay! The anonymous accuser immediately identified himself as George Kremer, a representative from a Pennsylvania Dutch district, "a manager of some originality and boldness," but chiefly distinguished for the crudeness of his manners and the eccentricity of his dress—he habitually wore a leopard-skin coat.[32] Impossible to duel with George Kremer. Besides, it was well known that Kremer was simply not literate enough to have written that rather skillful accusation in the *Columbian Observer*. Mr. Clay's impetuous "card," and his subsequent efforts to have the whole matter investigated in Congress, had merely given the accusation a wider publicity. Two days after Clay's fatal "card" had appeared, Adams made his last and most desperate venture. He called on Martin Van Buren, and told him that a young man whom Van Buren had recommended for the appointment of consul at Santiago, "would be nominated, but *perhaps not till after the election in the House.*" [33]

It was terrible for John Quincy Adams to be entangled politically with a man like Henry Clay. Clay's conscience was a political conscience: it was not necessarily bad or corrupt, it was simply elastic. Clay honestly believed that little good could be expected from a military President (and, Washington and Jackson excepted, American history scarcely contradicts him); and he saw nothing wrong in defeating Jackson by persuading his Congressional colleagues to vote against the recommendation of their own legislature. Nor, knowing that he had something to gain from the election of Adams, would he have persuaded them with less conviction. But Adams's conscience was not political at all. It was, indeed, the great enemy of his political ambitions; and with its unwelcome but persistent help he had managed hitherto to persuade himself that his integrity had been proof against all the evil allurements of public life. His knowledge of the past would have informed him that this was not true, and could not be true, of any statesman; but he had convinced himself that George Washington was the exception. And George Washington was his ideal.[34] Now, however, like a dram-drinker, whose ordinary life is usually spent in dull sobriety, he swallowed one intoxicating expedient after another; and the more intoxicated he grew, the more his doleful inner voice assured him that nothing good would come of it. Those who read his answer to the Committee of the House which came to inform him of his election, know that it is not really ungracious: it is really tragic.

VII

By February, almost everything had been done that could be done. Daniel Webster, dreaming of the Court of St. James, had persuaded the Federalist representatives from Maryland to vote for Adams. Clay had secured Ohio, Kentucky, and Louisiana. Cook of Illinois and Scott of Missouri were still wavering, but wavering towards Adams.[35] The Crawford men, if they could not succeed with their own candidate, were determined to switch to Jackson. By this time, the story that Clay had sold his support in return for a promise of the State Department had spread far beyond the boundaries of Washington and Philadelphia. "I have been in the habit of considering Jackson and Adams as honest men and feel persuasion that they would frown on all improper influence," De Witt Clinton wrote to Stephen Van Rensselaer, a Representative from New York "—but so it is—the acceptance of Office from the person selected as President by the person voting for him, would convey the most odious imputations." [36]

The imputation was obvious; and so, too, was the character of the man to whom it was addressed. Stephen Van Rensselaer was a Federalist who embodied in a very striking manner at least two of the three Federalist virtues —he was rich and he was good: but he was not wise. His was the kind of drowsy mind that records, with a faithful imprecision, the last argument that has been addressed to it. He was supposed to be undecided between Jackson and Crawford; and since he lived in the same boarding house as Van Buren, McLane of Delaware, and Cuthbert of Georgia, all good Crawfordites, it was believed that his vote would finally go to Crawford. Now the persuasions of Mr. Clay had worked upon the New York delegation to this effect: seventeen representatives were for Adams, and seventeen were still under the control of Van Buren. This meant that when the delegation polled its members to decide which way its single vote would go, the result would be a deadlock, and no vote would be cast at all. Mr. Adams needed the vote of New York if he was to win on the first ballot; and if he could not win on the first ballot, it was known that Maryland would desert him on the second, that other states would follow, and that he would never be President.[37] All seemed to depend upon that upright but fuzzy-minded old gentleman, Stephen Van Rensselaer of New York; as late as February 4, in spite of his known aversion, Van Rensselaer had gone calling upon John Quincy Adams.[38]

February 9 was the day set for the election in the House of Representatives. Long before noon, the chamber was crowded; not only with people but with memories. There were men there who recalled the terrors and the savageries of the seven-day contest between Jefferson and Burr, a quarter of a century before. As a Constitutional device, the election of a President by the House might not survive a second ordeal of that kind. "At ten minutes before twelve, a North Carolina member, 'with a countenance discovering deep concern,' besought a colleague from Maryland, 'I hope to God you may be able to terminate the election on the first ballot.' " [39]

That morning, at breakfast, Van Rensselaer had assured his fellow lodgers that all was well: nothing could induce him to vote for Adams. He drove to the Capitol; he was seized upon by Clay, and, in the privacy of the Speaker's room, was formidably confronted with Daniel Webster. If he did not vote for Adams, said Clay and Webster, and thus assure a decision on the first ballot, chaos would follow. What could one old landowner do against two of the most persuasive voices in American history? He staggered away into the Hall of Representatives and, passing McLane of Delaware, told him of his agony of mind. The rest may be simply folklore: how Van Rensselaer, when the New York delegation began to ballot for its choice, bent his head in prayer for guidance and, the prayer ended, saw at his feet an Adams ballot; how he took this for heavenly answer and hurriedly dropped it into the New York box. This was the story that, in his old age, Van Buren remembered as coming from Van Rensselaer himself.[40] Van Rensselaer had another version. "Dear Sir," he wrote to Clinton on February 10. "The long agony is over. M. Adams was elected on the first ballot. Mr. Clay's combination could not be resisted and to allay the excitement we agreed to vote for Adams. . . . I hope his administration will be more fortunate than his Father's and more liberal." [41]

Whether it was by prayer or by persuasion, the "good and true gentleman, Patroon Van Rensselaer" cast the decisive vote for Adams. When the results of the first ballot were announced by the tellers, Daniel Webster and John Randolph, it was revealed that Adams had received the votes of thirteen states, Jackson of seven, and Crawford of four.[42] "It was impossible to win the game, gentlemen," said John Randolph too loudly. "The cards were packed." [43] Blandly, Mr. Speaker Clay rose in his seat and declared that: "John Quincy Adams, having a majority of the votes of these United States, is duly elected President of the same."

VIII

And so, when the House Committee came to inform him of his good fortune, John Quincy Adams received the news with anguish. He had been elected by methods he thought deplorable, and with which, to his inmost horror, he had personally involved himself. Moreover, the understanding with Mr. Clay was still incomplete. That night, at Mr. Monroe's levee, all the leading figures in the drama were present. Clay walked about with a smiling face and a fashionable belle on each arm; and there was Van Rensselaer, "poor man his messmates wouldn't speak to him"; and Adams, upon whose face an Englishman who was present professed to see an "air of low cunning & dissimulation, which I believe has not been much belied by the course of his political career." [44] At length Adams and Jackson came face to face. The General had a lady on his arm, but, reaching out a hand to his success-ful rival, he said: "How do you do, Mr. Adams? I give you my left hand, for my right as you see is devoted to the fair; I hope you are very well, sir." It was gallantly done. "Very well, sir," answered Adams, seizing the General's hand, "I hope Gen. Jackson is well." [45] Since the days when Secretary Adams had written his great letter to Erving in defense of General Jackson, the two men had held each other in great respect; these were the last friendly words that either was to speak to the other in all the many days that were left to them.

IX

On February 11, at four o'clock, Adams called on the President, and gave him to understand that the State Department had already been offered to Henry Clay. Monroe felt that this precluded him from giving any advice; but he spent a sleepless night, turning many things over in his mind. Had not the people of Kentucky preferred Jackson to Adams? Was this not true of other Western states, whose delegations had been persuaded to vote for Adams? Would Adams construe Monroe's silence as meaning that he ap-proved the selection of Henry Clay? This latter consideration bore so heavily upon the President that on the morning of February 12 he sent Major-General Jacob Brown to Adams, "to make known to him, the public sentiments respecting it." [46] Brown was unduly tactful, and never hinted to the Secretary that he was Monroe's emissary; instead, he suggested that the State Department should be offered to De Witt Clinton, and was told that Mr. Clay had already been given the first refusal of it.[47] On Febru-ary 14, Adams called on Monroe again, and informed him that Clay had accepted his offer; and the President, courteous to the end, uttered no word of criticism.

Ever since the election in the House Jackson's behavior had been that of a man who considered himself honestly beaten and who held no grudges. He suspected Henry Clay, no doubt—who did not?—but he did not nurse his suspicions, and probably would have been glad enough to discover that they were unfounded. When he heard the news, however, he was more angry than astonished. "So you see," he wrote to Major Lewis, "the Judas of the West has closed the contract and will receive the thirty pieces of silver. his end will be the same." [48] Long before John Quincy Adams, drawn and melancholy after two successive sleepless nights, was driven to the Capitol for his inauguration, the whole West had taken up the cry.[49]

X

The accusation that he had obtained the State Department by "bargain and corruption" was one that Henry Clay refuted over and over again. Indeed, it might be said that he spent the rest of his life in the effort to argue it away. Nowadays, we readily admit that "corruption" is not a word that can be used lightly about men like Adams and Clay; and that if corruption existed, it was the corruption that is inseparable from all political arrangements. To condemn the two statesmen for their understanding of January 9 is really to make an *ex post facto* judgment . . . one might as well condemn them for criminal complicity in the Fall of Man. But it was precisely this element in the situation—this intrusion of human fallibility into high affairs of state—that distressed and horrified John Quincy Adams, who never could forgive himself for being a man of the world. Believing as he did that the election of Jackson would be a calamity, that he himself was fittest for that high office, and that Clay's presence in the State Department would give his Administration both stability and symmetry, he might have soothed his conscience with these beliefs if that organ had been amenable to persuasion. But his conscience was his infirmity, and his conduct of the Administration had, in that respect, a purely clinical significance: it is one long testimony to the weakening after-effects of the Presidential fever.

As for Henry Clay, he was genuinely surprised when the "bargain and corruption" clamor—which he had perhaps anticipated—did not die down. From his point of view, not to have accepted the State Department would have been a confession of weakness. Worse still, it would have been a betrayal of all his followers. Having told himself that Adams was the best of the three candidates, was it not his duty to use all his influence on Adams's behalf, and, after succeeding in his endeavors, was he then to stigmatize the Administration by declining to have any part of it? [50] Naturally, he hoped to become the ruler of the Republican Party, and the successor to Adams; it was here that he made what must be called a fatal miscalculation.

He was a popular man who placed himself in a highly unpopular light; and who did this deliberately, one might almost say wantonly. His mind was fundamentally conservative, and he fell victim to that peculiarly conservative form of "hubris" which consists in flouting popular opinion in the belief that popular opinion is something that registers the decisions of its leaders but rarely makes its own. Political democracies frequently encourage this belief, sometimes to the ruin of those who hold it. And Henry Clay's act of "hubris" was followed in due course by the classical nemesis, approaching in a most unclassical form. "Expired at Washington," said one Jacksonian newspaper, "on the ninth of February, of poison administered by the assassin hands of John Quincy Adams, the usurper, and Henry Clay, the virtue, liberty, and independence of the United States." [51] If he read this passage, as no doubt he did, Henry Clay probably dismissed it as cant; but cant which happens to express a profoundly popular sentiment is very dangerous. When Clay tampered with the delegations of Kentucky, Louisiana, and Ohio he was going against all the signs and portents of the election of 1824. He was not, to be sure, the only guilty man. Daniel Webster had persuaded Maryland to vote for Adams, though seven of its eleven electoral votes had been given to Jackson.[52] North Carolina, with all its fifteen electoral votes committed to Jackson, had switched its vote in the House to Crawford.[53] If the election of 1824 had a meaning, it was an attack upon the old political machines, the politicians with a vested interest in the past, the stubborn supporters of the reactionary and the out-of-date. When Jackson, the popular candidate, was defeated in the House, it seemed as if these old-line politicians had brought about his defeat; as if Henry Clay, by accepting the State Department, had openly proclaimed himself their leader and exemplar; as if he had deliberately mocked the feelings of "the people" of the United States—the debtors, the small farmers, the mechanics, the men with little property or none, now visibly crowding together upon the verge of national politics, ready to break in. It is true that Henry Clay was loved in the years that followed; but was he ever forgiven for his tragic offense in 1825? Or should one just say that he lusted for the Presidency too openly and too violently ever to have been allowed to have it? There is, after all, a thin but very marked line between political ambition and political concupiscence.

CHAPTER TWO

The Perilous Experiment

WHETHER we take John Quincy Adams's Administration to be the solution to the theme of Monroe's policies, or look at it as an unsuccessful coda to the Era of Good Feelings, it must be admitted that, in either case, it got completely out of hand. It was intended to be played, as it were, *adagio* and ended by becoming an agitated *prestissimo*. Under these circumstances, its values for us are not analytical but narrative and preceptive. It tells a story; it offers a homily; it requires but a brief relation.

I

In forming his Cabinet, Adams attempted to be conciliatory. Vice-President Calhoun's friend, Samuel L. Southard, was retained in the Navy Department. John McLean, another Calhoun man, remained as Postmaster General—not a Cabinet post, but a great source of patronage. The War Department went to James Barbour of Virginia, a follower of Crawford, an appointment that for the time being split the powerful Crawford forces in Virginia. As a formality, the Treasury was offered to Crawford and was, of course, refused; it was then given to the protectionist Richard Rush, who had done his duty as Minister to England with such conspicuous success during the days of George Canning's "flirtation" with America.[1] Here conciliation ended, as it was bound to do. With Rush in the Treasury, and Clay in the State Department, the Administration seemed to be weighted in favor of Clay's American System; to be resting on a geographical basis which ran from New England, through Pennsylvania, and into the new industrial regions of the Ohio Valley. Eastern finance, moreover, could comfort itself with the thought that Henry Clay, before entering the State Department, had been one of the attorneys of the Bank of the United States.[2]

346

In his Inaugural Address, Adams announced that he was not very much of a party man. "There still remains," he had said, "one effort of magnanimity, one sacrifice of prejudice and passion, to be made by individuals throughout the nation who have heretofore followed the standards of political party. It is that of discarding every remnant of rancor against each other, of embracing as countrymen and friends, and of yielding to talents and virtue alone that confidence which in times of contention for principle was bestowed only upon those who bore the badge of party communion." [3] This was language which might have been used by James Monroe; but it soon became evident that the effort of magnanimity and the sacrifice of prejudice and passion were to be exacted rather from the friends of Mr. Adams than from his enemies. No group in the Union had helped him more than had the Tallmadge-Weed faction in New York State; but one of his first acts as President-elect was to offer De Witt Clinton the post of Minister to England—Clinton, who had not raised a finger to help him but had favored the cause of Jackson.[4] When Clinton refused, the offer was made to Rufus King, undoubtedly with a view to Federalist support; and King became Minister.[5] Tallmadge, Weed, and their friends were very disturbed at these developments; and when they heard that the federal judgeship of the Northern District of New York was to be given to the Clintonian Alfred Conkling, they hardly knew whether they were standing on their heads or their heels. "Mr. Adams is pursuing a steady course," Tallmadge wrote sarcastically to Weed, "but will he succeed to keep old friends & buy up old enemies? He began by an attempt on Clinton—who sniffed at him—I suppose the price was too low. Next he selected King—a minister recalled by Jefferson for cause as head of the Federalist party—their candidate against Tompkins:—against whom all republicans are committed on printed hand bills to rise up against him—and who is now without influence in either party— Next comes Conklin for District Judge, a quondam federalist, now a mere page to Clinton. . . . His old friends cannot retain the power to give him the votes of this state & make him President a second time as they have the first if he pursues the course he has begun." [6] Weed himself made a trip to Washington to explain to President Adams that he was deserting his friends in New York, and that some post at least equal to the English mission ought to be given to Tallmadge; but though he was warmly received by Henry Clay, whom he had done as much as any man to hurt, he was greeted by the President with a chilling indifference.[7] It is possible that Adams had never known—it is more probable that he was trying to forget— the stratagem which had won him the electoral votes of New York.

It was in this spirit of Olympian detachment that Adams sat down to write his first Annual Message. To many worthy citizens this Message, which was written with the purest motives, stamped his Administration indelibly with the mark of Cain.

II

The draft of this Message was discussed in the Cabinet on November 25, 1825. With the exception of Richard Rush, every Secretary seems to have been filled with dismay. Mr. Adams had recommended a national university, the financing of scientific explorations, the establishment of a uniform standard of weights and measures, the building of an astronomical observatory, the creation of a Department of the Interior, the reform of the patent laws, and the inception of a program of internal improvements on a huge scale. Even Henry Clay, the champion of internal improvements, shuddered away from so bold a design. He did not much care for the national university, or for the new executive department, or for any tampering with the patent laws; but it was in Adams's final enumeration of the purposes of internal improvements and the powers of Congress that he saw the gravest danger. He "approved the general principles," he said, "but scrupled a great part of the details"; his political instincts, which had certainly been dormant during the late elections, were now fully awake.[8]

These were the words that so alarmed Henry Clay and that—coming as they did from a minority President—can be described only as an extraordinary, perhaps a unique, example of the art of suicide by manifesto:

> "If the power to exercise exclusive legislation in all cases whatsoever over the District of Columbia; if the power to lay and collect taxes, duties, imposts, and excises, to pay the debts and provide for the common defense and general welfare of the United States . . . and to make all laws which shall be necessary and proper for carrying these powers into execution—if these powers and others enumerated in the Constitution may be effectually brought into action by laws promoting the improvement of agriculture, commerce, and manufactures, the cultivation and encouragement of the mechanic and of the elegant arts, the advancement of literature, and the progress of the sciences, ornamental and profound, to refrain from exercising them for the benefit of the people themselves would be to hide in the earth the talent committed to our charge—would be treachery to the most sacred of trusts. The spirit of improvement is abroad upon the earth. It stimulates the heart and sharpens the faculties not of our fellow-citizens alone, but of the nations of Europe and of their rulers. While dwelling with pleasing satisfaction upon the superior excellence of our political institutions, let us not be unmindful that liberty is power; that the nation blessed with the largest portion of liberty must in proportion to its numbers be the most powerful nation upon earth, and that the tenure of power by man is, in the moral purposes of his Creator, upon condition that it shall be exercised to ends of beneficence, to improve the condition of himself and his fellow-men. While foreign nations less blessed with that freedom which is power than ourselves are advancing with

gigantic strides in the career of public improvement, were we
to slumber in indolence or fold up our arms and proclaim to
the world that we are palsied by the will of our constituents,
would it not be to cast away the bounties of Providence and
doom ourselves to perpetual inferiority?" [9]

In modern times, such language would be called not merely axiomatic but
mild in the extreme. It was, to be sure, not very tactful of the President to
warn the Congress against being palsied by the will of its constituents, when
great numbers of its constituents already believed that their will had been
palsied by the election of the President. But it was not tactlessness of which
Mr. Adams was now to be accused: it was tyranny. He had described the
abstention of the general government from using all its powers as "treachery
to the most sacred of trusts"; but many Americans, in those simpler days,
believed that the most sacred of trusts consisted in curbing the powers of
the general government. His analogies seemed frightful. When he recommended scientific expeditions and astronomical observatories, he explained
that monarchical governments were far ahead of the United States in these
respects; and he summoned the people to the feast of internal improvements
by citing the example of "the people of Europe and their rulers." [10] With
a mad magic he had resurrected the old dead canard that "all Adamses are
monarchists"; and had informed everyone that he—the son of the President
who had signed the Alien and Sedition Acts—had even more perilous ideas
of consolidation and central government. Thomas Jefferson saw the Message as a new chapter in Federalist history. "Their younger recruits," he
wrote, ". . . having nothing in them of the feelings and principles of '76,
now look to a single and splendid government of an aristocracy, founded on
banking institutions, and moneyed incorporations under the guise and cloak
of their favored branches of manufactures, commerce and navigation, riding
and ruling over the plundered ploughman and beggared yeomanry. This
will be to them a next blessing to the monarchy of their first aim, and perhaps the surest stepping stone to it." [11] Four years later, W. H. Crawford
remembered the Message as being "replete with doctrines which I hold to
be unconstitutional." [12] Thomas Ritchie bitterly assailed it in the Richmond
Enquirer; Francis Preston Blair, who had supported Clay in the Kentucky
Argus of Western America, went over to Jackson; and William Branch
Giles denounced it as leading to "an admitted despotism of the worst tendencies." [13]

In the Cabinet, men like Barbour, Wirt, and Clay had anticipated these
denunciations; and Adams, on his own confession, was persuaded to disregard their warnings only by the enthusiasm of Richard Rush. "Rush approved near the whole. . . ." he wrote. "Thus situated, the perilous experiment must be made." [14] It need only be added that Rush completed the
fabric of the Message by submitting a letter with his annual Report on the
State of the Finances which was nothing less than a dithyramb in honor of
protective tariffs. "By a flourishing state of manufactures," he wrote, "we
shall see rising up a new class of capitalists, rivaling in the extent and use-

fulness of their operations, and in the amount of their gains, the wealthiest of our merchants. . . . When to the complete establishment of manufactures, the internal improvements of the country shall have been superadded, the farmer of the United States cannot but perceive that the measure of his prosperity is made potentially full." [15]

III

The Message was, for its time, Caesarean; but John Quincy Adams, to his honor, was the mildest of Caesars. He had told his Cabinet that it was not very material to him whether he should present his views in his first or his last Annual Message; but simply that, in one Message or the other, "I should feel it my indispensable duty to suggest them." [16] This was the language not of a tyrant, but of a teacher.

The Message, indeed, suggested that one-party government must end either in dictatorship or the dissolution of party; and it seemed to lean toward the former conclusion by showing how the general government might interfere in every phase of the national life. But to support these dictatorial views one would have to indulge in the most downright and savage use of patronage and the power of dismissal. And John Quincy Adams could not bring himself to strengthen his hand by these means: or, at any rate, could not bring himself to do so in the early and formative days of his Administration.[17] When Henry Clay complained that the principal customs-house officers at Philadelphia and Charleston were hostile to the Administration and were appointing hostile subordinates—that the friends of the Administration were forced to contend, not only against their enemies, but against the Administration too—Adams admitted that there was truth in his complaint. But he said that he saw no reason "sufficient to justify a departure from the principle with which I entered upon the Administration, of removing no officer for merely preferring another candidate for the Presidency." Clay returned to the attack with a denunciation of McLean, the Postmaster-General, who was bitterly hostile to the Administration, and who was giving his extensive patronage to men who were known to be its enemies. Adams admitted the truth of this—but McLean, he said, was an efficient Postmaster, he had committed no decisive offense—and he refused to dismiss him.[18] "I will not dismiss, or drop from Executive offices, able and faithful political opponents to provide for my own partisans." [19] Nothing in Henry Clay's life is more pleasant to contemplate than his gentle, courteous, and faithful relations with President Adams—a man who, he was convinced, was bent upon destroying himself and all who had mixed their fortunes with his.

Adams's scruples give some force to his grandson's contention that he was not a political man, actuated by ordinary political feelings, but an "idealistic philosopher." [20] But the immediate past—it was as true of Thomas Jefferson as of the Tsar Alexander—suggested rather strongly that philosophers in government must either cease to be philosophers or cease to govern. President Adams, in the end, ceased to govern.

It is, therefore, of some interest to discover what was really in his mind when he composed his first Annual Message, his "perilous experiment."

"The great effort of my administration," he wrote some years later, "was to mature into a permanent and regular system the application of all the superfluous revenue of the Union into internal improvement which at this day would have afforded high wages and constant employment to hundreds of thousands of laborers, and in which every dollar expended would have repaid itself fourfold in the enhanced value of the public lands. With this system in ten years from this day the surface of the whole Union would have been checkered over with railroads and canals. It may still be done half a century later and with the limping gait of State legislature and private adventure. I would have done it in the administration of the affairs of the nation. . . . [But] the Sable Genius of the South saw the signs of his own inevitable downfall in the unparalleled prosperity of the North, and fell to cursing the tariff, and internal improvement, and raised the standard of free trade, nullification and state rights." [21]

The theory he strove to perfect had been advanced by George Washington in the days of the Potomac Company. It was a topographical theory, which proclaimed that if the American community was to have the energy to cohere it must be the product of a social system resting on converging highways—specifically upon the Ohio and Potomac Rivers connected by a canal. This would have turned the city of Washington into the center of American exchanges, industry, and thought. The conditions necessary to the health of this theory were removed one by one: by the Presidency of Washington, which forced him to sever his connection with the Potomac Company; by the existence of a natural break in the Appalachians, which was bound to produce the great competing highway of the Erie Canal; and, above all, by the invention of the cotton gin, which decreed that Virginia should not become an industrial state but a slave-selling one. [22]

IV

The idealistic philosopher, subjected to political analysis, was doomed to undergo a dismal metamorphosis. Adams himself, it is true, sincerely believed that his Creator thought according to certain fixed laws, which were called scientific laws: "that these laws may be discovered by human intelligence and when discovered may be adapted to human uses." [23] This mechanistic faith rested on the assumption that a law, discovered and stated through human agencies, implies a lawgiver willing to abide by these discoveries and statements: or conversely, that Nature always obeys the "law" of nature. The fallacy of trusting to legislative analogies is tragically demonstrated in the life of a man like Adams, truly a good man, who, when his Creator's will—as expressed in the first Annual Message—was abused and ridiculed by the American people, began to lose faith in his Creator. [24]

The American people did not and could not share the President's theology. His Message rested upon the public lands—"the richest inheritance [he said, years later] ever bestowed by a bountiful Creator upon any national community"—as a source of revenue with which to finance his public improvements. He did not, it is true, suggest any enhancement of their price; but his diary shows how bitterly he opposed any effort to cheapen them.[25] He remembered his land schemes with particular regret in 1838 when the mood of the House of Representatives seemed to him "something akin to the thirst of the tiger for blood . . . in the rapacity with which the members of the new states fly at the public lands." Were not these members all enormous speculators and land-jobbers, and their constituents all settlers, or tame and careless spectators of the pillage?[26] But how was he to prevent the contractor and the enterpriser and the speculator from descending with an equal rapacity upon his plan for a huge scheme of roads and canals? He thought himself that the general government—or at least its executive branch—should be the very vicar upon earth of his mechanistic Deity, dispensing justice and contracts in the most pure and implacable manner. But it seemed unlikely that a President who would not dismiss a hostile Postmaster-General, because he had scruples against judging his own cause in his own favor, would ever create so formidable an entity.

Certainly the American people in 1825 did not share his views about the functions and majesty of the general government. It contented itself with laughing at his description of astronomical observatories—"these light-houses of the skies"—but underneath this laughter there lay a profound suspicion.[27] To finance a scheme of internal improvements through the public lands meant raising the price of those lands; and would not this deter the poor man from pioneering into the West and throw him into a pool of cheap labor in the East, where he would lie at the mercy of the industrialist? And of an industrialist who was to become the most powerful man in the country through the help of protective tariffs? President Adams mentioned protective tariffs only indirectly in his first Annual Message; but here, as we have seen, he allowed his Secretary of the Treasury to speak for him. Mr. Rush's Treasury Reports grew more flagrantly industrial until, in the 1827 report, he said as much in dispraise of the pioneer—as a consumer of capital and a drain on the labor market—as any man could have said without being hounded from office. Of this report, Adams wrote in his diary: "It will, of course, be roughly handled in and out of Congress. But the policy that it recommends will outlive the blast of faction and abide the test of time."[28] Adams said in after years that he was no worshiper of the tariff.[29] During his Presidency he permitted Richard Rush to do the worshiping for him.[30] In spiritual life, there is a great difference between worship in person and worship by proxy: in political life, the distinction is scarcely visible.

One cannot argue with the statement that John Quincy Adams, as President, misunderstood democracy. He believed that he could bring about a marriage between the democratic theory of equality and his scientific plans for collective administration. The American people believed that it was not a marriage but a rape. His planned economy—his policy of conservation—was out of place in those simple and expanding times. In spite of his high ideals and his pure motives, he had announced himself the President, not of the whole country, but of its industrial and financial classes. He had completed the work Monroe had so unwillingly begun: he had underwritten the American System of Henry Clay.[31]

Considering the dubious circumstances surrounding his election, and the fearful impact of his Message, one might say that the story of John Quincy Adams's Administration was written—even to the word "Finis"—in the first year.

CHAPTER THREE

Blifil and Black George

THE most vehement assault upon the principles of the First Annual Message was delivered in the Senate on March 30, 1826. The speaker was John Randolph of Roanoke, and the speech was—it was only to be expected from such an orator—wandering, far-fetched, and brutal. For John Randolph, more than any of his contemporaries, had the gift of divining, not so much the logical weakness in an enemy's position, as the emotional terrors that could be brought to bear upon it. He was an alarmist, who brought to his task a certain amount of genius, a good deal of madness, and something that, in combination with both, was more terrifying than either—a great deal of sincerity. And this sincerity, in turn, made itself felt in those intelligent and concentrated phrases which, out of the cloudy irrelevancies of his oratory, dropped upon his opponents like thunderbolts.

John Randolph would appear in Congress dressed in riding clothes, with a riding whip in his hand, and followed by a little Negro boy carrying a jug of porter; and he would often stride up and down as he made his speeches, accompanying his more hateful words with a smack of the whip against his boot. This behavior was not appreciated by Northern Congressmen, when it came, as it did, from a man who owned nearly four hundred slaves.

In appearance, Randolph was tall and slim and, from a distance, singularly boyish: on closer inspection, his parchment face was seen to be lined with a thousand fine wrinkles, so that at times he resembled a mummy whom some transient demon had animated with a violent and pointless energy. But in the midst of his wildest speeches there would be inserted a passage of invective, exact, pointed, and terrible; or a paragraph of exquisite construction; or a phrase so brilliantly apt as to remind his hearers that however close he may have been to madness (and he lived in constant fear of it), he had not lost his command of method. Except for a brief stay in the Senate, from 1825 to 1827, his career was spent in the House of Representatives—where he was feared and hated. But it must be admitted, too, that he was sometimes loved.

For this strange Virginian could inspire his friends with affection and with faith. In his private life, he often showed that genial and simple courtesy which was typical of Virginians at their best; when his face would light up with an irresistibly sweet expression, his voice—so shrill and piercing when he was angry—would grow almost musical, and his flashing dark eyes would soften into candor and mildness. Men like Nathaniel Macon, whose friendship was not easily given, were his friends for life. To most of the world, however, he was arrogant and posturing; or shy, crabbed and morose; or insanely irrelevant; or a sadistic dialectician, who could ring the changes of torture on a human victim with a skill worthy of a Grand Inquisitor. The miseries of his school days under Walker Maury, the illness that deprived him of the chance of normal relations with a woman, the scandal that his brother Richard brought upon the family—all these were fragments in the portrait of a tormented human being, whom neither his friends nor his enemies understood, who was so brilliant, so cruel, and so bewildered, who was so tender to his relatives, and who lived his whole life in the flickering light of what he conceived to be the truth.[1]

And what he conceived to be the truth was contained, politically, in the dogmas of Old Republicanism. Or, if not contained, at any rate protected by them. He was not a philosopher, or a scholar, or a jurist: still less was he a simple agrarian. He clung passionately to the fundamental tenets of Old Republicanism: that political power tends to grow at the expense of human liberty; that human liberty on the American continent depended upon resistance to the supreme central power called national sovereignty; and that this resistance could best be organized by supporting the individual states in the exercise of all their reserved rights. But he construed human liberty as meaning liberty for the Virginian gentleman and slave-holder to pursue his own way of life without interference; and his hatred of despotism, though deep and sincere, was somewhat akin to that of an English Whig—it was a hatred of despotism which had, for its ultimate purpose, the protection of an aristocracy. Thus the doctrine of State Rights became with him, not the doctrine of human liberty, but the rationale of chattel slavery. It was true that he abominated slavery; but it was also true that slavery was inseparable from his way of life. He desired the political mirror always to reflect the same images in the same exact relationships: like other and very different men—like Tecumseh, the Indian warrior, like Castlereagh, the English diplomat—he sought to impose static principles upon dynamic events. This fallacy, working upon a temperament as unstable as his, drove him almost to madness. One cannot be a political Joshua, forever commanding the sun to stand still in the heavens, without being horribly disturbed by its refusal to do so. Nor, by perpetually prophesying doom to those who believe in change, can one fail, in the end, to be a prophet.

I

It was as a prophet that John Randolph made his speech of March 30, 1826. President Adams's First Annual Message had naturally struck him as a mass of dangerous and threatening innovations; while for the President himself he entertained an aversion which exceeded even the distaste he felt for the President's father. "The cub," he said, "is a greater bear than the old one." [2] Ever since that distant day in New York, when John Adams had taken his seat as vice-president, and the Adams coachmen had thrust his brother Theodoric Randolph—"a mere skeleton, worn out with excesses"—away from the arms emblazoned on the vice-presidential coach, John Randolph had made the Adams family the very embodiment of despotism.[3] He called it "the American House of Stuart," but he spoke these words with a sneer: to him the Adamses were not only despots but upstarts. As for Henry Clay, in John Randolph's mind he was something even more objectionable—an ex-Virginian, a slave-holding gentleman from Kentucky, who had become a renegade from the one way of life by engineering the Missouri Compromise, and by giving his name to the American System. The combination of Adams and Clay was peculiarly dreadful to John Randolph; and the circumstances of Adams's election, followed so soon by the heresies of the Annual Message, filled him with a terror that was inevitably transformed into terrorism. He waited for his opportunity, and he did not have to wait long.

President Adams, having accepted an invitation to send representatives to the Congress of American Republics soon to assemble at Panama, met with an unexpected resistance in the Senate. At the moment, it is enough to say that Senator Van Buren of New York offered two rather mischievous resolutions on February 15, 1826, which requested the President to state whether all the documents submitted by him might be made public, or only a portion of them; and to specify which portion, if any, must remain confidential.[4] The President's reply was anything but tactful. "In answer to the two resolutions of the Senate of the 15th instant," he wrote, "marked executive, and which I have received, I state respectfully that all the communications from me to the Senate relating to the Congress at Panama have been made, like all other communications upon executive business, in confidence, and most of them in compliance with a resolution of the Senate requesting them confidentially. Believing that the established usage of free confidential communication between the Executive and the Senate ought for the public interest to be preserved unimpaired, I deem it my indispensable duty to leave to the Senate itself the decision of a question involving a departure hitherto, as far as I am informed, without example, from that usage, and upon the motives for which, not being informed of them, I do not feel myself competent to decide." [5] The Senate's motives were undoubtedly questionable; but it was hardly statesmanlike of Adams, at this juncture, to call them into question.

The arguments and protests that followed this message must be noticed separately; but they had scarcely died away when Senator Branch of North Carolina reopened the whole quarrel by combating the President's cautious assertion that he had the right to appoint Ministers independently of the Senate.[6] His speech contained a more direct assault upon Adams. "He came into office in opposition to three-fourths of the American people, in opposition to seventeen or eighteen states out of the twenty-four. He came in by the prostration of our dearest principles. He came in by the total disregard of the right of instruction, the basis of a Republic. He came in, sir, in opposition, not only to the sovereign will of the people, but he overcame the most formidable of all difficulties: He came in in opposition to the will of the Representatives too." [7] It was now John Randolph's turn. A week or two before, sitting in his room at "Dawson's" on Capitol Hill, Randolph had told Josiah Quincy that of all writers Henry Fielding best held the mirror up to nature. "His characters are flesh and blood. There are Blifil and Black George types of character repeated in every age." [8] With these two types for a text, John Randolph rose to his feet on March 30. People used to say in those days that he was more than half demented; but demented or not, he was certainly demoniacal. "Our name, too, is Legion," he began, appropriately enough. Then, his voice growing shriller and shriller, he began to ramble from one topic to another. He acknowledged no nation, only a Confederate Republic— The Administration's internal improvement program was an attempt to buy up Congress with its own money— Now that Judas had received his thirty pieces of silver, let him buy a potter's field with them in which to inter the Constitution— He himself had known about the Adams-Clay bargain as far back as January 1824— Old President Adams was the Apostle of Monarchy. Thus, by degrees, he approached his text for the day. "Sir, in what book is it—you know better than I—in what parliamentary debate was it, that, upon a certain union between Lord Sandwich, one of the most corrupt and profligate of men in all the relations of life, and the sanctimonious, puritanical Lord Mansfield, and the other ministerial leaders—on what occasion was it, that Junius said, after Lord Chatham had said it before him, that it reminded him of the union between Blifil and Black George?" * Vice-President Calhoun, gazing impassively at the speaker, betrayed no surprise at this monstrous innuendo. Randolph went on to utter what must still be called the strangest accusation ever to be made on the floor of the Senate. He declared that the Colombian and Mexican invitations to the Panama Conference had not, in fact, existed at all: that, with the connivance of the President, they had been forged in the State Department; that "they have the foot-prints and the flesh-marks of the style of that office, as I shall show on a future occasion." Even then, he said, he would not have opposed the President's right to hold a confidential communication with the Senate, if it had not been for the President's mes-

---

* In Fielding's *Tom Jones*, Blifil is a canting hypocrite; Black George is a blackguardly gamekeeper, who has, however, something of a kind heart.

sage of February 16, with its suggestion that the Senate's motives were bad. "That moment did I put, like Hannibal, my hand on the altar, and swear eternal enmity against him and his politically. . . . Here I plant my foot—here I fling defiance right into his teeth before the American People. Here I throw the gauntlet to him and the bravest of his compeers to come forward and defend these miserable dirty lines: 'Involving a departure, hitherto, so far as I am informed, without example, from that usage, and upon the motives for which, not being informed of them, I do not feel myself competent to decide.' Amiable modesty! . . . In spite of the remonstrances of my friends, I went away, not fearing that anyone could doubt what my vote would have been had I staid. After twenty-six hours exertion, it was time to give in. I was defeated, horse, foot, and dragoons—cut up—and clean broke down—by the coalition of Blifil and Black George—by the combination, unheard of till then, of the puritan with the black-leg." [9]

Any reader of *Tom Jones* would rather be compared to Black George than to Blifil: it was the word "blackleg" that Henry Clay found insupportable. He challenged Randolph to a duel, and Randolph, waiving his privilege not to be held responsible for words uttered in debate, accepted the challenge in "brief, terse, and superlatively decorous language." The two men met on April 8, on the right bank of the Potomac, within the state of Virginia. Randolph had privately determined not to fire at Clay: in this way, he argued, he would not be violating Virginia's statute against dueling, nor would he be waiving his Senatorial right to say what he pleased in debate. The argument was eccentric, but so was the duelist. When he reached the dueling ground, he had changed his mind, having heard that the Secretary of State was determined to kill him.[10] At the first exchange of shots, both men missed. Thomas Hart Benton, who had come as a spectator and conciliator, hurried out of the woods where he had hidden himself, and demanded that the duel should cease. Clay brushed him aside: "This is child's play," he said angrily. Randolph agreed that they must shoot again; but he whispered to Benton that he did not intend to return Clay's fire. And so he stood calmly while Clay put a bullet through the skirt of his long white flannel overcoat. Then, firing into the air, Randolph threw his pistol away and came forward with his hand outstretched. "You owe me a coat, Mr. Clay," he said. Clay grasped his hand. "I am glad that the debt is no greater," he replied. The two men, fundamentally so generous, had probably never liked each other so well.[11]

But if Clay owed Randolph a coat, Randolph owed Clay a reputation. The words "Blifil and Black George . . . the puritan with the black-leg" were never forgotten.

II

When we claim, as perhaps we may, that Randolph spoke in the Senate in a prophetic vein, it is because most prophets have, not only a skill in invective, but a deep attachment to the past. Their predictions are founded, as often as not, upon this attachment; and their warnings against the following of new paths are generally predicated upon the hypothesis that safety lies only in the old ones. Randolph was hardly a Hannibal, but he might have been a Habbakuk. His language was dreadful; but had he not summoned up all the wonderful faithfulness of Old Republicanism to bear witness against the new Administration? Politically, this faithfulness was a dead letter; yet it lingered—and still lingers—in the American conscience as a warning against the misuse of power.

Old Republicanism alone could have made little impression upon the Administration. But Old Republicanism was willing to make allies; and Randolph, when he made his speech of March 30, was simply in the forefront of a coalition that was gradually forming itself against Adams. It was composed of the followers of Calhoun and Jackson, and the Northern and Southern friends of Crawford; and its leading spirit was Martin Van Buren of New York.

Ever since his defeat over the electoral vote in the New York legislature, Van Buren had determined upon the ruin of Adams. And Van Buren, though he had been badly outwitted by Thurlow Weed, was still one of the most astute political managers in the country. He was a deadly opponent, who assassinated quietly and with a smile. Often it was not until his designs had succeeded that his victims realized who had been responsible for their downfall. He "rowed to his object with muffled oars," said John Randolph, in one of his happiest phrases.[12] When all was over, Van Buren would greet his enemy with the utmost kindness; or, if he himself chanced to be defeated, without any signs of chagrin. He was one of those detached personages who can separate the social from the political in everyday life. Short, plump, flaxen-haired, beautifully dressed, he was a poised, a charming, a witty companion; and no man realized that he was preyed upon by the gnawing conviction that he had been insufficiently prepared for public life. A man of humble birth, he was largely self-educated and had never gone to college.[13] This feeling of inadequacy may account for a certain lack of originality in his political thinking: even at the end of his career, when his practices as a statesman had carried him far beyond the Jeffersonian pale, he contented himself, as a thinker, with a dry repetition of the Jeffersonian dogmas. It may account in some measure for his singular unwillingness ever to commit himself. "Mr. Knower, Mr. Knower," an Albany wool merchant once said to Benjamin Knower, at the conclusion of one of Van Buren's tariff speeches, "that was a very able speech." "Very able," replied Knower. There was a pause. "Mr. Knower," said a wool merchant, "on what side of the tariff question was it?" With a characteristic relish, Van Buren often told this story against himself.[14]

Van Buren had already given signs that he was to be something more than a political manager; that he had dreams of becoming a statesman; and that his political creed was to be a liberal one. He had fought for the end of imprisonment for debt; and he had fought for the extension of the suffrage. His Albany Regency, though its behavior in 1824 was anything but liberal, usually favored the small farmer and the poor man. He was still one of Crawford's Radicals, and had not yet made up his mind whether or not he would give his support to Andrew Jackson; he was merely determined that Adams should never be President again. He realized that the House of Representatives, by voting John W. Taylor into the Speaker's chair, was safe for the Administration until the next election. But the Senate was less friendly. In the Senate, therefore, this plump and smiling Cassius made his preparations for the assassination of the most vulnerable of Caesars.

III

The Panama Conference gave him his first opportunity. In the first place, he could argue that the President should not have accepted an invitation to it without asking for the advice and consent of the Senate. In the second place he could contend, or get others to contend for him, that the Panama Conference was not the sort of gathering to which the United States should send plenipotentiaries.

The idea of a Conference was originally Bolivar's. Simon Bolivar was certainly the most Byronic figure ever to exist outside the pages of Byron. He had, it is true, few if any of the Byronic traits: he was neither scornful nor melancholy nor detached. He was no Childe Harold, though he might have been a Mazeppa. But he was Byronic in the sense, at least, that he stood magnificently silhouetted against the ruins of empire and the wonders of nature. His individual exploits were on so huge, so heroic, so almost impossible a scale that the world is still amazed at them; his statecraft, though its objectives were and always will be debatable, had the merit of a grand design; and his life, from its violent alternations of triumph and disaster down to the smallest personal details, from its aristocratic beginning to its embittered end, was a supreme evocation of the Age of Romance. But if the word "Byronic" can be applied to so vital a hero, then one might go further and say that, like Byron himself, Bolivar concealed a core of robust eighteenth-century realism beneath his panoply of romantic attributes. He was convinced that the Polignac Memorandum, backed by the British fleet, was of more consequence to Latin America than the Message of President Monroe; and he was not anxious for the United States of America to take a seat at his new version of the amphictyonic council. Moreover, the Liberator's genius was more suited to the idea of liberation than to the concept of liberty, which is apt to demand that Liberators should be self-effacing; and it may be that he hoped to exercise over his projected Conference a monocratic rule that would have been quite impossible if representatives from the northern Republic had been seated there.[15]

But Bolivar was busy in Arequipa from May 1825 to January 1826; and it was in his absence and behind his back that the governments of Colombia and Mexico put out feelers to the United States, with regard to a possible attendance at Panama.[16] These invitations were delivered by the Ministers of Colombia and Mexico on November 2 and 3, 1825. The Mexican note made a rather pointed reference to the principles of the Monroe Doctrine, as a protection against European interference with Latin America. The Colombian note tactfully admitted that some questions to be aired at the Conference would be of interest to Latin-American belligerents; but it suggested that the United States might profitably join in the discussion of the following topics: the clarification of international law, the possibilities of an inter-American alliance based on Monroe's Non-Colonization principle, the abolition of the slave trade, and the correct behavior to be adopted towards the black Republic of Haiti. The Colombians had also taken the precaution of approaching the British government with the suggestion that the presence of a British representative at Panama might help to create an equilibrium between the New World and the Old. This effort to play the British off against the Americans—or the Monroe Doctrine against the Polignac Memorandum—was well received by George Canning, who wanted nothing less than a division between the two worlds.[17]

To the Americans, as a recent and illuminating study has shown, the two notes could only have meant that Mexico and Colombia wished to convert the Monroe Doctrine into a "conditional multilateral alliance among the states of the Western Hemisphere." [18] The question was: could the United States be usefully represented at Panama while avoiding such an open breach with the past? As Secretary of State, John Quincy Adams had been what today we should call an isolationist: he had adapted his remarkable diplomacy to the needs of the continental republic as it strode westward, and had steadily guarded it from the distractions and pitfalls of foreign alliances. He had never departed from the sacred text of George Washington's Farewell Address. He had, however, read that text with more care than was usually bestowed upon it; and he knew that George Washington had admitted that the nation, as it grew stronger, could disregard his warnings.[19] Certainly there was nothing in the Address to preclude an understanding with the Latin-American republics; there had been no Latin-American republics when the Address was written. And there was something very attractive in the thought, so shrewdly suggested by Colombia, that the United States might impose upon the whole Western Hemisphere its principles of maritime, belligerent, and commercial law. There was also the chance that Colombia and Mexico, in their campaign against Ferdinand VII and the Holy Allies, might attempt to liberate or colonize the island of Cuba; and Adams believed that Cuba should remain Spanish until the time had come for it to join itself to the United States. The Cuban question was to be aired at the Panama Conference. Without wishing to commit himself to a system of American alliances, Adams decided that United States representatives should be seated at the Conference. We cannot question the wisdom of such a decision. On December 26, 1825, he submitted to the Senate the names of Richard C. Anderson of Kentucky and John Sergeant of Pennsylvania as Envoys Extraordinary and Ministers Plenipotentiary to the Assembly of American Nations. In his accompanying message, he explained that the United States would take no part in deliberations of a belligerent character, and that no alliances would be contracted. "We have laid the foundations of our future intercourse with the southern republics," he wrote, "in the broadest principles of reciprocity and the most cordial feelings of fraternal friendship. To extend those principles to all our commercial relations with them and to hand down the friendship to future ages is congenial to the highest policy of the Union." [20] Adams's views as to the future of Cuba, though Jeffersonian, were not very liberal; but the language of his message to the Senate was quite unexceptionable.

IV

The Senate, however, did not quite see it in this light. The Committee on Foreign Relations was unable to reconcile the President's message with the documents that accompanied it. The President said that he contemplated no alliance, but was it not obvious that an alliance was just what the South Americans had in mind? The President had said nothing about relations with Haiti, nothing about the slave trade, nothing about the dangerous position of Cuba and Porto Rico. On the whole, said the Committee, four of whose members were Southern Senators, it thought that the President's purposes could better be carried out by individual negotiators than by Ministers Plenipotentiary and Envoys Extraordinary to some mysterious and bellicose international congress.[21]

The opposition Senators, led by Martin Van Buren, first attacked the President by passing resolutions to the effect that the Senate ought to act with open doors and to publish documents that had been submitted to it in confidence.[22] It was to these mischievous resolutions that President Adams made his untactful reply, questioning the honesty of the Senate's motives.

Other resolutions, chiding the President for his reply, were submitted by Rowan of Kentucky, Woodbury of New Hampshire, and Holmes of Maine: they were all negatived by a vote of 24 to 19 or 20. The same vote dismissed the Foreign Relations Committee's resolution: "That it is not expedient at this time for the United States to send any Ministers to the Congress of American Nations assembled at Panama." [23] Thus the President was still able to command a majority. The minority of nineteen was not exactly sectional: twelve of its members were from the South; one, Elias Kent Kane of Illinois, had been a proslavery leader in his state's Convention battle of 1824; the rest were Senators from New Hampshire, Maine, New Jersey, Pennsylvania, and New York.[24] It would seem as if a ghostly world was arising against Adams. Was it not the same alliance between Northern and Southern democrats, supported by the same New York-Pennsylvania-Virginia axis, which had brought in Jefferson and Burr in 1800? The debate, however, was monopolized by the Southern opposition, which had already rejected a treaty with Colombia designed to suppress the slave trade; and which had done so because it descried a connection—invisible to less prejudiced eyes—between the suppression of the slave trade and the emancipation of slaves.[25] It now professed to see emancipation written large over the Congress of

Panama. The Senate was familiar with its arguments, but astounded at its language. Men like Randolph of Virginia, Hayne of South Carolina, Berrien of Georgia, and White of Tennessee loaded the Latin Americans with insults, which culminated in White's description of them as "an ignorant and vicious people." As for John Sergeant, who had been nominated as one of the plenipotentiaries at this Congress of emancipators, he was "an acknowledged abolitionist." [26] And, indeed, the choice of John Sergeant—a friend and attorney of the Bank of the United States, an ardent protectionist, and an antislavery leader in the Missouri debates—was not one that would have recommended itself to any Southern legislator.

On March 14, the Senate at length consented to the nomination of Richard C. Anderson by a vote of 27 to 17; of John Sergeant by 28 to 18; and of William B. Rochester of New York, for Secretary to the mission, by 28 to 16.[27] On March 15, Adams sent a special message to the House, requesting appropriations. It was written in his most eloquent vein. It was a masterly summation of every argument that could be devised against an appeal to George Washington's Farewell Address. On April 22, the House voted the necessary forty thousand dollars by an overwhelming 134 to 60.[28] Surely the Administration could pride itself upon its victory. But could it? Before the House could record its vote, John Randolph had made his deadly Blifil-Black George speech in the Senate, and had stood the fire of the Secretary of State. A victory under these conditions was a Pyrrhic affair: like the victor of Asculum, President Adams might well have remarked, "One more such, and we are lost."

V

Vice-President Calhoun had sat through John Randolph's speech like Harriet Martineau's "iron man"; not a flicker of surprise had disturbed his impassive features; not one word of expostulation had escaped his lips. He himself explained that he was not a member of the Senate, that he was merely its presiding officer, and that only another Senator could call a Senator to order. The argument was at least arguable. But some people—and President Adams was naturally among them—decided that Calhoun's silence through the Blifil-Black George speech, with its endless breaches of parliamentary usage, was nothing less than evidence of inveterate enmity to the Administration. On May 1 an article appeared in the Washington *National Journal*, bitterly attacking the vice-president for not exercising a power that was inherent in his office, and for not exercising it because he was "the residuary legatee of General Jackson's pretensions to the Presidency." The article was signed "Patrick Henry," and its style suggested that the author was none other than the President himself. The editor of the *National Journal* was Peter Force, who had established the paper in Adams's interest in 1823; and when Calhoun wrote an answer, under the *nom de guerre* of "Onslow," Force declined to publish it. It appeared in the *Intelligencer* on May 20. "Onslow's" style was as recognizable and as trenchant, and his argument as bitter and sarcastic, as that of "Patrick Henry," who returned to the attack in the *Journal* of June 7. The two kept it up, on and off, until the middle of October. After the edifying duel between the Secretary of State and the Virginia Senator, the public was now treated to the spectacle of the President and the vice-president of the United States blazing away at each other in the Washington newspapers. The spectacle was unprecedented; but by then everything had got out of hand.[29]

CHAPTER FOUR

Burial at Sea

THE Congress of Panama was to meet in June 1826. John Sergeant, who knew something about Panamian summers, absolutely refused to venture his life upon the Isthmus during the hot months. He was given permission to postpone his departure. The brilliant and courtly Richard Anderson did indeed come down from his legation at Bogotá, but he was seized by some tropical pestilence as his steamboat lay grounded on a sand bank near Cartagena: and at Cartagena he died on July 24. Because of this tragic event, no envoy from the United States was present at Panama. The Congress became just another example of the failure of the conference system in the early nineteenth century. Of the American nations invited, only Colombia, Mexico, Peru, and Guatemala appeared. One of the Peruvian delegates, Viduarre, announced in the press: "This will probably be the last attempt to ascertain whether Mankind can be happy. Companions! The field of glory . . . is before us. Our names are about to be written either in immortal praise or in eternal opprobrium." [1] His companions did not share these views. Hastily writing a treaty for a common army and mutual defense, they fled the fever-haunted city, agreeing to meet again in Tucubaya when their respective governments had ratified their work. Only the government of Colombia took the trouble to do so.

There was a British representative at Panama, named Edward J. Dawkins. He had been instructed to obtain the most regular and correct information of the proceedings of the Congress; to let it be known that Great Britain would frown upon any project of putting the United States at the head of an American Confederacy; and to suggest, as forcibly as possible, that the South Americans should adopt those principles of British maritime law—paper blockades, the right of search, the inability of the neutral flag to cover the goods of an enemy, the formidable list of contraband, and so forth—which had done so much to bring about the War of 1812.[2]

Mr. Dawkins, who did not actually attend the formal deliberations of the Congress, but who held a number of informal conferences, interpreted these instructions as meaning that he was to create such misunderstanding as he could between the United States and the Latin Americans. In this he was successful. Ever since a French fleet, in 1825, had appeared in West Indian waters, ostensibly to collect a debt from Haiti, Canning's anxieties about Cuba had arisen all over again. He thought that he could handle the French; though a nation that had prefaced its invasion of Spain in 1823 by announcing that its army had been assembled merely for the purpose of preventing an epidemic of yellow fever from crossing into France might easily assault Cuba on the plea of collecting a debt from Haiti. None the less, what Canning feared chiefly was that the United States might intervene; and these fears were increased by the threats of Colombia and Mexico that they intended to liberate Cuba from the rule of Ferdinand VII. Dawkins told the Mexican and Colombian delegates that Great Britain would not interfere with such a project; but he pointed out that the United States most certainly would, and by force. Let them contrast the ambitions of the United States with the moderation of England! [3] He directed this ingenious argument especially at Pedro Gual of Colombia, whose country was the arsenal of South America, and who of all the delegates was most friendly towards the United States. On the Cuban question, he believed that he had succeeded. He could not, it is true, shake Gual's stubborn fondness for American principles of maritime law; but the Mexican and Peruvian delegations declared that they would have nothing to do with them, and the Guatemalans were divided.[4]

When it came to calling attention to the disparaging remarks of Randolph and Berrien in the Senate; to refuting the story that Great Britain was lukewarm in her efforts to obtain Spanish recognition for the Spanish-Americans; or to pointing out that Adams's message to the House of Representatives gave evidence of a blighting attitude to the aspirations of the Congress—here Dawkins was in his element.[5] His conduct, said Briceño Mendez of Colombia, who had been greatly flattered by his attentions and his mischievous confidences, was "noble, frank and loyal." He was invited to attend the projected meeting at Tucubaya; but his instructions did not cover such a journey; and he returned to London to make his report. His mission had cost the British government sixteen thousand dollars, and was probably cheap at the price.[6]

I

The personal success of Dawkins was superficial; perhaps it was even hollow. The Congress never came to anything. It scarcely survived the death of Anderson, the defection of Sergeant, and the absence of Chile, Brazil, and Buenos Aires; the indifference of Simon Bolivar extinguished it altogether. In January 1827 a few delegates reached Mexico City on their way to

Tucubaya: they went no farther. But, representing the contest between the Monroe Doctrine and the Polignac Memorandum, Dawkins was a suggestive figure. It is true that Canning never sought exclusive commercial privileges in South America and that Adams never seriously considered the organization of an American League of Nations headed by the United States.[7] The issue lay deeper. The Monroe Doctrine was a grave and noble pronouncement, but its strength lay in the future: the Polignac Memorandum was an immediate pledge of British naval assistance, and it was backed by British loans and British manufactures. British exports to South America (Cuba excepted) were at least three times greater than those of the United States.[8] Under these circumstances, Mr. Dawkins was transformed into the herald of a commercial hegemony that Great Britain, the heiress of imperial Spain, was to exercise over Latin America for many years to come.

Territorially, the Monroe Doctrine was still astray in the mysterious immensities of Oregon; economically, it had reached its logical conclusion in the Tariff Act of 1824, and had no more to say for the time being. From the British point of view, it had already said more than enough. Lord Liverpool is the best register of the sensibilities of Liberal Toryism; and Lord Liverpool, in the winter of 1824, had grown very angry. The Non-Colonization principle, followed by a protective tariff, had been too much for him; and he began to remember that Great Britain and the United States were rivals in a navigation controversy. "The views and policy of the North Americans," he said, in language that was (for him) positively menacing, "seem mainly directed toward supplanting us in navigation in every quarter of the globe. . . . Let us recollect that as their commercial marine is augmented, their military marine must proportionately increase." [9] In 1825, Huskisson harshly criticized the United States in the House of Commons.[10] In 1826, George Canning insisted that the British version of maritime rights should be proclaimed at Panama with much of the arrogance of Napoleonic days. This progression indicates that the United States had so agitated Liberal Toryism that its Liberal mask was beginning to slip.

II

But the Congress of Panama, in the story of Anglo-American relations, was little more than a suburban incident. The real issue had already been revealed in 1824, when Richard Rush opened a general negotiation in London with Stratford Canning and William Huskisson. The negotiation was to some extent sweetened for the British by the signing of a Convention on March 13, designed to suppress the African slave trade, and allowing each country the right to search the other's merchant ships under certain very carefully defined conditions.[11] But the Senate refused to ratify this Convention, or, what was much the same thing, ratified it with crippling amendments; and the news of this refusal reached London in June, much to the discomfort of Mr. Rush. In other respects, he was even less successful. He was instructed to discuss the boundary questions that had been left unsettled by the Treaty of Ghent and the Convention of 1818—specifically, the Northeast boundary between Maine and New Brunswick, and the Northwest boundary between the Rockies and the Pacific. The Northeast boundary question had been complicated from the beginning by the language of the definitive Treaty of Peace (1783) between the United States and Great Britain, which had been quite unable to define a boundary of any kind. Arguing from two dissimilar maps, the British and American commissioners had reached a point in 1821 where their different interpretations of the phrases "northwest angle of Nova Scotia" and "northwesternmost head of the Connecticut River" involved, in the first instance, more than seven and a half million acres, and, in the second, a small tract of valuable timberland.[12] In order to arrive at this impasse, they had collected a formidable and quarrelsome miscellany of books, maps, surveys, and documents; they had then adjourned in disgust. Since the whole British Empire demanded a military road between New Brunswick and Quebec across the state of Maine, it was unlikely that Rush would succeed where the two commissioners had failed. He was offered an exchange—the northern portion of the state of Maine to become British, and the Americans to be allowed to navigate the St. Lawrence. He replied that the Americans already had the right to navigate the St. Lawrence—a pretension that angered the British almost as much as the Non-Colonization principle had done; and so the Northeast Boundary remained as mysterious as ever. As to the Oregon boundary, Rush was willing to accept the parallel of 49° from the Rockies to the Pacific. But George Canning was (in the American sense of the term) a continentalist—more so, indeed, than any Foreign Secretary before or after him. He wanted nothing less than the Columbia River from its mouth to the parallel of 49°, and then a line eastward along that parallel to the Rockies— or about half the present state of Washington (including, of course, Puget Sound) with the Columbia thrown in. If subsequent Foreign Secretaries had persisted in this policy, the upshot would have been another Anglo-American war. It remained for Polk's Administration, that stormy reservoir of the ambitions, mistakes, and dreams of these years, to settle the Oregon question; in 1824, Richard Rush left it where it was—a "joint occupation" by Great Britain and the United States.

But it was not, really, the boundary problems that counted in this negotiation. Behind all Rush's discussions with William Huskisson and Stratford Canning there loomed John Quincy Adams's great version of the Freedom of the Seas. Nowadays, the Freedom of the Seas is a concept one examines as one would a graveyard—it is the crowded repository of beautiful dead hopes. In 1824, however, it could be humane and hopeful. John Quincy Adams believed that privateering should be abolished, and that all private property on the seas, neutral or belligerent, should be immune from capture by public cruisers: these great and luminous principles, supported by the old theories of "free ships, free goods," no impressment, no fictitious blockades, limited lists of contraband, and so forth, would have made warfare upon the sea exceedingly unprofitable; and there was little reason to suppose that the world's greatest sea power would look upon them with favor.[13] This does not, of course, detract from their innate nobility, nor weaken the claim that the United States in the 1820's was a leader in the development of a system of free navigation.[14] It is not Mr. Adams's idealism, however, which has to be examined; but rather the weird tempo that was signed upon his efforts to impose it on the British. Here, also, *adagio* became *prestissimo,* to the confusion and defeat of Mr. Adams.

Richard Rush discovered that the British were still immovable on the subject of impressment; that they were indisposed to abandon their compact between the living and the dead because of the ideals of an American statesman. Impressment had been a great source of manpower during Nelson's days—and surely then the British navy had done pretty well. When Huskisson and Stratford Canning made this clear to Richard Rush, he declined to enter upon the general subject of the Freedom of the Seas and turned to a more specific issue—the controversy over the West Indian trade. Here, as has been shown, the American Act of 1823 had imposed certain duties upon British vessels in this trade until such time as the British would grant the United States equal trading rights with the mother country and her dominions; and the British had replied by imposing similar duties upon American cargoes and vessels. Stratford Canning and William Huskisson now declared themselves willing to accept a reciprocal suspension of these duties, if the Americans would only forego their claim to equal trading rights. Richard Rush's instructions, however, did not permit him to agree to this reasonable solution. He demanded complete freedom of intercourse in the West Indies; and this demand, however idealistic it may have been, was scarcely statesmanlike, for the British still believed that their system of colonial preferences was essential to the maintenance of their sea power; and any government in the 1820's that abandoned this system would certainly have been abandoned by the House of Commons.

Mr. Rush persisted, none the less. And so, when at length he returned to England to become Secretary of the Treasury under John Quincy Adams, the United States and Great Britain had not changed their positions. The United States still clung to the word "elsewhere," backed by discriminating duties. Great Britain still continued to lay countervailing duties upon United States vessels entering her ports in North America and the West Indies.

III

When we attempt to assess the importance of the United States in the schemes of George Canning, we have to remember that Canning's greatest work as Foreign Secretary was his successful effort to discredit the Holy Alliance. He had begun this task at Verona; he went on to drive a wedge between Austria and Russia by giving the Greek rebels the status of belligerents; he recognized Brazil without consulting any of his allies. All this occurred between 1822 and 1826; as a result of it he made Tory Great Britain, strange to say, the leader of European liberalism, the champion of nationality. Europe, therefore, occupied the first place in his thoughts. In 1824 he was already a very ill man—the Foreign Office was badly understaffed and British Foreign Secretaries were apt to sicken from overwork—who lay in bed for days at a time, tortured by gout. (He was to die in three years; and this hastening death had already restored to his face, with a mocking irony, some of the sharpness that had marked it in his *Anti-Jacobin* youth.) The United States, having rebuffed his advances with the Monroe Doctrine, might well have become with him (as once with Lord Castlereagh) just another afterthought. In 1824, he had few dealings with Richard Rush, leaving the negotiation to Stratford Canning and William Huskisson.

But George Canning's diplomacy was the diplomacy of early liberalism, which was more concerned with the release of energy than the rights of man; and his foreign policy was the foreign policy of a commercial and industrial country that had become, or was becoming, the center of world exchanges. He was an imperialist who conceived that the termini of the British Empire were India and America; who announced that Singapore (then inhabited only by fisherfolk) was "the *unum necessarium* for making the British Empire in India complete"; and who coveted the Oregon country because of the future prospects of a trade with China.[15] To such a mind, the United States could never be an afterthought. After 1824, the language of the Liberal Tories became prophetic whenever they spoke of the United States. They looked into the future, and conjured up visions of gigantic rivalries. By driving too hard at Great Britain's concept of maritime rights in the negotiation of 1824, John Quincy Adams had put the United States into the position of a challenger to Great Britain's future. It was not the negotiation itself that was at fault; it was the tempo of the negotiation, the thudding persistent effort in 1824 to force from Great Britain the sacrifice of a system that, however outdated, however unpopular with enlightened thinkers, was far too deeply rooted in the past to be plucked out all at once.

IV

When John Quincy Adams became President, Richard Rush's place at the Court of St. James was taken by Rufus King. King was now an old man, nor was he in good health; and, in any case, his hands were tied because he had received no instructions. "My present entry upon the duties of the Department of State," wrote Henry Clay, "and the great pressure of the mass of other business which called for immediate attention, have not allowed me to bestow on those objects the time which is indispensably necessary to the formation of a satisfactory judgment. I am not, therefore, now ready to communicate to you the instructions of the President. . . . I have, therefore, the approbation of the President in requesting that, without waiting for them, you proceed on your voyage.[16] Minister King proceeded on his voyage. Weeks passed, months passed, a whole year passed, and still he had received no instructions. Then he asked to be recalled on a plea of ill health; and so nothing was done.

Henry Clay had accepted the State Department because in those days it carried with it the succession to the Presidency. He was not equipped to be a great or even a good Secretary of State. It is true that the instructions he wrote for the envoys to the Panama Conference—though they may have seemed to the contemporary reader a mere congregation of clichés—have the note of statesmanship: today we can recognize that they were founded upon great and progressive principles; but the writing of these instructions seems to have exhausted his energies.[17] After the Blifil-Black George duel with Randolph, moreover, he realized that he had allied himself to a ruined cause; he grew despondent and sick, and often thought of retiring. His genius, in any case, was social and personal; in the State Department it was in exile, too near and yet too far from its appropriate haunts.

None the less, President Adams could himself have drawn up the instructions to King if he had wished to do so. He seems to have been quite content to let the matter rest. And his passivity was founded upon a natural but fatal misconception. He assumed that the pressure of West Indian interests in Parliament would force the British government to give way on the West Indies issue. He failed to take into full consideration the possibility that the West Indies might be supplied indirectly by way of the French, Danish, and Swedish islands; nor was this all. He was an extraordinarily clearsighted man, but even he could not see that British statesmen were less interested in colonies than they had been. It was true that after the Napoleonic Wars, Great Britain had not restored to their owners the Cape of Good Hope, Mauritius, Demerara, Trinidad, St. Lucia or Tobago; but she had kept these places for strategic rather than commercial reasons.[18] Her most characteristic thinkers were beginning to doubt whether colonies, as colonies, were worth the cost of upkeep; and as for the West Indies, they were dependent upon slave labor, and slavery was growing more and more distressful to the English conscience.[19] India, of course, was in a different category, for India was already a great market for cheap cotton goods; and Canada was treasured for her lumber, fish, and furs. But an expanding industrial economy, with a leaning towards free trade, is not colonially minded; nor does it become so until it has exploited or been denied all the obvious markets —in other words, until it has begun to contract or is in danger of contraction. This did not happen until long after Lord Palmerston's reign at the Foreign Office. Thus, President Adams's hope that George Canning and Lord Liverpool would yield to him on the West Indies question was based on a misunderstanding of the importance of the West Indies to George Canning and Lord Liverpool. He assumed that things were as they had been in 1818 and 1820, when American navigation laws had made such an impression upon the British. Having announced his great theme of the Freedom of the Seas with a full orchestra in 1824, John Quincy Adams now laid down his baton, and waited in triumphant silence for the British to reply.

But much had happened since 1818 and 1820. On the British side, there had been the Parliamentary attack upon the navigation laws, the formation of Lord Liverpool's "economic cabinet," the great Free Trade budgets of 1822 and 1823, and George Canning's flirtation with the United States. On the American side, there had been the "elsewhere" Act of 1823, the Monroe Doctrine, the crippling of the Slave Trade Convention, and the Tariff Act of 1824. It was time for the British to strike back; their reply, when it came, was rude and shocking—and would have been even more so if anyone had been able to understand precisely what it meant.

This reply was prefaced—it was only to be expected—by certain remarks from Lord Liverpool, who was still the touchstone of Liberal Toryism. Lord Liverpool could not have realized that the Senate's amendments to the Slave Trade Convention were simply maneuvers in a Presidential campaign. He assumed that they were directed at Great Britain. The Tariff of 1824, no doubt, was not an immediate threat—American manufacturers were still incapable of supplying America's needs—but it was a promise of future and most drastic prohibitions. He was now both old and ill, and his usual fidgety good humor was often more fidgety than good humored.[20] He was reported in America as having told the House of Lords that European powers should be invited to share with the United States in the West Indian trade, because this would give them an increase of naval power which would be of great service to Great Britain in the event of a war.[21] This strange prevision of a naval Armageddon, with the New World pitted against the Old, might be put down to the irritable fancies of an ill, old man; but it hinted that Liberal Toryism was now ready to chastise the United States.

This chastisement began on June 27, 1825, with an Act "for further regulating the trade of His Majesty's possessions in America and the West Indies, and for the warehousing of goods therein." The Act contained an unprecedented invitation to the countries of Europe, Africa, and Western Asia to compete with the United States in the British West Indies; and it established five free warehousing ports—in Kingston, Halifax, Quebec, St. Johns, and Bridgetown—which would take from the United States some part of its trade with South America. The great object of this Act was to see whether or not the British West Indies could be supplied from sources other than the United States; its secondary object was to demonstrate that the Monroe Doctrine, if its purpose was to establish a political and commercial leadership over the New World, could not possibly succeed.[22] So far, everything was clear enough. Since this Act was repealed on May 26, 1826, we may assume that the British were still open to offers on that date.[23]

Then, on July 5, there came three more Acts which seemed to defy interpretation. The acute and perspicacious Gallatin himself confessed that he was baffled by them; historians have shuddered away from them; and even the most lucid of modern students has failed to elucidate them entirely.[24] If they are mentioned now, it is because they had and have a rather dreadful fascination: they seemed to the contemporary mind to be laboring with some kind of monster, whose shape no man could predict; and to modern observers their convulsions—no other word seems to answer—are part of the obscure birth-pangs of nineteenth-century liberalism.

The first was called "an Act to regulate the trade of the British possessions abroad." [25] Since at first sight it appeared merely to repeat the provisions of the Act of June 27, it might have been taken for another example of the relentless redundancy of admiralty lawyers. In its fourth section, however, it made a distinction between nations with colonies, and nations without them. The latter were required to place the navigation and commerce of the United Kingdom and its possessions upon the footing of "the most favored nation" in their ports. The United States was the only country, not possessing colonies, to have any considerable trade with British possessions; so that this fourth section appeared to be—and presumably was—a direct blow at President Adams.[26] The preamble to this fourth section gave the Act of June 27 a very liberal appearance as regards the export trade between British colonies and European countries; at least, George Canning interpreted it in this light. Lord Stowell, however, sitting in the High Court of Admiralty, handed down a decision that entirely contradicted the language of Canning. Thus, it was quite impossible to discover whether the Act of June 27, as redefined by the first Act of July 5, was or was not a liberal piece of legislation.

This inner confusion was increased by a second Act of July 5, called "An Act for the encouragement of British shipping and navigation," which explained what the law of navigation for the British Empire should be; but in language so imprecise, and with provisions so full of lacunae, that it could be made to support any interpretation whatsoever.[27] Its eleventh section, however, made it clear that goods could not be *imported* into British possession in Africa, Asia, or America in foreign ships, unless these ships were ships of the country of which the goods were the produce and from which they were imported.[28] If Lord Stowell was correct, the Act of June 27 forbade *exportation* of goods from British possessions except in vessels of the country for which they should clear out. There was nothing in this second Act of July 5, however, to give explicit support to Lord Stowell, and much that appeared to contradict him; so that the general effect of these first two Acts of July 5 was to make the navigation law of the British Empire as fluid and stormy as the sea itself.

And then, on the same day, July 5, there appeared a third Act, entitled "An Act to repeal the several laws relating to the customs," which did away with some 450 statutes—some relating to the customs, some to navigation—dating back to the reign of Richard II.[29] To remove so much dead underbrush, so many ancient and intertwined anomalies, and all at one stroke—this was a task for which Liberal Toryism felt itself peculiarly fitted. But it so happened that the 359th section repealed the Act of June 24, 1822, which had been so favorable to the United States.[30] Since the third Act of July 5 was to come into force on July 25, 1826, this meant that American vessels might be prohibited from trading to the West Indies after that date—

if, indeed, they had not already been prohibited by the first Act of July 5, which was to come into force on January 6.

On the whole, the three Acts of July 5, 1825—with all their circumlocutions, all their odd and interminable contradictions—might best be compared to a whirlpool formed by the meeting of two adverse currents. For if any truth can be extracted from such a heaving confusion, it would seem to be that the effort to liberalize the navigation laws in favor of free trade had clashed head on with the effort to use the navigation laws as a weapon against the United States. Such was the effect of Adams's stubbornness during the negotiation of 1824.

The four Acts of June 27 and of July 5 were not communicated officially to the United States. They were, of course, known and studied; and President Adams seems to have reached the conclusion—by no means an unreasonable one—that the British would certainly withdraw by Order-in-Council the reprisals they had threatened by Act of Parliament. January 6 arrived and passed, and nothing had taken place which could make him believe that he was wrong. But he was growing uneasy. Could it be that he had overreached himself; that in his demand for a suspension of colonial preferences he had pushed the British too far? In April, there were complaints in the Senate that the grain-growing states were suffering from these quarrels over the West Indian trade—complaints that were coupled, rather ominously, with eulogies of Mr. Huskisson and his colleagues for "opening the eyes of the world to the advantages of a free trade." [31] Clay had never been quite happy about the uncompromising attitude of the United States; and it may have been his pressure that induced the President at length to agree that the word "elsewhere" must be sacrificed. [32] The sacrifice was laudable, but once again the timing was wrong. When Rufus King was recalled, and Gallatin was asked to go to London in his place, it was agreed that he should demand no more than what the British themselves had wanted in 1824—a reciprocal suspension of alien and discriminatory duties upon vessels, and an American withdrawal of the pretension that the produce of America should be admitted into British colonies upon the same terms as the produce of the mother country and her possessions. [33] Gallatin was one of the most brilliant negotiators that the United States has ever possessed; but what profit or fame or pleasure could he obtain as the agent of surrender? Forgetting his unhappy experiences during the campaign of 1824, his dislike of the government's protective policies, and his longing for retirement, he loyally consented to undertake this thankless task. He set sail in July 1826; arrived in August; and arrived too late. He was met—it was an "unhappy coincidence," said George Canning—by an Order-in-Council, which interdicted trade in United States vessels with *all* British colonies except those in North America; and even this North American trade, whether inland or by sea, was subject to a heavy countervailing duty. It was a terrible blow. Moreover, George Canning absolutely declined to resume the negotiation where Rush had left it off unless the American Congress repealed the "elsewhere" Act of 1823. And so the door was slammed in Adams's face. [34] When news of the Order-in-Council reached Adams, he called it "a new trial through which we are to pass, and the issue of which is with higher powers." [35]

V

The British government explained, succinctly and truthfully, that it had shown a very "liberal disposition . . . towards the United States," that it had been disappointed by the American government's failure to reciprocate, and that it had issued the Order-in-Council with great reluctance.[36] Indeed, it seems that it would never have made so drastic a use of the Acts of July 5, if it had not been shaken by a panic and depression which struck Great Britain in the winter of 1825-6. Prosperity had been returning ever since 1822; and this had made even the most reactionary of merchants and ship-owners fairly tolerant towards Liberal Toryism. Between 1824 and 1825, however, prices rose very sharply, owing to a banking policy that permitted a glut of gold to form itself in the vaults of the Bank of England; and this rise in prices was celebrated by a dance of speculation, which grew more and more vertiginous. In March 1825, gold, following its simple laws, had seeped out of England to such an extent that a decline set in; and the directors of the Bank grew fearful about their dwindling reserve, and sharply contracted their issues. Speculation gave place to hoarding. In November, the inevitable crash took place. Country bankers were ruined by the dozens; "for forty-eight hours it was impossible to convert even government securities into cash"; and the Bank of England was saved from closing its doors, and reducing England to a state of barter, only by the fortunate discovery, in one of its refuse cellars, of a box full of old one- and two-pound notes.[37] This absurd predicament forced the directors to change their policy; the panic died away; but Britain's foreign trade had been seriously damaged. The year 1826 marks the decline of the Liberal Toryism of Lord Liverpool and William Huskisson.

Upon no one had the blow fallen more heavily than upon William Huskisson. Reactionary opinion decided that the panic and depression—which were evidently due to hysterical overtrading on the one hand, and timorous banking on the other—should be blamed upon the liberal policies of the president of the Board of Trade. He was the most vulnerable member of the government, a mere middle-class reformer at whom the great Whig and Tory magnates had always looked askance; and all through 1826 he was under attack from the shipping interest, which had overextended itself in anticipation of an increase in foreign trade. The Order-in-Council, interdicting American trade with British colonies, was not entirely due to the obstinacy of Adams in 1824 and his silence in 1825; it was also an effort to placate the shipping interest. In May 1827 the House of Commons was the scene of a strange and violent debate on the condition of the shipping industry. All the most antiquated arguments were heard once more. General Gascoigne declared (it was a good definition of the battle between the old mercantilism and the new industrialism) that "the carrying trade of the country was being ruined for the sake of exports"; and Admiral Sir Joseph Yorke shouted that the government's relaxation of the Navigation Laws, "if it had been proposed thirty years ago, would have been deemed a qualification for the proposer's entry into Bedlam." All were agreed, however, that the Order-in-Council must not be suspended or revoked.[38] Huskisson bent to the storm. The Order-in-Council was the only measure of his that anyone seemed to like; and now, crouching behind it as behind some obsolete barricade, he hurled his defiance at the United States. The Americans, he said, were "building ships of war of the largest class . . . and looking forward to the time when they expect to wrest from this country its sway upon the ocean. I cannot say [he continued] that, with a view to the interests of our navigation, *I regret the course which the policy of the American Government has forced us to adopt.*" This language was not entirely insincere—Huskisson had been outraged by Adams's demand for a suspension of colonial preferences—but it was chiefly designed to smooth the ruffled feathers of Gascoigne, Yorke, and the shipping interest in general. Huskisson's real feelings came out by accident, as it were, towards the end of his long speech when, defending his policy of reducing tariff schedules, he complained that "a formidable rival" had just arisen in America's new textile industry—a rival who could be defeated only by admitting raw materials as cheaply as possible into England's ports.[39] These remarks passed almost unnoticed. It was evident from the debate that the stars in their courses were fighting against President Adams—for Adams, though he might have known that British statesmen would be angered by his obstinacy in 1824, could not have foreseen the panic of 1825-6, which was to make the British, in their turn, even more obstinate than he.

VI

When the news of the Order-in-Council arrived in the United States, public opinion was immediately aroused. The controversy had been so dry, confused, and almost pointless that no one had bothered about it; now, at last, here was something definite. The President's Second Annual Message, which his Cabinet had examined with extreme suspicion and concern, was chiefly taken up with an effort to put the British in the wrong. To the modern reader, it does not appear either candid or successful.[40] The opposition newspapers attacked the Administration for the folly and confusion which seemed to attend every one of its measures. "Heaven grant," said the pious Ritchie of the Richmond *Enquirer*, "it may be drawing to a close." [41]

According to the "elsewhere" Act of 1823, President Adams might have declared a retaliatory interdict upon British shipping. He chose instead to go to Congress for support and advice. On February 21, 1827, the Senate Committee on Commerce reported a Bill that was designed to save the Administration's face by forcing the British to recede first.[42] Opposition Senators attacked it for not being conciliatory. Smith of Maryland said that the British Act of 1822 "gave us all that we wanted. It was truly a boon—it gave us that which Great Britain had not given to any other nation . . . and we wanted that good sense which would have induced us to accept a favor so every way desirable." He accused Monroe's Administration of drafting the Act of 1823, and imposing it on the Senate by stealth. "Few of us," said Smith, "understood what was the real meaning of the word 'elsewhere.' " He now proposed an amendment that, by suspending the Act of 1823, would have forced the Administration to yield to Great Britain; but an amendment so subtly contrived that it altered the original Bill only to the extent of shaming the Administration.[43] This amendment was agreed to, on February 24, by a vote of 29 to 19, which proved that the President had lost control of the Senate. On that day Martin Van Buren made a speech that attacked the government, supported the Smith Amendment, and then announced that this amendment was exactly what the government's supporters had asked for in the first place! [44] It was a remarkable example of the art of assassination by double talk. "My dear friend," Van Buren was writing the next day, "the administration have to say the least been very unfortunate in this affair & will find it difficult to resist the imputation of having trifled with a very valuable portion of our commerce. I spoke at some length upon the subject and was gratified by the declaration of very many of the Senators that they had not before understood the merits of the dispute. *You may rest assured that the re election of Mr. Adams is out of the question.*" [45]

Van Buren's political instincts were usually sound. The Nineteenth Congress had only a few more days to run; and the House of Representatives, with a pro-Adams Speaker in John W. Taylor, and with a majority still willing to support the Administration in an emergency, refused to concur with the Senate's amended bill. The Senate disagreed with the House's amendment, which would have saved the Administration for the time being, and which was passed by a majority of 71 to 47; a conference came to nothing; the House declined to give way by a vote of 75 to 67; and Congress adjourned without anything being done at all.[46] Adams had been abandoned to the mercies of the British.

After two or three anxious Cabinet meetings he issued a proclamation —which, by the Act of March 1, 1823, he was bound to do—closing American ports against all British vessels coming from any British colony in the Western Hemisphere.[47] The accompanying Treasury Orders were lenient, and the interdict was not wide in scope.[48] Just as he had refrained from supporting the principles of the First Annual Message with a show of power, so now, in this narrower field, Adams would not push the controversy to its logical conclusion. For surely either the situation called for a more formidable interdict, or else the United States should have been satisfied in the first place with the friendly advances of the British in their Act of 1822.

Everything was now left to Gallatin in London. But Gallatin found that he could make no impression on the British. He was authorized to make concessions that would have been more than satisfactory in 1824; he discovered that Adams's obstinacy had provoked the British into a mood where no concession would satisfy them. Their refusals grew more and more staccato:

once more, the timing was all wrong. "I only discovered," he wrote, "irritation, not yet extinguished, on account of the United States not having met, especially in 1823 and 1824, the overtures of Great Britain." [49] Here indeed was sufficient punishment, not only for navigation acts and for "elsewhere" pretensions, but for the Monroe Doctrine and the Tariff of 1824! When Gallatin left England at the end of 1827 the Order-in-Council was still popular and still unrevoked; and newspapers like the London *Times* and *Bell's Weekly Messenger* were using language that would not have been out of place in the War of 1812. Englishmen rarely approved of the United States in those days. "America would not show a legitimate descent from her European parent," said Alexander Baring, as tactfully as he could, "if she did not carry herself with something more of haughtiness than is agreeable to those she has to deal with." [50]

Time itself, in its most obvious shape, had already taken a hand in these events. Liberal Toryism, severely shaken by the panic and depression of 1825-6, was soon to be visited by an even more terrible antagonist. The Earl of Liverpool was stricken by paralysis in February 1827; and George Canning, who succeeded him as Prime Minister, died after only five months in office. Overwork and gout were the proximate causes of Canning's death; the immediate cause would seem to have been the funeral of the Duke of York, held in a church so cold and damp that the Bishop of Lincoln died of exposure, and half the dignitaries present (Canning included) took to their beds. [51]

State funerals, in those days, were often murderous. Few Americans lamented Canning—this brilliant, insolent, enigmatic man, whose discussions with Rush had touched off the train of events which led to the Monroe Doctrine, who had fought the Holy Allies to a standstill, but who despised republics and coveted the Oregon country. On the whole, the United States owed more to him, as a stimulant, than to his predecessor Lord Castlereagh, who was an opiate; but Castlereagh was always considered a friend, and Canning an enemy. "An implacable, rancorous enemy of the United States," wrote John Quincy Adams, when he heard of Canning's death. "May this event, in the order of Providence, avert all the evils which he would, if permitted, have drawn down upon us." [52] Only Huskisson was left of the great trio, and Huskisson had not been friendly to the United States since 1824. Moreover, his nerve had been shaken by the attacks that were being made upon him; and his work was almost done. He and his two late colleagues had been sketching out a policy that would lead to unrestricted commerce, to an unimpeded exchange of commodities, to customs duties levied for revenue only; when they vanished from the scene, the policy was still only a sketch or a premonition. The customs duties were not drastically reduced, the Navigation Laws and Corn Laws were not totally repealed until the late 1840's, when the pressure of British industry was too strong to be resisted and Free Trade became the oriflamme of the victorious middle classes. In 1827, after Canning had with difficulty formed an Administration, Huskisson was described in Parliament as the leader of "a crowd of visionary theorists, of political economists, and the professors of what are called the liberal principles of the present day." [53] He had never succeeded in presenting himself to pre-Reform England as anything more than that. Three years later he, too, was gone—crushed to death by a runaway railroad engine in the sight of his great enemy, the Duke of Wellington.[54]

None the less, a policy that ends only with a premonition has its strength. "The march of Liberalism (as it is called)," Charles Greville said after Canning's death, "will not be stopped, and this he knew. . . ." [55] Canning's liberalism was an unlovely affair, quite blind to the horrors of England's factory towns, quite deaf to pleas for a wider suffrage and a reformed Parliament; but in foreign affairs it was truly formidable. The Holy Allies discovered this; and so too, in the end, did President John Quincy Adams. Under Monroe and Adams the United States was being urged—quietly under Monroe, loudly under Adams—into a policy of neo-mercantilism: protection of industry, conservation of resources, isolationism. It was policy designed (perhaps undesignedly) to place the government's powers at the disposal of the young business community; and it was naturally and instinctively hostile to the industrial and commercial supremacy predicted by men like Canning, Huskisson, and Liverpool. The navigation controversy became the most plausible arena for a parade of this hostility—plausible because Adams, after all, was doing battle for the freedom of the seas. But Adams, pushing his theories too hard both at home and abroad, aroused the deep suspicion of his countrymen on the one hand and the dogged imperialism of Canning on the other. The West Indies controversy, just as Van Buren predicted, helped to ruin the Administration, for Adams's loss of the West Indies trade in 1826 and his failure to regain it in 1827 became one of the leading issues in the Presidential campaign.[56]

VII

In the Senate debate in 1827, the opposition to Adams was partly and perhaps chiefly due to the skillful management of Martin Van Buren; but throughout the debate one detects a note of genuine bewilderment. Why had the President, whether as President or as Secretary of State, refused to accept the reasonable terms the British were prepared to offer him? Neither defenders nor opponents could find an explanation. In the House, James Hamilton of South Carolina—a good example of the conservative agrarian mind—was at length reduced to describing the Administration as "a set of drivellers." [57]

It was the agrarian conscience, bewildered and angry, that could be heard most clearly in Congress during those navigation debates. To the agrarian mind—to the mind, that is to say, which liked to think of American society as a society of independent property-owners—the crisis of the 1820's was beginning to take a recognizable form. The government was helping the industrialist with protective tariffs, and the speculator with subsidies to internal-improvement corporations; but the people wanted economic independence and equal rights. There seemed to be no connection between the government and the people. The President's First Annual Message appeared to advertise this disconnection in the most Olympian manner; and the President's passiveness in the face of a navigation crisis of his own making was merely an extension of his failure to recognize the greater crisis all around him. This was the drift of agrarian thinking, and it had begun to take the shape of an opposition in Congress which was drawn from every quarter of the Union—not a sectional opposition but a class opposition. Agrarianism, whenever it went to battle on class rather than on sectional terms, was a very dangerous foe—"terrible as an army with banners." The agrarian mind, it is true, had no appreciation of the true worth of a man like Adams; but Adams—inexcusably for a President in the 1820's—was quite out of touch with the agrarian mind.

VIII

After Andrew Jackson, the agrarian candidate, had become President, the West Indies quarrel was settled without any difficulty. History has foreborne to point out the obvious moral. Both sides made the necessary concessions. The British, on the one hand, abandoned their historic stipulation that all commerce between the United States and the West Indies must be carried on in British ships only; they no longer limited imports from the United States into the West Indies to a small list of articles; they gave up their plan to make their North American colonies a vestibule for the West Indian trade; and they permitted United States vessels to clear from West Indian ports for any foreign port in the world. The American government, on the other hand, ceased to claim that the products of the United States, when imported into the British West Indies, should be subject to no higher duties than those imposed upon goods from Great Britain and other parts of the British Empire; it no longer insisted that British vessels, exporting United States goods to the West Indies, must first prove that they had come directly from those islands; and it submitted to the British demand that the disagreement should be adjusted, not by convention, but by mutual legislation. In other words, Adams's claim that the United States should be granted privileges without making an equivalent concession was given up; and the British, in their turn, made very important modifications in their navigation laws. The agreement was less surprising than the language that accompanied it. Martin Van Buren, as Jackson's Secretary of State, actually instructed the American Minister in London to inform the British government that: "To set up the acts of the late Administration as the cause of the forfeiture of privileges which would otherwise be granted to the people of the United States, would, under existing circumstances, be unjust in itself, and could not fail to excite their deepest sensibility." [58] This humiliating disavowal of Adams and Clay, in the name of the American people, was described by Webster as "derogatory to the character and honor of the United States"; and perhaps it was.[59] But it showed how sincerely the Jacksonians believed that there was no connection between the people of the United States and the Administration of John Quincy Adams.

The West Indies controversy—so dry, complicated, and repulsive—becomes in retrospect merely the focus of that queer, shadowy battle between early American protectionism and early British free trade; but it was also the burial ground of the hopes and ambitions of President John Quincy Adams.

CHAPTER FIVE

Ferment

THOMAS JEFFERSON and John Adams died on July 4, 1826—the fiftieth anniversary of the Declaration of Independence. The coincidence, then and thereafter, seemed a majestic one. Its wonderful pathos left everyone breathless, even exhilarated, and quite convinced that there was something providential about it; in the course of time folklore crowned the occasion by insisting that John Adams's last audible words had been a whispered "Thomas Jefferson still survives." [1] Whether or not it was true in fact, this dying speech was faithful to the spirit of a classical friendship. The two patriots, who had fought so bitterly in the early Federalist-Republican battles, made their peace in 1812, preferring to remember that they had once fought upon the same side. They never met again; if they had, would Adams's rather testy "delight in social intercourse," and Jefferson's urbanity have survived this difficult test? Their friendship was confined to letters, however, and epistolary bonds are commonly more lasting than physical ones. Their letters were discursive; each man feeling free to say what he pleased, with the certainty (rare in those days) that what he wrote would not reappear in the columns of some polemical newspaper. Each was erudite and inquisitive, and each had had a supremely practical experience of the world: the mixture is always and necessarily rare; with very old men, who have lost most of their illusions and gained serenity, it is apt to be enchanting.

They could not always agree. Was there, for example, or was there not a distinction to be made between "natural" and "artificial" aristocracy? Mr. Jefferson said yes, Mr. Adams no. [2] This disagreement went to the very heart of their political philosophies; yet they never permitted it to become bitter or ill-natured: indeed, their whole correspondence seems to insist that society is nurtured by the disputes of intelligent and honest men. They

382

did not, of course, carry toleration to the point of supposing that their own enemies had always been either intelligent or honest; but their own political differences, they agreed, were due "to the circumstances of the times in which we happened to live, and the partiality of our friends at a particular period, [which] placed us in apparent opposition." [3] This curious, unlikely, and beautiful agreement between the signer of the Alien and Sedition Acts and the author of the Kentucky Resolutions was "sweetening to the evening of our lives." [4]

In religion, Adams, who was a Unitarian and an agnostic, and Jefferson, who was a Deist, found much in common. They were convinced that "the Sermon on the Mount is the key to true Christian teaching." [5] Adams, however, could never give up his hope in an after-life, though he did not believe that it would be eternal; while Jefferson was content with the thought that immortality was a concept "useful" only as a deterrent to crime and immorality. But when Adams lost his wife, Abigail, who was the very center of his existence, Jefferson forgot his prejudices, and, in the course of an infinitely tender letter, offered the pretense (it could be no more than a pretense with him) that "the term is not very distant, at which we are to deposit in the same cerement, our sorrows and suffering bodies, and to ascend in essence to an ecstatic meeting with the friends we have loved and lost, and whom we shall still love and never lose again." [6]

Tenderness, indeed, was the bond that united these two old men—a tenderness not so much personal as patriotic; a pride in the other's achievements and survival; melting at last into an identification, each of the other, with an American destiny that seemed to them the most important thing in the universe. Thus Jefferson's famous "We are all Republicans, we are all Federalists" found, at any rate, consummation here. [7]

The magic of this correspondence lies in the fact that it is almost the only occasion upon which the early American dream of unique republican virtue, uniquely residing in the United States of America, becomes a reality. Here it is—with all its wisdom, its toleration, its amplitude, its fresh and astringent individualism—an actual and palpable event.

I

In one of his later letters to Jefferson, Adams described his son John Quincy, whose career he had watched with extreme solicitude and immense pride, as "our John." "I call him our John [the old man continued] because, when you were at the Cul de Sac in Paris, he appeared to me almost as much your boy as mine." [8] What Jefferson felt when he read these words, and discovered that so strange a foster-child had been wished upon him, must be left to the imagination; he had rarely expressed anything but dislike and suspicion of John Quincy Adams, though to be sure he had been far too kind to give the elder Adams so much as a hint of this. A few weeks after this letter was written, John Quincy Adams became President under circumstances which made it unlikely that Jefferson's feelings towards him would grow more paternal. On the whole, "our John" was by no means the happiest phrase in that great correspondence.

And yet, when it came to republican virtue, John Quincy Adams had as good a claim to that as any man in the country. It is only just to him to say that when he became President his great object was to improve the condition of all parties to the social compact.[9] The trouble was that he suggested—or seemed to suggest—that this could best be effected by first improving the lot of those who stood in the least need of help. The conservation he planned could not be accomplished without changing the very nature of American expansion, which modified environment swiftly and wastefully and through the medium of speculation. It is arguable, after all, that the pioneers did less damage in fifty years than a modern lumber corporation could do in one-fiftieth the time; and as for land speculation, it was so endemic in early American history that to check it by legislation would have been as impossible in the 1820's as the suppression of drinking proved to be in the 1920's. Mr. Adams's plans for the public lands might have driven out the small speculator only to make room for the big one; and though he himself was the last man to wish for such a consummation, those who read his First Annual Message may well have read it in that light. With a rather heart-breaking confidence in their willingness to share his ideals, he told the American people that they would eventually get what they wanted through his scheme of internal improvements. The people responded by calling him every bad name under the sun. What then did the people want—always supposing that the people's collective wants could be formulated at all? The answer would have to be made in agrarian terms—the people wanted universal free education, abolition of imprisonment for debt, prohibition of special privileges for corporations.[10] In short, the people wanted equal rights. They had not yet made any bargain with destiny. Every man, in his heart, still longed to be his own master; and this longing, like a rainbow, arched the country from the cities of the Northeast to the margins of the "Great Desert."

For such a longing—so delusive but so creative—John Quincy Adams had no sympathy at all. He conceived of progress in America as of something that moved swiftly in terms of consolidation and control, and slowly in terms of waste; and this concept was counter to the dreams of whole masses of his countrymen. To say that his planned economy was ahead of his times is really to beg the question: the truth was that it was out of step with them.

II

The President himself was the least ostentatious of men. No arms were emblazoned on his coach; no guards surrounded him. When a poor mad ex-army doctor, convinced that he had been cheated of his rights by a court martial, conceived the notion that he could revenge himself upon a hostile universe by slitting the President's throat, Adams received him in his study alone.[11] Every summer morning, in the first year of his Presidency, he might have been observed (and Thurlow Weed did in fact observe him) emerging from the Potomac, dressed in the simple costume of the Garden of Eden; and these swims were abandoned only because he very nearly drowned himself. Washington in those days, and the President too, did not seem to think that Presidential lives were more valuable than any other kind.[12] Sometimes in winter, before sunrise, a solitary squat menacing figure, he "raced" around Capitol Square. He would return to light his fire, read a passage from the Bible, and write until breakfast.[13] No man was more faithful to the rule of republican simplicity. The executive mansion, to be sure, was rather more social than it had been in the days of Monroe: partly because Louisa Catherine Adams was a more successful hostess than the beautiful Elizabeth Monroe, who was an invalid; partly because the growing consequence of the United States required more display. "I dined yesterday at the President's," wrote Horatio Greenough in 1828. "The party consisted of about twenty members of Congress and twenty gentlemen from different parts of the country. . . . The furniture was in the gout Francais. An enormous gilt waiter, with many vases, temples, and female figures in different attitudes holding candles, gave light to the whole table. We sat down at six o'clock, and had every variety of fish, flesh and fowl. I cannot pronounce on the canvas-backs, for they had been boned and cut in slices. I took them for cake. We had macaroni! Every drinkable under the sun—porter, cider, claret, sherry, Burgundy, champagne, Tokay, and the choicest madeira that ever passed my larynx. We came away about ten." The young sculptor, fresh from Harvard College, was only giving a description of a typical Washington banquet.[14] But, somehow or other, people got it into their heads that the President had been seriously corrupted by his long absence near the courts of Europe; and when Congress was informed —erroneously as it turned out—that Adams had spent sixty-one dollars of the public money on a billiard table and twenty-one dollars on a set of chessmen, there was a good deal of oratory wasted upon the topic of "gambling at the President's palace."[15] To accuse that forbidding Puritan in the executive mansion of carousing all night with wastrels and sharpers was a feat even for the Nineteenth Congress; but the accusation was, after all, no more than the *reductio ad absurdum* of the people's case against him.

III

The death of John Adams in 1826 was possibly the saddest moment in John Quincy Adams's career. He loved his father deeply and tenderly; and his father gave him in return, not only love, but an unqualified support and approval. There was no one to take his father's place; while, on the other hand, the whole of America seemed to have transformed itself into a conspiracy to frustrate his highest aims and mock his most serious language. In his First Annual Message, for example, he had described astronomical observatories as "light-houses of the skies," and the laughter that greeted these words, though it was the symptom of a profound exasperation, was not only maddening but must have seemed a little mad. Many years later, when he was a very old man, worn out by a long, taxing, and honorable service in the House of Representatives, he traveled by railroad, steamer, and canal boat to Cincinnati to lay the cornerstone for a new observatory; and then the people of America cheered him all the way. Then at last he was forgiven for having been President and for having been out of place.

In July 1826, standing by his father's grave at Quincy, he already knew that, as a President, he was a failure. "My father and mother have departed," he wrote. "The charm which has always made this house an abode of enchantment to me is dissolved. . . . I feel that it is time for me to set my house in order, and to prepare for the churchyard myself." [16] The soil of Quincy—"the stoniest glacial and tidal drift," said his grandson Henry, "known in any Puritan land—" was suited to a desolate mood: and not all the memorial exercises for John Adams, nor the eulogies of Edward Everett and Daniel Webster, nor the solemn occasion upon which, standing up in the family pew in the Congregational meeting house, he united himself formally to the church of his fathers, could have offered him any consolation.[17]

July 1826, therefore, seems an appropriate time, and Quincy an appropriate place from which, looking backward and forward, to sum up the Administration of John Quincy Adams. On the surface, events were moving towards that parody of consolidation which came to be known as the Tariff of Abominations; beneath the surface there was a ferment, painful and violent and not pretty, such as—in the natural world—usually presages the coming of spring.

IV

The President's Massachusetts offers us a somewhat eccentric, though dignified, idea of this ferment. Massachusetts had experienced one curious revolution as far back as the period 1815-19, when the orthodox Congregationalists and the Unitarians came to a final parting of the ways. It is true that the most prominent Unitarian, William Ellery Channing, the elder, bore little resemblance to a revolutionary: for social innovations he had no use at all, and his mysticism and his rationalism were both too cloudy to shape themselves into a system of theology. His influence was less doctrinal than imaginative. In those rather didactic sermons, which the Bostonians who thronged his Federal Street Church did not take amiss, he summoned the imagination to a new reading of the old scriptures and dared the individual mind to assert, not its weight or its consequence, but its originality. He was to become a far more important man in the 1830's, when his *Remarks on American Literature* was the preface to Transcendentalism; but in the early 1820's, by teaching that the Church was not, after all, the terrible monitress of a mankind dead in sin, but the enchantress daughter of a God of love; and that the world was not the woeful vestibule to an almost certain damnation, but was actually to be the scene of human happiness and perfectibility, he did break the warlock grip of the old Federalist clergy.[18] There was never any connection between Unitarianism and democracy in those days, but Channing at least proved that Massachusetts might, one day, accept innovations that were not merely imaginative. One could even see signs of this in 1826 and 1827 when David Henshaw, a wealthy druggist and the leader of urban democracy, and the more upright Marcus Morton, the rural democrat, organized the "Friends of Jackson" in Massachusetts. The merchants, the professional men, the big new banker-industrialists like Nathan Appleton and Amos and Abbot Lawrence—with the Lawrences' protégé, Daniel Webster, to do the talking—were all for Adams, even though he had not been forgiven by State Street for deserting the Federalists in 1808. But men noted with surprise that members of the old Salem aristocracy, like George and Theodore Lyman, and former Hartford Conventionists like Harrison Gray Otis, were supporting the Hero for President. The Lymans, who loudly denounced all Western migrants as "the refuse of society . . . thieves and insolvents" were ludicrously out of place in the camp of the Western Jackson: it was even more ludicrous to suppose that they would co-operate with men like Henshaw and Morton. But the fact that both political extremes in the Bay State had turned towards Jackson was in itself a portent.[10]

In Massachusetts one could look for no more than portents; Henry Clay's Kentucky was easier to read. Here was a story of the politics of debt, which was given a national character because the general government—or two of its three co-ordinate branches—turned its back on the Kentucky debtor. Kentucky had been very hard hit by the Panic of 1819, and its debtors had been especially enraged by the usurious behavior of the two branches of the Bank of the United States at Lexington and Louisville. When the United States Supreme Court, in *McCulloch v. Maryland*, rescued the Bank of the United States from the individual state taxing power; and when Monroe, in his Message of 1820, referred to the prostration of the farmer as a "mild and instructive admonition," the people of Kentucky began to lose faith in the general government. Even before being abandoned by the Supreme Court, the debtors of Kentucky had turned to their own legislature for relief. The culmination of their efforts was an Act of December 25, 1820, prohibiting the sale of property by order of a court for less than three quarters of its value as appraised by a jury of neighbors, unless the plaintiff would consent to receive notes of the Bank of the Commonwealth or the Bank of Kentucky in discharge of the execution. If the plaintiff did not consent to receive these notes, the debtor might replevy for two years. The two banks were devices for allowing debtors to pay their debts in cheap money; and from a creditor's point of view the Bank of the Commonwealth, which had a nominal capital of two million dollars, but which went into business with nothing more substantial than a legislative appropriation of seven thousand dollars for books, paper, and plates for printing, was a mere swindle. By May 1822 its paper was worth little more than fifty cents on the dollar. The effect of the Act of December 25 was singularly mixed: debtors were temporarily relieved, property under execution was ultimately

placed at the mercy of the few men who had saved some money for investment, and creditors were obliged to accept paper money that represented
about half what they had lent, or else to wait for two years, when things
might have become worse.[20]

Stay laws and replevin laws in those days were rarely more than incanta-
tions to quiet the delirium of debt. Creditors naturally claimed that they
were flagrant violations of contract. But Kentucky creditors were often not
citizens of Kentucky, and Kentucky debtors were the backbone of the state.
When the state Court of Appeals declared that the Act of December 25 was
un-Constitutional, the Relief (or debtor) Party succeeded in passing a bill
through the legislature, creating a new Court of Appeals. This was on December 24, 1824.[21] From a judicial point of view, the situation was nothing
less than a nightmare. There were now two parties in the state, the Old
Court and the New Court party, the former supported by the large land-
owners, the professional men, and the two branches of the Bank of the
United States, the latter representing the more desperate of the debtor
classes. There were also two Courts of Appeal—one of which refused either
to resign or to do business, the other deriving its existence from a very
dubious piece of legislation. The circuit judges, with four exceptions, sent
cases in appeal to both courts. The people, less judicious, began to lose their
respect for all courts, and "it was about this time that . . . the term 'lynch
law' first appeared in Kentucky." New Court justices went armed to church
in Frankfort, and "if what is told me is true [wrote Hezekiah Niles] there
is a greater show of feeling than has caused the revolution of an empire."
For a whole year, it seemed as if the quarrel between the Old Court and
the New Court parties could have no issue but civil war.[22]

But Kentuckians, though individually high-spirited and lawless, were col-
lectively "mild." In the elections of 1825 and 1826, asked to choose between
a group of men whom they mistrusted and a state of anarchy, they returned
Old Court majorities to the legislature. Good times, moreover, were slowly
returning to Kentucky. Debtors were less desperate, creditors less grasping.
By the end of 1825, the Old Court quietly resumed business; by the end
of 1826 all traces of the New Court had been obliterated.

What is really important about this bizarre story is that the Kentucky
debtor, during the course of it, began to realize that he would get no sympathy from the federal government. The Supreme Court had disappointed
him in *McCulloch v. Maryland,* and in *Green v. Biddle* (1823) had blandly
exposed him to the mercies of the land laws of Virginia. In 1824, the Federal District Court decreed that every judgment it issued in execution of
a debt should be paid in silver or gold and that no replevin of more than
two months should obtain. In 1825, the New Court majority in the legislature instructed Henry Clay to vote for Jackson in the House of Representatives; and Clay disobeyed them and went on to become Secretary of State.
Thereafter, he and President Adams notoriously gave their patronage only
to Old Court men. Clay's American System and Adams's First Annual Message called for strong central government; but what sort of central govern-

ment was this? In 1828 Kentucky deserted Adams and Clay, her favorite son, and gave her electoral vote to Jackson. The Kentucky debtor had been saved from prostration, not by state laws or federal laws, but by the return of good times. What would happen when the lean years came back again? Hitherto, most Kentuckians had been Jeffersonian Republicans. In their Presidential vote of 1828, one can discern the beginnings of a cleavage between Jeffersonian democracy and Jacksonian democracy; between the assumption that all strong central government was bad, and the hope that a central government might be devised which would be strong enough to redress the balance between those who produced the wealth and those who exploited it.

V

State politics in the 1820's were singularly introverted, and much that happened took place without any reference to national events. There was some truth in Ninian Edward's complaint that Jackson men in his own state of Illinois—men like William Kinney, Emanuel West, John Reynolds, and Shadrach Bond—who "insist upon making the Presidential question control every election . . . in effect . . . proscribe and disfranchise every man who happens to differ in opinion with them." [23] What Edwards really meant, however, was that the Jackson men (who had not themselves been guiltless in this respect) were attacking him for having opposed a reduction in the price of public lands, which would have damaged his own large holdings in real estate, and those of his son-in-law, Daniel P. Cook. Indeed, the popular Cook had been defeated for Congress in the election of 1826 partly because he had voted for Adams in the House of Representatives and partly because it was thought that he and his father-in-law, who was governor, were running the state in the interests of a personal clique. The inference to be drawn was that Edwards and Cook represented an old political order, able but "aristocratic," and intent upon exacting a personal allegiance in return for their services. [24] Though the factional disputes of Illinois scarcely permitted anyone to speak of clear-cut issues, except the slavery issue in the Convention battle of 1824, the desire to overthrow the old order underlay them all; and it was this which united Illinois to the rest of the nation. The same was true of Pennsylvania, where most men supported the tariff and internal-improvement features of the American System; but where local jealousies, obscure factions, and distrust of the Administration made it almost impossible for the American System to form a party. The Jackson politicians in Pennsylvania were themselves divided into two parties, at least as anxious to cut each other's throats as to elevate the General; but in Pennsylvania the gatherings "in the farm kitchens, on river rafts and among carters and field hands in the taverns" were more Jacksonian than the politicians. It was all very well for Governor Shulze, who committed himself to President Adams in his Annual Message of December 1826, to announce in his peroration, "What a happy state of things! What a blessed country!"—it is clear that the Pennsylvania Germans (and S¹ 'ze himself was of Pennsylvania

German stock) were convinced that Adams stood for aristocracy, extravagance, and even a revival of the Alien and Sedition Laws.[25] The Pennsylvania Germans, it is true, carried their devotion to Jackson so far that many of them are said to have voted for him years after he was dead; but their conviction that Adams was an aristocrat and Jackson a democrat is what counts. The extreme confusion of Pennsylvania politics—where men who held much the same opinions on national issues fought one another with an unremitting ferocity—only partly conceals the strong desire, here as elsewhere, to do away with the old order and to look for a new one.

VI

The ferment of the late 1820's, on one occasion at least, went far beyond the range of this good desire. Georgia was then a frontier commonwealth, a remote and unreasonable satrapy of the cotton empire, with the mysteries of Florida real estate to the south and the unassimilated Creeks and Cherokees to the west. For years the state had been distracted by the factions of George Michael Troup, a graduate of the College of New Jersey (Princeton), and of John Clark, an unlettered Indian fighter. Troup represented the cotton planters who cultivated the red loam of "middle" Georgia and spread up the navigable rivers; Clark was the leader of the small subsistence farmers of the northwest, southwest, and south. In 1824, the Clark party was able to take the election for governor away from the legislature and give it to the people; and though the people responded by electing Troup as governor, 1824 may be taken as the year when the small farmer of Georgia entered the main stream of American history. Otherwise the battles between the Clark and Troup factions were curiously aimless; and only the class conflict that lay at the very heart of them could explain their peculiar virulence.[26]

When the two factions united on any issue, however, the virulence, instead of abating, was apt to become extreme. They were quite united on the issue of expelling the Creeks and Cherokees from the good cotton lands between the Flint and the Chattahoochie rivers, directly in the road of Georgia's westward march; and in the Treaty of Indian Springs they believed they had found the means of doing so. The Treaty was made on February 12, 1825, by United States Commissioner Duncan G. Campbell and a handful of Creek chieftains. It took from the Creeks 4,700,000 acres of their best land without any adequate return.[27] It was clearly fraudulent; and when the Adams Administration decided that it was null and void, and made a new arrangement, only a little less inhumane, called the Treaty of Washington, the whole of Georgia was in an uproar. The Treaty of Washington had been submitted to the United States Senate on January 31, 1826; it was publicly proclaimed in April; and, such as it was, it was now one of the supreme laws of the land. It returned to the Creeks about one million acres of the land wrested from them at Indian Springs.[28] In December 1826, neglecting the fact that Indian treaties were federal business, the General Assembly of Georgia protested against this "violation" of State Rights by the federal government. "It is a sovereign, and not a subject, that sues," said the General Assembly, "it is an equal, and not an inferior, that remonstrates." [29] Governor Troup told the Secretary of War that if an attempt was made to prevent him from carrying out the provisions of the Treaty of Indian Springs, the whole state would strike back. "I feel it my duty [he wrote] to resist to the utmost any military attack which the Government of the United States shall think proper to make upon the territory, the people, or the sovereignty of Georgia." [30] He had already issued orders to the Major Generals of militia commanding the Sixth and Seventh divisions to be ready to repel a hostile invasion, when the Administration yielded. As was usually the case with Adams, he had pressed too hard at the beginning, and had failed to press at all at the end.[31] The Cherokees and the Creeks were abandoned. In 1828 the wealthier (and more venal) among them set out for the eastern part of Oklahoma. The less prosperous followed them across the Chattahoochie into Alabama, but went no farther. In Alabama, they starved to death.[32]

In such cases the commonplaces of the moral judgment are best left unuttered, and we are obliged to fall back on the mechanics of civilization. The law of inertia is resistance to something; and since Indian inertia resisted a superior force, the result was bound to be tragic for the Indian. There is, however, a smaller lesson to be extracted from these violent and melancholy events. It is probably true that if Georgia had fought a war with the United States, the rest of the South would not have supported her; but since both Alabama and Mississippi began to adopt an extreme State Rights position with regard to their Indians, it would be unwise to assume that the example of Georgia went unheeded.[33]

VII

Ferment in another and more rational form reveals itself in the statistics of the growth of cities. Between 1820 and 1830 the number of cities with over eight thousand inhabitants had increased from eleven to twenty-four; the percentage of urban population from 4.9 to 6.7.[34] It was inevitable that such a growth should be accompanied by efforts to improve the conditions of the working man; and these figures and percentages, in terms of vocabulary, mark the transformation of the early labor "societies" and "associations" into "unions."

In 1823, the New York stonecutters went on strike for a $1.62½ a day uniform wage; and in the same year the cabinetmakers of that city assembled in mass meeting to discuss the threat to their trade of the introduction of prison-made goods. In 1825 the Boston house-carpenters staged a great strike for a ten-hour day, with overtime pay. Their arguments represent them as crushed between the merchant-capitalist who supplied the raw materials, financed the production expense, and marketed the finished product, and the merchant-employer, who had sunk to the status of a small contractor, making his profits solely out of wages and work.[35] The skilled journeyman saw his chances of himself becoming an independent employer being gradually extinguished; and the strike was in some measure a protest against the status of propertyless wage-earner which he saw being thrust upon him. The merchant-employers and merchant-capitalists, uniting for the first time, responded with sentences of shocked surprise. Was it possible, they said, that the "industrious sons of Massachusetts" were really demanding a change in "the time of commencing and terminating their daily labor, from that which has been customary from time immemorial"? What snares would the Devil not lay for them if they cease to work from sunrise to sunset! What infection might not seize upon Boston, the early rising and industry of whose inhabitants were universally proverbial! Behind these arguments lay the simple fact that the building trade was so entirely in their grip that they could stop all construction everywhere for the whole season; and it was this simple fact that broke the strike.[36]

In 1827 there was a movement in Philadelphia which was, in effect, a milestone in the history of the nineteenth century. It seems to have started with the circulation of a pamphlet that demanded the establishment in every city of a free press and a library with reading, lecture, and debating rooms; and protested against the sunrise-to-sunset hours of labor. As a result of this, about six hundred journeymen carpenters of Philadelphia went on strike in June, declaring that the "sun to sun" system condemned them to unemployment during the short winter days and to twelve or fifteen hours of labor during the spring, summer, and early fall. The strike—it was the usual fate of strikes in those days—came to nothing; but in the course of it there was formed the Mechanics' Union of Trade Associations, the first city-wide federation of workers in the history of the United States. And in 1828 there appeared the weekly *Mechanics' Free Press*, the first labor newspaper of which any issues have been preserved.[37]

The Mechanics' Union lasted only for two and a half years, but before its death—of precocity—it had fathered the Working Man's Party. And though the Working Man's Party, in turn, perished within three years, chiefly from poison administered by the old-line party politicians, it became the focus for all the agitations of the late 1820's. In its city and county conventions, held in and around Philadelphia in 1828, it gave a very clear expression to the grievances, not only of working men, but of poor men everywhere. The first of these grievances was that state legislatures had the power of creating corporations by special charter; and that these special charters were rarely granted to men with little capital or political influence. Business enterprise, therefore, was falling into the hands of a small clique of capitalists, who were able to charge high prices while at the same time they forced down wages.[38] The worst of all these monopolies was the banking monopoly, not only because it tended to deny credit to the small businessman and aspiring journeyman, but also because wages were invariably paid in depreciated bank notes, which merchants purchased at a discount but which wage-earners were forced to accept at their face value. All wage-earners were "hard money" men; all were opposed to banks of issue; some were opposed to banks of any kind. Another grievance was the lack of a mechanics' lien law, which meant that employers who went bankrupt were not obliged to pay their workmen any part of the wages due to them; so that some employers declared themselves bankrupt solely for the purpose of pocketing unpaid wages.[39] Since wages were often paid monthly, and in some cases even semi-annually, a mechanics' lien law did not seem too much to ask for.

A more universal grievance, voiced by the Working Man's Party, was the hopeless inefficiency of the public school system. At the heart of this inefficiency lay the fatal identification of free education with pauperism; the unwillingness of the taxpayer to be taxed for the maintenance of schools; the awful calamity of administrative indifference. Conditions varied from state to state; but even in New York, which was probably the most advanced state in this respect, it was known in 1829 that more than twenty-four thousand children between the ages of five and fifteen were not attending any school at all. In New England, some attempt was made to provide free schooling for children of all classes; to the south of New England, land and money were usually spent upon academies and colleges of use to none but the prosperous, while the children of the poor were educated as paupers or not educated at all.[40] For the working man, this state of affairs was rendered even more disgraceful by the employment of children in factories, where they labored from sunup to sundown in conditions that, at their best, were monotonous and unhealthy and, at their worst, unspeakable. Parents were threatened by their employers with the dismissal of the whole family if they attempted to withdraw even one child for education; and manufacturers and master carpenters were inclined to believe that a ten-hour day would have an unhappy effect upon these children by "reducing them from that course of industry and economy of time" in which they were so anxious to bring them up! [41]

Yet another grievance, and perhaps the greatest, was imprisonment for debt. In 1829 it was estimated that seventy-five thousand debtors were annually imprisoned in the United States. In Indiana, Illinois, Mississippi, and Alabama no one could be imprisoned for debt unless he first refused to surrender his estate; but most farmers preferred to go to prison and keep their farms for their families to run. In Kentucky, owing to the efforts of Richard Mentor Johnson and of the Relief Party, all imprisonment for debt was abolished. In some other states, it was not permitted for sums of less than fifteen dollars (Vermont), thirteen dollars and thirty-three cents (New Hampshire), and twenty-five dollars (New York); but these provisions were often disregarded; and in Massachusetts, which forbade imprisonment for less than five dollars and required the creditor to pay the debtor's board, a blind man with a dependent family of six was imprisoned for six dollars, while in Rhode Island a woman was imprisoned for sixty-eight cents by the very man whose property had been saved by her husband from a fire, at the cost of her husband's life. Debtor's jails were usually overcrowded and unsanitary. In New York "there is no settled allowance in this Jail for the prisoners, nor have they even bedding. But the *Humane Society* has benevolently stepped forward to their relief, and allows each poor prisoner half a pound of meat, 3 pints of soup, 2 potatoes, and an Indian corn dumpling, every 24 hours. During winter, they frequently receive donations of firewood . . . The health of the prisoners is greatly promoted by their having permission to walk on the roof of the building at all seasonable hours." The wretched condition of the imprisoned debtor, and the impracticable scheme of shutting him away from all opportunity of making money and thus extinguishing his debt, both owed their existence to the prevailing worship of sanctity of contracts. It was not until 1832 that Congress passed a bill abolishing imprisonment for complaints of debts in the federal courts; and it was not until 1840 that all states had done the same thing.[42]

It would seem that the Working Man's Party in its conventions of 1828 and 1829 had offered a program that was more humanitarian, more concerned with the relief of distress, more a mirror of the general discontents of the country than an actual formulation of a labor philosophy. The skilled mechanics, who were the backbone of the party, still hoped to be themselves employers and creditors; this hope somewhat dazzled and confused them in their quest for an economic democracy. When the issue in 1828 lay between Adams and Jackson for President, they usually chose Jackson; but they chose him chiefly because they mistrusted Adams. Adams's ideal of a great scheme of internal improvements financed by the public lands seemed to the working man merely a device for creating a cheap labor market in the manufacturing states; his national bank was considered (mistakenly but inevitably) nothing more than the apotheosis of a system of depreciated paper money; and the system of protective tariffs which his Secretary of the Treasury urged upon Congress was the system, in the language of the *Mechanics' Free Press*, "most prone to reduce the wages of workmen."[43] The American System was filled with the great vision of Henry Clay; but somehow or other it seemed more than anxious to commit this vision to the sole guidance of the business community. Adams's Administration, which was primarily the Administration of the American System, had done little or nothing for the debtor; and in 1831, when all was over, Adams himself confessed that imprisonment for debt was necessary to the "security of property and fidelity to contracts, as well as . . . credit."[44] Whereas Jackson in his First Annual Message announced that "some more liberal policy than that which now prevails in reference to this unfortunate class of citizens is certainly due to them, and would prove beneficial to the country. . . . All experience proves that oppressive debt is the bane of enterprise, and it should be the care of the republic not to exert a grinding power over misfortune and poverty."[45] Jackson's philosophy did not carry him much beyond an attack upon monopoly in the interest of the small businessman and the small property-owner; but his "hard money" policy was a working-man's policy; he destroyed the bank after a Homeric struggle; and he was no friend to internal improvements or to a high tariff. He was an enigmatic figure, both to himself and to others, in the campaign of 1828: at most a herald of change. But the working man who voted for him, and whose thinking was still bound up with the agrarian demand for equal rights, was not in the event disappointed by his vote. And so the agitation in the industrial districts and the larger cities, which produced the Working Man's Party in 1828, also showed that the Administration of John Quincy Adams was helplessly poised over a mass of fermenting grievances, which was slowly shaking it to pieces.

CHAPTER SIX

Abominations

STANDING beside his father's grave at Quincy, lonely and sorrowful, in the summer of 1826, John Quincy Adams already knew that his Administration was in danger of collapsing. There was still a chance, of course, that the will of Providence, as expressed in the First Annual Message, might not be disobeyed by the American people. But the will of Providence would have to be supported by the most forthright use of patronage and the power of dismissal; and Adams, though he was human enough to ignore the patronage dispensed in his interests but behind his back, did not himself change his views on this subject until 1828. Even then he did not change them radically; and by then it was too late. In the summer of 1826, however, many people professed to believe that Andrew Jackson's magnetism might prove insufficient to attract all the fragments of opinion hostile to Adams; even as late as December there were rumors that Van Buren had gone over to the Administration.[1] The fall elections were hard to read: the one-party system had not entirely dissolved; and state politics, as a mirror of national events, were dark and confusing. But Scott of Missouri and Cook of Illinois went down to defeat on the "bargain and corruption" issue; New York, Ohio, Virginia, and the old Crawford territories in the South gave promise of being more Jacksonian than before; and in Kentucky, of the eight delegates who had disobeyed their orders and voted for Adams in the House, four did not care to run and one was defeated. When the new Congress assembled in December 1827 these scarcely legible signs were immediately transcribed into actualities. John W. Taylor, the Administration's Speaker, was ousted from his chair by a vote of 104 to 94, and his place was taken by the hostile Andrew Stevenson of Virginia; while the Senate chose for its printer the ebullient Duff Green, whose Washington *United States Telegraph* was violently abusive of Adams. For the first time in American history, both House and Senate had majorities hostile to an Administration only two years old. "Desperation is their only hope," Sam Houston wrote to Jackson.[2]

I

Adams's reaction to the defeat of John W. Taylor was typically gloomy and suspicious. Taylor had recently been accused of sexual irregularities; and "the difficulty of his situation was," Adams wrote, "that the falsehood could not be refuted without bringing the truth to more conspicuous light, and there was of truth enough to sully his fair fame. I deeply lament it; for Taylor has been one of the few men in whom I had hoped to find a friend of whom I could be proud, as well as a virtuous politician." [3] This self-righteous statement hardly conceals the President's neurotic suspicion that his friends were all preparing to desert him; and it was singularly unfair to Taylor, who seems to have been one of the early victims of a form of political mud-slinging which was to reach its climax in the campaign of 1828. The accusation was that Taylor, as he himself put it, "had brought my girl from Baltimore, established her in quarters & lodged with her every night since the commencement of the previous session"; but the "girl" happened to be two ladies, whom the mildly philandering Taylor met by chance while taking the stage at Baltimore and whom he never saw again after he and his friends had alighted at the Queen's Hotel in Capitol Hill. Such slanders, he was convinced, were "part of a system to calumniate & vilify every man in distinguished station connected with the present administration"; and, lacking any evidence to the contrary, we can only give him (which Adams conspicuously did not) the benefit of the doubt.[4]

Taylor himself attributed his defeat partly to Southern unforgiveness for his part in the Missouri debates, but chiefly to lack of support in the New York delegation.[5] De Witt Clinton's victory in the gubernatorial election of 1826, and his known preference for Jackson, had forced Van Buren to make up his mind. Hitherto, Van Buren had been simply an enemy of Adams; and his support of Jackson did not become an open one until the middle of 1827, when he seemed (or was said to be) not unwilling to join forces with Clinton.[6] These maneuvers were enough to turn the New York delegation into a Jacksonian group—at least to the extent of being hopelessly divided on the Speakership issue. But Taylor might have added that Adams himself had done nothing to help him in New York.

In December 1826, for example, the President decided to nominate the genial and learned Judge Samuel Rossiter Betts to the United States district court of the southern district of New York; and though the choice was a conspicuously wise one, considering the great work Betts afterwards performed in the restatement and illumination of admiralty law, it was made over the heads of James Tallmadge and Henry Wheaton, two of Adams's staunchest friends during the election of 1824.[7] Tallmadge had already protested that "we put *our all* at stake to get the President's election—& his friends cannot again succeed against all candidates unless they are sustained

& acknowledged. . . . Those who have been known friends of Mr. Adams find themselves unpleasantly placed at present—The Clintonians scoff at them as unrecognized by the man they support—the Bucktails condemn them as renegades from the Republican Party. . . . At the close of the Session they will break up." [8] When Taylor informed Tallmadge that the prize he sought for had gone to Judge Betts, he could only add: "Your name has often been mentioned in the conversations with which he [the President] has favored me & always with respect and friendship." Taylor was too much of a politician not to know that respect and friendship, unless they were accompanied by some tangible proof, were perfectly meaningless to a New Yorker in search of patronage. "You may tell the President," replied the angry Tallmadge, "we have only two men in the State (Gov C–& V. Buren) who envy him his situation." [9]

But when the Third Annual Message was sent to the Twentieth Congress on December 4, 1827, the indignation of Adams's supporters in the New York delegation boiled over. Not a word had been said in the Message in favor of protective tariffs! [10] When the news reached New York, the consternation among the President's followers was extreme. "This state is becoming outrageously tariff-mad," wrote Ebenezer Sage, who was reduced to punning, "and Mr. Adams's silence on that subject in his late missusage is considered by them as an electioneering matter and that he is with the Boston merchants—his best friends here find a great difficulty in getting over the thing; the more so as they had promised us he would unquestionably recommend the support of the American System. . . . I fear this tariff thing, by some strange mechanical contrivance or legerdemain, will be changed into a machine for manufacturing Presidents, instead of broadcloth and bed blankets." [11]

II

Adams had, on his own confession, written the Message "in such agony of mind, proceeding from causes relating to both public and private affairs, that I am ashamed of it, and almost afraid to read it to my confidential advisers." [12] And certainly the Message was not very confident. The President was able to tell the Congress that a convention had been signed with Great Britain on November 13, 1826, by which $1,204,960 were to be paid to those who, under the first article of the Treaty of Ghent, had claimed indemnity from the British for carrying off their slaves during the War of 1812. He announced that the Conventions of 1815 and 1818, regulating the direct commercial intercourse between Great Britain and the United States on terms of perfect reciprocity, had been renewed, subject only to the agreement of the Senate. He showed that the Oregon question had been quieted by "a temporary compromise" and that the vexatious problem of the Maine-New Brunswick border would be (the Senate concurring) submitted to an arbitrator. But he had to confess that the British still refused to negotiate on the vital question of the West Indies trade; that France still declined to pay her bill for depredations committed during the Napoleonic Wars;

and that the Panama Conference had come to nothing. Only the tariff-minded Secretary of the Treasury and the hostile Postmaster-General were praised. There was a brief panegyric on internal improvements; there was a plea for a continued relaxation of the land laws, not in terms of reducing the price of the public lands (Adams would never have urged that) but in terms of the remission of forfeitures. "It can never be in the interest or the policy of the nation," said Adams, speaking directly to the debtors of the West, "to wring from its own citizens the reasonable profits of their industry and enterprise by holding them to the rigorous import of disastrous engagements." And he added a rather cold little phrase recommending "the amelioration in some form or modification of the diversified and often oppressive codes relating to insolvency." [13]

The entrance of the debtor in any form into an Adamsite message was, of course, significant and cheering; but any consolation his followers may have derived from it was altogether dissipated by his failure to mention protective tariffs. As Adams said himself, he considered that the extreme recommendations of Secretary Rush in this respect would prove sufficient. "The report of the Secretary of the Treasury upon the finances would with my entire approbation recommend the protection of the manufacturing interest." He would not himself "interfere improperly for the purpose of exercising an influence over the House." [14]

III

The House might have replied that it had long since passed the stage when it could be influenced by the President. The Twentieth Congress, restless and mischievous, and preoccupied with the coming Presidential contest between Adams and Jackson, was an extraordinary example of the jealousy that always exists between the Executive Mansion and Capitol Hill. Yet it did, in the end, and in spite of its best endeavors, offer the nation a strange parody of the wishes of the Administration.

It was impossible to ignore the tariff question. The high-tariff propagandists had done their work so well that farmers everywhere outside the South and the Southwest were in a condition of doubt which bordered upon frenzy. The merchants and bankers of Massachusetts had been converted to the cause, as was evident in the Nineteenth Congress, when Daniel Webster drove a bill through the House which gave the New England woolen manufacturer all the protection that he asked for.[15] When the Bill came up to the Senate, Martin Van Buren found himself in a singular predicament. He had decided that the opposition to Adams must be founded upon "the most natural and beneficial combination . . . that between the planters of the South and the plain republicans of the North . . . weakened, if not destroyed by the amalgamating policy of Mr. Monroe." [16] The planters of the South were opposed to protective tariffs in any form; but this was not held to be true of the plain republican farmers of western New York. Never was a politician in a more odious dilemma. Van Buren solved it by not voting at all: he was absent from his seat, he explained long afterwards, because he had "promised to accompany a friend on a visit to the Congressional Cemetary." [17] Other Senators found it convenient to disappear. When the roll was called in the Senate, the result was a tie; and Vice-President Calhoun, whose tariff views were still unknown, killed the bill by his casting-vote. A casting-vote, in either direction, was bound to hurt him as a national figure. It was a very courageous action. Calhoun's position in Jackson's new Democratic Party was still so insecure—for he had aroused the jealousy of Van Buren—that he might well have been excused if he also had gone sight-seeing on that day. [18]

The narrow defeat of the woolens bill was merely an incitement. In the summer of 1827, the Pennsylvania Society for the Promotion of Manufactures called a convention together at Harrisburg "to take into consideration the present state of the wool growing and wool manufacturing interests, and such other manufactures as may require encouragement." Delegates from thirteen of the twenty-four states were present—a powerful congregation of wool-growers, manufacturers, politicians, and editors. [19] The convention deliberated for five days, and then came out for increased duties on imports of manufactured cotton, hemp, flax, iron, and glass; but its chief demand was for an ad valorem duty on imported woolens, to begin at 40 per cent and rise gradually to 50 per cent, and for a duty of 20 cents a pound on imported wool, to be raised yearly by 2½ ¢ until it reached 50 cents. [20] With this agreement between the growers of wool and the manufacturers of woolens, the early tariff movement reached its height.

IV

The convention was sometimes called an Adams maneuver, sometimes an anti-Jackson demonstration; but in truth it was neither. The manufacturing interest knew that it had Adams in its pocket, but it believed itself strong enough to bully the Jacksonians. In this moment of victory, it was sure that no President could be elected who dared to say that he would fight protective tariffs; and the careful arguments of so worthy a man as Hezekiah Niles in his "Address to the people of the United States" gave this assurance an air of respectability. [21] The Harrisburg men believed, however, that what they lacked was a competent political economist: their own report had been sadly muddled, and their chief publicists—Hezekiah Niles and Mathew Carey—were, after all, only journalists. In Georg Friedrich List they believed that they had found such a man. List had been a professor of "administration and politics" at the University of Tübingen; but his views on internal free trade and external tariffs for the German states had mysteriously enraged the authorities of Württemberg, and, after a brief incarceration in the fortress of Aspern, he fled to the United States. In Pennsylvania, he was a farmer, a promoter, and an editor of the *Readinger Adlinger*, the German-American weekly—"the Bible of Berks County." Hanging around the Harrisburg Convention, he brought himself to the attention of Charles Jared

Ingersoll, one of the vice-presidents of the Pennsylvania Society for the Promotion of Manufactures. Here was a find! A genuine German Professor! Very soon List was writing a series of letters on the philosophy of the American System for the editor of the Philadelphia *National Gazette*. These were reprinted in other protectionist journals and were spread throughout the country in pamphlet form as *Outlines of American Political Economy*. His views at the time were not particularly original, but they were pungent and promotional. He advocated, among other things, the swelling of the Pennsylvania Society into a national chamber of businessmen which should supply Congress with information and guide it in the matter of legislation.[22]

The bustling eager List, who was one day to become the tragic saint of German economic nationalism, probably gave the home-market argument its best publicity; but he had one disadvantage; he was a foreigner. "We appear to have imported a professor from Germany," sneered James Hamilton of South Carolina, "in absolute violation of the American System." [23] There was Daniel Raymond, however, a product of Connecticut and of Baltimore, whose *Thoughts on Political Economy* was founded upon "the effort to break loose from the fetters of foreign authority—from foreign theories and systems of economy, which from the dissimilarity of the nature of the governments, renders them altogether unsuited to our country." [24] Raymond was original, too original perhaps: his harsh Ricardian views upon banks of issue were not likely to make him popular with protectionists. But his anonymous pamphlet, *The American System*, a ringing defense of protective tariffs, was widely read; and it had the additional merit of exciting the wrath of Governor William Branch Giles of Virginia, whose polemical writings usually did more service to his enemies than to his friends.[25] Or there was Willard Phillips, a lawyer of Boston, who had given way to his "excessive passions and appetites" while at Harvard College, but had subsequently repented in a course of abstemious living and wide and varied reading. Once a free-trader and a worshiper of Adam Smith, he had found the flow of Massachusetts capital towards industry an irresistible one; and in 1828 he published his protectionist *Manual of Political Economy*, much to the comfort of the manufacturing interest. And then, in spite of his theoretical weakness, there was always Mathew Carey of Philadelphia—Mathew Carey who had exposed the "fallacies" of Adam Smith in his *Addresses of the Philadelphia Society* (1819) without having—so he claimed—spent as much as three days on the study of political economy.[26] A native of Dublin, a friend of Irish Revolution, of Benjamin Franklin, and of Lafayette, Carey had assailed the British authorities so enthusiastically in his *Volunteer's Journal* that in 1783 he was shut up in Newgate Prison. After his release, he thought it best to take ship for the United States; and since he went on board disguised as a woman it must be assumed that the British had decided that his stay in Newgate had been far too short. Printer, editor, publisher, bookseller, a pious Catholic, a beloved humanitarian, whose wide affections embraced both the poor working man and the banks of issue, Carey was chiefly known for his indefatigable writings in favor of the protective system. For although, with a characteristic modesty, he confessed himself totally inferior to men like Raymond and List, with an enthusiasm no less characteristic he refused to allow this inferiority to dam his output. His simple arithmetical arguments were condemned by McDuffie of South Carolina as "statistical nonsense"; but he, and the equally simple Hezekiah Niles, of *Niles's Register*, were very popular. Moreover they were said to be entirely disinterested. This was probably not true of a promoter like List, or of lawyers like Raymond and Willard.[27]

V

In the end, of course, the tariff question would be settled, not by the theorists but by the practical men. In the spring of 1827, Martin Van Buren, accompanied by Churchill C. Cambreleng, the New York free trader, went traveling in the South. His object seems to have been chiefly to see if he could bring the Crawford Radicals into Jackson's fold; and this was easily accomplished by promising Crawford, who was slowly and angrily dying in Georgia, that everything would be done to bring about the ruin of Calhoun, who was Crawford's great bugbear. Calhoun himself had gone over to Jackson as early as June 1826; and Jackson had accepted him with the words "we shall march hand in hand." [28] Van Buren was far too wise to break with Calhoun at this stage of the game; but he knew that he could not rise in the new Democratic Party if Calhoun were to remain Jackson's heir-apparent. The obvious means of removing Calhoun lay ready to hand: by February 1827, it was already known that he would be accused of attempting to disgrace the General during the Seminole crisis of 1818.[29] But all that would have to wait till after the election. In May 1827 Van Buren returned from the South, plump and smiling. "He is now acting over the part in the affairs of the Union," wrote John Quincy Adams, who had glumly observed his progress through the South, "which Aaron Burr performed in 1799 and 1800; and there is much resemblance in character, manners, and even person, between the two men." [30]

Although he allowed his own hand-picked delegate, Samuel Young, to appear at the state convention in Albany which preceded the Harrisburg Convention, Van Buren would not allow Young to go to Harrisburg itself. He was not sure that the Convention would not end by advancing the fortunes of Henry Clay. In the meantime, he was being bombarded by letters from Thomas Cooper, the scientific president of South Carolina College, whom he had met at Columbia on his way to Charleston. Cooper was not a man to be disregarded. He was one of the ablest economists in the South; and, what was more to the point, he was an economist with a following. The simple argument that the Southern exchange of domestic staples for foreign manufactures would be ruined by protective tariffs would not, in itself, have stirred the planter to frenzy if it had not been for men like Cooper. Various, scholarly, fiery, controversial—he was exactly what the cotton kingdom admired in the way of an intellectual. Whether, in his long jumble of a career, he had not carried variety too far was another question. Born in eighteenth-century England, he was educated at Oxford but did not take a degree because of "an unwillingness to sign the Thirty-Nine Articles"; and this healthy dislike of authority turned him into an agitator-scientist, the friend of Joseph Priestley on the one hand and of the French Jacobins on the other. The English reaction to the French Revolution was no more disgusting to him than the French Terror; and, convinced that there would be no peace for him in Europe, he came searching for freedom in the United States. Here he was an outstanding example of the pressure that necessity will sometimes exert upon intelligence. He was imprisoned in Pennsylvania under John Adams's Sedition Act, yet he became an ardent admirer of John Adams's *Defence of the Constitutions*, he was a Jeffersonian in 1800 and very nearly a Federalist in 1811, a supporter of protective tariffs in the War of 1812 and their bitter foe after 1819, an antislavery man in England and a proslavery man in the United States: in brief, he was something between a calendar and a chameleon, a curious register of temporary fads and local prejudices. But Thomas Jefferson always supported him; perhaps because he needed Cooper's intelligence and hoped to make him useful, perhaps because he believed that Cooper at heart was a foe to tyranny. We cannot say whether he was right or whether he was wrong. Cooper experienced no difficulty in adjusting himself to the mental coloration of South Carolina. "We of the South," declaimed this ex-Englishman and ex-Pennsylvanian in 1827, who had then been in the South about six years, "hold our plantations . . . as the serfs and operatives of the North." He had recently published his *Lectures on the Elements of Political Economy*, which was chiefly remarkable for its ingenious handling of Ricardo's theory of rent in the interests of the conservative landowner; and which, of course, sternly denounced the doctrine of protectionism. He supported these lectures with a flood of speeches and articles; and in 1827 he was a famous man in South Carolina, an oracle who did not even wait for the formality of a consultation before bursting into advice and prophecy.[31]

On July 5, 1827, he was writing to Van Buren to say that if a new tariff on wool was passed—if "the *American system* is pushed"—"the next step, which I think will be adopted by this time twelve month . . . will be, to separate & declare Charleston a Free Port."[32] On July 31, his tone grew more menacing. "From what I can gather," he wrote, "on perusing the imperfect reports of the meeting at Albany, you incline to support the principle of a Tariff of protection. I regret it, for it is unworthy of your good sense, & political fitness. . . . You are treading on the crust of a Lava not yet solid. . . . The manufacturers will make the woollens bills a sectional question: you will be hurried on with the multitude. The measure will be carried; perhaps with some slight modification as to the quantum of the impost. In one twelve month from that period, South Carolina will be an independent State and her ports will be free ports. . . . Where will New York in that case derive her trade from? . . . Let your own manufacturers tax your own consumers as much as you choose to permit: we cannot stand under the system that transfers our money into your pockets without an equivalent." Van Buren was probably not disturbed by these threats: what followed, however, came a little too close to home. "I have taken it into my head [Cooper continued] that will all yr reputation for management, your management hitherto has been nothing but the clear sighted views of plain good sense, & honesty of intention. Therefore I venture to state to you with all freedom my own views. If you oppose decidedly (as I shd in your situation) not merely the woollens bill, but the principle of a protecting Tariff, your present popularity will sink, to rise with redoubled strength & full permanence." ³³ Van Buren was playing too delicate a game to allow his present popularity to sink; but Cooper had shown how weak was the alliance between the planters of the South and the plain republicans of the North. Van Buren kept his skirts clean by removing his own delegate from the Harrisburg Convention. But his failure to vote for the wool tariff early in the year had not made a very good impression in New York. "There was last spring," wrote William L. Marcy, state comptroller of New York and one of the leaders of the Albany Regency, "a more than half formed opinion that you were hostile to the tariff; this opinion was settling down into a conviction accompanied with some excitement and was doing infinite mischief to the cause of General Jackson in this state. . . . With . . . a manufacturing excitement rageing all over the State (except the city of New York) which will, I apprehend, be got up if Jackson's friends from this state do not all that mortal men can do for the success of such a measure [a high protective tariff], we shall have a difficult and doubtful conflict at the next election." ³⁴

Van Buren believed that Jackson himself was the only solution to the problem. Jackson was becoming so popular, one might almost say so mythical, a figure that he simply transcended differences; or, rather, floated above them as if he had been provided with a magic cloud or carpet. On his record as a Senator in 1824, he was a friend to tariffs and internal improvements; yet even his record seemed to have been forgotten where it would be dangerous to him, and remembered where it would do him good. As Van Buren put it, in a letter to Jackson, advising the General not to come to Washington, "I am entirely confident that all that is necessary to make the election perfectly safe is *that we be discreet.*" ³⁵ Jackson's indiscretions were famous; but Van Buren had not yet realized that they were almost always purposeful. Jackson did not deny what he had done in 1824—"I have nothing in my political career to keep secrete," he said, and he meant it—but he was not very discursive on the tariff question.³⁶ On the whole, people were quite satisfied with the publication of a letter he had written back in 1824, in which he had declared himself in favor of a "judicious examination and revision" of the tariff.³⁷ Obviously, this could mean one thing in South Carolina, and just the opposite in Pennsylvania, Ohio, and New York. Van Buren knew that he would have to declare himself on the tariff question before very long; but he felt pretty safe behind a leader who was not, in fact, either mendacious or opportunistic, but whom circumstances had endowed with the happy and effortless gift of being all things to almost all men.

VI

When the Twentieth Congress met in December, 1827, the manufacturing interest was in high hopes. The Western farmers appeared to have accepted the home-market argument, even though they did not approve of Clay's American System when it touched upon banking and the public lands. The home-market idea, however, was the farmer's hope of escaping from distresses that he attributed chiefly to the Administration—Henry Clay's favorite doctrine was being turned against Henry Clay.[38] To the manufacturing interest, this meant little. It had been assured by the Secretary of the Treasury's Reports that the Administration was on its side; but the Administration itself was visibly tottering. The business community has never been conspicuous for political loyalty; it will use any party that offers to be useful; and on this occasion it was ready to do business with anyone. After the Harrisburg Convention, the Twentieth Congress would have to do something; and although the Twentieth Congress was notoriously anti-Adams, this did not mean that it was necessarily anti-tariff.

The most important committees were naturally packed with opposition members. Even John Randolph was made chairman of the House Committee of Ways and Means; and although he proved to be too sick in mind and body to retain his chairmanship, his place was taken by McDuffie of South Carolina, who was just as intransigent. The House Committee on Manufactures had a protectionist chairman in Rollin Mallary of Vermont, and Mallary supported Adams, but the majority of its members were Jacksonians. None the less, the lobbyists who moved into Washington were not dismayed. There were manufacturers of all kinds from a dozen states; there were journalists from fifty newspapers; there was "a group of some thirty 'wool growers and other friends of the protecting principle,'" fresh from their triumph at Harrisburg; and behind them and around them there flowed a steady stream of memorials and petitions.[39]

The debate in the House began on March 4, 1828, when Rollin Mallary reported out the bill of his committee, which he said was not his own work and which he confessed himself determined to amend, so as to bring it more in line with the proposals of the Harrisburg Convention. He would not support it as it was: it was the work, he said, of Silas Wright of New York. With the mention of Wright's name, the bill ceased to be a serious piece of legislation, and became an ingenious but rather frantic stratagem, referring, as John Randolph put it, "to manufactures of no sort, but the manufacture of a President of the United States."[40]

The bill was framed to satisfy all the hopes of the Jacksonian tariff men in Pennsylvania, Ohio, and New York; but it bore very heavily upon New England, where the Administration was strongest. Thus the duty on raw wool was high, but the duty on imported woolens was low; and molasses, hemp, and iron were protected so thoroughly as to outrage the feelings of the New England rum-distillers, shipbuilders, and manufacturers of machinery. The Southern Jacksonians, all violent antitariff men, were to be asked to vote against any amendment designed to give relief to New England; New England would be forced to defeat the bill; and the Jacksonian tariff men would be able to tell their followers that it was not they but the New Englanders who had done the deed. The ruin of the Administration would be the inevitable result. Whether the Administration, which was already ruined, was worth such an elaborate stratagem was another question. But politicians are often timorous on the eve of triumph; and it was still feared that Adams and Clay would rescue themselves on the tariff issue. The Southern Jacksonians, of course, would only agree to vote for high tariffs on hemp, iron, and molasses upon the understanding that the Northern Jacksonians would—if the Administration's followers still persisted in voting for the bill—turn around and vote against it. It was upon this understanding that the plot was concerted.

The leading spirits were probably Martin Van Buren and his loyal henchman Silas Wright, both of whom were destined to play far worthier roles in the future; and the shrewdness of the plot bears all the signs of Albany politics. But Albany politics, with all their cleverness, were sometimes transparently innocent. It was easy to invent a stratagem to defeat a tariff; but would the tariff consent to be defeated?

VII

It was never difficult to justify protective tariffs on the patriotic grounds that "infant" industries needed a nurse. But protective tariffs have a life of their own, derived not from patriotism but from self-interest in its hungriest form; and tariff debates, which attempt to conceal the latter derivation, have a dull and ugly appearance, like an alligator pretending to be a log. John Taylor complained that "day after day passes without any sensible advance in the public business. One dull prosing speech after another & arguments for the fiftieth time repeated are hashed up & dished in new covers." [41] And one can imagine the House of Representatives as it was in those days—the members "lolling back in armchairs, laughing, coughing, spitting, rattling newspapers, while some poor speaker tried to talk above the din." [42] The Senate was more dignified: and the Senate offered at length one of the most extraordinary spectacles of the decade—the spectacle of Daniel Webster rising to his feet to explain that he was about to unsay all the great free-trade arguments he had made in the House in 1824. His oratory was not needed on this uninspiring occasion; never had he been less "the great cannon loaded to the lips." But never had he been more honest. He did not try to justify himself on moral or intellectual grounds: he simply said that he had changed his mind because New England had accepted the protective system as the established policy of the government, and after

1824 had built up her manufacturing enterprise on that basis. It was a profession of allegiance which the American people never forgot.[43]

In the meantime, the Southern and Northern Jacksonians in the House had obediently united in suppressing all amendments that would have given some comfort to the New England manufacturer. There were increased duties on pig iron and rolled bar iron, though no iron manufacturer had asked for them.[44] Flax was subjected to a duty of $60 a ton; hemp to $45 a ton—a direct blow at ropemakers and users of cordage, and therefore eventually at shipbuilders and shipowners. Wool was burdened with an ingenious mixture of specific and ad valorem duties—the specific duty raising the cost of coarse wools, used in the manufacture of carpets, and imported mainly from Asia Minor and South America, the ad valorem duty reaching the high grades of wool, much to the comfort of the domestic wool-grower. The low duty on coarse woolens was maintained, however, because coarse woolens were imported chiefly for the use of slaves in the Southern plantations. The whole point of the new duties on woolens was to defeat the provisions of the Harrisburg Convention, which had asked for the same duty on goods 40¢ to $2.50, thus taxing cheap goods at a far higher price than dear ones. The House now inserted a minimum point of $1.00 between these two valuations, which meant that woolen goods imported at $1.00—and a very large part of the imported woolens were worth, abroad, about that price—were now subjected only to a duty of 40¢, instead of the prohibitory duty suggested at Harrisburg. Since a very large part of domestic woolens were of the same character and value, it was not surprising that John Davis of Massachusetts should have lamented that "the dollar minimum falls at a point the most favorable that could be fixed for the British manufacturer." [45]

It only remains to add that the duty on molasses was raised from five to ten cents a gallon. The Bill was not unfavorable to the protectionists of the Middle and Western States, and although 22 of the 39 representatives of New England were against it, it passed the House by a vote of 105 to 94 on April 22, and was sent up to the Senate. The division in New England seemed decisive. As George McDuffie of South Carolina put it years later: "We saw this system of protection was about to assume gigantic proportions, and to devour the substance of the country, and we determined to put such ingredients in the chalice as would poison the monster and commend it to his own lips." [46] Everyone supposed that the New England Senators would now unite with the South to kill the measure out of hand.

VIII

But monsters, alas, have a certain tolerance for poison. On May 5, the Senate Committee on Manufactures reported the House's bill out with fourteen amendments, designed to restore that harmony between the grower and the manufacturer which the protectionist interest had created at Harrisburg. Vice-President Calhoun presided over the Senate on May 5 with an easy mind. He was not exactly in Van Buren's plot, but he knew and approved of it.[47] He supposed that all these amendments would be voted down. He soon realized to his horror that the arch-plotter was busily engaged in destroying his own plot. Years later, when Van Buren had become President-elect, Calhoun reviewed the whole scene in a bitter speech. "Relying on the assurance on which our friends acted in the House," he said, "we anticipated with confidence and joy that the bill would be defeated and the whole system overthrown by the shock. Our hopes were soon blasted. A certain individual, then a Senator, but recently elected to the highest office in the Union, was observed to assume a mysterious air in relation to the bill, very little in accordance with what, there was every reason to believe, would have been his course. The mystery was explained when the bill came up to be acted upon. I will not give in detail his course. It is sufficient to say, that, instead of resisting amendments, which we had a right to expect, he voted for all which were necessary to assure the votes of New England; particularly the amendments to raise the duties on woollens which were known to be essential for that purpose. All these amendments, with one or two exceptions, were carried by his votes. . . ."[48]

The accusation was substantially correct. "Why a course," he continued, "which good faith, as well as the public interest, so obviously dictated, was avoided, and the opposite pursued, has never been explained." The explanation, perhaps, is not very difficult. Those who play with high tariffs are apt to discover that high tariffs, in the end, will play with them. The language of the plot, of course, could still sometimes be heard in the Senate. Thomas Hart Benton, for example, mockingly asked for a duty on indigo in "gratitude" to the Southerners who had voted with the West against striking out the duty on hemp. But Benton was not mocking anybody when he moved for a forty-five per cent duty on furs; or when he pleaded with the Senate for a duty on lead, the only demand (he said) that Missouri had to make. The antiprotectionist Levi Woodbury of New Hampshire asked for and obtained a duty on all manufactured goods made of silk. Mahlon Dickerson of New Jersey, who had discovered that a solitary vermicelli factory was doing business in his State, wanted a fifty per cent duty on vermicelli: and so it went. And if all this was done in the open, one can easily imagine what was going on behind the scenes. What was meant to be a preposterous jest had suddenly become serious. Van Buren, at any rate, was unable to resist the forces he himself had set loose. The crucial day was May 5, when an amendment was offered that increased the duties on woolens to an ad valorem of forty-five per cent and was just enough to placate the manufacturers of New England. This amendment was passed by a vote of 26 to 21, with Van Buren and Woodbury voting with the protectionist majority; and thus the great plot was ended. Even then Daniel Webster, who spoke for the conservative businessmen of New England, could not make up his mind. The bill was still a bad bill; but then was it not better than no bill at all? In his perplexity, he consulted the President; and although what passed between the two men is unknown, Webster went on to make his speech, and to carry with him just enough New England Senators to pass the bill by a vote of 26 to 21. The Senate's amendments were accepted by the House, and the bill was signed by the President on May 19.[49]

Adams's signature meant only that he believed the bill to be Constitutional: like his predecessors, he did not consider himself justified in vetoing a piece of legislation merely because it was inexpedient. Known as the Tariff of Abominations, it satisfied nobody: it was a mere farrago of political tricks and undisguised appetites. None the less, protectionists preferred it to no bill at all, if only because it asserted the protectionist principle. This was the weakness of the American System: it called on self-interest to strip off all disguises, even the disguise of common sense; and when it triumphed, as in 1828, it triumphed at the cost of proving that it was probably unworkable.

IX

The country's disgust at this monstrous parody was well reflected in the columns of that sober protectionist, Hezekiah Niles.[50] But it was in South Carolina, which had become the leader of the seaboard South, that this disgust took the shape of an almost uncontrollable agitation. South Carolina had been nationalist when cotton prices were high and production was relatively small; she had become progressively less nationalist as prices declined and production increased. There had been a sudden price rise in 1825, which was a "good" year everywhere in the United States and a year of speculative buying in Great Britain; but the British panic in the winter of 1825-6 was hard on everyone in the United States and particularly hard on the planter. Liverpool worked its usual necromancy; the price of cotton fell from a high of 29.5 cents a pound in June 1825 to an average of 12 cents in 1826 and of 8.8 cents in 1827. South Carolinian planters were singularly articulate, not only in themselves but in their spokesmen, and as their purchasing power decreased and the new tariff movement threatened to raise the price of everything that they purchased, their grievances overflowed in the violent speeches of Thomas Cooper and the agitated pages of Robert J. Turnbull's *The Crisis*.[51]

After the passage of the Tariff of Abominations, South Carolina broke out into a new rash of "protest meetings and intemperately worded memorials."[52] In Washington, the South Carolinian delegation met at the house of Senator Robert Y. Hayne and agreed—not without some violent arguments—to keep their seats in Congress until its adjournment, and not to do anything extreme until after the Presidential election. Vice-President Calhoun was not present at these meetings; but he influenced them, and their final decision was in keeping with his wishes. He was, after all, in an exceedingly difficult position. He had killed the woolens bill in 1827; but even then he was assailed by Turnbull as a "moderate" and a "nationalist"; and while he did not wish to lose his character as a nationalist, he could not bear to see his own section slipping away from him.[53] He hoped that the election of Jackson would "reverse the precedent that brought Mr. Adams into power . . . arrest the protective system . . . overthrow the principles in which it originated." In after years, he declared that his opinion of Jackson was not very high. The opponents of the protective system, he said, were "compelled to select someone whose position, in relation to the Tariff, was not well defined; and who had a popularity in the States, friendly to the protective system, unconnected with politics. General Jackson united these advantages, to which he added others, which recommended him to the confidence of the South. He was a cotton planter and a slave holder; and as such, it was believed, would use his power and influence to halt the further progress, and to correct the excess, of a system so oppressive to the Staple States." [54] This statement, made in 1837, after he and Jackson had become mortal enemies, was more cold than incorrect. In 1828 Calhoun believed that he himself was to be Jackson's successor.

It was necessary for him that South Carolina should be kept under control until after the election; and that he, in the meantime, should not lose the confidence of South Carolina. When Congress adjourned on May 22, he hastened back to his plantation in the South Carolina uplands; and here, in the intervals of conferring with state politicians, he composed what was afterwards known as *The South Carolina Exposition and Protest.* This document was printed by the legislature on December 19, and scattered throughout the Union in pamphlet form. It was an extraordinary composition, a mixture of conventional arguments and metaphysical disquisitions, a plea for caution and a plan of action, at once reactionary and prescient, and informed with Calhoun's unique gift for stripping the disguise from sectional differences and showing them as the class differences they really were.

His arguments against the tariff were based upon the familiar theme that it was an unjust tax upon the South's exchange of domestic staples for foreign manufactures; that it was levied for the benefit of Northern profiteers; and that it would provoke such retaliation from the rest of the world that American exports—which were largely agricultural—would be ruined by it. Since the South was responsible for two thirds of the nation's exports, but was politically only one third of the Union, the tariff was a clear case of oppression by the majority. Granted his premises, Calhoun could follow out their implications with all the rigor of a medieval monk. But he was often unfortunate in his choice of premises, and in this case the premise that the tariff was solely responsible for the miseries of South Carolina was, to say the least, open to some doubt. There were other factors involved. Nothing was said in the *Exposition*—nothing could be said—about exhausted Carolina soils, which could not compete with the "buckshot" cotton lands in the new Southwest; about a one-crop slave-labor economy, depending more and more for its subsistence upon the produce of the West; about the inherent inefficiency of this economy, which made it the servant of Northern bankers and Northern shipowners, and a perpetual apprentice to the sorcery of

Liverpool and the world cotton market. If the Tariff of Abominations was indefensible, the economy of South Carolina was scarcely less so.

Calhoun's remedies were equally open to attack. Abandoning the old agrarian earthenworks of the natural law, he sought refuge in the concept of law as something dictated by the will of the majority. How then was it to be resisted if—as was the case with the tariff of 1828—it appeared to South Carolina to be tyrannous and un-Constitutional? Calhoun's answer was the doctrine of the unity of sovereignty. There was no division of sovereignty, he said, between the states and the federal government. Government was one thing; sovereignty another. Government was strictly limited in its application; sovereignty belonged solely to the people of the several states. This doctrine was derived from all sorts of fragments, dealing with the reserved rights of the sovereign states, in the writings of John Taylor of Caroline, James Turnbull, Judge Spencer Roane, and in the Virginia and Kentucky Resolutions. For a fixative to hold these fragments together in their new shape of the unity of sovereignty, he chose the old "compact" theory of the Constitution—the theory which held that the Constitution was nothing more than the articles of compact between sovereign states. According to his reading of this theory, each of these states could peacefully prevent the operation of any disputed law within its own limits, pending a decision by the same power that could amend the Constitution—namely, three fourths of the states. In this sense the *Exposition* was merely a threat of what South Carolina would do if the tariff was not repealed or modified; but it was a threat that contained a clear plan of action. It suggested caution for the present; and counseled the extreme, the rebellious, the treasonable step of nullification, if caution went unrewarded.

Calhoun was destined all his life to be a politician; but some ironical fairy seems to have bestowed upon him at his birth precisely the kind of mind—conventual, metaphysical, dedicated—which could never make its politics intelligible to the ordinary man. To most people his distinction between sovereignty and government was totally invisible—at best the dialectical splitting of Constitutional hairs. And the Hartford Convention had taught the lesson that the compact theory of the Constitution was something people pulled out of its pigeonhole when they were disgruntled or rebellious, and thrust back again when times got better and feelings were less exacerbated.

To the modern reader the *Exposition* may possibly seem of purely antiquarian interest—a mere piece of bric-à-brac, gathering dust in the attics of history. But suddenly, in the midst of his arguments, Calhoun comes forth with a paragraph that is not antiquarian at all.

> "The [protective] system [he writes] has not been sufficiently long in operation with us, to display its real character in reference to the point now under discussion. To understand its ultimate tendency, in distributing the wealth of society among the several classes, we must turn our eyes to Europe, where it has been in action for centuries,—and operated as one among the

efficient causes of that great inequality of property which prevails in most European countries. No system can be more efficient to rear up a moneyed aristocracy. Its tendency is, to make
the poor poorer, and the rich richer. Heretofore, in our country, this tendency has displayed itself principally in its effects,
as regards the different sections,—but time will come when it
will produce the same results between the several classes in
the manufacturing States. After we [the Southern planters] are
exhausted, the contest will be between the capitalists and operatives; for into these two classes it must, ultimately, divide society. The issue of the struggle here must be the same as it has
been in Europe. Under the operation of the system, wages
must sink more rapidly than the necessaries of life, till the operatives will be reduced to the lowest point,—when the portion
of the products of their labor left to them, will be barely sufficient to preserve existence."

The South Carolina legislature did not see fit to publish this particular paragraph—and small wonder. If it was to break with the Union, it was upon
sectional and not class terms that it proposed to do so. The paragraph,
written when Karl Marx was still a little boy in Trèves, is a strange, rude,
compelling prevision (borrowed in part from John Taylor of Caroline) of
some of the ideas that one day Marx was to raise into a system. But whereas
Marx's dialectic led him to the conclusion that the battle between the capitalist and the laborer must end in social revolution and the victory of the
working class, Calhoun in the course of time took the position that revolution was impending but that it need not take place. What he wanted was
an alliance not between the planters of the South and the plain republicans
of the North but between the planters of the South and the conservative
businessmen of the North. The Northerners would promise not to interfere
with slavery in the South, and the Southern planters would give all the assistance in their power to put down labor agitation in the North. This alliance
has to some extent been realized in our day; but Calhoun, more happy with
abstractions and predictions than with the actualities of his own time, and
concerning himself more and more exclusively with his "arresting defense
of reaction, a sort of intellectual Black Mass," never seems to have realized
that the Northern laborer might not make his bargain with destiny, might
not accept the postulates of proletarianism, but might content himself with
agitation as a substitute for revolution.

All this, however, was in the future. In 1828, the *Exposition* was published, without the offensive paragraph, and without any reference to Calhoun as the author. It was considered that a vice-president's name upon such
a document would have an odd and unseemly appearance. None the less,
Calhoun's style and mind were too forceful not to be recognized at once;
and whatever good the *Exposition* may have done him in South Carolina,
it did him little but damage as a national figure. To Martin Van Buren this
was manna from heaven.[55]

X

Van Buren had voted for the passage of the Tariff of Abominations, but he had taken the sensible precaution of demanding explicit instructions from his own legislature before he did so. Thus he retained his position with the protectionists of New York, but avoided any odium in the national sense. Although the plot had exploded in his face, although the engineer had been hoist with his own petard, that fortunate man had merely risen, as it were, gracefully upward. Moreover, the sudden and unexpected death of Governor De Witt Clinton on February 11—"he had only time to say, Charles I feel a stricture across my breast & departed"—had left Van Buren supreme among New York Jacksonians.[56] What was to prevent him from running for the governorship as a step toward Jackson's Cabinet and the Presidency itself? Senators, indirectly elected, could not truly be called popular men. "Being a candidate at this time," said one of his correspondents, "would make the justices, constables, & all the minor active men in the towns familiar with your name. . . . Indeed I lay it down as certain that unless a man has performed military service or been before the people in such a way as to make them familiar with his name, he can never have a well founded popularity." [57] *The justices, constables & all the minor active men in the towns:* here was a new force in national politics. Advice like this was too sound to be disregarded; nor was it.

As for Andrew Jackson, no matter what obscure roles his friends had played in it, he himself was not in the least damaged by the Tariff of Abominations. The American people took it for granted that he stood a little apart from such things. Jackson's mind lay fallow, ready to be seeded with the ideas that dealt with the protection, not of manufactures, but of small businessmen and small property-holders; so that the popular instinct was undoubtedly correct. But the Tariff—pushed through by New England Senators and signed by a New England President—did the Administration whatever damage there was left to be done. The Administration, after all, was unashamedly protectionist. "Harmony and concord among the friends of the American System," said Henry Clay, "can only be preserved by the adherence to what has been done, although some of it has been ill done." [58] Ever since John Marshall had smitten the rock in *McCulloch v. Maryland,* and the waters of economic nationalism had gushed forth in all their plenitude, the Executive had been carried along with them—Monroe with some signs of protest, Adams willingly. Adams's Secretary of the Treasury had invited the manufacturers to a feast of sound and dignified protectionism; the manufacturers had accepted the invitation; and the Administration had suffered its usual fate. Once again, *adagio* had become *prestissimo;* once again, and for the last time, everything had got out of control.

And to all this there was a curious and ironical pendent. The Tariff of Abominations was an absurd and unlooked-for conclusion to Adams's long argument with British coal and iron; but it was a conclusion, none the less. When Jackson was elected President, James Brown, who had succeeded Gallatin as Minister at Paris, wrote from that city to announce that "the British are delighted with the choice." How could they be delighted with the choice of the backwoods general, the frontier imperialist, the victor of New Orleans, the executioner of Arbuthnot and Ambrister? "They say [Brown explained] Jackson will repeal the Tariff." [59]

CHAPTER SEVEN

Finale

IN APRIL 1828 Henry Clay, complaining of "a paralytic numbness and
torpidity" of his left leg, thought that he must go home "and die or get
better." When Brigadier General Winfield Scott, his own choice, was not
nominated for the vacant major-generalship on April 17, the place being
given to Alexander Macomb, he offered to resign, and the "paralytic numbness and torpidity" crept up towards his hip. Adams perceived the connection between these two events. "This is in every point a disastrous occur-
rence," he wrote of Clay's illness, "and is among those of deep humiliation
which are thickening around me." Were not all his lieutenants about to
desert him, on one excuse or another, in order to seek "a shelter from the
storm with which they are in fear of being overwhelmed?" There were
Secretaries Rush and Barbour, both asking for the vacant post at London,
which no man in his senses would have wanted at such a time, except as
a refuge. He did not blame them. But he was sure that their "anxiety to
save themselves from the wreck" and "Mr. Clay's recent propensities to resign" were one and the same thing.[1]

In the end, Clay proved to be too loyal and, indeed, too mercurial to
give up. He agreed to take a short holiday, in order to consult the eminent
Dr. Philip S. Physick of Philadelphia. And although he still announced that
he had few hopes of surviving and set little value on life, he was soon writing
from Philadelphia, with all his usual vigor, to urge the immediate dismissal
of Postmaster-General McLean. Nor did he neglect, that spring, to do a
little brisk electioneering in Kentucky.[2] Rush also—too fastidious and high-
minded to turn his back on a losing cause—consented to run for vice-president on Adams's ticket.[3] But James Barbour went to London, and McLean—
though he continued to express his devotion to Adams, and managed his
department with great efficiency—was believed to be so Jacksonian in his

sympathies and appointments that John W. Taylor, for one, thought it hardly safe to entrust a private letter to his own post office at Ballston Spa.[4] Adams himself had long since decided that "the base and profligate combination against Clay and me would succeed in their main object. . . . General Jackson . . . will be elected." [5]

I

It was, indeed, a contest between David and Goliath, with both the characters and the outcome reversed. David advanced, slow, sullen, unarmed and unloved; Goliath, growing more gigantic by the minute, was universally applauded. David's slingshot bounced harmlessly off the forehead of his adversary; and then the great arm was raised and the terrible spear did its work.

John Quincy Adams depended chiefly upon a reputation for public service very nearly unique in the annals of the republic; but it was service performed in foreign lands or behind the walls of the State Department. Andrew Jackson had a military reputation that consisted only of victories, and would probably have been sufficient; but he had reinforced it with a constant reiteration of the "bargain and corruption" cry. This was his real strength, for the "bargain and corruption" cry went very deep. Superficially, it meant (and Andrew Jackson most sincerely believed that it did mean) that the American people had been cheated of their rights by two individuals called Adams and Clay; but in another and more persuasive sense it implied that the Adams-Clay coalition represented the sway of an old, creaking, and privileged political machine, which could no longer do the work that was required of it.

This might seem a little unjust to Adams and Clay, both men of vision; yet the fact remained that Adams's planned economy and Clay's American System both seemed to place the state at the service of one special interest. The coalition might call itself "National Republican"; but a more lucid title would have been "Neo-Federalist," since the old Federalist emphasis on commercial capital had been replaced by a new emphasis on industrial capital. Andrew Jackson, on the other hand, had no program, almost no ideas: he offered—on an ascending scale of values—his personal vendetta against Adams and Clay, a willingness to place himself at the service of the American people, and a profound and ingrained respect for their judgment. This respect, it is true, would have been seriously modified if the popular judgment had not consistently rewarded Jackson with offices and honors. To this extent, it would be true to say that he supported democracy "primarily because it supported him." [6] But, having realized in 1824 and 1828 that he was the popular candidate, he was ready to "support democracy" with all the intensity of his extraordinary character. His great "Protest to the Senate" in 1834 defines his ultimate position as well as anything can; and these words, in particular, are peculiarly illuminating:

"In the history of conquerors and usurpers, never in the fire of youth nor in the vigor of manhood could I find an attraction to lure me from the path of duty, and now I shall scarcely find an inducement to commence their career of ambition when gray hairs and a decaying frame, instead of inviting to toil and battle, call me to the contemplation of other worlds, where conquerors cease to be honored and usurpers expiate their crimes. The only ambition I can feel is to acquit myself to Him to whom I must soon render an account of my steward-ship, to serve my fellow-men, and live respected and honored in the history of my country. No; the ambition which leads me on is an anxious desire and a fixed determination to return to the people unimpaired the sacred trust they have confided to my charge; to heal the wounds of the Constitution and pre-serve it from further violation; to persuade my countrymen, so far as I may, that it is not in a splendid government sup-ported by powerful monopolies and aristocratical establish-ments that they will find happiness or their liberties protection, but in a plain system, void of pomp, protecting all and grant-ing favors to none, dispensing its blessings, like the dews of Heaven, unseen and unfelt save in the freshness and beauty they contribute to produce." [7]

This restatement of agrarian ideals was as far as Jackson needed to go; for in his time economic relations had not attained that terrible impersonality which requires the close and persistent intervention of the government. Jackson still believed in the Jeffersonian creed of weak government: "a plain system, void of pomp." But when he did intervene, he did so in a positive manner, without excusing himself, and always in what he believed to be the interest of an expanding economy. In his Farewell Address the same enemies appear as in the Protest—"great moneyed corporations," "monopoly," "exclusive privileges": he strove to defeat these because he believed them to be (as in the days of special charters they certainly were) checks upon sound business enterprise; because the American "common man" of his time was the small capitalist, the small farmer, the skilled crafts-man; because American democracy was still conceived of itself as the democ-racy of independent property-holders.[8] Jacksonian philosophy sometimes went further than that: Jackson himself never did.

In 1828, however, he stood before the American people merely as the symbol of change. He promised nothing more than that he would be dif-ferent from Adams; and the American people construed this to mean that he would put an end to political privilege and inaugurate an era of oppor-tunity. The real nature of the crisis confronting them—the effort of the business community to dominate the government—had been concealed rather than revealed by the Tariff of Abominations, because the Tariff had orig-inally been designed to defeat itself, and had outwitted this design only at the price of becoming absurd. The secondary crisis—that a slave-holding state might resist this effort in the name of State Rights and to the verge of rebellion—had not yet emerged from the pages of Calhoun's *Exposition*. The ferment which preceded the election of 1828, and which Calhoun had the insight to translate into a class conflict, arose from the profound belief that there was "something radically wrong in the administration of the government." The one specific charge against Adams was that he had destroyed the West Indies trade; otherwise the campaign was allowed to remain on the level of personalities.

Here Adams, who so conspicuously lacked the public personality, had no chance. The result was a foregone conclusion; and few Jacksonians in the summer of 1828 thought otherwise. Both sides already had national general committees in Washington, state central committees, and local committees of correspondence; but the Jacksonians had been steadily at work since 1825 drumming up enthusiasm for the General at militia musters, fish frys, and barbecues—a form of frontier electioneering which jovially supplemented the work of their pamphleteers and editors. The Jacksonian press was certainly the more forceful: Peter Force's *National Journal* in Washington was not equal to Duff Green's *United States Telegraph*, Charles King's New York *American* never got the better of Mordecai Noah's New York *Enquirer*; and no editor on the Adams side could equal Isaac Hill of the *New Hampshire Patriot*, Thomas Ritchie of the Richmond *Enquirer*, or Amos Kendall of the *Argus of Western America*.[9]

A campaign between personalities is bound to degenerate into mere abuse; but the degeneration of the 1828 campaign has rarely been equaled. To call Jackson a gambler, a drunkard, and a duelist, and Adams a monarchist, a gourmandizer, and a spendthrift was one thing: it was part of the give and take of an election and, like the dead cats and rotten eggs with which the free and independent electors of Great Britain pelted their candidates in pre-Reform days, might be taken by both men as an unpleasant but unavoidable necessity. Even the "Coffin Handbill," put out by John Binns of the Philadelphia *Democratic Press*, and accusing the General of the murder of six militiamen during the War of 1812, came just within the verge of political license—at least in the sense that the General could defend his own reputation. But in 1827 a story was printed in the Cincinnati *Gazette* accusing Jackson of having knowingly lived in adultery with Rachel Jackson before she was divorced from her first husband. (The facts, of course, were that Jackson and Rachel Robards had been married in 1791 in the belief that she had been legally divorced from Lewis Robards in Virginia; and that they had been living together for two years before they discovered, to their horror, that that divorce had never been granted. They had then remarried.) The slander almost entered the campaign of 1824; it was being whispered about in 1825; in 1826, Charles Hammond, editor of the Cincinnati *Gazette*, was doing all that he could to spread it around by word of mouth; and in 1827 it was given a semiofficial sanction by its appearance in the columns of the Administration's leading newspaper, the Washington *National Journal*.[10]

That one of the happiest and most unexceptionable marriages in the United States should have been dragged into the campaign in this foul way must be taken as an example of the strange desperation that surrounded Presidential contests in those days. Charles Hammond was one of the leaders of the Ohio bar; he had been praised by Chief Justice Marshall for his "acuteness and accuracy of mind"; he had been offered a seat on the Supreme Court of the United States; yet, when a dignified refutation of the slander, prepared by a Nashville committee, was published in the Washington *United States Telegraph*, Hammond was unmoved. He replied with the unforgivable question: "Ought a convicted adultress and her paramour husband be placed in the highest offices of this free and christian land?" [11] Jackson writhed in agony. "How hard it is," he wrote to his friend John Coffee, "to keep a cowhide from these villains." [12]

The villains were not just Charles Hammond and Peter Force. The President could have kept the *Journal* from encouraging Hammond if he had wished to do so. In order to let the story go on, he had first to believe it; and this, it seems, the Puritan in him was only too ready to do.[13] Clay, too skeptical to believe such a tale, and far more skilled in the management of editors than Adams, could and should have killed it; but Clay's ambition pursued him like a Fury. The *National Journal* repeated the slander; the Adams "National General Committee" in Washington circulated Hammond's *A View of General Jackson's Domestic Relations:* and the President and the Secretary of State, protesting with perfect truth that they had had no hand in starting the slander, stood by and let it go on. Slander is infectious; and Duff Green of the Washington *United States Telegraph* was soon printing in his columns some nonsensical story about premarital relations between President and Mrs. Adams. He wrote in triumph to Andrew Jackson to tell him of what he had done. "Let Mrs. Jackson rejoice," he said, "her vindication is complete." How one reputation could be vindicated by the blackening of another is a question that seems not to have disturbed the florid Mr. Green, who, whatever his faults, had never been accused of over-subtlety; but Jackson's reply was calculated to make him sink into the ground. "*I never war against females,*" wrote the General, "and it is only the base and cowardly that do." [14] No more was heard about Mrs. Adams; but in January 1828 Isaac Hill of the *New Hampshire Patriot* announced that John Quincy Adams, while Minister at St. Petersburg, had prostituted a beautiful American girl to the lusts of the Tsar Alexander. This accusation was ludicrous; but with it the campaign, as far as the editors and pamphleteers could push it there, had disappeared into the mud.[15]

The immediate victim was Rachel Jackson. When she heard the stories that were being told against her, her heart was nearly broken. The thought that she might be dragged out of her privacy into the social glare of Washington completed the damage that the charges of adultery had begun. To the outsider, Rachel Jackson would not have seemed fitted to follow in the steps of Dolly Madison, Elizabeth Monroe, and Louisa Catherine Adams: she was short, she was stout, she was swarthy, she was careless in her dress; her manner were the manners of the frontier; she smoked her pipe of an evening. Beside her tall husband, with his air of the high, fine gentleman, she made an incongruous appearance. But Jackson, who loved her better than anything in the world, thought her perfect. And in Donaldson County, and widely throughout Tennessee, "Aunt Rachel"—with her piety, her benevolence, her selflessness, her acute sensitivity to the feelings and needs of other people—was known for the great lady she really was. Had she survived, the city of Washington might have made the same discovery. After the excitement of the election, her spirits sank lower and lower—"I had rather be a doorkeeper in the house of God," she was heard to murmur, "than to live in that palace in Washington"—and within a month she was dead. Ten thousand people came to her funeral: and they did not come for the show, or to honor a President-elect. Standing by her grave, Andrew Jackson whispered, more to himself than to the bystanders: "In the presence of this dear saint I can and do forgive all my enemies. But those vile wretches who have slandered her must look to God for mercy." [16] He had grown, it was said, "twenty years older in a night."

II

The circulation of all these scandals showed what an abyss there still was between the politicians and the people. The effort to discredit the General was ignored by the voters, and ended only in the death of the General's wife. Abandoning issues, the politicians came up with innuendoes that grew more and more desperate: the voters had already formulated the issues, at least to the extent of believing that Adams was indifferent to their grievances and that Jackson was not. The politicians told one another that Jackson was too old, tired, and inexperienced to do much: the voters believed that he could do a great deal.

Politically, Jackson represented a release of energy. In the campaign of 1824, six states chose their electors in the legislature, and in seven others the choice was made by districts and not by a general ticket. In the campaign of 1828, only two states committed the choice to the legislature, and only four states retained the district system.[17] Moreover, the qualifications for voting had grown less severe, and the population had increased. It was a Jacksonian belief that Adams would not have succeeded in the campaign of 1824-5 if the people had had a proper access to the polls; and it was assumed that if Jackson triumphed in 1828 it would be because the polls had become accessible.

A release of political energy in early nineteenth-century America meant also a release of aspiration. The American ideal was still a nation of independent property-holders; and it was still believed that this ideal could be realized through simple political mechanisms. Adams's plan of progress through privilege (high tariffs, a national bank, costly public lands, internal-improvements corporations) and Jackson's belief in progress through opportunity (a "judicious tariff," no national bank, cheap public lands, hostility to internal improvements at the federal expense) were not rigidly exclusive: they suggested no more than modifications of a *laisser-faire* economy which

Jackson always supported and which Adams disliked but would never have been able to overthrow. The question was, in whose favor was this economy to be modified? And to what extent?

The question could not be answered under the one-party system; and from the ferment of the late 1820's, which was an instinctive and delirious effort to find an answer, there emerged two parties—the National Republicans and the Jacksonian Democrats—which at least promised that the question might be debated.[18] The need for a debate was critical, as Jackson afterwards discovered when he was confronted with disunion in South Carolina; when he found himself obliged to veto a bill for improving the road from Maysville to Lexington; when he fought his great battle with the Bank of the United States. By "debate" one means the continual effort of American democracy to settle economic differences without recourse—in Jackson's day to tyranny, in ours to totalitarianism. Jackson's methods of debating were in themselves debatable; and no one would suggest that he settled the crisis he was called upon to face, for the crisis would emerge, in different shapes and circumstances, as long as liberal capitalism survived. But he placed himself squarely upon the side of the small property-holder—"the planter, the farmer, the mechanic and the laborer . . . the bone and sinew of the country, men who love liberty and desire nothing but equal rights and equal laws"—and he did so in part because he had retained a Jeffersonian belief in the freedom and dignity of the individual, the uncommonness of the common man.[19] From the simple and personal relations of his time to the complex and impersonal ones of ours is a long and difficult journey; and Jeffersonian beliefs have found the battle for survival progressively more difficult. Moreover, what had Jackson to offer us but an example? History never repeats itself; what is gone is gone: and if history teaches anything, it is that we invariably disregard what it has to teach. In Jefferson's election in 1800 and Jackson's in 1828 we observe the emergence of a great leader in a time of crisis, who founded his leadership on a respect for liberty and democracy; and we would say the same thing of Lincoln, Wilson, and Franklin Roosevelt. But these great men do not necessarily represent some American continuum; they are illustrations, not proofs; analogies, not precedents; and we have reason to hope but no reason to *assume* that an analogous leadership will always be found when it is needed. The choice has always to be made, and it is never the same choice. Jackson offers an example because he and his followers championed certain liberal "freedoms" that are still recognizable— that is to say, are analogous to the ones we ourselves profess. Whether the future will have any use for such freedoms is uncertain; but contemporary experience suggests that a future without them will hardly be worth living in.

As the nation moved towards the election of 1828, it seemed to be wrapt in anticipation. The Era of Good Feelings was mortally smitten by the Panic of 1819; it was probably buried by the Missouri debates; and its obsequies were recited by John Taylor of Caroline. It was succeeded (one might say) by the Era of Suspense. Neither period was very kind to the creative mind, for the personal myth was still ensnared in politics. Utopias came and went:

Robert Owen's New Harmony was submerged by the acquisitive frontier, as if the jungle had been let into it; Frances Wright's Nashoba succumbed to the very slave atmosphere it had sought to dispel. The imagination hibernated. In architecture, it is true, the dawn of the romantic movement already stirred among façades and roofs; but architecture still offered mainly curiosities—such as the head office of the United States Bank in Philadelphia, which was an exact replica of the Parthenon, a union of finance and chastity more fascinating than persuasive. Painters painted portraits. The most forceful writers divided their energies between political philosophy and political polemics. Even Washington Irving's remarkable observation was becoming filmy and insipid. But the transition from the Era of Good Feelings to the Era of Suspense is suggested in two novels by an unabashed romantic—*The Spy* (1821) and *The Pilot* (1823) by James Fenimore Cooper. Both were products of the postwar nationalism of the Era of Good Feelings; and in both the nationalist figures—George Washington and John Paul Jones—are, as it were, veiled. Both move about in disguise.[20] Cooper's purpose was no more than to compose two patriotic romances; but American writers who, like Cooper, made no effort to evaluate the social forces of their time often produced symbols that did this work for them. Cooper was no Melville; but Cooper at least interpreted the prevailing nationalism of the 1820's. Everybody believed that the nation was destined to be great (John Taylor of Caroline, perhaps, would have said that it was destined only to be big); but who was to profit by this greatness? American destiny was obscure, until some leader could arise who would restore its features. Cooper's own and obvious answer can be found, no doubt, in *The Prairie* (1827), a novel about life beyond the Mississippi, in a land which Cooper had never seen, and which he filled with stereotypes—superhuman scouts, benevolent and reflective pioneers, and Indians who were either noble savages (if they were on our side) or red devils (if they were not). Cooper himself despised the real frontier—the frontier of raw settlements and shiftless settlers; for he was nothing if not a country squire.[21] But the massive amount of misinformation *The Prairie* conveyed is as nothing when compared to its misty revelation of the agrarian ideal. As long as the frontier advanced into unknown or half-known country, then even land-speculation, however gross and extortionate, became simply the mechanics of surmise; and the nation of independent property-holders and of equal rights was always a remote possibility, all the more alluring because it was remote. Calhoun, who predicted social revolution in the North, never seemed to have realized that this mysterious and hopeful frontier, the very symbol of surmise, was itself the antidote to revolution.[22] But Calhoun was a sternly logical agrarian: no one has ever suggested that he was a romantic one. . . . Calhoun who, it was said, made an attempt at writing poetry, produced the single word "Whereas," and never tried again.

John Quincy Adams, who presided over the Era of Suspense, made the strange mistake of turning his back on surmise—strange in a man who, as Secretary of State, had drawn that great line to the Pacific. His planned economy was intended to be above the reach of special interests; but contemporary circumstances molded it into a plan of conservation and privilege. He seemed, to the majority of his countrymen, a living obstacle, an image of frustration. The battle between the Adamsites and the Jacksonians, therefore, was like a battle between the dam and the flood, with the dam already weakened by political earthquakes. The election was held between October 31 (Pennsylvania, Ohio) and November 14 (Tennessee); and when the returns were in, it was discovered that Adams had carried all New England, New Jersey, Delaware, and Maryland; and that the rest of the country had gone to Jackson. The popular vote was 647,276 for Jackson and 508,604 for Adams, reflecting large majorities for Adams in New England and a close contest in New York. The electoral vote was 178 to 83, revealing Jackson's immense popularity, which gave him, indeed, every electoral vote in Pennsylvania and in the huge stretches of country west of Pennsylvania and south of the Potomac.[28]

Adams had been predicting defeat for some time; but when the defeat came, its size astonished and horrified him. He spoke of "the ruin of our cause . . . the overwhelming ruins of the Administration." "The year begins in gloom," he wrote on January 1, 1829. "My wife had a sleepless and painful night. The dawn was overcast, and, as I began to write, my shaded lamp went out, self-extinguished. It was only for lack of oil; and the notice of so trivial an incident may serve to mark the present temper of my mind. . . . I began the year with prayer, and then, turning to my Bible, read the first Psalm. It affirms that the righteous man is, and promises that he shall be, blessed. This is comfort and consolation." [24] But was it? He had endeavored to guide the nation into the paths of righteousness—to teach it those scientific laws which he believed to be manifestations of the thought of his Creator. The nation had responded by electing General Jackson, who was anything but scientific and whom Adams believed to be both malignant and lawless. Was this because Adams had not duly served his Creator? Or had his Creator abandoned him? Or could the election of Jackson mean that Adams's concept of a watchful Providence, benevolent but mechanistic, was totally astray? From that time on he was a prey to those "involuntary but agonizing doubts, which I can neither silence nor expel." [25]

He decided that it would be unbecoming for him to attend the inauguration of a man who for three years had accused him of bargain and corruption; and all the Cabinet, except Mr. Rush, agreed with him.[26] As the day approached, all were stricken. Mr. Clay was thin and pale, and his eyes were "sunk in his head," Mr. Rush was "alarmingly ill," Mr. Southard was bedridden, General Peter B. Porter, who had taken Barbour's place in the War Department, was "almost blind from an inflammation of the eyes," and Attorney-General Wirt suffered from vertigo. Such was the report of Mrs. Harrison Smith, who went everywhere and knew everyone. About the health of Postmaster-General McLean she had nothing to say; we may assume it was flourishing. As the friends of the Administration prepared to depart she noted, too, "so many changes in society—so many families broken up, and those of the first distinction." Washington's best drawing-rooms were "empty, silent, dark, dismantled. Oh! 'tis melancholy." [27]

But while the drawing-rooms were deserted, the inns and the boarding houses were spilling over with human beings, not only in Washington but in Georgetown and in Alexandria. The new President had, in one way or another, nearly eleven thousand offices in his gift; and the office-seekers, the reverse side of the dispensation of opportunity, came to greet the dispenser, a hungry and unmanageable mob. Jackson arrived on February 12— a sad, emaciated old man, in deep mourning for his Rachel. He was not expected to serve for more than four years: the scramble for offices was all the more relentless. The siege of Gadsby's Hotel, where Jackson stayed, was so disorderly, and the appearance of the besiegers so *farouche* and forbidding, that anti-Jacksonians called the hotel "The Wigwam." As for Inauguration Day itself: "recall to your recollection," Henry Clay told the Senate three years later, "the 4th of March, 1829, when the lank, lean, famished forms, from fen and forest, and the four quarters of the Union, gathered together in the halls of patronage; or stealing by evening's twilight into the apartments of the president's mansion, cried out, with ghastly faces, and in sepulchral tones, "give us bread! Give us treasury pap! Give us our reward!" [28] Clay's imagery was more alliterative than accurate; but the mob that followed Jackson back from the Capitol to the President's mansion (soon to be called the White House), and burst into the East Room, was long remembered. "Orange punch by barrels full was made, but as the waiters opened the door to bring it out, a rush would be made, the glasses broken, the pails of liquor upset, and the most painful confusion prevailed. . . . Wines and ice-creams could not be brought out to the ladies, and tubs of punch were taken from the lower story into the garden, to lead off the crowd from the rooms. On such an occasion it was certainly difficult to keep any thing like order, and it was mortifying to see men, with boots heavy with mud, standing on the damask satin chairs, from their eagerness to get a sight of the President." The President himself, "listless with exhaustion," was rescued with some difficulty and spirited away by a back entrance. "A regular Saturnalia," wrote James Hamilton of South Carolina: "It would have done Mr. Wilberforce good to have seen a stout black wench eating a jelley with a gold spoon on the lawn of the President's House." Not all, it would seem, were office-seekers. "People have come five hundred miles to see General Jackson," Webster remarked, "and they really seem to think that the country had been rescued from some dreadful danger." He may have been right.[29]

III

While the crowd gathered around the Capitol, and watched Andrew Jackson take the oath from Chief Justice Marshall (a formidable encounter), John Quincy Adams rode out from Meridian Hill, whither he had removed his family, and entered the city. Through deserted F Street he rode, as far as the Rockville Turnpike, and then came back by way of College Hill. Towards the end of this morose pilgrimage, "near the Post Office I was over-taken by a man named Dulaney, who first inquired of me whether I could inform him how he could see John Quincy Adams." [30] Well, there he was: a great man certainly, and possibly a very good one; but a President who had planned for the people, without ever trying to understand them.

IV

Years later, Martin Van Buren was to write that the people of the United States were Andrew Jackson's "blood relations—the only blood relations that he had." [31] In 1829, the real distinction between him and Adams lay in this feeling of relationship. On the record, Jackson was still a conservative. One could search his past and produce nothing more positive than an aver-sion to paper money; but this aversion, significantly enough, he shared not with the Westerner but with the working man of the East. He came to the Presidency, as it were, to learn from the only source of learning available to him—his feeling for the people. The political aspects of his Presidency, the steps by which he seized and maintained a firm control of his own party, present this education as being far from idealistic: it would be sentimental to suppose that it was. It was often harsh and sometimes relentless. But with every year, every month of his Presidency, he grew in stature, because his education as President was founded upon a simple idealism—one might almost say a simple faith—that "a plain system, void of pomp, protecting all and granting favor to none" was the system that "the genius of our people re-quires." As Van Buren put it, in words curiously strong, he thought that "to labor for the good of the masses was a special mission assigned to him by his Creator." [32]

In 1829, however, it was often said that he was too old, too sick, and too heartbroken to last out his four years; and no one supposed that he would run for re-election. Van Buren, who had been elected governor of New York, lingered on in Albany to go through the formalities of resigning be-fore he took up his duties as Secretary of State. He did not arrive in Wash-ington until the end of March. He had been seriously warned by friends—both before he left and while he was on his way—that he was about to attach himself to a doomed Administration; that Jackson's Cabinet was mediocre and disunited; that Jackson himself was an ignoramus. On the night of his arrival, having politely disposed of a crowd of office-seekers, whose gross importunities were not very heartening, he made his way to the President's House. He found Jackson sitting in his office with Major William B. Lewis, a picture of weariness and dejection. But no sooner had they begun to talk than he watched with pleased surprise the vitality flood-ing back into the President's face and body. [33] It was by the light of a single candle, we are told, that he was able to observe this reassuring transforma-tion: in a sense, that candle has never gone out.

NOTES

BIBLIOGRAPHY

INDEX

Notes

PART ONE

CHAPTER ONE

1. John Quincy Adams to John Adams, July 7, 1814; John Quincy Adams, *Writings*, Worthington Chauncey Ford, ed., V, 57n.
2. Louisa Catherine Adams to John Quincy Adams, June 10, 1814; John Quincy Adams to Louisa Catherine Adams, July 22, 1814; *ibid.*, V, 66 and 66n.
3. Viscount Castlereagh to the Earl of Liverpool, August 28, 1814; Wellington, *Supplementary Despatches*, IX, 190.
4. Henry Goulburn to Earl Bathurst, September 2, 1814; *ibid.*, IX, 217.
5. W. A. Dunning, *The British Empire and the United States*, 5.
6. Gallatin to Badollet, May 4, 1789; Henry Adams, *The Life of Albert Gallatin*, 72.
7. *The Diary of James Gallatin*, Count Gallatin, ed., 32.
8. Adams, *The Life of Albert Gallatin*, 17.
9. *American State Papers, Miscellaneous*, I, 724-41.
10. Gallatin to Jean Charles Leonard de Sismondi, June 10, 1842. "Je ne regrette point que telle ait été ma destinée; je n'avais pas des talents nec-essaires pour cultiver avec succès les les lettres ou les sciences; et mes facultés ont été probablement employées plus vitalement dans la vie active ou j'ai été jetté, et pour laquelle j'étais plus propre." Gallatin *MSS*, New York Historical Society.
11. John Jacob Astor to Gallatin, October 9, 1815; Gallatin *MSS*. In 1830, however, Gallatin *did* accept the presidency of the National Bank (later Gallatin Bank) of New York, of which J. J. Astor was one of the principal stockholders.
12. Hon. W. H. Lyttleton to Sir Charles Bagot, January 22, 1827; *George Canning and his Friends*, Capt. Josceline Bagot, ed., II, 362.
13. John Quincy Adams, *Memoirs*, IV, October 12, 1818, 131-2.
14. *Ibid.*, IV, June 4, 1819, 388.
15. Christopher Hughes to Gallatin, November 16, 1821; Gallatin, *MSS*. Hughes, who was on good terms with John Quincy Adams, but who congratulated himself on the exquisite amenity of his own address, added rather waspishly, "*Quaere*, does such *touching up* do any good?" See also *Holmes-Pollock Letters*, I, 95, Holmes to Pollock,

July 16, 1899. Samuel Gilman Brown, *The Life of Rufus Choate*, 417.

16. *The Duplicate Letters, the Fisheries, and the Mississippi* (Washington, 1822). This pamphlet is said to have hastened Russell's death.

17. For his "recall" see W. C. Ford, "The recall of John Quincy Adams in 1808," *Mass. Historical Society, Proceedings*, XLV, 354-75.

18. Taylor to Monroe, November 8, 1809; *John P. Branch Historical Papers*, II, 346.

19. Adams, *Memoirs*, VI, August 9, 1823, 170.

20. *Ibid.*, V, December 25, 1820, 222.

21. *Ibid.*, V, February 22, 1821, 291.

22. *Memoirs of John Quincy Adams, comprising portions of his Diary from 1795-1848*, Charles Francis Adams, ed., 12 vols., 1874-7.

23. Brooks Adams, "The Heritage of Henry Adams" in Henry Adams, *The Degradation of the Democratic Dogma*, 35.

24. Adams, *Memoirs*, VI, December 23, 1824, 453.

25. Bennett Champ Clark, *John Quincy Adams*, 139.

26. John Quincy Adams to Louisa Catherine Adams, December 16, 1814: Adams, *Writings*, V, 239.

27. Gamaliel Bradford, *As God Made Them*, 55.

28. Harriet Martineau, *Retrospect of Western Travel*, I, 242.

29. Bradford, *op. cit.*, 49.

30. The Diary—it is really little more than an appointment book—is in the *MSS* collection of the New-York Historical Society. The entry is undated.

31. Bradford, *op. cit.*, 62. Rogers, *The True Henry Clay*, 163.

32. Bradford, *op. cit.*, 61. However, it is generally conceded that Clay was not an excessive drinker.

33. Adams, *Memoirs*, III, 32, 39.

34. J. J. Astor to Gallatin, December 22, 1814, "I have not a Doubt that unless we have a Peace there will be a great Depression—the apointment of Mr. Clay had an effect to depress stocks about 3 or 4 pct from as I hope a false impression that it is unfavourable to an arrangement." Gallatin *MSS*.

35. He had already had some training as Speaker in the Kentucky Legislature.

36. William W. Story, *Life and Letters of Joseph Story*, I, 423.

37. Bernard Mayo, *Henry Clay: Spokesman of the New West*, 112. Daniel Webster called his legal knowledge "superficial," *ibid.*, 111, and John Quincy Adams declared that he was "half-educated," *Memoirs*, V, 325.

38. Gallatin to James Gallatin; Adams, *Gallatin*, 623.

39. Mayo, 46, 100. Sarah Bolton, *Famous American Statesmen*, 241. Noah Brooks, *Statesmen*, 13.

40. Clay, *Works*, Colton, ed., VII, 491.

41. Mayo, 91.

42. *Ibid.*, 62.

43. *Ibid.*, 194.

44. Joseph M. Rogers, *The True Henry Clay*, 302. Bradford, *op. cit.*, 57.

45. Henry Adams, *A History of the United States During the Administrations of Jefferson and Madison*, 1930 ed., I, 172-6.

46. Henry Adams, *op. cit.*, IX, 15.

47. *Am. Hist. Assoc. Reports, 1913*, II, 165.

48. John Quincy Adams to Louisa Catherine Adams, Dec. 16, 1814: Adams, *Writings*, V, 238.

49. *Ibid.*

50. Henry Adams, *A History &c.*, IX, 14.

51. *Diary of James Gallatin*, 27. John Quincy Adams to Louisa Catherine Adams, August 1, 1814; Adams, *Writings*, V. 69. Samuel Flagg Bemis in his notable *John Quincy Adams* calls it the Hotel Lovendeghem, following John Quincy Adams, *Writings*, V, 262, etc.

52. Adams, *Writings*, V, 73.
53. John Quincy Adams to Louisa Catherine Adams, July 19, 1814; *ibid.*, V, 64.

CHAPTER TWO

1. *Lectures on Rhetoric and Oratory*, (2 vols., 1810).
2. Jefferson to Adams, January 21, 1812; Jefferson, *Writings*, Paul Leicester Ford, ed., XI, 219-20.
3. John H. Latané and David W. Wainhouse, *A History of American Foreign Policy*, 89. For the Order-in-Council and its predecessor of June 9, pre-empting foodstuffs conveyed in neutral bottoms, see J. B. Moore, *Digest of International Arbitrations*, I, 299-305.
4. I refer to Thucydides' superb boast concerning the Peloponnesian War in Book I, Chapter I: "This was the greatest movement that had ever stirred the Hellenes, extending also to some part of the Barbarians, *one might say even to a very large part of mankind.*"
5. See Richardson, ed., *Messages and Papers*, I, 499 ff.; *Annals of Congress*, 12 *Cong.*, 1 *Sess.*, 1714-19.
6. Bowers, *Jefferson in Power*, 483.
7. *Statutes at Large of the United States*, I, 570, 577, 596.
8. Elliot's *Debates*, IV, 528-9.
9. *Ibid.*, IV, 532-9.
10. Madison, *Writings*, Hunt, ed., VI, 402.
11. *Ibid.*, IX, 491. *Letters and Other Writings of James Madison* (hereafter cited as *Works*, Congressional ed.), IV, 229, 232.
12. Adams, *Memoirs*, I, 544. Margaret Bayard Smith (Mrs. Harrison Smith), *The First Forty Years of Washington Society*, 59-63. Richardson, *Messages and Papers*, I, 466-8.
13. Henry Adams, *History*, I, 189. Gaillard Hunt, *Life of James Madison*, 300.

14. Henry Adams, *History*, I, 190.
15. Adams, *Memoirs*, I, 416. A. C. Clark, *Life and Letters of Dolly Madison*, 65.
16. Henry Adams, *History*, VI, 222.
17. For the reports in Washington of British gifts of weapons, etc., to the Indians, see *ASP, Indian Affairs*, I, 799. The connection between the British gifts and Tippecanoe is vaguely suggested in *Report on the MSS of Earl Bathurst* (Historical Manuscripts Commission, London, 1923), 192. Report of Warlike Indians in Canada, by Francis Gore, Lieutenant-Governor of Upper Canada. "The Miamis, Tuscaroras, Wyandots, Shawanoes, Potowotamies, and Delawares . . . and some others, whose names I do not recollect, receive their annual presents at Amherstberg [Malden]. They reside, however, chiefly within the line ceded to the United States, but have no attachment to the Americans, of which occurred a strong instance— the attack on the Wabash River. The Potowotamies, Shawanoes, and Delawares attacked, or rather surprised, Governor Harrison's army." Gore's report is dated August 4, 1812. Early in 1812, the British withheld the gift of ammunition. Morrison & Commager, *Growth of the American Republic*, I, 413.

CHAPTER THREE

1. Part of this correspondence is to be found in Gallatin, *Writings*, Henry Adams, ed., I; part in the unpublished Gallatin Papers.
2. John Badollet to Albert Gallatin, May 19, 1812; Gallatin *MSS*.
3. Badollet to Gallatin, August 5, 1812; *ibid.*
4. Note: With its pendant, the Treaty of December 9, 1809.
5. John B. McMaster, *A History of the People of the United States*, III, 529. Adams, *History*, VI, 83. Moses

Dawson, *A Historical Narrative of the Civil and Military Services of Maj.-Gen. Wm. H. Harrison*, 1824, 11.

6. Adams, *History*, VI, 75.
7. Secretary Eustis to Governor Harrison, July 15, 1809; *ASP, Indian Affairs*, I, 761.
8. Daniel J. Boorstin, *The Lost World of Thomas Jefferson*, 174.
9. Jefferson to Harrison, February 27, 1803; Adams, *History*, VI, 74. Jefferson to Hawkins, February 17, 1803; Jefferson, *Works*, Ford, ed., IX, 449.
10. *Dictionary of American Biography*, XVIII, "Tecumseh."
11. McMaster, III, 529-30. Adams, *History*, VI, 79. *DAB*, XVIII, "Tecumseh." Harrison to Armstrong, March 22, 1814; Benjamin Drake, *Life of Tecumseh*, 161.
12. McMaster, III, 531.
13. Dawson, *Harrison*, 173-4.
14. McMaster, III, 532.
15. Dawson, 179
16. Adams, *History*, VI, 91. McMaster, III, 535.
17. De Tocqueville, *Democracy in America*, 1945 ed., I, 25.
18. Dawson, 190-1.
19. *Ibid.*, 253.
20. Adams, *History*, VI, 96.
21. Dawson, 196.
22. Adams, *History*, VI, 98. Dawson, 206.
23. *ASP, Indian Affairs*, I, 776.
24. Badollet to Gallatin, December 4, 1811; Gallatin MSS.
25. Adams, *History*, VI, 101-2. McMaster, III, 533.
26. *ASP, Indian Affairs*, I, 779.
27. McMaster, III, 534.
28. Adams, *History*, VI, 107.
29. Harrison to Eustis, December 4, 1811; *ASP, Indian Affairs*, I, 779.
30. Badollet to Gallatin, April 29, 1812; Gallatin MSS.
31. *ASP, Indian Affairs*, I, 808.
32. *Ibid.*, I, 806.
33. Dawson, 266.

CHAPTER FOUR

1. C. M. Wiltse, *Calhoun: Nationalist*, 53.
2. *DAB*, XV, "Porter," 99. D. S. Alexander, *Political History of the State of New York*, I, 138, 147.
3. McMaster, III, 475.
4. Adams, *History*, IV, 435, 451.
5. *DAB*, IV, "Cheves," 63.
6. Adams, *History*, V, 342.
7. For Bacon see Adams, *History*, IV, 432 ff.
8. Richardson, *Messages and Papers*, I, 491-6.
9. *Ibid.*, I, 494.
10. McMaster, III, 420.
11. *Annals of Congress*, 12th Cong., 1 Sess., 373-7. This report may have been written by Monroe, who was then under War Hawk influence; *Am. Hist. Rev.*, XIII, 303-10. In *Am. Hist. Rev.*, XLIX, 253-9, C. M. Wiltse makes out a case for the authorship of Calhoun.
12. Wiltse, *Calhoun: Nationalist*, 55-6.
13. Adams, *History*, VI, 136, 141. McMaster, III, 432.
14. Charles A. Beard and Mary R. Beard, *The Rise of American Civilization*, 1942 ed., I, 412.
15. See Part II, Chapter 4, *note* 19, *infra*.
16. For a discussion of the story that Clay forced Madison to write a war message in return for the nomination—a story that seems to have been quite untrue—see Theodore Clark Smith, "War Guilt in 1812," *Proc. Mass. Hist. Society*, LXIV, 319-45.
17. Wiltse, *Calhoun: Nationalist*, 54.
18. W. Lowndes to Elizabeth Lowndes, December 7, 1811; Harriott H. Ravenel, *Life and Times of William Lowndes*, 90.
19. Adams, *History*, VI, 114.
20. Division Orders, 2nd Military Division of the State of Tennessee, March 7, 1812; *Correspondence of Andrew Jackson*, Bassett, ed., I, 221-2.

21. Adams, *History*, VI, 142.
22. *Annals of Congress*, 12 *Cong.*, 1 *Sess.*, 803 ff.
23. McMaster, III, 542.
24. Joseph Dorfman, *The Economic Mind in American Civilization*, I, 345; citing Elijah Parish, *A Protest Against War* (Newburyport, 1812), 16.
25. Dwight, *Travels*, II, 458 ff.

CHAPTER FIVE

1. Napoleon's Berlin Decree will be found in *American State Papers, Foreign Relations* (hereafter identified as *ASPFR*), III, 289 and *Annals of Congress*, 10 *Cong.* 2 *Sess.*, 1749-51. His Milan Decree will be found in *Annals of Congress*, 10 *Cong.*, 2 *Sess.*, 1751-2. The first of the British Orders-in-Council, of May 16, 1806—known as "Fox's blockade" because the man responsible for it was that marvelously attractive Whig, Charles James Fox, was conciliatory. *ASPFR*, III, 267. The second of the Orders-in-Council, of January 7, 1807, was not conciliatory, but was inoperative because it omitted the shallow coasting trade. *Annals of Congress*, 10 *Cong.* 2 *Sess.*, 1695 and *ASPFR*, III, 267. The Orders-in-Council to which I refer were a group of Orders, with supporting parliamentary enactments, issued on November 11, 1807. *ASPFR*, III, 269. Samuel F. Bemis, *Diplomatic History*, 149-50. Though certain modifications were made both in the Decrees and the Orders-in-Council of November 11, they represent the essence of the Continental System of Napoleon, and of the British system of making the war pay for itself by (a) monopolizing the carrying trade and (b) thrusting their goods upon Napoleon through their own blockade.
2. Jefferson's concept of the Freedom of the Seas had its origin in the Model Plan of 1776. *Journals of the Continental Congress*, V, 768. It was developed in his great and famous Instructions of 1784, and section 4 of these Instructions is peculiarly illuminating. Jefferson, *Writings*, Ford, ed., VIII, 354-5. In *ibid.*, VIII, 120 he explains the origin of the principle that "free bottoms make free goods." That it was directly opposed to international law as expounded by Vatel, the great Neufchâtelois, in *Droit des Gens*, III, Cap. VII, secs. xv, xvi, he freely admitted; but since his principle of "free ships free goods"—i.e., that the property of an enemy found on a neutral ship could not be seized—was adopted by all the powers of Europe and embodied by them in the Declaration of Paris of 1856, we cannot doubt that he was correct. See section 6 of the Instructions in Jefferson, *Writings*, Ford, ed., VIII, 356. W. E. Hall, *International Law*, ed. of 1904, 591-3 and W. F. Reddaway, *The Monroe Doctrine*, 15 say that Jefferson opened a new epoch in the usages of neutrality. For the Embargo Message see Richardson, *Messages and Papers of the Presidents*, I, 433, October 18, 1807. The Embargo Act was signed on Tuesday, December 22, 1807. *Statutes at Large of the United States*, II, 451-3. It was preceded by the Non-Importation Act of 1806, which proscribed the importation of certain essential British goods, McMaster, III, 230-6, and this Act was in force during the Embargo, making the Embargo a self-blockade. Madison's less forceful methods were the Non-Intercourse Act of 1809. *Statutes at Large* &c., II, 528-33. It was followed by Macon's Act No. 2, of May 1, 1810, which repealed the Non-Intercourse Act, but threatened to renew it against either power should the other modify its Orders or Decrees

in favor of the United States. *Ibid.*, II, 605-6. This was the single piece of economic legislation that really affected Napoleon. He instructed his Foreign Minister, the Duc de Cadore, to inform General Armstrong, the American Minister, that the Decrees of Milan and Berlin were revoked. Cadore to Armstrong, August 5, 1810; *ASPFR*, III, 386-7. Since a decree could be revoked only by another decree, he was at length forced to pretend, in 1812, that he had issued a decree at St. Cloud to this effect on April 28, 1811. He had never done so; nor had he ceased confiscating American ships. Joel Barlow to James Monroe, May 12, 1812; *ASPFR*, III, 603. Duc de Bassano to Serurier, French Minister at Washington, May 10, 1812; Adams, *History*, VI, 257. Madison was not deceived by Napoleon, but he was making his choice; he pretended to believe him; the Non-Intercourse Act was revived against Great Britain as early as March 2, 1811, seriously curtailing her market in the United States; and on June 16, 1812, the Orders-in-Council were repealed. For the British panic and depression of 1809-10 see Brooks Adams, *Law of Civilization and Decay*, 305 ff. W. S. Jevons, *Investigations in Currency and Finance*, 144.

3. Adams, *History*, IV, 1931 ed., 98-9, citing Perceval to Speaker Abbot, November 30, 1807; *Diary and Correspondence of Lord Colchester*, II, 134.

4. R. G. Collingwood and J. N. L. Myers, *Roman Britain*, 42-51.

5. George Santayana, *Character and Opinion*, 194.

6. Harold Nicolson, *The Congress of Vienna*, 6.

7. The figures on impressment will be found in James F. Zimmerman, "Impressment of American Seamen," *Columbia University Studies in History, Economics and Public Law*,

CXVIII, No. 1, 255, 268 (Appendix). Of these American seamen, impressed between 1803 and 1812, only 1,995 were listed as discharged or ordered to be discharged; perhaps another 1,500 were imprisoned during the war because of their refusal to fight against their country. The fate of the rest is unknown. These figures are, of course, tentative: but Zimmerman is the authority on this subject.

8. Bemis, *Diplomatic History*, 156. The reader is also referred to Julius W. Pratt's authoritative *Expansionists of 1812*.

9. Richard Rush to Benjamin Rush, June 20, 1812; Adams, *History*, VI, 229.

10. Ellen Churchill Semple, *American History and its Geographic Conditions*, 135. McMaster, III, 541-2.

11. Yeo to Viscount Melville, May 30, 1815; "An American Plan for a Canadian Campaign," *Am. Hist. Rev.*, XLVI (January 1941), 348-58.

12. *Ibid.*

13. Secretary Eustis suggested such an attack to Dearborn and Dearborn already had it in mind; but both of them seem to have considered it merely a feint. Dearborn to Eustis, December 15, 1812; Eustis to Dearborn, December 15, 1812. Adams, *History*, VI, 340-1.

14. *ASP, Military Affairs*, I, 315.

15. Madison to Henry Wheaton, February 26, 1827; Madison, *Works*, Congressional ed., III, 555.

16. John Quincy Adams, *Writings*, IV, 238.

17. John Quincy Adams to Robert Smith, April 19, 1810; John Quincy Adams to James Monroe, August 2, 1811; *ibid.*, III, 419-20, IV, 166-7.

18. Brooks Adams, *The New Empire*, 161 ff.

19. Madison to Henry Wheaton—*v.* note 15 *supra.*

20. Philippe Paul de Ségur, *Histoire et Memoires*, IV, 93.
21. Harold Nicolson, *op. cit.*, 4.
22. *With Napoleon in Russia*, George Libaire, ed., 45-70.
23. Hull surrendered on August 16, 1812.
24. *With Napoleon in Russia*, 77.
25. *Ibid.*, 196.
26. Sometimes he went even further and along a different route. In his *Advice to the Privileged Orders*, a work that deserves to be remembered more than it is, he put forth the suggestion, absurd at the time, that the state should actually make itself responsible for the welfare of its citizens. Vernon Parrington, *Main Currents*, 1927 ed., I, 385. However, his speculating activities with the *Compagnie de Scioto* in France and his later dealings in the commercial claims of American citizens against the French Government suggest that he might not have been too comfortable in a state whose sense of responsibility tried to extend itself, without a specific invitation, into the realm of the financier and the entrepreneur. Monroe dismissed the rumor that Barlow had advance information that the Louisiana Treaty would include the settlement of such claims. Monroe to Madison, December 17, 1803; Monroe, *Writings*, IV, 119-20. Dorfman, *Economic Mind*, I, 467, *n.*30, says that this was "charged but never clearly substantiated."
27. Adams, *History*, VI, 264-5.
28. Dorfman, I, 471 citing Leon Howard, *The Connecticut Wits*, 50.
29. Monroe to Jonathan Russell, June 26, 1812; *ASPFR*, III, 585-6.
30. Russell to Castlereagh, August 29, 1812; *ibid.*, III, 589. He did not of course mention the Orders since they already stood repealed.
31. Castlereagh to Russell, August 29, 1812; *ibid.*, III, 589-90.

32. Monroe to Russell, July 27, 1812; *ibid.*, III, 586.
33. *Ibid.*, III, 595-6.
34. Daschkoff to Monroe, March 8, 1813; *ibid.*, III, 625.
35. Monroe to Daschkoff, March 11, 1813; *ibid.*, III, 625.
36. For these instructions see *ibid.*, III, 695-700.
37. *Statutes at Large of the United States*, II, 809-11.
38. For the debate on this bill see *Annals of Congress*, 12 *Cong.*, 2 *Sess.*, 960-1055.
39. Henry Adams, *Gallatin*, 493.
40. Adams, *Memoirs*, II, 51-3, 226, 268.
41. John Quincy Adams to Monroe, June 26, 1813; Adams, *Writings*, IV, 492. The British told Count Lieven that their differences with the United States "were of a nature involving the principles of the internal government of the British nation, and which it was thought were not susceptible of being committed to the discussion of any mediation." This language could mean simply that their maritime principles could not be submitted to the arbitration of a Baltic power. Or it could mean that the British government considered the War of 1812 a family affair —a dispute between the Mother Country and her semicolonial offspring. Adams himself wrote: "I *do not* consider the questions at issue between the United States and Great Britain as questions in which the continent of Europe has no interest—not even the question of impressment. In every naval war waged by Great Britain, it is to the interest and right of her adversary that she should not be permitted to recruit her navy by man-stealing. . . ." Adams to Monroe, April 15, 1814; *Writings*, V, 38 and Gallatin *MSS*.
42. Castlereagh to Cathcart, July 5 and July 13, 1815; Adams, *History*, VII, 340-3.

43. Adams to W. H. Crawford, November 15, 1813; *Writings*, IV, 531.
44. Adams, *History*, VII, 360.
45. The Federalists made their decision in spite of two Federalist precedents—both Jay and Ellsworth, when Chief Justices of the Supreme Court, had been sent abroad as envoys. Senator Joseph Anderson of Tennessee, chairman of the committee on Gallatin's nomination, changed his vote. Cf. W. H. Crawford to Gallatin, Paris, April 20, 1814. "Anderson . . . declared he would vote for the nomination. I have no doubt he voted against it in the end. The desire to get Mr. Cheves into the Treasury had some influence upon one or two Senators." Gallatin *MSS*. Langdon Cheves, one of the War Hawks, did not get the Treasury. The Senators mentioned were William B. Giles of Virginia, Michael Leib of Pennsylvania, and Samuel Smith of Maryland.
46. Adams, *Gallatin*, 502.
47. J. J. Astor to Hannah Nicholson Gallatin, July 15, 1813. Astor writes that on this day he had had a long conversation with Mrs. Madison, who had been asked by the President to find out from him "whether I thought Mr. Gallatin would prefer a confirmation of the nomination or Remain in the Department, for it apares that the Senate will confirm if he will call an other Secretary." Gallatin *MSS*.
48. Adams, *Gallatin*, 502.
49. John Quincy Adams, *Memoirs*, II, 549. Gallatin to Adams, March 6, 1814. "I will ever retain a grateful sense of yours and Mrs. Adams' civilities; I fear that bad health and worse spirits made me still more dull than usual," *Writings*, V, 24n.
50. James Gallatin, *Diary*, 13, says January 26.
51. John Quincy Adams to John Adams, January 2, 1814. In this letter he states that he has had no

communication from America later than June. "The communications are nearly annihilated." See also John Quincy Adams to Abigail Adams, December 30, 1813. "We have not a line from our own government dated later than 23 June." Adams, *Writings*, V, 3 and IV, 535.
52. S. Browne, United States agent at Amsterdam, to Gallatin and Bayard, February 11, 1814; Gallatin *MSS*.
53. Adams to Galatin and Bayard, February 6, 1814; Gallatin *MSS*.
54. So Adams, *Gallatin*, 504. They arrived on March 4. James Gallatin —*Diary*, 13—says that Gallatin heard of his appointment on March 20; but this seems almost impossible, since the appointment was not made until February 18.
55. Dolly Madison to Hannah N. Gallatin, May 22, 1814. Madison has just heard from Mr. Beasely, the agent in London, that he had "dispatched" to Gallatin his official notification. Gallatin *MSS*.
56. Napoleon abdicated on April 6, 1814.
57. James Gallatin, *Diary*, 14. Bentham left his hermitage at Queen's Square Place especially to visit Gallatin, but was not received. He had ideas of peace which he wished to present to Tsar Alexander. Jeremy Bentham to Gallatin, June 16, 1814; Gallatin *MSS*. Christopher Hughes to Gallatin, January 19, 1827. "Do you remember the visit he had the impertinence to make to Mr. Bayard in 1814, in Albemarle Street. Mr. Bayard sent *me*, to announce to you the fact, and to report all the *sweep* had said: You were at Oxford Street; I scarcely knew you *then!* However I went, and I gave my message, faithfully, to you. You sent me back, drily! 'Go back, if you please, Mr. Hughes, give my compliments to Mr. Bayard, with my felicitations, on the distinguished honour he has enjoyed, in

a visit from *Wm. Cobbett.*' " Gallatin *MSS.* James Gallatin, *Diary*, 14, says that the dinner with Lord Bathurst took place on April 14; and, *ibid.*, 21, the dinner with Lord Liverpool, May 2. Lord Bathurst was Secretary for War and Colonies. Lord Liverpool became Prime Minister early in 1812, after Spencer Perceval had been assassinated in the House of Commons by a madman who was sufficiently insane to have no political reasons for his deed.

58. Bathurst to Bayard and Gallatin, May 16, 1814. Bayard and Gallatin to Bathurst, May 17, 1814. Gallatin *MSS.*

59. John Quincy Adams to Levett Harris, July 9, 1814. "I am not surprised that the Emperor should inquire pourquoi *Gand?* et pourquoi Gothenburg? but these questions can be answered only by the British government. Both places were proposed by them." Adams, *Writings*, V, 58. Levett Harris, American consul at St. Petersburg, had been secretary to the mediation commission, and had accompanied Bayard and Gallatin on their journey to London. S. F. Bemis, *John Quincy Adams*, 188*n.*

60. Adams to Louisa Catherine Adams, July 2, 1814; Adams, *Writings*, V, 55.

61. Wellington, *Supplementary Despatches*, IX, 290-1.

62. Crawford to Gallatin, May 12, 1814; Gallatin *MSS.*

63. Lafayette to Gallatin, May 26, 1814; Henry Adams, *Gallatin*, 512 and Gallatin *MSS.*

64. Harold Nicolson, *op. cit.*, 109-17.

65. James Gallatin, *Diary*, 25.

66. Gallatin to Monroe, June 13, 1814; Gallatin, *Writings*, Henry Adams, ed., I, 627.

67. Dallas to Gallatin, February 14, 1814; Gallatin *MSS.*

68. Dolly Madison to Hannah N. Gallatin, May 22, 1814; *ibid.*

69. Clay and Russell to Adams, April 16, 1814; *ibid.*

70. Clay and Russell to Monroe, April 20, 1814; *ibid.*

71. Clay to Russell, May 1, 1814. Clay says that he has no objection to Holland but will not negotiate in London. *ibid.* Ghent was not finally decided upon until May 16, *v. n.*58, *supra.*

72. Adams to Monroe, May 28, 1814; Adams, *Writings*, V, 47. Adams to Louisa Catherine Adams, May 31, 1814; *ibid.*, V, 45.

73. Adams to Louisa Catherine Adams, June 25, 1814; *ibid.*, V, 50.

74. Adams, *Memoirs*, II, 639.

75. Adams to Monroe, May 28, 1814; Adams, *Writings*, V, 47.

76. Adams, *Memoirs*, II, 640.

77. *Ibid.*, II, 649.

78. Adams to Louisa Catherine Adams, June 25, 1814; Adams, *Writings*, V, 50.

79. Adams to Louisa Catherine Adams, October 28, 1814. "The hatred of the English is . . . universal, and . . . bitter." Of course an *ex parte* statement. *Ibid.*, V, 174.

80. Winston Churchill, *Marlborough*, V, 362. J. M. Deane, *A Journal of the Campaign in Flanders, 1708*, 4.

81. John Quincy Adams to Abigail Adams, June 30, 1814; Adams, *Writings*, V, 54*n.*

82. John Quincy Adams to Louisa Catherine Adams; *ibid.*, V, 68.

83. *Memoirs and Correspondence of Lord Castlereagh*, X, 67.

CHAPTER SIX

1. James Gallatin, *Diary*, 72.

2. Monypenny & Buckle, *The Life of Benjamin Disraeli*, III, 260. "That weird Sybil!" is Disraeli's description of him in *ibid.*, III, 446.

3. *Ibid.*, III, 67, 437.

4. *Letters of Queen Victoria*, 1 series, II, 369. Memorandum of Prince Albert, February 27, 1851. Concerning

the efforts of Lord Stanley to form an administration. "At one time Lord Ellenborough had accepted, but having been sent on a mission to Mr. Goulburn to see whether he could convert him, he came home himself converted, and withdrew his acceptance again."

5. Goulburn to Bathurst, December 13, 1814. "As the Americans *entre nous* have rather hoaxed us for the number of our references home, we should be glad if you could send a provisional instruction in answer to our despatch of today, without waiting for the American note itself." *Report on the Manuscripts of Earl Bathurst*, 306.

6. Henry Adams, *History*, IX, 14.

7. Adams to Louisa Catherine Adams, August 30, 1814; *Writings*, V, 107. Frank A. Updyke, *The Diplomacy of the War of 1812*, 196, citing *Dictionary of National Biography*, I, 108.

8. Adams, *Writings*, V, 106-7.

9. Monroe to plenipotentiaries, June 25, 1814 and June 27, 1814; *ASPFR*, III, 704.

10. Monroe to plenipotentiaries, April 15, 1813; *ibid.*, III, 700; also Monroe to plenipotentiaries, January 28, 1814; *ibid.*, III, 701-2.

11. Gallatin had always believed that the subjects of impressment and neutral rights should be omitted. Gallatin to Monroe, August 28, 1813 and June 13, 1814; Gallatin, *Writings*, I, 568, 627. Gallatin to Emperor Alexander, June 19, 1814, *ibid.*, I, 629-31. Henry Clay had also reached the same conclusion. Clay to Crawford, July 2, 1814; "Letters Relating to the Negotiations at Ghent," *Am. Hist. Rev.*, XX, No. 1, 111.

12. This was granted in Article III of that Treaty, ratified and proclaimed January 14, 1784, in Malloy, ed., *Treaties, Conventions &c.*, I, 586 ff.

13. Updyke, *op. cit.*, 202.

14. *"Don't give up the ship."* Adams to Louisa Catherine Adams, August 16, 1814; Adams, *Writings*, V, 83.

15. Castlereagh to Liverpool, August 28, 1814; Wellington, *Supplementary Despatches*, IX, 192-3. James Gallatin in his *Diary* says (p. 30) that Lord Castlereagh arrived on August 23, and had a conference with Gallatin on the 24th; from which it has been deduced that Gallatin visited Castlereagh behind his colleagues' backs. However, Lord Castlereagh was in Paris on August 24, Cf. Nicolson, *op. cit.*, 126; and certainly his word that he did not see the Americans can be accepted against James Gallatin's that he did. Bemis, *John Quincy Adams*, 203n.

16. For the first instructions see *Memoirs and Correspondence of Castlereagh*, X, 67-72; for the second, see *ibid.*, X, 90-1.

17. Adams to Louisa Catherine Adams, August 23, 1814. "We did not see him [Lord Castlereagh], but at the conference it is scarcely a figure of speech to say that we felt him. Our opponents were not only charged fourfold with obnoxious substance, they threw off much of the suavity of form they had observed before." *Writings*, V, 90. Here Adams misjudges Castlereagh, who was always courteous, and had tried to instill courtesy into the British commission. See Castlereagh to Liverpool, Aug. 28, 1814, quoted above.

18. This treaty right was accorded by Jay's Treaty with Great Britain in 1794, apparently withdrawn in Pinkney's Treaty with Spain in 1795, and then restored by an "additional" article to Jay's Treaty, signed and ratified in 1796.

19. *ASPFR*, III, 708-10.

20. Adams, *Memoirs*, III, 17-18.

21. Castlereagh to Liverpool, Aug. 28, 1814; Wellington, *Suppl. Desp.*, IX, 192-3. His government had already

decided, if necessary, though the necessity of course was still remote, to make peace on the basis of *status quo ante bellum.* Bemis, *John Quincy Adams,* 202, citing Memorandum of Cabinet, December 26, 1813, *British Diplomacy, 1813-1815, Select Documents &c.,* C. K. Webster, ed., 123-6.

22. A part of this draft appears in Adams, *Writings,* V, 93.

23. Adams, *Memoirs,* III, 21-3.

24. Note of August 25, 1814; *ASPFR,* III, 711-13.

25. Adams, *Memoirs,* III, 23.

26. Goulburn to Bathurst, August 23, 1814; Wellington, *Suppl. Desp.,* IX, 189.

27. Castlereagh to Goulburn, August 28, 1814; *Memoirs and Correspondence of Lord Castlereagh,* X, 102.

28. Liverpool to Castlereagh, September 2, 1814; Wellington, *Suppl. Desp.,* IX, 214.

29. Liverpool to Bathurst, September 14, 1814; *Report on the MSS of Earl Bathurst,* 287.

30. For the new instructions see Wellington, *Suppl. Desp.,* IX, 245.

31. Liverpool to Wellington, September 2, 1814; *ibid.,* IX, 212.

32. *ASPFR,* III, 713.

33. Updyke, *op. cit.,* 178-9.

34. Adams to Monroe, September 5, 1814; Adams, *Writings,* V, 110-20. Cf. especially p. 112-13. "I answered that the conquest of Canada had never been an object of war on the part of the United States. . . . It was an effect and not a cause of war. . . . The American Government, I said, had never declared the intention of conquering Canada. He referred to General Hull's proclamation. I answered that the American government was not responsible for that." This conversation took place on September 1.

35. Adams, *Memoirs,* III, 31.

36. September 9, 1814; *ASPFR,* III, 715.

37. Liverpool to Bathurst, September 15, 1814; *Report on the MSS of Earl Bathurst,* 288.

38. Draft of September 16; Wellington, *Suppl. Desp.,* IX, 263-5.

39. Philip Coolidge Brooks, *Diplomacy and the Borderlands, University of California Publications in History,* Vol. XXIV, 25.

40. British note of September 19, 1814; *ASPFR,* III, 717-8.

41. Adams, *Memoirs,* III, 41; Brooks, *op cit.,* 32.

42. Adams to Louisa Catherine Adams, September 27, 1814; *Writings,* V, 147.

43. *Idem.*

44. *ASPFR,* III, 719-21.

45. Liverpool to Bathurst, September 30, 1814; *Report on the MSS of Earl Bathurst,* 294.

46. Madame de Staël to Gallatin, September 30, 1814. Her holdings amounted to 1,500,000 francs. Gallatin *MSS.*

CHAPTER SEVEN

1. Gallatin to Madame de Staël, October, 1814; Adams, *Gallatin,* 532-3.

2. Adams, *Memoirs,* III, 52-3.

3. *ASPFR,* III, 721 3.

4. Updyke, *op. cit.,* 274.

5. Adams to Louisa Catherine Adams, October 14, 1814; Adams, *Writings,* V, 158 ff.

6. *ASPFR,* III, 724.

7. Updyke, *op. cit.,* 276.

8. *ASPFR,* III, 724-5.

9. Henry Adams, *History,* IX, 34, 37.

10. Prevost to Bathurst, October 6, 1814; *ibid.,* VIII, 112.

11. Account of Major General Sir Frederick Philipse Robinson, September 22, 1814; *Report on the MSS of Earl Bathurst.*

12. Updyke, *op. cit.,* 167. *ASPFR,* III, 622-3.

13. American note of October 24; *ASPFR,* III, 725.

14. The reply did at first drive the Earl of Liverpool into the very mercantilist thickets which he had already forced his own commissioners to abandon. "The Americans are disposed," he told the Duke of Wellington, "to advance the extravagant doctrine of some of the revolutionary governments of France, viz., that they will never cede any part of their dominions, even though they shall have been conquered by their enemies. This principle they bring forward during a war in which one of their chief efforts has been to conquer and annex Canada to the United States. . . . We still think it desirable to gain a little time before the negotiation is brought to a close." Liverpool to Wellington, October 27, 1814; Wellington, *Suppl. Desp.*, IX, 385. On the question of annexation as an original American objective, Lord Liverpool was undoubtedly correct; but annexation had long since ceased to enter into the calculations of the War Department; it had never been advanced by the American commissioners as a possible claim; and to propose a compensatory seizure of territory was a revenge scarcely worthy of Lord Liverpool, and not in accordance with his government's proposals of October 18. Lord Liverpool changed his mind on November 2.

15. Liverpool to Castlereagh, November 2, 1814; Wellington, *Suppl. Desp.*, IX, 401.

16. The only plenary session of the Congress was the one that announced its conclusion.

17. Liverpool to Wellington, November 8, 1814; Wellington, *Suppl. Desp.*, IX, 404.

18. Wellington to Bathurst, November 4, 1814; *Report on the MSS of Earl Bathurst*, 303.

19. This is borne out by his comments on Sir George Prevost. On October 30, he says flatly: "It is very obvious to me that you must remove Sir George Prevost," and suggests Lord Niddry as his successor. Wellington to Bathurst, October 30, 1814; *Report on the MSS of Earl Bathurst*, 303. On December 22, he says: "I am inclined to think that he [Prevost] was right. I have told the ministers repeatedly that a naval superiority on the Lakes is a *sine qua non* of success in war on the frontier of Canada, even if our object should be wholly defensive." Wellington to Sir George Murray, December 22, 1814; Henry Adams, *History*, VIII, 113. Murray succeeded Sir George Prevost as Governor General of Canada.

20. British note of October 31, 1814; *ASPFR*, III, 726.

21. *ASPFR*, III, 733-4.

22. Goulburn to Bathurst, November 14, 1814; Wellington, *Suppl. Desp.*, IX, 432-3. F.O. Despatches of November 21 and 22, 1814, in Updyke, *op. cit.*, 315.

23. Baring to Gallatin, November 15, 1814; Gallatin *MSS*.

24. Liverpool to Castlereagh, November 18, 1814; Wellington, *Suppl. Desp.*, IX, 438 ff.

25. *ASPFR*, III, 740 ff.

26. Baring to Gallatin, November 29, 1814; Gallatin *MSS*.

27. Baring to Gallatin, December 2, 1814; Gallatin *MSS*.

28. Jefferson to Madison, June 29, 1812; Jefferson, *Writings*, Ford, ed., XI, 263. See also *id.* to *id.*, April 17, 1812; *ibid.*, XI, 235.

29. *Am. Hist. Rev.*, XXVIII, No. 1, 24-44.

30. *Statutes at Large of the United States*, III, 88-93.

31. McMaster, IV, 236. For circulation difficulties one need go no farther than this letter from Lewis Salomon to Gallatin, written on December 3, 1814, from Washington. "I need not say that money is scarce, because there is not any to be seen. . . . It is

a fact that there is not a piece of silver in circulation but to make up the deficiency, we have notes of from one cent, to 25: notes of one dollar cut in two, making two half Ds & those of two Ds with the same operation, making two notes of one dollar. You see the general ingenuity has not diminished." Gallatin *MSS.*

32. Henry Adams, *History*, VIII, 261-2. A. J. Dallas to Eppes, January 17, 1814; *ASP, Finance*, II, 885. *Life, Letters and Journals of George Ticknor*, 1876 ed., I, 31.

33. Liverpool to Castlereagh, November 2, 1814; Wellington, *Suppl. Desp.*, IX, 401-2.

34. McMaster, III, 490-1, citing Montreal *Gazette*, July 3, 1809; Baltimore, *Evening Post*, August 3, 1809; *True American*, July 25, 1809.

35. Ellen C. Semple, *op. cit.*, 257.

36. Adams, *Memoirs*, III, 72.

37. Protocol of Conference, *ASPFR*, III, 742.

38. McMaster, IV, 271. Samuel Eliot Morison, *Maritime History of Massachusetts*, 137.

39. Bathurst to commissioners, December 6, 1814; Castlereagh, *Memoirs and Correspondence*, X, 214. Adams, *Memoirs*, III, 93.

40. Goulburn to Bathurst, December 13, 1814; *Report on the MSS of Earl Bathurst.*

41. John Quincy Adams to John Adams, December 26, 1814; Adams, *Writings*, V, 253. Albert Gallatin went even further. The day before Adams wrote these words, Gallatin wrote to his wife: "For not having had a better peace, and six months sooner, the United States are indebted solely to the New England traitors. To the last moment the hope of a fatal issue to their movements and designs have [*sic*] operated against us." Gallatin to Hannah N. Gallatin, December 25, 1814. Gallatin *MSS.*

42. H. V. Ames, *State Documents on Federal Relations*, II, 34.

43. Adams to Louisa Catherine Adams, November 29, 1814; *Writings*, V, 221.

44. Carl Schurz, *Life of Henry Clay*, I, 196.

45. Henry Adams, *History*, VII, 389.

46. *Ibid.*, VIII, 17, citing Boston *Gazette*, April 14, 1814 and Boston *Chronicle*, April 14, 1814.

47. Ames, *State Documents;* II, 10-42, citing Connecticut, August 25, 1812, *Report of Committee . . . on that part of the Governor's Speech which relates to his correspondence with the Secretary of War* (New Haven, 1812), 1-12; *ASP, Mil. Aff.*, I, 325, 326, 614-22; *Records of the Governor and Council of the State of Vermont*, VI, 80, 85, 89, 92, 420, 492 ff.

48. Madison's Special Message of December 9, 1813; Richardson, *Messages and Papers*, I, 541.

49. Henry Adams, *History*, VIII, 22.

50. The blockade of New England was instituted in April 1814.

51. J. S. Martell, "A Sidelight on Federalist Strategy during the War of 1812"; *Am. Hist. Rev.*, XLIII, No. 3, 553-66.

52. Wellington to Bathurst, October 30, 1814. "[Sir John Sherbrooke] is the most violent tempered person I ever met with, and there are no bounds to his folly when he is in a passion." *Report on the MSS of Earl Bathurst*, 303. Liverpool to Castlereagh, December 23, 1814; Wellington, *Suppl. Desp.*, IX, 495. Adams, *Writings*, V, 246-7n.

53. This is the language of the Massachusetts memorial against War and Embargo of December 17, 1813, cited in Ames, *op. cit.*, II, 29.

54. Ames, *op. cit.*, II, 39-42. *Proceedings of a Convention of Delegates convened at Hartford, December 15, 1814* (Hartford, 1815).

55. *Jacobin and Junto . . . The Diary of Dr. Nathaniel Ames*, Charles

Warren, ed., entry for January 4, 1815, 279-80.

56. *Parturient montes, nascetur ridiculus mus.* Horace, *Ars Poetica,* 139.

57. John Quincy Adams to John Adams, December 26, 1814: Adams, *Writings,* V, 253.

58. *ASPFR,* III, 743. Adams, *Writings,* V, 231 ff.

59. Adams, *Memoirs,* III, 118.

60. Instructions of December 19, 1814; *Memoirs and Correspondence of Lord Castlereagh,* X, 221.

61. Adams to Louisa Catherine Adams, December 30, 1814; Adams, *Writings,* V, 257.

62. Hunter Miller: *Treaties and Other International Acts of the United States,* II, 574-84. It called for a cessation of hostilities as soon as it had been ratified by both parties; for the release of prisoners; for the restoration of all territory captured during the war by both parties, except for the disputed islands in Passamaquoddy Bay; for a better definition of boundaries; for the pacification of the Indians; for the return of Negro slaves carried away by British armed forces; and for both nations to do their best to help abolish the slave trade. As to boundaries —it arranged for four boards of commissioners, composed in each case of one commissioner from each country, to decide (a) the title to

Moose Island and the islands in Passamaquoddy Bay; (b) the boundary line from the source of the St. Croix River to the point where the 45th degree of latitude meets the St. Lawrence; (c) the water boundary from the St. Lawrence to Lake Huron, and between Lakes Huron and Superior; (d) the latitude and longitude of the line to "the most northern point of the Lake of the Woods." As Professor Bemis points out, the provisions of the first ten articles of Jay's Treaty, the "permanent" articles, which stipulated, among other things, the free navigation of the Mississippi, were not renewed. "The lapse of these articles," he says, "was a great advantage for the United States." Bemis, *John Quincy Adams,* 215n.

63. Hansard, *The Parliamentary Debates,* 2d series, I, 571.

64. On one occasion, Count Grote, Grand Master of the Wardrobe to the King of Prussia, was obliged to write to Gallatin, asking for the return of the marble monument to the late Queen, which had been seized on its way from Italy by *"le corsaire Américain Leo."* Grote to Gallatin, December 6, 1814; Gallatin *MSS.*

65. Liverpool to Castlereagh, November 9, 1814; Wellington, *Suppl. Desp.,* IX, 438.

PART TWO

CHAPTER ONE

1. *The Tour of James Monroe, President of the United States, Through the Northern and Eastern States in 1817,* by Samuel Putnam Waldo, Hartford, 1817.

2. *Ibid.,* 62, 68.

3. *Ibid.,* 149.

4. Jefferson to Monroe, January 10, 1803; Jefferson, *Writings,* Ford, ed., IX, 416.

5. William E. Dodd, *Life of Nathaniel Macon,* 198-9.

6. For Monroe's dealings with Randolph see William Cabell Bruce, *John Randolph of Roanoke,* I, 329 ff. and Henry Adams, *John Randolph,* 199 ff. "This coquetry be-

tween Monroe and Randolph continued all winter [of 1807-8]." *Ibid.*, 230.

7. Randolph to J. M. Garnett, Jr., March 19, 1811; Bruce, *op. cit.*, II, 747*n.* John Taylor of Caroline, however, whose orthodoxy cannot be questioned, advised Monroe to take this step; Henry Adams, *History*, V, 369. "His argument," Adams says, "seemed to place Monroe in a position where, if he could not convert Madison, he would have no choice but to let Madison convert him."

8. Adams, *History*, VIII, 161.

9. Randall, *Life of Jefferson*, III, 255.

10. V. Birdseye to J. W. Taylor, March 13, 1816. Report of a conversation with Daniel Tompkins, who subsequently ran for vice-president in the 1816 election, and received the same number of electoral votes as Monroe. "Tompkins felt that the President ought no longer for the present to come from Virginia . . . that if the Republicans of this state [New York] and our delegation in Congress thought proper to make an effort to effect what they conceived a necessary change of dynasty—he was willing to be at their service." John W. Taylor *MSS.*, New-York Historical Society. This sentiment, of course, increased with time. For example, M. Ulshoeffer to Martin Van Buren, February 17, 1822. Correspondent has lately received a long letter from a friend in Ohio, saying that state is willing to support De Witt Clinton, "or any one else we may think fit, who will put down Virginia dictation." Van Buren Papers, Library of Congress.

11. *Literary History of the United States*, ed. by Spiller, Thorp, Johnson, Canby, I, 285.

12. Tudor to Monroe, February 22, 1817; Monroe Papers, LC.

13. Boorstin, *The Lost World of Thomas Jefferson*, 123, cites *Writings*, National Ed., XIII, 279 ff. Also, *ibid.*, "The same political parties which now agitate the United States, have existed through all time."

14. Jefferson to Horatio Gates, March 8, 1801; *Writings*, Ford, ed., IX, 205.

15. Richard Hofstadter, *The American Political Tradition*, 41.

16. Jefferson to Cooper, July 9, 1807; Jefferson, *Writings*, Ford, ed., X, 450-1.

17. Sullivan to Monroe, July 10, 1817; Monroe Papers, LC. A note attached to this letter says that George W. Erving wrote from New York on February 24, 1816, to say that no faith could be placed in Mr. Sullivan.

De Witt Clinton, whose Federalist alliances in the War of 1812 made him suspect among New York Republicans, wrote in April 1817: "That great disinterest existed with respect to the late administration cannot be denied. The officers of the late general Govt. here were a set of political janissaries whose object appeared to be to paralyze the energies of the State and to destroy by calumny . . . some of our most decided republicans. . . . Having been in the habit of cherishing a favorable opinion of the President [Monroe] I cannot believe that he will in the remotest degree countenance such unhallowed practices and having openly avowed and decidedly supported him for the presidency in preference to the other candidates (as my letters to members of Congress and as my communications to my friends in the State Legislature will shew) I have every predisposition to afford him all the aid and support in my power in the discharge of his high functions." Clinton to N. J. Ingraham,

Albany, April 10, 1817. *MS.* New-York Historical Society.

18. Monroe, *Writings*, VI, 29*n*.

19. Charles M. Wiltse, *Calhoun: Nationalist, 1782-1828*, 140.

20. William Wirt to Judge Carr, January 18, 1818: "My single motive for accepting the office was the calculation of being able to pursue my profession on a more advantageous ground—i.e. more money for less work." John P. Kennedy, *Memoirs of the Life of William Wirt*, II, 67. So also Wirt to Mrs. Wirt, November 13, 1817. "They all [Monroe and the Cabinet] assure me that there is nothing in the duties of the office to prevent the general practice of my profession in the place." *Ibid.*, II, 29.

21. Crawford to Gallatin, April 23, 1817; Gallatin, *Writings*, II, 36.

22. J. E. D. Shipp, *Giant Days*, 142. Crawford declared that he could not run against so venerable a figure: but even then the Congressional caucus gave 54 votes for Crawford as against 65 for Monroe. Shipp quotes Jabez Hammond to the effect that only Irving, Throop, and Bridges among the New York delegation gave their votes to Monroe. Another New York voice, politically a voice from the dead, protested against Monroe's choice. *Memoirs of Aaron Burr*, II, 433. Presumably Burr also was for Crawford, as against the "stupid and illiterate" Monroe, as he called him. The story of Crawford's abnegation was printed, with embellishments, in the *Savannah Daily Republican*, January 10, 1824. See also *DAB*, IV, 528. "Crawford."

23. Theory of concurrent majorities. Cf. "Disquisition on Government," Calhoun, *Works*, I, 1-107. For dual executive, see *ibid.*, I, 392 ff.

24. Harriet Martineau, *Retrospect of Western Travel*, I, 149.

25. W. H. Crawford to James Tall-madge, Jr. Private (A Copy), July 12, 1819. "Indeed, it is difficult I think even now for the President to avoid giving his approbation to any law appropriating money for a road or canal. It may be even more difficult to induce him to sign an act embracing a system. But a few years in the age of nations is nothing. A system will be introduced gradually, if not directly at once." John W. Taylor *MSS.* Here Mr. Crawford, it will be noticed, refers only to appropriation and not to application of money. Americanus (Thomas Cooper) in *Sketches of the Life and Character of William H. Crawford* (1824), 37, places him more certainly in the Internal Improvement ranks.

26. J. E. D. Shipp, *Giant Days*, 46, 50.

27. *Ibid.*, 72-4.

28. Margaret Bayard Smith (Mrs. Harrison Smith), *First Forty Years &c. passim.* Mrs. Smith was one of his most ardent supporters. For his "want of refinement" see *The Life and Times of William Harris Crawford of Georgia. An address delivered by Charles N. West, A.M., before the Georgia Historical Society . . . May 2, 1892* (Savannah, 1892), p. 9.

29. W. E. Dodd, *Life of Nathaniel Macon*, 333. Jefferson to Crawford, February 15, 1825. "The disappointment will be deeply felt by our state generally, and by no one in it more seriously than myself. I confess that what we have seen in the course of this election has very much dampened the confidence I had hitherto reposed in my fellow citizens." In Shipp, *op. cit.*, 192.

CHAPTER TWO

1. Semple, *American History and Its Geographic Conditions*, 371.

2. W. J. Cash, *The Mind of the South*, 18-19.

3. Zebulon Pike, *An Account of Expeditions to the Sources of the Mississippi and Through the Western Parts of Louisiana*, 1810. *History of the Expedition under the Command of Captains Lewis and Clark*, 2 vols., 1814. Bernard De Voto, *Across the Wide Missouri*, 1-2.

4. Bidwell and Falconer, *History of Agriculture in the Northern United States*, 157, 158.

5. Cobbett, *A Year's Residence in the United States*, 3rd ed., London, 1822, II, 182.

6. Bidwell and Falconer, *op. cit.*, 158.

7. *Ibid.*, 159.

8. *Ibid.*, 162. Birkbeck, *Notes on a Journey in America from the Coast of Virginia to the Territory of Illinois*, 1818, 26.

9. "Yet another family, consisting of man, wife, and five children, passed through Woodbury, New Jersey, with all their household goods in a wheelbarrow. They were walking to Ohio." McMaster, IV, 386-7.

10. Cobbett, *op. cit.*, III, 305, 319, 332. However James Stuart—*Three Years in America*, 1833—says that log cabins, though rude, are far better than the cottages provided for farm overseers in Great Britain.

11. "Flavia" to Monroe, May 30, 1820; Monroe Papers, NYPL. Adam Hodgson, *Letters from North America*, I, 315. (Letter XIX, an account of a visit with Jefferson on June 2, 1820.)

12. F. J. Turner, *The Rise of the New West* (The American Nation, Vol. XIV), 80-2.

13. *Ibid.*

14. *Ibid.*, 91.

15. Charles S. Sydnor, *Development of Southern Sectionalism*, 4-5.

16. Semple, *op. cit.*, 152-3.

17. Turner, *op. cit.*, 84, citing William Kingdon, Jr., *America and the British Colonies*, London, 1820, 10, 54. $50 or $60 in addition to the government price of the land was commonly charged to later comers for 40 acres of such land.

18. At the edge of the Illinois prairie, in 1830, the price of fencing a 160-acre farm into 40-acre fields was $160; for breaking it up with a plow, $2 an acre. J. M. Peck, *Guide for Emigrants*, 1831, 183-8, estimates that the price of an improved farm would be $1000 for 320 acres. In the 1820's, an Indiana farm of 80 acres, cleared by the farmer and his sons, and adding the value of articles of husbandry and livestock (2 horses, 2 or 3 cows, a few hogs and sheep) to the original cost of the land, represented an outlay of $400. Turner, *op. cit.*, 87. Even in western New York, which retained its pioneer character until after the completion of the Erie canal, farmers would often exhaust their land and lay it down in grass and buy new land, or would sell their cleared land and move on. James Stuart, *op. cit.*, I, 258.

19. "Not far from 822,000,000 acres were orginially forested. Of this amount about five-sixths was in the eastern half of the country. A glance at a forest map will show that until settlement reached Iowa nearly all farms were of necessity cleared out of forest land." Bidwell & Falconer, *op. cit.*, 531; citing *Timber Depletion, &c.* Bulletin of Forest Service: *Report on Senate Resolution 311*, 1920, 32.

20. Birkbeck, *op. cit.*, 94. Turner, *op. cit.*, 85. Turner points out that when the pioneer in the Southwest invited his slave-holding neighbor to such an occasion, the man arrived in gloves, and directed a gang of slaves to do the work, greatly to the disgust of everyone else. 91.

21. Bidwell & Falconer, 168.

22. This was noted by Bernhard of Saxe-Weimar with some astonishment: he remarked, in soldierly fashion, that the cattle and swine "biv-

ouacked" in the woods. Bernhard, Duke of Saxe-Weimar, *Travels Through North America, during the Years 1825 and 1826*, II, 98.

23. J. Ford, *History of Illinois*, 1854, 41.

24. Bidwell & Falconer, 163.

25. E.g., of Indiana in 1825. "With the exception of some miserable, filthy lodgings in Canada, I do not recollect in any part of the United States, even among the Creek Indians, to have found myself so wretchedly situated in every respect as here." Saxe-Weimar, II, 126.

26. *Narrative of Richard Lee Mason in the Pioneer West, 1819* (Heartman's Historical Series, No. 6: 1915), 51. *The Diaries of Donald MacDonald, 1824-1826*, Indiana Historical Society Publications, Vol. XIV, No. 2, 237. A. J. G. Perkins and Theresa Wolfson, *Frances Wright: Free Enquirer*, 190.

27. Adlard Welby, *A Visit to North America and the English Settlements On the Illinois*, London, 1821, 73. *Narrative of Richard Lee Mason*, 34, 56. Frederick Fitzgerald De Roos, *Personal Narrative of Travels in the United States and Canada*, London, 1827, 88.

28. Carl Sandburg, *Abraham Lincoln: The Prairie Years*, I, 30 ff.

29. *Ibid.*, 76.

30. W. W. Sweet, *Religion on the American Frontier: The Baptists, 1783-1830*, 62.

31. Sweet, *Religion on the American Frontier, 1783-1840, The Methodists*, 65.

32. *Ibid.*, 44.

33. *Ibid.*, 68, citing Peter Cartwright, *Autobiography of Peter Cartwright, The Backwoods Preacher*, W. P. Strickland, ed., 81.

34. *Ibid.*, 730.

35. Sweet, *Baptists*, 69.

36. *Ibid.*, 69-70, citing Daniel Parker, *A Public Address to the Baptist Society*, 1820.

37. J. Q. Adams, *Memoirs*, V, 128-9.

38. Birkbeck, *op. cit.*, 25.

39. Jefferson to Joseph Priestley, June 9, 1802; Jefferson, *Writings*, Ford, ed., IX, 380-1. So also Jefferson to John Dickenson, March 6, 1801; *ibid.*, IX, 202.

40. James Tallmadge, Sr., to James Tallmadge, Jr., January 7, 1819; Tallmadge *MSS.*, New-York Historical Society.

41. *ASP, Finance*, III, 718.

42. B. H. Hibbard, *A History of the Public Land Policies*, 98, citing *Annals of Congress*, 15 *Cong.*, 2 *Sess.*, 216.

43. *ASP, Public Lands*, III, 561. The act of 1820 did not provide relief for those who had bought on credit, and who were charged interest on delinquent payments. An Act of March 2, 1821, provided for the relinquishment of a portion of land in payment for the balance due; 37½% discount for prompt payment; remission of accrued interest; and extension of time of payment. A further relief law was passed on February 28, 1824. As a result of this, the debt stood at only $6,322,-766 in June 1825, or about twice what it was in 1815, before the land boom had set in. The ultimate liquidation took place in 1832. Hibbard, *op. cit.*, 94-5. Ernest L. Bogart, *Economic History of American Agriculture*, 48.

44. The Act of 1807 was very hard on the squatter, largely due to Southern influence, since the squatter was supposed to hinder the development of the plantation; and this act lasted nominally until 1830. Hibbard, *op. cit.*, 148, citing *Ann. Cong.*, 9 *Cong.*, 2 *Sess.*, 664, 672. The Act of 1820 made some provision for pre-emption, but only for those who had made payment on land, and then relinquished part of it. *Ibid.*, 151. When actually faced with enforcing the Act of 1807, however, Congress

temporized again and again, and allowed pre-emptions in state after state; Bidwell & Falconer, *op. cit.*, 155. The measure of Western influence after the apportionment of 1822 may be gauged by the fact that the House Committee on Public Lands in 1824 spoke against the squatter; whereas the House Committee on Public Lands in 1828 was entirely on his side. "It is just and proper that he who renders a benefit to the public, who by his enterprise and industry has created to himself and his family a home in the wilderness, should be entitled to his reward." *ASP, Public Lands,* III, 619; V, 401. In 1830 the House Committee on Public Lands favored a reduction in price and a relinquishment of public lands to the states, but the Committee on Manufactures in a classical report held that this would be unfair. *ASP, Public Lands,* VI, 445-7. See Hibbard, *op. cit.,* 148-91; Bogart, *op. cit.,* 48 ff.; Bidwell & Falconer, *op. cit.,* 95 ff.; Sato, *The Land Question in the United States,* Johns Hopkins University *Studies in Historical and Political Science,* IV, Nos. 7-9.

45. For the Homestead movement see St. G. L. Sioussat, "Andrew Johnson and the Early Phases of the Homestead Bill," *Mississippi Valley Historical Review,* V, 280 ff. For the manufacturers' opposition to liberalization of the land laws, see Thomas Hart Benton in United States Senate, March 20, 1832, *Register of Debates,* 22 *Cong.,* 1 *Sess.,* 666. See also Andrew Jackson's Eighth Annual Message, December 5, 1836; Richardson, *Messages and Papers,* III, 249-50; and Martin Van Buren's First Annual Message, December 5, 1837, *ibid.,* III, 384-9, for executive approval of liberalized land laws.

46. These are startling enough. In 1820, one quarter of the population of the United States, which exceeded nine million, lived west of the Alleghenies. U.S. *Census* (1820). Ratios of increase show, for example: between 1810 and 1820, Indiana, an increase of 500%; Illinois, 349%; Ohio, 151%; Missouri, 219%; Western New York, 250%; Mississippi, 86.9%. Bidwell & Falconer, 151.

47. James Monroe, Second Annual Message, November 16, 1818. "By increasing the number of states the confidence of the State Governments in their own security is increased and their jealousy of the National Government proportionally diminished. The impracticability of one consolidated government for this great and growing nation will be more apparent and will be universally admitted." Richardson, *Messages and Papers,* III, 46. This opinion was typically Monrovian. A fervent State Rights man would not have wished for any diminishment of the jealousy of the national government; nor would the impracticability of a consolidated government have impresesd him so much as would its undesirability. After the Missouri Compromise there was always some fear that new states, carved out of the public lands, would come into conflict with the national government on the public-land issue. Martin Van Buren, First Annual Message, "The practicability of retaining the title and control of such extensive domains in the General Government, and at the same time admitting the Territories embracing them into the Federal Union as co-equals with the original States, was seriously doubted by many of our wisest statesmen. All feared that they would become a source of discord, and many carried their apprehensions so far as to see in them the seeds of a future dissolution of the Confederacy." *Ibid.,* III, 384.

48. James Madison said: "Were they [the new states] numerous and

weak, the government over the whole would find less difficulty in maintaining and increasing subordination." Madison to Judge Roane, May 6, 1821. He clung however to his theory of equilibrium. "It happens, that while the power of some is swelling to great size, the entire number is swelling also. In this respect, a corresponding increase of centripetal and centrifugal forces may be equivalent to no increase of either." Madison, *Works*, III, 218.

49. Richard Rush, "Report on the State of the Finances," December 8, 1827, 20 *Cong.*, No. 786, *ASP, Finance*, V, 638.

50. See Part III, *infra*.

51. *Works of Henry Clay*, Calvin Colton, ed., VI, 74-80, 108-10, 117-35, 218-37, 254-94, VII, 388-91, 393-415, 437-86. The formulation of this System might be said to begin with his address of 1816 on the Bank of the United States. It reached a climax in his tariff speech of 1824. It was completed by his great apologia of February 1832.

52. The flow of Western produce, from the Ohio Valley to the Southwest, is indicated by the following table of receipts of produce at New Orleans. Averages from 1822-4; and from 1825-8. Bacon and hams, lbs., 853,453; 9,871,054. Pork, lbs., 3,-062,000; 7,828,000. Lard, lbs., 1,217,-000; 3,895,000. Beef, dried, lbs., 12,-900; 42,700. Beef, pickled, lbs., 495,-467; 1,026,420. Hides, lbs., 12,300; 14,900. Butter, lbs., 308,900; 428,400. Flour, barrels, 111,900; 142,700. Corn, bushels, 94,638; 168,400. Whiskey, barrels, 10,200; 27,900. Tobacco, hogsheads, 24,700; 26,200. Potatoes, barrels, 2,000; 3,600. Some of this increase can be ascribed to increase in acreage under cultivation and increase in population. But the increase in the exported surplus of pork and pickled beef shows very clearly that Southern and Southwestern slavery

was beginning to consolidate around a one-crop system and that it was no longer willing to subsist its slaves from the produce of its own plantations. The figures are taken from Bidwell & Falconer, 173, a digest from U.S. Bureau of Statistics (Treasury Department), *Report on the Internal Commerce of the United States*, 1887, 195, 196, 200-2. The internal market otherwise still showed a flow rather from east to west, in shipments of manufactures, than in a flow of produce from west to east. The cost of transportation was prohibitive, except for cattle, which was made more profitable by a complicated operation, allowing the cattle, wherever raised, to be fattened in Ohio, and then driven slowly across the mountains, arriving in Eastern stockyards between April 15 and August 1. *Ibid.*, 178. It was estimated by W. Faux in *Early Western Travels*, R. G. Thwaite, ed., XI, 291, that in Indiana the usual price for land carriage was 50¢ for 100 lbs. for every 100 miles. Flower in *ibid.*, X, 142, says that land carriage to the Wabash, a distance of nine miles, was 16¢ for every 100 lbs. At this rate, corn could not have stood the expense of moving 20 miles, even though produced at no cost. Corn was exported to the East, but always in the form of animals. Freight rates were reduced by the construction of the national road, and the introduction of steam navigation up the Mississippi cut the water rates to as much as one third of the former charge. Turner, *op. cit.*, 100, citing *Ann. Cong.*, 18 *Cong.*, 1 *Sess.*, I, 991. The completion of the Erie Canal in 1825 was followed by (a) the great migration of wheat towards the Western plains and (b) the invasion of the Eastern farmer's domain by a flow of Western produce. But this may not have made itself felt until after 1830. On the whole, therefore, it may be argued that the internal market for Western domestic produce was still organizing itself down the Ohio and the Mississippi towards the Southern and Southwestern slave-holder; and that it was still in a very primitive condition.

53. T. P. Abernathy, "Andrew Jackson and the Rise of Southwestern Democracy," *Am. Hist. Rev.,* XXXIII, 64-77.

CHAPTER THREE

1. Jackson to Don Matteo Gonzalez y Manrique, August 24, 1814; Jackson, *Correspondence,* Bassett, ed., II, 29.
2. Marquis James, *Andrew Jackson: Border Captain,* 94.
3. Parton, *Jackson,* II, 333-6.
4. James, *op. cit.,* 304.
5. Correspondence, II, 273-5, 277-82, 291-2, 319, 320-1, 320-32, 343. Emory Upton, *The Military Policy of the United States,* 145-7. Niles' *Register,* XIII, 342. Wiltse, *Calhoun: Nationalist,* 150-1. James, *op. cit.,* 302, 306.
6. *ASP, Mil. Aff.,* I, 690.
7. "Early History of the Creek Indians and their Neighbors," by John R. Swanton in Bureau of American Ethnology, Bulletin 73, Washington, 1922, 398 ff. Jedediah Morse, *A Report to the Secretary of War, on Indian Affairs, Comprising a Narrative of a Tour Performed in the Summer of 1820,* New Haven, 1822, 311. John T. Sprague, *The Origin, Progress, and Conclusion of the Florida War,* 19.
8. Parton, II, 399.
9. *Ibid.,* 402-7.
10. General D. Mitchell, when governor of Georgia in 1817, said that the first outrage committed after the Treaty of Fort Jackson was by white banditti—"a set of lawless and abandoned characters." Parton, II, 409. So also Mitchell to the Secretary of War, 24 February, 1817—"some worthless white men who reside on the frontiers of East Florida, and who live by plunder." *ASP, Ind. Aff.,* I, 156.
11. Maj.-Gen. E. P. Gaines to Secretary of War, October 1, 1817; *ASP, Ind. Aff.,* I, 159.
12. *ASP, Mil. Aff.,* I, 687.
13. Secretary Calhoun to Gaines, December 16, 1817; *ibid.,* I, 689. The italics are inserted.
14. *Ibid.,* I, 690.
15. Jackson to Monroe, January 6, 1818; *Correspondence,* II, 345.
16. Parton, II, 408.
17. Bemis, *J. Q. Adams,* 303. Parton, II, 307. *ASPFR,* IV, 50.
18. Nicholls to Benjamin Hawkins, May 12, 1815; *ASPFR,* IV, 34.
19. Proclamation of October 27, 1810; Richardson, *Messages and Papers,* I, 480-1.
20. *Statutes at Large of the United States,* II, 708, 734. In 1804, Congress passed two Acts: one, of February 4, for laying and collecting duties in these disputed areas; the other, of March 6, erecting Louisiana into two territories, the Territory of Orleans to contain the disputed areas. *Ibid.,* II, 251, 285.
21. The No-Transfer Resolution, which declared that the United States, "taking into view the peculiar situation of Spain and her American provinces; and considering the influence which the destiny of the territory adjoining the southern border of the United States may have upon their security, tranquillity, and commerce . . . cannot without serious inquietude see any part of the said territory pass into the hands of any foreign power." *Annals of Congress,* 11 *Cong.,* 3 *Sess.,* 374-6. The resolution declared that any occupation of territory should be temporary. And President Madison's Proclamation of October 27, 1810, while it asserted that West Florida as far

as the Perdido was part of the Louisiana Purchase, also said that the occupation of West Florida would not cease "to be a subject of fair and friendly negotiation and adjustment."

22. Brooks, *Borderlands*, 17. Rippy, *Rivalry of the United States and Great Britain over Latin America*, 252-3. Richardson, *Messages and Papers*, I, 488-9, gives President Madison's Special Message of January 10, 1811, which speaks of "misrepresentations and suggestions" in a letter from Onís to the captain-general of Caracas, and the general tendency of his correspondence "to promote in foreign councils at a critical period views adverse to the peace and best interests of our country."

23. Brooks, *op. cit.*, 62.

24. The University of Texas published this treatise in four volumes between the years 1931 and 1947. The editor and translator is Charles W. Hackett.

25. *ASPFR*, IV, 450 ff.

26. Onís to Adams, January 24, 1818; *ASPFR*, IV, 464-7. As Brooks shows, Onís in his dispatch to Pizarro of January 28, 1818, admitted that he knew that Adams meant the Colorado of Texas. Brooks, *op. cit.*, 95.

27. Adams to Onís, March 12, 1818; *ASPFR*, IV, 468.

28. Onís to Adams, March 23, 1818; *ibid.*, IV, 480 ff.

29. For Mr. Clay's speech, see *Annals of Congress*, 15 *Cong.*, 1 *Sess.*, 1482 ff.

30. Brooks, *Borderlands*, 87.

31. *Ibid.*, 92.

32. Jackson to Calhoun, January 20, 1818; *ASP, Mil. Aff.*, I, 696.

33. Parton, II, 441.

34. Jackson to Calhoun, February 26, 1818; *ASP, Mil. Aff.*, I, 698.

35. *Ibid.*

36. Parton, II, 443.

37. Jackson to Calhoun, March 25, 1818; *ASP, Mil. Aff.*, I, 698.

38. See Part I, Chapter 6, *supra*.

39. *Ibid.*, I, 698.

40. *Ibid.*, I, 699.

41. *Ibid.*, I, 700.

42. Parton, II, 450.

43. James, *op. cit.*, 311. *ASP, Mil. Aff.*, I, 700.

44. *Ibid.*, I, 701.

45. Parton, II, 462. Parton quotes from the MS journal of J. B. Rodgers, of the Tennessee Volunteers.

46. *ASP, Mil. Aff.*, I, 701.

47. *Ibid.*, I, 702.

48. For the gist of Arbuthnot's correspondence see *ASP, Mil. Aff.*, I, 682, 723-6, 729.

49. Arbuthnot to J. Arbuthnot, April 2, 1818; *ibid.*, I, 722.

50. James, *op. cit.*, 313.

51. *ASP, Mil. Aff.*, I, 731. For the belief that he was plotting with Gregor McGregor, the Venezuelan patriot who had once occupied Amelia Island, to make an invasion of Tampa Bay, see Brooks, *Borderlands*, 94, citing Davis T. Frederick, "McGregor's Invasion of Florida," Florida Historical Society *Quarterly*, VII, 4-5.

52. For the trial, see *ASP, Mil. Aff.*, I, 721-34.

53. *Ibid.*, I, 734.

54. *Ibid.*

55. Parton, II, 477.

56. Parton, II, 480.

57. So Benjamin F. Butler in his eulogy of Jackson delivered at New York after Jackson's death. *Ibid.*, II, 485.

58. Jackson to Calhoun, May 5, 1818; *ASP, Mil. Aff.*, I, 702.

59. Jackson to Rachel Jackson, April 20, 1818. "I am advised that there are a few red sticks west of the appelachecola, should this be true, I will have to disperse them, this done, I shall commence my Journey home." *Correspondence*, II, 360. Jackson to Calhoun, April 20, 1818. "I shall order, or take myself, a

reconnaissance west of the Appe-
lachicola at Pensacola Point, where
I am informed there are a few sticks
assembled." However, he adds a
little ominously that the Seminoles
"are fed and supplied by the Governor of Pensacola." *Ibid.*, II, 362.
60. Parton, II, 489.
61. Masot to Jackson, May 23, 1818;
ASP, Mil. Aff., I, 712.
62. Jackson to Masot, March 25, 1818;
ASPFR, IV, 562; Masot to Jackson,
April 16, 1818; *ASP, Mil. Aff.*, I, 706
(also in *ASPFR*, IV, 506, with some
verbal alterations and dated April
15, 1818); also May 18, 1818, denying that he has encouraged Indian
hostilities. Jackson to Masot, April
27, 1814, attempting to implicate the
governor in the murder of Lieutenant Scott in 1817, *ibid.*, I, 709.
63. *ASP, Mil. Aff.*, I, 716-17.
64. Masot to Jackson, May 24, 1818.
Jackson replied, May 25, 1818, ap-
plauding the governor's feelings as a
soldier, but assuring him that the
sacrifice of a few brave men would
be "an act of wantonness." *ASP,
Mil. Aff.*, I, 712-13.
65. *Ibid.*, I, 719-20.
66. *Correspondence*, II, 374. Proclamation of May 29. The army with
Jackson when he attacked Barancas
was as follows: 4th Battalion United
States Artillery—52 officers and men;
Fourth Infantry Regiment—137 officers and men; 1st and 2nd Regiment of Tennessee Volunteers—837
officers and men; Kentucky and Tennessee Lifeguards, 55 officers and
men; Staff officers—11. Total: 1,092.
ASP, Mil. Aff., I, 718. Jackson told
Monroe that the men were "liter-
anny barefoot" from continued
wading of water. Jackson to Monroe, June 2, 1818; *Correspondence*,
II, 378. Captain Isaac McKeever of
the U.S. Navy also landed two guns
and was prepared to bring his vessel
before the water battery in the event

it was deemed necessary to storm
the upper works. Parton, II, 503.
67. *Niles' Register*, XIV, 399.
68. James Tallmadge, Sr., to James
Tallmadge, Jr., January 7, 1819;
Tallmadge *MSS.*, NYHS.

CHAPTER FOUR

1. Adams, *Memoirs*, IV, 102.
2. Onís to Adams, June 24, 1818;
ASPFR, IV, 495-6. Onís had just
written, *ibid.*, IV, 495, demanding a
restitution of St. Marks to the military commander.
3. *Memoirs*, IV, 104. Monroe himself
declared that he was waiting until
he could avail himself "of the aid
of the heads of departments." Monroe to Madison, July 10; Monroe,
Writings, VI, 53.
4. *Memoirs*, IV, 105.
5. Monroe actually wrote to the General, suggesting that his dispatches
should be rewritten. Monroe to
Jackson, July 19, 1818; Monroe,
Writings, VI, 54-61.
6. *Memoirs*, IV, 109-15.
7. Adams to Onís, July 23, 1818;
ASPFR, IV, 497.
8. *Memoirs*, IV, 115.
9. Jackson's explanation was written
at the White House in 1831, but not
published until 1854, when it appeared in Thomas Hart Benton's
Thirty Years' View, I, 169-80. The
notations on Jackson's private copy of
his letter of January 6 reads: "Mr.
J. Rhea's letter in answer is burnt
this 12th April, 1818." The General
meant 1819. James, 410.
10. Monroe to Calhoun, May 18, 1830;
Monroe, *Writings*, VII, 209-10. In
his annotation of the original Rhea
letter, Monroe distinctly states that
no word was passed from him to
Mr. Rhea on the subject, and that
Mr. Rhea, himself, "declared that he
had never heard of the subject before." Monroe Papers, NYPL.

11. Bassett, *Life of Andrew Jackson*, I, 247.

12. Monroe, *Writings*, VII, 234-6.

13. Rhea to Monroe, June 3, 1831; Jackson, *Correspondence*, IV, 288. This was the letter that reached Monroe on his deathbed.

14. Rhea to Jackson, December 18, 1818; *ibid.*, II, 403.

15. Rhea to Jackson, January 12, 1818; *ibid.*, II, 348.

16. Wiltse, *Calhoun: Nationalist*, 158.

17. Parton, II, 506.

18. Henry Adams, *History*, VI, 240-2. Julius W. Pratt, *Expansionists of 1812*, 115.

19. Monroe to Jackson, July 3, 1816; cited in James, 304.

20. Monroe to Jackson, December 28, 1817; cited in *ibid.*, 307.

21. Calhoun to Charles Tait, July 20, 1818; Wiltse, 417, *n*.13. Gadsden to Jackson, September 18, 1818; James, 411, *n*.18.

22. Richard R. Stenberg in "Jackson's Rhea Letter Hoax," *Journal of Southern History*, II, 480-96, brings evidence to show that Jackson knew of Calhoun's stand against him as early as 1819. See also Jackson, *Correspondence*, IV, 233.

23. John Quincy Adams to John Adams, February 14, 1819. "There was no other member of the Administration who had less or even so little concern with General Jackson's acts, or agency over them, until long after they were past and irretrievable. The orders by which he was authorized to enter Spanish Florida had issued from the War Department, without my being consulted, and without my knowledge. His correspondence was entirely with that department." John Quincy Adams, *Writings*, VI, 530.

24. Adams, *Memoirs*, IV, 106-7. In his diary Adams says merely that he insisted upon the Colorado from source to mouth. Onís, in a dispatch to Pizarro, July 18, 1818, declared

that it was during this meeting of July 11 that Adams suggested the line to the source of the Missouri and so west. Bemis, *J. Q. Adams*, 319.

25. Adams, *Memoirs*, IV, 110.

26. Bemis, *J. Q. Adams*, 310. Professor Bemis quotes from a memorandum in Monroe's handwriting bound between two documents dated February 5 and 23, 1818, in a volume of letters from Monroe to Adams, 1798 to 1831. He believes that Monroe was simply recording and sanctioning what the two men had agreed to; and that the idea of drawing a boundary line through to the Pacific originated with Adams.

27. Monroe to Madison, July 10, 1818. "I shall return to Washington on Monday next, the 13th." Monroe, *Writings*, VI, 53.

28. Monroe to Gallatin, May 26, 1820. "So strong is the inclination, in some, to seize on Texas, particularly, that I should not be surprised, if we should be compelled to act, on that principle, & without a treaty, if that province, at least as well as Florida, should be taken possession of. Internal considerations, of which the discussion of the late Missouri Question, will have given you a just view, are favorable to moderate pretentions on our part. With me they have much weight, as I am persuaded they have with many others, but still so seducing is the passion, for extending our territory, that if compelled to take our address, it is quite uncertain within what limit it will be confined." Gallatin *MSS*. This may be taken as Monroe's considered judgment. By "moderate pretensions" he evidently means pretensions that did not include Texas. See also Monroe to Jefferson, May 1820, Monroe, *Writings*, VI, 119-23. Even when Secretary of State, he had been willing if necessary to take as a western point the Sabine

River, which then, as now, ran between Texas and Louisiana.

29. Duc de Richelieu to Count Fernan Nuñez, September 11, 1817, says that Neuville is to be a "conciliator"; and this is repeated in Richelieu to Neuville, September 1, 1818. Brooks, *Borderlands*, 125, 127. Bemis, *J. Q. Adams*, 320, shows that Hyde de Neuville was much afraid of British intrusion into the Caribbean. Neuville wrote to Onís on July 14, saying that he could not support Onís's claims *in toto*. Brooks, 125. Onís to Pizarro, July 12, 1818, complains of Neuville's attendance at July 4 banquet. *Ibid.*, 126.

30. Erving to Adams, July 13, 1818; in Brooks, *op. cit.*, 137.

31. G. W. Erving to Gallatin, February 1, 1845. "The blundering of Adams added to the ineptitude of Monroe, and the gullibility of both under the small arts of Onís & Hyde, engendered this "Florida Treaty"— hence all the embarrassments which belong to the Texas question." In this letter Erving encloses two pamphlets. (A) *Letter from George W. Erving to A Friend*, Paris, December 12, 1844. *Imprimerie de E. Briere, Rue Ste-Anne*, 55. (B) Second *Letter from George W. Erving to A Friend*, Paris, January 6, 1845. *Imprimerie*, &c. In (A) Erving declares that, according to John Q. Adams in his speech to the young men of Boston in the fall of 1844, Mr. Monroe "was more than indifferent to any acquisition West of the Sabine, he thought that it would weaken us, &c. &c." "It was on intimate acquaintance with the character of Pizarro," Erving adds in (A), "his conciliatory disposition, his frankness and good faith, that I founded the opinion which I afterwards expressed and still maintain, that the limit of the 'Colorado' (with the desert) might have been finally agreed to at Madrid, and ought to

have been insisted on. . . ." As for his republican manners, Erving says in (A) that the deportment of a United States Minister should be free from "the bowing and cringing of a servile courtier." (B) is more or less a repetition of the arguments in (A). It is in (B) that he refers to "my excellent and zealous friend, Mr. Crawford, then Secretary of the Treasury." This would in itself account for Erving's hostility to Adams. Gallatin *MSS*.

32. Adams, *Memoirs*, IV, 219.

33. C. C. Griffin, *The United States and the Disruption of the Spanish Empire*, 191. Brooks, 180, citing Henry Wellesley to Castlereagh, June 24, 1819 in PRO, FO, 72/224.

34. Bemis, *J. Q. Adams*, 336.

35. Griffin, *op. cit.*, 191.

36. Adams, *Memoirs*, IV, 289.

37. Griffin, *op. cit.*, 171, 173.

38. Monroe to Adams, August 10, 1818; Monroe Papers, LC.

39. Onís to Adams, October 24, 1818; *ASPFR*, IV, 526-30. Onís offered a line between the Calcasieu and Mermentau rivers, up the Arroyo Hondo, across the Red River at 32° north latitude, thence north to the Missouri and up that river to its source. This offer, he told Madrid, was intended only to delay matters. Onís to Pizarro, October 31, 1818; Griffin, 181.

40. Adams, *Memoirs*, IV, 144.

41. Adams to Onís, October 31, 1818; *ASPFR*, IV, 530-1. The line was as follows: the Sabine from its mouth to 32° north latitude; thence due north to the Red River, and up the Red River to its source. According to Melish's map, the source of the Red River was just beneath the Sangre de Cristo Mountains at 37° 25' north and 106° 15' west. He then proposed to follow the Sangre de Cristos (or Snow Mountains as he called them) as far north as 41° and "follow that parallel of latitude to

the South Sea." This offer, as Bemis points out, would have obtained for the United States the entire Columbia River with all its southern tributaries. Bemis, *J. Q. Adams*, 324. At any rate, it would have done so according to Melish's map. Adams in his *Memoirs* says that this was the first time the line to the Pacific was introduced in a written proposal. *Memoirs*, IV, 275.

42. Brooks suggests that Adams's interest in the Oregon country was much increased by the influence of J. J. Astor. It is true that Astor was a friend of Gallatin's; that he was not without influence in the State Department; and that he welcomed Adams on his return from Europe with a banquet for 100 people. Brooks, 151-2. Adams was, of course, incorruptible; but he was of a centralizing mind, and the interests of the fur trade would seem to him to be important ones.

43. Onís to Adams, November 16, 1818; *ASPFR*, IV, 531-3.

44. *Memoirs*, IV, 172 (November 17, 1818). Adams to Onís, November 30, 1818; *ASPFR*, IV, 545.

45. Adams to Erving, November 28, 1818; *ASPFR*, IV, 539-45. Adams, *Writings*, VI, 474 ff.

46. Richard Rush to Gallatin, April 22, 1818; Gallatin *MSS.*

47. Gallatin to Rush, July 30, 1818; Rush *MSS.*, NYHS.

48. Rush to Gallatin, January 20, 1819; Gallatin *MSS.*

49. Castlereagh to Bagot, British Minister at Washington, January 2, 1819; PRO, FO, 115/34, cited in Brooks, 117.

50. Richard Rush, *Memoranda of a Residence at the Court of London* (1845 ed.), 153. Of those words, which he had printed in capitals, Mr. Rush confessed, "I thought them memorable at the time. I think so still." *Ibid.*

51. Rush to Gallatin, April 22, 1818.

See *n.46 supra*. In this letter Rush tells Gallatin that Lord Castlereagh had expressed the hope that the United States and Great Britain would be actuated by the same policy as regards trade privileges with the Spanish colonies. At this point, Castlereagh seems to have believed that an unfriendly attitude towards the United States would intensify competition between the two countries in their trade with South America.

52. Rush, *Memoranda*, &c., 231.

53. "Of all the powers on earth, America is the one whose increasing population and immense territory furnish the best prospects for British produce and manufactures. Every man, therefore, who wishes prosperity to England, must wish prosperity to America." The Earl of Liverpool in the House of Lords, May 16, 1820; *Hansard*, 2d series, I, 575. By "America" Lord Liverpool meant the United States.

54. Second Annual Message, November 16, 1818; Richardson, *Messages, and Papers*, II, 39-43.

55. Jefferson to Monroe, January 18, 1819; Jefferson, *Writings*, Ford, ed., XII, 114.

56. Clay, *Works*, Colton, ed., VI, 184. This was the second of two speeches; the first has not survived.

57. McMaster, IV, 451-6. One would not dispute McMaster's claim that Clay's speech was "greatly and justly admired."

58. Cf. Abner Lacock to Monroe, Confidential, January 30, 1820. Mr. Lacock says that in the early part of the preceding winter (i.e., the winter of 1818-19) a particular friend showed him a letter of General Jackson's "in which the Gen speaks of taking the posts in Florida *on his own responsibility* and denounces the administration violently as 'weak & pusillanimous' for giving them up." Monroe Papers, LC. The italics are

mine. Mr. Lacock could not produce this letter. Moreover, he was a friend of Mr. Crawford, and his words must be read with that in mind. If such a letter existed, it would of course upset the theory that Jackson seized Pensacola because of a communication from Mr. Rhea.

59. Irujo to Onís, October 10, 1818; Brooks, *op. cit.*, 155.
60. Adams to Onís, January 29, 1819; *ASPFR*, IV, 616.
61. Adams, *Memoirs*, IV, 261.
62. *Ibid.*, IV, 264-9.
63. The text of the treaty will be found in Hunter Miller, *Treaties and Other International Acts of the United States*, III, 3-18. Its most important provisions were as follows: Article II stated: "His Catholic Majesty cedes to the United States, in full property and sovereignty, all the territories which belong to him, situated to the Eastward of the Mississippi, known by the name of East and West Florida." The absence of a comma between the words "territories" and "which" supported the Jeffersonian claim that West Florida was not the property of the King of Spain, but part of the Louisiana Purchase. Article III stated: "The boundary Line between the two Countries, West of the Mississippi, shall begin on the Gulph of Mexico, at the mouth of the River Sabine in the Sea, continuing North, along the Western Bank of that River to the 32d degree of Latitude; thence by a Line due North to the degree of Latitude, where it strikes the Rio Roxo of Natchitoches, or Red-River, then following the course of the Rio Roxo Westward to the degree of Longitude, 100 West from London and 23 from Washington, then crossing the said Red-River, and running thence by a Line due North to the River Arkansas, thence, following

the course of the Southern bank of the Arkansas to its source in Latitude 42, and thence by that parallel of Latitude to the South-Sea. . . ." Article XI stated: "The United States, exonerating Spain from all demands in future, on account of the claims of their Citizens, to which the renunciation herein contained extends, and considering them entirely cancelled, undertake to make satisfaction for the same, to an amount not exceeding Five Millions of Dollars."

64. Adams, *Memoirs*, IV, 275.
65. *Ibid.*, IV, 277.
66. *Ibid.*, IV, 289.
67. *Ibid.*, IV, 287.
68. Brooks, *op. cit.*, 176. Griffin, *op. cit.*, 195.
69. *Memoirs*, IV, 290.
70. *Ibid.*, IV, 288.
71. Forsyth to Gallatin, June 13, 1819; Gallatin *MSS*.
72. Forsyth to Gonzalez Salmon, June 21, 1819; *ASPFR*, IV, 654-5.
73. Brooks, *op. cit.*, 179.
74. *Ibid.*, 180.
75. Forsyth to Gallatin, June 23, 1819; Gallatin *MSS*.
76. Forsyth to Gallatin, July 22, 1819; Gallatin *MSS*.
77. Rush to Gallatin, June 30, 1819; Gallatin *MSS*.
78. Rush to Gallatin, July 25, 1819; Gallatin *MSS*.
79. Forsyth to Gallatin, September 11, 1819; Gallatin *MSS*.
80. Forsyth to Gallatin, October 31, 1819; Gallatin *MSS*.
81. Brooks, *op. cit.*, 178.
82. *Ibid.*, 183.
83. Forsyth to Gallatin, October 31, 1819; Gallatin *MSS*.
84. Rush to Gallatin, June 30, 1819; Gallatin *MSS*.
85. Brooks, 186.
86. Griffin, *op. cit.*, 224.
87. G. H. Campbell to Gallatin, October 26/November 7, 1819; Gallatin *MSS*.

88. Richardson, *Messages*, II, 58.
89. *Ibid.*, II, 69-70.
90. *Annals of Congress, 16 Cong.*, 1 Sess., 1819-20, 1719.
91. Brooks, *op. cit.*, 189; *ASPFR*, IV, 696-701.
92. Richardson, *Messages*, II, 83-4. *Senate Journal of Executive Proceedings*, III, 242-4; Brooks, 189.
93. Adams, *Memoirs*, V, 283, 289.

CHAPTER FIVE

1. Thomas Moore, "To Thomas Hume, Esq., M.D.: from the City of Washington." *The Poetical Works of Thomas Moore*, A. D. Godley, ed., 1910, 117.
2. Adams, *Memoirs*, IV, 17.
3. "Mrs. Monroe's drawing room is open this evening. . . . Her parties are always dull & I presume they will be no better this season—she is a formal uninteresting woman —she receives her company as if she considered it an irksome task, which although necessary to be performed, may be lawfully conducted in such manner as to invite as few visitors as possible." J. W. Taylor to Mrs. Taylor, January 9, 1822. J. W. Taylor *MSS.* The beautiful Elizabeth Monroe was an invalid, and Taylor, when he wrote this letter, had no very friendly feelings to Monroe.
4. Macon to Bartlett Yancey, February 8, 1818; W. E. Dodd, *The Life of Nathaniel Macon*, 300.
5. Adams, *Memoirs*, IV, 481, 483. Adams to Daniel D. Tompkins, December 29, 1819; *Writings*, VI, 569 ff.
6. W. P. Cresson, *James Monroe*, 369.
7. Brooks Adams, "The Heritage of Henry Adams," in Henry Adams, *The Degradation of the Democratic Dogma*, 43.
8. Adams, *Memoirs*, IX, 185.
9. *Report of the Secretary of State upon Weights and Measures*, Washington, 1821, 29, 30, 59.
10. *Ibid.*, 69.

11. *Ibid.*, 48.
12. Brooks Adams, *loc. cit.*, 52.
13. 4 Wheaton, 192 ff.
14. *Ibid.*, 625 ff.
15. Holmes, *Collected Legal Papers*, 269.
16. One of the great exceptions is his attack on imprisonment for debt in *Sturges v. Crowninshield*, 4 Wheaton, 200-1.
17. Max Lerner, "John Marshall and the Campaign of History," *Columbia Law Review*, XXXIX, No. 3, 419.
18. Beveridge, *John Marshall*, III, 586 ff. A case argued before the Supreme Court as *Fairfax's Devisee v. Hunter's Lessee* in 1812 and as *Martin v. Hunter's Lessee* in 1814 was connected with the early speculations of Marshall and his brother. Though Marshall had no personal interest in the actual tract of land involved in this litigation, he very rightly refused to sit on both occasions. He did not, however, show the same nicety with regard to *Fletcher v. Peck*, which had some bearing upon these two later cases.
19. *Ogden v. Saunders*, 12 Wheaton, 334 ff. This was one of Marshall's rare dissenting judgments.
20. 4 Wheaton, 192.
21. *Ibid.*
22. Felix Frankfurter, *The Commerce Clause*, 17 ff. To this book, and to Max Lerner's illuminating article cited above, this chapter is much indebted.
23. *Willson v. The Black-bird Creek Marsh Company*, 2 Peters, 245; cited in Frankfurter *op. cit.*, 28-9.
24. 4 Wheaton, 407.
25. Beveridge, IV, 60 ff. E. S. Corwin, *John Marshall and the Constitution*, 40.
26. *Harriet Martineau, Retrospect of Western Travels*, I, 150. Beveridge, IV, 67-8. For his feelings towards women see Marshall to Joseph Story, October 29, 1828, *Mass. Hist. Soc.*, *Proceedings*, 2 ser., XIV, 337-8.

27. Lerner, *loc. cit.*, 423, citing Warren, *The Supreme Court in U.S. History*, I, 529*n.*
28. *Ibid.*, 424.
29. Bray Hammond, "Jackson, Biddle, and the Second Bank of the United States," *The Journal of Economic History*, VII, No. 1, 1.
30. Bray Hammond, *loc. cit.*, 2, citing E. R. Taus, *Central Banking Functions of the U.S. Treasury, 1789-1941*, Appendix III and IV.
31. *Ibid.*
32. William Gouge, *A Short History of Paper Money and Banking in the United States*, 1833, I, 90.
33. Vera C. Smith, *Rationale of Central Banking*, 40.
34. Biddle to Monroe, May 28, 1824; Monroe Papers, LC. The italics are inserted.
35. Beveridge, IV, 87.
36. Jefferson to Henry Dearborn, July 16, 1810. "I ascribe all this"—the repeal of the Embargo—"to one pseudo-republican, Story." Jefferson, *Writings*, Ford, ed., XI, 143.
37. Warren, *op. cit.*, II, 129.
38. Frankfurter, *op. cit.*, 43. He refers specifically to *Gibbons v. Ogden*, but does not exclude other decisions.
39. *Life and Letters of Joseph Story*, I, 325.
40. S. G. Brown, *Life of Rufus Choate*, I, 516. This story was told to Rufus Choate by Chauncey A. Goodrich, who heard Webster's argument. The famous peroration, or post-peroration, runs as follows: "Sir, you may destroy this little Institution; it is weak; it is in your hands! I know it is one of the lesser lights in the literary horizon of our country. You may put it out. But if you do so, you must carry through your work! You must extinguish, one after another, all those great lights of science which, for more than a century, have thrown their radiance over our land! It is, Sir, as I have said, a small College. And yet, there

are those who love it. Sir, I know not how others may feel, but, for myself, when I see my Alma Mater surrounded, like Caesar in the Senate-house, by those who are reiterating stab upon stab, I would not, for this right hand, have her turn to me, and say, '*Et tu quoque, mi filii!*' "
41. Lerner, *loc. cit.*, 417.
42. E. S. Corwin, *op. cit.*, 124
43. 4 Wheaton, 407.
44. *DAB*, XII, "John Marshall," 323.
45. Bryce, *The American Commonwealth*, 1891 ed., I, 363.
46. 4 Wheaton, 417.
47. *Ibid.*, 421.
48. *The Federalist*, 1937 ed., 294.
49. Madison to Spencer Roane, September 2, 1819; Madison, *Works*, Congressional ed., III, 144-5.
50. February 23, 1791; *Works of Alexander Hamilton*, J. C. Hamilton, ed., IV, 104 ff.
51. Niles, XVI, 41-4.
52. Beveridge, IV, 311, citing Niles, XVI, 104.
53. Ames, *State Documents on Federal Relations*, III, 3 ff.

CHAPTER SIX

1. 4 Wheaton, 408. The italics are inserted.
2. A. J. G. Perkins and Theresa Wolfson, *Frances Wright: Free Enquirer*, 1939, 12.
3. A. H. Cole, *Wholesale Commodity Prices in the United States*, 85.
4. McMaster, IV, 341.
5. Robert Chesebrough to John W. Taylor, December 8, 1820; John W. Taylor *MSS*.
6. "The energies of the American merchants, are prostrated by the Auctioneer; after giving a judicious order for goods, adapted to the wants and custom of the country, the British manufacturer avails himself of the information, and immediately ships the same goods, of inferior fabric and texture, and with the fa-

cilities of Auction sales drives the American out of the trade, leaving the foreigner to furnish our supply of goods . . . which leads him . . . to injure our domestic manufactures." *An Address to the Honorable the Legislature of the State of New York:* by Aaron Leggett. Albany, February 5, 1829, p. 5.

7. J. & P. Hone & Co. of New York City, in 1819, paid a tax of 1½% on sales equal to nearly $3,000,000 for which they received a commission of 2½%. Hoffman, Glass & Co., and Roggs, Thompson & Co. made sales of $1,300,000 and $800,000 respectively; and there were many lesser firms. In 1820, Leggett, Shotwell & Fox made sales of nearly $1,500,000. In 1818-19 the nine leading New York auctioneers made sales of nearly $8,500,000. John W. Taylor *MSS.* In 1827, it was estimated that all the auctioneers of New York City between them must have disposed of goods to the value of $20,000,000. *Historical and Chronological Account of the Origin and Progress of the City of New York,* 1828, 453-5. There is, of course, no way of telling what proportion of these goods was of British manufacture.

8. Hansard, 1 ser., XXXIII, 1098; speech of April 9, 1816.

9. McMaster, IV, 346.

10. *Ibid.,* IV, 348, citing *N. Y. Evening Post,* May 1, 13, June 3, 7, 1816.

11. L. C. Gray, *History of Agriculture in the Southern United States,* II, 697. This was at Savannah in October 1818. The *average* annual price of cotton at New Orleans reached its peak of 30¢ in 1817-18.

12. J. Marshall, *A Digest of all the Accounts,* London, 1833, 112.

13. Gray, *op. cit.,* II, 698.

14. Turner, *Rise of the New West,* 137.

15. Astor to Gallatin, March 7, 1817; Gallatin *MSS.*

16. Astor to Gallatin, March 14, 1818; Gallatin *MSS.*

17. Holdsworth and Dewey, *The First and Second Banks of the United States,* 176. R. C. H. Catterall, *The Second Bank of the United States,* I, 32n. *ASP, Finance,* III, 341-2. Gouge, II, 87, 88. Niles, XVI, 104. *Annals of Congress,* 15 *Cong.,* 2 *Sess.,* 1292—for Lowndes's attack on discounts on a pledge of stock. *Life and Correspondence of Rufus King,* VI, 38, 39—for King's protest.

18. Catterall, *op. cit.,* 28.

19. *Ibid.,* 32, 160n.; quoting HR 121, 22 *Cong.,* 2 *Sess.,* 140.

20. Gouge, II, 93. Catterall, 34. *ASP, Finance,* IV, 351-9.

21. Gouge, II, 94, 95. He says that the specie imported from Europe or purchased in the West Indies amounted to more than $7,000,000 at a cost of $500,000.

22. *ASP, Finance,* IV, 832.

23. Catterall, *op. cit.,* 44-50.

24. Nicholas Biddle to James Monroe, July 5, 1819; Monroe Papers, LC.

25. Catterall, 51. *ASP, Finance,* III, 325, 326.

26. Gouge, II, 96.

27. *Ibid.* "In other words, the merchants were called on to pay four or five millions, and were not allowed the privilege of paying debts due to the Bank itself in the paper of the bank."

28. Gouge, II, 104. *ASP, Finance,* III, 325, 326.

29. Catterall, *op. cit.,* 47.

30. Niles, XV, 125.

31. Astor to Gallatin, September 5, 1818. "Alltho trade is not Brisk the country at large seems to be doing well. Speculations in lands to the westward & South are running very high here property apears not to fall." Gallatin *MSS.*

32. Catterall, 57.

33. Gouge, II, 95.

34. Jefferson to John Adams, November 7, 1819. "The paper bubble is

then burst. . . . We were laboring under a dropsical fullness of circulating medium." *Writings*, Ford, ed., XII, 144-5.

35. Niles, XIV, 2.

36. Beveridge, *Marshall*, IV, 186.

37. An example of this, taken from the State of New York and the year 1828, will serve to illustrate the banking mind vis-à-vis the legislator. Charles Wilkes to Luther Bradish, September 23, 1828. Trusts that Mr. Bradish [an assemblyman from Franklin County, New York], "always so obliging where the interests of the Bank of New York is concerned" will bring up the Bank of New York Bill "if any bill whatever is brought up for the renewal of any charter of a bank, town or country." Luther Bradish to Charles Wilkes, September 25, 1828. ". . . You may rely upon my best efforts in favor of the renewal of the charter of the Bank, believing as I most sincerely do that such renewal is intimately connected with the Public Good. . . . I addressed a letter, on the 23rd inst, to your Mr. Heyer, inclosing my note endorsed for $1000, and offering the same for DisT. at your Bank. I don't know whether Delicacy would not have restrained me from doing this, had I previously recd. your letter. But as I feel persuaded the Decision of your Bank upon the subject of my letter will be given as if yours had not been written, I think I may safely trust that you and all others will believe me in no danger of having my conduct upon the subject of your letter in any degree influenced by such decision, whatever that may be." Mr. Heyer, Cashier of the Bank of New York, to Luther Bradish, September 27, 1828: informs Mr. Bradish that he has discounted his note for $990. Mr. Bradish is obviously innocent of any connection between his vote on the Bank Bill and his note for $1000. What is fascinating is that the cashier waited until Mr. Bradish's letter of September 25 was received before he discounted the note. Luther Bradish *MSS.*, NYHS.

38. *ASP, Public Lands*, III, 460; *Ibid., Finance*, III, 718.

39. This premium might be as high as 14% or even 20%; McMaster, IV, 486. Davis R. Dewey, *State Banking Before the Civil War*, 100.

40. Gouge, II, 157.

41. Faux's Journal, October 11, 1818; *Early Western Travels*, Thwaites, ed., XI, 171, cited in Beveridge, IV, 192.

42. Niles, XV, 60.

43. Beveridge, IV, 179.

44. Gouge, II, 130. "All this, however, availed nothing," Gouge remarks. "It went with the rest."

45. *Ibid.*, II, 167-8.

46. Niles, XIV, 428, cited in Beveridge, IV, 196.

47. Gallatin, *Considerations on the Currency and Banking System of the United States*, 68.

48. *ASP, Finance*, IV, 903.

49. Gouge, II, 106: "The revenue was principally paid off in branch paper, as well at Boston and New York as at Philadelphia, and while the duties were thus paid off at one counter, in branch paper, the debentures, which amounted to one million dollars every three months, were demanded and paid off at the other, in specie or its equivalent—money of the place."

50. Catterall, 68; citing Niles, LIII, 8.

51. Cheves, *Exposition of the Bank*, 1822, 21.

52. Gouge, II, 109.

53. It is in this period, McMaster notes, that "a general movement in behalf of temperance and morals swept the United States." IV, 530.

54. Samuel Rezneck, "Depression of 1819-1822." *Am. Hist. Rev.*, XXXIX, 31.

55. Sydnor, *The Development of Southern Sectionalism*, 111-12.
56. *Ibid.*, 112.
57. Catterall, 65 ff.
58. Benton, *Thirty Years' View*, I, 198.
59. Catterall, 78*n*.
60. Mr. Jones permitted himself, in his genial and muddleheaded way, to receive a gift from Buchanan and Smith—from the profits of their speculation in Bank stock. *ASP Finance*, III, 364.
61. Richardson, *Messages*, II, 75.
62. These prices were quoted by Niles on September 2, 1820; Gouge, II, 130.
63. Miller, *Banking Theories in the United States*, 20.
64. Gouge, I, 135-40. Webster's definition of a bank is instructive. "What is it, then, without which any institution is not a bank, and with which it is a bank? It is a power to issue promissory notes with a view to their circulation as money!" *Writings and Speeches*, XI, 127. Cited in Schlesinger, *The Age of Jackson*, Appendix, 525.
65. Miller, *op. cit.*, 114.
66. Catterall, 83, 84*n*.
67. Indiana, Illinois, North Carolina, Kentucky, and Georgia.
68. The case was *Osborn et al. v. The Bank of the United States*. 9 Wheaton, 738.
69. He owned two other plantations—Hayfield and Mill Hill.
70. Avery O. Craven, "The Agricultural Reformers of the Antebellum South," *Am. Hist. Rev.*, XXXIII, No. 2, 308. L. C. Gray, *History of Agriculture in the South to 1860*, II, 801, points out that horizontal plowing had to make its way against much ridicule at least until 1825, and that deep plowing was popularly supposed to work injury to the soil.
71. Craven, *loc. cit.*, 306. Gray, II, 780.
72. *Arator*, 188.

73. Nothing in the history of early soil conservation is more ironical than the fact that Edmund Ruffin, a reformer even more distinguished than John Taylor, was happy in his old age to fire the first gun against Fort Sumter. Craven, *loc. cit.*, 311.
74. Taylor to Jefferson, March 5, 1795; cited in Craven, *loc. cit.*, 305.
75. *Arator*, 35-6.
76. Henry H. Simms, *Life of John Taylor*, Richmond, 1932, 15.
77. Benton, *Thirty Years' View*, I, 45.
78. Taylor to Monroe, January 31, 1811; *Branch Historical Papers*, II, 316.
79. *Ibid.*, 352.
80. *Tyranny Unmasked*, 291.
81. Taylor to Monroe, November 8, 1809; *Branch HP*, II, 301.
82. *Inquiry*, 242.
83. *Ibid.*, 397.
84. *Ibid.*, 559.
85. *Ibid.*, 167.
86. E. T. Mudge, *The Social Philosophy of John Taylor of Caroline*, 1939, 2 ff. citing Jefferson, *Writings*, 1907, XVI, 14.
87. *Construction Construed*, 109.
88. Mudge, *op. cit.*, 118.
89. *Construction Construed*, 150.
90. *Ibid.*, 96.
91. 4 Wheaton, 424-5.
92. *Construction Construed*, 161.
93. 4 Wheaton, 408. *Construction Construed*, 87.
94. "Let the end be legitimate, let it be within the scope of the constitution, and all means which are appropriate, which are plainly adapted to that end, which are not prohibited, but consist with the letter and spirit of the constitution are constitutional." 4 Wheaton 421.
95. *Construction Construed*, 216.
96. *Inquiry*, 550, 552 ff.
97. *Construction Construed*, 291 ff.
98. *Inquiry*, 354.
99. *Ibid.*, 548.

PART THREE

CHAPTER ONE

1. J. Tallmadge, Sr., to Matthias B. Tallmadge, February 3, 1819. Tallmadge MSS, NYHS.

2. Jackson to Major M. B. Lewis, January 30, 1819; Parton, *Jackson*, II, 543.

3. Laura Tallmadge to Mrs. M. B. Tallmadge, January 22, 1819. Tallmadge MSS.

4. *Annals of Congress*, 15 *Cong.*, 2 *Sess.*, I, 1170. James D. Woodburn, "The Historical Significance of the Missouri Compromise," Am. Hist. Assoc. *Annual Report, 1893*, 255, points out that the words of the Annals of Congress "shall be free at the age of twenty-five" are incorrect.

5. James Tallmadge, Jr., to J. W. Taylor, September 14, 1819, in which he says that at Washington he and Taylor are looked upon as Clintonians, while in New York they do not have "the good will of Clinton's influence." J. W. Taylor MSS. Diary of De Witt Clinton, Volume for March 13, 1822-September 12, 1823, entry undated. "Speaking of a son of Judge Tallmadge it was observed that the more he is like his mother and the less like his father, the better." Judge Tallmadge is Matthias B. Tallmadge, brother of James Tallmadge, Jr., who died in 1819. MSS, N.Y.H.S.

6. Jabez D. Hammond, *History of Political Parties in the State of New York*, II, 184. T. Rudd to J. W. Taylor, February 27, 1828; J. W. Taylor MSS. So also W. L. Marcy to Martin Van Buren, December 27, 1826. "I suppose I shall not give you any news by informing you that his [Tallmadge's] talent for mischief as

[*sic*] quite equal to his inability." Van Buren Papers, LC.

7. *Ann. Cong.*, 15 *Cong.*, 2 *Sess.*, I, 1204.

8. The Bill creating the new Territory of Arkansas, which was successfully enacted during the last days of the Fifteenth Congress, very nearly received the same treatment. Only the efforts of Henry Clay prevented John W. Taylor of New York from adding a similar amendment to this Bill. The difference between the two amendments was that Tallmadge's amendment enjoined the adoption of the nonslavery principle upon the Constitution of Missouri, while the Taylor amendment imposed a condition on a Territorial government. It was during the debate on the Taylor amendment that the doctrine later known as "squatter sovereignty" was distinctly avowed by Southern opponents. Cardinal Goodwin, *The Trans-Mississippi West*, 96.

9. McMaster IV: Trenton, Worcester, Hartford, Albany, Philadelphia, Boston, and New York held citizens' meetings. The legislatures of Pennsylvania, Vermont, Massachusetts, and New Jersey sent memorials to Congress.

10. Ames, *State Documents on Federal Relations*, V, 4-9. Virginia and Kentucky were the two Southern states most vociferous in their opposition to restriction.

11. Albert F. Simpson, "The Political Significance of Slave Representation, 1787-1821," *Journal of Southern History*, VII, 330, 332.

12. H. A. Trexler, *Slavery in Missouri*, 102, citing *Missouri Gazette*, October 26, 1816 and June 9, 1819; St. Louis *Enquirer*, November 19, 1819. New settlers "came almost exclu-

sively from the states south of the Potomac and the Ohio bringing slaves and large herds of cattle."

13. Flint, *Recollections of the Last Ten Years*, 1932 ed., 173.

14. Caleb Atwater, *Remarks Made On A Tour to Prairie du Chien, thence to Washington City in 1829*, Columbus, 1831, 232.

15. U.S. *Census of 1820*, Washington, 1821.

16. Alabama was admitted on December 14, 1819; Maine's admission as a free state was made to depend upon that of Missouri as a slave state.

17. Timothy Flint, *op. cit.*, 195-6.

18. These are the States south of the Mason-Dixon line and the Ohio River: Maryland, Virginia, North Carolina, South Carolina, and Georgia on the Atlantic coast; Mississippi, Louisiana, and Alabama on the Gulf; Kentucky and Tennessee inland.

19. *Annals of Tacitus*, XIV, xliv, is generally considered the classical example of the fear of slavery. Pedanius Secundus, city prefect of Rome in the first century A.D., was murdered by one of his own slaves. The Senate, urged on by Gaius Cassius the jurist, voted for the harsh but traditional revenge of putting all the slaves of Pedanius to death. "*To our ancestors,*" said Gaius Cassius, "*the temper of their slaves was always suspect, even when they were born on the same estate or under the same roof, and drew in affection for their owners with their earliest breath.* But now that our households comprise nations—with customs the reverse of our own, with foreign cults or with none, you will never coerce such a medley of humanity except by terror." 1937 ed., John Jackson, translator.

20. James Monroe to The Speakers of the General Assembly, December 5, 1800; Monroe, *Writings*, III, 234 ff.

21. M. B. Hammond, "Correspondence of Eli Whitney Relative to the Invention of the Cotton Gin," *Am. Hist. Rev.*, III, 90-127, shows that in Eli Whitney's manuscript copy of the original specifications—dated and certified October 28, 1793—there is mention in a footnote of "Teeth set in right lines like a number of saws" as a possible substitute for his cylinder with inserted wires. This shows that he had anticipated (though without approval) the circular saws Hodgin claimed as his own invention. L. C. Gray, *History of Southern Agriculture*, II, 674 ff., says that roller-gins had been in use long before Whitney's invention appeared, but had not been developed, perhaps because of the superior profitableness of rice and indigo. For the British textile demand see Baines, *Cotton Manufacture in Great Britain*, 215, 346; Ure, *Cotton Manufacture of Great Britain*, I, 222; Bishop, *American Manufactures*, I, 397; Gray, op. cit., II, 677-8. It is to be noted, also, that one year after Whitney patented his gin, Jean Etienne Boré revolutionized the making of sugar in Louisiana. *DAB*, II, "Boré, J. E.," 461.

22. Gray, *op. cit.*, II, 683.

23. *Ibid.*, II, 691.

24. Avery O. Craven, *The Coming of the Civil War*, 36.

25. Sydnor, *Development of Southern Sectionalism*, 14.

26. *Ibid.*, 21.

27. Jefferson to John Adams, October 28, 1813; Jefferson, *Works*, Ford, ed., XI, 347.

28. Jefferson to John Taylor, May 28, 1816; *ibid.*, XI, 530-1.

29. Sydnor, *op. cit.*, chapter 2, *passim*.

30. W. C. Bruce, *John Randolph of Roanoke*, II, 203.

31. Gray, *op. cit.*, II, 666.

32. D. A. Tompkins, *American Commerce*, Charlotte, 1900, 111, 125. According to the Census of 1810 the

manufactured products of Virginia, the Carolinas, and Georgia exceeded those of all the Northeastern states with New York thrown in. See also Victor S. Clark, *The South in the Building of the Nation*, J. C. Ballagh, ed., Richmond, 1910, 169, 170.

33. Wilbur J. Cash, *The Mind of the South*, 70.

34. Adams, *Memoirs*, V, 10: entry for March 3, 1820.

35. Edward Field, *State of Rhode Island and Providence Plantations*, Boston, 1902, II, 403. This is undoubtedly the speech to which Nathaniel Macon—who was a member of the House in 1800—referred in his Senate speech of January 20, 1820, when he said that the only time he had ever heard the African slave trade defended was by "a member from the same state with the gentleman from Rhode Island." *Ann. Cong.*, 16 *Cong.*, 1 *Sess.*, I, 229.

36. *Ann. Cong.*, 16 *Cong.*, 1 *Sess.*, II, 1325. Speech of Charles Pinckney of South Carolina in House of Representatives, February 14, 1820.

37. *Jarman v. Patterson*, 7 T. B. Mon. 664, December 1828: cited in that great and invaluable compilation, *Judicial Cases Concerning American Slavery and the Negro*, Helen T. Catterall, ed., I, 311.

38. 2 Peters, 150-6.

39. Justice Mills of the Kentucky Court of Appeals in *Rankin v. Lydia*, 2 A. K. Marsh 467, October 1820. So also the Mississippi Supreme Court in *Harry et al. v. Decker and Hopkins*, R. J. Walker, *Reports, &c.*, 36, declared that "Slavery is condemned by reason and the laws of nature. . . . It can only exist through municipal regulations." This point of view prevails in the federal Constitution, which refers to slaves as "persons held to service in one State, under the laws thereof." *Judicial Cases*, I, 294 and III, 283.

40. Josiah W. Goodall to John W. Taylor, August 24, 1819. Goodall, who was bred in Massachusetts, said that he was at the time "persecuted by the slaveholders of Virginia with unrelenting fury." This language scarcely strengthens his story. John W. Taylor *MSS*.

41. *State v. Mann*, 2 Devereux, 263. December 1829. Italics inserted. *Judicial Cases*, II, 57.

42. *State of North Carolina v. Reed*, 2 Hawks 454, June 1823, where the death sentence passed upon Reed was sustained by the Supreme Court of N.C. *State of South Carolina v. Raines*, 3 McCord 533, May 1826, where Raines cleared himself of an atrocious killing of a sullen Negro. *Judicial Cases*, II, 44, 334.

43. In *Lee v. Lee*, 4 McCord 533, January 1827, an owner was said to be so terrified after killing a slave that he fled from Georgia into South Carolina; but since this man habitually dresed himself in "a negro cloth short coat" and "would sometimes send for all his negroes to throw dirt upon the roof . . . to keep off the witches," his standing in the community may have had something to do with his flight. The statement that the slave was "the most valuable species &c." was made by Judge Abraham Nott of South Carolina in *State v. Miles*, 2 Nott & McCord 460, January 1819. No Southern jurist would have contested it. *Judicial Cases*, II, 312, 336.

44. Thomas R. Dew, *The Pro-Slavery Argument*, 1852, contains his "Review of the Debate in the Virginia Legislature of 1831 and 1832," published as a pamphlet in 1832. Chancellor William Harper, *A Memoir On Slavery*, 1838. George Fitzhugh, *Sociology for the South*, 1854.

45. *Ann. Cong.*, 16 *Cong.*, 1 *Sess.*, I, 1024; Robert W. Reid of Georgia, February 1, 1820.

46. *Negro George v. Corse,* 2 Harris and Gill 1, June 1827; Court of Appeals of Maryland. *Judicial Cases,* IV, 69.

47. *Cannon v. Jenkins,* 1 Devereux Eq. 422, June 1830. *Judicial Cases,* II, 59.

48. *Girod v. Lewis,* 6 Martin La. 558, May 1819. *Judicial Cases,* III, 461.

49. Harper, *op. cit.,* 56.

50. James F. Rhodes, *History of the United States,* I, 336.

51. *Johnston v. Sprigg,* 12 Martin La., 328, April 1822, overseer is paid $600 per annum for a good crop, $500 otherwise. In *Lazare v. Peytavin,* 9 Martin La., 566, April 1821, a particularly brutal overseer was paid $800 per annum. In *Ritchie v. Wilson,* however, 3 Martin n.s., 585, May 1825, we find that the overseer was not paid his yearly $628 because his brutality caused a Negro girl, worth $1,000, to commit suicide. All this was in the sugar country. Cotton overseers, however, were not much more humane. *Judicial Cases,* III, 467, 471, 479.

52. Richard Hofstadter, "U. B. Phillips and the Plantation Legend," *Journal of Negro History,* XXIX, No. 2, 109-24.

53. A. H. Stone, "The Cotton Factorage System of the Southern States," *Am. Hist. Rev.,* XX, No. 3, 561.

54. L. C. Gray, *op. cit.,* II, 715. A. H. Stone, *loc. cit.,* 562.

55. Norman S. Buck, *The Development of the Organization of Anglo-American Trade,* 79, citing DeBow, *Review,* 1849, VII, 411.

56. *Ibid.,* 78.

CHAPTER TWO

1. Stratford Canning to W. Fazakerly, 14 November, 1820; S. Lane-Poole, *Life of Lord Stratford de Redcliffe,* 100-1.

2. McMaster, IV, 583. See also *Annals of Congress,* 16 *Cong.,* 1 *Sess.,* I, 832.

3. James J. Woodburn, "The Historical Significance of the Missouri Compromise," *AHA Annual Report,* 1893, 260. See also *Ann. Cong.,* 16 *Cong.,* 1 *Sess.,* I, 92.

4. *Ann. Cong.,* 16 *Cong.,* 1 *Sess.,* I, 85-6.

5. *Ibid.,* I, 99.

6. *Ibid.,* I, 107, 114.

7. *Ibid.,* I, 116, 127.

8. Federal Constitution: Ninth Section of the First Article.

9. Cotten, *Life of the Hon. Nathaniel Macon,* 60. Dodd, *The Life of Nathaniel Macon,* 42.

10. *Ann. Cong.,* 16 *Cong.,* 1 *Sess.,* I, 225.

11. *Ibid.,* I, 228.

12. *Ibid.,* I, 226.

13. *Ibid.,* I, 274.

14. *Ibid.,* I, 269, 270.

15. Jabez D. Hammond, *History of Political Parties,* I, 484-6. In 1819, the Bucktail and Clintonian factions in the New York Republican Party caucused together for the last time.

16. J. Q. Adams, *Memoirs,* V, 204.

17. It proposed that slavery and involuntary servitude should not be permitted in Missouri, and allowed children born of slave parents after Missouri's admission to statehood to be free immediately.

18. *Ann. Cong.,* 16 *Cong.,* 1 *Sess.,* I, 965-6.

19. *Ibid.,* I, 1001-2.

20. Madison to Monroe, February 10, 1820; *Works,* Congressional ed., III, 165.

21. *Ann. Cong.,* 16 *Cong.,* 1 *Sess.,* I, 1012.

22. *Ann. Cong.,* 16 *Cong.,* 1 *Sess.,* II, 1325—Charles Pinckney of South Carolina said that, as a member of the Constitutional Convention, he could aver that the word "migration" applied wholly to free whites. James Madison, whose memories of the Convention were reinforced by his own voluminous notes, declared that "the term 'migration' . . . referred exclusively to a migration

... from other countries into the United States," and that nothing in the subsequent state Conventions—unless it was the language of Mr. Walsh in that of Pennsylvania—indicated any other construction. Madison to Robert Walsh, November 27, 1819; *Works*, III, 150-1.

23. *Ann. Cong.*, 16 *Cong.*, 1 *Sess.*, I, 1092.

24. *Ibid.*, I, 1243.

25. *DAB*, X, "King, Rufus," 399; citing William Sullivan, *Familiar Letters*, 21.

26. Benton, *Thirty Years' View*, I, 57.

27. Jabez D. Hammond, *op. cit.*, I, 480.

28. King to J. A. King, February 20, 1820; Rufus King *MSS*, NYHS.

29. *Id.* to *id.*, February 25, 1820; *Life and Correspondence of Rufus King*, VI, 284.

30. Van Buren to M. M. Noah, December 17, 1819; Van Buren Papers, LC.

31. Mr. Tallmadge protested that when he left Washington in March 1819 he found himself "Opposed by Tammanies as a Clintonian—opposed by Federalists as a friend of Munroe—suspected & squinted at by Clinton"; and his only reference to King that has survived is one to "an infirm old Federalist." Tallmadge to John W. Taylor, April 4, 1819. *Id.* to *id.*, May 13, 1826. John W. Taylor *MSS*. In January 1820, he was quite sure that both he and Taylor had nothing to expect from "either State or Genl Government—The one hates us—the other is jealous of us—So we go." *Id.* to *id.* January 11, 1820; John W. Taylor *MSS*. John W. Taylor was a politician through and through; but he was neither a very distinguished man nor a very pleasing man; and though he gained the Speakership in 1820, he was not adept at managing a Congress, nor close to the centers of power. In 1819, he would have been content with the District Judgeship of the Northern District of New York; and in 1820, he seems to have realized that his efforts to restrict Missouri had lost him the good will of Monroe, and that he would have to be satisfied with Mr. Tallmadge's thought that "you have in this business a monument to your fame." *Id.* to *id.*, March 2, 1820; John W. Taylor *MSS*. From Tallmadge to J. Q. Adams and from Tallmadge to William H. Crawford—suggesting Mr. Taylor for the Judgeship. These are dated June 21 and July 7, 1819, *ibid*. No doubt Taylor hoped to gain popularity in his own state through his efforts in the Missouri debates.

32. Adams, *Memoirs*, IV, 522.

33. *Ibid.*

34. Draft of a letter to the editors of the *National Intelligencer*, in which King complains that the reports of speeches, whether taken by the *Intelligencer's* stenographer, or furnished by the speakers themselves, often contain opinions and arguments, ascribed by one speaker to another, and enclosed in inverted commas, leaving readers to suppose "such reports to be correct to ye letter." Thus Senator Smith is made to say that Rufus King felt himself "degraded" in the Senate, when King had said nothing of the sort. This draft is in the Rufus King *MSS*, apparently dated July 20. Mr. King's speeches were not reported; but his speeches in the Fifteenth Congress will be found in *Substance of two Speeches delivered in the Senate of the United States on the subject of the Missouri Bill, (by the Hon. Rufus King of New-York. New-York, 1819)*, and in the Sixteenth in *Life and Correspondence of Rufus King*, VI, 690-703.

35. Memorandum of January 7, 1820; Rufus King *MSS*.

36. "Humanitas" to King, March 10, 1820; Rufus King *MSS*.

37. *Ann. Cong.*, 16 *Cong.*, 1 *Sess.*, I, 405.

38. *Ibid.*, I, 407.
39. King to Charles Gore, February 17, 1820; *Life, &c.*, VI, 276.
40. *Ibid.*, VI, 339.
41. Thomas first offered his amendment on February 3 and withdrew it on February 7. On February 16, his amendment proposed that the sixth article of the Ordinance of 1787 should apply to all the Louisiana Purchase, excepting Missouri, north of 36° 30′ north latitude. On February 17, he withdrew this amendment, and substituted the one he had first offered on February 3. This read: *And be it further enacted,* That in all the territory ceded by France to the United States under the name of Louisiana, which lies north of 36° and 30′ north latitude, excepting only such part thereof as is included within the limits of the State contemplated by this Act, slavery and involuntary servitude, otherwise than in punishment of a crime whereof the party shall have been duly convicted, shall be and hereby is forever prohibited." *Ann. Cong.*, 16 *Cong.*, 1 *Sess.*, I, 428.
42. King to J. A. King, March 4, 1820. King to O. Wolcott, March 3, 1820. *Life, &c.*, VI, 287, 289.
43. *Ann. Cong.*, 16 *Cong.*, 1 *Sess.*, II, 1455-7.
44. *Ibid.*, II, 1553, 1556.
45. *Ibid.*, II, 1572.
46. John Mott to Rufus King, March 7, 1820; Rufus King *MSS.*
47. Rufus King to John A. and Charles King; *Life, &c.*, VI, 291.
48. *Ann. Cong.*, 16 *Cong.*, 1 *Sess.*, II, 1429.
49. J. Q. Adams, *Memoirs*, V, 4.
50. Jefferson to Holmes, April 22, 1820; Jefferson, *Writings*, Ford, ed., XII, 158.
51. *Ibid.*
52. Madison to Monroe, February 10, 1820; *Works*, III, 168.
53. Monroe to Jefferson, May 1820; Monroe, *Writings*, VI, 122-3.

54. *Congressional Globe*, 30 *Cong.*, 2 *Sess.*, Appendix 64-7.
55. E. S. Brown, *The Missouri Compromises and Presidential Politics*, 10.
56. Hay to Monroe, February 17, 1820; Monroe Papers, LC.
57. *Ibid.*, Friday morning, February 18.
58. Adams, *Memoirs*, V, 5 ff.
59. McMaster IV, 592.
60. Joseph Charles to J. W. Taylor, April 19, 1819; John W. Taylor *MSS.*
61. For Benton's land claim activities see John Baptiste Charles Lucas to J. W. Taylor, January 4, 1822; John W. Taylor, *MSS.* Lucas also accuses him in this letter of dishonest actions as a director of the Bank of Missouri. Lucas is, of course, a most prejudiced witness. For Benton's connection with Astor see Porter, *J. J. Astor*, II, 711, 713; H. M. Chittenden, *The American Fur Trade of the Far West*, I, 12-16.
62. Hodder, *loc. cit.*, 153. Sydnor, *op. cit.*, 130.
63. Trexler, *op. cit.*, 110.
64. Poore, ed., *Federal and State Constitutions*, II, 1108.

CHAPTER THREE

1. *Gibbons v. Morse*, 2 Halstead 253, November 1821. *Fox v. Lambson*, 3 Halstead 275, May 1826. Cited in Catterall, IV, 335, 337.
2. *Annals of Congress*, 16 *Cong.*, 2 *Sess.*, 10, 26.
3. *Ibid.*, 43, 44. Offered on December 6.
4. *Ibid.*, 48. Speech of December 8.
5. *Ibid.*, 67.
6. *Ibid.*, 55 ff.
7. *Ibid.*, 105 ff.; speech of December 11.
8. *Ibid.*, 1135.
9. Boorstin, *op. cit.*, 92; citing *Transactions of the American Philosophical Society*, IV, 289 ff., read July 14, 1792.

10. *Ann. Cong.*, 16 *Cong.*, 2 *Sess.*, 119.
11. *Ibid.*, 454-5.
12. *DAB*, XI, 474, "Lowndes, William."
13. Benton's *Abridgement*, VII, 12*n*.
14. *Annals of Congress*, 16 *Cong.*, 2 *Sess.*, 517-31.
15. *Ibid.*, 580, 991.
16. *Ibid.*, 670.
17. *Ann. Cong.*, 16 *Cong.*, 1 *Sess.*, II, 1426. Speech of William Plumer, Jr., of New Hampshire in HR, February 21, 1820.
18. *Ibid.*, 982.
19. *Ibid.*, 986.
20. *Ibid.*, 1019, speech of February 2.
21. *American Daily Advertiser*, November 4, 1820.
22. McMaster, IV, 598.
23. *Ibid.*, 600. *Annals of Congress*, 16 *Cong.*, 2 *Sess.*, 1147-66.
24. *Ann. Cong.*, 16 *Cong.*, 2 *Sess.*, 1027.
25. *Ibid.*, 1116.
26. *Ibid.*, 1195 ff.
27. *Ibid.*, 1219.
28. *Ibid.*, 1238-40.
29. *Ibid.*, 1228.
30. Richardson, *Messages and Papers*, II, 96.
31. Hodder, *loc. cit.*, 161; citing R. L. Mo., 1825, p. 600 and R. S. Mo., 1855, p. 1101.
32. Edwin C. Holland and others, *A Refutation of the Calumnies against the Southern and Western States, Respecting the Institution and Existence of Slavery Among Them*, Charleston, 1822. Richard Furman, *Exposition of the Views of the Baptists, Relative to the Coloured Population of the United States*, Charles-

ton, 1823. This kind of literature, marking a gradual change from defense to justification and from justification to eulogy, increased throughout the decade.
33. Early L. Fox, *The American Colonization Society* (Johns Hopkins Studies in Historical and Political Science, XXXVII, No. 3), 66, citing *African Repository*, I, 107.
34. Tocqueville, *Democracy in America*, I, 368*n*. These words were written after 1830, but are none the less true for most non-slave-holding States in the previous decade.
35. Carter G. Woodson, *The Negro in Our History*, 250.
36. *DAB*, "Vesey, Denmark," XIX, 258.
37. Herbert Aptheker, *American Negro Slave Revolts*, 270.
38. *Ibid.*, 272.
39. Joseph C. Carroll, *Slave Insurrections in the United States*, 94, gives details of the plot.
40. Aptheker, *op. cit.*, 271, says that Peter, the slave of Colonel J. C. Prioleau, first informed his master of what was on foot: this occurred between May 25 and May 30.
41. Carroll, *op. cit.*, 100. *DAB*, XIX, 259 puts the number of hanged at 35 and of transported out of the state at 34. Aptheker, 271, puts the number arrested at 139.
42. Holland, *op. cit.*, 86.
43. *The Savannah Republican*, August 29, 1822.
44. Aptheker, 272.

PART FOUR

CHAPTER ONE

1. Adams, *Memoirs*, V, 317.
2. Canning to Edward Planta, March 8, 1821; Stanley Lane-Poole, *The Life of the Right Honourable Stratford Canning*, I, 318. Adams, *Memoirs*, V, 317, 318. Adams describes the "queer sounds from the gallery" as "disorder and agitation in the gallery."

3. Richardson, *Messages and Papers*, II, 86 ff.

4. Adams, *Memoirs*, V, 180.

5. *Annals of Congress*, 16 *Cong.*, 1 *Sess.*, 615 ff., 1914 ff.

6. Macaulay, "Gladstone on Church and State," *Critical and Historical Essays*, 1900 ed., IV, 244.

7. W. R. Brock, *Lord Liverpool and Liberal Toryism*, 1941, 45.

8. Hansard, 1 ser., XXXVIII, 548.

9. *The Greville Memoirs*, 4th ed., *Reigns of George IV and William IV*, I, 90.

10. E. L. Woodward, *The Age of Reform* (Oxford History of England, XIII), 51.

11. Brock, *op. cit.*, 76.

12. *Annual Register*, LII, Appendix, 627.

13. *The Private Letters of Princess Lieven to Prince Metternich*, Peter Quennell, ed., 37, 160.

14. *ASPFR*, IV, 10.

15. F. Lee Benns, *The American Struggle for the West Indian Carrying Trade* (Indiana University Studies, X, Study No. 56), p. 37, citing *Annals of Congress*, 14 *Cong.*, 2 *Sess.*, 781-2.

16. *Ibid.*, 47. *Statutes at Large of the United States*, III, 351.

17. *Annals of Congress*, 15 *Cong.*, 1 *Sess.*, 341, 1720. Benns, *op. cit.*, 51-2, citing Niles, XIV, 106, 217.

18. *ASPFR*, IV, 382, 406.

19. *ASPFR*, IV, 405. Interview of September 16, 1819. Italics inserted.

20. Benns, *op. cit.*, 65, 66.

21. *Ibid.*, 64. W. W. Bates, *American Navigation*, 1902, 183.

22. Richardson, *Messages and Papers*, II, 60.

23. Benns, *op. cit.*, 70. The Act of May 15, 1820, is in *Statutes at Large of the United States*, III, 602-4.

24. *Annals of Congress*, 16 *Cong.*, 1 *Sess.*, I, 491, for Senator King's resolutions. *Ibid.*, I, 557, 586, for favorable report of Senate Foreign Affairs Committee, all of whom were Southerners. Senator Macon of North Carolina, however, expressed some doubts; he said that Great Britain would not give way till she saw how we got along with our own affairs; nor would the other Powers. Had not their Ministers attended the Missouri Debate (i.e., the first Missouri Debate) as constantly as he had done? And he was not absent an hour. "They were not there for nothing." Adams, *Memoirs*, V, 40.

25. Adams, *Memoirs*, V, 41. *ASPFR*, IV, 371, where Adams tells Rush officially of the reluctance of Monroe.

26. *Memorial of the citizens of the borough of Norfolk*; *ASP, Commerce and Navigation*, II, 523. Benns, *op. cit.*, 77, 78, citing *Charleston Mercury* editorial quoted in *New England Palladium and Commercial Advertiser*, January 29, 1822.

27. *ASPFR*, V, 84. Interview of July 13, 1820.

28. Benns, *op. cit.*, 71.

29. Hansard, 2 ser., I, 168, 424, 432, 478.

30. *Ibid.*, I, 184. Alexander Brady, *William Huskisson and Liberal Reform*, 1928, 74 ff. G. N. Clark, *The Later Stuarts*, Oxford History of England, XIII, 51.

31. Hansard, 2 ser., I, 574-5. In *ibid.*, I, 547-54 the Marquis of Lansdowne made a mild free-trade speech, in the course of which he said: "Their Lordships, he was sure, were well aware that in the year previous to the commencement of the unfortunate war which terminated in the establishment of American independence, our exports to the United States did not amount to more than £3,000,000, whereas at present they amounted to no less a sum than £30,000,000. Was this great and amazing increase the result of restrictive laws and provisions? Certainly not; *it was the result of the*

increased prosperity and population of those states, and of their becoming, in consequence of it, great consumers of our produce and manufactures." Lord Lansdowne was a Whig—the Liberal Tories were not alone in favoring free trade; but the Whigs at this time were more interested in political than in economic reform.

32. *Ibid.*, VI, 1418. Speech of April 1, 1822.

33. 3 Geo. IV, ch. 44.

34. Benns, *op. cit.*, 84.

35. Hansard, 2 ser., VI, 1428.

36. Benns, *op. cit.*, 84, citing *Edinburgh Review*, XXVIII, 487.

37. A. G. Stapleton, *Political Life of George Canning*, III, 14.

38. Canning to Gallatin, September 11, 1826; *ASPFR*, VI, 251.

39. *Greville Memoirs, Reigns of George IV and William IV*, II, 49.

40. Brock, *op. cit.*, 55.

41. *Ibid.*, 164.

42. *Ibid.*, 168-9. The Chancellor of the Duchy of Lancaster was N. Vansittart, who had previously yielded the Exchequer to the more able Robinson, and who became Lord Bexley. The Master of the Mint was the Duke of Wellington's brother, Lord Maryborough. Woodward, *op. cit.*, 633.

43. Richardson, *Messages and Papers*, II, 184-5.

44. Niles, XXIII, 87.

45. *Statutes at Large of the United States*, III, 740-2.

46. Hansard, 2 ser., XII, 1106.

47. Adams to Rush, June 23, 1823; *ASPFR*, VI, 228. Adams says that the Act was fully discussed in the Senate and the Cabinet.

48. Benton, *Thirty Years' View*, I, 125.

49. *ASPFR*, VI, 221, 228.

50. Adams, *Memoirs*, V, 411; entry for November 23, 1821. Cf. *n.*47 *supra* and Part V, Chapter 4, *n.*43.

CHAPTER TWO

1. H. W. V. Temperley, *The Foreign Policy of Canning*, 5. Harold Nicolson, *Congress of Vienna*, 250.

2. C. K. Webster, *The Foreign Policy of Castlereagh*, II, 413, 419. Wellington, *Supplementary Despatches*, XII, 805. Dexter Perkins, "Russia and the Spanish Colonies," *Am. Hist. Rev.*, XXVIII, 667.

3. *Cambridge History of Foreign Policy*, II, 662, for Castlereagh's Memorandum of May 15, 1820, drawing a famous and hitherto unprecedented distinction between constitutional and autocratic states. Lieven to Nesselrode, May 16, 1820, in Webster, *op. cit.*, II (Appendix), 565, tells of the division in the Cabinet (Ultra v. Liberal) concerning this Memorandum.

4. C. K. Webster, "Castlereagh and the Spanish Colonies," *English Historical Review*, XXVII, 78-95, XXX, 631-45. Webster, *Foreign Policy of Castlereagh*, II, 405 ff.

5. *Memoirs*, V, 250-2. Canning argued, among other things, that such a settlement (it had originally been J. J. Astor's Pacific Fur Company post sold to the Canadian Northwest Company during the War of 1812 and returned by the British in 1817, conformably to the Treaty of Ghent) violated the 3rd Article of the Convention of 1818, which left the whole Northwest coast free and open to the vessels, citizens, and subjects of either country for a term of ten years. Castlereagh to Stratford Canning, April 10, 1821, in Bemis, *J. Q. Adams*, 493 and *n*. (citing PRO, FO, 5, Vol. CLVI), instructs Stratford Canning not to contest Adams's remarks. The British government did not wish to call attention to the Hudson Bay Company which, about to merge with the Northwest Company, was a great power in the Oregon country. Professor Bemis, *ibid.*,

358, shows that Stratford Canning actually admired Adams's anti-British harangue of July 4, 1821.

6. Hughes to Gallatin, Stockholm, November 16, 1821. Gallatin *MSS.*

7. Adams to Robert Walsh, July 10, 1821, July 27, 1821. Adams to Edward Everett, January 31, 1822; *Writings*, VII, 113 ff., 127 ff., 197 ff.

8. Richardson, *Messages and Papers*, II, 116-18.

9. Bemis, *Latin American Policy*, 46.

10. *Works of Henry Clay*, Colton, ed., VI, 145-6.

11. W. S. Robertson, *Rise of the Spanish American Republics*, 235.

12. Giberto Freyre, *Brazil*, 171, points out that the four great heroes of the war against the Dutch belonged to different races: one was a Negro, one a Portuguese, one a white Brazilian, and one an Indian.

13. Adams, *Memoirs*, V, 325. Conversation of March 9, 1821.

14. *ASPFR*, IV, 217 ff. The members were John Graham, Caesar A. Rodney and Theodoric Bland. See also William R. Manning, *Diplomatic Correspondence of the United States Concerning Independence of the Latin-American Nations*, I, 382 ff., which also contains the independent observations of Joel R. Poinsett.

15. Adams to Anderson, May 27, 1823; Adams, *Writings*, VII, 441 ff. The deleted paragraph will be found on pp. 442-3.

16. *Annals of Congress*, 17 *Cong.*, 1 *Sess.*, 825-6; January 30 and 31, 1822.

17. George Watterston and N. B. Van Zandt, *Tabular Statistical Views*, Washington, 1828, 95. Pitkin, *A Statistical View*, 230, gives the details of the Cuban Trade.

18. July 19, 1822.

19. Monroe to John Quincy Adams, August 27, 1818; Monroe to Thomas Jefferson, November 23, 1818; Monroe to Andrew Jackson, May 23, 1820; Monroe to Albert Gallatin,

May 26, 1820: Monroe, *Writings*, VI, 72-3, 84-5, 128-9, 132-3, are examples of Monroe's thinking on Spanish-American affairs. It is summed up in "Sketch of Instructions for Agents for South America," March 24, 1819; *ibid.*, VI, 92 ff.

20. Webster, *op. cit.*, II, 484-5. The most terrible indictment of Castlereagh was written by Shelley in two lines from *The Masque of Anarchy*, 1819: "I met Murder on the way/ He had a mask like Castlereagh."

21. *Private Letters of Princess Lieven*, 189-90.

22. Earl Stanhope, *Conversations*, 126, 272.

23. Webster, *op. cit.*, II, 486.

24. Von Schultze-Gavernitz, *The Cotton Trade in England and on the Continent* (London, 1895), 99. J. A. Hobson, *The Evolution of Modern Capitalism*, 82. Hansard, 2 ser., XII, 1198: statement of March 25, 1825, that British cotton goods are underselling native manufactures in India.

25. Temperley, *op. cit.*, 33.

26. J. A. R. Marriott, *George Canning and his Times*, 13.

27. Temperley, *op. cit.*, 441.

28. Virgil, *Georgics*, IV, lines 86-7.

29. Temperley, *op. cit.*, 234, citing Marcellus, *Politique de la Restauration*, 15-17.

30. Nicolson, *op. cit.*, 271. One of George Canning's first statements was "For *Europe* I shall be disposed now and then to write *England*." This shows very clearly the trend of his diplomacy—the diplomacy, that is to say, of competition not of conferences. Algernon Cecil, *British Foreign Secretaries*, 1927, 57.

31. Temperley, "British Secret Diplomacy from Canning to Grey," *Cambridge Historical Journal*, VI, 1938, No. 1, p. 3.

32. Harold Laski, *The Rise of Liberalism*, 222 ff.

33. Brock, *op. cit.*

34. J. W. Croker to Robert Peel, August 25, 1822; *Croker Papers*, I, 213. See also Gallatin to Clay, August 31, 1827. "Influenced by Mr. Huskisson in all that related to commerce and commercial relations . . . Canning had the exclusive lead when they became clearly affected by political considerations." *Senate Docs.*, 22 *Cong.*, 1 *Sess.*, III, 132.

35. Temperley, *op. cit.*, 73.

36. Wellington to Canning, September 21, 1822: Wellington, *Despatches, Correspondence and Memoranda*, I, 288 ff.

37. Canning to Wellington, September 27, 1822; Temperley, *op. cit.*, 64.

38. *Ibid.*, 80. E. J. Stapleton, *Some Political Correspondence of George Canning*, I, 73-4.

39. *British and Foreign State Papers*, X, 64-70, dispatch of March 31, 1823.

40. Temperley, *op. cit.*, 92-3.

41. *Ibid.*, 72. Dexter Perkins, *The Monroe Doctrine, 1823-1826*, 111 ff.

42. Woodward, *op. cit.*, 198. Temperley, *op. cit.*, 88.

43. *Private Letters of Princess Lieven*, 274.

44. *Ibid.*, 273.

45. *Speeches in the House of Commons on Friday the 24th of February, 1826*, London, 1826, 95-6.

46. Adams, *Writings*, VII, 372.

47. Adams to Nelson, April 28, 1823; *ibid.*, VII, 372-3, 381.

48. *Ibid.*, VII, 373n.

49. Bemis, *J. Q. Adams*, 373-4.

50. Adams, *Memoirs*, VI, 138.

51. Stratford Canning to George Canning, May 8, 1823, in Perkins, *op. cit.*, 60.

52. *Memoirs*, VI, 151 ff.

53. Adams to Rush, July 28, 1823; Monroe, *Writings*, VI, 359.

CHAPTER THREE

1. *ASP, Commerce and Navigation*, II. Annual Report of the Secretary of the Treasury on the State of the Finances, 1824. H.R., *Misc. Doc.*, No. 117, 52 *Cong.*, 2 *Sess.*, 1893, x-xi, gives the percentage of total U.S. imports for 1821-5 coming from the United Kingdom only as 40.39 per cent.

2. Pitkin, *Statistical View*, 183. Marshall, *A Digest of All the Accounts*, 124. G. R. Porter, *The Progress of the Nation*, 1912 rev. ed., App. 477, shows that in 1820 this had sunk to about one twelfth.

3. Norman S. Buck, *The Development of the Organization of Anglo-American Trade*, 135. L. H. Jenks, *The Migration of British Capital to 1875*, says that 80% of Lancashire cotton supplies came from the American cotton fields in the period 1820-30.

4. Benns, *op. cit.*, 99.

5. Bemis, *Adams*, 378, citing *Speeches of George Canning*, V, 374.

6. McMaster, V, 328 ff., citing Sidney Smith's review of Seybert's *Statistical Annals*, in the *Edinburgh Review* for January-March 1820.

7. Greville, *Memoirs: Reigns of George IV and William IV*, I, 249. "Washington Irving wants sprightliness and more refined manners." *Journal of Washington Irving*, Stanley T. Williams, ed., 171. "Greville noisy & talkative–spoiled the dinner party." Robert E. Spiller, *Fenimore Cooper*, 118. Cooper on Scott: "It struck me that he wanted the ease and *aplomb* of one accustomed to live with his equals." Scott on Cooper: "This man, who has shown so much genius, has a good deal the manner, or want of manner, peculiar to his countrymen." See also Cooper to editor of *The New Monthly*, May 21, 1831; *Correspondence of James Fenimore Cooper*, New Haven, 1922, 227.

8. Bemis, *Adams*, citing *Speeches of George Canning*, VI, 414. Sir Charles Bagot to Canning, October 29, 1823; *George Canning and his Friends*,

Josceline Bagot, ed., II, 199. For Hughes's customary attitude towards American "republicans" see Hughes to Gallatin, January 19, 1827: a violent attack upon the "republicanism" of Alexander H. Everett. Gallatin *MSS.*

9. Canning to Bagot, January 22, 1824; *George Canning and his Friends*, II, 215 ff.

10. Rush to Adams, August 19, 1823; Monroe, *Writings*, VI, 361 ff., gives the substance of this conversation. See also Richard Rush, *Residence at the Court of London*, 399 ff.

11. Madame de Lieven to Metternich, August 18, 1823; *Private Letters*, 281-2.

12. *Ibid.*, 271, 283-4.

13. Canning to Rush, August 20, 1823; Monroe, *Writings*, VI, 365-6.

14. Rush to Canning, August 23, 1823; *ibid.*, VI, 366-7.

15. Canning to Rush, August 23, 1823; *ibid.*, VI, 369.

16. Rush to Canning, August 27, 1823; *ibid.*, VI, 370.

17. Rush to Adams, August 28, 1823; *ibid.*, VI, 371.

18. Rush to Adams, September 8, 1823; *ibid.*, VI, 374.

19. Rush to Monroe, September 15, 1823; *ibid.*, VI, 374-7.

20. Rush to Adams, September 19, 1823; *ibid.*, VI, 377 ff.

21. Rush to Adams, October 2, 1823, October 10, 1823; *ibid.*, VI, 386-90.

22. Canning to Wellington, September 24, 1823; Wellington, *Despatches, Correspondence and Memoranda*, II, 137. Wellington to Canning, December 10, 1822; *ibid.*, I, 639, shows that this was in Villèle's mind as early as December 1822. Temperley, *op. cit.*, 109, cites Villèle, *Mémoires*, IV, 200-1 to show that in July 1823 Villèle told the Duc d'Angoulême of similar plans.

23. C. D. Yonge, *Life and Administration of the 2d Earl of Liverpool*, 1868, III, 231-3, quotes an unsigned and undated Cabinet Memorandum, which he claims to be Liverpool's, but which was probably written by Canning, to the effect that France, if successful in Spain, might put "her fleets and armies" at the command of Spain to assist Spanish operations in South America, but that "we have the means of easily and effectually preventing any such projects." Brock, *op. cit.*, 238*n.*

24. Monroe, *Writings*, VI, 413-19. British and Foreign State Papers, XI, 49-53. Temperley, *op. cit.*, 115-17. The full text is in Cambridge History of Foreign Policy, II, 633-37.

25. Perkins, *op. cit.*, 118.

26. Temperley, *op. cit.*, 119.

27. *Ibid.*, 115. The Memorandum was known, in substance, at least, to Austria, Russia, and Prussia, as well as France, by the third week in October.

28. Monroe, *Writings*, VI, 364.

29. Canning to A'Court, December 31, 1823; Stapleton, *George Canning and His Times*, 394-5.

30. Hansard, 2 ser., X, 731, 737, 800 ff.

31. Hansard, 3rd ser., I, 479; gives a minute by Huskisson discovered at the Board of Trade, asserting that duties must be retained for the protection "absolutely requisite for the maintenance of your own internal industry."

32. Temperley, *op. cit.*, 115.

33. Perkins, *op. cit.*, 68-9.

CHAPTER FOUR

1. Bemis, *J. Q. Adams*, 382.

2. Monroe to Jefferson, October 17, 1823; Monroe, *Writings*, VI, 324.

3. Jefferson to Monroe, October 24, 1823; Jefferson, *Writings*, Ford, ed., XII, 318-19.

4. Madison to Monroe, October 30, 1823; Madison, *Works*, Congressional ed., III, 339.

5. Mrs. Harrison Smith, *The First*

Forty Years, 162. J. E. D. Shipp, *Giant Days*, 174n.

6. C. M. Wiltse, *Calhoun: Nationalist*, 278. Bemis, *J. Q. Adams*, 385.

7. W. C. Ford, "John Quincy Adams and the Monroe Doctrine," *Am. Hist. Rev.*, VIII, No. 1, 1902, 32.

8. *Memoirs*, VI, 177-79.

9. *Ibid.*

10. *Ibid.*, VI, 185.

11. *Ibid.*, VI, 186.

12. Two dispatches arrived on this day from Mr. Rush. One, No. 334, of October 2, dealt with Canning's desire for a joint declaration on the understanding that Great Britain would acknowledge the independence of the Spanish-American states at some future date. The other, No. 336, of October 10, said that Canning "said nothing of Spanish affairs." In Monroe, *Writings*, VI, 386, 388, the date of arrival is given as November 19: In Adams, *Memoirs*, VI, 187, as November 16.

13. *Memoirs*, VI, 190. Ford, *loc. cit.*, 34 ff.

14. *Ibid.*, VI, 190.

15. *Ibid.*, VI, 194.

16. *Ibid.*, VI, 194.

17. Bemis, *J. Q. Adams*, 388.

18. *Memoirs*, VI, 196.

19. *Ibid.*, VI, 197, 199.

20. *Ibid.*, VI, 201, 203.

21. *Ibid.*, VI, 201.

22. Ford, *loc. cit.*, 39-40.

23. As a leading authority has shown, though not included in the President's message, this principle was joined to the Monroe Doctrine by Hamilton Fish, President Grant's Secretary of State. Bemis, 395, citing Dexter Perkins, *The Monroe Doctrine, 1867-1907*, 25. *Memoirs*, VI, 222.

24. Adams to Rush, November 29, 1823; Manning, *Diplomatic Correspondence*, I, 210-12. Monroe, *Writings*, VI, 405-8.

25. Canning to Rush, December 13, 1823; Monroe, *Writings*, VI, 409.

26. Rush to Adams, February 9, 1824; *ibid.*, VI, 426. This interview took place on February 2.

27. Adams to Rush, December 8, 1823; Bemis, *J. Q. Adams*, Appendix 2, 578.

28. Richardson, *Messages and Papers*, II, 209, 217-19. Bemis, *Latin American Policy*, 63-4, quotes the original manuscript copy in the Senate archives, and this version is followed here.

29. Richardson, *Messages*, IV, 398; "The United States, sincerely desirous of preserving relations of good understanding with all nations, can not in silence permit any European interference on the North American continent, and should any such interference be attempted will be ready to resist at all hazards."

30. Perkins, *The Monroe Doctrine, 1823-1826*, 166.

31. *Ibid.*, 168.

32. *Ibid.*, 178.

33. Bemis, *Latin American Policy*, 68, citing W. S. Robertson, "South America and the Monroe Doctrine, 1824-1828," *Political Science Quarterly*, XXX, 82-105.

34. The five states were Chile (1824), Colombia (1824), Brazil (1825) for alliance. Mexico (1825) and the United Provinces (1826) for assistance. *Ibid.*, 68.

35. Clay to John M. Forbes, chargé d'affaires at Buenos Aires, January 3, 1828; Manning, *op. cit.*, I, 292. See also Adams to José Maria Salazar, Colombian Minister to the United States, August 6, 1824; *ibid.*, I, 224-6.

36. A. G. Stapleton, *George Canning and His Times*, 395.

37. *British and Foreign State Papers*, XI, 58-62.

38. Hughes to Gallatin, Brussels, January 19, 1827; Gallatin MSS.

39. Anna Lane Lingelbach, "William Huskisson as President of the Board of Trade," *Am. Hist. Rev.*, XLIII, No. 4, 769.

40. Bemis, 522, 524; In 1821, a Russian ukase, dated September 4/16, prohibited all foreign vessels from coming within 100 Italian miles of the northwest coast between the Bering Straits and 51° north latitude, and granted whaling and fishing rights exclusively to Russian subjects. The question was easily settled by The Convention of April 5/17, 1824. *ASPFR*, IV, 861-4.

41. Temperley, *op. cit.*, 132.

42. Private Letters, 339.

43. Temperley, *op. cit.*, 147.

44. *Ibid.*, 152.

45. Woodward, *op. cit.*, 201. The speech was made on December 12, 1826.

CHAPTER FIVE

1. Perkins, *op. cit.*, 145.

2. *Memoirs*, VI, 224. *Ann. Cong.*, 18 *Cong.*, 1 *Sess.*, I, 2204.

3. Perkins, *op. cit.*, 147, citing *Register of Debates*, 19 *Cong.*, 1 *Sess.*, II, 2446.

4. A sixth, De Witt Clinton, hovered on the outskirts; but Clinton was, if anything, a Clintonian.

5. Thomas L. McKenney to Phillip Milledoler, December 13, 1821. Milledoler *MSS*, NYHS.

6. John McClean to John W. Taylor, October 25, 1824. John W. Taylor *MSS*, NYHS.

7. Lowrie to Gallatin, February 21, 1824; Gallatin, *MSS*, NYHS.

8. Sydnor, *Southern Sectionalism*, 164-5.

9. Taylor to Monroe, April 29, 1823; "Although I believe Mr. Calhoun and Mr. Adams entertain some opinions which I think erroneous, yet I discern no proofs that either would invest a coalition between political craft and pecuniary speculation with a power of making presidents." He says that when it comes to moral rectitude and frugality, both may be classed with the best

men. Monroe Papers, LC. This letter seems to have been written in a mood of deep distrust of Crawford who had recently been accused in the "A.B." letters (written by Ninian Edwards) of willful mismanagement of the public funds in his dealings with the banking institutions of the West. The accusations were not well founded.

10. Jackson to A. J. Donelson, August 6, 1822; *Correspondence*, III, 174.

11. Jackson to John Coffee, March 10, 1823; *ibid.*, III, 192.

12. Temperley, *Foreign Policy of Canning*, 38.

13. Marquis James, *Andrew Jackson: Portrait of a President*, 44.

14. Jackson to H. W. Peterson, February 23, 1823; *Correspondence*, III, 189.

15. Jackson to G. W. Martin, January 2, 1824; *ibid.*, III, 222.

16. J. H. Eaton to Rachel Jackson, December 18, 1823; *ibid.*, III, 217.

17. Jackson to John Coffee, December 31, 1823; *ibid.*, III, 222.

18. *Ibid.*

19. Jackson to Rachel Jackson, December 21, 1823; *ibid.*, III, 217-26.

20. *Report of the Debates and Proceedings in the Convention of the State of New York*, New York, 1821. The debates on the right of the free Negro to vote—pp. 98 to 106 particularly—were the most impassioned of this convention, although the supporters of property qualifications put up a very stiff battle. *Journal of Debates and Proceedings in the Convention of Delegates Chosen to Revise the Constitution of Massachusetts*, Boston, 1853. The speech of Josiah Quincy, p. 251, is a peculiarly ingenious defense of property qualifications. Only in Illinois, Ohio, Indiana, Missouri, Vermont, New Hampshire, New Jersey, Alabama, Maryland, and Kentucky was there no relation-

ship between voting on the one hand, and real property or taxation, on the other.

21. District tickets prevailed in Maine, Massachusetts, Maryland, Tennessee, Missouri, and Illinois. The legislatures chose electors in Vermont, New York, Delaware, South Carolina, and Georgia. McMaster, V, 75n.

22. *Niles' Register*, XXVI, April 3, 1824, 65-6.

23. Edward Stanwood, *American Tariff Controversies in the Nineteenth Century*, I, 172-3. F. W. Taussig, *The Tariff History of the United States*, 55 ff. Chester W. Wright, *Economic History of the United States*, 391 ff. Edward C. Kirkland, *A History of American Economic Life*, 319-21.

24. Kirkland, 332-4. F. A. Shannon, *Economic History of the People of the United States*, 252. Wright, 388.

25. ASP, Finance, V, 792-832.

26. Stanwood, I, 237.

27. *Ann. Cong.*, 18 *Cong.*, 1 *Sess.*, II, 1857-59. Report of the Committee on Agriculture—a faithful résumé of the home-market argument.

28. Niles, XXVI, March 18, 1824, 29 ff. *Ann. Cong.*, 18 *Cong.*, 1 *Sess.*, II, 1751 ff.

29. *Ann. Cong.*, 18 *Cong.*, 1 *Sess.*, II, 1859.

30. Gray, *History of Agriculture in the Southern United States*, II, 746.

31. *Report of the Committee of Merchants and Manufacturers of Boston on the proposed Tariff, January 1824*, Boston, 1824.

32. *Ann. Cong.*, 18 *Cong.*, 1 *Sess.*, II, 2026-82.

33. Ames, *State Documents*, IV, 6.

34. *Ann. Cong.*, 18 *Cong.*, 1 *Sess.*, I, 1372.

35. Ames, *op. cit.*, IV, 4. Niles, XXIX, 293.

36. *Ann. Cong.*, 18 *Cong.*, 1 *Sess.*, II, 1962-2001. Clay, *Works*, Colton, ed., VI, 293. *Ann. Cong.*, 18 *Cong.*, 1

Sess., II, 1569 for Cambreleng's speech of February 18.

37. *Ann. Cong.*, 18 *Cong.*, 1 *Sess.*, II, 1515.

38. Niles, XXVI, April 24, 113.

39. Turner, *Rise of the New West*, 242.

40. Some of the chief duties were: the duty on pig iron—raised from 50¢ to 56¢ a hundredweight, hammered bar iron from 75¢ to 90¢, rolled bar iron from $1.50 to $3.00. Hemp was protected with a duty of $35 a ton instead of the old $15. Cotton fabrics received a duty of 33⅓% instead of 25%.

41. Taussig, *op. cit.*, 75n. Stanwood, *op. cit.*, I, 202, 203. Wiltse, *Calhoun: Nationalist*, 289.

42. *Statutes at Large of the United States*, IV, 25-30.

43. Crawford's treasury *Report* of 1819 seems to favor a protective tariff; his *Report* of 1820 is doubtful. His subsequent *Reports* do not mention the subject at all. Jackson voted for the Bill in the Senate, Clay sponsored it in the House, and Adams's friends let it be known that he was also in favor.

44. McMaster, V, 239. Clay, *Works*, VI, 283.

45. Hansard, 2 ser., XII, 1209.

46. Richardson, *Messages*, II, 215-16. Italics inserted.

47. Anna L. Lingelbach, *loc. cit.*, 759-75. ASPFR, VI, 245, 567. Benns, *op. cit.*, 101.

CHAPTER SIX

1. Jefferson to Richard Rush, June 5, 1824; Jefferson, *Writings*, Ford, ed., XII, 355.

2. Taylor, *Tyranny Unmasked*, 201.

3. Richardson, *Messages*, I, 584-5. Madison's Veto Message of March 3, 1817.

4. *Ibid.*, II, 142-3.

5. W. P. Cresson, *James Monroe*,

390-1, citing Madison, *Writings*, Hunt, ed., VIII, 404-5.

6. Richardson, *Messages and Papers*, II, 173.

7. The "Views" are in *ibid.*, II, 144-83.

8. Turner, *Rise of the New West*, 233.

9. Turner, *op. cit.*, 234, citing *Ann. Cong.*, 18 *Cong.*, 1 *Sess.*, I, 1315.

10. Kirkland, *op. cit.*, 272-8. Ellen C. Semple, *American History and its Geographic Conditions*, 267-71. Shannon, *op. cit.*, 178.

11. Turner, *op. cit.*, 235.

12. *Statutes at Large of the United States*, IV, 629.

13. Martin Van Buren, *Inquiry into the Origin and Course of Political Parties in the United States*, 51, 54.

14. *Statutes at Large of the United States*, IV, 124.

15. Cresson, *James Monroe*, 498.

16. Adlard Welby, *A Visit to North America and the English Settlements in Illinois*, London, 1821, 209.

PART FIVE

CHAPTER ONE

1. Mrs. Harrison Smith, *First Forty Years of Washington Society*, 186. Clark, *John Quincy Adams*, 228. Richardson, *Messages and Papers*, II, 292-3—answer to the Committee, February 10, 1825.

2. Henry Adams to Brooks Adams, February 18, 1909; Henry Adams, *The Degradation of the Democratic Dogma*, 10.

3. Adams, *Memoirs*, VI, 442, 450-2, 458, 472. Everett S. Brown, ed., *The Missouri Compromises*, 119.

4. *Education of Henry Adams*, 1931 ed., 146-7.

5. Dennis T. Lynch, *An Epoch and a Man*, 266. Hammond, *op. cit.*, II, 143 ff. W. L. Marcy to Martin Van Buren, December 14, 1824. Marcy says that the "enlightened republicans" were against a change in electoral law but that "the current of public opinion was so strong that it cannot be resisted." Van Buren Papers, LC. However, it was resisted.

6. Van Buren, *Autobiography*, 144, calls the removal of Clinton a "very unexpected and badly devised step," and says that he "had no knowledge, being in Washington, of the intention to make it." Judge Roger W. Skinner, one of the Regency, was thinking about it as early as January 1824. "Judge Skinner behaves quite well; now and then he indulges his spleen against certain persons for keeping Clinton in the board of canal commissioners, but that is seldom." W. L. Marcy to Martin Van Buren, Van Buren Papers. For such motives behind the removal of Clinton as can be discerned see Hammond, *op. cit.*, II, 167. The resolution was introduced in the New York Senate by Bowman of Monroe County, but was handed to him by Silas Wright, Jr., one of the Regency leaders. Clark, *op. cit.*, 212.

7. "At a numerous and respectable meeting of citizens of the Village of Geneva and its vicinity held pursuant to notice, at Faulkner's Hotel on the 1st May 1824 to express their sentiments on the subject of the removal of De Witt Clinton from the Office of Canal Commissioner.

"Resolved that the majority of the Legislature, in voting for the removal of De Witt Clinton from the Office of Canal Commissioner, have manifested malignant feelings unworthy of Statesmen, a contempt for public opinion and a disregard for the public interests, calculated to fix upon the people of this state the stain of ingratitude towards an enlightened and patriotic public benefactor, and to render the state an object of contempt in the eyes of the foreign nations and of our Sister States."

This is a good example of the public feeling. Clinton *MSS*, NYPL. Hammond, II, 175. Clinton's majority was 16,906; Tallmadge's 32,409.

8. Benjamin F. Butler to Van Buren, March 27, 1824. Crawford will receive the "united vote of the State . . . provided we succeed in the Govs election." Van Buren Papers, LC.

9. The Clay forces were led by Peter B. Porter.

10. Judge Skinner to Van Buren, December 1, 1824. "Hammond and others openly declare that the Adamsites have violated the most solemn obligations to Clay, that they stood pledged to give Clay from the Adams list eight votes in consideration of Clay's friends supporting the successful ticket. . . . Lockwood said openly yesterday that Genl Tallmadge for himself and in behalf of his friends declared in his presence that Clay should have the eight votes." Van Buren Papers, LC.

11. Van Buren to Crawford, November 17, 1824. A draft. Van Buren Papers, LC.

12. Clark, *op. cit.*, 218.

13. Albert R. Newsome, "The Presidential Election of 1824 in North Carolina," *James Sprunt Studies in History and Political Science*, XXIII, No. 1, 164. Newsome says that the People's Ticket was not a fusion Jackson-Adams affair, as McMaster V, 74, seems to think; but that it was, in all but name, a Jackson ticket. 153.

14. Lowrie to Gallatin, September 25, 1824; Gallatin *MSS*. Gallatin to Van Buren, October 2, 1824; Van Buren Papers.

15. William Plumer, Jr., to William Plumer, Sr., December 16, 1824; Everett S. Brown, ed., *Missouri Compromises*, 123.

16. Clay, *Works*, Colton, ed., VI, 302. "I seemed to be the favorite of every body. Describing my situation to a distant friend, I said to him, 'I am enjoying, while alive, the posthumous honors which are usually awarded to the venerated dead.' . . . I found myself transformed from a candidate before the people, into an elector for the people." "Mr. Clay's Address to his Constituents," March 26, 1825.

17. Marquis James, *Andrew Jackson: Portrait of a President*, 105. Thomas H. Benton, *Thirty Years' View*, I, 48.

18. Adams, *Memoirs*, VI, 447.

19. Adams, *Memoirs*, VI, 452, 453, 457.

20. Philip S. Klein, *Pennsylvania Politics, 1817-1823*, 176, 180, citing Buchanan to the editor of the *Lancaster Journal*, August 8, 1827. Cf. Moore, *Works of James Buchanan*, I, 263-67; Curtis, *Life of James Buchanan*, I, 41-4. For Clay's account see Clay, *Works*, Colton, ed., I, 440.

21. Jackson to Carter Beverly, June 5, 1827; *Correspondence*, III, 355.

22. The two versions disagree as to dates. Buchanan says that he interviewed the General on December 30, 1824; the General says that he saw Buchanan "early in January," 1825. Mr. Clay, in his version, says that Buchanan came to him "some time in January." The dates have no special significance, except that they seem to support Jackson's version by a vote of two to one.

23. George T. Curtis, *Life of Daniel Webster*, I, 222.

24. Adams, *Memoirs*, VI, 464, 465.

25. "Mr. Clay's Address to his Constituents," Clay, *Works*, Colton, ed., VI, 311.

26. McMaster, V, 75.

27. James, *op. cit.*, 118. Adams, *Mem-*

oirs, VI, 469. Plumer called on January 17.

28. *Memoirs*, VI, 474.

29. *Ibid*. Both these calls were made on January 21.

30. *Ibid*., VI, 475.

31. *Ibid*., VI, 476.

32. Klein, *op. cit.*, 184.

33. *Memoirs*, VI, 487. Italics inserted.

34. Brooks Adams in Henry Adams, *The Degradation of the Democratic Dogma*, 13, 14.

35. Daniel P. Cook, an Adams man at heart, was under constant attack from Ingham of Pennsylvania and McDuffie of South Carolina, Calhoun's supporters, who wished him to vote for Jackson. Scott was threatened with terrible reprisals by Thomas H. Benton, as late as February 8. Adams, *Memoirs*, VI, 496. Benton to John Scott, February 8, 1825. "Tomorrow is the day for your self-immolation. If you have an enemy, he may go and feed his eyes upon the scene." Parton, *Jackson*, III, 62, 63.

36. Clinton to Van Rensselaer, February 1, 1825; *MS.*, New York State Library. Adams was persuaded that Clinton was working on the New York delegation, "particularly Gen Van Rensselaer," to vote for Jackson. Adams, *Memoirs*, VI, 470. Clinton was personally a supporter of Jackson for President. Hammond, *op. cit.*, II, 188, 189.

37. Van Buren, *Autobiography*, 152.

38. Adams, *Memoirs*, VI, 493.

39. James, *Andrew Jackson: Portrait of a President*, 124.

40. Van Buren, *Autobiography*, 152. Mrs. Harrison Smith, *The First Forty Years*, &c., 191, tells of the meeting of Van Rensselaer and McLane. The notion that the voting in the House might be dragged out indefinitely and result in Calhoun, the elected vice-president, becoming President by default was current as early as October 17, 1824; "N" to

Samuel Smith, October 17, 1824. Van Buren Papers.

41. Van Rensselaer to Clinton, February 10, 1825; Clinton *MSS.*, NYPL. This was dated March 10, evidently a mistake. It does not, of course, refute Van Buren's version. However, J. Gales to Gallatin, February 28, 1825—"In N.Y. the vote depended on Genl Van Rensselaer, & on the morning of the 9th he would have challenged any man that would have said he would vote for Adams. Not five minutes before his vote was taken he was firm against him, but finally gave way to the fears with which it was attempted to alarm him."—Supports Van R's version. Gallatin, *MSS.*

42. For Adams: Maine, New Hampshire, Vermont, Massachusetts, Rhode Island, Connecticut, New York, Maryland, Louisiana, Kentucky, Missouri, Ohio, Illinois. For Jackson: New Jersey, Pennsylvania, South Carolina, Alabama, Mississippi, Tennessee, Indiana. For Crawford: Virginia, Delaware, North Carolina, Georgia. McMaster, V, 81*n*.

43. Mrs. Harrison Smith, *op. cit*, 181.

44. Wiltse, *Calhoun: Nationalist*, 307-8. James, *Andrew Jackson: Portrait of a President*, 128-9. Mrs. Harrison Smith, 181, 183. Edward Stanley, *Journal of a Tour in America, 1824-25*, 313.

45. James, 129, citing Samuel G. Goodrich, *Recollections of a Lifetime*, II, 403.

46. *Am. Hist. Rev.*, XLII, No. 2, 273-6. Actually, Adams did not offer the State Department to Clay until some hours after his interview with Monroe. Adams, *Memoirs*, VI, 508.

47. *Memoirs*, VI, 508-9. This may explain Dennis Tilden Lynch's insistence that the State Department was first offered to Clinton. Lynch, *An Epoch and a Man*, 282.

48. James, *op. cit.*, 130. Jackson to W.

B. Lewis, February 14, 1825; *Correspondence*, III, 276.
49. *Memoirs*, VI, 518.
50. Clay to Crawford, February 18, 1828. Clay, *Works*, Colton, ed., IV, 193.
51. McMaster, V, 489.
52. However, Adams had gained 14,-632 popular votes in Maryland to Jackson's 14,523. *Ibid.*, V, 75n.
53. The North Carolina delegation probably intended to change to Jackson on the second ballot. Newsome, *loc. cit.*, 169-70.

CHAPTER TWO

1. Adams said that he would never have offered the Treasury to Crawford if he had known that Crawford, his mind befuddled and half-maddened by illness, had threatened Monroe with personal assault in the winter of 1824. Monroe, on that occasion, had seized a poker in order to defend himself. Adams, *Memoirs*, VI, 81.
2. Wiltse, *Calhoun: Nationalist*, 313, 317-18.
3. Richardson, *Messages and Papers*, II, 296-7.
4. Adams to Clinton, February 18, 1825. "The Minister of the U.S. at London has long been wishing to return home. I am desirous, if it may suit your views, to obtain your assistance in the administration of the General Government about to commence; and believe it would be useful to the nation, in the Mission to Great Britain. . . ." Clinton *MSS.*, NYPL. It has been contended that if Clinton had accepted, the Governorship of New York would of course have gone to Lieutenant Governor James Tallmadge—that the offer of the Mission was simply a way of removing Clinton. Wiltse, 318. Tallmadge, however, did not see it in that light—see Tallmadge to Weed, below.

5. J. H. Powell, *Richard Rush: Republican Diplomat*, 1942, 181. Powell, the most informed and eloquent defender of the Adams Administration, calls this "the only sheerly political appointment he made."
6. Tallmadge to Weed, September 3, 1825; *MS.*, NY State Library.
7. Clark, 254-5. Thurlow Weed, *Autobiography*, I, 177-181. (The Autobiography, edited by Harriet A. Weed, comprises Vol. I of the 2 vol. *Life of Thurlow Weed*, 1883-1884.)
8. Adams, *Memoirs*, VII, 63.
9. Richardson, *Messages and Papers*, II, 315-16.
10. Adams, *Memoirs*, VII, 64. William Wirt, Adams's Attorney-General, said in Cabinet that the reference to voyages of discovery and scientific researches in monarchies would be cried down as partiality to monarchies.
11. Jefferson to W. B. Giles, December 26, 1825; Jefferson, *Writings*, Ford, ed., XII, 427.
12. Crawford to Clay, February 4, 1828; Clay, *Works*, Colton, ed., IV, 192.
13. *Niles's Register*, XXXV, November 15, 1828, 190. Richmond *Enquirer*, December 8, 1825. Adams, *Memoirs*, VII, 76. Madison to Ritchie, December 18, 1825; Madison, *Works*, III, 506. Wiltse, *Calhoun: Nationalist*, 321, citing William E. Smith, *The Francis Preston Blair Family in Politics*, I, 38.
14. *Memoirs*, VII, 63.
15. *A Letter From the Secretary of the Treasury Enclosing the Annual Report on the State of the Finances*, Washington, 1825.
16. *Memoirs*, VII, 63.
17. Towards the end, he began to compromise with his conscience. "The right," he said, "must . . . yield to the expedient." *Memoirs*, VIII, 5.
18. *Memoirs*, VII, 163-4, 343, 349, 364.
19. *Ibid.*, VII, 390. The notion that

Adams was above the use of patronage is scouted in Wiltse, *Calhoun: Nationalist*, 327. "Adams had a convenient way of not knowing exactly what his lieutenants were doing, and of failing to mention in his diary all that he did know."

20. Brooks Adams in Henry Adams, *The Degradation of the Democratic Dogma*, 11.

21. Adams to the Rev. Charles Upham, February 2, 1937; *ibid.*, 24-5.

22. Dorfman, *The Economic Mind in American Civilization*, I, 256-7, for Washington's hope that a great industrial empire would arise close to Alexandria. See also Brooks Adams, *loc. cit.*, 17-22 for Adams's extension of Washington's theory.

23. Brooks Adams, *loc. cit.*, 31, 32.

24. *Ibid.*, 33, 34, citing *Memoirs*, XI, 340-1—Adams's expression in his old age of "agonizing doubts, which I can neither silence nor expel."

25. *Memoirs*, VII, 188. Adams says that Thomas Hart Benton's scheme of graduated prices for the public lands—which would have made them more accessible to the pioneer —was supported by a speech "the whole drift of which was to excite and encourage hopes among the Western people that they can extort the lands from the Government for nothing."

26. Brooks Adams, *loc. cit.*, 32.

27. Richardson, *Messages and Papers*, II, 313

28. Arthur M. Schlesinger, Jr., *The Age of Jackson*, 62, citing James K. Polk in the House of Representatives, March 29, 1830; *Register of Debates*, 21 *Cong.*, 1 *Sess.*, 698-9. ". . . The policy . . . is, to sell your lands high, prevent thereby the inducements to emigration, retain a population of paupers in the East, who may, of necessity, be driven into manufactories to labor at low wages for their daily bread. The second branch of the system

is high duties . . . first, to protect the manufacturer, by enabling to sell his wares at higher prices, and next to produce an excess of revenue. The third branch of the system is internal improvements, which is to suck up the excess of revenue." Adams did not see high tariffs as revenue producers; and, indeed, the excess of revenue produced by high tariffs forced those protectionists who believed in a high price for public lands to change their public-land policy. For Rush's antipioneer report see "Report on the State of the Finances," December 8, 1827. 20 *Cong.*, 1 *Sess.*, No. 786; *ASP, Finance*, V, 638. For Adams's praise of this report see *Memoirs*, VII, 361.

29. Brooks Adams, *loc. cit.*, 21.

30. *Memoirs*, VII, 365. When New York protectionists begged him to mention tariffs in his Third Annual Message he declined on the grounds that it would appear to be an improper interference with the decision of the House. "I added, however, that the Report of the Secretary of the Treasury upon the finances would with my entire approbation recommend the protection of the manufacturing interest in the most effective manner."

31. "There is such a thing," said Martin Van Buren, when he heard that the Regency had forced De Witt Clinton out of the Board of Canal Commissioners, "as killing a man too dead." Henry Clay might have said, when he examined the draft of the first Annual Message, that there is such a thing as making a man too alive. The rage for internal improvements was so great that all the Administration had to do was to say nothing about them: by championing them in so open a way, Mr. Adams had made a bogey out of Henry Clay and his American System. It is true that his Administration has been called the period of

Internal Improvements; but, considering the generosity with which he asked the Congress to take their fill of internal improvements, one can only comment upon Congress's unwillingness to do so. Far more public money was spent on improvements than in any previous administration; but it was nothing compared to the money voted in the Presidency of Andrew Jackson, an unequivocal foe of internal improvements, whose enmity was defeated by the system of riders—the system, that is to say, of attaching objectionable appropriations to a general appropriations bill, thus forcing the President either to veto the whole bill or to accept the objectionable appropriations. It seems that Adams's imperious invitation had actually frightened away all but the greediest of legislators, while at the same time it raised against him an irresistible opposition. *Statement of Land Grants Made by Congress to aid in the Construction of Railroads, Wagon Roads, Canals and Internal Improvements, Compiled from the Records of the General Land Office by Order of the Secretary of the Interior,* Washington, 1908, 22-7. E. C. Nelson, "Presidential Influence on the Policy of Internal Improvements," *The Iowa Journal of History and Politics,* IV, 1906, 33 ff. *Cyclopaedia of Political Science,* John L. Lalor, ed., Chicago, 1883, II, 570. Aside from land grants, the appropriations for internal improvements under J. Q. Adams amounted to $2,310,475. Under Jefferson they were $38,000; under Madison, $250,000; under Monroe, $707,621; under Jackson, $10,582,882.

CHAPTER THREE

1. These descriptions are taken *passim* from Joseph G. Baldwin, *Party Leaders,* 1855; Gerald W. Johnson,

Randolph of Roanoke, 1929; William Cabell Bruce, *John Randolph of Roanoke,* 2 vols., 1922; Henry Adams, *John Randolph,* 1898.
2. Henry Adams, *John Randolph,* 26.
3. Henry Adams, *op. cit.,* 19. Bruce, *op. cit.,* I, 74. H. A. Garland, *The Life of John Randolph,* 1850, II, 248.
4. *Register of Debates,* 19 *Cong.,* 1 *Sess.,* II, part i, 142.
5. Richardson, *Messages and Papers,* II, 327.
6. In his message of December 26, 1825, Adams said: "Although this measure was deemed within the constitutional competency of the Executive, I have not thought it proper to take any step in it before ascertaining that my opinion of its expediency will concur with that of both branches of the Legislature, first, by the decision of the Senate upon the nominations to be laid before them, and, secondly, by the sanction of both Houses to the appropriations without which it can not be carried into effect." Richardson, *Messages and Papers,* II, 318.
7. *Register of Debates,* 19 *Cong.,* 1 *Sess.,* II, part i, 388.
8. Josiah Quincy, *Figures of the Past,* M. A. deW. Howe, ed., 180.
9. *Register of Debates,* 19 *Cong.,* 1 *Sess.,* II, part i, 390-401.
10. Here he was wrong. The Secretary of State was so unfamiliar with firearms that he had asked that the time permitted for firing should be measured by a slow rather than a quick count of "one, two, three"; otherwise he feared he would not be able to discharge his pistol at all. Henry Clay was brave, but not bloodthirsty.
11. Benton, *Thirty Years' View,* I, 71-7. Clark, *John Quincy Adams,* 245.
12. Bruce, *op. cit.,* II, 203.
13. Van Buren, *Autobiography,* 11-12.
14. Schlesinger, *Age of Jackson,* 49. Van Buren, *Autobiography,* 171.

15. Bemis, *J. Q. Adams*, 549.
16. Bemis, *op. cit.*, 546-7. *ASPFR*, V, 835-9. Adams, *Memoirs*, VI, 542.
17. *ASPFR*, V, 836-7. Bemis, *J. Q. Adams*, 547-9. C. K. Webster, *Britain and the Independence of Latin America*, I, 400-2.
18. Bemis, *J. Q. Adams*, 549.
19. Richardson, *Messages and Papers*, I, 222. "If we remain one people, under an efficient government, the period is not far off when we may defy material injury from external annoyance; when we may take such an attitude as will cause the neutrality we may at any time resolve upon to be scrupulously respected; when belligerent nations, under the impossibility of making acquisitions upon us, will not lightly hazard the giving us provocation; when we may choose peace or war, as our interest, guided by justice, shall counsel."
20. Richardson, *Messages and Papers*, II, 318-20.
21. *Register of Debates*, 19 *Cong.*, 1 *Sess.*, II, part i, 92-100. Committee's report of January 16, 1826.
22. *Ibid.*, 142, resolutions of Martin Van Buren, agreed to 23-20, February 15, 1826.
23. *Ibid.*, 143-6, 150.
24. Levi Woodbury of New Hampshire, John Chandler and John Holmes of Maine, Mahlon Dickerson of New Jersey, William Findlay of Pennsylvania, Martin Van Buren of New York. "Southern" Senators included Rowan of Kentucky and Benton of Missouri. The two Louisiana Senators, however, consistently supported Adams.
25. This treaty was rejected on March 9, 1825, a few days after Adams had taken office.
26. *Ibid.*, 112, 166, 208, 290.
27. *Ibid.*, 150.
28. Richardson, *Messages and Papers*, II, 329-40. The House debate is in

Register of Debates, 19 *Cong.*, 1 *Sess.*, II, part ii, 2009-2399.
29. Wiltse, *Calhoun: Nationalist*, 333, 334. Adams never admitted the authorship of the "Patrick Henry" letters, and they have subsequently been attributed to Phillip R. Fendall, a clerk in the State Department. Wiltse's authoritative work says that Calhoun, and Adams's contemporaries in general, believed that Adams himself was "Patrick Henry." This view is adopted by Clark, *John Quincy Adams*, 246. "The pretense of anonymity," Clark adds, "had also the advantage of permitting each to laud himself with somewhat more warmth than would have been entirely seemly if he had been writing under his own name."

CHAPTER FOUR

1. H. W. V. Temperley, "The Late American Policy of George Canning," *Am. Hist. Rev.*, XI, No. 4, 786.
2. J. Fred Rippy, *Rivalry of the United States and Great Britain over Latin America, 1808-1830*, 229.
3. In October of 1826, during the height of his misunderstanding with Spain over Portugal, Canning had some idea of a forcible seizure of Cuba. Canning to Liverpool, October 6, 1826; E. J. Stapleton, *op. cit.*, II, 144. This was only a passing fancy; in general he favored Spanish rule for Cuba.
4. Rippy, *op. cit.*, 242-4.
5. T. Watts, chargé d'affaires at Bogotá, to Clay in Manning, *Diplomatic Correspondence*, II, 1302-3. Alexander Hill Everett, writing to Clay on October 20, 1825, said that Frederick Lamb, the British Minister at Madrid, was not seriously attempting a settlement between Spain and the Spanish Americans on the basis of recognition. This letter was circulated at Panama and refuted

by Dawkins. *Sen. Doc.* No. 68, 19 *Cong.*, 1 Sess., ser. 127, 84-5.

6. Rippy, *op. cit.*, 245.

7. *Ibid.*, 124.

8. Temperley, *Foreign Policy of Canning*, 198. W. S. Robertson, *Hispanic American Relations*, 197. *British and Foreign State Papers*, XIV, 877-89. L. A. Lawson, *Relation of British Policy to the Monroe Doctrine*, 84-6.

9. C. D. Yonge, *The Life and Administration of the 2d Earl of Liverpool*, II, 301.

10. *Hansard*, 2 ser., XII, 1107. It was in the course of this speech, delivered on March 21, that Huskisson gave this definition of the word "elsewhere": "They imposed alien duties in their ports upon all British ships trading between those ports and our colonies, to be levied until the productions of the United States should be admitted into British colonies upon the same terms and duties as the like productions of any other country, meaning, thereby, the like productions not of any other foreign country, but of our country, or of our own provinces in North America. This is a pretension unheard of in the commercial relations of independent states." *Ibid.*, 1106.

11. Hugh G. Soulsby, "The Right of Search and the Slave Trade in Anglo-American Relations," *Johns Hopkins University Studies in Historical and Political Science*, Ser. LI, No. 2, 35.

12. Bemis, *J. Q. Adams*, 472.

13. *Ibid.*, Appendix 3, gives the full text of Adams's "Project of a Convention for Regulating the Principles of Commercial and Maritime Neutrality."

14. John G. B. Hutchins, "The American Maritime Industries and Public Policy," *Harvard Economic Studies*, LXXXI, Cambridge, 1941, 253.

15. Temperley, *op. cit.*, 41.

16. Clay to King, May 10, 1825; *Sen. Docs.*, 22 *Cong.*, 1 Sess., III, No. 132, pp. 2-3.

17. *Register of Debates*, Appendix, 38-49. Instructions dated May 8, 1826. Again, when Gallatin went to England as Minister in 1826, we find Clay writing to him privately: "As you have examined more than I have yet been able to do, the question of our North Eastern boundary, I should be glad to receive your view of the grounds and state of the controversy, briefly exhibited, prior to your departure, if convenient." Clay to Gallatin, June 21, 1826; Gallatin *MSS*.

18. Woodward, *Age of Reform*, 350.

19. Morley, *Life of Gladstone*, I, 22 ff., gives an interesting account of the British attitude toward slavery in these years. The great Gladstone's father was an extremely rare phenomenon—a strict evangelical churchman who was also a large West Indian slave-holder.

20. Brock, *op. cit.*, 111.

21. Benns, *op. cit.*, 105, citing *New York American* (for the country), August 12, 1825.

22. 6 Geo. IV, c. 73.

23. 7 Geo. IV, c. 648. Act of May 26, 1826.

24. Gallatin to Clay, October 27, 1826; *Sen. Docs.*, 22 *Cong.*, 1 Sess., III, 132, pp. 14-5. The "most lucid of modern students" on this subject, is, of course, F. Lee Benns, whose monograph on the West Indies controversy is invaluable.

25. 6 Geo. IV, c. 114.

26. Since the United States had a number of particular arrangements with various countries, some by treaty, others by separate and reciprocal acts, she would have found it exceedingly difficult to put Great Britain upon the footing of the most favored nation in her ports. Benns, *op. cit.*, 109, 111.

27. 6. Geo. IV, c. 109.

28. *Sen. Docs.*, 22 *Cong.*, 1 *Sess.*, III, 132, p. 13.
29. 6 Geo. IV, c. 105.
30. *Sen. Docs.*, 22 *Cong.*, 1 *Sess.*, III, 132, p. 14.
31. *Register of Debates*, 19 *Cong.*, 1 *Sess.*, II, part i, 576, 579, April 18, 1826.
32. Adams, *Memoirs*, VI, 540.
33. *ASPFR*, VI, 248, 262.
34. Benns, *op. cit.*, 119, 122. Gallatin to Clay, August 19, 1826; *Sen. Docs.*, 22 *Cong.*, 1 *Sess.*, III, 132, p. 6.
35. Adams, *Memoirs*, VII, 150.
36. Benns, *op. cit.*, 122.
37. Brooks Adams, *Law of Civilization and Decay*, 312. Lord Overstone, *Tracts*, 1858, 325.
38. *Hansard*, 2 ser., XVII, 599, 619.
39. *Hansard*, 2 ser., XVII, 620 ff. Huskisson's speech was made on May 7, 1827. Gallatin wrote: "Mr. Huskisson is assailed from every quarter, and, above all, by the shipping interest . . . and it is not likely that he will recede from the ground taken on the colonial intercourse . . . the only measure of his which is approved by those who are dissatisfied with his general policy. . . . Mr. Huskisson's policy towards the United States, so far as relates to commerce and navigation, has appeared to me not to accord with his avowed general opinion on those matters. He has also been compelled, on account of the opposition of the shipping interest, to take, in some respects, some retrograde steps." Gallatin to Clay, April 21, July 20, 1827. *Sen. Docs.*, 22 *Cong.*, 1 *Sess.*, III, 132, pp. 19, 25.
40. Richardson, *Messages and Papers*, II, 354.
41. Benns, *op. cit.*, 135.
42. *Register of Debates*, 19 *Cong.*, 2 *Sess.*, III, 399-402.
43. *Ibid.*, 403-17.
44. *Ibid.*, 474-80.
45. Martin Van Buren to H. Bleecker, February 25, 1827; *MS.*, NY State Library.
46. *Register of Debates*, 19 *Cong.*, 2 *Sess.*, III, 1503-6, 1514-17, 1522-7, 1528-30.
47. Richardson, *Messages and Papers*, II, 376; proclamation of March 17, 1827. Adams, *Memoirs*, VII, 236, 237, 239.
48. Benns, *op. cit.*, 145.
49. Gallatin to Clay, October 3, 1827; *Sen. Docs.*, 22 *Cong.*, 1 *Sess.*, III, 132, p. 31.
50. Baring to Galatin, September 20, 1827; Gallatin *MSS.*
51. Greville, *Memoirs: Reigns of George IV and William IV*, I, 89.
52. Adams, *Memoirs*, VII, 328. The perspicacious (and anti-protectionist) Gallatin, however, used very different language. He said that he missed Canning's "sagacity, quickness, self-confidence, and decision"; and that he was convinced that he could have made terms with him, if he had lived. Gallatin to Clay, August 31, 1827; *Sen. Docs.*, 22 *Cong.*, 1 *Sess.*, III, 132, p. 27. *Ibid.*, pp. 1-36 gives a clear picture of Gallatin's negotiations. See also *ASPFR*, VI, 248, 251-66.
53. *Hansard*, 2 ser., XVII, 560. Speech of W. Peel, May 4, 1827.
54. Greville, *Memoirs: Reigns of George IV and William IV*, II, 48. "As to the Duke of Wellington," Greville wrote gloomily on that occasion, "a fatality attends him, and it is fatal to cross his path." As if Wellington, and not a railway engine, had crushed poor Huskisson.
55. *Ibid.*, 42.
56. Benns, *op. cit.*, 162.
57. *Register of Debates*, 19 *Cong.*, 2 *Sess.*, III, 1507. Webster, in his speech of March 2 deliberately—and, to do him justice, explicitly—declined to discuss the word "elsewhere." *Ibid.*, 1524.

58. Van Buren to Louis McLane, July 20, 1829; *Sen. Docs.*, 21 *Cong.*, 2 *Sess.*, I, No. 20, p. 11.
59. *Works of Daniel Webster*, III, 357.

CHAPTER FIVE

1. Adams, *Memoirs*, VII, 133.
2. Adams to Jefferson, November 15, 1813; *Correspondence of John Adams and Thomas Jefferson*, Paul Wilstach, ed., 98-100.
3. Jefferson to Adams, October 12, 1823; Jefferson, *Writings*, Ford, ed., XII, 314.
4. *Ibid.*
5. *Selected Writings of John and John Quincy Adams*, Adrienne Koch and William Peden, eds., xxx.
6. Jefferson to Adams, November 13, 1818; Jefferson, *Writings*, Ford, ed., XII, 103.
7. Richardson, *Messages and Papers*, I, 322.
8. Adams to Jefferson, January 22, 1825; Adams, *Works*, X, 414.
9. *Selected Writings*, xxxiii.
10. Henry Bamford Parkes, *The American Experience*, 154.
11. Clark, *op. cit.*, 270.
12. *Memoirs*, VII, 27-8, 36, 38.
13. *Ibid.*, VII, 171, 365. Adams said he could make it around the Square in one hour.
14. *Letters of Horatio Greenough to his Brother Henry Greenough*, Frances Boott Greenough, ed., 36.
15. McMaster, V, 504: citing *Register of Debates*, 19 *Cong.*, 2 *Sess.*, II, part ii, 2655-6.
16. Clark, *op. cit.*, 262.
17. *Ibid.*, 263.
18. Henry Adams, *History*, IX, 176 ff. *Literary History of the United States*, Spiller, Thorp, Johnson, Canby, eds., I, 286, 346-7. Jarvis Means Morse, *A Neglected Period of Connecticut History*, 1933, 3.
19. Arthur B. Darling, *Political Changes in Massachusetts, 1824-1828*, 1925, 2 ff. R. G. Thwaites, ed., *Early Western Travels*, I, 60, 61.
20. Arndt M. Stickles, *The Critical Court Struggle in Kentucky*, 1929, 24. Robert M. McElroy, *Kentucky in the Nation's History*, 1909, 385. Lewis Collins, *History of Kentucky*, I, 30.
21. 4 Littell, 1824, 34-87. Collins, *op. cit.*, I, 322. Stickles, *op. cit.*, 53, 57. *Letters on the Condition of Kentucky in 1825, reprinted from the Richmond Enquirer*, R. G. Swemm, ed. (Heartman's Historical Series No. 22), 15, 3, 27. George Robertson, *Scrapbook on Law and Politics*, 1855, 127. Arndt M. Stickles, "Joseph R. Underwood's Fragmentary Journal on the New and Old Court Contest in Kentucky," *The Filson Club History Quarterly*, October, 1939, XIII, No. 4, 308.
22. Stickles, *Critical Court Struggle*, 73. Niles, XXVIII, 277.
23. Edwards to John McClean, June 24, 1828; "The Edwards Papers," E. B. Washburne, ed., *Chicago Historical Society's Collection*, III, 1884, 352.
24. "Memoir of the Late Hon. Daniel P. Cook," by W. H. Brown in N. W. Edwards, *History of Illinois from 1778 to 1833*, 1870, 273. John Marshall of Shawneetown to Ninian Edwards, September 2, 1826; "The Edwards Papers," *loc. cit.*, 255. For the contest about whether or not a Convention should be held which would introduce a limited slavery into Illinois, see Elihu B. Washburne, *Sketch of Edward Coles*, C. W. Alvord, ed., *Collections of the Illinois State Historical Library*, XV, Biographical Series No. I. "Correspondence of Edward Coles," *Journal of Negro History*, III, No. 2. McMaster, V, 187-88. Coles was the ex-Virginian, antislavery governor of Illinois during this Convention battle, which the antislavery forces

won by 6,640 to 4,972 in a statewide
vote in 1824.
25. Klein, *Pennsylvania Politics*, 120,
250. For the Governor's Message of
December 6, 1826, see *Pennsylvania
Archives*, 4 ser., V, 667. His Message of December 3, 1827, was even
more outspoken for Adams. "May
the Giver of all Good," he said in
his opening, "fill our hearts with
gratitude that our lot has been cast
in such a country and at such times
as these." *Ibid.*, 747.
26. Amanda Johnson, *Georgia as Colony and State*, 1938, 209. For a to-
pography of the two parties see U. B.
Phillips, "Georgia and State Rights,"
AHA, Annual Report, 1901, 104,
and Paul Murray, "Economic Sectionalism in Georgia, 1825-1855,"
Journal of Southern History, X, No.
3, 293-307.
27. *ASP, Indian Affairs*, II, 563-4. *Statutes at Large of the United States*,
VII, 237. Adams signed the Treaty
of Indian Springs, a holdover from
the previous Administration, on
March 5, 1825. He had not then
heard the rumors of its fraudulence.
28. *U.S. Sen. Doc.*, 57 *Cong.*, 1 *Sess.*,
1903, No. 452. *ASP, Indian Affairs*,
II, 612-14.
29. *Acts of Georgia, 1826*, 277. *ASP,
Indian Affairs*, II, 731-4.
30. Edward J. Harden, *Life of George
M. Troup*, 1859, 484-6. Troup to
James Barbour, February 17, 1827;
ibid., 485.
31. Richardson, *Messages and Papers*,
II, 370-3 for Adams's Message to
Congress of February 4, 1827. Adams
could have excused himself for
yielding to Georgia on the grounds
that Congress offered him no real
support in this crisis.
32. Angie Debo, *The Road to Disappearance*, 95-6.
33. Coulter, *op. cit.*, 215. Sydnor, *Development of Southern Sectionalism*,
184, citing T. P. Abernethy, *Formative Period in Alabama*, 116-19,

and *Mississippi Acts, 1829*, 81-3,
January, *1830*, 5-6.
34. John R. Commons and Associates,
*History of Labor in the United
States*, I, 176-7.
35. *Ibid.*, I, 158.
36. *Ibid.*, I, 159-60. Philip S. Foner,
*History of the Labor Movement in
the United States*, 102. *Columbian
Centinel*, April 20, 1825.
37. Foner, *op. cit.*, 102-3. The *Journeymen Mechanics' Advocate* was published in 1827, but all trace of it
had disappeared. The *Mechanics'
Free Press* was organized on April
19, 1828. Commons, *op. cit.*, I, 190.
38. *Mechanics' Free Press*, August 23,
1828.
39. Foner, *op. cit.*, 124.
40. McMaster, V, 343 ff. William
Oland Bourne, *History of the Public School Society of the City of
New York*, 1870, 111. Commons, *op.
cit.*, I, 181-2.
41. Commons, *op. cit.*, I, 174-5.
42. McMaster, IV, 535. Stickles, *Critical Court Struggle*, 22. Kentucky
forbade the imprisonment of women
for debt in 1820, and all imprisonment for debt in the Act of December 17, 1821. *Kentucky Gazette*, December 14, 1821, shows how this
Act was opposed by many of the
creditor class. Commons, *op. cit.*, I,
179, citing *Prison Discipline Society
of Boston, Fourth Annual Report*,
1829, 16-18. *Historical and Chronological Account of the Origin and
Progress of the City of New York*,
1829, 452. Philadelphia *National Gazette*, November 15, 1827, quoting
New York *Courier*, said that in New
York 1,972 persons were reported
imprisoned for debt, in some cases
for sums of less than $3; and that
they were provided neither with
food nor bedding and given only
a quart of soup every twenty-four
hours. Arthur M. Schlesinger, Jr.,
Age of Jackson, 134-6.

43. *Mechanics' Free Press*, May 15, 1830.
44. *Memoirs*, VIII, 428.
45. Richardson, *Messages and Papers*, II, 454.

CHAPTER SIX

1. W. L. Marcy to Van Buren, December 27, 1826. Van Buren Papers. Marcy, of course, scouts these rumors, which were totally unfounded.
2. Jackson, *Correspondence*, III, 329. Adams, *Memoirs*, VII, 367: "There is a decided majority of both Houses of Congress in opposition to the Administration, a state of things which has never occurred under the Government of the United States." In *ibid.*, VII, 370, Adams calls the *United States Telegraph* "a scurrilous and abusive print set up by the opposition."
3. *Memoirs*, VII, 368.
4. Taylor to R. M. Livingston, May 3, 1826. In this letter, Taylor tells of another story to the effect that he had gone one evening "to visit a female of easy virtue, that I found a Creek chief in company with her in the room, that I turned the chief out of doors & caned the girl. . . . I have never to my knowledge been under the same roof with an Indian in this city except in the Hall of Representatives & in the Presidents drawing room—I have never received a blow or an unkind word from an Indian in my life." John W. Taylor *MSS*. This chief was reported to be Chilly McIntosh, who had come to Washington to demand indemnification for his father's execution by the Upper Creeks; Taylor to Samuel Bunch, August 15, 1828. *Ibid*. In November 1828 Taylor was accused of picking up a woman of bad fame in New York and bringing her to Washington, where he introduced her to

members of Congress as his wife. Taylor to Joseph Richardson, October 2, 1830. *Ibid*.
5. Draft of an article, dated December 22, 1827; John W. Taylor *MSS*.
6. Van Buren to Thomas Ritchie, January 13, 1827: "Genl Jackson has been so little in public life that it will be not a little difficult to contrast his opinions with those of Mr. Adams." This is still somewhat lukewarm. On July 15, 1827, J. Schermerhorn writes to Van Buren to say that he wishes Van Buren and his friends would "accede to the nomination of Gov Clinton as V President & give him your support. . . . I view Gov C and his friends, if they cannot essentially aid the election of the Gen, they certainly can defeat it. . . . Gen J is apprized that I have written to you on the Presidential question, but you know the man & he cannot be committed beforehand to do anything but what is right." This puts Van Buren in the Jackson camp. By November, 1827, Van Buren was writing to Jackson—Van Buren to Jackson, November 4, 1827—to ask him not to come as yet to Washington, since this would "impair our good prospects." Van Buren Papers. In April 1827 John W. Taylor believed that, while Van Buren's election to Senator in that year was not a Jacksonian portent, yet "mournful as is the truth yet it must be told that Clinton has descended to playing second fiddle to Martin Van Buren." Clinton, Taylor said, "has always been for Genl Jackson." Taylor to Charles Miner, April 16, 1827. John W. Taylor *MSS*.
7. Tallmadge to Taylor, December 4, 1826, says that he has written to the President asking for the district judgeship, which he feels should be given him as "a token of friendship." John W. Taylor *MSS*.

8. Tallmadge to Taylor, January 17 and March 4, 1826; John W. Taylor *MSS.*

9. Taylor to Tallmadge, December 23, 1826. Tallmadge to Taylor, February 3, 1827. John W. Taylor *MSS.*

10. It is true that they had had some warning; for when Representative Henry C. Martindale called upon him on the 3rd to recommend protection in his Message, in order to quiet the fears of western New York, Adams had replied that he would allow the Secretary of the Treasury's report to speak for him. *Memoirs,* VII, 365. But no doubt they had hoped that he would change his mind at the last minute.

11. Sage to Taylor, February 17, 1828; John W. Taylor *MSS.* So also A. Spencer to Taylor, January 12, 1828. Referring to the President's silence in his Message, Spencer says: "I wish it could be known beyond a doubt that President Adams is favourable to the American System as now understood, & that Genl. Jackson's adherents are inimical to that system." Spencer adds that the agriculturalists of the State favor the American System, as it enhances the price of their product and creates a home market. *Ibid.* So also Tallmadge to Taylor, December 18, 1827: At a Duchess County meeting, held on December 17, which passed protariff resolutions, "it was difficult to calm the murmurs against Mr. Adams for omitting the Tariff in his speech." *Ibid.* For an opposition opinion—Charles Butler to A. C. Flagg, Genesee, New York, December 15, 1827: "Mr. Adams can now drink the bitter waters of disappointed ambition to the end of his term. His country's curse resting upon him—the silence of the message on the tariff affords striking proof of the heartlessness and policy of the man." A. C. Flagg Papers, NYPL.

12. Adams, *Memoirs,* VII, 362.

13. Richardson, *Messages and Papers,* II, 378-92. The arbitrator for the Northeast Boundary was chosen in 1828: he was the king of the Netherlands. In 1831, the award he made was disputed by both sides. The question was not finally settled until the Webster-Ashburton Treaty of 1842, and then the settlement was very adverse to the United States. Bemis, *J. Q. Adams,* 478-81—a very searching account of the Webster-Ashburton Treaty.

14. Adams, *Memoirs,* VII, 365.

15. By an ingenious system of minimum valuations, the bill made the most important domestic goods, worth about $1 a yard, subject to a protective duty of 83⅓¢ a yard, while retaining nominally the existing duty of 33⅓ per cent. Taussig, *op. cit.,* 82. Stanwood, *op. cit.,* I, 254 ff. The agitation for this bill was started by a meeting of woolen manufacturers at the Exchange Coffee House in Boston in September, 1826. *Ibid.,* citing Niles, XXXI, 105.

16. Van Buren to Thomas Ritchie, Washington, January 13, 1827; Van Buren Papers, LC.

17. Van Buren, *Autobiography,* 169. Stanwood, *op. cit.,* I, 258, declares that he was in his seat but did not vote: Stanwood, however, is very disparaging about Van Buren during this stage in his career. Wiltse, *Calhoun: Nationalist,* points out Van Buren "moved a vote on another measure a few minutes earlier." 437, n.30.

18. *Register of Debates,* 19 Cong., 2 Sess., 496.

19. Stanwood, *op. cit.,* I, 264. There were no delegates from Indiana or Illinois, but delegates came from Virginia, Delaware, and Maryland. Niles, XXXII, 385, contends that the majority of the assembly was composed of "farmers"—he neglects to say that these farmers were all

wool-growers. His list of delegates is in *ibid.*, 388-96. Taussig, *op. cit.*, 83, insists that the composition of the Convention was mostly of manufacturers and editors, with a few politicians. See also Wiltse, *op. cit.*, 354.

20. Taussig, *op. cit.*, 83. The Convention also suggested minimum valuations on imported woolens of 50¢, $2½, $4, $6. Raw wool under 8¢ was to be admitted free. *Ibid.*, 84.

21. Niles published this Address in October, 1827.

22. Dorfman, *Economic Mind*, II, 576 ff. *DAB*, XI, "List, George Friedrich," 292.

23. Dorfman, *op. cit.*, II, 582.

24. *Thoughts on Political Economy*, 1820, I, v, vi. Dorfman, *op. cit.*, II, iv, *n.*1, points out that the second edition and third edition (1823, 1836) bore the title *The Elements of Political Economy*, and that the fourth edition (1840) was called *The Elements of Constitutional Law and Political Economy*.

25. Dorfman, *op. cit.*, II, 572. Thomas Ritchie to Van Buren, March 11, 1828. "What think you of Gov Giles's message & writings? His friends, however, must manage him better. I will make the Enqr. a sealed book to him hereafter." Van Buren Papers, LC.

26. Dorfman, *op. cit.*, I, 385.

27. Mathew Carey, *Appeal to the Wealthy of the Land*, and *Letters on the Condition of the Poor*, show his humanitarian side. *DAB*, III, "Carey, Mathew," 489-90. On February 5, 1827, answering McDuffie's remark that Mathew Carey published "statistical nonsense," Andrew Stewart of Pennsylvania told the House of Representatives that "he would not give one page of the 'statistical nonsense' of Mathew Carey on this subject for all the theories of Adam Smith." Niles, XXXII, 173.

28. Calhoun to Jackson, June 4, 1826; Jackson to Calhoun, July 26. Jackson, *Correspondence*, III, 304-5, 307-8.

29. Wiltse, *Calhoun: Nationalist*, 363.

30. *Memoirs*, VII, 272.

31. Dorfman, II, 527 ff.

32. Cooper to Van Buren, July 5, 1827; Van Buren Papers, LC.

33. Cooper to Van Buren, July 31, 1827. *Ibid.*

34. Marcy to Van Buren, 29 January, 1828; *ibid.*

35. Van Buren to Jackson, November 4, 1827; *ibid.* Italics inserted.

36. Marquis James, *Andrew Jackson: Portrait of a President*, 162, citing Jackson to James K. Polk, December 27, 1826, in Bassett, II, 396.

37. Jackson to L. H. Coleman, April 26, 1824; Parton, *Jackson*, III, 35.

38. As has been shown—Part II, Chapter 2, *n.*52—the produce of the West was still supplying the slave-holding South. Hence the basis of the home-market argument was a little shaky.

39. Wiltse, *Calhoun: Nationalist*, 367-8. *ASP, Finance*, V, 778-845.

40. *Register of Debates*, 20 *Cong.*, 1 *Sess.*, IV, part ii, 1749-54 for Mallary's speech of March 3, 1828. *Ibid.*, 2472, for John Randolph's motion that the bill be called "A Bill to Manufacture a President of the United States."

41. Taylor to Mrs. Taylor, April 3, 1828; John W. Taylor *MSS.*

42. Schlesinger, *Age of Jackson*, 5.

43. *Register of Debates*, 20 *Cong.*, 1 *Sess.*, IV, part i, 750-70. Speech of May 9, 1828.

44. Taussig, *op. cit.*, 90*n. ASP Finance*, V, 784-92 gives the testimony of the iron manufacturers before the House Committee on Manufactures.

45. *Register of Debates*, 20 *Cong.*, 1 *Sess.*, IV, part ii, 1878-99. Davis, who came from Worcester, and spoke for the textile manufacturers, was supporting Mallary's amendment—*ibid.*, 1729 ff.—which would

have restored the provisions of the Harrisburg Convention. Mallary offered his amendment on March 4; Davis made his speech on March 13.

46. Wiltse, *Calhoun: Nationalist*, 369, citing *Congressional Globe*, 28 *Cong.*, 1 *Sess.*, appendix 747. Niles, XXXV, 53-5, gives an analysis of the vote, delegation by delegation, on all the leading amendments. For New England speeches against the Bill see especially John Anderson of Maine, *Register of Debates*, 20 *Cong.*, 1 *Sess.*, IV, part ii, 1772-84; Jonathan Hunt of Vermont, *ibid.*, 1784-9; Isaac Bates of Massachusetts, *ibid.*, 1998-2014; Peleg Sprague of Maine, *ibid.*, 2054-79; Ralph J. Ingersoll of Connecticut, *ibid.*, 2123-31.

47. Wiltse, *Calhoun: Nationalist*, 369.

48. *Speeches of John C. Calhoun*, Richard K. Crallé, ed., 1859, III, 47-51. Speech delivered in the Senate, February 23, 1837.

49. *Register of Debates*, 20 *Cong.*, 1 *Sess.*, IV, part i, 726-7, 730, 734, 783, 786.

50. Niles, XXXIV, 33, 84, and XXXV, 52-7, offer good examples of his attack.

51. Turnbull's *The Crisis* was published in October, 1827, under the pen name of Brutus. Some of it had already appeared in the columns of the Charleston *Mercury*. For its effect on South Carolina see James Hamilton, *An Eulogium on the Public Services and Character of Robert J. Turnbull, Esq.*, 1834, 15, and D. F. Houston, *A Critical Study of Nullification in South Carolina*, 1896, 50. Also Wiltse, *Calhoun: Nationalist*, 356.

52. Wiltse, *op. cit.*, 374.

53. Turner, *Rise of the New West*, 323.

54. Calhoun, *Speeches*, Crallé, ed., III. 51. Speech of February 23, 1837.

55. Calhoun, *Works*, VI, 1-59, gives the full text of the *Exposition and Protest*. For helpful discussions of

it, see Turner, *Rise of the New West*, 326-30, and Wiltse, *Calhoun: Nationalist*, 390-7. A recent and illuminating study of Calhoun will be found in Richard Hofstadter's *The American Political Tradition*, 1948, 67-91, to which the reader is referred. It is in Hofstadter that one finds the sentence: "A brilliant if narrow dialectician, probably the last American statesman to do any primary political thinking, [Calhoun] placed the central ideas of 'scientific' socialism in an inverted framework of moral values and produced an arresting defense of reaction, a sort of intellectual Black Mass." Hofstadter takes issue with Professor Wiltse on the latter's statement that Calhoun went on to become "the supreme champion of minority rights and interests everywhere." (*Calhoun: Nationalist*, 398.) "It is true," says Hofstadter, "that Calhoun superbly formulated the problem of the relation between majorities and minorities, and his work at this point may have the permanent significance for political theory that is often ascribed to it. But can the same value be assigned to his practical solutions? Not in the slightest was he concerned with minority rights as they are chiefly of interest to the modern liberal mind—the rights of dissenters to express unorthodox opinions, of the individual conscience against the State, least of all of ethnic minorities. At bottom, he was not interested in any minority that was not a propertied minority." *American Political Tradition*, 90.

56. S. Demarest to John W. Taylor, February 12, 1828; John W. Taylor, *MSS*.

57. J. Clark to Van Buren, April 18, 1828; Van Buren Papers.

58. Clay to John W. Taylor, November 13, 1829; John W. Taylor *MSS*.

59. Brown to Gallatin, December 13, 1828; Gallatin *MSS*.

CHAPTER SEVEN

1. Adams, *Memoirs*, VII, 474, 483, 511, 525.
2. *Ibid.*, 521, 535.
3. As late as December 1827, the suggestion was made that James Monroe should run for vice-president! Samuel L. Southard to Monroe, December 16, 1827. "It would be a pleasant employment," said Southard, "& a handsome yearly income for the next ten [*sic*] years." Monroe Papers.
4. John W. Taylor to Charles Miner, August 18, 1828: "P.S. Private . . . Will you do me the favor to mail the enclosed letter at your P. O. & pay the postage. The person to whom it is directed is now at Washington on private business. The postmasters here are violent Jacksonians & I have reason to believe no correspondence is safe in their hands." John W. Taylor *MSS*.
5. Adams, *Memoirs*, VII, 382-3, December 17, 1827.
6. *DAB*, IX, Jackson, 534.
7. Richardson, *Messages and Papers*, III, 92-3.
8. *Ibid.*, 305-6.
9. Duff Green and Mordecai Noah, however, were attached primarily to Calhoun; and Ritchie was always afraid of Jackson, whom he considered a firebrand.
10. Anonymous to John W. Taylor, January 22, 1825. The anonymous writer, who addressed his letter from New York, says that Jackson lived with his wife near Natchez for some time before marrying her. The writer has no personal knowledge of the facts, but has heard them from "two persons of respectability," one from Tennessee, one from New Orleans. John W. Taylor *MSS*. Taylor was never involved in circulating the story. For a detailed account of the spreading of this slander, see Marquis James, *Andrew Jackson: Portrait of a President*, 152-8.
11. *DAB*, VIII, Hammond, Charles, 202, citing E. O. Randall and D. J. Ryan, *History of Ohio*, III, 329. Hammond's most celebrated argument was delivered before the U.S. Supreme Court in the case of *Osborn v. Bank of the United States*. He became editor of the *Cincinnati Gazette* in 1825. For the offer of a seat on the Supreme Court (made by President John Quincy Adams) see C. T. Greve, *Centennial History of Cincinnati*, I, 806. Charles Hammond asked his question in a pamphlet called *A View of General Jackson's Domestic Relations* (1828), reprinted from his *Truth's Advocate and Monthly Anti-Jackson Expositor*, a campaign sheet which he edited. James, *op. cit.*, 156. This pamphlet was said to have been distributed under the franks of Administration Congressmen.
12. Jackson to John Coffee, June 2, 1828, *Correspondence*, III, 409.
13. Clark, *John Quincy Adams*, 282, 283.
14. Green to Jackson, July 8, 1827; *Correspondence*, III, 372. Jackson to Green, August 13, 1827, in James, *op. cit.*, 158. The story was published in the *United States Telegraph* on June 16, 1827: *ibid.*, 528, n.70.
15. Adams, *Memoirs*, VII, 415, 416. "Martha Godfrey"—chambermaid and nurse to the Adamses—"was a girl of irreproachable conduct."
16. Parton, *Jackson*, III, 154 ff. James, *op. cit.*, 164-75.
17. McMaster, V, 75, 518.
18. The rise of the Anti-Masonic Party in New York shows how desperate was the effort to break the one-party system. Neither Adamsites nor Jacksonians could make much of

the Anti-Masons in the election of 1828. W. L. Marcy to Van Buren, January 29, 1828. "The antimasonic excitement in the west [of New York] will be turned in favor of Mr. Adams." Van Buren Papers. L. B. Langworthy to John W. Taylor, July 10, 1828. "The antimasons are doing Mr. A more harm than anything you can imagine." John W. Taylor *MSS.* The party had the brief career usually reserved for causes founded on a negation.

19. Richardson, *Messages and Papers,* III, 305.

20. Washington is thinly disguised as "Mr. Harper," and his identity is revealed at the end. John Paul Jones is always impenetrably The Pilot. Hervey Birch in *The Spy* is almost always in disguise; but he is also always Hervey Birch.

21. Vernon L. Parrington, *Main Currents in American Thought,* 1930 ed., II, 232, shows that Ishmael Bush in *The Prairie* typifies this dislike of the physical frontier.

22. The frontier today is not geographical but technological: it is still an antidote.

23. McMaster, V, 518-20, tabulates the popular and the electoral vote. Rush obtained the same number of electoral votes as Adams. Calhoun lost the seven votes of Georgia to William C. Smith of South Carolina, so

that his electoral vote was 171. Of the New York election Van Buren wrote: "The result has been uniform success in Democratic counties by large majorities & defeat in old Federal counties by very small ones. The manor influence here was exerted to an extent unknown for the last 20 years." Van Buren to C. C. Cambreleng, November 7, 1828. Van Buren Papers.

24. Adams, *Memoirs,* VIII, 79, 89.

25. Henry Adams, *Degradation of the Democratic Dogma,* 33, 34. J. Q. Adams, *Memoirs,* XI, 340, 341.

26. *Ibid.,* VIII, 104.

27. Mrs. Harrison Smith, *The First Forty Years,* 257.

28. Clay, *Works,* Colton, ed., VII, 463-4.

29. Parton, *Jackson,* III, 170-1. James, *op. cit.,* 187. James Hamilton, Jr., to Martin Van Buren, July 16, 1829; Van Buren Papers. (William Wilberforce was the great English abolitionist.) Webster to Mrs. Ezekiel Webster, March 4, 1829; Webster, *Private Correspondence,* I, 473.

30. *Memoirs,* VIII, 105.

31. Van Buren, *Autobiography,* 255.

32. *Ibid.*

33. Van Buren, *Autobiography,* 229-31. Arthur M. Schlesinger, Jr., *The Age of Jackson,* 7. Marquis James, *Andrew Jackson: Portrait of a President,* 188-90.

$\mathcal{B}ibliography$

MANUSCRIPTS

Luther Bradish Papers, New-York Historical Society

De Witt Clinton Papers, New York Public Library

A. C. Flagg Papers, New York Public Library

Gallatin Papers, New-York Historical Society

Rufus King Papers, New-York Historical Society

Miscellaneous Manuscripts, New York State Library

Monroe Papers, Library of Congress

Monroe Papers, New York Public Library

Tallmadge Papers, New-York Historical Society

John W. Taylor Papers, New-York Historical Society

Van Buren Papers, Library of Congress

NEWSPAPERS

(From the Collection of the New-York Historical Society)

Albany (N.Y.) *Argus*

Baltimore *Niles' Weekly Register*

Boston *Columbian Centinel*

Charleston *Gazette and Commercial Daily Advertiser*

Concord (N.H.) *New Hampshire Patriot*

Frankfurt *Argus of Western America*

New York *American, Columbian, Daily Advertiser, Enquirer, Evening Post, Morning Courier*

Philadelphia *National Gazette, Poulson's American, United States Gazette*

Richmond *Enquirer*

Washington *National Intelligencer, National Journal, United States Telegraph*

BOOKS AND PERIODICALS

Abernethy, T. P.: *The Formative Period in Alabama, 1815-1828* (1922).
——: *From Frontier to Plantation in Tennessee* (1932).
——: "Andrew Jackson and the rise of Southwestern Democracy," *American Historical Review*, XXXIII (1927-8), 64-77.
Adams, Brooks: *The New Empire* (1902).
——: *The Law of Civilization and Decay* (1943 ed.).
——: "The heritage of Henry Adams," in Henry Adams, *The Degradation of the Democratic Dogma*.
Adams, Henry: *History of the United States of America* (9 vols., 1889-91).
——: *The Life of Albert Gallatin* (1879).
——: *John Randolph* (1882).
——: *The Education of Henry Adams* (1918).
——: *The Degradation of the Democratic Dogma* (1919).
Adams, John: *The Works of John Adams*, C. F. Adams, ed., Vol. X, General Correspondence, 1811-1825 (1856).
Adams, John Quincy: *Writings of John Quincy Adams*, W. C. Ford, ed. (7 vols., 1913-17).
——: *Memoirs, comprising portions of his Diary from 1795-1848*, Charles Francis Adams, ed. (12 vols., 1874-7).
——: *The Diary of John Quincy Adams*, Allan Nevins, ed. (1 vol., 1928).
——: *Lectures on Rhetoric and Oratory* (2 vols., Cambridge, 1821).
——: *An address, delivered at the request of the Committee of arrangements for celebrating the anniversary of independence at the city of Washington on the fourth of July 1821, upon the occasion of reading the Declaration of Independence* (Cambridge, 1821).
Adams, John Quincy: *The Duplicate Letters, the Fisheries and the Mississippi* (1822).
Albion, Robert G.: *Square-Riggers on Schedule: The New York Sailing Packets to England, France and the Cotton Ports* (1938).
Alexander, H. M.: *The American Talleyrand: The Career and Contemporaries of Martin Van Buren, Eighth President* (1935).
Ambler, Charles H.: *Sectionalism in Virginia from 1776-1861* (1910).
——: *Thomas Ritchie, a Study in Virginia Politics* (1913).
American State Papers. Documents, legislative and executive, of the Congress of the United States (38 vols., 1832-61).
Ames, Fisher: *Works of Fisher Ames*, S. Ames, ed. (2 vols., 1854).
Ames, H. V.: *State Documents on Federal Relations* (1900-6).
"An American Plan for a Canadian Campaign," *American Historical Review*, XLVI (1941), 348-58.
An Exposition of the Causes and Character of the Late War [attributed to the pen of Mr. Secretary Dallas] (Washington, 1815).
"Anglicanus": *A Letter to P. Bastard, Esq., M. P. for the County of Devon, on the Expediency and Necessity of a Parliamentary Reform* (London, 1817).
Annals of Congress: Debates and Proceedings, First Congress, First Session to Eighteenth Congress, First Session, May 27, 1824 (42 vols., 1834-56).
Anonymous: *Idea of a Patriot President* (Washington, 1823).
Aptheker, Herbert: *American Negro*

Slave Revolts. Columbia University Studies in History, Economics and Public Law, No. 501 (1943).

Atwater, Caleb: *Remarks Made on a Tour to Prairie du Chien, thence to Washington City in 1829* (Columbus, 1831).

Babcock, L. L.: *War of 1812 on the Niagara Frontier.* Buffalo Historical Society (1927).

Bagnall, William: *Textile Industries of the United States* (1893).

Baldwin, Joseph G.: *Party Leaders* (1853).

Baldwin, Leland D.: *The Keelboat Age on Western Waters* (1941).

Bassett, John S.: *Anti-Slavery Leaders in North Carolina.* Johns Hopkins University Studies . . . XVI, No. 6 (1898).

——: *Slavery in the State of North Carolina.* Ibid., XVII, Nos. 7 & 8 (1899).

——: *Life of Andrew Jackson* (2 vols., 1931).

Bates, W. H.: *American Navigation* (1902).

Beard, Charles A.: *Economic Origins of Jeffersonian Democracy* (1915).

—— with Mary R. Beard: *The Rise of American Civilization* (1942 ed.).

Beaumont, Gustave de and Alexis de Tocqueville: *On the Penitentiary System in the United States,* Francis Lieber, trans. (1833).

Bemis, Samuel F.: *Latin American Policy of the United States* (1943).

——: *A Diplomatic History of the United States* (1943 ed.).

——: *John Quincy Adams and the Foundations of American Foreign Policy* (1949).

Benns, F. Lee: *The American Struggle for the British West Indian Carrying Trade, 1815-1830.* Indiana University Studies, X (1930).

Benton, Thomas Hart: *Thirty Years' View: or, A History of the Working of the American Government for Thirty Years from 1820 to 1850* (2 vols., 1854-6).

Bettle, Edward: *Notices of Negro Slavery as connected with Pennsylvania.* Pennsylvania Historical Society Memoirs, I, 351-88 (1826).

Beveridge, Albert J.: *Life of John Marshall* (4 vols., 1916-19).

Biddle, Nicholas: *The Correspondence of Nicholas Biddle,* Reginald C. McGrane, ed. (1919).

Bidwell, Percy W. and John I. Falconer: *History of Agriculture in the Northern United States, 1620-1860.* Carnegie Institution of Washington, Publication No. 358 (1941).

Binkley, Wilfred E.: *American Political Parties* (1943).

Birkbeck, Morris: *Notes on a Journey in America, from the Coast of Virginia to the Territory of Illinois* (London, 1818).

Bishop, J. L.: *A History of American Manufactures from 1608 to 1860* (3rd ed., 3 vols., 1868).

Bogart, E. L.: *The Economic History of the American People* (1907).

——: *The Economic History of American Agriculture* (1923).

——: *The Economic History of Europe, 1760-1939* (1942).

Bolton, Sarah: *Famous American Statesmen* (1888).

Boorstin, Daniel J.: *The Lost World of Thomas Jefferson* (1948).

Boudin, Louis: *Government by Judiciary* (1911).

Boyd, William K.: *History of North Carolina . . . 1783-1860* (1919).

Brackenridge, H. M.: *Voyage to South America, Performed by Order of the American Government in the Years 1817 and 1818* (2 vols., 1819).

Brackett, J. R.: *The Negro in Maryland.* Johns Hopkins University Series, Extra Vol. VI (1889).

Bradford, Gamaliel: *As God Made Them* (1929).

Brady, Alexander: *William Huskisson and Liberal Reform* (1928).

Brebner, John B.: *North Atlantic Triangle* (1945).

Brindoff, S. T. with E. F. Malcolm-Smith and C. K. Webster: "British Diplomatic Representatives, 1789-1852," Royal Historical Society. Publications. Camden, 3rd Series. Vol. L (1934).

Brock, W. R.: *Lord Liverpool and Liberal Toryism* (1941).

Brooks, Philip C.: *Diplomacy and the Borderlands, the Adams-Onis Treaty of 1819.* University of California Publications in History, XXIV (1939).

Brown, Edward: *Notes on the Origin and Necessity of Slavery* (Charleston, 1826).

Brown, Everett S.: "The Presidential Election of 1824-25," *Political Science Quarterly*, XL (1925), 384-403.

—: Ed. *The Missouri Compromises and Presidential Politics, 1820-1825* (1926).

Brown, James: "Letters of James Brown to Henry Clay," *The Louisiana Historical Quarterly*, XXIV (1941), No. 4.

Brown, W. G.: *The Lower South in American History* (1902).

Bruce, William C.: *John Randolph of Roanoke* (2 vols., 1922).

Buchanan, James: *Works*, J. B. Moore, ed. (12 vols., 1908-11).

Buck, Norman S.: *The Development of the Organization of Anglo-American Trade, 1800-1850* (1925).

Bullock, W.: *Sketch of a Journey Through the Western States* (London, 1827). In *Early Western Travels*, R. G. Thwaites, ed., XIX.

Burkett, C. W.: *History of Ohio Agriculture* (1900).

Butler, N. M.: *Influence of the War of 1812.* Johns Hopkins University Series, V (1888).

Calhoun, John Caldwell: *Works*, Richard K. Crallé, ed. (6 vols., 1854).

—: *Correspondence of John C. Calhoun*, J. Franklin Jameson, ed. American Historical Association Annual Report, 1899, II (1900).

Callahan, James M.: *Cuba and International Relations, an Historical Study in American Diplomacy* (1899).

Callender, G. S.: "Early Transportation and Banking Enterprises of the States in Relation to the Growth of Corporations," *Quarterly Journal of Economics*, XVII (1912), 3-54.

[Cambreleng, Churchill C.]: *An Examination of the New Tariff Proposed by the Hon. Henry Baldwin, A Representative in Congress, by "One of the People"* (1821).

Campbell, W. C.: *Life and Writings of De Witt Clinton* (1854).

Candler, Isaac: *A Summary View of America* (London, 1824).

Canning, George: *The Speeches of George Canning*, R. Therry, ed. (6 vols., 1828).

—: *George Canning and his Friends*, Josceline Bagot, ed. (2 vols., 1909).

Carey, Mathew: *The New Olive Branch* (2nd ed., 1821).

—: *To the Citizens of the Commonwealth of Pennsylvania* (1825).

—: *Appeal to the Wealthy of the Land . . .* (2nd ed., 1833).

—: *A Plea for the Poor* (2nd ed., 1836).

Carpenter, Jesse T.: *The South as a Conscious Minority, 1789-1861* (1930).

Carroll, Eber M.: "Politics during the Administration of John Quincy Adams," *South Atlantic Quarterly*, XXIII (1924), 141-54.

Carroll, Joseph C.: *Slave Insurrections in the United States, 1800-1865* (1938).

Cash, Wilbur: *The Mind of the South* (1941).

Castlereagh, Robert Stewart, Viscount, 2nd Marquess of Londonderry: *Memoirs and Correspondence of Viscount Castlereagh, second Marquess of Londonderry* (12 vols., 1848-53).

Catterall, Ralph C. H.: *The Second Bank of the United States* (1903).

Caulaincourt, Armand Augustin Louis, Marquis de: *With Napoleon in Russia . . . from the original Memoirs as edited by Jean Hanoteau*, abridged, edited and with an introduction by George Libaire (1935).

Cecil, Algernon: *British Foreign Secretaries* (1927).

Channing, Edward: *A History of the United States, 1700-1861* (6 vols., 1905-25).

Channing, William Ellery: *A Letter to the Rev. S. C. Thacher, on the aspersions contained in a late number of the Panoplist . . .* (Boston, 1815).

——: *A Sermon delivered at the ordination of the Rev. Jared Sparks . . . May 5, 1819* (Baltimore, 1819).

Chapelle, H. I.: *The History of American Sailing Ships* (1935).

Chateaubriand, François Auguste René, Vicomte de: *Le Congrès de Vérone* (2 vols., 1838).

Chinard, Gilbert: *Thomas Jefferson, the Apostle of Americanism* (1929).

Chittenden, H. M.: *The American Fur Trade of the Far West* (3 vols., 1902).

Clay, Henry: *Speeches*, Daniel Mallory, ed. (2 vols., 4th ed., 1844).

——: *The Works of Henry Clay*, Calvin Colton, ed. (10 vols., 1904).

——: *An Address of Henry Clay to the public; containing certain testimony, in refutation of the charges against him, made by Gen. Andrew Jackson, touching the late presidential election* (Washington, 1827; New Brunswick, 1828).

Clark, Bennett Champ: *John Quincy Adams* (1932).

Clark, J. Reuben: *Memorandum on the Monroe Doctrine* (Government Printing Office, 1930).

Clark, Victor S.: "The Influence of Manufactures upon Political Sentiment in the United States from 1820 to 1846," *American Historical Review*, X (1916), 58-64.

Clark, Victor S.: *History of Manufactures in the United States* (3 vols., 1929).

Cobbett, William: *A Year's Residence in the United States* (3rd ed., 1822).

Cochran, Thomas C. and William Miller: *The Age of Enterprise* (1942).

Coffin, Joshua: *An Account of Some of the Principal Slave Insurrections* (1860).

Coggeshall, George: *History of American Privateers and Letters of Marque, during our war with England, 1812, '13 and '14* (1856).

Cole, Arthur H.: *Wholesale Commodity Prices in the United States, 1700-1861* (1938).

Coles, Edward: "Correspondence of Edward Coles," *Journal of Negro History*, III (1918), 159-86.

Collins, Lewis: *History of Kentucky*, rev. Richard H. Collins (2 vols., 1874).

Collins, W. H.: *The Domestic Slave Trade of the Southern States* (1904).

Commager, Henry S.: *Majority Rule and Minority Rights* (1943).

—— with Samuel E. Morison: *The Growth of the American Republic* (2 vols., 1942).

Commons, John R. and associates: *History of Labour* (4 vols., 1918-35).

Cooper, James Fenimore: *Correspondence of James Fenimore Cooper*, James F. Cooper, ed. (1922).

——: *America and the Americans* (2nd ed., 1836).

——: *The Spy* (1821).

——: *The Pilot* (1823).

——: *The Prairie* (1827).

Corwin, E. S.: *John Marshall and the Constitution* (1921).

Cotten, Edward R.: *Life of the Hon. Nathaniel Macon, of North Carolina* (1840).

Coulter, E. M.: *Georgia, A Short History* (1947).

Craigmyle, Lord: *John Marshall in Diplomacy and in Law* (1933).

Craven, Avery O.: "The Agricultural Reformers of the Ante-Bellum

South," *American Historical Review*, XXXIII (1928), 302-14.

Craven, Avery O.: "The 'Turner' Theories and the South," *Journal of Southern History*, V (1939), 291-314.

——: *The Coming of the Civil War* (1942).

Cresson, W. P.: *James Monroe* (1946).

Croker, James Wilson: *The Croker Papers* (2 vols., London, 1884).

Curtis, George Ticknor: *Life of James Buchanan* (2 vols., 1883).

——: *Life of Daniel Webster* (2 vols., 1870).

Cutler, James E.: *Lynch Law* (1905).

Dallas, G. M.: *Life and Writings of A. J. Dallas* (1871).

Danhof, Clarence H.: "Economic Validity of the Safety-valve Doctrine," *Journal of Economic History* (Supplemental Issue, 1941).

Darling, Arthur B.: *Political Changes in Massachusetts, 1824-1828* (1925).

Dauer, Manning J. and Hans Hammond: "John Taylor; Democrat or Aristocrat?" *Journal of Politics*, VI (1944), 381-403.

Davis, Charles S.: *The Cotton Kingdom in Alabama* (1939).

Dawson, Moses: *A Historical Narrative of the Civil and Military Services of Major-General William H. Harrison* (Cincinnati, 1824).

Day, Clive: "The Early Development of American Cotton Manufacture," *Quarterly Journal of Economics*, XXXIX (1925), 450-68.

Deane, Charles: *Letters and Documents Relating to Slavery in Massachusetts* (1877).

Debo, Angie: *The Road to Disappearance* (1941).

Dennison, Eleanor E.: *The Senate Foreign Relations Committee* (1942).

Derby, Edward George Smith Stanley, 14th Earl of: *Journal of a Tour in America, 1824-1825* (1930).

De Roos, Hon. Frederick F.: *Personal Narrative of Travels in the United States and Canada in 1826* (London, 1827).

Dewey, Davis R.: *Financial History of the United States* (12th ed., 1934).

Digest of Accounts of Manufacturing Establishments in the United States and their Manufactures (Washington, 1823).

Documents of American History, Henry S. Commager, ed. (1940 ed.).

Dodd, William E.: "John Taylor of Caroline, Prophet of Secession," *John P. Branch Historical Papers*, II (1905).

——: "Chief Justice Marshall and Virginia," *American Historical Review*, XII (1907), 776-87.

——: *The Life of Nathaniel Macon* (1903).

——: *The Cotton Kingdom* (1919). Vol. XXVII in Allen Johnson, ed., The Chronicles of America Series (50 vols., 1918-21).

Donaldson, Thomas: *The Public Domain: Its History with Statistics* (HR Misc. Doc., 45, pt. 4, 47 Congress, 2 Session, XIX, 1884).

Donnell, E. G.: *History of Cotton* (1872).

Dorfman, Joseph: *The Economic Mind in American Civilization* (2 vols., 1946).

Douglas, David: *Journal Kept by David Douglas during his travels in North America, 1823-1827* (London, 1914).

Drake, Benjamin: *Life of Tecumseh, and of his brother the Prophet* (1858).

Drewry, W. S.: *Slave Insurrections in Virginia* (1900).

DuBois, W. E. B.: *Suppression of the African Slave Trade to the United States, 1638-1870* (1896).

Dunn, J. P., Jr.: *Indiana, or Redemption from Slavery* (1888).

Dunning, W. A.: *The British Empire and the United States* (1914).

Dwight, Timothy: *Travels in New-England and New-York* (4 vols., New Haven, 1821-2).

Eaton, Clement: *Freedom of Thought in the Old South* (1940).

Edwards, Ninian: "The Edwards Papers," E. B. Washburne, ed. Chicago Historical Society's *Collection*, III (1884).

Edwards, Ninian W.: *History of Illinois from 1778-1833; and Life and Times of Ninian Edwards* (1870).

Ellet, E. F.: *Court Circles of the Republic from Washington to Grant* (1870).

Elliot, J.: *Debates* (5 vols., 1836).

Elliott, O. L.: *The Tariff Controversies in the United States, 1789-1833.* Leland Stanford University. *Monographs, History and Economics*, No. 1 (1892).

Ely, R. T.: *The Labor Movement in the United States* (3rd ed., 1892).

Emmerick, Charles F.: *The Credit System and the Public Domain.* Vanderbilt Southern History Society, *Publications*, No. 3 (1899).

Farrand, Livingston: *Basis of American History.* The American Nation, Vol. II (1906).

Flint, Timothy: *Recollections of the Last Ten Years* (1826).

——: *History and Geography of the Mississippi Valley* (2nd ed., 2 vols., 1832).

Follett, M. P.: *The Speaker of the House of Representatives* (1896).

Folmsbee, Stanley J.: *Sectionalism and Internal Improvements in Tennessee, 1796-1845* (1939).

Ford, Worthington C.: "John Quincy Adams and the Monroe Doctrine," *American Historical Review*, VII (July, 1902), 676-96, and VIII (October, 1902), 28-52.

Foreman, Grant: *Indians and Pioneers* (1930).

Fox, Dixon Ryan: *The Decline of Aristocracy in the Politics of New York* (1919).

Fox, Early L.: *The American Colonization Society, 1817-1840.* Johns Hopkins University Studies in Historical and Political Science, XXXVII, No. 3 (1919).

Frankfurter, Felix: *The Commerce Clause under Marshal, Taney and Waite* (1937).

Franklin, John H.: *The Free Negro in North Carolina, 1790-1860* (1943).

——: *From Slavery to Freedom* (1947).

Fuess, Claude M.: *Daniel Webster* (2 vols., 1930).

Furman, Richard: *Exposition of the Views of the Baptists, Relative to the Coloured Population of the United States, in a Communication to the Governor of South-Carolina* (Charleston, 1823).

Gabriel, Ralph: *The Course of American Democratic Thought* (1940).

Gallatin, Albert: *The Writings of Albert Gallatin*, Henry Adams, ed. (3 vols., 1879).

——: "Bank of the United States," *American Quarterly Review*, IX (1831), 246-82.

——: *Considerations on the Currency and Banking System of the United States* (1831).

——: *Memorial of the Free Trade Convention* (Senate Docs. No. 55, 22 Congress, 1 Session, 1832).

Gallatin, James: *The Diary of James Gallatin*, Count Gallatin, ed. (1924).

Gates, Charles M.: "The West in American Diplomacy," *Mississippi Valley Historical Review*, XXVI, (1940), 499-510.

Geiser, K. T.: *Redemptioners and Indentured Servants in Pennsylvania. Yale Review*, X, 21, Supplement (1901).

Gilman, Daniel C.: *James Monroe* (1883; 1895).

Goebel, Dorothy Burne: "British Trade to the Spanish Colonies, 1796-1823," *American Historical Review*, XLIII (1938), 288-320.

Goldsmith, Lewis: "Observations on the Appointment of the Right Hon. Geo. Canning to the Foreign Department," *The Pamphleteer*, XXII, No. 44 (London, 1823), 299-362.

Good, H. G.: "To the Future Biographer of John Quincy Adams," *Sci-*

entific Monthly, XXXIX (1934), 247-51.

Goodrich, Samuel G.: *Recollections of a Lifetime* (2 vols., 1886).

Goodwin, Cardinal L.: *The Trans-Mississippi West* (1926).

Gouge, William M.: *A Short History of Paper Money and Banking in the United States* (1833).

Gouverneur, Marian: *As I Remember, Recollections of American Society during the Nineteenth Century* (1911).

Graham, Gerald S.: *Sea Power and British North America, 1783-1820* (1941).

Gray, Lewis Cecil, assisted by Esther Katherine Thompson: *History of Agriculture in the Southern United States to 1860* (2 vols., 1933).

Green, Fletcher M.: *Constitutional Development in the South Atlantic States, 1776-1860: A Study in the Evolution of Democracy* (1930).

Griffin, C. C.: *The United States and the Disruption of the Spanish Empire, 1810-1822.* Columbia University, Studies in History, Economics and Public Law, No. 429 (1937).

Haar, Charles: "Legislative Regulation of New York Industrial Corporations, 1800-1850," *New York History*, XXII (1941), 191-207.

Hailperin, Herman: "Pro-Jackson sentiment in Pennsylvania, 1820-1828," *Pennsylvania Magazine of History and Biography*, L (1926), 20-44.

Hall, Basil: *Travels in North America in the Years 1827 and 1828* (2 vols., Philadelphia, 1829).

Hall, Mrs. Basil: *The Aristocratic Journey*, Una Pope-Hennessy, ed. (1931).

Hall, W. E.: *International Law* (1904 ed.).

Hammond, Bray: "Jackson, Biddle, and the Bank of the United States," *Journal of Economic History*, VII (1947), 1-23.

Hammond, Jabez D.: *The History of*

Political Parties in the State of New-York* (2 vols., 1842).

Hammond, M. B.: *The Cotton Industry.* American Economic Association, Publications, n.s., No. 1 (1897).

Hansard. See *The Parliamentary Debates.*

Harden, E. J.: *Life of George Troup* (1859).

Harrison, N. Dwight: *History of Negro Servitude in Illinois* (1904).

Hart, Albert Bushnell: *Slavery and Abolition.* American Nation, XVI (1906).

Hay, Thomas R.: "John C. Calhoun and the Presidential Campaign of 1824; some unpublished Calhoun letters." *American Historical Review*, XL (1934-5), 82-96, 287-300.

Hesseltine, William B.: *The South in American History* (1943).

Hewitt, D.: *The American Traveller; or, National Directory Containing an Account of all the Great Post-Roads and Most Important Cross roads in the United States* (1825).

Hibbard, Benjamin A.: *A History of the Public Land Policies* (1939).

Hickock, C. T.: *Negro in Ohio, 1802-1870* (1896).

Hidy, Ralph W.: "Anglo-American Merchant Bankers," *Journal of Economic History*, I (December Supplemental Issue, 1941), 53-66.

Higginson, T. W.: *Travellers and Outlaws* (1889).

Hill, C. E.: *Leading American Treaties* (1922).

Hinsdale, B. A.: *Old Northwest* (2 vols., 1888; 1899).

Historical and Chronological Account of the Origin and Progress of the City of New York (New York, 1829).

Hobson, John A.: *The Evolution of Modern Capitalism* (1917).

Hockett, Homer C.: "Rufus King and the Missouri Compromise," *Missouri Historical Review*, II (1907-8), 211-20.

Hodder, F. H.: *Side Lights on the Missouri Compromise*. American Historical Association, *Annual Report 1909*, 153-61.

Hodgson, Adam: *Letters from North America* (London, 1824).

Hofstadter, Richard: *The American Political Tradition and the Men Who Made It* (1948).

——: "U. B. Phillips and the Plantation Legend," *Journal of Negro History*, XXIX (1944), 109-24.

Holland, Edwin C.: *A Refutation of the Calumnies circulated against the Southern and Western States, respecting the institution and existence of slavery among them* (Charleston, 1822).

Holmes, Isaac: *An Account of the United States of America* (London, 1824).

Holmes, Oliver Wendell, Jr.: *The Common Law* (1881).

——: *Collected Legal Papers* (1920).

Hooker, Richard J.: "John Marshall on the Judiciary, the Republicans, and Jefferson, March 4, 1801," *American Historical Review*, LIII (1948), 518-20.

Hosack, David: *Memoir of De Witt Clinton* (1829).

Houck, L.: *A History of Missouri from the Earliest Eastern Explorations and Settlements until the Admission of the State into the Union* (3 vols., 1908).

Howells, W. C.: *Recollections of Life in Ohio* (1895).

Hulbert, A. B.: *Historic Highways of America* (16 vols., 1902-5).

Hunt, Gaillard: *Life of James Madison* (1902).

——: *John C. Calhoun* (1908).

Hunter, Louis C.: "The Invention of the Western Steamboat," *Journal of Economic History*, III (1943-4), 201-20.

Hurd, John Codman: *The Law of Freedom and Bondage* (2 vols., 1862).

Huskisson, William: *Free Trade Speech . . . in the House of Commons . . . the 23rd of February, 1826, on Mr. Ellice's motion . . . to inquire into . . . the various petitions from persons engaged in the silk manufacture* (London, 1826).

——: *Speech of the Right Honourable W. Huskisson in the House of Commons, Friday the 12th of May, 1826, on the Present State of the Shipping Interest* (London, 1826).

——: *Substance of Two Speeches delivered in the House of Commons on the 21st and 25th of March, 1825* (London, 1825).

——: *The Huskisson Papers*, Lewis Melville (Lewis S. Benjamin), ed. (1931).

Hutchins, John G. B.: *The American Maritime Industries and Public Policy*. Harvard Economic Studies, LXXI (1941).

Irving, Washington: *Journal of Washington Irving, 1823-1824*. Stanley T. Williams, ed. (1931).

Jackson, Andrew: *Correspondence of Andrew Jackson*, John S. Bassett, ed. (6 vols., 1926-33).

James, Marquis: *Andrew Jackson: The Border Captain* (1933).

——: *Andrew Jackson: Portrait of a President* (1937).

Jefferson, Thomas: *The Writings of Thomas Jefferson*, Paul L. Ford, ed. (12 vols., 1904-5).

——: *The Writings of Thomas Jefferson*, Andrew A. Lipscomb, ed. (20 vols., 1903-4).

——: *Correspondence of John Adams and Thomas Jefferson*, Paul Wilstach, ed. (1925).

Jenks, Leland H.: *Migration of British Capital to 1875* (1927).

Johnson, Amanda: *Georgia as Colony and State* (1938).

Johnson, T. C.: *Life and Letters of Robert Lewis Dabney* (1903).

Judicial Cases Concerning American Slavery and the Negro, Helen Honer Tunnicliff Catterall, ed., with additions by James J. Hayden. Carnegie Institute of Washington, Publication No. 374 (5 vols., 1926-37).

Kappler, Charles J.: *Indian Affairs, Laws and Treaties* (5 vols., 1903-41).

Kendall, Amos: *Autobiography of Amos Kendall*. Wm. Stickney, ed. (1872).

King, Rufus: *The Life and Correspondence of Rufus King*, Charles R. King, ed. (6 vols., 1894-1900).

Kirkland, Edward C.: *A History of American Economic Life* (1932).

Klein, Philip S.: *Pennsylvania Politics, 1817-1832* (1940).

Koch, Adrienne: *The Philosophy of Thomas Jefferson* (1943).

— with William Peden: *The Life and Selected Writings of Thomas Jefferson* (1944).

Krout, John A. and Dixon Ryan Fox: *The Completion of Independence, 1790-1830* (1944).

Lane-Poole, Stanley: *The Life of the Right Honourable Stratford Canning, Viscount Stratford de Redcliffe* (2 vols., 1888).

Laski, Harold: *The Rise of Liberalism* (1936).

Latané, John H. and David W. Wainhouse: *A History of American Foreign Policy* (1934).

Laws of the State of New York, in Relation to the Erie and Champlain Canals, together with the Annual Reports of the Canal Commissioners (Albany, 1825).

Lawson, L. A.: *The Relation of British Policy to the Declaration of the Monroe Doctrine.* Columbia University Studies in History, Economics and the Public Law, CIII (1922).

Leggett, Aaron: *An Address to the Honorable the Legislature of the State of New York* (Albany, 1829).

Lerner, Max: "John Marshall and the Campaign of History," *Columbia Law Review*, XXXIX (1939), 396-431.

Letters on the Condition of Kentucky in 1825 . . . Paul G. Swemm, ed., Heartman's Historical Series No. 22 (1916).

Letters of Theodore Dwight Weld, Angeline Grimké Weld and Sarah Grimké, 1822-1844. Gilbert H. Barnes and Dwight L. Dumond, eds. (2 vols., 1934).

Lieven, Princess: *The Private Letters of Princess Lieven to Prince Metternich*, Peter Quennell, ed. (1945).

Lindsay, William Schaw: *History of Merchant Shipping and Ancient Commerce* (4 vols., London, 1876).

Lingelbach, Anna Lane: "William Huskisson as President of the Board of Trade," *American Historical Review*, XLIII (1938), 759-75.

Liverpool, Robert Banks Jenkinson, 2nd Earl of: *The Speech of the earl of Liverpool, in the House of Lords* . . . *the 26th of May, 1820, on a motion of the Marquis of Lansdowne, "That a select committee be appointed to inquire into the means of extending and securing the foreign trade of this country"* (London, 1820).

Lockey, J. B.: *Pan-Americanism* (1920).

Lodge, Henry Cabot: "International Events which precipitated the Monroe Doctrine," *Congressional Digest*, VI (1927), 115-16.

Longstreet, A. B.: *Georgia Scenes* . . . *by a Native Georgian* (1897).

Lynch, Dennis T.: *An Epoch and a Man; Martin Van Buren & his Times* (1929).

Lynch, William O.: *Fifty Years of Party Warfare, 1789-1837* (1931).

MacDonald, Donald: *The Diaries of Donald MacDonald, 1824-1826.* Introduction by Caroline Dale Snedeker. Indiana Historical Society *Publications*, XIV, No. 2 (1942).

McCarthy, Charles: *The Antimasonic Party.* American Historical Association, *Annual Report, 1902*, I.

McConachie, L. G.: *Congressional Committees* (1898).

McCulloch, J. R.: *A Dictionary, Practical, Theoretical and Historical of Commerce and Commercial Navigation.* H. Vethake, ed. (2 vols., 1852).

McDougall, Marian G.: *Fugitive Slaves, 1619-1865.* Fay House Monographs, No. 3 (1891).

McDuffie, George: *Defence of a Liberal Construction of the Powers of Congress as regards Internal Improvements* etc. . . . *Written by George McDuffie, Esq., in the year 1821, over the signature "One of the People"* (1831).

McGregor, John: *Commercial Statistics of America: A Digest of Her Productive Resources, Commercial Legislation, Customs, Tariffs, Shipping, Imports and Exports, Monies, Weights and Measures* (London, 1847).

McLaughlin, Andrew C.: *A Constitutional History of the United States* (1935).

McMaster, John Bach: *The History of the People of the United States From the Revolution to the Civil War* (8 vols., 1883 1913).

McPherson, J. H. T.: *History of Liberia.* Johns Hopkins University Studies in History and Political Science, 9th Series, No. 10 (1891).

Madison, James: *Letters and Other Writings of James Madison* (Congressional ed., 4 vols., 1865), cited as *Works.*

——: *The Writings of James Madison,* Gaillard Hunt, ed. (9 vols., 1900-10).

Mahan, A. T.: *Sea Power in its Relations to the War of 1812* (2 vols., 1905).

Mallory, W. M.: *Treaties, Conventions, International Acts, Protocols, and Agreements between the United States of America and Other Powers, 1776-1904.* Senate Docs., 61 Cong., 2 Sess., No. 357 (2 vols., 1910).

Malone, Dumas: *The Public Life of Thomas Cooper, 1783-1839* (1926).

Manning, W. R.: *Early Diplomatic Relations Between the United States and Mexico* (1916).

——: *Diplomatic Correspondence of the United States Concerning Independence of the Latin-American Nations* (3 vols., 1925).

Marcellus, Marie J. J. A. C. D. du Tyrac, Comte de: *Souvenirs Diplomatiques* (Paris, 1858).

Marriott, J. A. R.: *George Canning and his Times* (1903).

——: *Castlereagh* (1936).

Marshall, J.: *A Digest of all the Accounts Relating to the Population, Productions, Revenues, Financial Operations, Manufactures, Shipping, Colonies, Commerce &c &c. of the United Kingdom of Great Britain and Ireland. . . . Arranged by J. Marshall . . .* (London, 1833).

Martell, J. S.: "A Side Light on Federalist Strategy during the War of 1812," *American Historical Review,* XLIII (1938), 553-66.

Martin, W. E.: *Internal Improvements in Alabama.* Johns Hopkins University Studies in Historical and Political Science, XX, No. 4 (1902).

Martineau, Harriet: *Retrospect of Western Travel* (2 vols., New York, 1838).

Marvin, W. L.: *The American Merchant Marine: Its History and Romance from 1620 to 1902* (1902).

Mason, Richard Lee: *Narrative of Richard Lee Mason in the Pioneer West, 1819* (New York, 1915).

Mayo, Bernard: *Henry Clay: Spokesman of the New West* (1937).

Meigs, W. M.: *The Life of Charles Jared Ingersoll* (1897).

——: *The Life of Thomas Hart Benton* (1904).

——: *The Life of John Caldwell Calhoun* (2 vols., 1917).

Melish, John: *A Geographical Description of the United States* (1822).

Meyer, Balthasar H.: *History of Transportation in the United States before 1860* (Washington, 1917).

Miller, Harry E.: *Banking Theories in the United States before 1860* (1927).

Mitchell, S. A.: *Compendium of the Internal Improvements of the United States* (1835).

Monroe, James: "Monroe on the Adams-Clay Bargain," *American Historical Review*, XLII (1937), 273-6.

——: *The Writings of James Monroe*, Stanislaus M. Hamilton, ed. (7 vols., 1898-1903).

Moore, Glover: *The Missouri Controversy* (1937).

Moore, James M.: *A Neglected Period of Connecticut's History* (1933).

Moore, John B.: *History and Digest of . . . international arbitrations* HR Misc. Docs. 212. 53 Congress, 1 Session (5 vols., 1898).

——: *A Digest of International Law* (8 vols., 1906).

Moore, Thomas: *Poetical Works*, A. D. Godley, ed. (1910).

Morgan, Edward V.: *Slavery in New York*. American Historical Association, *Papers*, V (1891).

Morgan, George: *Life of James Monroe* (1921).

Morison, Samuel Eliot: *The Life and Letters of Harrison Gray Otis, Federalist, 1765-1848* (2 vols., 1913).

——: *The Maritime History of Massachusetts, 1783-1860* (1921).

—— with H. S. Commager: *The Growth of the American Republic* (2 vols., 1942).

Morris, C. N.: *Internal Improvements in Ohio*. American Historical Association, *Papers*, III (1889).

Morse, Jedediah: *A Report to the Secretary of War, on Indian Affairs, Comprising a narrative of a tour performed in the summer of 1820* (New Haven, 1822).

Mott, Frank L.: *A History of American Magazines* (3 vols., 1938).

Mudge, Eugene T.: *The Social Philosophy of John Taylor of Caroline* (1939).

Murray, Paul: "Economic Sectionalism in Georgia Politics, 1825-1855," *The Journal of Southern History*, X (1944), 293-307.

Nelson, E. C.: "Presidential Influence in the Policy of Internal Improvements," *Iowa Journal of History and Politics*, IV (1906), 3-69.

Nevins, Allan: *America Through British Eyes* (1948).

Newsome, Albert R.: *The Presidential Election of 1824 in North Carolina*. James Sprunt Historical Studies, XXIII, No. 1 (1939).

——: "Correspondence of Calhoun, McDuffie and Charles Fisher, relative to the Presidential Campaign of 1824," *North Carolina Historical Review*, VII (1930), 477-504.

Nicolson, Harold: *The Congress of Vienna* (1946).

Nock, Albert J.: *Jefferson* (1926).

North, S. N. D.: *A Century of Wool Manufacture*. Association of Wool Manufacturers, *Bulletin* (1894).

Olmsted, Denison: *Memoir of Eli Whitney, Esq.* (1846).

Ostrogorski, M.: *Democracy and the Organization of Political Parties* (1902).

Page, William: *Commerce and Industry, A Historical Review of the Economic Conditions of the British Empire from the Peace of Paris in 1815 to the Declaration of War in 1914, based on Parliamentary Debates* (2 vols., 1919).

Parrington, Vernon L.: *Main Currents in American Thought* (3 vols., 1927-30).

Parton, James: *A Life of Andrew Jackson* (3 vols., 1859-60).

Paxson, F. L.: *The Independence of the South American Republics* (2nd ed., 1916).

Pease, Theodore: *The Frontier State, 1818-1848*. The Centennial History of Illinois, II (1918).

Peck, J. M.: *Guide for Emigrants* (1831).

Pelzer, Louis: "The Negro and Slavery in Early Iowa," *Iowa Journal of History and Politics*, II (1904), 471-84.

Perkins, A. J. G. and Theresa Wolfson: *Frances Wright: Free Enquirer* (1939).

Perkins, Dexter: "Russia and the Spanish Colonies, 1817-1818," *American Historical Review*, XXVIII (July, 1923), 656-72.

——: *The Monroe Doctrine, 1823-1826.* Harvard Historical Studies, XXIX (1927).

Phelan, J.: *History of Tennessee* (1888).

Phillips, U. B.: *Georgia and State Rights.* American Historical Association, *Annual Report, 1901*, II (1902).

——: "The Origin and Growth of the Southern Black Belts," *American Historical Review*, XI (1906), 798-816.

——: *American Negro Slavery* (1918).

——: *Life and Labor in the Old South* (1929).

Pierson, George W.: *Tocqueville and Beaumont in America* (1938).

Pitkin, Timothy: *A Statistical View of the Commerce of the United States of America* (1835).

Plumer, William, Jr.: "Extracts from the Journal of William Plumer, Jr.," *Pennsylvania Magazine of History and Biography*, VI (1882), 357-9.

Poor, H. V.: *Sketch of the Rise and Progress of Internal Improvements*, in *Manual of the Railroads of the United States for 1881* (1882).

Porter, G. R.: *The Progress of the Nation in its Various Social and Economic Relations from the Beginning of the Nineteenth Century* (London, 1838).

Porter, Kenneth W.: *John Jacob Astor* (2 vols., 1931).

Porter, Kirk H.: *A History of Suffrage in the United States* (1918).

Pound, Roscoe: *The Formative Period of American Law* (1939).

Poussin, Guillaume Tell: *Travaux d'améliorations intérieures, projetés ou exécutés par le gouvernement général des États-Unis d'Amérique, de 1824 à 1831* (Paris, 1834).

Powell, J. H.: *Richard Rush, Republican Diplomat, 1780-1859* (1942).

Pratt, Julius W.: *Expansionists of 1812* (1925).

Public Statutes at Large of the United States, Richard Peters, ed., III (1856) and IV (1856).

Quincy, Edmund: *Life of Josiah Quincy* (1867).

Quincy, Josiah P.: *Figures of the Past* (1883).

Ragatz, L. J.: *The Fall of the Planter Class in the British Caribbean* (1928).

Rammelkampf, C. H.: *Campaign of 1824 in New York.* American Historical Association, *Annual Report, 1904*, 175-202.

Randall, Henry S.: *The Life of Thomas Jefferson* (3 vols., 1858).

Ravenel, Harriott H.: *Life and Times of William Lowndes of South Carolina, 1782-1822* (1901).

Reddaway, William F.: *The Monroe Doctrine* (1898).

Register of Debates in Congress (14 vols., 1825-37).

Renwick, James: *Life of De Witt Clinton* (1854).

Reports of Cases Argued and Adjudged in the Supreme Court, 1 Wheaton (1816) to 12 Wheaton (1827), 1 Peters (1828).

[First] Report from the Select Committee on the Navigation Laws. Ordered by the House of Commons . . . (London, 1847).

Report on the Manuscripts of Earl Bathurst. Great Britain, Historical Manuscripts Commission (London, 1923).

Reynolds, J.: *My Own Times* (1854-5).

Rezneck, Samuel: "The Depression of 1819-1822, A Social History," *Amer-*

ican Historical Review, XXXIX (1933), 28-47.

Richardson, James D.: *A Compilation of the Messages and Papers of the Presidents* (10 vols., 1907).

Ringwalt, J. L.: *Development of the Transportation System in the United States* (1888).

Rippy, J. Fred: *Rivalry of the United States and Great Britain over Latin America, 1808-1830* (1929).

Roane, Spencer: "Letters, 1788-1822," New York Public Library *Bulletin*, X (1906), 167-180.

Robert, Joseph C.: *The Tobacco Kingdom: Plantation, Market and Factory in Virginia and North Carolina, 1800-1860* (1938).

Robertson, George: *Scrapbook on Law and Politics, Men and Times* 1855).

Robertson, W. S.: *Rise of the Spanish American Republics* (1918).

—: "South America and the Monroe Doctrine, 1824-1828," *Political Science Quarterly*, XXX (1915), 82-105.

Rogers, Joseph M.: *The True Henry Clay* (1904).

Roseboom, Eugene H.: "Ohio in the Presidential Election of 1824," *Ohio Archaeological & Historical Quarterly*, XXVI (1917), 153-225.

Rowe, Kenneth W.: *Mathew Carey: A Study in American Economic Development*. Johns Hopkins University Studies in Historical and Political Science, LI, No. 4 (1933).

Rowland, Dunbar: *History of Mississippi: The Heart of the South* (2 vols., 1925).

Rush, Richard: *Memoranda of a residence at the court of London, 1817-1819* (2nd ed., 1833).

—: *Residence at the Court of London, 1817-1825* (3rd ed., 1872).

Sargent, Nathan: *Public Men and Events* (2 vols., 1875).

Sato, Shoshuke: *History of the Land Question in the United States*. Johns Hopkins University Studies in His-

torical and Political Science, IV, Nos. 7-9 (1886).

Saxe-Weimar, Bernhard, Duke of: *Travels Through North America, during the years 1825 and 1826* (2 vols., Philadelphia, 1828).

Schafer, Joseph: *The Social History of American Agriculture* (1936).

Schaper, W. A.: *Sectionalism and Representation in South Carolina*, American Historical Association, *Annual Report, 1900*, I, 237-463.

Scherer, James A. B.: *Cotton as a World Power* (1916).

Schmidt, George P.: "Intellectual Crosscurrents in American Colleges," *American Historical Review*, XLII (1936), 46-67.

Schlesinger, Arthur M.: *New Viewpoints in American History* (1928).

Schlesinger, Arthur M., Jr.: *The Age of Jackson* (1945).

Schoolcraft, Henry R.: *Narrative of Travels through the Northwestern Regions of the United States . . . in the year 1820* (1821).

Schouler, James: *History of the United States of America under the Constitution* (7 vols., 1880-1913).

Schurz, Carl: *The Life of Henry Clay* (2 vols., 1887).

Secretary of the Interior: *Statement showing Land Grants Made by Congress to Aid in the Construction of Railroads, Wagon Roads, Canals and Internal Improvements* (Washington, 1908).

Secretary of the Treasury: *Report, 1854-1855*. Exec. Docs., 34 Cong., 1 Sess., No. 10, 86-92. Statistics on Manufactures.

Ségur, Louis Phillipe, Comte de: *Mémoires ou souvenirs et anecdotes* (Paris, 1825).

Ségur, Philippe Paul, Comte de: *Histoire et Mémoires* (8 vols., Paris, 1873).

Selekman, Benjamin M. and Sylvia K.: "Mathew Carey," *Harvard Business Review*, XIX (1941), 326-41.

Semple, Ellen C.: *American History and its Geographic Conditions* (1903).

Setser, Vernon G.: *The Commercial Reciprocity Policy of the United States, 1774-1829* (1937).

Shannon, F. A.: *Economic History of the People of the United States* (1934).

Shipp, John E. D.: *Giant Days: or, The Life and Times of William H. Crawford* (1909).

Shoemaker, F. C.: *Missouri's Struggle For Statehood* (1916).

—: *The First Constitution of Missouri* (1912).

Simkins, Francis B.: *The South Old and New: A History 1820-1947* (1947).

Simms, Henry H.: *Life of John Taylor* (1932).

Simpson, Albert F.: "The Political Significance of Slave Representation," Vanderbilt University Department of History (1940). Private Edition, distributed by The Joint University Libraries (1941) and *Journal of Southern History*, VII (1941), 315-42.

Smith, Culver H.: "Propaganda Technique in the Jackson Campaign of 1828," *East Tennessee Historical Society Publications*, No. 6 (1934), 44-66.

Smith, Margaret Bayard (Mrs. Harrison Smith): *The First Forty Years of Washington Society*, Gaillard Hunt, ed. (1906).

Smith, Theodore C.: "War Guilt in 1812," *Proceedings*, Massachusetts Historical Society, LXIV (1932), 319-45.

Smith, Vera C.: *Rationale of Central Banking* (London, 1936).

Soltau, R. H.: *An Outline of European Economic Development* (1935).

Soulsby, Hugh G.: *The Right of Search and the Slave Trade in Anglo-American Relations, 1814-1862* (1933).

Sparks, Edwin E.: *Expansion of the American People* (1900).

Stanwood, Edward: *A History of Presidential Elections* (2nd ed., 1888).

—: *A History of the Presidency*, C. K. Bolton, ed. (rev. ed., 2 vols., 1928).

—: *American Tariff Controversies in the Nineteenth Century* (2 vols., 1903).

Stapleton, A. G.: *Political Life of the Right Honourable George Canning* (3 vols., 1831).

—: *George Canning and his Times* (1859).

Stapleton, E. J.: *Some Official Correspondence of George Canning* (2 vols., 1887).

Stenberg, Richard R.: "Jackson, Buchanan and the Corrupt Bargain Calumny," *Pennsylvania Magazine of History and Biography*, LVIII (1934), 61-85.

—: "Jackson's Rhea Letter Hoax," *Journal of Southern History*, II (1936), 480-96.

Stickles, Arndt M.: *The Critical Court Struggle in Kentucky* (1929).

—: "Joseph R. Underwood's Fragmentary Journal on the New and Old Court Contest in Kentucky," *The Filson Club History Quarterly*, XIII (1939), No. 4.

Stone, Alfred H.: "Cotton Factorage System of the Southern States," *American Historical Review*, XX (1915), 557-65.

Story, Joseph: *Commentaries on the Constitution of the United States* (5th ed., 2 vols., 1891).

—: *Life and Letters of Joseph Story*, W. W. Story, ed. (2 vols., 1851).

Stuart, James: *Three Years in America* (Edinburgh, 1833).

Sumner, William G.: *Andrew Jackson* (1882).

—: *A History of Banking in the United States* (1896).

Swank, J. M.: *History of the Manufacture of Iron* (rev. ed., 1892).

Swanton, John R.: *Early History of the Creek Indians and Their Neighbors*. Bulletin No. 73, Bureau of American Ethnography (1922).

Sweet, William W.: *Religion on the American Frontier: The Baptists, 1783-1830* (1931).

——: *The Presbyterians, 1783-1840* (1936).

——: *The Methodists, 1783-1840* (1946).

Switzer, W. F.: *Report on Internal Commerce of the United States*. Treasury Department, Bureau of Statistics, January 1888, part ii, Doc. No. 10396.

Sydnor, Charles S.: "The One-Party Period of American History," *American Historical Review*, LI (1945-6), 439-51.

——: *The Development of Southern Sectionalism, 1819-1848*: Vol. V of *A History of the South*, W. H. Stephenson and E. Merton Coulter, eds. (1948).

Tatum, Edward L.: *The United States and Europe, 1815-1823* (1936).

Taus, E. R.: *Central Banking Functions of the United States Treasury, 1789-1941* (1943).

Taussig, Frank W.: *The Tariff History of the United States* (8th ed., 1931).

Taylor of Caroline, John: *Arator* (Georgetown, 1814).

——: *Inquiry into the Principles and Policy of the Government of the United States* (Fredericksburg, 1814).

——: *Construction Construed and Constitutions Vindicated* (Richmond, 1820).

——: *Tyranny Unmasked* (Washington, 1822).

Temperley, H. W. V.: "The Later American Policy of George Canning," *American Historical Review*, XI (1906), 779-97.

——: "Canning, Wellington and George IV," *English Historical Review*, XXXVIII (1923), 206-25.

Temperley, H. W. V.: "Documents Illustrating the Reception and Interpretation of the Monroe Doctrine in Europe," *English Historical Review*, XXIX (1924), 590-3.

——: *The Foreign Policy of Canning, 1822-1827* (1925).

——: "British Secret Diplomacy from Canning to Grey," *The Cambridge Historical Journal*, VI (1938), 1-11.

The Parliamentary Debates, published under the superintendence of Thomas Curson Hansard, 2nd Series (New Series), I, II, V, VI, XII, XVIII (cited as "Hansard").

The Record of American Diplomacy, Ruhl J. Bartlett, ed. (1947).

The South Carolina Rice Plantation as Revealed in the Papers of Robert F. W. Allston, James H. Easterby, ed. (1945).

Thomas, E. S.: *Reminiscences of the Last Sixty-five Years* (2 vols., 1840).

Ticknor, George: *Life, Letters and Journals*. Compiled by E. S. Hilliard (1876).

Tocqueville, Alexis de: *Democracy in America*. With introduction, editorial notes and bibliographies by Phillips Bradley (2 vols., 1945).

Tompkins, D. A.: *American Commerce, Its Expansion* (1900).

Treat, Paysan J.: *The National Land System, 1785-1820* (1910).

Tremain, Mary: *Slavery in the District of Columbia*. University of Nebraska, Seminary Papers, No. 2 (1892).

Trexler, H. A.: *Slavery in Missouri, 1804-1865* (1914).

Tuckerman, H. T.: *America and her Commentators* (1864).

Turnbull, Robert J.: *The Crisis: or, Essays on the Usurpations of the Federal Government. By "Brutus"* (1827).

Turner, Frederick Jackson: *The Frontier in American History* (1921).

——: *The Rise of the New West* (1906).

United States Bureau of Labor Statistics: Bulletin 367, pp. 235-48; Average Annual Prices of all Commodities in the United States, 1801-40.

——: *Bulletin 499*; History of Wages in the United States from Colonial Times to 1928, prepared by Estelle M. Stewart and J. C. Bowen.

Updyke, Frank A.: *Diplomacy of the War of 1812* (1915).

Upton, Emery: *The Military Policy of the United States* (1917).

Van Buren, Martin: *The Autobiography of Martin Van Buren*. American Historical Association, *Annual Report*, 1918, II (1920).

——: *Inquiry into the Origin and Growth of Political Parties in the United States of America*; edited by his sons (1867).

Van Deusen, Glyndon G.: *The Life of Henry Clay* (1937).

Villèle, Comte Jean de: *Mémoires et correspondence* (5 vols., 1888-90).

Von Halle, E.: *Baumwollproduktion und Pflanzungswirtschaft in den Nordamerikanischen Südstaaten*. Staats und socialwissenschaftliche Forschungen, XV, No. 1 (Leipzig, 1897).

Von Holst: *John C. Calhoun* (1900).

——: *The Constitutional and Political History of the United States*. J. J. Lalor, trans. (8 vols., 1888-90).

Von Schulze-Gavernitz, G.: *The Cotton Trade in England and on the Continent* (1895).

Waldo, Samuel Putnam: *A Narrative of a Tour of Observation, made during the summer of 1817 . . . through the North Eastern and North Western departments of the Union with a view to the examination of their several military defenses* (1820).

Wallace, David D.: *The History of South Carolina* (4 vols., 1934).

Walters, Raymond: *Alexander James Dallas* (1943).

Warren, Charles: *The Supreme Court in United States History* (3 vols., 1922).

Warren, Charles: *Jacobin and Junto, or Early American Politics as Viewed in the Diary of Nathaniel Ames, 1758-1822* (1931).

Watkins, James L.: *Production and Price of Cotton for One Hundred Years*. United States, Department of Agriculture, Division of Statistics, Misc. Ser., Bulletin No. 9 (1895).

——: *King Cotton* (1908).

Watterston, George and Nicholas Biddle Van Zandt: *Tabular Statistical Views of the United States* (1828).

——: *Continuation of the Tabular Statistical Views* (1833).

Webster, C. K.: *British Diplomacy, 1813-1815. Select Documents* (1921).

——: *The Foreign Policy of Castlereagh, 1815-1822* (2nd ed., 1934).

——: *Britain and the Independence of Latin America, 1812-1830*, C. K. Webster, ed. (2 vols., 1938).

Webster, Daniel: *Writings and Speeches of Daniel Webster* (18 vols., 1903).

——: *The Works of Daniel Webster . . .* (6 vols., 1877).

Weed, Thurlow: *Autobiography of Thurlow Weed*, Harriet A. Weed, ed. (1883).

Weeks, Stephen B.: *Southern Quakers and Slavery* (1896).

——: "Anti-Slavery Sentiment in the South," Southern History Association, *Publications*, I (1898), 87-130.

Welby, Adlard: *A Visit to North America and the English Settlements in Illinois . . .* (London, 1821).

Wellington, Arthur, Duke of: *Supplementary Despatches and Memoranda*, Arthur Richard, Duke of Wellington, ed. (15 vols., 1858-72).

——: *Despatches, Correspondence and Memoranda* id. ed. (8 vols., 1867-80).

Wells, D. A.: *Our Merchant Marine* (1882).

Wertenbaker, Thomas J.: "The Molding of the Middle West," *American Historical Review*, LIII (1948), 223-34.

Weston, Florence: *The Presidential Election of 1828* (1938).

Whitaker, Arthur P.: *The United States and the Independence of Latin America, 1800-1830*. The Albert Shaw Lectures on diplomatic history (1941).

White, G. S.: *Memoir of Samuel Slater* (1836).

Whitney, Eli: "Correspondence of Eli Whitney, Relative to the Invention of the Cotton Gin," M. B. Hammond, ed., *American Historical Review*, III (1897), 90-127.

Wilson, C. H.: *The Wanderer in America* (Thirsk, 1823).

Wilson, E. M.: *The Congressional Career of Nathaniel Macon*. James Sprunt Historical Monographs No. 2 (1900).

Wilson, W.: *Division and Reunion*. Cambridge Modern History, VII (1906).

Wiltse, C. M.: "The Authorship of the War Report of 1812," *American Historical Review*, XLIX (1944), 253-9.

——: *The Jeffersonian Tradition in American Democracy* (1935).

Wiltse, C. M.: *John C. Calhoun: Nationalist, 1782-1828* (1944).

Winsor, Justin: *The Westward Movement* (1897).

Wirt, William: *Memoirs of the Life of William Wirt*, John P. Kennedy, ed. (2 vols., 1860).

Woodburn, J. A.: *The Historical Significance of the Missouri Compromise*. American Historical Association, *Annual Report, 1893*.

Woodson, Carter G.: *The Negro in Our History* (8th ed., 1945).

Wright, B. F.: *Growth of American Constitutional Law* (1942).

Wright, C. W.: *Economic History of the United States* (1941).

Württemberg, Paul Wilhelm, Herzog von: *Erste Reise nach den nördlichen Amerika in den Jahren 1822 bis 1824* (Stuttgart und Tübingen, 1835).

Yonge, C. D.: *The Life and Administration of Robert Banks, second Earl of Liverpool* (3 vols., 1868).

Young, J. S.: *Political and Constitutional Study of the Cumberland Road* (1904).

Zimmerman, James F.: *Impressment of American Seamen*. Columbia University Studies in History, Economics and Public Law, CXVII, No. 1 (1925).

Index

[Superior numbers refer to the Notes]